KEYS TO *THE GIFT*

A Guide to Nabokov's Novel

STUDIES IN RUSSIAN AND SLAVIC
LITERATURES, CULTURES AND
HISTORY

Series Editor: Lazar Fleishman
(Stanford Universtity)

KEYS TO *THE GIFT*

Yuri Leving

A Guide to Nabokov's Novel

Boston
2011

Library of Congress Cataloging-in-Publication Data:
A catalog record for this book is available from the Library of Congress.

Copyright © 2011 Academic Studies Press
All rights reserved

ISBN 978-1-934843-11-6 (hardback)
ISBN 978-1-934843-97-0 (paperback)

Cover design: Andrey Bashkin

The companion website for this book is www.keystogift.com

Published by Academic Studies Press in 2011
28 Montfern Avenue
Brighton, MA 02135, USA
press@academicstudiespress.com
www.academicstudiespress.com

*To Ella,
Lola and Leva (Arieh Levi),
for their love and patience*

Contents

How to Use This Book xi
Acknowledgments xvii
References xix
Note on Spellings of Names xx
The Gift: A Biography of the Novel xxi

Chapter One
COMPOSITION AND PUBLICATION

Writing 3
The Manuscript 5
Editing 10
The Unwritten Part Two 12
The History of Publication 30
The Market Value 61
Towards the Variorum Edition 72
References 75

Chapter Two
HISTORICAL CONTEXT

Imperial Russia and the Golden Age 81
Aesthetic Theories and Literary Criticism 86
The Plot of *What to Do?* 96
St. Petersburg: Turn of the Century 105
Berlin: The Russian Émigré Community Between the Two World Wars . . 113
References 121

Chapter Three
STRUCTURE

Title	127
Plot	133
Narrative	135
Development of Themes	136
Calendar	143
Setting	152
Characters	162
Structure	205
Themes	213
References	236

Chapter Four
STYLE

Method	245
Form	249
Style	252
Transitions	257
Points of View	265
Sources	270
Allusions	277
Intertextuality	286
References	305

Chapter Five
COMMENTARY

The Gift as Hypertext: Digital Databases	313
What Constitutes a Footnote?	315
Playing with Readers	318
Types of Commentary	322
Visual Aids to Commentary	333
The Opening Scene	337
Author's Name, Dedication, Epigraph	338
Close Reading	343
References	368

Chapter Six
ENGLISH TRANSLATION

"I Am Still Looking For Somebody…"	373
A Sheer Happenstance	377
Passing the Test	379
Collaboration by Correspondence	380
Some General Principles of Translating *The Gift*	381
Challenges in Translating	385
Nabokov's Revisions of Scammell	389
What Had To Be Compromised?	397
References	411

Chapter Seven
CRITICAL RECEPTION

Contemporary Critics: 1937–38	415
Contemporary Critics: 1938–56	424
Contemporary Critics: 1962–77	436
Critical Reception: 1977–2000s	474
References	480

Appendixes

Appendix I	487
Appendix II	503
Appendix III	508
Appendix IV	515
Index	518

How to Use This Book

"Where are the keys? Keys, my keys!"
Alexander Pushkin,
The Covetous Knight (1830)

To critically interpret a text means to read it in order to discover, along with our reactions to it, something about its nature. To use a text means to start from it in order to get something else, even accepting the risk of misinterpreting it from the semantic point of view. If I tear out the pages of my Bible to wrap my pipe tobacco in them, I am using this Bible, but it would be daring to call me a textualist—even though I am, if not a strong pragmatist, certainly a very pragmatic person.
Umberto Eco, *The Limits of Interpretation*

— 1 —

Imagine purchasing an expensive coffee maker without a user's manual, or trying to run an outdated word processing program on a brand new iPad. You would probably be able to produce a simple cup of coffee to sip while gazing at the green block letters on your screen, but what is the point of this elementary task if the machines are designed for excellence? Reading Vladimir Nabokov's novel *Dar* (*The Gift*) without a critical guide is comparable to the unwelcome prospect of trying to enjoy Joyce's *Ulysses* without a single line of commentary. Current English-language editions of *The Gift*, however, seem to produce just this sort of blundering. *The Gift* is a difficult novel, and requires an especially meticulous and expansive scholarly guide.

How to Use This Book

My own reading of the novel was not easy and, therefore, typical. The first encounter occurred in the early nineties, when an old friend presented me with a small copy of the novel published in the provincial Russian town of Omsk (much to my chagrin, I later discovered that this particular edition was peppered with monstrous errata). At the time, I was studying abroad in Israel and could have afforded the hardbound 1975 Ardis edition, lovingly printed on vellum paper, but the tiny red paperback easily carried in a pocket served well for an undergraduate student working odd jobs. A few times I glanced through the opening pages of the book, but could hardly force myself beyond that point. My attention dwindled easily; I found the painfully long sentences irritating. Given the abundance of parenthetical digressions, by the time I reached the end of a paragraph I would often forget how it had begun, which provoked multiple readings. I tried to cheat by snatching fragments at random, but this grew tiresome and only made me want to put the book aside. I felt perplexed. I liked Nabokov's other novels, but *The Gift* was somehow different.

I remember how I tried to engage with the fourth chapter, Chernyshevski's biography, while working as a guard at the maternity ward in the Hadassah Ein-Kerem hospital. Unfortunately, the moments of peace between attacks from irritated expectant fathers and importunate relatives were too brief to allow time for the novel to truly beguile me. I will refrain, however, from drawing any conclusions or seeking symbolism in the fact that I was impregnated with the seed of this book while working at the labor ward, especially since my devotion was not then carried to full term, as I did not finish the novel.

It is possible that the very structure of *The Gift* discouraged me in my half-hearted courtship and challenged me to hold out for a true romance. As ironic as this may sound, the first spark flared during my own honeymoon, which was not even remotely romantic. When I had just returned from a summer of military training, my new bride and I, finding ourselves short of money, decided to spend the month after our wedding at an Israeli kibbutz, where we harvested apples next to the sloping Jerusalem Mountains. For some reason, I decided to shove Nabokov's misleadingly petite book into my bag. Along with another young couple, we shared a room divided by an oversized wardrobe that barely blocked a third of the space needed for privacy; for the rest we strung makeshift curtains. As in the Shchyogolev apartment in Berlin, one could easily hear the neighbors' toilet splashes (and not only that), and right outside the entrance to our dwelling was an improvised zoo complete with garrulous monkeys, a couple of goats, and a flabby iguana.

Despite (and perhaps because of) these eclectic circumstances, I found myself unexpectedly captivated by the world of *The Gift*. I began to immerse myself in it as soon as the hard days of physical labor had ended, lying on my bed or on the ground under the pomegranate bushes and...feeling increasingly happy. I stepped into Zina and Fyodor's universe as imperceptibly as the protagonist of Nabokov's novel crossed the realities between his own dreams and daily Berlin life, just as Godunov-Cherdyntsev Senior entered the rainbow. Inevitably came the afternoon when I finished the book. I closed my eyes, refusing to believe that the novel I had hungered for, that I had wanted so much to continue devouring, could end so suddenly.

As often happens, I hesitated for a long time to analyze my feelings rationally and examine the source of my delight under any sort of intellectual magnifying glass. Then, in 1996, Professor Roman Timenchik (my beloved teacher at the Hebrew University) offered for the very first time his graduate seminar entitled "The Russian Nabokov."

That first semester we only read about twenty-five pages of the opening chapter (the entire novel is over three hundred pages). Usually we looked at several sentences per class, but in the case of some particularly complex constructions, we might spend up to two sessions on a single phrase. Practicing the method of close reading (and our readings were very close indeed!) we brainstormed about the text. We began by discussing a simple understanding of the pragmatic message of each sentence, then moved toward dissecting the syntax, before finally attempting to crack the metatextual codes and track down the implicit literary allusions. I audited the same course the following year and our progress turned out to be even more modest: we managed to get through only the first fifteen pages. By the time I left Israel, I had attended Timenchik's seminar three times (twice from start to finish and then less regularly in the third year due to other commitments), and our intense discussions almost never duplicated the debates of the previous years, proving to be just as interesting, stimulating, and refreshing.

During the seminars, some of us questioned whether Nabokov could have possibly kept *consciously* in his mind such a multiplicity of allusions and reminiscences, fusing them in packed images that so deftly entrapped his readers and laying semantically explosive mines in the dense field of his prose. Could our overzealous interpretations lead us to unintentionally presumptuous fallacies? One of the puzzled students, unable to restrain himself, once exclaimed: "But even if half of what we discover here is true, then Nabokov's mind had to be a kind of computer!"

Timenchik instantly retorted: "Then a computer he *was*."

———————————— How to Use This Book ————————————

— 2 —

The structure of the present book follows the conventions of current literary guides.

In Chapter One the reader is taken on a historical journey from the creation of the novel through its publication and beyond. There I bring together the scattered data pertaining to writing and publishing the novel, from its serialization in the émigré press to the most recent editions. Before the present book, this work had yet to be done in a systematic way, though I greatly appreciate the field work of many colleagues who over the years have studied and copiously annotated the archival discoveries, published Nabokov correspondence, and other documents relevant to the history of *The Gift*. To this I add my own research on Nabokov's original manuscripts and archival materials at the Library of Congress in Washington, D.C., and in the Berg Collection of the New York Public Library. From issues related to the manuscript and paleography (sample textological analysis will be provided in the fifth chapter of the monograph) I move to discussion of the phantom "second part" of *The Gift*.

It is almost impossible, especially for a beginner, to fully appreciate *The Gift* and its numerous subtleties without some basic knowledge of Russian and European (German, in particular) history and artistic culture of the nineteenth and early twentieth centuries. Chapter Two, using a montage of material, is designed to provide the necessary introduction: a series of brief sections sketches Chernyshevski's Russia of the late nineteenth century, followed by excursions into the life and mores of pre-Revolutionary St. Petersburg and the Russian émigré community in Berlin between the two World Wars. This historical milieu will be familiar terrain for Slavists and native speakers of Russian, but should provide those who are less conversant in Russian culture with much of the essential data necessary for a deeper understanding of Nabokov's work. I have tried to gather and arrange the available sources in such a way as to introduce readers to the most important landmarks of the intricate landscape against which *The Gift* swiftly and majestically unfolds.

The guide proceeds then with two further parts on "Structure" and "Style" (Chapters Three and Four, respectively). The former outlines the basic components of *The Gift* (its plot and characters) and reconstructs the internal chronology of the novel. Other literary elements are explored in such sections as "Setting" and "Themes." The latter chapter deals with "Method," "Points of View," and "Form." Intertextuality is one of the main principles of poetic structure in Nabokov's oeuvre and it is treated in a separate section of Chapter Four.

Without annotating the entire text of *The Gift*, Chapter Five, nonetheless, discusses the general principles for providing commentary on the novel and provides a variety of examples of the novel's challenging riddles and their solutions. The history of the novel's English translation is covered in Chapter Six.

It is widely understood that *The Gift* provokes mixed reactions from readers. Although the number of responses to the work during Nabokov's lifetime, especially at the time of its initial Russian-language publication during 1937–38, was limited—what material there is has still not been studied sufficiently and remains somewhat opaque. A detailed account of the history of critical reception of the novel is given in Chapter Seven. In this last chapter of the book I mainly describe and quote publications prior to the author's death; after this, the survey becomes less comprehensive since the more recent works are readily available to anyone interested in retrieving the full texts.

The guide ends with an appendix, "Firing Practice to *The Gift*" (I borrow Fyodor's own definition of his work on Chernyshevski as preparation for the "real" novel, that is *The Gift* itself[1]). For the first time, it introduces the English-language reader to a lengthy letter written by Nabokov in 1937 to his friend and former classmate at Tenishev School, Samuil Rozov, who later moved to Palestine. From a literary point of view, this letter (kept by the Rozov family for three generations now) is probably one of the most valuable documents in the entire corpus of Nabokov's European correspondence, excluding family letters. It offers deep insight into his intimate world and his artistic laboratory, and demonstrates that the author provided a generous autobiographical layer for Fyodor's childhood (as described in the first chapter of *The Gift*). With the kind permission of both heirs, Dmitri Nabokov and Arieh Rozov, the publication of the original Russian document was made possible after two successive summers of research at the Central State Historical Archive in St. Petersburg.

The other appendices and indexes (*Dramatis personae*, *Flora and fauna*, *Color distribution*, and *Toponymy*) are available as a supplement to this printed edition at the website (www.keystogift.com), which is designed to provide the reader with a quick and convenient reference regarding various technical aspects of the narrative.

— 3 —

The next step in the study of *The Gift* should be the publication of a facsimile of the manuscript along with variant texts placed on the opposite pages (the kind of work that has been done for other English and Russian classics). The necessity of a variorum edition of *The Gift*, akin to the authoritative editions

---

[1] Vladimir Nabokov. *The Gift*. New York: Vintage International, 1991, 196. Throughout the book I refer to this edition by a letter G following the page number.

in series such as The Library of America, Pléiade, or Literaturnye Pamiatniki (Literary Monuments) is self-evident. However, its implementation will most likely take years of collaborative scholarly effort. The current study is something of a compromise: an introductory attempt to gather comprehensive data on the novel from a variety of available sources. Using both referential and analytical approaches, it merely paves the way to future academic editions and invites more extensive work on what can truly be called one of the masterpieces of twentieth century modernist literature.

The rare emotional catharsis that accompanied my first serious reading of *The Gift* is unforgettable, and it is for this bliss that I am grateful to Nabokov. Below is my humble attempt to look beyond *the skyline of the page*, to catch, weigh and deconstruct the very *haze*, which cannot *terminate the phrase*.

Halifax, 2010

Acknowledgments

The goal of this book is to systemize in a coherent and clear way the main data available on Nabokov's *The Gift*, from passing mentions in private correspondence to newspaper reviews and scholarly articles accumulated during the seven decades since its first appearance in print, and to make the novel ultimately accessible to any interested reader without prior deep knowledge of Russian history or literature.

I have tried not to burden the reader with too many references to sources; however, I have felt it appropriate to include a bibliography of critical works at the end of each chapter and to credit the researchers who first came up with original answers to the riddles of *The Gift*, although since so much has been written on the novel in the past twenty years there are inevitable repetitions in some articles. And if at times the book reads like a collage of scholarly citations, it can be said to mimic the very method of Nabokov in his composition of *The Gift*; in my case this can be justified by one simple reason—the guide is an attempt to summarize and serve as a compendium of sorts for the many fine studies of Nabokov's puzzling novel. Unattributed information will, I trust, be uncontroversial, and will derive either from general investigative work or from Nabokov papers in the Library of Congress and Berg Collection at the New York Public Library.

In addition to the published labors of Nabokov scholars I am grateful to many friends and colleagues: Keith Blasing—not just for his help with editing and translation of parts of this manuscript, but also for pulling plums out of a pot-pie of metaphors; John Barnstead for translating Nabokov's letter to Rozov; Frederick White, Olga Gurin, and Dana Dragunoiu for making my English more elastic; Lazar Fleishman for coming up with the idea of this book and Igor Nemirovsky for his patience; Roman Timenchik for being my teacher; Omry Ronen for encyclopedic insights into Nabokov and beyond; Savely Senderovich for ongoing support; Alexander Dolinin for constant inspiration; Leona Toker for serving as the ideal of an almost legalistic structure of argumentation; Maria Malikova for her sense of elegance and style; Boris Katz for two musical consultations; Norman G. Pereira for preventing me from blunders in sketching Russia's history; Stephen Blackwell for an intellectually charging breakfast in Kyoto; Michael Scammell for a surprisingly candid interview; Michael Katz, the translator of *What to Do?*, for supporting my—still unrealized—project of the annotated English edition of this Nabokov novel; Brendan Rutherford for compiling the index to this book and providing copy-editing; and, finally, to all of the students in my "Nabokov" classes taught at Dalhousie University since 2007, who enthusiastically contributed to the electronic concordance to *The Gift*, an online educational project (www.keystogift.com), which, thanks to Andrei Bashkin, has acquired a sleek skin worthy of competing with high-end 3D computer games.

Without the cooperation of Dmitri Nabokov in giving me access to materials in archives and permission to make use of them, this book would be a much poorer thing. Indeed, the very idea of studying Nabokov could not be imagined without his benign and stimulating presence. I am grateful to Dmitri Vladimirovich and the Nabokov Estate for permission to quote from the writer's works, published and unpublished.

Isaac Gewirtz of the Berg Collection at the New York Public Library and Alice L. Birney of the Manuscript Division at the Library of Congress have greatly facilitated my work with the Nabokov materials.

Parts of this research appeared in *The Nabokovian* (39, 1997; 45, 2000; 48, 2002; 64, 2010); in *The Real Life of Pierre Delalande. Studies in Russian and Comparative Literature to Honor Alexander Dolinin* (Ed. by David M. Bethea, L. Fleishman, and A. Ospovat. Stanford: Stanford Slavic Studies. Vol. 34 (2), 2007); as well as in the *Nabokov Online Journal* (Vol. I, 2007), reprinted by permission.

I am indebted to Alexander Dolinin for reading the draft of this book; his specific comments saved me from a number of errors, while his general observations have helped me to refine the overall thesis. If I have not followed all of his suggestions, the fault is mine alone.

The author of the first ever monograph-length study of the novel, Stephen H. Blackwell, lamented: "What is *The Gift*, which many consider the century's greatest Russian novel? Why is it not automatically included in 'Great Books' courses?" His response to his own question was that perhaps it is because of the bizarre sedateness of its plot, the sense that "nothing happens," or its esoteric focus on artistic creation (Blackwell 1). And even though Nabokov, this "emphatically Eurocentric male writer of aristocratic background and demanding high cultural standards," has not yet had "a comparable place in academe, for many reasons, including his inherent difficulty, especially for students who now spend less time reading books than their forebears; his straddling the disciplinary boundaries between English and Russian; and his being deeply unfashionable in an age committed to canonical revisionism and increased attention to women, minorities, the non-Eurocentric and the demotic" (Boyd 32), my hope is that the present guide will make questions such as those above at least more approachable.

Finally, I wish to acknowledge the support of the Social Sciences and Humanities Research Council of Canada, which made this research possible.

References

Blackwell, Stephen H. *Zina's Paradox: The Figured Reader in Nabokov's* Gift. New York, New York: Peter Lang, 2000.

Boyd, Brian. "Literature, Pattern, Lolita: Or Art, Literature, Science," *Transitional Nabokov*. Ed. by Duncan White and Will Norman. New York: Peter Lang, 2009: 31-53.

Note on Spellings of Names

Throughout this book I am using the spelling of Russian names based on the Library of Congress system, with the exception of certain conventional departures from that system (Tolstoy, Dostoevsky, etc.). However, in order to be consistent with the primary text, I have decided to keep "Chernyshevski," "Fyodor," and Nabokov's other idiosyncratic versions as they appear in the authorized translation of *The Gift*.

THE GIFT:
A BIOGRAPHY OF THE NOVEL

1933 *January.* Nabokov begins gathering materials for what will become his last novel written in Russian.
November 11. Reports to Fondaminsky and Rudnev, the editors of *Sovremennye zapiski* (*Contemporary Annals*), that he is still busy doing preparatory work and has not even begun writing the novel.

1934 *January–February.* Composes a short story, "The Circle," orbiting around the still emerging universe of *The Gift*.
June. Breaks off writing "The Life of Chernyshevski," a fictional biography of the legendary Russian revolutionary, to switch to the anti-totalitarian novel, *Invitation to a Beheading*, completed in just a few weeks.

1935 *June.* Begins Chapter Two of *The Gift* (about the butterfly expeditions into Central Asia).
Late summer. Writes a short autobiographical piece in English.
April. Reads parts of *The Gift* at the home of Iosif Gessen, the former editor of the journal *Pravo* (*Law*) and friend of V. D. Nabokov.

1936 *March 15.* Informs Gleb Struve from Berlin that he is back to writing a major novel. Composes lyrical verse that will later be included in the first chapter.
Late spring–summer? Writes a few chapters (all lost) of an autobiography in English.
August. Begins Chapter One.
October 2. Confides to Mikhail Karpovich that the work is so intensive that he feels aches in his writing hand.

1937   *January.* A public reading of two excerpts from *The Gift* in Paris.
       April. Chapter One of *The Gift* is published in the literary magazine *Sovremennye zapiski*, though remaining chapters remain incomplete.
       July. Moves to Cannes.
       August 6. Proposes to Rudnev, the editor of *Sovremennye zapiski*, that Chapter Four ("The Life of Chernyshevski") be published instead of Chapter Two, which is not yet ready.
       August 10-16: Exchanges letters with Fondaminsky in which he expresses his anger at the journal's unwillingness to publish Chapter Four.
       September 4. Writes a private letter to Samuil Rozov in Palestine that contains many autobiographical glimpses related to the novel in progress (reprinted in the Appendix).
       Mid-October. Moves to Menton. Works on Chapter Three.

1938   *January.* Completes *The Gift*.
       Spring. Sends the manuscript to Altagracia de Jannelli, his American literary agent, who forwards it to Bobbs-Merrill publishing house for consideration.
       Early summer. Critic Alexander Nazaroff submits the first written review of the novel to Bobbs-Merrill: "In its general type, *Gift* sharply differs from that which hitherto was the common run of Nabokoff's novels...*Gift* is not a realistic novel. I even am not sure that it can be called a novel at all. It is an ultra-sophisticated and modernist piece of introspective, almost 'non-subjective' writing which, in composition, may be likened to James Joyce's *Ulysses*."
       July 14. Comments to Altagracia de Jannelli: "On the whole I rather liked N[azaroff]'s description of *The Gift*, although it is very superficial—there is a lot more in my book both for the connoisseur and the lay reader...My style and methods have nothing in common with Joyce (though I greatly appreciate *Ulysses*)."
       October. Moves to Paris. Final installment of *The Gift* appears in *Sovremennye zapiski*.
       November. Abram Kagan, co-owner of the émigré publishing house "Petropolis," negotiates to have the novel published in two volumes.

1939   *May 28.* Sergei Rachmaninoff becomes involved in a possible publication of the book.
       Fall. The outbreak of the World War in Europe ruins the prospects of publishing *The Gift* as a monograph for the foreseeable future.
       December 31. One of the final issue of the émigré Parisian newspaper *Bodrost'* (*Cheerfulness*) features an extract from the novel's omitted chapter ("The Arrest of Chernyshevski").

1940 Contemplates writing the continuation of *The Gift*, but completes only a draft of addendum on lepidoptera as well as a rough plan for the second part, which was never to be finished.
May. The Nabokovs move to the United States, leaving most of the writer's archive in Europe.

1941 *July 25*. Suggests that Peter Pertzoff, who earlier translated a number of his short stories from Russian to English, undertake the translation of *The Gift*, granting him exclusive rights for the project until December 1, 1941. Pertzoff's translation was never completed.

1942–1943 Active efforts to elicit interest in *The Gift* on the part of American publishing industry. Among the potential translators—writers and scholars—Yarmolinsky, Wilson, Werth, Muchnic, and Guerney.

1944 *May*. Discusses with Zenzinov a prospective literary evening in New York and entertains the idea of publishing *The Gift* independently.

1945 *October 25*. Véra Nabokov inquires with Zenzinov again: "The last thing I would like to ask you, concerns the odds of publishing *The Gift*. We want to print it ourselves."

1951 *July 18*. Mark Aldanov recommends that Nabokov's novel be published by a new émigré Russian press, the Chekhov Publishing House, in New York.

1952 *April*. Reads the proofs of the first Russian-language edition of his novel.
Early May. The Chekhov Press issues *The Gift*.
May 27. Edmund Wilson receives a complimentary copy of the novel, but apparently never reads (or finishes reading) it.
July. Review of the Russian edition of *Dar* in the émigré journal, *Posev*.

1958–1959 Donates manuscript materials relating to *The Gift* to the Library of Congress in Washington, D.C.

1961 *February*. Anna Feigin, Véra's cousin, recommends Michael Scammell as the translator of *The Gift* into English.
July–August. Scammell finishes translating Chapters Four and Five. Véra writes Scammell to say that her husband is "amazed at the speed with which you work."

1962 Praises the forthcoming English edition of *The Gift* in an interview to BBC: "It is the longest, I think the best, and the most nostalgic of my Russian novels."

1963 *March–April.* Two excerpts from *The Gift* appear in English translation in *The New Yorker* magazine.
May 27. *The Gift* is published in the United States while the Nabokovs travel in Europe.
July–December. Over 100 reviews of *The Gift* appear in various periodicals. The reception is mixed: most critics cautiously praise the novel but also project that it won't repeat the success of *Lolita* or *Pale Fire*.
September. Unequivocally claims in an interview for the *Television 13* educational program in New York: "My best Russian novel is a thing called, in English, *The Gift*. My two best American ones are *Lolita* and *Pale Fire*."

1967 *Fall.* Gallimard in Paris publishes the French translation of *The Gift* by Raymond Girard.

1975 *Spring.* Ardis Publishers begins reprinting Nabokov's Russian works, including *The Gift*.

1979 The first scholarly paper on *The Gift* is published in the USSR: its author, Mikhail Lotman, pretends that he is writing about an obscure Russian poet named Godunov-Cherdyntsev, and does not mention the still forbidden Nabokov's name.

1988 *March.* The Soviet magazine *Ural* (3-6) begins a serialized publication of what is announced as an unabridged version of *The Gift* (it includes the controversial Chapter Four, as well as some omissions and alterations).

1989 The novel is printed in a book edition in the Soviet city of Sverdlovsk (now Yekaterinburg) in the Urals. A Russian Americanist scholar A. Zverev contributes an introduction to this edition, whose print run amounts to a quarter of a million copies.

1990 The Berg Collection (New York Public Library) acquires materials relating to the translation of *The Gift* into English, among other Nabokov's manuscripts.
Two different annotated Russian editions of *Dar* are published for the first time with extensive commentary (by O. Dark and A. Dolinin respectively).

1993 D. Zimmer presents his German translation of the novel (the Rowohlt edition contains commentary translated from Russian with a few additions).

1999 *Spring.* $35,000 is the listing price of the inscribed edition of *The Gift* (New York: The Chekhov Publishing House, 1952) for sale by the American book dealer Glenn Horowitz (lot № 71 in the catalogue).

2000 *January.* St. Petersburg publishing house Symposium produces the first copyrighted post-Soviet edition of *The Gift*, by arrangement with the Estate of Vladimir Nabokov, incorporating Alexander Dolinin's thorough commentary in Volume 4.
April. Publication of "Father's Butterflies" in *The Atlantic Monthly*; the same magazine had introduced Nabokov to his first extended audience in the English-speaking world more than half a century earlier.
July. The first monograph-length study of the novel, *Zina's Paradox*, by Stephen H. Blackwell appears in print.

2002 *Summer—winter.* Exhibitions devoted to the fiftieth anniversary of the publication of *The Gift* held at the Russian National Library (St. Petersburg) and the Libriary of Russia Abroad (Moscow); Dr. Galina Glushanok, curator (concept and design). It features émigré editions of the novel as well as samizdat copies, serialized excerpts, and reproductions of the correspondence between Nabokov and Scammell pertaining to the translation of *The Gift*.

2007 *October.* The launch of the online *Gift Project*—concordance and visual commentary, an English-language scholarly resource featuring concordance, annotations, bibliographic information and abstracts of academic articles devoted to the novel, as well as the covers of international editions and photographic reproductions of various journal publications of the novel.

2009 *July.* The manuscript of *The Gift* becomes available for research as part of the Nabokov Collection in the Library of Congress upon the expiration of the 50 year term during which public access was not allowed.

2010 *January.* The Russian-language editions of *The Gift* (Azbooka) begin to include "Father's Butterflies," still without the short story "The Circle," but closer to Nabokov's own master plan for addenda.
April. The second translation of the novel into Japanese comes out (translated from the Russian by Mitsuyoshi Numano; the earlier version was based on the English translation).

June. *The Gift* is being rapidly re-discovered by readers and scholars alike: the latest printed monograph devoted to the writer, Eric Naiman's *Nabokov, Perversely* (Ithaca: Cornell University Press, 2010), features a chapter entitled "Blackwell's *Paradox* and Fyodor's *Gift*," which ends as follows:

> The reward for reading *The Gift* well is the absence of the anxiety that necessarily characterizes "good reading" of other novels by Nabokov. The 'price' is a loss of self. As Zina says in the novel's final quoted line of dialogue, uttered as she and Fyodor prepare to leave a café, "We have to pay. Call him over." (178)

2011 *December. The Gift* in the English translation is to be released as an unabridged audiobook by *Brilliance Audio* on CD. Reader to be announced.

Chapter One
COMPOSITION AND PUBLICATION

Writing

The Gift was an entirely new kind of a novel and composing it required new skills and a much longer timeframe even from an author as productive as Sirin (Vladimir Nabokov's pen name during his career as a Russian-language writer). When, in late 1933, Vadim Rudnev, an editor of the journal *Sovremennye zapiski* (*Contemporary Annals*) and former political activist, heard from a mutual friend, Ilya Fondaminsky, that Nabokov had started working on a new novel, he inquired as to whether it would be possible to examine the manuscript for consideration. "Unfortunately, I am unable to oblige you," Nabokov politely declined, "for, as I mentioned to Ilya Isidorovich [Fondaminsky] the other day, I have not even begun writing the new novel. For the past half year I have been busy doing preparatory work, and this work is not yet finished. I apologize for the somewhat belated reply" (November 11, 1933; Nabokov Papers in the University of Illinois Archives; trans. by Gene Barabtarlo). It was logical for Rudnev to ask this of Nabokov, who was a regular contributor to that journal and a rising star in Russian émigré literature. Ironically, it will be the same Rudnev who tried to secure the novel in progress for *Sovremennye zapiski* who would reject *The Gift* in its final form four years later.

A few months later, by mid-1934, Nabokov was hard at work on writing Fyodor Godunov-Cherdyntsev's fictional biography of the nineteenth century Russian revolutionary and philosopher, Nikolai Chernyshevski (Boyd, *Russian Years* 416). Shortly before that, a rough draft of Chernyshevski's novel *What Is To Be Done?*, lacking sections of Chapter Five and all of Chapter Six (discovered in the archive of the Peter and Paul Fortress), had been published in 1929; it is possible that this publication reached Nabokov and attracted his attention to the vagaries of the controversial book.[1]

---

[1] We know almost all the major sources that Nabokov studied for Chapter Four. Beside Chernyshevski's complete works, two books by Steklov and one by Volynsky (they are mentioned in the text), he used a three-volume collection of annotated biographical materials edited by N.A. Alekseev, M.N. Chernyshevski and S.N. Chernov (*N.G. Chernyshevskii.*

Chapter One. COMPOSITION AND PUBLICATION

Nabokov had not yet composed Chapter Five of *The Gift* when he wrote another novel, *Invitation to a Beheading*. Brian Boyd explains that this brief side project was motivated by Nabokov's research on Chernyshevski, which revealed to him the nightmares of the Russian penal system (Chernyshevski was sentenced to fourteen years of hard labor in Siberia and was forced to undergo a ritual mock execution). After reading all of Chernyshevski's works that he could track down—a feat in itself—Nabokov creatively absorbed the material ("I had to...digest all this my own way, so that now I have heartburn," as he writes to Khodasevich; April 26, 1934; Boyd, *Russian Years* 406-7). The same letter provides an interesting clue as to why Nabokov would bother spending his time on this seemingly thankless task; every one of Chernyshevski's books, he confesses, was "utterly dead" by the 1930s and Chernyshevski "had less talent than a lot of people, *but more courage than many*...He was thoroughly tormented" (Ibid.).[2] At the early stage of composition he also confides to his friend Gleb Struve:

> The idea of a new novel has germinated with me and it will have direct relation to—guess who?—Chernyshevski! I read his correspondence, *What Is To Be Done?*, etc., etc., and I see this curious gentleman large as life. I hope this little piece of news will amuse you. My book, for certain, will in no way resemble the most insipid and, in my opinion, pseudo-intellectual [*poluintelligentnye*] biographies romancées a la [André] Maurois. (August 23, 1933; Struve 251; *cf.* in *The Gift*: "You know those idiotic '*biographies romancées*' where Byron is coolly slipped a dream extracted from one of his own poems?"; G200)

A year later Nabokov mentioned his work to Struve again: "My Chernyshevski grows up, revolts and, hopefully, will kick the bucket soon" (Ibid.). *The Gift* turned out to be, without a doubt, the most labor-intensive of Nabokov's novels. The author wrote to Vladislav Khodasevich that it was "monstrously difficult," explaining that he had to undertake Fyodor's research for him before composing the Chernyshevski biography. He tackled that chapter first, establishing a precedent of writing the most difficult sections of a novel before the rest—a practice he would return to for both *Pale Fire* and *Ada*. After completing Fyodor's semi-historical sketch, Nabokov turned back to chapter two in mid-1935 (Boyd, *Russian Years* 419). His aim now was to recreate an account of the life and the Asian journeys of Godunov-Cherdyntsev senior, the protagonist's father. The

---

Literaturnoe nasledie. Moscow and Leningrad: 1928-1930); a three-volume collection of Chernyshevski's letters from Siberia edited by E.A. Liatsky and annotated by M.N. Chernyshevski (*Chernyshevskii v Sibiri. Perepiska s rodnymi*. Saint Petersburg: 1912-1913), and M. Lemke's book on political trials of the 1860s in Russia: M.K. Lemke. *Politicheskie protsessy v Rossii 1860-kh godov (Po arkhivnym materialam)*. Izd. 2-e. Moscow and Petrograd, 1923.

[2] Unless specifically mentioned, all italics in quotations are mine.

work with documentary sources for the life of Chernyshevski proved to be useful experience, though Nabokov used totally different material to construct his colorful mosaic of the Asian flora and fauna. Nabokov then directed his attention back to the unseasoned poet, Godunov-Cherdyntsev, whose poems, according to the plan, were to have been interspersed throughout the first chapter of the book (Boyd, *Russian Years* 426). This task required a subtle approach: verses had to present a careful mixture of banal style and epigone lyricism through which Fyodor's future poetic gift could be discerned.

A reading of parts of *The Gift* in April of 1935 at the home of Iosif Gessen — former editor of *Pravo* (*Law*) and a friend of the writer's father, Vladimir Dmitrievich Nabokov, — received a positive response, as did public readings of excerpts in Paris in late December 1936 and January 1937.

In a letter to Struve (March 15, 1936) Nabokov reported that, as he had resettled in Berlin, he was back to writing *The Gift*. Chapter Four, which would cause him so much trouble later, had been finished, and it is probable that a tentative outline of the third chapter had also been completed. Three and a half years after the work on *The Gift* began, its most challenging parts were ready. The author could now use the drafts (which have not survived) to write out the book in a linear way. Armed with the samples of Fyodor's youthful poetry, Nabokov started putting the novel together on August 23, 1936. This work was so intensive that Nabokov's writing hand soon started aching (as he confided in a letter to Mikhail Karpovich, a historian and an older friend, on October 2, 1936; Boyd 429). By September 1937 Chapters Three and Five existed in draft form; Nabokov continued to revise them while residing at Cannes. After completing Chapter Two he continued straight to Chapter Three.

Around mid-October 1938, Nabokov moved to Menton in the French Riviera (Boyd, *Russian Years* 445). Due to the subtropical climate there, winter is practically unknown in Menton (hotels and villas in this resort, which was popular up until 1914, welcomed rich guests from England, Russia and all over the world during the beautiful mild days of winter). The Nabokovs enjoyed the beautiful sea and the nearby sunny mountains; it was in this garden paradise that the writer concluded the final chapter of *The Gift* in January 1938.

THE MANUSCRIPT

Problems of Paleography

Vladimir Nabokov was extraordinarily careful when making any statements that might provide the casual reader with details about his life as a writer. In the English-language period of his work, he deliberately created a mythologized and somewhat eccentric picture of his laboratory--index cards kept in shoe boxes. As is well known, Nabokov was skeptical about the possibility of gaining insight into an author's intentions by analyzing his manuscripts. In the introduction to his translation of *Eugene Onegin*, he writes: "An artist should ruthlessly destroy his manuscripts after publication, lest they mislead academic mediocrities into thinking that it is possible to unravel the mysteries of genius by studying cancelled readings. In art, purpose and plan are nothing; only the results count" (Nabokov 1:15). Nevertheless, this conviction did not hinder the author himself (or those close to him) from solicitously preserving his own rough drafts and sketches (for example, for some of his short stories and poems). The accumulated manuscript corpus is fertile soil for studying the creative history of Nabokov's works, his artistic logic and his techniques.

Among the texts that have been preserved, the materials for *The Gift* occupy a special place in the legacy of the author, who considered this novel the culmination and literary peak of his Russian-language career. It is difficult to say at what stage of the novel's development the text available to researchers was written. Nabokov was clearly guided by a definite principle when choosing the materials (of which a significant portion was lost during the German occupation of Paris) to hand over to the state depository for archiving. In several cases, both the rough draft and fair copy of the published work have survived (for example, the drafts of the short story "A Busy Man"). Study and comparison of the different versions make it possible to trace the evolution of the text and the manner in which Nabokov wrote it, supplementing evidence from biographical sources and memoirs.

Iosif Gessen, who knew Nabokov quite well, said of the latter's professional habits (which did change over the course of his life) that he "rewrites his works several times, introducing more and more corrections or changes, and only after this, from his dictation, is the final text hammered out" (Gessen 181). Véra Nabokov, the author's full-time editor, secretary, and archivist throughout his life, typed up his compositions. Nabokov's own numerous statements about his ability to envision the plan of a novel at once and as a whole are famous; this capacity allowed him afterward to gradually implement on paper the plan that he held in his consciousness, as if he were developing camera film. It was just this technique, as Nabokov said, that made it possible for him to start work on any part of the novel, even chronologically nonconsecutive ones, because of the precision with which he had imagined the subject, plot, and composition of the work in process. At the same time, the texts of Nabokov's Russian-period works, in the form in which they have come down to us (in the present instance, we have in mind the conventional linear method of writing them down—that is, with pen on paper, and not in pencil on cards for indexing, as was the case from the mid-1940s onward), form a coherent narrative written from the first to the last line without any substantial gaps or insertions made at later stages. From the very beginning of his literary career, Nabokov also had the habit, like clockwork, of dating a finished work, and the majority of the Russian-period manuscripts in his archive are just such definitive texts with the date on the last page.

As mentioned above, it is known about *The Gift* that the Chernyshevski chapter and the poems that the author planned to attribute to his main character, Godunov-Cherdyntsev, were written earlier than the rest of the novel. As distinct from an interviewer, a textologist can and should verify the author's version of events by studying the manuscripts. In fact, the archival sources I have examined do not contain any of Nabokov's sketches or outlines for even a single work that contained any kind of preliminary working notes (lists of names for possible characters, plot outlines, and so on). This fact alone, however, should not lead one to conclude that such groundwork for complex plot constructions (with which it must be said that the multilayered novel *The Gift* is assembled) simply did not exist, but only that Nabokov, in keeping with his declared philosophy of creative work, was in fact able to destroy these early materials. In the assessment of Brian Boyd, Nabokov's archival legacy for the most part consists of either fair copies of the works or else very advanced-stage rough copies (Boyd, "Manuscripts" 345). The palimpsestic nature of the heavily revised manuscripts of some of the Russian novels will yield a great deal, although the English-language scholars of the American Nabokov are less fortunate: the erased and heavily crossed out text on the index-card manuscripts, written with a pencil equipped with an eraser (the writer's favorite feature of this tool), are not easily decipherable. In general, Nabokov's manuscripts appear to be quite accommodating: as opposed to those of Alexander Pushkin, there are practically no sketches or vignettes in the margins. Nabokov's work produces the impression of concentrated literary labor—of an artistic plan logically brought to life.

Description of an Archival Copy

> The safety of the rough draft is the statute assuring preservation of the power behind the literary work.
> Osip Mandelstam, *Conversation about Dante*

The manuscript of Nabokov's last Russian novel is a part of the "Papers of Vladimir Vladimirovich Nabokov" collection at the Manuscript Division of the Library of Congress. Nabokov began donating various documents and manuscripts to the state depository in 1958, and the papers pertaining to *The Gift* were among them. According to the terms of the Instrument of Gift signed by Nabokov and by the Librarian of Congress (June 23, 1959), the author or his wife or son had control of both access and copyright for fifty years. After that point, the collection was to be opened, and the as yet unpublished writings by Nabokov were transferred into the public domain as of July 2009.[3]

The incomplete materials relating to *The Gift* are distributed among eight folders (Box 2, folders 3-10). The condition of the manuscript is on the whole satisfactory—the text of the first chapter is written in blue and black ink, on one side of pages of yellowish rice paper;[4] the pagination (sometimes doubled) is in the upper right corner. Nabokov's handwriting is, as a rule, quite legible. The main difficulty for the textologist when deciphering Nabokov's hand is that in the rough drafts, the author had the habit of drawing a line through the original text and inserting corrections in minute handwriting, both between lines and above the basic text; it would be fair to say that they are written anywhere there is blank space, and thus the added text is often arranged vertically on the page.

As a result of numerous layers of palimpsest and the thick lines used to mark out the text, the manuscript is almost illegible in places. The contents of the manuscript corpus of *The Gift* in the Library of Congress are as follows (in passing, I will provide additional information about the format of the text in the documents):

Folder 3. Chapter One of the novel. Advanced draft, holograph, heavy revisions and edits by the author, pages numbered 1-83; A4 paper, writing in ink.

Folder 4. Chapter Four ("The Life of Chernyshevski"). A typescript (blue ribbon) with handwritten revisions, pages numbered 1-54.

Folder 5. Continuation of the Chapter Four, pages numbered 55-108.

Folder 6. The Pink Notebook—an exercise book containing unpublished drafts and notes for a continuation of the novel.

Folder 7. Second Addendum to *The Gift*. On the first page there is a bracketed note in Nabokov's hand: "First: a short story 'Circle' (*Posled*[*nie*] *novosti*, 1934)—omit this title."

---

[3] Additions were acquired by purchase in 1971 and 1991 and in gifts from Peter Pertzoff in 1964 and Jay Wilson in 1991. The papers of Nabokov were organized and described in 1969. They were reorganized in 2000 when additional material was integrated into the collection, with further processing and description completed in 2003. Until recently, Dmitri Nabokov was responding separately to each detailed application for access submitted through the Manuscript Division; presently it is still the prerogative of the Nabokov Estate to grant the rights for publication of any material cited from this and other Nabokov-related archives. Those items acquired by the Library from persons other than the author, which are located at the end of the collection, have no access restrictions.

[4] I have provided this physical description because the Nabokov Papers in the Library of Congress, including the manuscript of *The Gift*, have recently been microfilmed (2008-2009). For conservation purposes, the originals in a collection that has been microfilmed are usually withdrawn from general circulation.

The Manuscript

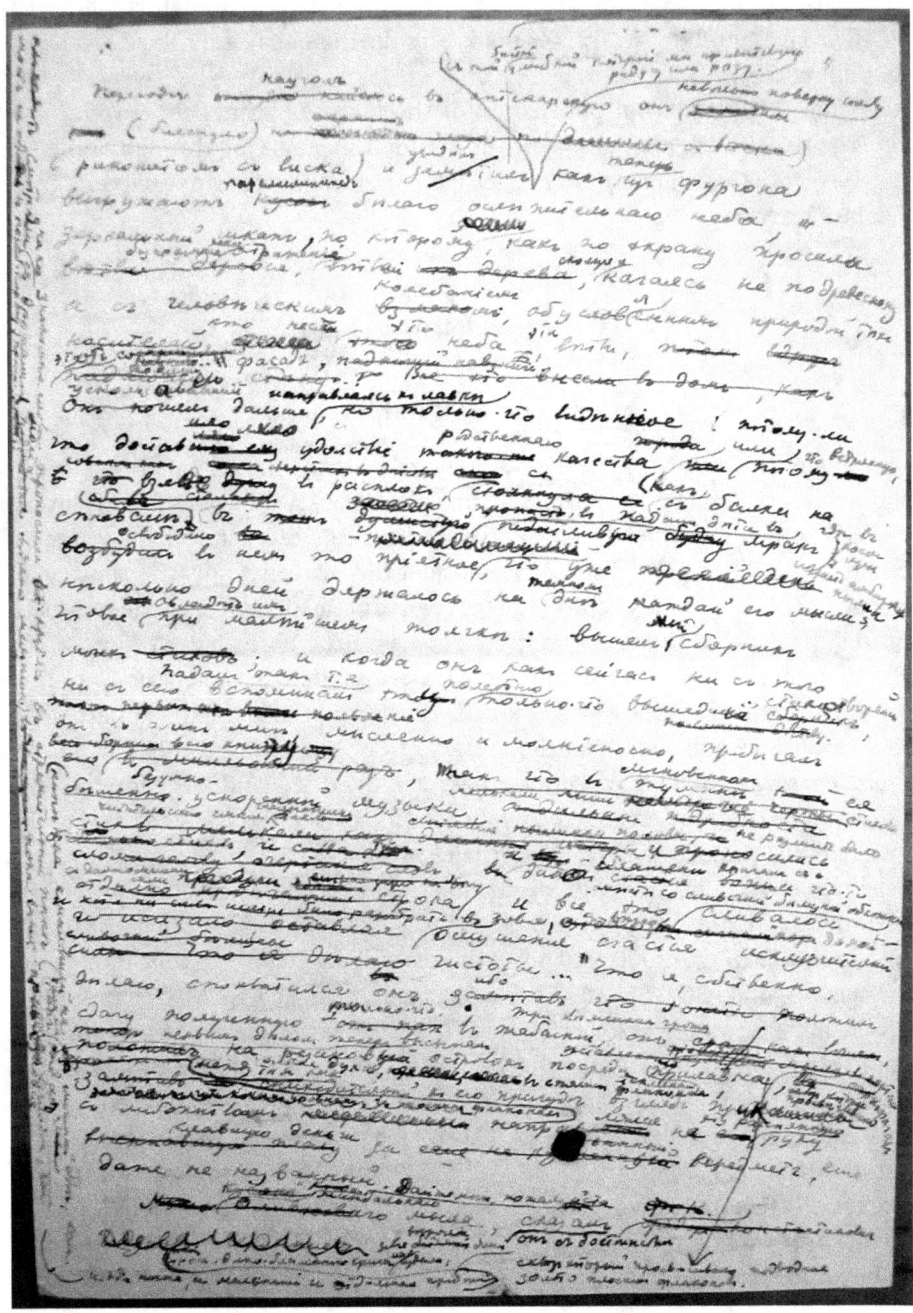

[Ill. 1-1] Page 5 of the manuscript of *The Gift*. Courtesy of the Manuscript Division, Library of Congress, Washington, D.C. Reprinted by arrangement with The Estate of Vladimir Nabokov

Folder 8. Typescript of an excerpt from the handwritten text in Folder 7 — five pages total (ends with the phrase "as the Russian headlines were making witticisms...").

Folder 9. The journal publication of the novel as printed in *Sovremennye zapiski* (1937), with minor edits by the author. Chapters One through Three.

Folder 10. Continuation of the journal publication, ending of Chapter Three, Chapter Five.

Editing

Textological Riddles

The manuscript history of *The Gift* deserves to be among the primary directions of future research on Nabokov's Russian prose of the 1930s. By general consensus, *The Gift* is the most difficult and stylistically intricate text that Nabokov created before he switched to English. Many consider this novel not only the pinnacle of Nabokov's oeuvre, but also one of the best works of Russian prose in the twentieth century. On can, without exaggeration, compare the unrivaled position of *The Gift* with that of Joyce's *Ulysses* in English literature of the same period.

Apart from the manuscript of *The Gift*, a few unpublished fragments pertaining to the novel have been held at the Library of Congress since the 1950s. One of them, consisting of 52 manuscript pages, is entitled "Second Addendum to *The Gift*." Dmitri Nabokov arranged a public reading of selected passages during the international Nabokov Festival at Cornell University in 1998. The draft has since been published in English translation under the title "Father's Butterflies" in *The Atlantic Monthly* (an excerpt) and then in *Nabokov's Butterflies: Unpublished and Uncollected Writings* (2000; full text); this was followed by the publication of the Russian original in the St. Petersburg journal *Star* (*Zvezda* 1, 2001).

In his "Note on the Translation of 'Father's Butterflies'" Dmitri Nabokov addresses the need for expertise that has arisen in deciphering Vladimir Nabokov's unpublished papers. Five initial sheets were typed by Véra Nabokov on the old Russian-language Adler, "through whose ribbons many Nabokov works had passed" (*Nabokov's Butterflies* 198). The remaining handwritten material was not entirely legible. In many places the text proved impervious even to the most discerning eyes and the text was deciphered only thanks to the efforts of Dmitri Nabokov, Brian Boyd and Jane Grayson. The problem was eventually resolved by Alexander Dolinin, who analyzed the remaining illegible portions, with the help of the Library's sophisticated equipment, which made it possible to peek under the edges of the refractory palimpsest and to identify with considerable confidence what was on the layers beneath. This work resulted in a typescript of extremely high quality, allowing the translator—Nabokov's son—to declare that "very few puzzles remain" (*Nabokov's Butterflies* 199). Parts of the archival materials in the Nabokov papers, especially those at the Library of Congress pertaining to *The Gift*, still present numerous puzzles to the researcher, who will need, in the words of Dmitri Nabokov, "to tug a remaining weed or two from the densest thickets" (Ibid.).

Around the same time that Nabokov started working on *The Gift*, Osip Mandelstam was pondering the universal challenges and individual secrets in the writer's laboratory in his *Conversation about Dante*:

> What can ignorant piety have to do with that? Dante is discussed as if he had the completed whole before his eyes even before he had begun work and as if he had utilized the technique of moulage, first casting in plaster, then in bronze. At best, he is handed a chisel and allowed to carve or, as they love to call it, "to sculpt." However, one small detail is forgotten: the chisel only removes the excess, and a sculptor's draft leaves no material traces (something the public admires). The stages of a sculptor's work correspond to the writer's series of drafts. Rough drafts are never destroyed. (Mandelstam 415)

Studying "the excess" is as valuable as following the stages of inspiration in the writer's work, especially in the case of Nabokov, who claimed that he always had "the completed whole" of the future work in his mind. Exploration of the textological riddles of *The Gift* and its immediate context (which includes the unpublished drafts, plans, sketches, printed materials that were edited, as well as Nabokov's private and business correspondence regarding publication of the novel), reveals, if not the secrets, then at least certain artistic principles that led to the writer's unique stylistic choices.

This preparatory study is intended to be the first step towards a future academic edition. Such an edition would include not only extensive commentary on the literary history, but also provide existing versions of the text that have been deciphered through careful perusal of the manuscripts. Ideally, this edition would also contain photographic reproductions of the handwritten originals, as was done with the recent publication of Nabokov's *The Original of Laura* (Knopf, 2009).

A thorough, scrupulous examination of the available parts of the manuscript of *The Gift* will enhance our understanding of how a creative genius operates, and will help to illuminate some of the more obscure parts of the work already known to us. The final product should be available both for research and for general interest, and would certainly help to increase interest in Nabokov's work among the non-Russian readership.

Chapter One. COMPOSITION AND PUBLICATION

THE UNWRITTEN PART TWO

A Satellite Story: "Krug"

The first offshoot of *The Gift* consisted of a smaller "satellite" (as Nabokov called it), "*Krug*," translated and published as a short story under the title "The Circle." It is told from the perspectives of episodic characters marginal to the main narrative of the novel (Tania, Fyodor's sister, and the schoolmaster's son, Innokentiy). The author explained the design years later:

> By the middle of 1936, not long before leaving Berlin forever and finishing *The Gift* in France, I must have completed at least four-fifths of its last chapter when at some point a small satellite separated itself from the main body of the novel and started to revolve around it. Psychologically, the separation may have been sparked either by the mention of Tanya's baby in her brother's letter or by his recalling the village schoolmaster in a doomful dream. Technically, the circle which the present corollary describes (its last sentence existing implicitly before its first one) belongs to the same serpent-biting-its-tail type as the circular structure of the fourth chapter in *Dar* [Russian title of *The Gift*] (or, for that matter, *Finnegans Wake*, which it preceded). A knowledge of the novel is not required for the enjoyment of the corollary which has its own orbit and colored fire, but some practical help may be derived from the reader's knowing that the action of *The Gift* starts on April 1, 1926, and ends on June 29, 1929 (spanning three years in the life of Fyodor Godunov-Cherdyntsev, a young émigré in Berlin); that his sister's marriage takes place in Paris at the end of 1926; and that her daughter is born three years later, and is only seven in June 1936, and not "around ten," as Innokentiy, the schoolmaster's son, is permitted to assume (behind the author's back) when he visits Paris in "The Circle." (*The Stories* 659)

In fact, Nabokov misinforms his readers by giving an erroneous date for the composition of "The Circle," which should be 1934. In an earlier letter to Roman Grynberg (November 5, 1952) Nabokov had been more sincere and admitted that he composed the story while working out the "scheme" of *The Gift* (Yangirov 378-79). Nabokov later gave a false version of the composition history of *The Gift*. He believed that, among readers familiar with the novel, the story would produce "a delightful effect of oblique recognition, of shifting shades enriched with new sense." This narrative displacement allows readers to observe the world of *The Gift* not through the eyes of Fyodor, but through those of an outsider. Innokentiy is closer to old Russia's idealistic radicals, while Fyodor's family obviously belongs to liberal aristocrats (*The Stories* 600), and thus the particular color of its perception does not always coincide with that of the main character.

The writer hoped to print this short story as the "First Addendum" to *The Gift*; the second would have been an entomological fragment suggesting yet another possible continuation that Nabokov had considered for his novel.

Catching Father's Butterflies

Although Nabokov had been producing new novels at the rate of one per year, the idea of continuing *The Gift* was still haunting his mind in the late 1930s, even after he had formally completed the novel. Brian Boyd estimates that Nabokov composed a long appendix to *The Gift* sometime in 1939 (Boyd, "Nabokov, Literature, Lepidoptera" 7). In this fifty-two page typescript, entitled "Second Addendum" in Nabokov's manuscript, the protagonist and narrator Fyodor Godunov-Cherdyntsev recounts his own early love for Lepidoptera and expounds his father's incisive but cryptic ideas on speciation and evolution, supposedly noted down in outline on the eve of his departure for the final expedition (Ibid.). Nabokov did not publish this appendix during his lifetime—first because he still hoped to expand *The Gift*, then later because of his switch to a new language—until finally he perhaps realized that the whole project was simply irrelevant in the alien cultural context.

[Ill. 1-2] The title page of the "Second Addendum" typed by Véra Nabokov

It is difficult to disagree with Boyd's assertion that those who have read "Father's Butterflies" will have noticed that it is an opaque text, though also unparalleled and unusually rewarding: "Many of its difficulties arise from its subject matter—Lepidoptera, taxonomy and evolutionary theory—and await explication from some impeccable and improbable scholar perfectly fluent in Russian and Nabokov and with an intricate knowledge of theories of speciation in the period between, say, 1890 (when Konstantin Godunov-Cherdyntsev supposedly began publishing) and 1939 (when Nabokov certainly finished writing *Father's Butterflies*)" (Boyd, "The Expected Stress" 22).

The addendum to the novel is written in the form of a scientific meditation and is framed as Fyodor's memoir. A very intimate experience for Nabokov, it was also his professional calling, as he confides to his sister Elena at a time when employment as curator of the Harvard University entomological collections seems more realistic than nebulous literary pursuits: "In a certain sense, in *The Gift*, I 'foretold' my destiny—this retreat into entomology" (November 26, 1945; *Selected Letters* 59). The hero leafs through the entomological encyclopedia, *Butterflies and Moths of the Russian Empire*, in four volumes, and reflects on both the contents and the stylistic idiosyncrasies of his father's imaginary book: "I liked the solidity of my father's method, for I liked sturdy toys. For every genus there was a supplementary list of Palearctic species that did not occur within the confines under examination, complete with precise 'references' to textual location. Each Russian butterfly was allocated from one to five pages of small print, depending on its obscurity or variability, i.e., the more mysterious or changeable, the more attention it received. In places a small map helped to assimilate the detailed description of a species' or its subspecies' distribution, just as an oval photograph in the text added something to the careful exposition of observations of the habits observed in a given butterfly" (*Nabokov's Butterflies* 209). Nabokov the entomologist dreamed of writing something such as this throughout his entire life and, actually, once came very close to fulfilling this plan in the mid-1960s; however, difficulties with finding the right publisher and the sheer scope of the project diverted him. In the preliminary sketches Nabokov teases his readers with numerous allusions to the superstructure of *The Gift* (cf. "the blue gifts" of Fyodor's childhood in the passage below). He places the roots of the protagonist's prose deeply in his father's fictitious discourse, which, for its own part, owes much to Pushkin's lucidity, linear English logic and the eloquence of the French philosophy—an ideal combination that one might suspect the writer strove for himself:

> Today, as I reread these four plump volumes (of a different color, alas, than the blue gifts brought for my childhood), not only do I find in them my fondest recollections, and revel in information that, at the time, was not as

comprehensible, but the very body, flow, and structure of the whole work touches me in the professional sense of a craft handed down. I suddenly recognize in my father's words the wellsprings of my own prose: squeamishness toward fudging and smudging, the reciprocal dovetailing of thought and word, the inchworm progress of a sentence—and even some embryos of my own parentheses. To these traits must be added my father's predilection for the semicolon (often preceding a conjunction—something one does find in the language of his university tutors: *'that scholarly pause'* an echo of unhurried English logic—but at the same time related to Montaigne whom he regarded so highly); and I doubt that the development of these traits under my frequently willful pen was a conscious act. (*Nabokov's Butterflies* 210)

According to Nabokov's chronology, *Butterflies and Moths of the Russian Empire* would have been published fifteen years prior to Fyodor's reminiscences, which took place around 1927. Fyodor confesses that because of the author's death, publication of the translation was delayed, and he has no idea where the manuscript is now. To a great extent the very feat of writing out this heavy research in four volumes can be considered a kind of *gift* from Fyodor's father to his beloved Russia—in a similar way Nabokov viewed his own novel as a paradigmatic gift to Russian literature: "The independence and proud stubbornness that had made my father write his work in his mother tongue, devoid even of the Latin synopses that, for the benefit of foreigners, were included in Russian scientific journals, did much to slow the book's westward penetration—which was a pity, for, in passing, it resolves a good number of problems regarding western fauna. Nonetheless, even if very slowly, and thanks more to illustrations than text, my father's views of relationships among species within various 'difficult' genera have to a degree already made their mark on the literature in the West" (*Nabokov's Butterflies* 212).

Between Politics, Prose and Science

Though he was seemingly detached from contemporary Soviet Russia, Nabokov remained attuned to its everyday problems and engaged in polemics with the regime much more proactively than has been presumed. An example of such latent criticism of Soviet science and its pre-revolutionary precursors is found in "Father's Butterflies":

When, on one occasion, Count B., the governor of one of our central provinces, a boyhood friend and distant relative of my father's, addressed to him an official, friendly request for a radical means of dealing with some highly energetic caterpillar that had suddenly gone on a rampage against the province's forests, my father replied, 'I sympathize with you, but do not find it possible to meddle in the private life of an insect when science does not require it.' He detested applied entomology—and I cannot imagine how he could work in present-day Russia, where his beloved science is wholly reduced to anti-locust campaigns or class struggles against agricultural saboteurs. This horrid debasement of 'sublime curiosity' and its hybridization with unnatural factors (social ones, for instance) explain (apart from the general numbing of Russia) the artificial oblivion that has befallen his work in his homeland. No wonder that even the crowning achievement among his biological reflections, that wonderful theory of 'natural classification'... has so far found no followers in Russia, and has penetrated abroad rather haphazardly and in incomplete, muddled form. (*Nabokov's Butterflies* 213)

In the original Russian text of *the addendum*, the last part of the sentence about anti-locust campaigns in the above-cited passage reads: "...*gde ego lyubimaya nauka splosh' svedena k pokhodu na saranchu ili klassovoi bor'be s ogorodnymi vrediteliami*," which is, as Victor Fet notices, an obvious pun on dual meaning of the ideologically loaded term "*vrediteli*" [saboteurs]. Agricultural (*ogorodnye*, i.e. vegetable garden) *vrediteli* are insect "pests." However, during the Stalin era the word "*vrediteli*" in general referred first of all to human "saboteurs" who were to be denounced, arrested and executed. In the original Russian phrase, the meaning is heavily weighted toward insects, thus creating a "class struggle against insects" (Fet 13). "Agricultural saboteurs" in English, as the scholar justly asserts, can only be humans, and not insects. Besides being a reference to a real problem which faced applied entomology in the south of Russia and the USSR, the anti-locust campaign ("*pokhod na saranchu*"), is also Nabokov's hidden reference to the famous incident involving Alexander Pushkin during his exile in the southern Russian city of Odessa. On May 22, 1824 Count Vorontsov, in writing, ordered young Pushkin (who was assigned to his office as a clerk) to make a report on a locust infestation. Pushkin reported, in verse:

> The locust flew, flew,
> And landed
> Sat, sat, ate all,
> And left again.

This verse is one of the few entomological poems in Pushkin's work (other than Prince Gvidon's triple metamorphosis into a mosquito, a fly, and a bumblebee in *The Tale of Tsar Saltan*). The Old World locust in question (*Locusta migratoria*, the eighth Egyptian plague) should not be confused with the "locust" found in the eastern United States, which is in fact not a locust (a type of grasshopper) but a cicada—as Shade once explained to Kinbote (*Pale Fire*, Commentary to Line 238) (Fet 14).

Pushkin's presence is not coincidental here. Fyodor had been inspired by Pushkin "while writing the now-abandoned life of his father, by the purity of Pushkin's prose and the clarity of his thought" (Boyd, "Nabokov's Butterflies" 55); he constantly contrasts Pushkin with Nikolai Chernyshevski, whose mock biography he composes. Brian Boyd sees this opposition largely in Hegelian terms, noting that Chernyshevski's life in exile in north-central Asia is as bleak and empty as Count Godunov's time "just a little farther south had been rapturous and rewarding":

> If the fulfillment Fyodor had tried to depict in his life of his father had been... a thesis not quite yet earned, and the life of Chernyshevski its antithesis, a life of frustration, Fyodor's story of his own life, *The Gift* itself, becomes a synthesis: it combines his initial chafing at his émigré existence with his retrospective realization that the apparent frustrations of the past now seem like the concealed but kindly design of a fate that has brought him his true love, Zina Mertz, and has developed his art to its full maturity. (Ibid.)

Toward the end of the "Second Addendum" this synthesis culminates in Fyodor's powerful metaphysical soliloquy: "Whatever may lie in store for the soul, however fully earthly mishaps may be resolved, there must remain a faint hum, vague as stardust, even if its source vanishes with the earth. That is why I cannot forgive the censorship of death, the prison officials of the other world, the veto imposed on the research envisioned by my father. It is not for me, alas, to complete it" (*Nabokov's Butterflies* 234). Indeed, Nabokov never completed or revisited the sequel to his last Russian novel.

In reading the addendum as a scientific manifesto, scholars have argued that the principal source of Nabokov's dissatisfaction with natural selection lay in the analogy he established between the creator of a fictional work and the Creator of the earth. This, as Leland de la Durantaye lucidly explains, should make clear to us why Nabokov never finished his "furious refutation": "Just as in the case of Goethe [and his essentially erroneous theory of colors], what motivated Nabokov's scientific claim regarding deception and mimicry was an aesthetic—or, perhaps, a theological—question. What he wished to demonstrate...was a fundamental analogy between the Book of the World and the book of the artist—and not just any artist, but himself" (de la Durantaye 155). The fact that Nabokov's hypothesis is incomplete or erroneous *as a scientific theory* takes nothing away from his art; in fact, the contrary might be asserted. Attacking natural selection was a way of attacking the utilitarianism of his age. In the addendum to *The Gift*, we read that "[n]ature found it amusing, or artistically valid, to retain, near a selected species, an elegant corollary" (*Nabokov's Butterflies* 226). Stephen Blackwell, in *The Quill and the Scalpel*, aptly supports this view of Nabokov as adopting a special strategy in his effort to explore alternative theories of speciation, based on doubts raised by mimicry: "Rather than represent the professional voice of a scientist directly, by means of his lepidopterist character, Nabokov instead has the scientist's son Fyodor, a poet and budding novelist, re-create a vision of the Russian scientific text indirectly... with the assistance of memory. Why all these added layers of complexity?... to have the technical prose grasped almost from the void, distilled, and refracted by an *artistic* mind" (Blackwell 14; italics in the original). What the reader finds in the story is not an isolated piece of scientific discourse, but "rather a scientific approach to nature that has been absorbed and interwoven with the very fabric of the artistic text itself, by means of the artist-son's consciousness and memory. Fyodor may not have fully grasped every aspect of the theory in his father's 'supplement,' but his intense urge to do so, and to integrate that experience into his art, tells us a great deal about Nabokov's ambitions for the nexus between his own scientific and artistic passions" (Blackwell 15), which cross traditional boundaries and defy typical classifications.

The Pink Notebook Mystery

The third alternative path is seen in Nabokov's possible contemplation of expanding the novel's Pushkinian conclusion and using his own completion of Pushkin's unfinished dramatic poem *Rusalka* (*The Water-Nymph*) as a transition to a sequel. In this unwritten second part the action is moved to Paris in the late 1930s (almost a decade after we leave our acquaintances in Berlin). Zina Mertz dies in a car accident and Fyodor Godunov-Cherdyntsev, as a consequence, withdraws into himself.

As with the second part of *The Gift* a century later, Pushkin's *The Water-Nymph* was left unfinished some time after 1832; it uses the familiar motif of the transformation of a drowned girl into a water spirit, combining it with the common theme of a poor girl whose upper-class lover abandons her for a more profitable marriage. Pushkin breaks off the short drama after a line in scene 6, by which time it is clear that the "little *rusalka*," the seven-year-old daughter of the Prince and the Miller's daughter, will somehow lure her father to his death in the Dnieper River and thus avenge her mother. All the works in Pushkin's cycle of "little tragedies" have non-Russian locales—France, Austria, Spain, England; *Rusalka* draws on elements of Russian folklore and the belief that a drowned girl may try to lure others to their death (Brown 134-35).

At least three scholars have attempted to decipher the cryptic contents of the modest lined exercise book with a pink paper cover (Boyd, *Russian Years* 516-20; Grayson; Dolinin, *Istinnaia zhizn'* 281-90). The lengthy entry in the front of the notebook covers 33 consecutive unnumbered sides; another entry, identified at the top of the first page as "last chapter" and ending with the single centered word "*Vse*" [meaning: "This is it"; "The End"], covers just three sides, also unnumbered, starts from the back of the notebook and proceeds in the reverse direction. The pioneering detailed description and analysis of the contents were produced by Jane Grayson (available in English); Alexander Dolinin, in a chapter of his excellent Russian-language book on Sirin, corrects some initial misreadings and, more importantly, attempts to provide a coherent interpretation and to place this unfinished draft in the context of other projects that Nabokov was working on at the time. The material in the pink notebook can be summarized as falling into four basic sections:

1) A visit by Shchyogolev's nephew, Mikhail Kostritsky, to Zina and Fyodor's Paris apartment (pages 1-15);
2) A draft of an ending to Pushkin's verse drama *Rusalka* (pages 16-19);
3) Fyodor's meetings with a French prostitute in Paris, blending prose fragments with poetic lines ("Meetings with Colette," pages 20-33);
4) The "last chapter," beginning with Zina's sudden death, featuring Falter, and ending with Fyodor reading his ending of *The Water-Nymph* to Koncheyev in Paris (back of the exercise book, pages 1-3).

The fragment is set almost a decade after the time when *The Gift* takes place. The heroes, like their creator, relocate from Berlin to Paris. Fyodor is about forty years old now, with his hair cut short, and looks slightly old-fashioned. Zina, on the other hand, is described having exactly "the same sliding, leggy walk" and "the same inclination of her narrow back" as fifteen years ago. It also becomes clear that Fyodor is now a recognized author with a few novels under his belt.

Jane Grayson is convincing in her evaluation that, while we are evidently facing a draft—"with a good deal of crossing-out, writing and re-writing"—it is at the same time clearly recognizable as a shaped piece of sequential narrative presented in a series of self-contained episodes (Grayson 28).

The Shchyogolevs, who left for Denmark at the end of the fifth chapter, are still in Copenhagen. Boris Shchyogolev's nephew, Kostritsky, appears; he is dressed untidily, with a missing tooth and bitten finger-nails. Like his uncle, the young man is engrossed in modern politics and his colloquial speech is strongly reminiscent of the style of Zina's stepfather. Kostritsky's visit in the first section turns into a distasteful conversation about politics and money between Zina and a pro-Nazi fellow at the Godunovs' tiny rented apartment. Fyodor intrudes upon that reality only to retreat from it into his poetic inner world. Kostritsky's last name derives from the words "*kostrit'*"—to lie or boast, and "*koster'*"—the tough bark of plants (see Dahl's dictionary) with possible connotations of "fiery" due to the similarity in sound to the word *kostyor* (campfire or bonfire). Kostritsky projects an ardent single-mindedness that identifies him as an heir to the Russian radical tradition established by Nikolai Chernyshevski and Turgenev's nihilists (the name of Ivan Turgenev is visible through one of the crossed-out lines in the notebook). Zina assures Kostritsky that she has nothing in common with her stepfather, that she herself is half Jewish, and that his rubbish annoys her, but the guest seems to pay little attention to these interpolations. Fyodor is less patient when he is introduced to Kostritsky. He has just come from a busy day and wants to write; seeing an irritating stranger in the house leads him to make a sharp remark to Zina and leave the apartment.

It is true, remarks Grayson, that in *The Gift* the young Fyodor at times is "shown to be arrogantly, comically at odds with his surroundings" (as when he launches into a mental diatribe against Germans on a Berlin tram, only to discover that the poor passenger who triggered this spontaneous vexation is in fact a Russian), but he is never depicted as divided against himself (Grayson 33). The scholar notes the narrative bifurcation and the character's ability to view himself as the "other," as well as the overall dark tone of this episode.

Fyodor and the Prostitute

Two episodes from the Pink Notebook, entitled "Rendezvous with Colette," are densely erotic and foreshadow future scenes in *Lolita* (although Colette is older than Dolores Haze; she is about 18-19 years old). The teasingly sexual passages may also, paradoxically, bring to mind another incomplete work by Nabokov, his last English-language novel, *The Original of Laura*. The excerpt about Fyodor and Colette is very much in tune with Gaito Gazdanov's *An Evening with Claire* (1929), a novel set mainly in Paris and telling a story of the protagonist's tormenting relationship with a young French woman named Claire. Contemporary critics compared Nabokov's prose with that of Gazdanov, who had emerged among the Russian émigré writers as the second most talented young prose writer after Sirin.

The quasi-memoir is written in "the aftermath of [Fyodor's] intense and destructive affair" (Grayson 34) with a woman, who introduces herself as Yvonne. Prostitution flourished in Paris in the 1930s and soon, during the World War II German occupation of France, twenty of the capital's leading brothels, including *le Chabanais*, *le Sphinx* and *le One Two Two*, would be reserved by the Wehrmacht for German officers and collaborating Frenchmen. During their first meeting, Fyodor takes the unknown prostitute to an adjacent hotel (a similar episode is found in Nabokov's earlier short story "The Return of Chorb," 1925). In a sort of an internal rhyme, Fyodor says his name is "Ivan"; like this false identity, "Yvonne" must also be Colette's alias for her interaction with clients. Two meetings between the protagonists take place; Fyodor arranges a third and Yvonne assures him, using the French idiom *"poser un lapin,"* that she never lets people down. However, Fyodor is either unwilling or unable to come at that point, and the affair ends as it started, in medias res.

The following episode has not been cited yet by either Grayson or Dolinin in their exceptionally thorough studies, so I will quote from it:

> He turned around and so did she. He took six steps towards her. She took three steps forward. A kind of dance. Both halted. Silence.
> The straight and transparent level of her eyes fell on the knot of his tie.
> "So, how much?" Fyodor Konstantinovich asked.
> She answered shortly and glibly.
> [crossed out: "hundred" [illegible]] listening to the echo of numbers he was able to realize, — French pun, "be carried away" [crossed out: *to take the bit between one's teeth*] — and a rhyme on a lance under the queen's window.
> And I answered: "A bit too much"
> Although I'd give mountains of gold,
> Although I knew I'd pay with my life,
> However much it takes—I will get it. [In the original the preceding four lines form a rhymed quatrain—*Y.L.*]
> Already walking away—just [out of] the corner of his eye, a moment and he will disappear... She said distinctly: *Eh bien, tant pis!* — the lady who taught music similarly forced me to strike with a little finger as if it was a small hammer when I was messing with keys.
> As soon as I gave in, she started moving—briskly and closely moving her heels—so the pavement immediately became awfully narrow and uncomfortable; then touching Fyodor Konstantinovich's elbow she led him across the street—a petite guide and a huge, sullen, exultant, terrible blind man.
> Life's comforts: straight from the street a door, yellow small hallway with a fence. She nodded to a clerk, number twelve, accompanied by the convoluted sound of a long bell.
> She went up the steep stairs rotating her slender, agile, forthright buttock. "La vie parisienne," only without a hat box.
> Such a room. A worn mirror and a bedsheet that was not fresh but had been assiduously ironed—everything as it should be, including the washstand with a single hair and a monumental bidet. A parody of a maidservant took the payment for the room and a tip, and in passing to her the money also turned counterfeit, into board game tokens, into chocolate coins. Enfin seuls.
> [Crossed out: *eighteen*; inscribed on the margins: *eighteen or nineteen?*] years old, light, diminutive, with a glossy black head, lovely greenish eyes, dimples, and dirty fingernails. It's wild luck, it's absolute luck, I can't, I am going to weep.
> "You're right," she said, "I am a slob," and started to wash her hands while singing.
> Singing and bowing, she took the banknote. And one wished to live so that no sound would be heard... – as some swarthy adolescent had written. [*In the margin*: Still, be careful: G....]

Brockhaus, same as the fifteen-year-old Efron,—is on his knees in the corner of the study.

To outwit or is it all the same? You are young and will remain young...

Noticing, anticipating, respectful and respecting his tenderness, she asked whether she should remove her lipstick.—Actually this happened during their second rendezvous. The first time it was not so important. How pretty you are! Seriously and politely she thanked for [a flattering remark?] cautiously [*deleted, and then restored*: tucking up] her net stockings to her ankles.

Her slender back [illegible] torn by darkness reflected in the mirror.

Unbelievable that this immense, dense, blind,—he didn't know how to define it—happiness, torture, a path in the remote youth—could be contained in this petite body. I will die right now. Survived but with such a groan. She commented [one detail] with short laugh:

– The one who invented this trick (ce truc-la) was pretty smart (malin).

She was not in a hurry to get dressed. Listening to the music of a barrel organ rising from the street [*deleted*: Turgenev would have recognized exactly what kind], she stood naked between the glass and the dirty muslin curtain, with one foot on the other, showing through the yellow-grey muslin.

Für die Reine alles ist Rein.[5]

Meanwhile he sat down on the undone edge of the deceived bed and started putting on his dear, comfortable shoes: the laces on the left one were still tied.

They honestly exchanged names: "Yvonne. Es toi?" "Ivan"

When they went out and said goodbye to each other she turned immediately into a boutique. Merrily: "Je vais m'acheter des bas!" which she pronounced almost like "bo"—because of delicious anticipation.[6]

The structure of this scene is obviously rather narrow compared to other parts of the Pink Notebook, especially, as Jane Grayson observes, in that there is just one viewpoint, Fyodor's, but "again his inner world is presented within the frame of an outer reality. In this case it is a remembered past framed by a narrative past" (Grayson 34). Nabokov employs the shifts between the third and first person narration so familiar to those who have read *The Gift*, and at certain moments he subjects his prose to a delicate metamorphosis into poetry.

Grayson goes on to highlight three narrative devices that mark the representation of the brief affair as evoked by Fyodor in all its forbidden intensity and beauty.

First, it is "an exercise of memory which is at the same time an exercise of the imagination and the transmutation of the raw stuff of experience into art,"

---

[5] An erroneous German quote from the New Testament: "All things are clean to the clean"—*Titus* 1:15.

[6] The Nabokov Collection, Library of Congress; the transcript and translation are mine. I am indebted to A. Dolinin and M. Malikova for their invaluable help with deciphering the original manuscript.

when an adulterous relationship with a common prostitute, sexual gratification obtained in the most tawdry fashion, becomes a subject of a powerful and inspiring experience transcending into a high art of poetry (Grayson 35).

The second device that Fyodor calls upon is irony: he "values and emphasizes the discrepancy, the complete mismatch between his arousal and the heavy emotional involvement" (ibid.) and Colette-Yvonne's blithe, routine professionalism.

Finally, "to keep his aesthetic and moral balance, and not slip into pornography or *poshlost*'" (Nabokov's favorite word for "triteness"; ibid.), Fyodor/narrator employs the literary pastiche, ranging from general musings on the nature of parody to concrete allusions to Alexander Blok's poem, possibly also about a prostitute, *"Neznakomka"* ("The Unknown Woman," 1906).

Alexander Dolinin greatly expands Grayson's list of literary allusions, showing how in this passage — compact but lavish with references — Fyodor summons the "Russian word, the dozing word" (this very quote demonstrates Nabokov's preoccupation with sheer sound play — *"russkoe slovo, solovoe slovo"*; Dolinin, "Znaki i simvoly" 512, n. 7). The episode, which hardly occupies two handwritten pages, includes references to Pushkin ("swarthy adolescent") and his works such as "Kniaziu A.M. Gorchakovu" ("To Count Gorchakov") and *The Stone Guest*; poems by Afanasii Fet; Evgenii Baratynsky; Vassily Zhukovsky, and it even parodies the name of the Soviet writer Maxim Gorky ("maksimal'no gor'kii," literally: "maximally bitter") (Dolinin, *Istinnaia zhizn'* 287). The profoundly "literature-centric" nature of the episode is also emphasized by the split appearance of the names Brockhaus and Efron (publishers of the Russian-language encyclopedia in 86 volumes, a counterpart of the Brockhaus Enzyklopädie and the Encyclopedia Britannica, which was printed in Imperial Russia in 1890–1906). Here Brockhaus and Efron are mentioned as the publishers of Pushkin's complete works, edited by Vengerov; most likely, a boy is reading Pushkin's erotic verses in this edition.

And again one cannot help noticing parallels between this fragmentary project and *The Original of Laura*, the last incomplete novel in English which Nabokov was struggling to finish before his death. Here Fyodor quotes from the dialogue between Don Karlos and Laura in Pushkin's short drama *The Stone Guest* (1830) — "You are young and will remain young" (Colette is "about eighteen years old"):

> Don Karlos:
> Tell me, Laura,
> How old are you?
>
> Laura:
> I am eighteen.

Chapter One. COMPOSITION AND PUBLICATION

Don Karlos:
> You are young... and will remain young
> For another five or six years during which
> Men will surround you,
> Fondle, foster, and present gifts,
> And entertain with nightly serenades... [...]

Laura:
> ...Come here, open the balcony. The sky is so silent.
> [...] While far off, in the north — in Paris —
> The sky perhaps is covered with black clouds...
>   (Pushkin 384-385; my translation)

Nabokov's Parisian girl of the same age is likewise seen standing near the window, between the glass and a muslin curtain. Blending Pushkin's Laura, who dreams of Paris, and Colette in that city in the present day, Nabokov links the past and present into a visual and poetic rhyme—"'La vie parisienne,' only without a hat box" may refer to the popular magazine of the same title, whose covers were usually adorned with sexually suggestive pictures. A transformative technique was possibly hinted at by the insertion of another clue in the title of Jacques Offenbach's opéra bouffe, "*La vie parisienne*" ("Parisian life"). The latter was turned by Robert Siodmak into a film around the same time (the French version premiered in January 1936 in Paris): the poster featured a frivolous image of a curvaceous leg pointing to a man's hat.

About a year later Fyodor returns to that corner of Paris where he had agreed to meet Yvonne. Godunov-Cherdyntsev has not written to her since they parted, despite having her address. Neither did he warn her that he was coming, although he knew that she regularly traveled up to Paris from Meudon, where her father worked as a gardener. Fyodor is tormented by unanswered questions ("Who is she? A girl in quotation marks, mid-priced, and because he is sad and intent, and obsessed with imagination which can be used to his disadvantage, most probably at an extra premium for him"; my translation). Grayson believes that this "reliance on chance is quite intentional, for he is well aware that he is engaging in a kind of moral and aesthetic brinkmanship" (35); deep down, Fyodor probably wishes this meeting would never occur.

As Fyodor walks past the urinals on the Paris street corners, mumbling a kind of panegyric to the French capital for all its mixture of lust and beauty, the "Yvonne-Ivan" combination playfully evokes another literary subtext—the poet Georgii *Ivan*ov's daring novella, *Disintegration of the Atom* (*Raspad atoma*, 1938). Published in Paris in a meagre edition of 200 copies, it provoked controversies in the émigré press ranging from attacks by Khodasevich to praise by Zinaida Gippius. One of the scornful responses came from Nabokov himself:

[Ill. 1-3] Maurice Pepin, "Nude in the Moonlight" (*Le Sourire*, 1923)

[Ill. 1-4] *La Vie Parisienne*. Cover of the magazine featuring a girl with a hat box next to her (France, 1925)

[Ill. 1-5] Poster for Robert Siodmak's movie *La Vie Parisienne* (1936)

> ...This miserable pamphlet with its amateur searches for God and banal renderings of street urinals (descriptions that might embarrass only green readers) is simply very bad. [...] Georgii Ivanov should never have been frolicking with prose. (*Sovremennye zapiski* 70, 1940: 284)

Celebrating "the pale advertisement bananas next to the multi-legged urinals on the street corner," Fyodor takes aim at Ivanov's *flâneur*, who pathetically reveals his spiritual and corporeal experiences:

> I am walking down the avenue, thinking about God, staring at the feminine faces. I like that one, she is pretty. I imagine how she washes her lower parts. Feet planted apart, knees slightly bent. Stockings slipping down her knees, her deep dark eyes look innocent and bird-like. I am convinced that an average Frenchwoman, as a rule, washes her lower parts fastidiously, but rarely washes her legs. What for? She is always in her stockings, frequently without even removing her shoes. I am thinking about France in general. About the nineteenth century, that still lingers on here...about baguettes getting wet in the public urinals [...] I am thinking about war [...] I am thinking about the banality of such thoughts...I am thinking about an epoch disintegrating in front of my eyes. About two basic kinds of women: either already prostitutes or those proud that they aren't yet in the business of prostitution. [...] Woman as a self does not exist. She is a body and a reflected light. But here you have absorbed all my light and left. And all my light is gone away too. (Ivanov 8-9; my translation)

The agile but slovenly Colette is also shown during her most intimate rituals; she disappears from Fyodor's life taking along "the light of his life, fire of his loins," to paraphrase a later work by Nabokov.

Omry Ronen calls Nabokov's strategy an "antiparody." After studying Nabokov's baffling "*Parizhskaia poema*" ("The Parisian Poem," printed in *Novyi zhurnal* 47, 1944; possibly started in the late 1930s, in France), Ronen pointed to Georgii Ivanov's *Disintegration of the Atom*, which is "subjected to fission in Nabokov's long poem by being bombarded with references to the utmost stage of Russian poetry's and Russian soul's decay" (the graphomaniac poet and assassin Gorgulov, beheaded in Paris for killing the French president Doumer in 1932; [Ronen 68]).

As the drafts from the Pink Notebook demonstrate, Nabokov's reading of his archenemy's work was quite careful. The fact that Nabokov transmits a parallel experience to one of his own closest authorial "representatives," Godunov-Cherdyntsev, makes us wonder whether, at least to some extent, he had also shared similar views.

Where Might All of This Lead?

The problem of the texts comprising the mysterious notebook does not lie exclusively in their fragmentary nature or in the unfilled gaps in the narrative; it also stems from certain arcane connections with Nabokov's other writings of the time. One such puzzling link leads us to the prophetic character Falter from the short story "Ultima Thule." The author later claimed that this story was to be the first chapter of the unfinished novel, *Solus Rex*. Nabokov worked on the story during the winter of 1939-40, but "except for two chapters and a few notes...destroyed the unfinished thing" (*The Stories* 663). Could Nabokov, in mentioning "a few notes," have been referring to the contents of the Pink Notebook? If, based on the fact that Falter makes an appearance there, the answer is yes, this hypothesis might shed a whole new light on the status and possible plot developments of the unfinished second part of *The Gift*.

Based on the outline of the "last chapter," featuring Falter and a conversation between Fyodor and Koncheyev (the three pages at the back of the notebook), Alexander Dolinin has put forth a compelling theory (*Istinnaia zhizn'* 281). According to his hypothesis, "Solus Rex" is the very beginning of the eponymous novel as it was published in *Sovremennye zapiski*, while "Ultima Thule" is a fragment of the novel whose position in the whole remains unknown. Later, when Nabokov translated them into English, he constructed a legend of their origins that did not correspond to the facts.

The two short stories, "Ultima Thule" and "Solus Rex," can be viewed not as sketches of a completely new novel but as embryonic texts that, along with the typescript of "Father's Butterflies," were to serve as inserted chapters in the continuation of *The Gift* — in the manner of "The Life of Chernyshevski" or the father-explorer's journey to Asia in the "first" volume.

The dominant mood of what was probably intended to become the last chapter of the second volume of *The Gift* is one of lost direction and a sense of futility (Grayson 45). Godunov-Cherdyntsev reads his ending of Pushkin's unfinished drama *The Water-Nymph* to Koncheyev, who is now a famous Russian poet-in-exile, during a German air raid in Paris. As Fyodor and Koncheyev speak, sirens begin sounding. As opposed to the two imaginary conversations contained in *The Gift*, this encounter is real. When Koncheyev is taking his leave Fyodor suddenly confronts him with a strange question: "*Donesem?*" (literally: "Shall we carry it through?"). Dolinin's interpretation of this is as follows: "contrary to what Koncheyev thinks, it refers not to their chances of physical survival in the war but to their obligation as Russian writers to keep alive the legacy of Russian literature bequeathed to them by their fathers and to pass it on to the next generations of writers. Fyodor's own attempt to complete Pushkin's unfinished work in a time of personal and social disasters is the ultimate symbolic gesture, an avowal of filial

Chapter One. COMPOSITION AND PUBLICATION

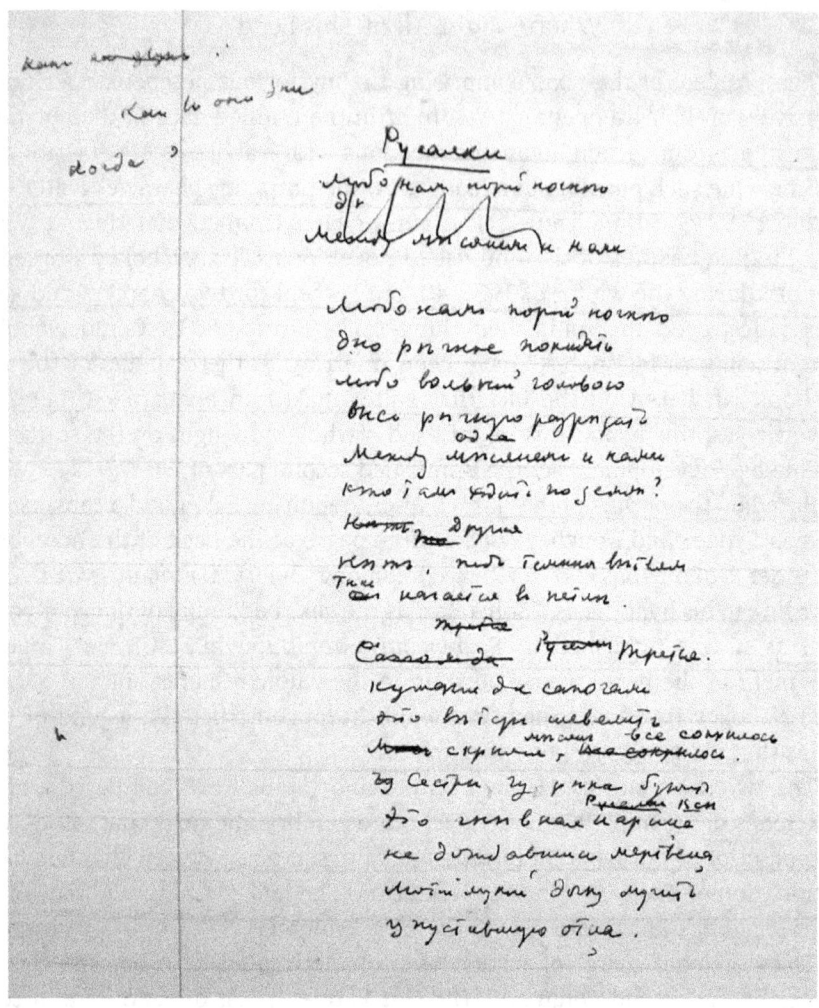

[Ill. 1-6] Page with the poem *Rusalka* from the Pink Notebook (Library of Congress)

loyalties that Nabokov himself later chose to forsake" ("Nabokov as a Russian writer," 62). Pushkin's 1827 poem, "*Akafist Ekaterine Nikolaevne Karamzinoi*" ("A Canticle to Ekaterina Karamzin"), contains another clue, a line about the messenger who "carries his gift with reverence"—"*Svoi dar neset s blagogoven'em.*" It was Nikolai Karamzin's *History of the Russian State* that provoked Pushkin to write his drama *Boris Godunov*, which was first printed in 1831, ironically with two scenes omitted due to the tensions with Czarist censorship.

In support of Dolinin's theory (*Istinnaia zhizn'* 288), it should also be noted that one of the rough plotlines in Nabokov's unrealized plan involves Fyodor's fleeting affair with a certain Madame Blagovo (*Muza Blagoveshchenskaia*), whose very aristocratic surname (meaning "good news" in the evangelical sense, and also connoting "awe," "veneration," and "bliss") echoes the last word of the quoted line from Pushkin's poem. The idea of cultural inheritance and artistic bliss was apparently intended as the third aesthetic pillar of the unwritten second volume. And although the sense of doom and the apocalypse of a civilization permeates this final chapter, moving from Fyodor's personal crisis to a large-scale political tragedy (more on a loss of direction and a sense of futility see Grayson 45), the "good news" is still part of the novel's legacy; that much, at least, is contained in the hope of perpetual literary renewal and historical continuity.

By the time Nabokov could shape any distinct vision for his characters' future, his mind had already turned to the task of writing fiction in English. *The Real Life of Sebastian Knight* was completed in January 1939. Although Nabokov "was still not ready to relinquish Russian," as Brian Boyd asserts, the spring of that year "seems the likeliest time" for him to have written the "Second Appendix to *The Gift*" (*Russian Years* 504; 505). None of the seeds sown for the continuation of *The Gift* were destined to blossom. The unfinished novel *Solus Rex*, perhaps the very nucleus of the second volume, if Dolinin's suggestion is correct, was left as a series of disjointed sketches that were printed as two separate short stories; some motifs later evolved into scenes in *Lolita* and *Pale Fire*.

Adolph Hitler's army was marching towards Paris when a German bomb hit the Nabokovs' apartment house on rue Boileau. The dreadful sound of sirens seems to have been echoed in the draft of the projected second part of *The Gift*. It was time for the Nabokov family to embark on the boat *Champlain* for the United States—the plan to continue *The Gift* was never realized. It remained as it was, with the existing complement of poems and butterflies.

In his new homeland Vladimir Nabokov submitted the "completion" of Pushkin's *The Water-Nymph* as a whole piece to *Novyi zhurnal* (*New Journal* 10, 1942). This Russian-language American thick journal would become the writer's primary venue for works written in his native language during his early years in the USA. The magazine was edited by the writer Mark Aldanov, who as late as mid-April 1941 would still inquire from New York: "Do not forget that you have definitely promised us your new novel—the continuation of *The Gift*" (Chernyshev 128). His friend had nothing to offer; the Pink Notebook remains the only slim testimony to what eventually might be seen as one of the most interesting, haunting sequels ever written by Nabokov.

Nabokov bid farewell to *Muza Blagovo* to make his fundamental decision to harness the English-language muse. As if to fold the patterned rug of life (resorting to Nabokov's favorite metaphor), Anna *Ivan*ovna Blagovo will resurface as the long-necked typist and wife of the Russian émigré writer vv in 1974, in Nabokov's final published novel before his death.

The History of Publication

Serialized in the Press

Throughout the 1930s Nabokov's major works usually appeared in the magazine *Sovremennye zapiski* (*Contemporary Annals*). It is not surprising that from the outset *The Gift* was intended for publication in installments in that journal.[7] The most prestigious and liberal mainstay on the spectrum of literary and political journalism in the Russian community abroad, the periodical was founded in Paris in 1920. The journal was enormously popular among the Russian-speaking diaspora from Prague to Shanghai, and was run by a group of Nabokov's older compatriots: Mark Vishniak, Vadim Rudnev, Alexander Gukovsky, Nikolai Avksentiev, and Ilya Fondaminsky-Bunakov. Although these were, for the most part, former Socialist Revolutionary party members, that fact rarely influenced the journal's tolerant political stance (The tsarist police considered the SRs extremely dangerous; between 1902 and 1905, their small, highly disciplined Combat Detachment assassinated two interior ministers, the Moscow governor-general, and other officials).

During the two decades of its existence, *Sovremennye zapiski* published seventy volumes (3-4 books annually, between 300-500 pages in each issue). Among the contributors were writers with established reputations such as Ivan Bunin, Vladislav Khodasevich, Georgii Adamovich, Mikhail Osorgin, Boris Zaitsev, Lev Shestov, Nikolai Berdiaev, and Dmitri Merezhkovsky. They were soon joined by a talented younger cohort—Nina Berberova, Vladimir Nabokov, Gaito Gazdanov, Boris Poplavsky, and others.

Chapter Four of *The Gift*, which consists entirely of Fyodor Godunov-Cherdyntsev's biography of Chernyshevski, was omitted due to editorial pressure. Nabokov agreed to the omission with great reluctance, realizing that this was the price he needed to pay to have the novel published at all. Vishniak writes in his memoirs that in the judgment of the editors, "the life of Chernyshevski was depicted with such naturalistic—and even physiological—particulars, that its artistic value became dubious" (Vishniak 180). Vishniak recalls the general principles applied by the journal to editing and revising:

> The editorial board viewed itself as something more than a mere mediator between an author and typography; it had every right *to edit* the material

---

[7] *Sovremennye zapiski* 63 (April 1937): 5-87 (ch. One); 64 (September 1937): 98-150 (ch. 2); 65 (December 1937): 5-70 (chs. Two [cont.]—Three); 66 (May 1938): 5-42 (ch. Three [cont.]); 67 (October 1938): 69-146 (ch. Five). Also see: Dolinin, "K istorii sozdaniia i tisneniia romana 'Dar'."

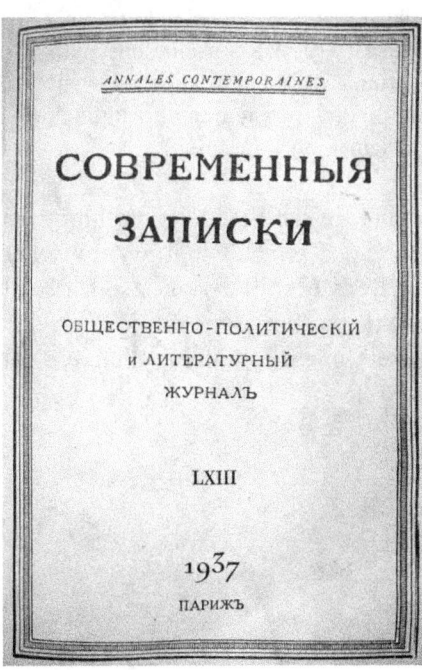

[Ill. 1-7] The cover of the issue of *Sovremennye zapiski* 63 (April 1937) in which *The Gift* was printed

[Ill. 1-8] Table of Contents

[Ill. 1-9] The first page of the novel as it appeared in the magazine

submitted to the journal. Often the editorial board preferred simply to omit the material deemed inappropriate without any special consultations with authors, who were informed about it post factum. This usually happened when the deleted text seemed inessential and could not seriously hurt the author's argument. (Vishniak 180, n. 2; italics in the original; my translation)

Nabokov's case was different, of course, because of the ideological motives behind this unprecedented censorship decision, which, contrary to what Vishniak said years later, clearly hurt the writer's overall design. After a brief but desperately exhaustive exchange between the author of the mock biography and the editors of *Sovremennye zapiski*, the installment containing Chapter Five appeared in Issue 67 of the magazine as follows:

Chapter 4

....
....

Chapter 5

Two weeks after the publication of "The Life of Chernyshevski" /.../

The accompanying explanatory note read: "See *Sovremennye zapiski* Nos. 63, 64, 65, 66. Chapter Four, consisting entirely of 'The Life of Chernyshevsky,' written by the novel's protagonist, has been omitted with the consent of the author." It was signed by the editors, but had actually been composed by Rudnev.

In addition to being serialized, incomplete, in *Sovremennye zapiski* (April 1937—October 1938), the novel was also excerpted in the authoritative Russian daily, *Poslednie novosti* (*The Latest News*).[8] Although "The Life of Chernyshevski" did not make it into either of these two major émigré media outlets, the marginal Parisian newspaper with the optimistic name *Bodrost'* (*Cheerfulness*) featured an extract from the omitted chapter ("The Arrest of Chernyshevski," *Bodrost'* 256, December 31, 1939: 3-4). It seems that Fondaminsky was behind this publication (Livak 828-29).

The Censored Fourth Chapter

Nabokov was not entirely naïve in his evaluation of the probable response when he submitted the controversial chapter to his peers, although he had certainly

---

[8] Excerpts appeared in *Poslednie novosti*, March 28, 1937; May 2, 1937; December 25, 1937; February 15, 1938; April 24, 1938.

Даръ *)

ГЛАВА 4.

. . . .
. . . .

ГЛАВА 5.

Спустя недѣли двѣ послѣ выхода «Жизни Чернышевскаго» отозвалось первое, безхитростное эхо. Валентинъ Линевъ (Варшава) написалъ такъ:

«Новая книга Бориса Чердынцева открывается шестью стихами, которые авторъ почему-то называетъ сонетомъ (?), а засимъ слѣдуетъ вычурно-капризное описаніе жизни извѣстнаго Чернышевскаго.

Чернышевскій, разсказываетъ авторъ, былъ сыномъ «добрѣйшаго протоіерея» (но когда и гдѣ родился, не сказано), окончилъ семинарію, а когда его отецъ, проживъ святую жизнь, вдохновившую даже Некрасова, умеръ, мать отправила молодого человѣка учиться въ Петербургъ, гдѣ онъ сразу, чуть ли не на вокзалѣ, сблизился съ тогдашними «властителями думъ», какъ ихъ звали, Писаревымъ и Бѣлинскимъ. Юноша поступилъ въ университетъ, занимался техническими изобрѣтеніями, много работалъ и имѣлъ первое романтическое приключеніе съ Любовью Егоровной Лобачевской, заразившей его любовью

---

*) См. «Совр. Зап.» № № 63, 64, 65, 66. — Глава 4-ая, цѣликомъ состоящая изъ «Жизни Чернышевскаго», написанной героемъ романа, пропущена съ согласія автора. — **Ред.**

[Ill. 1-10] Chapter 5 as it appeared in *Sovremennye zapiski* with the short editorial explanation as a footnote

underestimated it. He had at least a few opportunities to test the reactions of contemporaries among the émigré community to the scandalous biography while it was still in progress. On April 6, 1935, Nabokov read an excerpt from the recently composed "The Life of Chernyshevski" at Iosif Gessen's home, and over a hundred listeners turned up to hear Sirin on that day (Boyd, *Russian Years* 418). The fact that Nabokov had put so much more time into writing *The Gift* than any previous work made the refusal to publish it unadulterated all the more frustrating. Of Nabokov's six novels written over the course of the preceding five years, none had been subjected to forced revisions, let alone having any text declined.

Though in the novel Fyodor's publishers initially reject "The Life of Chernyshevski," Nabokov could hardly have imagined that his own colleagues would themselves hold back the corresponding part of *The Gift*. Chapter Three of the novel was written after the incident with Rudnev and Chapter Four. In fact, making Vasiliev refuse Chernyshevski's biography, Nabokov responded to Rudnev's rejection and parodied his arguments (Dolinin, "K istorii sozdaniia i tisneniia romana 'Dar'" 346). The fictional author ends up more fortunate than the real-life Nabokov: Fyodor does find an outlet for his work in Chapter Five, while Nabokov "was not allowed publicly to slaughter the holy cow of the Russian liberal intelligentsia" (Davydov 423). Later, in his foreword to the English translation of the novel (1962), Nabokov accurately described the history of the omission of Chapter Four by *Sovremennye zapiski* as "a pretty example of life finding itself obliged to imitate the very art it condemns." At the time of the refusal, however, Nabokov was not as pithy, as revealed by the tirades he addressed to the editors.

Nabokov's four letters to Vadim Rudnev and one to Ilya Fondaminsky unveil this exceptional case in the history of Russian émigré literature in great detail.[9] In the words of the translator and commentator, Gene Barabtarlo, these letters "show well how Nabokov's initially buoyant, if slightly assumed, surety that the chapter will be published in or out of sequence turns first to hopeful disbelief that it may not and then to bitter disappointment when he has realized that for reasons of camphor-ball ideology 'The Life of Chernyshevski' will not be placed in the *Sovremennye zapiski* and indeed anywhere else" ("Nabokov's Chernyshevski" 15). Let us recapitulate the events in the order in which they occurred.

On December 27, 1934, Nabokov addressed Rudnev:

---

[9] All four letters first appeared in Russian in the almanac *The Bygone* (*Minuvshee*) (Paris: Atheneum) 8, 1989: 274-81, with a Foreword and commentaries by Vladimir Alloy. The English version used here was published the following year in a translation by G. Barabtarlo ("Nabokov's Chernyshevski" 15-23); Nabokov's letter to Rudnev from August 10, 1937 is quoted in B. Boyd's translation (*Russian Years* 442). Translations from all of Vadim Rudnev's letters are mine, and are based on the originals in the Manuscript Division, Library of Congress, Washington, D.C.

Dear Vadim Viktorovich,

Very soon you should receive at last the manuscript [of *Invitation to a Beheading*]; I am only now completing the correction and revision. Anna Lazarevna [Feigin, Véra Nabokov's cousin] advised you of my financial situation. Thank you for offering an advance, it would be most welcome. Anna Lazarevna told me that some short piece of mine could be published in the next issue of C[ontemporary] A[nnals]); in talking with you she mentioned an excerpt from Chernyshevski. I, too, had been considering plucking a chunk out of it but upon examining what I had written I concluded that for the time being one could cull nothing either from Chernyshevski or from the novel of which it will be a component, without damaging the whole. One day soon I shall write a little story. I am afraid that it will be too late for the next issue but do let me know the deadline, just in case. [...] I wish you a pleasant holiday and shake your hand.

A few weeks later Nabokov tried to explain the importance of the research on Chernyshevski: "I have been working on the novel 'about Chernyshevski' for two years now but it is far from being ready for print, to say nothing of the fact that the range of readers able to comprehend it will be perhaps even more limited" (February 11, 1935).

The first chapter of *The Gift* was finally published in Issue 63 of *Sovremennye zapiski* after a two-year wait. It had been a common practice between the editors and their experienced authors, who understood the publication schedule, that a work in progress could be submitted on a chapter by chapter basis. This was certainly the case with Nabokov, who was a loyal contributor to the journal. None of the members of the editorial team could foresee the surprise that awaited them after the first chapter of Sirin's new novel had been delivered. When time came to submit the next chapter for Issue 64, instead of the expected Chapter Two Nabokov dispatched to Paris Chapter Four. Perplexed, Vadim Rudnev inquired about the reason for this:

Dear Vladimir Vladimirovich,

I just received your manuscript by mail and was quite happy. Without even reading the text I wanted to take it right away to the typography where they expect to work on it, but then I read your letter...and it caused me great chagrin...What happened?

Instead of the promised continuation of the novel begun in the last issue you sent us a chapter from the end of the book, and you suggest printing the novel in the order: 1, 4, –2, 3, —, 5...

How this can be possible? To start such a big and "Sirin-like" thing, i.e. a novel that is pretty complex in and of itself, in this strange order, — I assure you that the readers might interpret it simply as a mockery. Though you yourself, it seems, scarcely take the readers' opinions into consideration, but the editorial board, this humble editorial board, cannot permit itself to do that. I can hardly imagine that you have seriously thought that such a paradox really "suits" us and is to the good of the journal.

I am lost in guesses as to what might happen. It is clear to me that in our previous agreements and correspondence you referred to the second chapter, which you promised to send here any day. Trusting your word, I did little to press the other prospective authors in the literary section, and even gave some of them "time off"—and here I am now, in the very last days, when nothing can be done,—facing Volume 64 on the brink of a catastrophe...

Let's look together for a way out of this situation; I believe I have every right to rely upon you.

The only explanation for this whole mess that comes to my mind is that while working on the real continuation (Chapter Two) until very recently, you did not have enough time to polish it as intended. Therefore, instead of sending it in a raw form, you've opted to send Chapter Four, which you already had in reserve.

As the only feasible solution, may I suggest that you send us an excerpt from the second chapter for the forthcoming issue 64, at least a portion of it, or as much as you can finalize in the days remaining? We could even place your novel this time at the very end instead of the opening of the literary section, and if you keep sending me parts of the manuscript, the deadline can be extended until the 18th or even 20th [of August 1937]. I know how undesirable this fragmentation might be for you (and for the journal)—but I can't blame myself; if you send me the entire chapter by 20th, I am ready to print it in toto. Another possibility is to postpone the serialization of the entire novel until the December volume while we wait for the normal sequence to be resumed. However, what we shall do with the literary section in this issue remains a mystery to me. (August 4, 1937)

In conclusion, Rudnev, unable or unwilling to conceal his devastation, urged Nabokov to respond as quickly as possible. To this plight, Nabokov replied on August 6, 1937:

Just as I thought, the substitution of one chapter for another alarmed you at first blush. I do not doubt, however, that you are over the initial apprehension now that you have read the chapter, and that you have changed your opinion: after all, this is not a random chapter from the middle of the book, with a plot development yet unknown to the reader, but a completely separate piece of independent value. (My hero and I have worked at it for four years). This is precisely what I meant when I wrote that I considered placing "The Life of Chernyshevski" to be both valuable and profitable for the magazine. On the other hand, I can understand why you are reluctant to print the chapters in the sequence 1-4-2-3-5. Therefore, here is my proposition: 1. Either do not put any chapter number at all and make no mention of *The Gift* but rather entitle the thing simply "The Life of Chernyshevski," or 2. Print it under the title *The Gift* but head it with "Chapter Two" (instead of "Four").

As regards the second chapter: while working on it most rigorously here, I have come to the conclusion that its entire opening is in need of revamping, which should take me many more weeks of assiduous composition.

Sorry that I should have unwittingly upset you but what I propose seems to be a perfectly happy solution.

For Rudnev this proposition certainly did not appear to be a "perfectly happy" solution. "To tell you the truth," he wrote back, "I hoped that my suggestion would be acceptable and everything would be 'worked out' one way or another. To my enormous disappointment, I see this is not the case" (letter signed August 10-13, as dated in the original). Significantly, the technical problems were complicated by the fact that Rudnev had finally had a chance to familiarize himself with the contents of the chapter in question. What he discovered there was beyond all expectations. Although the editor tried to appease Nabokov, he also made clear that the chapter was so provocative that it may not be acceptable:

> I sincerely believe that "The Life of Chernyshevski" is *one of your most notable pieces*. The work is, without a doubt, venomous, scoffing from start to end, murderous for poor Ch[ernyshevski] — but devilishly strong at the same time. And it is precisely because Ch[ernyshevski] is not a fictional character but a historical figure, and what is more — one who played a crucial role in the Russian national liberation movement — for that reason, my dear Vladimir Vladimirovich, inevitably and regardless of either your or my wishes, one question arises: is it appropriate to judge *such* a work solely on the ground of its *artistic* merits and not to apply *social* criteria? (Italics throughout belong to Rudnev — Y.L.)

The question was largely rhetorical for Rudnev, who further explained that since two of his co-editors, Vishniak and Avksentiev, were currently away from Paris he was hesitant to take the sole responsibility for a "political" decision regarding the possible inclusion of this explosive material in the forthcoming issue.

The diplomatically stated rejection constituted a declaration of war for Nabokov. He wrote back saying that he had read the letter carefully and found its contents distressing:

> By your refusal for reasons of censorship to print the fourth chapter of *The Gift* you make it impossible for me to publish this novel at all with you. Do not be angry, but judge for yourself. How can I give you the second and third chapters (in which there already begin to show the images and evaluations rejected by you and developed in the fourth) and then the concluding chapter (in which among other things there are four complete reviews of "The Life of Chernyshevski" variously scolding its author for offending against the memory of "a great man

of the Sixties" and explaining how sacred his memory remains) when I know that *The Gift* will be not a whole but a hole [*v Dare budet dyra*] with no fourth chapter.... I'll tell you straight out, I can accept no compromises or joint efforts and have no intention of striking out or altering a single line. Your turning down the novel hurts all the more because I have always harbored a special feeling for *Sovremennye zapiski*. The fact that from time to time it has printed both creative work and articles developing views with which the editors plainly could not be in agreement has been a singular phenomenon in the history of our journals and a declaration of freedom of thought... that was a telling indictment of the situation of the press in present-day Russia. Why do you talk of "society's reaction" to my piece? Let me say, dear Vadim Viktorovich, that society's reaction to a literary work can only be a consequence of its artistic function, and not an a priori judgment. I do not intend to defend my "Chernyshevski"—the thing is, in my ultimate view, on a plane where it needs no defense. I merely note for your coeditors that as a fighter for freedom Chernyshevski is in no way belittled—and not because I have done this consciously (as you know, I am quite indifferent to every political party in the world) but no doubt because there was more justice in one camp and more evil in the other. If Vishniak and Avksentiev respected Chernyshevski not only as a revolutionary but as a thinker and critic (which is the main theme of the thing) then my researches could not fail to convince them. (August 10, 1937)

Nabokov then drew Rudnev's attention to the "curious situation" he himself was in: he would not be able to publish the ominous chapter with any Soviet publisher or rightist press; nor with *Poslednie novosti* or his customary thick journal: "You ask me to find some way out for *Sovremennye zapiski*: may I point out that my own situation has no exit at all" (Boyd, *Russian Years* 442). Nabokov concluded with the request "not to interpret this letter as a burst of authorial arrogance," adding that he writes his novels for himself and prints them for money, thus paraphrasing the famous Pushkinian formula that a poet's inspiration is not for sale, but the manuscript can be. "[T]he rest is but the folly of fortuitous fate, tasty tidbits, spring peas to go with my chickens. But it is sad that you should close for me the only magazine that I find suitable and of which I am very fond," Nabokov reiterated.

The implicit threat did not work—the editorial board stood firm.

A few days passed, and after receiving the unequivocal "no," the rejected author shared his anguish with another editor, the friendly but helpless Ilya Fondaminsky, who had just begun editing a new magazine entitled *Russian Annals* in 1937:

> Dear Ilya Isidorovich,
> You are probably aware of my correspondence with Rudnev regarding Chernyshevski. Today I received his letter, which left me no choice but to reply

as I did: I enclose a copy of my letter to him. I can't tell you how distressing I find the decision of *Sovremennye zapiski* to censor my art by applying old partisan prejudices.

Kindly let me know, by return post if possible, whether you intend to keep your promise to print "Chernyshevski" in the *Russian Annals*, if it comes to that. If so, could you then possibly publish it in the very next issue in place of the short story ["Cloud, Castle, Lake," in № 2, 1937]? Of course, the thing can be published only in its entirety. (August 16, 1937)

Fondaminsky could not. Short of money as never before, Nabokov had to yield to *Sovremennye zapiski* to ensure at least some honoraria for the months to come.

As the ensuing correspondence from the fall of the same year testifies, Rudnev and Nabokov quickly resumed their working relationship. Rudnev truly liked the new novel and confessed that he was thrilled by "the tempting black magic of [Nabokov's] stylistic artistry": "One watches you like an acrobat on the trapeze: a moment and a madman will fall off! — but then he shoots over a deadly abyss and here he is, once again, swinging light-heartedly" (November 26, 1937). Later Rudnev cautiously asked Nabokov to soften a few of the passages and change the characterization of the Russian literary critic Vissarion Belinsky, but this was nothing compared to the purged Chernyshevski story.

As if foreseeing the cut, Nabokov started the fifth chapter with several mock reviews of Fyodor's work. During the year leading up to its appearance in *Sovremennye zapiski* in the fall of 1938, Nabokov may have adjusted the opening to echo the earlier incident with Chapter Four even more directly.

Looking for a Publisher

Was the last-ditch effort to have Chapter Four published out of sequence at the last moment before the scheduled printing of *Sovremennye zapiski*, leaving Rudnev little choice but to accept it or else jeopardize the entire volume, simply part of Nabokov's scheme to have it published? After failed attempts to place "The Life of Chernyshevski" elsewhere, Nabokov turned his efforts to the possibility of publishing the entire novel in book form. Despite some harsh reactions, Nabokov was sure that the novel as a whole was worth it ("Volodya, I just read your *Gift* and I want to tell you — you are genius!" as Georgii Gessen opens his letter to the author; January 12, 1938).

The publishing business in Europe was crumbling, and embarking on such a controversial publication as a thick Russian novel was especially risky. Among the first people that Nabokov contacted was Abram Kagan, co-owner of the émigré publishing house "Petropolis" (Dolinin 2007). Founded in Petrograd, Kagan's publishing house was relocated to Berlin in 1924, and in the 1930s, when

Hitler came to power, to Brussels. It was printing belles-lettres of high quality and it is credited, for instance, with bringing out the first ever Russian translation of D. H. Lawrence's *Lady Chatterley's Lover* in 1932. The publisher initially agreed to have Nabokov's novel published and offered him financial terms on November 1, 1938. Kagan was to pay Nabokov starting after the first 200 copies of the print run were sold; the author insisted on doing this in reverse — he would waive his rights as soon as he received the proceeds from the sale of the first 200 copies. "Petropolis" compromised: payments to Nabokov would start immediately, but he was eligible for only 5% of the edition's list price. As soon as the first 400 copies of *The Gift* had been sold, the amount was to be paid out in full.

Kagan also suggested dividing the novel into two equal parts and issuing it simultaneously in two volumes. The practical reason for this was also financial — a larger volume costs more. Nabokov hesitated: since the first volume would include chapters one through three, the second book comprised of the two remaining chapters would have looked much thinner. At this point Nabokov decided to include the addenda: the short story "The Circle" and "Father's Butterflies." Late in 1939, despite heavy losses and the ongoing war, Kagan still hoped to print the novel and, therefore, kept a copy of the manuscript in his possession. As it turns out, these plans were never realized. In 1941 the co-owner of the bankrupted publishing house was fortunate enough to escape to the United States.

While still in Europe, perhaps as a backup plan to Kagan's two-volume venture, Nabokov was looking at other private publishing enterprises that could undertake the publication of the full text of *The Gift*. Composer Sergei Rachmaninoff (1873–1943) was an avid reader and liked Sirin's prose; no less important, Rachmaninoff was well known for his generosity and his financial support of Russian émigré artists. Rachmaninoff owned the publishing house "Tair" and Nabokov ended up trying to interest its editors in his new novel. The publishing company was founded by Rachmaninoff in Paris in 1925, and its title was formed from the first syllables of his daughters' names: Tatiana and Irina. Rachmaninoff's idea was to familiarize the émigré community with works by Russian writers who had trouble finding a suitable publisher. In addition, Rachmaninoff hoped that his children would make a useful contribution to society. Tatiana Rachmaninoff ran the business and Lollii L'vov (a former staff journalist for *Rul'* (*The Rudder*) who was now working on the Paris paper *Russia and Slavdom*) served as its literary consultant. Tatiana Rachmaninoff and L'vov discussed the publication *Glory* with Nabokov in 1930, but the author declined the offer. Nine years later, it was Nabokov who proposed the publication of his new novel, *The Gift*, to the Rachmaninoffs. The move came too late — when his publishing venture proved to be unsuccessful, in 1935, Rachmaninoff liquidated "Tair" (Leving 206).

> **LES EDITIONS PETROPOLIS**
> 27, RUE FÉLIX DELHASSE, BRUXELLES - ST GILLES TÉl. 37.06.40
>
> COMPTE CH. POSTAUX 199.423
> Reg. du Comm. 108767
>
> BRUXELLES, le 5.II.1938
>
> Господину
> В.В.Набокову
> Парижъ
>
> Дорогой Владимiръ Владимiровичъ,
> Подтверждаю полученiе Вашего открытаго письма отъ 24-го м/м.Отно-
> сительно раздѣла "Дара" можно договориться.На получловѣ нельзя,кон-
> ечно,обрывать,но можно выбрать и середину главы.Главное,чтобы обѣ
> части вышли почти одновременно.Соображенiе почему я хочу раздробить
> романъ на двѣ части только порядка цѣлесообразности.Если романъ бу-
> детъ дорого стоить,то его не будутъ покупать и наши взаимные инте-
> ресы пострадаютъ.Можетъ мы сдѣлаемъ съ Вами/одинъ томъ длиннѣе дру-
> гого.

[Ill. 1-11] A. Kagan's letter to Nabokov discussing the publication of *The Gift* (November 1, 1938)

Rachmaninoff, who at the time was in Villa Senar, his estate in Switzerland, had been informed of Nabokov's inquiry regarding publication of *The Gift* by "Tair." The composer responded immediately, sending on his own initiative a significant contribution:

> Dear Vladimir Vladimirovich,
> Only today, May 28, did I learn of your letter of May 10 to L. L'vov in which your two words—ghastly destitution (*dikaya nuzhda*)—stunned me. I am sending you 2500 francs by telegram, which you may repay me when those words no longer apply. And if this should not be soon—though God grant that this is not the case—it doesn't matter. The mere thought that I have been able to help you in a moment of need is sufficient repayment.
> I am afraid that the question of the publication of *The Gift* must be put off for a time. (May 28, 1938; Field 225)

Andrew Field, who published Nabokov's letter for the first time in translation, did not comment on this last line. The added sentence, however, strengthens the hypothesis that Rachmaninoff may have been somehow involved in resolving the fate of *The Gift*. In a more perfect world, Rachmaninoff would have assisted in this matter despite the formal closure of his publishing business. But it was the war in Europe that cancelled many plans, including the vague prospect of publishing *The Gift* as a monograph.

The Nabokov family's escape to the United States in 1940 was eventually made possible by the efforts of another prominent Russian-Jewish musician, Director of the Boston Symphony Orchestra Serge Koussevitzky, who arranged the affidavit and necessary paperwork for the Nabokovs (Leving 207).

On May 28, 1940, exactly two years from the day Rachmaninoff had sent him the telegram from Switzerland, the ship *Champlain* carried Nabokov and his family to New York. Though Nabokov often claimed that he was tone-deaf, he had enough of a musical sensibility to collaborate with Rachmaninoff on two unfinished projects in the early 1940s. At Rachmaninoff's request, Nabokov prepared the English text of *The Bells* (Symphony № 3, Op. 44) for performances in the United States. His goal was to eliminate the differences between the Russian and English texts and to make Rachmaninoff's music (based on the earlier translation by the Russian symbolist poet Konstantin Bal'mont) fit Edgar Allan Poe's original words (*The Bells*, 1849). Nabokov also specially adapted the monologue of *The Covetous Knight* from Pushkin's long poem for Rachmaninoff's opera, though this was subsequently never mentioned either by Nabokov or by his biographers. In retrospect, it would be safe to assume that this collaboration with the great composer—being part of Pushkin's cycle of the so-called "little tragedies"—*The Stone Guest, A Feast During the Plague,* and the unfinished "*Rusalka*" (*The Water-Nymph*)—somehow continued to stem from Nabokov's complex project surrounding *The Gift*.

Nabokov never abandoned his plans to print a full edition of the novel. As soon as the Nabokovs settled in America, the writer started looking for possible entrepreneurs and peers among the compatriots who had already gained some experience in the publishing business in their newly adopted homeland. Vladimir Mikhailovich Zenzinov (1880–1953) was a former professional terrorist and adventurous intellectual associated with the Socialist Revolutionaries who took part in the planning of several political assassinations prior to the Bolshevik revolution. Although he was much older and was a former SR party member who disapproved of the Chernyshevski chapter on ideological grounds (Glushanok, "Perepiska" 40), Zenzinov had been a good friend to Nabokov. In America Zenzinov was actively promoting Nabokov's art and helped support him financially from time to time by organizing his public readings for émigré compatriots. Zenzinov authored a dozen literary works, including one published at his own expense in New York, *Vstrecha s Rossiei* (*Meeting with Russia*, 1944 [1945]). In bringing this volume out, Zenzinov acted as his own publisher, vendor, and literary agent all at the same time. The venture turned out to be a success, surprising even the author himself. The book sold out and thus justified the financial risk. Zenzinov felt comfortable in his new homeland—soon after arriving to the United States he began publishing a political magazine *Za svobodu* (*For Freedom*).

It is in this role as editor that Nabokov sought out his older friend's advice regarding the possibility of publishing his last Russian novel in America. In a letter to Zenzinov discussing the idea of a literary evening in New York in the spring of 1944, Nabokov added toward the end:

> And here is another dream of mine: for quite a while now I have been preoccupied with the idea of publishing *The Gift* in a separate edition, and although I am aware that you disapprove one of its chapters, I am sure that this won't prevent you from lending a hand with the following. Would it be possible to attach to the newspaper ad for my public reading a notice announcing the launch of a subscription campaign for *The Gift*? The proclamation can mention that money will be deposited into the editorial fund of *Novyi zhurnal* or some other neutral place, and will be returned to subscribers if campaign does not cover the expenses for publication.
>
> The main impediment for me is that I don't know either the total amount needed, or what price to set. The book will be around 400 pages or more, but this is a good Russian cause. That's it. (May 2, 1944; Glushanok, "Perepiska" 70; my translation)

Nabokov also relied on the experience of Mikhail Tsetlin who had used the same technique to announce the forthcoming publication of his book on "The Mighty Handful" (the musical partnership of the five nineteenth-century Russian composers, including Mussorgsky and Rimsky-Korsakov). In Tsetlin's case the subscription ads ran starting with the journal's fourth issue until the book was published in April 1944, thus allowing the author and the publisher time to adequately prepare and accumulate funds. Nabokov obviously hoped to adopt the same method with *The Gift*.

However, Zenzinov reacted rather sourly and said, regarding Nabokov's plans for publishing *The Gift*, that "the omens do not look good" (May 8, 1944). Zenzinov even consulted with Tsetlin and Mark Aldanov, a writer of historical fiction, who were the founding editors of *Novyi zhurnal*; both were similarly skeptical. Nabokov's friends estimated that no more than two hundred copies of the book would have been sold, which meant it would not be practically possible to cover expenses. "Furthermore," continues Zenzinov, "all the printing houses at this time are overloaded with orders and will not print anything on credit—so 1,000 or 1,500 dollars must be spent at once, or almost concurrently, with no hope for return even in a year" (Ibid.).

Nabokov did not give up on his plans for *The Gift*, despite his colleagues' warnings and his own poor prospects (a succinct confession from that period bears witness to this: "I work a lot. Have financial troubles. Am looking for a good solid professorship somewhere"; Nabokov to E. Wilson, December 2, 1944; *Nabokov–Wilson Letters* 162).

A year later, Véra Nabokov included another inquiry among other matters in her letter to Zenzinov from Wellesley: "The last thing I would like to ask you concerns the odds of publishing *The Gift*. We want to print it ourselves. If possible, based on the experience with your own book, please let us know how to approach this, e.g. what press to turn to, where to get the paper, when to pay, and what are the costs of printing, binding, etc. I have never done this, and any advice will be appreciated" (October 25, 1945). Unfortunately Zenzinov misplaced this letter, so when he sent his answer with apologies to the Nabokovs almost six months later, he could only recall a question regarding the fates of their mutual friend, Ilya Fondaminsky, and Vladimir's brother, Sergei; both perished in the Nazi Germany during the war. By that time Véra must have made other inquiries about printing the book independently, and evidently concluded that the meager family budget would not succeed in funding such a project.

For years to come Nabokov would be attending to his English-language novels, *Bend Sinister*, *Lolita*, and *Pnin*, undertaking new translations, teaching at the universities, and saving money for his son's education. *The Gift* was to be put aside — though not forgotten.

The Chekhov Edition

Fifteen years after it was written, *The Gift* would finally appear in the full, unabridged, original version in the early 1950s. Before returning to reside permanently in post-war France, Mark Aldanov informed Nabokov that a new Russian press was to be founded in New York. Aldanov, whose strategic advice at the editorial board was in high demand, urged Nabokov to get in touch with the future head of the board, the scholar Nikolai Romanovich Wreden. "Of course, I spoke with him about *The Gift*," Aldanov assured Nabokov, who at the time was hunting for butterflies in West Yellowstone, Montana (July 18, 1951; Chernyshev).

Established by the Ford Foundation in affiliation with its East European Fund, the newly founded press was named after the famous playwright and writer of superb short stories, Anton Chekhov (1860–1904). The Chekhov Publishing House would publish over two hundred titles (including works by Bunin, Aldanov, Merezhkovsky, Mandelstam and Akhmatova) over a period of five years (1951-56). With its generous sponsors, the new publishing enterprise of the emigration intended to produce relatively cheap paperback editions and could afford to give fairly sizable advances (Boyd, *The American Years* 204).

"My appeal may seem premature to you," Nabokov wrote to Werden even before the press was officially running, "but I am really interested in publishing my novel among your first editions" (Véra Nabokov's draft; the Berg Collection, NYPL; August 8, 1951). As soon as Vera Alexandrova was appointed a literary editor of the Chekhov publishing house, she advised Nabokov to send the manuscript of *The Gift* to her home address in New York. The Board of Trustees' initial meeting was not scheduled until later that month (September 6, 1951). Nabokov immediately responded from Ithaca by sending a package with printed chapters, except "the fifth [sic], a precious typescript [that] has never been published" (September 13, 1951).

Nabokov was at this point more anxious than ever to bring his hidden treasure to the light of the day. In December, after some correspondence back and forth regarding the possibility of Nabokov writing the preface for a volume of Gogol's short stories prepared by the same publisher, the writer reminded them that he was still waiting for the formal decision to publish *The Gift*. His humble request was accompanied by an unobtrusive marketing ploy: "This novel is to be published in France in the French translation; I wish to arrange for its publication in Russian, the original language in which it was written, before it appears in French. Or in English, for that matter" (December 4, 1951). Although the prospects for the French publication were quite vague at the time, he mentioned the possible French edition again two weeks later. (The rights for *The Gift* had indeed been acquired by La Table Ronde, publishers of the English-language *Paris Review*, but the French edition would not in fact appear until fifteen years later.)

Finally, just a few days before the New Year, the Chekhov Press officially confirmed that *The Gift* would eventually get to the bookstands in 1952. Nabokov was expected to receive his contract shortly along with an advance payment of $500. Wreden stated that if Nabokov felt he could publish his novel in Europe sooner, he "most certainly will not stand in [Nabokov's] way" (December 27, 1951). Véra Nabokov quickly cleared the air regarding the available publication venues: "My husband asks me to thank you for your gracious letter and tell you that he is very glad that your firm decided to publish *The Gift*. Since the French translation is not done yet, I have no doubt that you will print the book before the French-language edition. My husband asks that you send him a contract to sign" (December 29, 1951).

The novel was expected to go to print in the spring of 1952. The terms of the deal were as follows: $1,500 for the first 3,000 copies printed, with additional payments on further quantities. The $1,500 was divided into three equal payments: one upon signing the contract, one upon publication, and one ninety days after publication. The retail cost of the book was set at $3.

As it turned out, applying some gentle pressure did not hurt. Nabokov wrote to Vera Alexandrova of the Chekhov Press: "I am told that, according to a notice—in the [newspaper] *Novoye Russkoye Slovo* (*The New Russian Word*), my *Gift* is to come out in May. I am delighted to learn this. May I ask you to include the enclosed paragraph as a foreword?" (March 31, 1952). The brief summary, in addition to some bibliographical data, notes that the novel "is written in the same vein as [Nabokov's] English memoir *Conclusive Evidence*" and that "the young Russian poet, Fyodor Godunov-Cherdyntsev, is an alter-ego of the author." Considering that Nabokov later reversed this statement and tried to disavow any potential similarity between the protagonist and himself, this admission is rather striking (the preamble was never published). The rest of the foreword looks quite familiar and predictable:

> Nabokov recreates in this novel the design of Fyodor's complex life, spending much time to introduce the reader to the creative laboratory of a poet. This is particularly well shown in the case of the novel that Fyodor writes about Chernyshevski, the great Russian critic of the Sixties (this novel forms Chapter Four of *The Gift*). Like Nabokov's Critical biography of Gogol, "The Life of Chernyshevski" is an original and somewhat risky interpretation of the great leader of the progressive-minded Russian intelligentsia. The entirely new psychological approach, based on intuition and little known facts from Chernyshevski's childhood[,] was one of the reasons why this chapter was not published in *Sovremennye zapiski*.

During April 1952, Nabokov read the proofs. Enclosing a list of 75 corrections, he asked: "I wonder if you would care to tell me something about the projected binding etc. I hope you are not planning to have any blurb or biographical note. But don't you think we should mention V. Sirin somewhere (in the foreword perhaps)?" (April 20, 1952).

The novel arrived fresh from typography in May. It bore a dedication in memory of Nabokov's mother, who had died exactly thirteen years before, on May 2, 1939. Except this one, all of Nabokov's novels are dedicated to the writer's wife, Véra Nabokov. The dedications in the Russian and English editions differ: "To the memory of my Mother" in the 1952 original edition became "To Véra" in the 1963 published translation.

The author was pleased with the final product. He shared his joy with the Editor-in-Chief: "I have just written Mrs. Dillon Plante [executive director of the Publishing House] telling her how much I like the appearance and presentation of DAR, but I would like to say it to you as well. I am very happy that DAR was at last published (fifteen years after it was written) in its entirety, and published so nicely and carefully" (May 27, 1952).

Nabokov gave the publisher a list of the people to whom he wished to present a copy of the novel. The list included relatives and close friends—Anna Feigin, Nicolas Nabokov, Elena Sikorski, Georgii Gessen, Roman Grynberg, Vladimir

 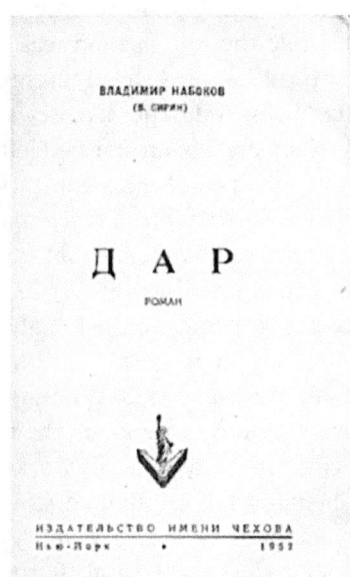

[Ill. 1-12, 1-13] The rare edition was recently available at Ozon.ru for 49,000 rubles ($1,775.04 USD, based on the conversion rate as of December 2008)

Zenzinov and Edmund Wilson. Nabokov does not forget his former art teacher, Mstislav Dobuzhinsky, as well as Mark Aldanov, who had given his blessing to this inaugural Russian-language edition. Remarkably, the inventory also included the widow of the former editor of *Sovremennye zapiski*, Vadim Rudnev (who had died in November 1940, after fleeing Paris on foot).

A year later it became evident that Nabokov had been correct in his assumption that some potential buyers might be confused about the Nabokov-Sirin connection. "A dealer in one of our largest markets has advised us that he is sure he could increase the sales of DAR greatly, if he were permitted to advertise the fact that it was written by 'Sirin,'" writes the representative of the Chekhov Publishing House, seeking to maximize the sales of the novel. "Would you have any objections to our using the name in this one market when advertising your book?" (April 27, 1953). The letter reached the Nabokovs in their "Arizona remoteness" (May 5, 1953). Of course, Nabokov had no objection whatsoever to the use of his old Russian pen name and he expressed his hope that the sales would be steady.

It is true that Nabokov was still popular among the émigrés who knew him better as Vladimir Sirin. However, despite an attractive binding, familiar name, and intelligent marketing (notwithstanding the quality of Nabokov's prose and the revolutionary structure of his last Russian novel), the book's commercial success was modest. The Russian communities in America and in Europe continued to shrink, while the iron curtain was still hermetically closed—at least until the Thaw of the 1960s and the breakthrough of samizdat in the 1970s.

After being told the sad news that the Chekhov Publishing House was closing, Nabokov sent an alarmed letter to the YMCA administration. In reply, Paul Anderson, secretary of the organization, denied the disturbing rumor concerning the possible destruction of the remaining books left at the Chekhov Publishing House. At the same time, he admitted that the storage facility was on the verge of being overstocked (November 27, 1957).

According to the contract, Nabokov was offered the option to buy out the remaining supply at cost. Five hundred seventy six copies (out of the total run of one thousand) still remained unsold on December 10. Nabokov made a few calculations in pencil on the margins of the letter trying to figure out the prime cost for all three of his works issued by Chekhov press (besides *The Gift* these included the Russian version of his memoirs, *Drugie berega* [*The Other Shores,* adapted as *Speak, Memory*], and a volume of short stories, *Spring in Fialta*). But clearly the total figure of $432 for *The Gift* alone (at $ 0.75 per book) was more than Nabokov could afford in order to rescue the books from the shredder.

Strikingly, the silence that followed the inaugural appearance of the complete text of *The Gift* was nearly identical to that which had ensued after its previous, serialized, incarnation. The literary critics were almost invisible, and even some of Nabokov's closest friends proved to be reluctant readers. Edmund Wilson confirmed receipt of Nabokov's opus on May 27, 1952, adding that the time is approaching when he is going to read Nabokov's "complete works and write an essay on them that will somewhat annoy" their author (*Nabokov–Wilson Letters* 276). "Are your reading *Dar*?," Nabokov asked, nudging Wilson to respond as he had promised two weeks earlier (June 14, 1952). As was often the case when some uncomfortable issue had been touched upon, Wilson never again returned to *The Gift* in their correspondence. He certainly did, however, write something that annoyed Nabokov, but the question of whether he actually *read* the novel remains open.

For others, the belated publication furnished an opportunity to read the novel in full for the first time. One such probing reader was Avraham Yarmolinsky (1890–1975), an excellent humanities scholar and translator who worked as curator of the Slavic collection at the New York Public Library for over three decades. On November 11, 1952 he enthusiastically reported to Nabokov: "Recently I've read *The Gift* almost in its entirety. This is a true gift to literature! During my reading I have repeatedly thanked the fates that it is my lot to know the Russian language" (Glushanok, "Rabota Nabokova nad perevodom" 334; my translation). In the same correspondence, Yarmolinsky wondered about the sources for the

The History of Publication

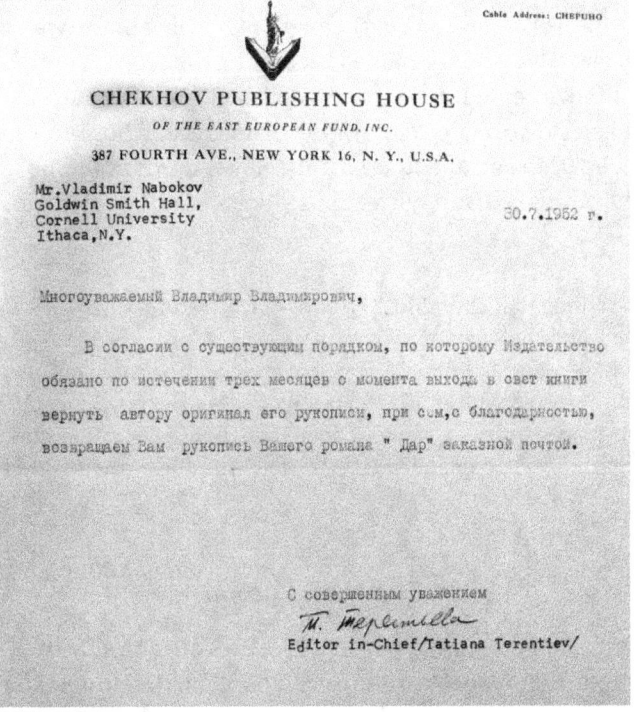

[Ill. 1-14, 1-15] Business correspondence pertaining to the publication of *The Gift* by Chekhov press (1952). *Berg Collection*, NYPL

Chernyshevski chapter, pointing out two specific episodes—"Is it all *realia* or a legitimate artistic fancy?" Even prior to receiving Nabokov's response, just four days later, Yarmolinsky rushed to tell Nabokov that he "randomly stumbled across the printed sources" [sic!] that served as documentary material for the episodes in question—one was found in Steklov's biography of the revolutionary, the other—in Evgenii Liatskii's edition of published correspondence, *Chernyshevski in Siberia* (St. Petersburg, 1912-13). In a letter sent from Cornell University, Vladimir Nabokov confirmed:

> Dear Mr. Yarmolinsky,
> Thanks for your two letters. Yes, you are right: all the factual information in the biography of Chernyshevski in my book is based on "sources." The few additions of my own are all pointed out as such in the following chapter.
> I am glad you like DAR. However, I quite agree with you that it would be well nigh impossible to translate. [...] (November 22, 1952; Glushanok, "Rabota Nabokova nad perevodom" 335-36)

A month after Nabokov's inquiry to Wilson, the journal *Posev* featured a positive but rather insignificant review of the first Russian edition of *The Gift* on July 13, 1952. The *Posev* [*Sowing*] émigré publishing house was set up in 1946 with this deliberately symbolic name (i.e. sowing the seeds of enlightenment and resurrection of legitimate Russia), and published books by authors belonging to the first and second waves of emigration. The critic, whose full name remains unknown, inclined to social and political debate, describes Nabokov as a direct disciple of the Symbolist and Formalist schools—and the stylistic continuation of both:

> One may assume that the "Silver Age" of our literature—the last years of the last century and the beginning of the current century... were only the search for new literary forms, answering our contemporary consciousness and our contemporary perception of life.... to my mind, in the novel *Dar*, V. Nabokov, having developed—as a writer—under free conditions, came closest to the Russian literary style demanded by our time. And this is the real reason of its importance. (G., A. 10)

The Ardis Edition

The Ardis Publishers was founded in 1970 by Carl and Ellendea Proffer, two enthusiastic American academics and, incidentally, admirers of Vladimir Nabokov. The very name Ardis comes from the novel *Ada*, in which an estate of this name is located in a mythical place that combines attributes of both Russia and America, a symbol of cultural exchange between two literary traditions. Ardis specialized in the publication of banned Russian literature and books by Soviet dissident authors. Ardis breathed new life into Nabokov's almost forgotten novel in the mid-1970s, and thus began the triumphant comeback of *The Gift*—albeit too late for its creator. The émigré literary magazine *Sovremennik* (*The Contemporary*), issued in Toronto, ran the following short announcement in 1977:

> In the year of Vladimir Nabokov's passing on, it is especially timely to turn our attention to works of this wonderful master of Russian prose and great Russian writer. The novel *The Gift*, written in the nineteen thirties, fully conforms to the view of Nabokov as a virtuoso of style and subtle psychology. (*Knizhnaia polka* 284)

Soon Ardis Publishers became the largest publisher of Russian works outside the Soviet Union. The Proffers were dedicated to Nabokov's art and would publish all of his works in Russian until the collapse of the Bolshevik system of ideological censorship. This compact but dynamic publisher could navigate easily in a niche too small and obscure for a giant like McGraw-Hill. The McGraw-Hill syndicate agreed to co-publish Russian editions of *Mary* and *Glory* with Ardis (earlier, when Nabokov signed on with them in 1969, they had issued a Russian-language edition of *King, Queen, Knave*, but the book sold poorly and the press was wary of future Russian undertakings). The endeavor encouraged further efforts on the part of the Proffers, and by the fall of 1974 the couple was preparing to republish more Russian Nabokoviana on their own (Boyd, *American Years* 647).

By mid-1975, Ardis had decided to reprint a complete edition of Nabokov's Russian works. This was a wise move because the political climate of Brezhnev's Soviet Union had become quite different from the Stalin era of high terror when Nabokov was composing *The Gift*. For the post-Thaw generation of the Soviet intelligentsia, Nabokov evolved into a hypnotic emblem of all that was forbidden and intellectual. What seemed to be of little significance for the disintegrating Russian Diaspora in the West turned out to be in great demand on the other side of the iron curtain.

In preparing the new Russian edition Nabokov used the experience he had gained from the first publication of the novel in the early 1950s. On the half-title of his personal copy of the Chekhov House edition, Nabokov listed several dozen corrections, by page number, in pencil—mostly typographical and printer's errors, but also spelling and punctuation. Many of these marginal ticks are crossed out and a few are erased. The only note on the half-title in English reads: *corrections checked on Aug[ust] 23, 1975, for Ardis edition.* The corrections have been made in ink, pencil, and colored pencil, suggesting multiple readings.

The émigré community at the time underestimated the developed network for disseminating illegal literature in the Soviet Union. As early as 1969 in Leningrad the fee for having *Lolita* for one night was six rubles—under the condition that the reader would not make copies of the rented book. Making a photocopy cost ten rubles. By 1980 the price for *The Gift* (a paperback edition) and *Lolita* amounted to 80 rubles (or 120 US dollars) on the black market (Paperno, Hagopian 113). This was approximately equal to the average monthly salary of a Soviet employee, who could also read Nabokov in the *samizdat*, as an informant tells: "[In the 1970s] officially functioning in society demanded your energy, which you tried to minimize and save for private life. One could be, let's say, a mid-level party functionary attending political briefings, coming back home and opening the Xeroxed copy of *The Gift*. And that was the main thing. [...] Cultural icons of the 1970s were really eclectic: [socialist realist prose writer Vladimir] Soloukhin could be right next to Nabokov" (Kolerov 81, 83).

After Perestroika

And when will we return to Russia? What idiotic sentimentality, what a rapacious groan must our innocent hope convey to people in Russia. But our nostalgia is not historical—only human—how can one explain this to them? It's easier for me, of course, than for another to live outside Russia, because I know for certain that I shall return—first because I took away the keys to her, and secondly because, no matter when, in a hundred, two hundred years—I shall live there in my books—or at least in some researcher's footnote. (G350)

Though Nabokov took away the keys to Russia, at the end of the last century Russia was eager to find the keys to Nabokov.

The Russian readership was once again officially allowed access to *The Gift* during the last years of the failing Soviet regime. In its March 1988 issue, the magazine *Ural* (№№. 3-6) began serialized publication of what was announced as an unabridged version of *The Gift* (it did include the controversial Chapter Four, but was marred by other omissions and alterations). An introductory editorial word of caution by Valentin Lukyanin warned that: "*The Gift* contains a concentrated expression of the very anti-democratic tendencies in Nabokov's creative output which—let us admit it quite soberly—are very much present, of course, in the 'harmless' works by the same author published in our country earlier, although perhaps in a less obvious form." Continuing to employ the tactic of political insurance, Lukyanin continued cautiously: "It would be a sacrilege to present to the Soviet reader the noblest figure of the Russian democratic movement [Nikolai Chernyshevski] as a caricature merely to add a realistic note to the understanding of the creative individuality of a writer not very close to us in spirit" (Barabtarlo, "...Et Dona Ferentesi" 15). This rhetoric on the part of the provincial functionaries to justify the printing of Nabokov's novel with the infamous Chernyshevski chapter was not a meaningful censure but rather a reflection on the fading power of the central authority.

There are only two omissions in the *Ural* publication for which the reasons can be plausibly surmised ("irreverent flippancy of tone when speaking of the noblest figures"). The first omission is the phrase, *"Lenin met a sloppy end"*; another is "waiting *for Cheryshevski to babble himself out and watching* what would come of it" (words in cursive were deleted). Most of the omitted or modified phrases, however, seem to be simply the result of hasty and careless typing coupled with inattentive proofreading, rather than of conscious censorship. The hallmark of the 1985–91 period was an explosion in publication of the hitherto unprintable writings of both Soviet and émigré authors. The process started on a rather modest scale in mid-1980s, accelerated rapidly, and reached its peak in 1989–91. According to Herman Ermolaev, before 1988, the publication policy seemed to favor the previously rejected works of Soviet writers and selected works of "first-wave" emigrants, such as Vladislav Khodasevich and Vladimir Nabokov. Passages concerned with the Soviet regime, the Stalinist terror, Lenin, and the Soviet Army constituted prime targets of censorship (Ermolaev 230) and *The Gift* was not the only work to suffer from such manipulation. Several passages condemning Lenin for creating a police state were eliminated in 1988 from Nabokov's memoir, *Other Shores*, during its serial publication in the journal *Druzhba narodov*. In addition to these overtly political cuts, the magazine got rid of Nabokov's evaluation of Lenin's aesthetic taste (Lenin disapproved of modernists). In the original text, Nabokov argued that "in his attitude toward art, Lenin was an absolute Philistine," and that he knew Pushkin from Tchaikovsky's librettos and Belinsky's pamphlets (Ibid. 241).

The early 1990s were seminal for the distribution of *The Gift* in the Soviet Union. The public was convulsively swallowing such hitherto forbidden intellectual fruits when the earliest legal publication of Nabokov's novel took place in 1989. The book came out in the provincial town of Sverdlovsk (now Yekaterinburg) in the Urals, where the first secretary of the Communist Party Committee until 1985 was Boris Yeltsin, later to become the first democratically elected President of Russia. The first Soviet edition was accompanied by an introduction by Alexei Zverev, a Russian specialist in American literature. More shocking is that its print run amounted to a quarter of a million copies (Martynov 88)! On the verge of its collapse, the Gorbachev state allowed long-awaited freedom of press, while virtually all systems of public control became dysfunctional.

Nabokov's *The Gift* saw six different editions between 1990 and 1997 (each declining in numbers, but still with an impressive figure for the total run of over 500,000 copies). These figures do not include the appearance of the novel as volume III of the inaugural Soviet edition of the writer's Collected Works: the 1990

Pravda edition, in four volumes, with a run of 1,700,000 copies — an unimaginable figure for an edition published without authorization from the Nabokov estate. The first post-Soviet edition published by special arrangement with the Estate of Vladimir Nabokov, *Collected Works of the Russian Period* in five volumes, was undertaken by the St. Petersburg publishing house Symposium, known for its intellectual refinement. In addition to the text of *The Gift*, the fourth volume incorporated a thorough commentary prepared by Alexander Dolinin (2000).[10] In 2008 the exclusive rights for publishing Nabokov in Russia were transferred to the publishing powerhouse Azbooka. Since then *The Gift* has again been printed without scholarly apparatus but — by way of an awkward compensation — in tandem with "Father's Butterflies," mistakenly referring to the Russian original as a translation from English, and in a glossy jacket design (the Penguin Classics edition of *The Gift* has also been featuring the entomological addendum as a supplement to the main text since 2001).

The English Editions

The Gift was published in English translation for the first time in 1963. Nabokov discussed the impending completion of the long-awaited project in an interview with the BBC, both praising the quality of the translation and declaring *The Gift* to be the pinnacle of his Russian-language career. Sparing no superlatives, isolating the novel's autobiographical strains and murky resemblance with his émigré reality, through shrewd promotion Nabokov created the anticipation of a masterpiece:

> ...I am very much concerned with things Russian and I have just finished revising a good translation of my novel, *The Gift*, which I wrote about thirty years ago. It is the longest, I think the best, and the most nostalgic of my Russian novels. It portrays the adventures, literary and romantic, of a young Russian expatriate in Berlin, in the twenties; but he's not myself. I am very careful to keep my characters beyond the limits of my own identity. Only the background of the novel can be said to contain some biographical touches. And there is another thing about it that pleases me: probably my favorite Russian poem is one that I happened to give to my main character in that novel. (*Strong Opinions* 13-14)

---

[10] Errata in this edition are minimal, but a few misprints altering the meaning must be noted: "pritvornuiu" (p. 227) should read "pritornuiu" [homonymous *feigned* instead of *luscious*]; "u stepnykh ural'tsev-staroverov" (p. 319) should read "u stepennykh" [*sedate* instead of *steppe*] (cf. in the texts of the *Sovremennye zapiski*, Chekhov and Ardis editions). I am grateful to Professor Mitsuyoshi Numano, the Japanese translator of *The Gift*, who noticed and shared with me these misprints.

Prior to coming out as a book, two segments from *The Gift* appeared in English in *The New Yorker* magazine, respectively under the titles "Triangle Within Circle" (March 23, 1963; in Dmitri Nabokov's translation) and "The Lyre" (April 13, 1963; in Michael Scammell's translation). Prepublication allowed for wider publicity and, moreover, being for the author of *Lolita*, was generously remunerated. After the April publication, Véra sent Scammell a handsome check for his share of the fee, which came as quite a surprise to the young translator.

Finding the Right Cover

When the time for a book edition of "the best and the most nostalgic" of his Russian novels finally came, Nabokov wanted as much control as possible over its appearance. One of the editions of *The Gift* in the author's private library (New York: G. P. Putnam's Sons, 1963) contains a leaf of tracing paper with Nabokov's color sketch of Putnam's dust-jacket cover. Nabokov was often at odds with dust-jacket art and artists throughout his career, and his correspondence testifies to the seriousness with which he addressed the issue, frequently offering his own detailed vision for the design.

Because this tracing paper design does not fit exactly over the printed dust-jacket, Sarah Funke, an expert bibliographer, presumes that it was not traced after the Putnam jackets were printed, but drawn before as a model. The paper design reproduced here courtesy of Cornell University was part of the acquisition made after 1999 along with a few rare editions of *The Gift* (the Berg Collection at the New York Public Library holds a similar example of a jacket sketch for *Speak, Memory: An Autobiography Revisited*). This lends credibility to the suggestion that Nabokov himself designed the emblematic Putnam jackets, beyond his verbal description of the design in a letter to his publisher (Funke 165). One may also compare this design with the first US edition of *Pale Fire*, which G. P. Putnam's Sons issued in the previous year. The front cover art for *Pale Fire* (1962) strongly resembles that which was chosen for *The Gift*, and probably meant to serve as a template for the entire Nabokov series.

[Ill. 1-16] The cover sketch in Nabokov's own hand (*From the collection of Cornell University*)

Apart from this authorial intervention, the subsequent story of the book jackets of *The Gift* is somewhat unfortunate. Nabokov was rarely satisfied with the artists who illustrated his works—he was annoyed by their simplistic figuration, flat realism or erroneous stylization. Some authors were luckier: for instance, in a 1963 American newspaper, next to a review of *The Gift*, there appeared an advertisement for the forthcoming publication of *The Collector* by John Fowles (B., "Nabokov Novel Not Up to Par" 11-C). By chance, the reproduction of the hardback cover featuring a lock of a lady's hair, a butterfly, and a key, looked most apt to Fyodor and Zina's romance. The beautiful dust jacket was designed by Tom Adams, who later admitted that this *trompe l'oeil* painting for *The Collector* was probably one of the most important paintings of his career. John Fowles attested that he had seen dozens more jackets on other editions since and "none comes within a mile of the original for beauty, subtle understatement" (Adams). Nabokov was not as fortunate in finding an ideal artistic alter ego who would channel his vision into a visual form.

Three years later, with the new edition of the novel in progress, Nabokov was still unsatisfied with jacket design of *The Gift*. He found the proposed drawings tasteless and tenuous in their relationship to the novel. In a letter sent from Montreux to Bud MacLennan, subsidiary rights director of Weidenfeld and Nicolson, Véra Nabokov conveyed her husband's visual blueprint for the model cover:

> THE GIFT, jacket design: This is one of the things on which my husband makes his own decisions. In the present case he asks me to say the following:
> 'The design for the jacket seems to me tasteless in the extreme. The only symbol a broken butterfly is of is a broken butterfly. Moreover, there is a grotesque clash between that particular peacock butterfly (which does not occur in the St. Petersburg region) and the Petersburg spring poem, while, on the other hand, in regard to the explorer father the peacock butterfly is pretty meaningless because it is one of the commonest butterflies in Asia, and there would have been no point in rigging up an expedition to capture it. The girl does not look like Zina Mertz at all. The entire conception is artistically preposterous, wrong and crude, and I cannot understand why they are not using the subtle and intelligent sketch I sent them, with the keys on the floor of the hall.'
> I am sorry that he should feel so strongly about this, but he does. (February 8, 1966; *Selected Letters* 383-384)

"The subtle and intelligent sketch" mentioned by Véra was actually drawn by Dmitri Nabokov. Dismayed with his publisher's inept efforts, Nabokov asked his own son, the translator of the first chapter, to provide an alternative drawing. Eventually it was used for the Panther paperback issued the same year.

Later covers, including international editions of the novel, turned out to be far from original; they either have presented a collage (made of butterflies or floral patterns, like in the Russian or British editions) or reproducing a painting borrowed from impressionist, expressionist, or strictly realistic styles. Aware of Nabokov's passion for lepidoptera, during his lifetime and even more so after the author passed away the publishers exploit the entomological motif in the jacket designs of his writings. The uniform Vintage-edition paperbacks of the early 1990s use the butterfly in a slightly subtler manner: the butterfly is often neither the dominating element nor expected to bear the bulk of the signifying force, and is more closely aligned with the author himself. The cover for *The Gift*, Juan Martinez believes, presents a special case: "[T]he protagonist's father was a lepidopterist, and the protagonist a writer, so that the images of butterfly net and typewriter (the latter about to be captured by the former) are less singular than the others. In being tied so closely to the actual story contained in the book, the butterfly and the butterfly net lose some of the connotative freight carried by the other covers" (Martinez).

[Ill. 1-17] The cover of the Panther paperback used Dmitri Nabokov's elegant and enigmatic drawing

A recent project taken on by John Gall has become the most creative and ambitious promotion of the Nabokov backlist in the history of Vintage International. As the art director for Vintage books at Random House, he individually commissioned Nabokov covers in 2009, following the loud publicity campaign surrounding the issue of the release of *The Original of Laura*. The new jacket designs have become collector's items in themselves: as an homage to the author's love for collecting butterflies, each cover was created using pins, paper, and butterfly boxes. Though *The Gift* (2010) is not the most extravagant among them, it certainly conveys the concept.

[Ill. 1-18 — 1-26]

Selected international paperback editions of *The Gift*, including the latest design by Rodrigo Corral (Vintage, 2010) and a graceful cover of the new Japanese translation

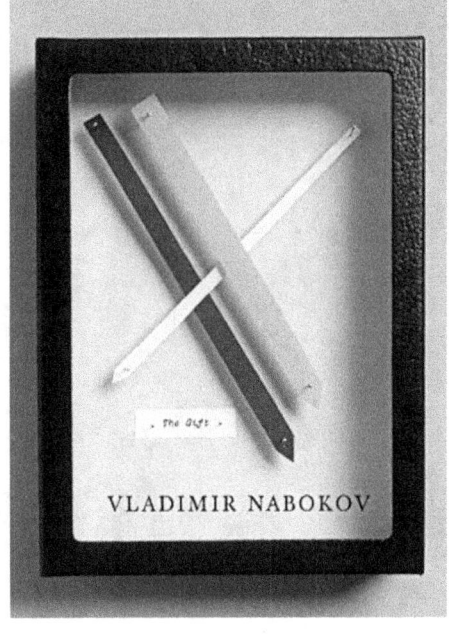

Chapter One. COMPOSITION AND PUBLICATION

The Market Value

Fifty Years Later: *The Gift* as a Collector's Item

Although Nabokov's manuscripts and correspondence related to *The Gift* are in the hands of institutional archives, signed editions of this novel have been offered at open auctions and it is this private sector of modern cultural economics that has determined the market value of *Gift*-related items. The first major donation of Vladimir Nabokov's manuscripts to the Library of Congress took place between 1958 and 1965; the second large set of papers was acquired in 1990 by the Berg Collection of the New York Public Library after the curators "spent many hours in the atom-proof Archive shelter and in a glassy arbor perusing materials... [later] transferred to new quarters without excessive disarray by a multinational team of movers and secretaries" (D. Nabokov, "History-to-be" 11-12).

In a 2004 interview, Glenn Horowitz of Horowitz Bookseller, Inc. claimed that his first big archive sale was to W. S. Merwin, for $185,000, in 1983. Since then he has also sold the archives of Kurt Vonnegut, Joseph Heller and Nadine Gordimer. But what really put him on the map, according to media reports, was the 1991 sale of Nabokov's literary estate to the New York Public Library, widely believed to have been the first archive sale to top $1 million.[11] Although both the Library and the Nabokovs were enthusiastic, it took two years to implement the complicated arrangement. Ultimately, Horowitz agreed to lower the purchase price, provided that the library paid Dmitri in full in one installment.

For Nabokov's hundredth birth anniversary the rare books that were still a part of the family collection were again entrusted to the same book dealer. The idea was to repeat the strategy that Horowitz had successfully enacted in 1996 when he took responsibility for the James Joyce materials. To stimulate public interest, he organized a museum-quality exhibition and catalog, including first editions and the proofs of the first English edition of what became *Finnegans Wake*; another exhibit on *Ulysses* at Horowitz's New York gallery in 1998 boasted a work on loan from the National Library of Ireland. The same elaborate approach was employed in the Nabokov sale, accompanied by the printing of an illustrated catalogue copiously edited by Sarah Funke.[12]

---

[11] Horowitz is known in the business for his creative deals, which include a combination of gifts and sales (under current tax law, living writers and artists derive no tax benefit from donating their work). He collects an agent's fee of ten to twenty percent on archive sales and had spent years winning over the executors to the estate, Nabokov's widow, Véra, who died in 1991, and then the couple's son, Dmitri (Donadio 2007).

[12] I wish to acknowledge that all the information on the editions in the Horowitz sale comes from this expertly prepared compendium (Funke 159-68).

Chapter One. COMPOSITION AND PUBLICATION

Among the detailed descriptions of over a hundred and thirty Nabokov first editions on sale—reproducing inscriptions, annotations and, in some instances, full-page color illustrations of Nabokov's drawings—the catalogue included seven different editions of *The Gift*.

The Russian-language *Dar* (New York: Chekhov Publishing House, 1952), the first publication of Nabokov's masterwork in the United States, was listed for $35,000 (lot no. 71). This volume, abundantly annotated by Nabokov and specially bound in grey pebbled cloth copy, was stamped in black and labeled by hand. It is inscribed to Véra in Russian on the first blank, in blue ink: "Dushen'ke moei dorogoi V." (*To my dear darling. V.*). Date and location in English: *Cambridge, Mass 16.V.1952*. And in Russian again: "Liubov' moia!" (*My love!*) in blue pencil. At the bottom of the dedication appears Nabokov's current address: *9 Maynard Place*, and in grey pencil in Vera's hand, *y May Sarton* (Russian for "at the house of May Sarton")—Mrs. Sarton had rented them her place in Cambridge.

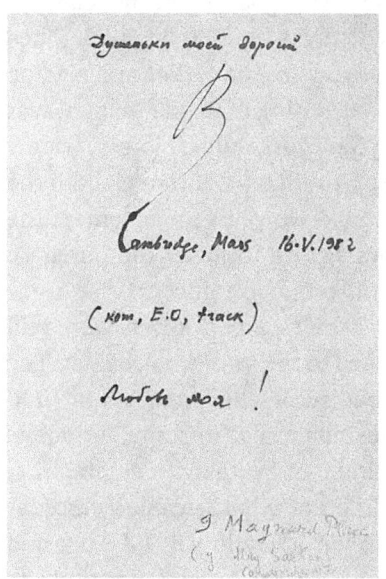

[Ill. 1-27] By permission of Cornell University, Rare Manuscripts collection.

The book contains four loosely inserted leaves—three are on Montreux Palace letterhead, one is blank—all sides covered with Dmitri's handwritten notes in Russian. These notes are mostly explanatory in nature but also feature a few explications of opaque allusions and cryptic quotes from Pushkin buried in the text of the novel, as well as suggestions for idiomatic translation of certain phrases.[13] The book, purchased by Cornell University, has minor abrasions to multiple pages due to the removal of post-it-style notes from the fragile, acidic paper; a few dozen post-its still remain.

Lot № 72 in Horowitz's price list was the 1963 Putnam edition of *The Gift* (black cloth; dust-jacket; minor wear to head of spine), with a foreword written specially for this publication. This dedication copy, inscribed *For Véra* in pencil on the half-title, was offered for $40,000, which makes it the most expensive among the editions of *The Gift* ever appraised. The flyleaf explains the high asking price: in addition to an autograph, the book is decorated with Nabokov's beautiful original drawing.

---

[13] I would like to thank Katherine Reagan of the Rare Books collection at Cornell University for providing me with the copies of these notes.

The sketch represents an imaginary butterfly with a drop shadow on the page (coloring pencils, 37 × 68 mm, page 1). Nabokov's hand was so heavy as he outlined the butterfly that some lead was transferred to the following page, the list of his works. The author signed beneath the image *Parnassius orpheus Godunov* and added the sign of Venus.[14] At least one element of the invented name does exist: Parnassiens include the Apollo and the Small Apollo butterflies. The name of the species is formed from the Latin name of Orpheus (the Greeks of the Classical age venerated this legendary figure as chief among poets and musicians), and also is a partial anagram of Fyodor's first name (the *ph* sound is rendered by the equivalent of the letter *f* in the Russian spelling of Orpheus' name). The discovery of the butterfly is attributed to Godunov who allegedly observed the mating habits within this genus.

To the left of the picture Nabokov indicated the page number. This reference is especially valuable: if we follow Nabokov's clue (page 124 in this edition), we can identify the particular passage of *The Gift* matching Nabokov's source for inspiration. In this excerpt, Fyodor evokes his father, entomologist Godunov-Cherdyntsev, and mentions his desire to reproduce *Parnassius orpheus* in the frontispiece of his work:

> [M]y father discovered the true nature of the corneal formation appearing beneath the abdomen in the impregnated females of Parnassians, and explained how her mate, working with a pair of spatulate appendages, places and molds on her a chastity belt of his own manufacture, shaped differently in every species of this genus, being sometimes a little boat, sometimes a helical shell, sometimes — as in the case of the exceptionally rare dark-cinder gray *orpheus* Godunov — a replica of a tiny lyre. And as a frontispiece to my present work I think I would like to display precisely this butterfly — for I can hear him talk about it... (G112)

The continuation of the passage describes the operation which allowed his father to preserve the specimen, "so that it dried that way forever." This pricey edition also bears an *ex libris* label: "From the library of Vladimir Nabokov. Palace Hotel Montreux. Switzerland."

Nabokov owned three identical copies of the 1963 edition, but, lacking the butterfly drawing, the other two (lots 73 and 74) have less value (priced $27,500 and $25,000 respectively). Both editions are Nabokov's corrected copies. The former preserves a pencil list on the front endpaper of eight misprints, with two more added by Véra; a typescript sheet, with handwritten revisions in either Vladimir's or Véra's hand, covering both sides, contains a side-by-side comparison of changes to be made to the hardcover and paperback editions, listed by page

---

[14] Funke's catalogue confuses it with the sign of Mars.

number. Many of the typescript revisions are crossed out, checked off, or bear manuscript notes next to them, and consist primarily of changes in spelling, the occasional addition, deletion or substitution of words, or simple marginal check marks.

The third and last Putnam edition of *The Gift* owned by the writer has a satin ribbon, its top edge gilt with the cloth in full brown morocco (instead of the regular black cloth), and stamped "V.N." in gilt on the front cover. This appears to be a unique printing of the book, in the publisher's presentation binding: it was produced on thicker paper than the regular edition, it is 5mm wider, and is trimmed 5mm shorter than any other copy examined by Glenn Horowitz and Sarah Funke. The emendations in this edition were insignificant (Nabokov altered a few words and corrected the spelling of Greek references).

The American Putnam copies in this sale were complemented by three editions from the British publishing house, Weidenfeld and Nicolson (1963). This first English edition from a new setting of type incorporated only three of the ten changes Nabokov made to his copy of the Putnam edition, but introduced multiple new printing errors. In Nabokov's centennial year the cost of the earlier of two dedication copies, inscribed in pencil on the front endpaper, *For Véra from the captor, Montreux 23.x.1963*, was appraised at $30,000. The edition features an elaborate imagined butterfly, *Vanessa atalurticae* Nab., which Kurt Johnson calls a "'hybrid' between two Brushfoots, *Vanessa atalanta* and *Vanessa urticae.*"[15]

The second dedication copy in the white dust-jacket was inscribed by Nabokov to Véra in Russian on the front endpaper on the occasion of their 43rd wedding anniversary: *Here is the tenderest of butterflies worthy of the anniversary. V. 1925–68*—the dates indicate the span of their marriage. This book is adorned with a large, elaborate pencil butterfly, meticulously colored in blue with red, orange, purple, and yellow highlights, named *Charaxes verae Nabokov* (female) and signed: Montreux, Vaud 15.iv.68. Nabokov wrote *for Véra* five times in red ink in various positions on the dust-jacket, labeled the spine with his Cyrillic initials and *Vé*.

According to Kurt Johnson, "the genus *Charaxes* is the well-known African and Indo-Australian genus of spectacularly colored butterflies of the Brushfoot family. All exotic collections have *Charaxes* and they are very popular among collectors as 'wow-bugs.'" Here Nabokov has combined aspects of at least three different groups of this genus, taking arched tails from one, the blue colors of another and the yellow margins from a third. "In nature," Johnson comments, "the broad blue basal colors and the yellow marginal colors occur in different groups of *Charaxes*, not together. Nabokov's magnificent *Charaxes verae* apparently illustrates how

---

[15] This and the immediately following entomological commentary by Kurt Johnson have been provided specially for the Horowitz catalogue.

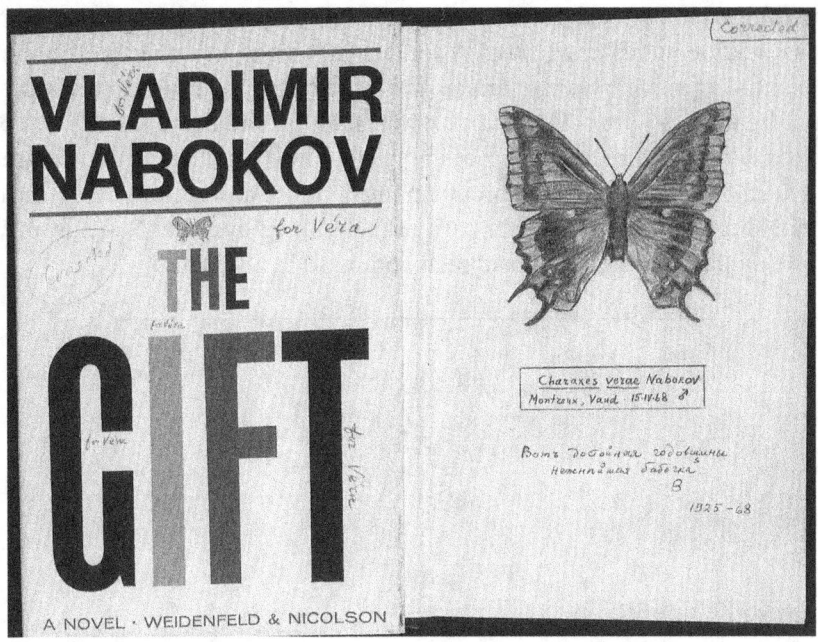

[Ill. 1-28] This 1963 first English edition of *The Gift* was inscribed by Nabokov to his wife on the occasion of their wedding anniversary

Nabokov would have imagined these bold colors aligned side by side." In this edition Véra notes one change on the dedication page and Nabokov makes twenty six minor revisions to wording, spelling, and spacing throughout (for example, "eighteenth" to *seventeenth*; "dinner" to *lunch*; "octavos" to *twelve-line poems*; "for" to *during*). A comparison of these corrections with those made earlier in the Putnam edition reveals that two suggested changes have been ignored and three were made by hand along with an additional twenty changes noted for later editions. This corrected copy, docketed in pencil on the cover and front endpaper, was offered in the Horowitz catalogue for $35,000.

The third and the last copy of *The Gift* (Weidenfeld & Nicolson, 1963, Lot 77, $15,000) in this collection is less remarkable for its contents (although its front endpaper filled with a list of misprints and mistranslations, along with some interesting word substitutions—*crude* for "disingenuous," for example) than for a loosely inserted index card. This index card bears more of Nabokov's notes on the text, corresponding to a series of X's and check-marks found throughout the book, concerning the temporal structure of the novel and the sequence of events, identifying specific dates and years in which the narrative develops.

The second Russian edition of *Dar* (Ann Arbor: Ardis, 1975; printed in blue cloth; 1000 copies) belonging to Nabokov incorporates approximately fifty

Chapter One. COMPOSITION AND PUBLICATION

corrections to the first edition of the complete text as published in 1952 by New York's Chekhov Publishing House. A presentation copy, inscribed to Véra on the first blank: *For you my DAR, my darling* [the last letter "g" is drawn to resemble the sign of Venus — ♀]/*from V./Montreux/Xmas/1975*. The inscription is complete with the detailed tropical Brushfoot in profile, drawn in blue ink and colored in red, blues, purple, orange, and brown, named *Verochka verochka*. With fourteen marginal lines and ticks in pencil (two of them noted by either Nabokov or Véra on the title page) this edition had been appraised at $30,000.[16]

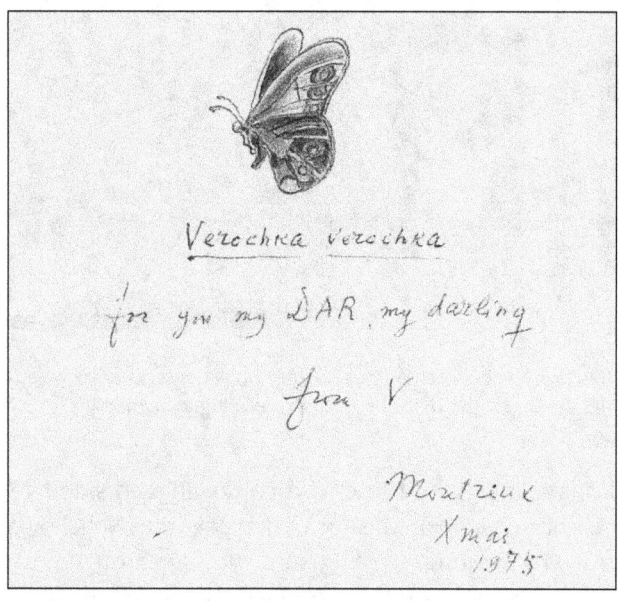

[Ill. 1-29] Author's 1975 Christmas present to his wife, drawing on the second Russian-language edition of *The Gift*

The same bookseller arranged the sale of the Morris and Alison Bishop collection of Vladimir Nabokov in 1999. It was accompanied by a handsome miniature catalogue, reproducing the texts of inscriptions and one photograph

---

[16] The total amount expected from the sale was $3,395.000, with editions of *The Gift* expected to gross $237,500 (hypothetically comprising 6.8% of the entire collection). Items 71, 73 and 77 from the catalogue were purchased by the Cornell University library; no. 74 by a private collector in New York; lots 72, 75, and 78 went back to Dmitri Nabokov, who presumably withdrew them to his private collection. Mr. Horowitz declined to comment on whether Cornell and the private buyer paid the prices as listed in catalogue.

on the frontispiece. Morris Bishop was a professor of comparative literature at Cornell University, and befriended the Nabokovs during the writer's tenure there. Nabokov presented and autographed many books for the Bishops, including *The Gift*. Part of the collection on sale, the novel in G. P. Putnam's Sons first edition (1963) once owned by Morris and Alison, was advertised for $25,000 (and was still available for sale a decade later). Originally sold for $5.95 per volume, it was issued in black cloth with a dust-jacket. The Bishops' presentation copy is inscribed on the half-title in pencil with Nabokov's hand-drawn chess-pieces: *for the* [drawing of two bishops] *from Vladimir Nabokov. April 2, 1964, Ithaca, NY*, with two butterflies and their shadows, and this annotation: *corrected: two misprints on p. 79/one misprint on p. 254*.

The most recent major sale of Vladimir Nabokov archive materials was arranged as an open auction by Tajan, one of the top three auction firms operating in France, in May of 2004. The Tajan Nabokov auction consisted of over 100 volumes and 30 titles, including five editions of *The Gift* (lots 22-26), including versions in Russian and French. Some of these items contain invaluable data regarding Nabokov's editing process and will be instrumental in establishing the definitive text of the novel for a variorum edition. For example, Nabokov's personal copy of the 1952 edition of the novel issued by the Chekhov publishing house (one of the six books sent to him as part of the honorarium) is peppered with Nabokov's remarks for Dmitri in preparation for his translation. Some of these preliminary suggestions were later revised, probably by the author himself, as in the case of Fyodor's poem (all fragments of Fyodor's poetic juvenilia were translated for the English-language edition by Nabokov himself). In the original the poem reads:

"…А потом, —
когда меняется картина,
и в детской сумрачно горит
рождественская скарлатина
или пасхальный дифтерит, —
съезжать по блещущему ломко,
преувеличенному льду
в полутропическом каком-то,
полутаврическом саду…"

In the margin of page 27 of the Russian edition Nabokov sketches Fyodor's poem in English (reproduced on the left). In the official printed edition of the English translation the same poem looks slightly differently (reproduced on the right):

"And when the picture exchanges, and darkly in the nursery glows a blend of Christmastide and scarlet fever or Easter and diphtheria— to ride down bright and brittle exaggerated slopes of ice in what is half a tropical mirage and half the city's Taurid gardens..."	"... and then When the scene underwent a grim change, And there somberly burned the nursery Scarlet fever on Christmas, Or, on Easter, diphtheria, One rocketed down the bright, brittle, Exaggerated ice hill In a kind of half-tropical, Half-Tavricheski park" (G20)

The edition containing the poem's draft was put on sale for 12,000 Euro (lot 22, *Dar*. New York: Izdatel'stvo imeni Chekhova, 1952). The dedication in Russian reads as follows: "Mitiushe, luchshemu moemu perevodchiku, ot V. Nabokova. Sent[iabr'], 1959. N.Y.C. vid na river" (*For Mitiusha [to Dmitri], my best translator, from V. Nabokov. Sept., 1959. New York, view of the river*).

The second edition of *The Gift* (New York: G P. Putnam's Sons, 1963) appears to be the same lot 72 that had been offered a few years earlier in New York and was later withdrawn by Dmitri Nabokov. Although the selling price was estimated at twice the amount of the Russian-language version in the same auction, its price dropped slightly compared to the earlier unsuccessful public bid. The book is tagged at 30,000 Euro now ($35,406 compared to unsold $40,000 in 1999).

The third American pocket format edition of *The Gift* (lot 24 in Tajan's catalogue) was modestly estimated at 3,000 Euro. This item has annotations handwritten by both Vladimir and his wife. It is described as having typographical corrections in pencil on about thirty pages, a list of references to the proofread pages at the back cover, and a loose page from a notebook. This sheet contains a drawing representing a stylized head wearing a hat with broad brim.

Even more affordable was the first British pocket format edition of the novel (lot 25; 2,500 Euro). The cover design reproduces Dmitri Nabokov's color drawing. This edition has typographical corrections on approximately 75 pages, with a list of references to the proofread pages entitled: "Correction of misprints (Feb. 1972) for next edition" (black pencil and red pencil, page 1).

The last edition of *The Gift* included in the 2004 auction was the French edition of the novel translated from English by Raymond Girard, with the exception of the poems rendered by the author himself (Paris: Gallimard, 1967; lot 26; 3,000 Euro). This book, one of the 36 numbered copies printed on pure vellum Lafuma-Navarre paper, has a few corrections and an *ex libris* label printed on the back cover.

The Tajan auction, except for a few items, was sold to various private collections, most from France and Switzerland, reportedly for nearly $750,000, a lower price than anticipated (Zanganeh). Dmitri Nabokov later admitted that "the Tajan auction was remarkably unprofessional and poorly prepared."¹⁷

The inscribed and lepidopterized copy of the novel that appeared on the market most recently is a 1952 Chekhov *Dar* that was presented to Véra Nabokov's sister, Sonia Slonim. The book still has the original printed wrappers and also contains (along with Slonim's signature in ink), the presentation inscription with a butterfly drawing on the front flyleaf

[Ill. 1-30] *Dar* (1952) with dedication to Sonia Slonim

in pencil and a small sketch of a flower beneath. At Christie's it was auctioned for $10,000 (estimated $10,000-15,000) on December 4, 2009, the same day when the 138 penciled index cards comprising the manuscript of Nabokov's last unfinished novel, *The Original of Laura*, failed to sell.

The last substantial group of books and manuscripts to come directly from Nabokov's family was scheduled for sale at Christie's on June 13, 2011. To draw the bidders in Dmitri Nabokov and Christie's decided to start out low (at about half what they would get at retail, according to collector and bibliographer Michael Juliar's estimate, who called it "an intriguing situation"). This strategy

---

17 In addition, Dmitri Nabokov shares his thoughts on rarity and value of his Father's editions: "The point, however, is not the edition, the inscription, or the chance object. The essence of a great writer is intangible and inestimable: it is what he has written, not the font or the format in which one enjoys it. Nor do the exact words scribbled on a football helmet or a baseball glove carry much weight for posterity. As for the value of autographed first editions, I can by chance give an example from a recent email. I and others on the Nabokv-L list recently received a request for help in finding an autographed copy of *Pale Fire* that was desired for gift-giving purposes. I was able to furnish some information because I happened to know that at least one such presentation copy exists on the rare book market. It can be bought for $17,500 or thereabouts. Certain exceptional rarities have been sold for sums well into six figures. Don [Barton] Johnson has contributed the authoritative comment that Nabokov's autographs are extremely rare and extremely expensive. Rarity, of course, generates value" (Stringer-Hye).

[Ill. 1-31] A copy of *The Gift* (1963) with dedication to Dmitri Nabokov

differed greatly from the Tajan sale in Geneva seven years before, when Dmitri consigned too many books at extremely high estimates. The intrigue, however, did not last long: Lots 291-401 have been withdrawn. Christie's announced that the entire fine collection (*Vladimir Nabokov: Books and Objects from the Collection of Dmitri Nabokov*) was sold prior to the auction by private treaty "to an important collector who appreciated the great cultural significance of this

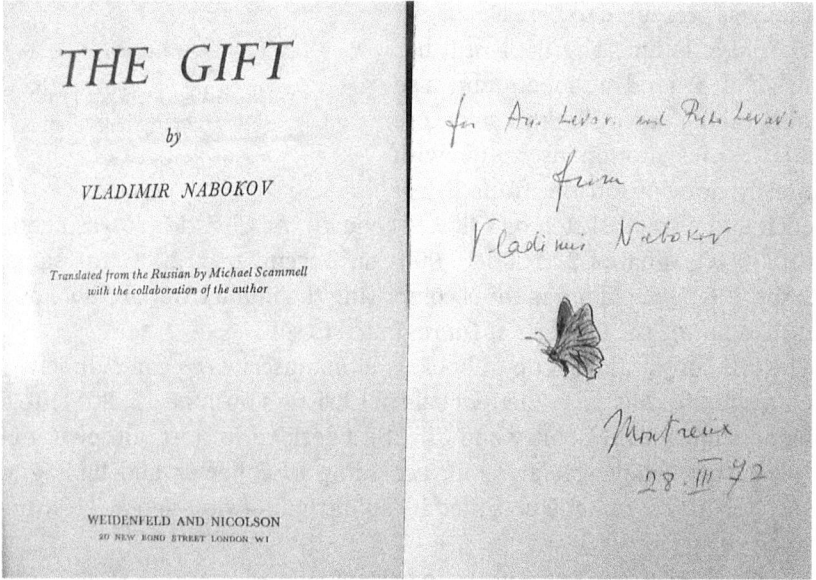

[Ill. 1-32] Nabokov's inscription on the book belonging to the former ambassador of State of Israel. Courtesy A. Levavi, photographed by author. Published by permission

group of books and objects, and the unique opportunity of acquiring en bloc the last substantial part of the Nabokov family archive. The price paid was in excess of £500,000."[18] Auction was to include the following earlier unsold editions of

---

[18] See the announcement on the official website (http://www.christies.com/ecatalogues/6332.aspx), as well as Michael Juliar's commentary in his own blog (http://www.vnbiblio.com/).

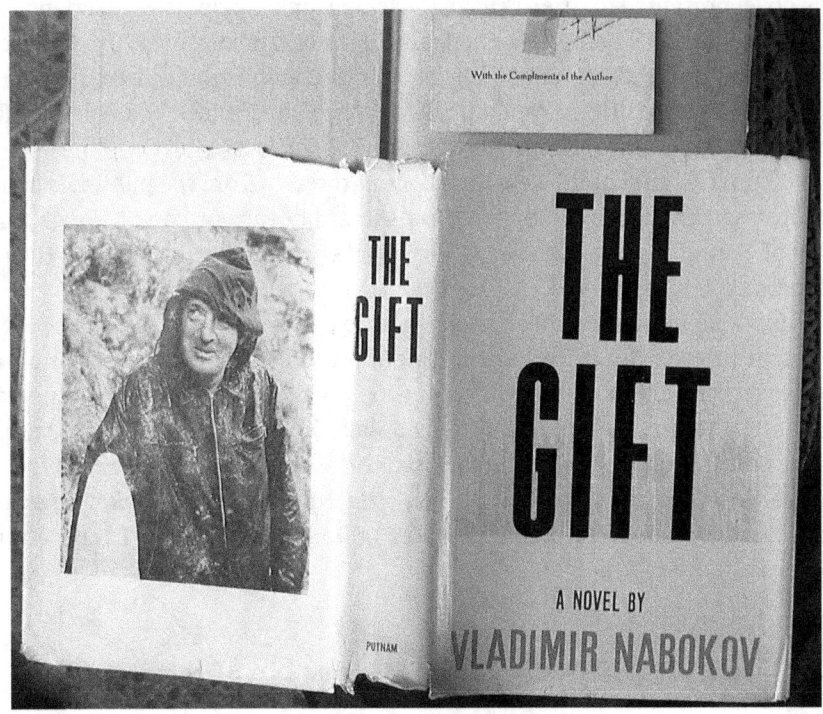

[Ill. 1-33] Complimentary copy of *The Gift* delivered by the publisher. Courtesy of the Rozov family, photographed by author. Published by permission

The Gift: the beautiful copy described as Lot 72 in Horowitz's sale (presently Lot 310 in the Christie's catalogue; US $4,500); *The Gift* (1963), reproduced on illustration 1-29, which reappeared as Lot 311 (US $4,500); Lot 312, the British 1963 edition of *The Gift*, inscribed by Nabokov ('For Véra from the captor') and offered now for only US $ 3,000 (described on p. 64 of this book). In addition to these items, a mysterious "important collector" has also acquired the first Russian edition of *Dar*: the Chekhov Publishing House (1952) presentation copy from the author with a butterfly drawing (Lot 309; US $3,800) inscribed to Anna Feigin, Nabokov's cousin by marriage, and a copy of *The Gift* (first edition, G. P. Putnam's Sons) with dedication to Dmitri Nabokov. It bears the following line under the title on the front page: *For my best translator, Dmitri Nabokov from his father. Montreux, May 1963*, and an elaborate drawing (ink and colored pencil) of an invented but scientifically plausible genus and species, *Babochka babochka* (*Butterfly butterfly*), with its taxonomically placed and abbreviated discoverer, and the sign of Mars denoting the sex.

Additionally, there are some interesting holdings in institutional archives and libraries, as well as in private collections. A rare personal treasure is a copy of the novel presented to Arieh Levavi, the Israeli ambassador to Switzerland, with whom the Nabokovs had a few entertaining meetings in the 1970s. A butterfly drawn in ink and red and blue pencils adorns the following inscription of the British paperback edition (Weidenfeld and Nicolson, 1963): *For Arie and Rika Levavi from Vladimir Nabokov Montreux 28.III.1972*

A number of gift copies were usually sent directly from the publisher to a list of addresses supplied by Nabokov. One such honorarium copy belongs to the family of Samuil Rozov, Nabokov's former classmate and dear friend (Leving, "Samuel Izrailevich" 13-17).

As for unsigned collectable Nabokoviana, bookshops currently offer relatively affordable prices. The price tag for an edition of *The Gift* with no autograph depends on the edition and condition of each specific item and usually fluctuates between twenty to two hundred fifty US dollars.[19] Although the market value of the rare editions of *The Gift* is still far from the record-breaking prices of the first Olympia French editions of *Lolita* (the *Lolita* edition from Nabokov's personal library was auctioned at Christie's for $273,500 in 2002), it will likely continue to rise.

Towards the Variorum Edition

The Vintage and Penguin Modern Classics editions are the most accurate English translations of Nabokov's Russian fiction; they have been reproduced photographically from the first English-language editions and have attempted to incorporate corrections recorded over the years by the Nabokovs, Elena Sikorski, Brian Boyd, and others who have submitted notes on errata. Unfortunately the pagination has sometimes been altered in the Vintage editions, as in *The Gift* and *Lolita* (both annotated and unannotated), although the page layout remains the same. The text of the first English-language edition of *The Gift*, for instance, begins at page 15, but in the modern Vintage edition it begins at page 3, so the difference is twelve pages throughout. Until a better redaction of *The Gift* is issued, scholars are encouraged to provide English citations from the Vintage edition and Russian citations from the Symposium edition.

There is as yet no edition of any of Nabokov's works that collates the published texts against manuscripts, typescripts, proofs and serial publications, which would be needed to ensure editions as close to definitive as possible; as

---

[19] For instance, one can get the first hardcover UK edition published by Weidenfeld and Nicolson (London, 1963) for $67.18, and the first US edition by G. P. Putnam's Sons (New York, 1963) for $129.19; the book in soft binding with Dmitri Nabokov's cover design (Panther, 1966) is traded for $20.64. Data is based on assessment through major online book vendors—Amazon.com and Alibris.com (Accessed on October 12, 2007).

Brian Boyd asserts, in the case of Nabokov, unlike Shakespeare or Joyce, they should be very close indeed ("Nabokov's Texts" 9). A bibliography that lists the manuscripts and other pre-publication versions, and the serial and book versions, and compares them textually, would be a necessary precursor to any such definitive, or at least variorum, edition (bilingual where necessary).

In the twenty-first century, such an edition is feasible, and the current state of the Joyce studies proves this. James Joyce specialists already have at their disposal all the relevant documents reproduced in the two beautiful volumes of color facsimiles of the Rosenbach *Ulysses* manuscript and the 63 large volumes of facsimiles of the *James Joyce Archive* (11 volumes for the early works, 16 volumes for *Ulysses,* 36 volumes for *Finnegans Wake,* including the 16 volumes representing the 14,000 pages of the Buffalo notebooks). Confronted with this overwhelming bulk, some scholars might even be tempted to ask the very basic question: why should we waste our time studying an author's manuscripts when we sometimes feel that his books are already more than we can handle? As Daniel Ferrer explains, one obvious answer is that "if we were afraid of difficulty, if we were not somehow attracted by difficulty, we would not be reading Joyce at all... the point of studying the drafts of *Finnegans Wake* was not that they would solve the obscurities of the book, but on the contrary that they provided us with an inexhaustible store of supplementary obscurity" (286). In other words, making sense of the maelstrom of a genius's drafts, though it may not answer many questions entirely, does open up many more enigmas and reveal hidden dimensions of the works.

In Russian philological scholarship, as early as the 1930s, it was demonstrated on the basis of Pushkin's materials that a rough-copy manuscript, as opposed to a fair-copy text, reflects the author's working process and is, consequently, a dynamic document. The methods applied to reading Pushkin's manuscripts demonstrate the concept of the rough-copy manuscript not as a static artifact but as a reflection of the process of creating a work of art through which one may trace the stages and progress of the work, the changes in ideas, and the author's development of chains of associations.

The preparation of a text of *The Gift* verified by scholars requires an *interpretation* of the novel: in other words, the hermeneutic task here cannot be separated from definitive scholarly editing. Yuri Lotman observed that in strictly textological work, researchers have long utilized structural models, regarding the manuscript as a "succession of synchronically balanced layers of intention" (206). In *The Gift,* as in no other novel, we have to deal with various models of generating text, on a meta-descriptive level as well. In the reader's perception, the author is accorded complete trust, and Nabokov-as-writer particularly insisted on the prerogative of his ultimate authorial will. The study of the real creative process is all the more interesting in scholarly perception when the textologist attempts, in the words of Dmitri Likhachev, to free himself from the hypnosis of "authorial will" in order to reconstruct the history of the text behind the final result imposed upon it by the author (29). The understanding of textology as something chiefly associated with the publication of texts has arisen out of a lack of understanding and artificial narrowing of the aims of textology (Grishunin 367). Studying the specific stylistics, poetics, language, and process involved in making *The Gift* during a period in which the investigative nature of literary research has largely subsided might partly compensate for the overgrowth of a new fashionable branch in Nabokov studies—theoretical criticism.

In accordance with the established goals, the publication of *The Gift* for a particular audience and with accompanying addenda seems optimal in the framework of the "Literary Monuments" academic series in Russian, or in a format similar to the Norton Critical Editions series in English. The reference apparatus should include various redactions of the text with a reconstruction of their origins and intentions, historical-literary data with an indication of the hidden quotations and allusions, attribution, dates, and linguistic peculiarities of the language of the work. In future editorial work, this type of publication will replace the hard-to-access original source and will become a special sort of encyclopedia for the given literary work. Considering the technology now available for photoreproduction, as well as the experience with facsimile publications in Pushkin or Joyce studies, the reproduction of the surviving manuscript fragments of *The Gift* as a separate supplement to an edition of the novel would serve as an effective documentary basis for further studies of Nabokov's text.

The composition of such an edition of *The Gift* might be particularly challenging because it will have to provide internal links and multilayered commentary for a range of hypertextual levels. Contemporary online tools make this complex task realistic (see, for instance, Brian Boyd's computerized project ADAonline devoted to Nabokov's novel, *Ada*), but paper editions will require different solutions. The experience gained from Biblical exegesis, namely the layout of the editions of Talmudic literature, offers an appropriate example: since 1523 the Talmud page in the Hebrew print tradition represents a hierarchically arranged system of text blocks emphasizing various elements graphically or through combinations of typescript styles. The source text is always reprinted in a larger font in the middle of the page, while wide margins usually contain assorted comments belonging to individual authors and schools of thought. The suggestion of this approach should not be misinterpreted as an attempt to identify the subject of our literary analysis with any sacred text or to force theological terminology and principles of interpretation into the humanities; I am simply proposing that borrowing of formal elements and applying them to less elaborate secular literature could be an efficient and productive methodology, especially in the unique case of *The Gift*.

References

Adams, Tom. "The Collector (hardback) by John Fowles," *Tom Adams Uncovered*. <http://www.tomadamsuncovered.co.uk/gallery.html> Accessed July 19, 2010.

B., A.G., "Nabokov Novel Not Up to Par," *News and Courier* (Charleston, South Carolina), July 28, 1963.

Barabtarlo, Gennady. "...Et Dona Ferentesi". *The Nabokovian* 23, 1989: 15-20.

____ "Nabokov's Chernyshevski in the *Contemporary Annals*: Letters to V. Rudnev and I. Fondaminski," *The Nabokovian* 24, 1990: 15-23.

Blackwell, Stephen H. *The Quill and the Scalpel: Nabokov's Art and the Worlds of Science*. Columbus: The Ohio State University Press, 2009.

Boyd, Brian. *Vladimir Nabokov: The Russian Years*. Princeton: Princeton University Press, 1990.

____ "Manuscripts," *The Garland Companion to Vladimir Nabokov*, ed. by Vladimir E. Alexandrov. New York: Garland, 1995.

____ "Nabokov's Texts," *The Nabokovian* 46, 2000.

____ "Nabokov's Butterflies." Introduction by B. Boyd. *The Atlantic Monthly* 4 (Vol. 285), April 2000.

____ "Nabokov, Literature, Lepidoptera" in *Nabokov's Butterflies: Unpublished and Uncollected writings*. Edited and annotated by Brian Boyd and Robert Michael Pyle; new translations from the Russian by Dmitri Nabokov. Boston: Beacon Press, 2000.

____ "The Expected Stress Did Not Come': A Note on "Father's Butterflies," *The Nabokovian* 45, 2000: 22-29.

Brown, William Edward. *A History of Russian Literature of the Romantic Period*, Vol. 3. Ann Arbor: Ardis, 1986.

Chernyshev, Andrei. "'Kak redko teper' pishu po-russki...' Iz perepiski V.V. Nabokova i M. Aldanova," *Oktiabr'* 1, 1996.

Davydov, Sergei. "Weighing Nabokov's *Gift* on Pushkin's Scales." *Cultural Mythologies of Russian Modernism from the Golden Age to the Silver Age*. Ed. Boris Gasparov, Robert P. Hughes, and Irina Paperno. Berkeley: University of California Press, 1992: 415-28.

Dolinin, Alexander. "K istorii sozdaniia i tisneniia romana 'Dar'," *Indiana Slavic Studies* 11, 2000: 339-47.

Donadio, Rachel. "The Papers Chase," *The New York Times* (Sunday Book Review). March 25, 2007.

_____ "Zagadka nedopisannogo romana," in *Istinnaia zhizn' pisatelia Sirina. Raboty o Nabokove* (St. Petersburg: Akademicheskii proekt, 2004): 278-293.

_____ "Nabokov as a Russian writer," *The Cambridge Companion to Nabokov*. Ed. by Julian W. Connolly. Cambridge: Cambridge University Press, 2005: 49-64.

_____ "Znaki i simvoly v 'Znakakh i simvolakh' Nabokova," *Imperia N. Nabokov i nasledniki*. Ed. by Yuri Leving and Evgeniy Soshkin. Moscow: NLO, 2006: 506-521.

Eidelman, Natan. "Sarancha letela...i sela," *Znanie–sila* 8-9, 1968.

Ermolaev, Herman. *Censorship in Soviet literature, 1917-1991*. Lanham: Rowland, 1997.

Ferrer, Daniel. "The Joyce of Manuscripts." *A Companion to James Joyce*. Ed. by Richard Brown. Hoboken: Blackwell Publishing, 2008.

Fet, Victor. "An Anti-locust Campaign in Nabokov (and Pushkin)," *The Nabokovian* 54, 2005: 13-14.

Funke, Sarah. *Véra's Butterflies: First editions by Vladimir Nabokov inscribed to his wife*. New York: Glenn Horowitz, 1999.

G., A. "Novoe slovo," *Posev*, July 13, 1952.

Gessen, I. "Iz knigi 'Gody izgnania: Zhiznennyi otchet'," *Pro et Contra. Lichnost' i tvorchestvo Vladimira Nabokova v otsenke russkih i zarubezhnykh myslitelei i issledovatelei*. Antologia. Vol. 1. St. Petersburg: Izdatel'stvo russkogo khristianskogo gosudarstvennogo universiteta, 1997.

Glushanok, Galina. "Rabota V. Nabokova nad perevodom 'Evgeniia Onegina' v perepiske s A. Ts. Yarmolinskim," *Pushkin i Nabokov: Sbornik dokladov mezhdunarodnoi konferentsii, 15-18 aprelia 1999*. St. Petersburg: Dorn, 1999: 321-40.

_____ "Perepiska V. Nabokova s V. M. Zenzinovym: 'Dorogoi i milyi Odissey...'" in *V. Nabokov: Pro et contra* II. St. Petersburg: Izdatel'stvo Russkogo Khristianskogo gumanitarnogo instituta, 2001: 34-123.

Grayson, Jane. "Washington's Gift: Materials Pertaining to Nabokov's *Gift* in the Library of Congress," *Nabokov Studies* 1, 1994: 21-67.

Grishunin, A. L. *Issledovatel'skie aspekty tekstologii*. Moscow: Nasledie, 1998.

Ivanov, Georgii. *Sobranie sochinenii v 3 tt*. Vol. 2. Moscow: Soglasie, 1994.

Knizhnaia polka ("The Book Shelf") [Unsigned], *Sovremennik* (Toronto, Canada) 35-36, 1977.

Kolerov, Modest. "Esli sistema vozroditsia, eiforiia prinadlezhnosti k vlasti proidet" [Kolerov's interview with E. Dyogot']. Moscow: Dom intellektual'noi knigi, 2001.

Leving, Yuri. "Singing 'The Bells' and 'The Covetous Knight': Nabokov and Rachmaninoff's Operatic Translations of Poe and Pushkin," *Transitional Nabokov*. Ed. by Duncan White and Will Norman. New York: Peter Lang Publishing Group: 205-228.

_____ "Samuel Izrailevich: Pnin's Character, Nabokov's Friend," *The Nabokovian* 39, 1997: 13-17.

Likhachev, Dmitri. *Tekstologiia. Na materiale russkoi literatury X–XVII vekov*. Moskva: Izdatel'stvo Akademii Nauk SSSR, 1962.

Livak, Leonid. "Le social contre l'esthétique. Le Zemgor dans la vie littéraire de l'émigration," *Cahiers du Monde Russe*, 46/4, October–Décembre 2005: 817-830.

Lotman, Yuri. "Stikhotvoreniia rannego Pasternaka i nekotorye voprosy strukturnogo izucheniia teksta," *Trudy po znakovym sistemam* 4 (Uchenye zapiski Tartuskogo gos. universiteta, No. 236), Tartu: Tartu State University, 1969.

Mandelstam, Osip. *The Complete Critical Prose and Letters*. Ed., trans. Jane Gary Harris and Constance Link. Ardis: Ann Arbor, 1979.

Martinez, Juan. "A Fold of the Marquisette: Nabokov's Lepidoptery in Visual Media." *The Goalkeeper: The Nabokov Almanac*. Ed. Yuri Leving. Boston: Academic Studies Press, 2010.

Martynov, G. *V.V. Nabokov: Bibliograficheskii ukazatel'*. St. Petersburg: Folio-Press, 2001.

Nabokov, Dmitri. "History-to-be: The Tale of the Nabokov Archive," *The Nabokovian* 29, 1991: 9-16.

Nabokov, Vladimir. *Eugene Onegin: A Novel in Verse by Alexander Pushkin*. Vol. 1. Trans. and comm. by V. Nabokov. Princeton: Princeton University Press, 1975.

_____ *Selected Letters: 1940-1977*. Ed. by Dmitri Nabokov, Matthew Joseph Bruccoli. New York: Harcourt, Brace, Jovanovich, 1989.

_____ *The Stories of Vladimir Nabokov*. New York: Vintage, 2002.

_____ *Strong Opinions*. New York: McGraw Hill, 1973.

_____ *Nabokov's Butterflies: Unpublished and Uncollected writings*. Edited and annotated by Brian Boyd and Robert Michael Pyle; new translations from the Russian by Dmitri Nabokov. Boston: Beacon Press, 2000.

_____ *The Nabokov–Wilson Letters: Correspondence Between Vladimir Nabokov and Edmund Wilson, 1941-1971*. Ed. by Simon Karlinsky. New York: Harper and Row, 1979.

Paperno S. and Hagopian J. "Official and Unofficial Responses to Nabokov in the Soviet Union." *The Achievements of Vladimir Nabokov*. Eds. George Gibian and Stephen Jan Parker. Ithaca, New York: Center for International Studies, Cornell University, 1984.

Pushkin, Alexander. *Polnoe sobranie sochinenii v 10 tt*. Vol. 5. Moscow: Nauka, 1964.

Ronen, Omry. "Emulation, Anti-Parody, Intertextuality, and Annotation," *Nabokov Studies* 5, 1998/99: 63-70.

Schiff, Stacy. *Véra (Mrs. Vladimir Nabokov)*. New York: Random House, 1999.

Stringer-Hye, Suellen. "*Laura* Is Not Even the Original's Name." An Interview with Dmitri Nabokov. *Nabokov Online Journal*, Vol. II, 2008. [http://etc.dal.ca/noj/volume2/articles/05_StringerDNabokov.pdf> Accessed July 19, 2010.

Struve, Gleb. "Vladimir Nabokov as I knew and I see him" [manuscript], Hoover Institute. Gleb Struve Archive. Box 50. Folder 54. Publication and commentary by M. Malikova. *Russkaia literatura* (St. Petersburg) 1, 2007: 236-257.

Tolstoy, Leo. *The Death of Ivan Ilych and Other Stories*. New York: Signet Classics, 2003.

Yangirov, Rashit. "Drebezzhanie moikh rzhavykh russkikh strun..." Iz perepiski Vladimira i Very Nabokovykh i Romana Grinberga (1940-1967). *In Memoriam. Istoricheskii sbornik pamiati A.I. Dobkina*. St. Petersburg; Paris, 2000.

Zanganeh, Lila Azam. "Butterflies and Other Bits of Nabokov's Life, Dispersed to the Wind," *The New York Times*. 6 May 2004.

Chapter Two
HISTORICAL CONTEXT

Imperial Russia and the Golden Age

The eighteenth century witnessed a remarkable ascendancy of Russia as a political power. During the reign of Catherine II some 200,000 square miles were added to the country's territory, and the population increased from 19 million to 36 million. By the end of that century Russia was "a full-fledged and, at times, leading member of the quarrelsome community of European states" (Florinsky 363). Despite these rapid developments, "there was no corresponding transformation in the field of cultural endeavor" in the Russian Empire (Ibid.). The cultural infrastructure of the era was meager and uninspiring: a few pretentious institutions with important-sounding names, such as the Academy of Science, the Academy of Arts, and the University of Moscow (it had a small number of students and bore little resemblance to a higher education institution); a few literary journals were run by a handful of professional historians and men of letters. Music, painting, and architecture were dominated by Western European influences, and the exponents of these arts were predominantly foreigners (Ibid.).

All of this began to change dramatically during the tense years of the Napoleonic Wars, which, in Russia as elsewhere, were notable for a surge of cultural creativity and artistic innovation. Indeed, the early decades of the nineteenth century (roughly 1810-30) have become known as the Golden Age of Russian culture. In the salons of St. Petersburg and Moscow, "poets, musicians, and intellectuals—most of whom were also officers in the imperial army—debated questions of literary form, translated the latest English and German romantic verse, and reflected on the question of Russian history, all with unprecedented intensity" (Goldfrank et al. 26). Numerous journals emerged in the two capitals, each with its own personality and literary direction. One particular feature of this Russian development, especially after the Decembrist uprising in 1825 (which sought at a minimum to establish a constitutional monarchy), was that the authorities regarded any manifestation of civil society "with deep suspicion" (Hosking 291). Philanthropy, educational initiatives, the formation of public interest groups and voluntary associations were seen as "the progenitors of subversion" (Ibid.). The government looked askance at literature too, especially since the literary community already possessed a network of printing presses and bookshops independent of the regime, and a good many enthusiastic customers. "Unlike music or painting, literature dealt in words and hence could comment directly on political or social matters; but at the same time its use of words was ambiguous and multi-layered" (Ibid.). Fiction posed tricky problems for the censorship apparatus: it was difficult for censors (who were themselves members of the educated public), "without appearing foolish before the educated public, to assign a single unambiguous meaning to a text and then in good conscience declare it unacceptable" (Ibid.).

The innovations and ferment of the Golden Age were concentrated primarily in three fields—language, literature, and religion. The 1810s and 1820s were, above all, the Golden Age of poetry, from which the modern Russian language emerged. At the center of the poets' circles, both in his years at the Lyceum and afterward, stood Alexander Sergeevich Pushkin (1799-1837). Pushkin is often considered a starting point in Russian literature. Born in Moscow, he was of African as well as Russian ancestry. Pushkin's early liberal verse not only gave him notoriety, but also earned him considerable influence and great popularity in educated society. In Russia in the nineteenth century literature came to play the role of what can loosely be termed an "alternative government." Given the lack of political democracy, "literature became the main forum for discussion of oppositional or even slightly critical ideas" (Andrew 9).

Tsar Alexander I (1801-25) exiled Pushkin for writing revolutionary epigrams that had come to his attention in the same year when Pushkin's first major publication, *Ruslan and Lyudmila*, met with resounding success (1820). Pushkin spent the remaining part of Alexander's reign moving constantly between the Caucasus, Bessarabia, and southern Ukraine, yet eventually coming to reside as an exile at his parents' estate, Mikhailovskoe, in 1824. Only Alexander's death and the accession of a new Emperor brought Pushkin back to Moscow and St. Petersburg in 1826.

The creator of modern literary Russian and the first truly national writer, Pushkin set the standard for nineteenth-century literature. He belonged to the era of Romanticism: an early admirer of Byron, Pushkin then outgrew his Romantic sensibilities and moved to Realism in several of his later works. As a modern writer with deep classical instincts, Pushkin had a sense of responsibility to tradition and to society: Russia, he thought, needed "Shakespearean" drama, and the result was his play *Boris Godunov*. He also produced "the best novel Walter Scott never wrote," *The Captain's Daughter* (Milner-Gulland 122). The importance of his novel in verse, *Eugene Onegin*, lay in its poetic creation of characters who were to become prototypes for the novels of Lermontov, Goncharov, and Turgenev. According to

Boris Gasparov it was Pushkin's own literary evolution that eventually connected Russian literature to European Romanticism: Russian authors mastered the formal accomplishments of the newest literary schools at the turn of the nineteenth century quickly and brilliantly (the elegy, the historical ballad, the friendly epistle, and the Byronic poetic monologue), but the romantic "poetry of life," the romantic struggle of thought with language, romantic reflexivity came significantly later, in the 1830s (Gasparov 545). Pushkin did not go as far as most romantics in his break with literary convention in overcoming fixed forms: "The reader himself is left to decide what lies concealed behind this faultless exterior. Peering into the smooth surface of Pushkin's verse, one begins to take note of more and more layers of implied meanings and interpretations, entirely new directions of his hints and allusions, dizzying intersections and collisions of disparate perspectives," reminiscent of a kaleidoscope (Ibid. 550). In a certain sense the complexity of Nabokov's texts is modeled after that of Pushkin's works. To use Gasparov's analogy, they do not "play hide-and-go-seek" with the reader "but instead really do refrain from showing him much, without the slightest concern for whether or not the 'right' reader, or any other kind of reader, will succeed in seeing the invisible. On the textual surface the reader does not detect the slightest trace that his understanding might differ from the quite obvious meaning offered by the surface with such aphoristic clarity and elegance" (551).

[Ill. 2-1] Nikolai Ge. "Pushkin in the village Mikhailovskoe" (1875, The Art Museum of Kharkiv collection)

The last decade of Pushkin's life was tinged with tragedy: some of his friends were involved in the Decembrist conspiracy and were exiled to Siberia. This left Pushkin feeling extremely isolated as he would, most likely, have been involved himself in the revolt had he not been forced to live at Mikhailovskoe. Although *Eugene Onegin* was completed in 1831, the new generation of poets and writers was distant from Pushkin and saw him as a venerable relic of an earlier age. Finally, his marriage, in 1831, to the beautiful and frivolous Natalia Goncharova, soon became a source of unhappiness. In 1837 Pushkin challenged his wife's admirer, Baron Georges D'Anthes (a French royalist in the Russian service) to a duel and was fatally wounded.

The cult of Pushkin, originating in the late nineteenth century, has lasted through the Soviet period and beyond: his poetry has been memorized by every educated Russian and continues to constitute a touchstone for literature, ideas, and political views. As the acclaimed essayist and critic Andrei Sinyavsky writes, in his light-hearted manner, "all themes, like women, were accessible to [Pushkin], and running through them he marked out roads for Russian letters for centuries to come. No matter where we poke our noses — Pushkin is everywhere, which can be explained not so much by the influence of his genius on other talents, as by the fact that there isn't a motif in the world he didn't touch upon. Pushkin simply managed to write about everything for everyone. As a result he became the Russian Virgil, and in this role of teacher-guide he accompanies us in no matter which direction of history, culture, or life we go" (Tertz 76).

If Pushkin's niche is that of the classic poet, then the great age of the Russian novel begins with Nikolai Gogol (1809–52). Pushkin welcomed Gogol's early stories, with their Ukrainian folk background. His next cycle, the so-called Petersburg tales, revealed an alarming underbelly beneath a surface of comedy and pathos. In a few years on either side of his thirtieth birthday, mostly spent abroad, Gogol produced his masterpieces: the play *The Inspector General*, "The Overcoat," and the first part of *Dead Souls*. Looked at in detail "these works are uproariously funny," while from a broader perspective they are terrifying "in their haunted soullessness" (Milner-Gulland 122). Gogol's "unruly genius deserted him, his projected [three-part] 'Divine Comedy,' *Dead Souls*, remained a fragment and he died in pitiful dejection" (Ibid.).

Russia and the West

Nabokov once stated that the reader "does not seek information about Russia in a Russian novel, for he knows that the Russia of Tolstoy and Chekhov is not the average Russia of history but a specific world imagined and created by individual genius" (*Lectures on Russian literature* 11). Nineteenth-century Russian literature is now part and parcel of the European canon. Nearly all Russian writers, as

Benedict Sumner writes, were deeply versed in French, German, and English literature—mostly in the originals, sometimes in translation; the range and quality of translations were wide and high. Similarly, Russian social thought and philosophy developed from European thinkers and were subject to influence from the same trends that were dominant in the West. Even Communism was born out of the West, out of Marx and Engels, and the Bolshevik revolution was international in its philosophy and appeal (Sumner 303). On the other hand, despite the fact that Russian literature belongs to "the great European heritage, there was in it, and still more in Russian social and religious thought, a persistent and often violent insistence that Russia was not and would not be Europe...Russia was regarded by many as a separate civilization, with its own basic foundations either in Orthodoxy or in the unique spirit of her people" (Ibid. 308). Peter the Great himself was reputed to have said: "Europe is necessary to us for a few decades, and then we can turn our backs on her."

Another important factor that shaped the Russian identity was its initial landlocked condition, which fueled expansionism in the form of a constant struggle to gain access to the oceans. Following the ideas of Russia's celebrated historian Vasilii Kliuchevskii, the philosopher Nicholas Berdiaev, in search of a metaphysical answer to the meaning of domestic history, recognized the formative significance of Russian geography. Self-preservation, he observed, "forced the Russians to push off invaders and to entrench themselves firmly in their habitat, but since it afforded them precious little natural protection they were constantly pressed to expand their borders to keep their enemies at bay" (Hunczak 20). Thus, the Russian identity can be seen in no small part as a product of the struggle for control of a vast territory: Nabokov's response to this spatial paradigm in *The Gift* to some extent defines the meaning of Fyodor's father's explorations.

Even as Russia struggled with its national identity, caught spatially and philosophically between Europe and Asia, the country produced a level of fiction that was equal to authors in the West. "That successful works of Russian literature would now be routinely translated into the languages of the West showed that Russia had arrived culturally, though it would take some time until the West realized that Tolstoy's *Anna Karenina* (1875–77) was a 'European event,' as Dostoevsky put it, and that the Russian novel of that period was one of the high points in all literature" (Terras 294).

The intellectual history of that period is marked by the ongoing debate between the so-called Slavophiles and Westernizers. Slavophiles believed that the nation needed to return to the purity and simplicity of early Russian society. Russia's ills, they believed, were caused by foreign influence and by the government's importation of Western institutions. The Slavophiles "had little patience with bureaucratic stupidity and autocracy," but they sought relief in Slavic equality and Christian brotherhood (Wren 391).

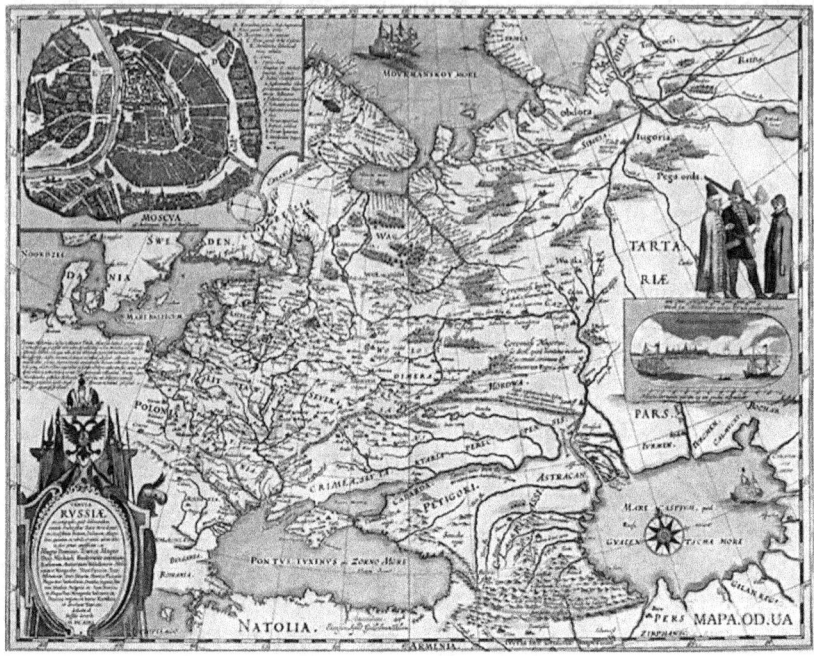

[Ill. 2-2] The Map of Russia published in Amsterdam in 1614 (Moskovyia, *Tabula Russiae ex autographo, quod delineandum curavit Foedor filius Tzaris Boris desumta*)

To the Westernizers, on the other hand, "Western Europe stood for enlightenment and freedom," while Russia embodied obscurantism and slavery (Ibid.). Russia suffered, they argued, "not from too much Western influence but from entirely too little. The West to them meant democratic government, economic progress, intellectual freedom, and moral dignity" (Ibid.). The radical Westernizers, although few in number, included such major figures as Alexander Herzen (1812–70) and Michael Bakunin (1814–76).

AESTHETIC THEORIES AND LITERARY CRITICISM

From the 1850s until well into the 1890s Russian literary criticism followed the example of social and literary critic Vissarion Belinsky (1811–48), seeing the principal role of criticism as that of a mediator between literature and society. These critics generally agreed that literature had a social responsibility. Their position as critics of the regime tended to determine their theoretical views on art. Using caustic and combative literary criticism they "advocated the anthropological principle that man was not divisible into soul and body but should be interpreted solely as a physical organism" (Freeborn, *The Rise of the Russian Novel* 130).

The four major literary critics were Nikolai Dobrolyubov (1836–61), Dmitri Pisarev (1840–68), Belinsky, and Nikolai Chernyshevski (1828–89). The first and the last were sons of priests and former seminary students; Pisarev was a member of the gentry. Dobrolyubov and Pisarev, who were principally critics, died quite young, while Chernyshevski, who lived on almost to the last decade of the nineteenth century, was also a novelist. Dobrolyubov "enjoyed the respect and admiration of his older colleagues for his unflagging revolutionary zeal, moral purity, amazing energy and remarkable talent" (Terras 300). His manner is "less arid, doctrinaire, and self-righteous than Chernyshevski's, but his style is awkward and prolix, in part because he was writing 'around' the censorship, using elaborate circumlocutions and Aesopian language to camouflage his message" (Ibid.). Pisarev was the *enfant terrible* amongst the Civic critics. He "served time in prison (as did Chernyshevski)" and once hypothesized that "the intellectual brilliance of the eighteenth century was due to the widespread drinking of tea and coffee (Voltaire is reported to have drunk seventy-five cups of coffee a day)" (Stacy 55). He was also one of the few Russian critics who have dared to challenge Pushkin. "Here is the ultimatum of our camp," Pisarev proclaimed, "What can be smashed should be smashed; what will stand the blow is good... at any rate hit out left and right" (Yarmolinsky 120). He condemned Pushkin despite the fact that Belinsky regarded *Eugene Onegin* as a realistic guide, as Russia's great national poem, calling it an "encyclopedia of Russian life," and indeed also of Russian history. According to Pisarev, as a painter may make himself most useful by illustrating a book on insect pests, so the writer best fulfills his calling by expounding positivist and scientific knowledge. "With all this, Pisarev was a lucid thinker, an elegant stylist, and a witty and entertaining writer" (Terras 304). Equally adept within utilitarianism, rationalism, and materialism, Pisarev died (by drowning or possibly by suicide) when he was twenty-eight.

Chernyshevski, whose aesthetics Pisarev accepted, "maintained that all art is subordinate to life, that it is dependent on the external world for both its content and its form" (Brown, "Pisarev and the Transformation" 152). Art, however imperfectly, does reflect life:

> Moreover, Russian novelists themselves seem to have accepted this notion without reflection. Gogol, who knew very little about Russia, believed that he was holding a mirror up to her, and that if the image seemed cracked or distorted, the fault was with the subject. Turgenev felt obliged to justify his behavior as a writer of novels by insisting on their importance as a kind of historical record. (Ibid.)

Young intellectuals were influenced by Chernyshevski and Dobrolyubov. Determined "to remake the world through reason, they turned enthusiastically to radicalism" (MacKenzie, Curran 349). These radical activists "gathered around a journal, *The Contemporary*. Soviet scholars regarded Chernyshevski, a leading contributor, as the chief precursor of Bolshevism and praised his materialism and his scorn for liberalism. Chernyshevski dreamed of changing history's course by building a perpetual motion machine to abolish poverty" (Ibid.). Pisarev, too, "believed that an educated elite with modern science and European technology would uplift the masses and destroy autocracy"; though they were ardent Westernizers, these intellectual revolutionaries posited that "Russia, unlike Europe, could avoid capitalism and move directly to socialism" (Ibid.).

The Conflict of Fathers and Sons

The theme of the father-and-son bond is one of the cornerstones of Nabokov's *The Gift*. It relies on a solid tradition that originated long before in the European epos (*cf.* Odysseus and Telemachus), and developed in a particular way in nineteenth-century Russian prose. While the intellectual history of Russia in the second half of the nineteenth century can be summarized through some aspects of Russian radicalism of the 1860s and 1870s, it has become customary to speak of the generation of the sixties as the "sons" (or "nihilists") and to contrast them with the "fathers" of the forties. The transformation in Russia was part of a broader change in Europe which has been associated with a transition from romanticism to realism. In Russian conditions the shift acquired an exaggerated and violent dimension.

[Ill. 2-3] Ivan Turgenev

The classic fictional exposition of the debate between the older moderate Westernizers and the younger militant ones is Turgenev's masterpiece *Fathers and Children* (1862; often translated, less accurately, as *Fathers and Sons*), with its portrait of the "nihilist" Evgenii Bazarov. Turgenev described Bazarov with a term that was not new but that was gaining currency at this time—*nihilist*—"on which the enemies of the younger generation and of democracy soon seized in order to give it an almost pejorative connotation" (Miliukov et al. 49). But Turgenev strove for impartiality: he depicted at once the virtues and the faults of the "son" (Bazarov) and of the "father" (Kirsanov). Later he was to explain that, "if Bazarov is called a *nihilist*, it is *revolutionary* that is meant"—indeed, it was at the same time as this novel was first published that the first revolutionary current stirred among the Russian youth (Ibid.). Alexander Herzen, a brilliant spokesperson of the old civilization, refused to consider these young men the representatives of true democracy:

The fates of the *fathers and sons* are strange! Clearly Turgenev did not introduce Bazarov to pat him on the head; it is also clear that he had wanted to do something for the benefit of the fathers. But, juxtaposed with such pitiful and insignificant fathers as the Kirsanovs, the stern Bazarov captivated Turgenev and, instead of spanking the son, he flogged the fathers.

This is why it happened that a portion of the younger generation recognized itself in Bazarov. But we do not recognize ourselves at all in the Kirsanovs...

There is no lack of moral abortions living at the same time in different strata of society, and in its different tendencies; without doubt, they represent more or less general types, but they do not present the sharpest and most characteristic aspects of their generation—the aspects which most express its intensiveness. (Herzen 222; see also Malia)

The nihilists' revolt began within their own family—they "questioned paternal authority, challenged social conventions and good manners, broke away from homes, and adopted brusque, often coarse ways of speech and behavior" (Slonim 115). Above all else "nihilism" meant a fundamental rebellion against received authority and accepted values: against abstract thought and family control, against structured lyric poetry and school discipline, against religion and romantic idealism. The term 'nihilism' soon became the symbol of anarchy and depravity. As Nabokov's émigré contemporary and his wife's distant relative, Marc Slonim, graphically put it: "Horrified mothers and fathers saw girls cut their hair, smoke cigarettes and treat males as equals, while boys wore peasant boots and Russian blouses, grew long whiskers, talked loudly without mincing their words and spoke of religion as 'a lot of trash.' The new fashion called for the strangest kind of attire: a bespectacled student with bobbed hair (if female) and with long hair (if male) represented the nihilist in the eyes of polite society; but for the authorities, nihilist meant 'an enemy of the established order'" (Slonim 116). Although nihilism was initially apolitical—under its disguise of rudeness and exaggeration lay a desire for work and practical action—the Russian government looked at this movement with unconcealed suspicion.

The key issue for Alexander II, the last royal ruler to make a concerted attempt to transform Russia, remained serfdom. This system of enslaved labor was decreasingly effective at meeting the economic needs of the Russian Empire, and the emancipation of the serfs in Russia occurred in 1861. However, "the government failed to resolve the fundamental dilemma of change: where to stop. The 'great reforms,' together with the general development of Russia and the intellectual climate of the time, led to pressure for further reform" (Riasanovsky 378). Dmitri Karakozov's attempt to assassinate the emperor in 1866 led to further reaction, which continued under Alexander III and Nicholas II at least until the revolution of 1905 (Ibid.). Nabokov's father, Vladimir Dmitrievich Nabokov, was among the Russian intellectuals who believed that the creation of a constitutional monarchy would have satisfied most of the demand and provided stability for the nation.

Despite the fact that the portrait of Fyodor Godunov-Cherdyntsev's father in *The Gift* was considered to be a very true likeness of V. D. Nabokov (assassinated in 1924 in Berlin), there is an important difference: one major area of his life that his author-son eliminated was Vladmir Dmitrievich Nabokov's lifelong dedication to legal reform, governmental service and constitutional law (Greenleaf 149). Boris Godunov's political battles in the Time of Troubles are replaced in the novel by Konstantin Godunov-Cherdyntsev's apolitical naturalism and exaggerated contempt for everything merely historical and human. Unlike his fictional reflection, as an editor of the émigré newspaper *Rudder* Nabokov's father continued to lead the politically fractured Russian Diaspora. Godunov-Cherdyntsev's professional and intellectual life inverts each of these details: a scholarly naturalist and explorer, he avoids the war in order to continue his monumental scientific quest.

Nabokov identified himself with the values of the "fathers." Asked once what he thought of the so-called "student revolution," his firm rejoinder was: "Rowdies are never revolutionary, they are always reactionary. It is among the young that the greatest conformists and Philistines are found, e.g., the hippies with their group beards and group protests. Demonstrators at American universities care as little about education as football fans who smash up subway stations in England care about soccer" (*Strong Opinions* 139).

The theme of the father-son relationship continues to play a role in the Chernyshevski biography, in which Fyodor "adopts an unusual compositional stance: he treats Chernyshevski almost as if the historical figure were a literary character" (Connolly 146). Fyodor does not fabricate events, but traces instead subtle repetitions in Chernyshevski's life and treats them as one would follow the "themes" found in fiction (the theme of "nearsightedness," the theme of "angelic clarity," and so on; G214-15). As Julian Connolly contends, the portrait of Chernyshevski emerging from this treatment is complex: "While Fyodor is unsparing in his criticism of the contradictions and confusion he finds in Chernyshevski's pronouncements on art, the reader also senses a certain degree of sympathy for Chernyshevski's consistent lack of good fortune in life" (Connolly 146). Connolly highlights several aspects of Chernyshevski's biography resonating with corresponding elements in Fyodor's life: they share a birthday (July 12, 1828 for Chernyshevski, and July 12, 1900 for Fyodor); Chernyshevski has a "mysterious 'something'" (G264) that recalls a trait Fyodor had perceived in his own father: "In and around my father...there was something difficult to convey in words, a haze, a mystery..." (G114; ibid.).

Nikolai Chernyshevski

In their views on society the radicals of the 1860s differed from the "fathers," reflecting the progressive democratization of the educated public in Russia (Riasanovsky 382). Many of them belonged to a group known in Russian as *raznochintsy* (pl.; usually translated as "commoners" or literally "of different ranks"), that is, people of mixed background below the gentry, such as sons of priests who did not follow the calling of their fathers, offspring of low-ranking officials, or individuals from the masses who made their way up through education and effort (Ibid.). For instance, Innokentiy, the protagonist of Nabokov's short story "The Circle," possesses traits linking him with this group.

[Ill. 2-4] Chernyshevski and Herzen pictured by a Soviet artist

A typical *raznochinets* (sing.), Nikolai Gavrilovich Chernyshevski, may have had a greater influence on the course of Russian history than any other major figure from Russian literature. The son of a parish priest in Saratov on the Volga, Chernyshevski earned a scholarship at Petersburg University. His master's thesis, "On the Aesthetic Relations of Art to Reality" (1855) was an attack on idealist aesthetics and charted the course of the new literature of the sixties. His *Essays in the Gogolian Period of Russian Literature* (1856) inaugurated the age of a socially conscious realism in Russian literature.

Chapter Two. HISTORICAL CONTEXT

[Ill. 2-5, 2-6] Chernyshevski's civil execution (St. Petersburg, 1864)

Chernyshevski's aesthetic was based on the premise that healthy art was no more and no less than imitation of nature, a substitute for real objects, useful for when those real objects were absent. He insisted that even the greatest work of art was inherently inferior to the real object it represented and saw the role of art in utilitarian terms.

Chernyshevski attacked the 1861 settlement that emancipated the serfs as grossly inadequate and mockingly cruel to the hopeful peasants (most peasants hardly understood the issues and were apolitical). He called himself a "socialist," a term and a doctrine that he picked up not from Marx but from the Utopian Socialists of France and Britain. The socialist future, according to Chernyshevski, would be provided by a free, democratic, republican state, strengthened by a network of cooperatives and communes (Randall 9).

In July 1862 Chernyshevski was arrested on suspicion of subversive activities and authorship of an inflammatory revolutionary pamphlet. He was held at Saint Peter and Paul Fortress for two years, during which he wrote his socialist Utopian novel *What to Do?*

After his trial in May 1864, he was subjected to a so-called civil execution in St. Petersburg: Chernyshevski was placed upon a scaffold and a placard reading "State Criminal" was hung from his neck. Then a policeman broke a sword over the convict's head and read his sentence aloud. Deprived of his civil rights, Chernyshevski was transported to Siberia to serve seven years of hard labor. He was allowed to return to European Russia in 1883 and to his native Saratov in 1889, just four months before his death. Chernyshevski was revered as a martyr by the radical Russian intelligentsia, which embraced his materialist, rationalist, and positivist philosophy.

Nabokov was aware of the episode tying his own family to Chernyshevski's ill-fated story. It was Dmitri Nabokov, the writer's grandfather, who, as a Minister of Justice in the Tsar's cabinet, made the report on which Alexander III acted in allowing Chernyshevski to transfer to Astrakhan (Boyd, *Russian Years* 22).

Chernyshevski and the Literary Scandal

The book that Chernyshevski wrote "so laboriously in his cell in the fortress, on parsimoniously doled out sheets of paper" (Randall 104), was entitled *Chto delat'?*. This is usually translated as *What Is To Be Done?*, but the implied message of the title is better rendered by Nabokov's choice: *What to Do?*, which is "more literal, save for dropping the question mark, which did not imply any genuine doubt on Chernyshevski's part" (Ibid.). Coming from such an author in such a place, the title heightened political expectations; this was reinforced by the subtitle, *From Stories about the New People*, "for everyone knew that the 'new people' were the revolutionary youth" (Ibid.).

Nabokov playfully inserts the title of Chernyshevski's novel early in the narrative ("What am I doing! [*Chto ia sobstvenno delaiu!*] he thought, abruptly coming to his senses"; G6), in the middle of the long sentence, in which the "syntactic flow, ecstasy, foam, and creamy white cover, ends with a verbal ejaculation" (Naiman 167). This exclamation by Fyodor is a rephrasing of the title of Chernyshevski's novel, and "as such this is just one of many moments that link Fyodor to the somewhat abject target of his own work—either by direct opposition or through parodic similarity. The adverb *sobstvenno* ('as a matter of fact,' but literally meaning 'properly,' with reference to the self, *sebia*) emphasizes further that here the action is all Fyodor's; this is not, as with Chernyshevski's title, a question for everyone" (Ibid.). To Naiman's contemplative remark we should add that Tolstoy's *War and Peace* provides an even closer utterance: in the very finale of the novel (just before the epilogue) the two protagonists repeat the same existential self-inquiry using an infinitive construction as in Chernyshevski's title: "But what shall I do?" [Pierre: *No chto zhe mne delat'?*] and "But what's to be done?" [Princess Mary: *No chto zhe delat'!*] (Tolstoy 414-15).

Few novels have been written in circumstances as dramatic as those in which Chernyshevski produced *What to Do?*. It is easy to understand why he would want to write when imprisoned in the fortress; there was little else that he could do, and fiction stood a far better chance of seeing the light of day than any other form of writing by a prisoner. The mere fact that Chernyshevski "was able to write the entire novel in under four months suggests that the ideas and concerns expressed therein had been germinating in his mind for a long time and had, at the first opportunity, spilled forth in a veritable torrent of verbal images. His arrest effectively removed the main constraint on [his] creativity" (Pereira 76).

There is "no direct reference in the novel to the burning political questions of the day" and, although the clever reader can find a number of Aesopian comments on public events (such as Negro slavery in the USA and Brazil and, thus, apparently the author's denunciation of Russian serfdom), by and large, *What to Do?* "is not even covertly a novel about politics" (Randall 104). Nonetheless, as Francis B. Randall admits, it is still surprising that the censorship passed the work when it was known to have been written by a political prisoner (Ibid. 105).

The story of the novel's publication seems to be a spectacular but typical example of tsarist bureaucratic bungling: in late 1862 Chernyshevski asked the prison commandant for permission to begin work on a novel. His request granted, Chernyshevski set to work and "the first part of the manuscript was then submitted to the prison censor, who, whether carelessly or for devious purposes, passed it to the literary censor" with a letter to the effect that the manuscript had no bearing on the legal case at hand (Katz, Wagner 22). It appears the censor "assumed that the police had thereby approved the manuscript for publication for reasons of their own. Not daring to overrule so dreaded a body, the [second]

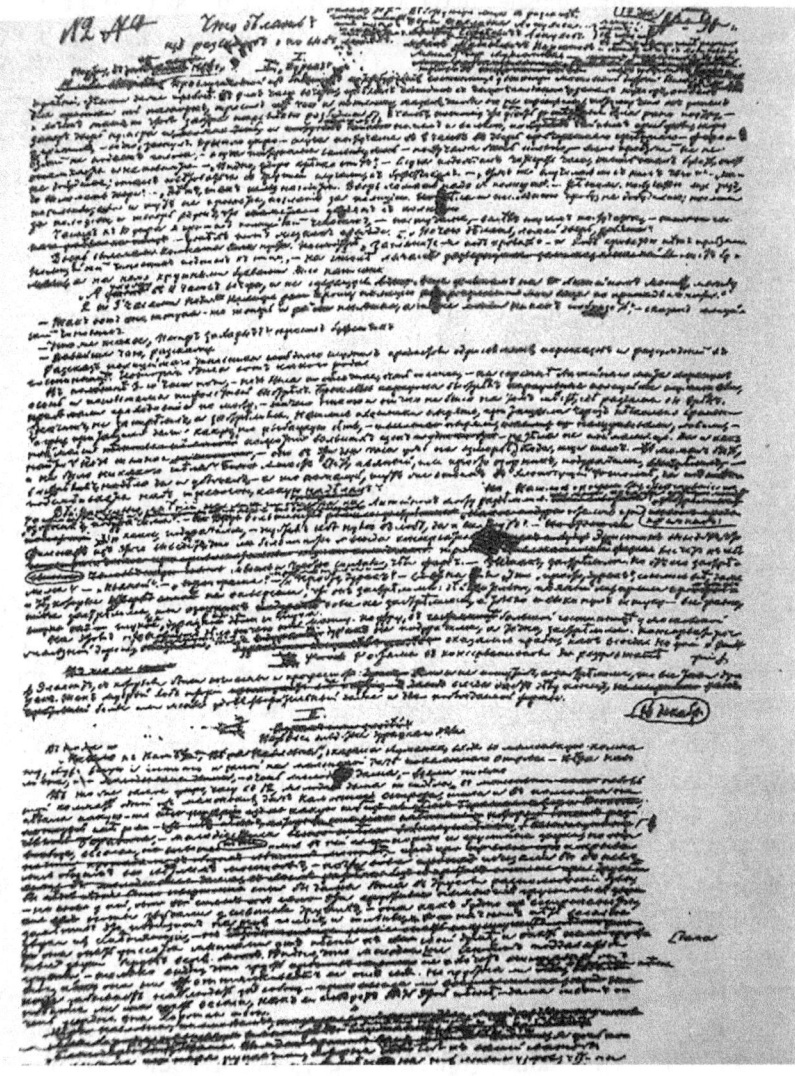

[Ill. 2-7] The manuscript of *What to Do?*

censor passed the manuscript, thinking he was merely rubber-stamping a high-level bureaucratic decision" (Randall 105).

Passed again, the novel was forwarded to the journal's editor, Nikolai Nekrasov, "who promptly lost it in a cab. He managed to recover the manuscript only after advertising in the official gazette of the St. Petersburg police. In what is perhaps the greatest irony of Russian letters, the novel that the police helped to retrieve turned out to be the most subversive and revolutionary work of nineteenth-century Russian literature" (Katz, Wagner 22-23). So, after this series of missed signals, the novel was actually published in the March, April, and May (1863) issues of *The Contemporary*. Only when permission was sought later to publish it in book form was it completely prohibited—as it would remain until the revolution of 1905. "But by then it was already the most influential of Russian novels" (Randall 105).

For contemporaries, "the novel was a bombshell and created a tremendous public uproar" (Paperno 26). Because the book was considered in official circles to be a serious threat to the stability of the existing social order, and despite the fact that the central issue of *What to Do?* was ostensibly the reorganization of relations between the sexes, both the author and readers projected the novel onto the reform of all social relations (Ibid.).

The Plot of *What to Do?*

What to Do? does not appear to be revolutionary at the start. The bulk of the action takes place in St. Petersburg from 1852 to 1856. The novel opens with "the mysterious disappearance and presumed suicide of Vera Pavlovna Lopukhov's husband" (Freeborn, *The Rise of the Russian Novel* 132). Vera is a typical lower-middle-class Russian girl, but, finding Lopukhov intellectually her inferior, she prefers the young doctor, Kirsanov, whom she marries after Lopukhov's disappearance. The novel ends by quite unsubtly showing Lopukhov's return to St. Petersburg under a pseudonym and the magnanimous reunion of the participants in a *ménage à trois* arrangement. The theme of female emancipation, Richard Freeborn observes, "is illustrated by the new morality, based on mutual respect between the sexes, that informs Vera's relations with her two husbands" (Lopukhov is a man of the new sort, who allows Vera to develop her full human potential) (Ibid.). Vera organizes communal cooperatives for seamstresses, and "the vision of a world transformed as a result of socialism is linked with the theme of female emancipation...She is finally granted, in her famous fourth dream, a utopian revelation of what a socialized industry in an era of Crystal Palaces could do for mankind" (Ibid.). Indeed, women would soon play a vital and growing role in the Russian revolutionary movement, both in its populist phase and later in the Marxist movement. Women "composed about one-eighth of revolutionary populists in the 1870s, most of them well educated," assuming the responsibilities undreamed of by traditional society (MacKenzie, Curran 353). About one-third of the Executive Committee of the People's Will (a Russian terrorist organization, best known for the successful assassination of Tsar Alexander II in 1881) was female, and they were subsequently incarcerated in the worst prisons alongside male terrorists (Ibid.).

The setting of *What to Do?* is "entirely realistic and quite specific" (Moser 142). The initial events described are dated precisely: Lopukhov arrives at a St.

Petersburg hotel on the evening of July 10, 1856 and asks to be awakened at eight the next morning. At three in the morning a shot is heard on the Liteiny Bridge on the Neva River, although nothing is found on the bridge thereafter:

> In the morning Lopukhov's room is broken into and found to be empty except for a suicide note in which he speaks of planning to take his own life in the early morning on the Liteiny Bridge. The chapter then offers some discussion as to whether a suicide has actually occurred, but the circumstantial evidence seems persuasive. Section 2 then goes back in time to provide background on the supposed tragedy: after discovering that his wife, Vera Pavlovna, has fallen in love with Kirsanov, Lopukhov proposes to make it possible for Vera to marry Kirsanov by removing himself from the scene through suicide. (Moser 142-43)

Chernyshevski seems to have developed a conventional Romantic novel spiced with a touch of forbidden radicalism. The novel's first two sections contain a concretely realistic description of a dramatic situation with a bit of mystery, in the established tradition of the popular crime novel genre. Indeed, according to Charles Moser, the author "deliberately designed the book's opening as a hook to seize his readers' attention" (Ibid.). Substantially past the novel's midpoint, in a brief passage filled with contempt for the implied reader (section 28 of Chapter Three), Chernyshevski openly "informs us that Lopukhov was the anonymous man involved in both the first and second sections (however, even at this point he does not make it clear that the suicide he had described so painstakingly and realistically was a hoax: he only does that at the novel's conclusion)" (Ibid.). In a similar way the reader of Nabokov's *The Gift* will learn significantly later in the narrative that the girl whom Fyodor dates is the very same daughter of his landlords whom we had observed earlier.

The Novel about Novels

Though Chernyshevski's major objective in writing *What to Do?* was to make certain essential political points, he also wished to make a statement on the nature of literature, and on the genre of the novel in particular (Moser 140). For this latter purpose he worked out what may be regarded as a new form of the contemporary novel, and it is true that very few of his contemporaries realized what he was doing. Most contemporary critics of whatever persuasion evaluated the book in terms of its social and political ideas while paying little or no attention to its artistic character, an approach that has persisted in Soviet and Western scholarship. A careful reading of *What to Do?* demonstrates that "Chernyshevski wished, among other things, to make an implicit statement about literature through the novel's form and an explicit one in certain passages of the text" (Ibid.).

The beginning of *What to Do?* is curiously arranged: it opens *in medias res*, in the best style of a mystery novel. The first section, numbered 1, is entitled "A Fool" and "describes the putative suicide; the second section, numbered 2 and entitled 'The First Consequences of the Idiotic Affair,' goes into the Vera Pavlovna Lopukhov-Kirsanov triangle" (Ibid. 143). And then Chernyshevski

> suddenly smashes the traditional structure of the Romantic novel: Section 3 is entitled—and is—a "Preface." "The subject of this novel is love," it begins, "and its principal character is a young woman." These statements turn out to be true, but their promise of conventionality, which the intelligent reader must by this time distrust, is very misleading. (Randall 108)

Only after the "Preface" in section 3 comes the first of six "chapters," all except the last of which are quite lengthy and themselves divided into numerous sections (Moser 143). This structural "incongruity" will later be employed fullscale in *The Gift*: recognizing its literary predecessor allows us to appreciate the literary depth of Nabokov's devices, which both mock and derive from Chernyshevski's experiment.

Chernyshevski worked without taking notice of the fact that he was explicitly distancing his own oeuvre from that of "the great Russian novelists." The salient feature of Chernyshevski's work is its persistent parodic commentary on the conventional expectations of readers of fine literature; some scholars go even further, claiming that it has been called a "novel" for no reason except that it is prose fiction of a certain length (Brown, "So much depends..." 379). Apart from allegedly being badly written (a contemporary critic called *What to Do?* "the most atrocious work of Russian literature," and Turgenev commented that Chernyshevski's style aroused physical revulsion in him), most critics agree that the novel abounds in "banal situations" and plot developments; it is "clumsy and awkward in style" (Paperno 26). It is clear though that one cannot judge this work as a regular piece of fiction. As Saul Morson notes, *What to Do?* consists of a constant alternation of narrative and metanarrative. In Chernyshevski's work the experience of reading is a self-reflexive and highly self-conscious process—the author repeatedly interrupts the story with interrogations of the reader and essays about the harmfulness of aesthetics: "So common are these metanarrative intrusions that the work often resembles a kind of socialist Sterne, a didactic *Don Quixote*. 'Baring' by exaggeration the devices it employs, Chernyshevski's work can be taken as a kind of textbook model of the utopian genre's techniques, particularly its techniques of didactic frame-breaking" (Morson 99-104). The same "frame-breaking," of course, is frequently featured in Nabokov's mature prose.

At the very start of the "Preface" Chernyshevski inserts himself into the novel as a participant, if not a character. Such a device was by no means unprecedented;

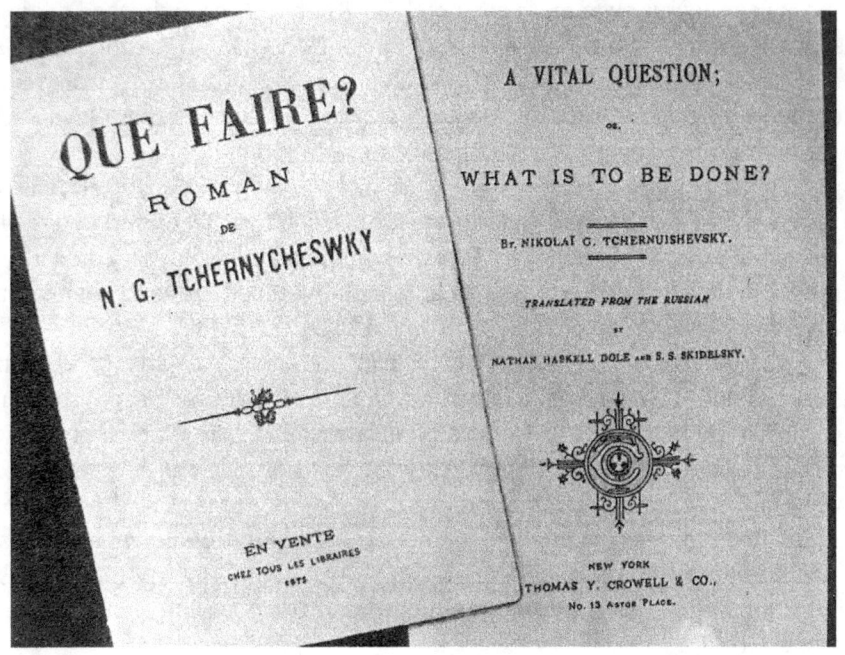

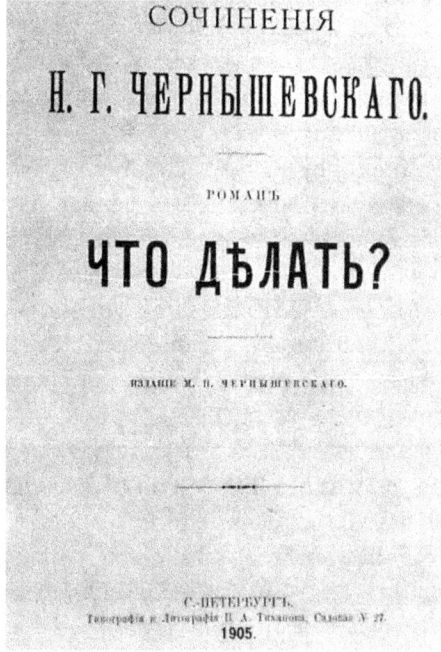

[Ill. 2-8, 2-9] The foreign and Russian editions of *What to Do?*

Charles Moser reminds us that Pushkin "uses it extensively in *Eugene Onegin*, and Pisemsky employs it even more concretely in *Troubled Seas*, published at almost exactly the same time as Chernyshevski's novel" (Moser 143). But this device has the effect of emphasizing a work's fictional nature by shifting away from reality, and underlining the fact that it is merely an intellectual construct. Beyond that the author as participant plays a didactic role, as Moser maintains: he is a mentor who tells his readers precisely what to think, comments sarcastically on their more blatant stupidities, and generally leads his ideologically uninitiated readers by the hand. Chernyshevski decisively takes up the mantle of literary didacticism: "since he believes that literature can and should be instructive, he deliberately sets out to compose a didactic novel" (Ibid. 144).

Chernyshevski connects the issue of plot predictability with the epistemological problem of how one "knows" anything in literature: "The only source of information in a literary work, says Chernyshevski, is its creator himself: a reader cannot properly bring outside information to bear on the fictional world" with which he is interacting (Ibid. 145). *What to Do?* is, then, not only a central document in the intellectual history of modern Russia, but also a major contribution to the continuing debate over the nature of literature in the Russia of the 1860s, and Chernyshevski's demolition of the novelistic genre by means of a novel itself.

The Age of Realism

Although Chernyshevski wanted "literature to serve as a blueprint for social and political change, in Tolstoy and Dostoevsky the impulse towards change suggested a philosophy of right conduct...based on complex choices" (Freeborn, "The Nineteenth Century" 330). Neither Tolstoy nor Dostoevsky avoided confrontation with the most intractable issues of the day, and the answers they offered have not lost their vital relevance since their own time (Ibid.). Because of censorship restrictions, writings often circulated in manuscript; sometimes "works were published abroad or printed on hidden presses. Occasionally authors gave up the struggle against social injustice and succumbed to the threats or rewards of the government" (Wren 391). The police were on their way to arrest the critic Belinsky when he died. Dostoevsky was condemned to death in 1849 and while he was on the scaffold his sentence was commuted to ten years in Siberia—strikingly similar to the scenario replayed with Chernyshevski just over a decade later.

The age of realism in nineteenth-century Russian literature was the age of the realistic novel. In the second half of the nineteenth century, "the positivist and materialist orientation of many educated Russians alienated them from a large part of Europe's [...] cultural heritage" (Terras 294). The themes, imagery, and sensibilities of the Golden Age poets were largely derived from Western literature; in sharp contrast, the major Russian novelists joined world literature on their own terms (Ibid.). Typical examples of the genre are those created by Tolstoy and Dostoevsky in the 1860s and the 1870s, especially *Anna Karenina* and *The Brothers Karamazov* (Nabokov seriously contemplated translating both into English). As exemplary realistic novels "they create a sense of multifaceted and multidimensional reality based on detailed description [and] character-enhancing dialogue" (Freeborn, "The Nineteenth Century" 329). As "socially orientated works of fiction, they mirrored the reality of their day" using a variety of milieus, but beyond this limited topicality their realism has achieved a universal appeal (Ibid.). Fyodor Dostoevsky cultivated his image of Russia as "that of a supernation whose mission was to create the conditions under which other nations could develop and resolve their conflicts, so long as they acknowledged Russia's leading role" (Hosking 310). Vladimir Nabokov, however, remained suspicious of and distant from Dostoevsky's idea that suffering had endowed Russians with distinctive and humble wisdom, enabling them to bring the light of salvation to other peoples.

The nineteenth-century "tradition of realism was maintained in the closing decades of the empire," but at the same time there were new cutting-edge literary movements—symbolism and futurism—making their appearance (Florinsky 373). The prominent authors of the realistic school, in addition to Leo Tolstoy, were Chekhov, Maxim Gorky, Leonid Andreev and Ivan Bunin. Anton Chekhov (1860–1904), son of a former serf who became a merchant, qualified as a physician but devoted himself to literature and theater instead. It is his works which Nabokov "would take on a trip to another planet" (*Strong Opinions* 286).

In *The Gift* Nabokov perfectly balances the polyphony achieved by Tolstoy and Dostoevsky with the structural complexity and formal conventionality of literary devices used by Proust and Joyce; Chekhov's dramatic tension and Bunin's elegiac beauty. Nabokov's last Russian novel catalogues and sums up the best developments achieved in modernist fiction written during the first quarter of the twentieth century in the major European languages.

Nabokov and the Chernyshevski Legacy

It is easy to see why Nabokov had a negative attitude toward Chernyshevski, or, more accurately, toward the tradition that crude Marxist and Soviet philosophers built up around Chernyshevski subsequently. Nabokov belonged to the younger generation of Russian émigrés and did not share the leftist sentiments of the old guard (the editorial board of the journal *Sovremennye zapiski* was composed of the latter group). Chapter Four of *The Gift* is nothing more than a comic, largely accurate, well-researched, concise biography of Chernyshevski. It introduces an imaginary authority named Strannolyubski (meaning "Strangelove") who reports that during Chernyshevski's Siberian exile "once an eagle appeared in his yard...It had come to peck at his liver but did not recognize Prometheus in him" (G289). Fyodor's (and Nabokov's) purpose is "to expose Chernyshevski as the false Prometheus of Russian tradition, a savant whose sincere good intentions and abundant sufferings in the cause of righteousness cannot excuse the dullness, dogmatism, and anti-aesthetic bias of his judgments and influence" (Moynahan 39).

The profound influence of *What to Do?* on the lives of contemporary readers and the generation immediately following them was unprecedented in the history of Russian literature. The most fascinating literary response that it provoked appeared shortly after the novel was published—Dostoevsky's *Notes from Underground* (1865) explored the role of the underground man, a parodic persona whose life exemplified "the tragicomic impasses resulting from his acceptance of all the implications of reason in its then-current Russian incarnation, especially those that Chernyshevski chose to disregard" (Joseph Frank quoted in Katz, Wagner 33). In the eyes of the younger cohort, the "men of the forties" were notoriously weak in having no concrete or workable program for either reform or revolution. The "men of the sixties," however, "were not only devotees of a veritable cult of Reason, Science, and Progress, but militant activists as well" (Stacy 56). Therefore, as militants, Chernyshevski and his allies were often regarded as forerunners of the Bolsheviks. Karl Marx was inspired to study Russian by a desire to read Chernyshevski's writings on economics. At least to some extent, Chernyshevski persuaded him in the 1880s that Russia might avoid the capitalist stage of history and move directly from tsarist "feudalism" into socialism, yet the message of *Capital* was the exact opposite: capitalism was inevitable (Priestland 72).

After its absurd blunder of allowing the publication of *What to Do?*, the government "had in fact achieved its objective, even though at considerable cost to its own reputation, of making Chernyshevski suffer for his affront and threat to the established order and traditions of Russian society. Moreover, the direct line of his influence was cut, never to be re-established. What remained was the legacy of his earlier published writing and a myth of the man based on his martyrdom for the radical cause" (Woehrlin 322). No new writing appeared in Russia over Chernyshevski's name until well after his death and an edition of his collected works in ten volumes was published legally only after the revolution of 1905.

All of the various revolutionary groups regarded Chernyshevski as a giant of the past, but there were more current documents to argue about and to inspire the youth. Marc Slonim, who participated in the populist movement as a member of the Socialist Revolutionary party, recalled that the young people in the early years of the twentieth century no longer read much of Chernyshevski, or thought very seriously about his novel (Slonim 105-107). Chernyshevski's slide into neglect was reversed by the Bolshevik revolution in 1917.

A catechism of the Russian revolutionary, *What to Do?* provided a "pattern for several generations of Russians to organize their emotional lives and personal relations," and this aspect of the novel's influence "has been compared with that of Rousseau's *La Nouvelle Héloïse* and *Emile* on the emotional life of the people of the eighteenth century" (Paperno 31). Lenin read *What to Do?* in early adolescence and adored the works of Chernyshevski. He was "determined to make for others what Chernyshevski had been for him — an exemplar of genius" (Tumarkin 35). Lenin even accepted the novel's program for preventing marital conflicts: separate rooms for complete privacy and the rational handling of love triangles. Not by accident did Lenin call his famous pamphlet on the necessity of disciplined, underground party of dedicated professional revolutionaries, "What is to be Done?" (1902; in Russian the title is identical to that of Chernyshevski's novel), in which he states: "Give us an organization of revolutionists, and we will overturn the whole of Russia."

During the Civil War, Lenin "found time to begin the process of Chernyshevski's official canonization" (Randall 146). The statue of Tsar Alexander II in Saratov was replaced by one of Chernyshevski, who was henceforth described as the Great Predecessor, the title of St. John the Baptist. Although Stalin "had been less influenced than Lenin by Chernyshevski, he was a great admirer of the man and his works, stating that *What to Do?* was the greatest novel ever written" (Ibid.). With an obelisk and a museum in the writer's hometown, the canonization of Chernyshevski was completed (Ibid.). In the year when Nabokov began his scandalous biography, the article on Chernyshevski appeared in the first edition of the Great Soviet Encyclopedia in 1934. This officially sanctioned article was given forty columns (as compared to eighty-two on Karl Marx). It defined Chernyshevski as "the great Russian savant and critic, publicist and revolutionary," sparing no praise for the author of *What to Do?* as a philosopher, economist, historian, and political activist. Nabokov's crow quill could not ask for a more suitable target.

Did Nabokov Really Hate Chernyshevski (and Did Chernyshevski Hate Pushkin)?

Some critics believe that the time is ripe to rescue Chernyshevski both from the Soviet icon frame and from the iconoclastic image of a long-bearded, impenetrable bore found in the West (Brown, "So Much Depends..." 373). It cannot be overemphasized, Edward Brown states, that the most important and influential novel of the Russian nineteenth century was not by Dostoevsky or Turgenev, but Chernyshevski's *What to Do?*, a novel that combined the features of a Biblical text and a guide to practical behaviour.

Foreign radicals who turned to the Russian revolutionary movement studied Chernyshevski in order to learn how to set up labor cooperatives in Chicago and

New York. A translation into English of *What to Do?*, authored by Benjamin R. Tucker, appeared in Boston in 1886. Tucker was a socialist leader in close touch with events in Chicago at the time, who had serialized his translation in his own periodical, *Liberty* (1884-86). Edward Brown lays out a series of interesting historical examples: apparently, *What to Do?* was the favored reading matter of the anarchist and socialist leaders involved in the McCormick reaper strike and the tragic Haymarket riot in Chicago in May 1886 (an event commemorated in labor circles by the traditional labor holiday, the first of May). In her New York apartment, Emma Goldman, a famous American anarchist leader, set up a sewing cooperative for young, possibly wayward, and in any case poor and helpless girls that was modeled directly on Vera Pavlovna's enterprise, the operation of which is meticulously described in Chernyshevski's novel. Goldman's associate, Alexander Berkman, when he went off to assassinate the steel magnate Henry Clay Frick during the brutal Homestead strike in 1892, used the pseudonym Rakhmetov, the name of the one of the characters in Chernyshevski's novel (see also Drozd, *A Reevaluation* 13). In other words, the novel was not, as some have said, a "peculiarly Russian phenomenon." Brown is emphatic: "Even some of those who execrate its message and deplore it as a literary performance (a futile exercise...) have sometimes betrayed some sympathy for it as a powerful human document. Nabokov, who wrote... a devastating fictional biography of Chernyshevski... felt in the end a kind of perverse sympathy for the man. [Fyodor] reports at one point that 'he cannot help feeling a thrill' (G277) as he touches the old and withered pages of that issue of the journal *The Contemporary* for 1863 where the first installment of the novel *What to Do?* appeared" (Brown 374-75).

There is no contradiction between Nabokov's treatment of Chernyshevski in the novel and Nabokov's (or his character's) possible sentiments toward the historical figure. Still, however, some critics believe that Nabokov is unfair in his representation of Chernyshevski's attitude to Pushkin. David Rampton claims that the "evidence" presented in *The Gift* is almost non-existent (Rampton 73-78) and argues that Chernyshevski did not dismiss Pushkin in the way that Fyodor implies; what he did say about the Byronic aspects of his work, regardless of the "method" he was using, constitutes genuine criticism (76). Although Rampton's handling of the Chernyshevski chapter has recently come under criticism (Boyd 578; Meyer 572), the image of Chernyshevski as Pushkin-hater in *The Gift* continues to bother scholars. Nabokov's "Chernyshevski vs. Pushkin" case was recently tried again and dubbed an "exercise in distortion" (Drozd, "Chernyshevski and Pushkin" 286, n. 6). According to Andrew Drozd, Chernyshevski is presented as a man who dismissed Pushkin as "only a poor imitator of Byron" (G255) by means of mixed quotations, guilt by association and outright fabrications. Drozd maintains that this passage, "rather selectively pulled out of context," seems to establish that Chernyshevski had a low opinion of Pushkin (Drozd 282). However, when reproduced in full, Chernyshevski's passage (occurring in a letter he writes to his wife while in Siberia) is rather ambiguous: "The thing is that until now Russian literature is still very poor. Our famous poets, Pushkin and Lermontov, were only weak imitators of Byron. No one denies this" (Liatskii 203). Chernyshevski makes this statement in the context of advising his wife on the education of their sons, therefore it is apparent from the start that he is not concerned with Pushkin in particular but with Russian culture as a whole. In addition, Drozd questions the very relevance of this passage, which did not appear in print until after Chernyshevski's death and long after his period of public activity was over (it in no way figured in the nineteenth-century debates between Russian intellectuals over the Pushkinian and the Gogolian trends in Russian literature). The fact that Nabokov had to resort to such an obscure passage to support his distortion of Chernyshevski should, by itself, force us to re-examine the image of Chernyshevski as having been entirely negative toward Pushkin.

Ironically, Nabokov himself contributed to Chernyshevski's revival in the twentieth and twenty-first centuries through what might be called today "negative publicity," commemorating the author of the revolutionary novel in one of the most vivid and unjust biographies ever written.

ST. PETERSBURG: TURN OF THE CENTURY

The Cultural Renaissance

In the 1880s Leo Tolstoy began to preach his ethical Christianity, which became the first point of contact between the religious rationalism of the intelligentsia and the rationalist dissent of the people. But on the whole Tolstoy's religious influence was stronger abroad than in Russia. In the words of Nabokov's contemporary, "the eighties, though a period of general gloom and disillusion that reflected the economic depression and political reaction of the time, produced a beautiful Indian summer of realistic fiction in the work of Anton Chekhov, an intellectual of plebeian birth, and an artist of unsurpassed ethical delicacy" (Mirsky 272). This period was followed by the livelier pre-revolutionary nineties. In literature this decade introduced Maxim Gorky, the last great realist of pre-Soviet Russia, and the only major writer who came out of the ranks of the genuinely revolutionary intelligentsia.

Even before 1905 the leadership in most cultural endeavors had begun to pass from the old civic liberal and radical intelligentsia to a new elite, aggressively individualistic and "highbrow," art-loving and anti-social. On the eve of the revolution a second generation of Modernists and Symbolists in arts and literature was growing, "more bohemian than bourgeois, less sophisticated and freer from the influence of Dostoevsky, free also from all *fin de siècle* aestheticism, and, for the most part, from all ideas and philosophies" (Mirsky 273). The distinct voice of this younger generation became especially apparent after 1917, but the aesthetic revival strongly affected all the arts even earlier. In music it first produced "the gushing expressionism of Skryabin, but afterwards the severe constructive formalism of Stravinsky, one of the Russians who had the greatest influence on European art" (Ibid.). In painting and in the decorative arts Russian modernism "did not show itself to be very creative," although Mikhail Vrubel must be considered the country's first original painter prior to the Russian futurists' invasion. It is clear that during this time the level of artistic culture rose in Russia, "art became a vital element in the cultural make-up of the intelligentsia, and understanding native and foreign beauty became the duty of every educated citizen" (Ibid.). The Moscow Art Theatre, with its psychological realism, achieved its record triumphs in the early years of the century in staging the plays of Chekhov; this theatrical success was soon catapulted to even greater achievements by one of Russia's most famous entrepreneurs, Sergei Diaghilev. The best composers and stage designers worked for Diaghilev, who succeeded in producing and developing a whole galaxy of dancers surpassing anything ever seen on a European stage. Next to the Russian novel, Diaghilev's ballet was perhaps the most spectacular success of Russian culture in the West.

Petersburg and the Rise of Russian National Identity

The cultural construction of citizenship in Russia had largely foreign underpinnings. Nabokov remembers his own family with its traditional leaning toward "the comfortable products of Anglo-Saxon civilization" ("I learned to read English before I could read Russian"; *Speak, Memory* 79). Citizenship in the Russian "republic of letters" presupposed a cosmopolitan upbringing, the sense that one's roots were as much in Paris, London or Gottingen (the romantic poet Lensky in Pushkin's *Eugene Onegin* is said to have a "Gottingen soul") as they were in Moscow or St. Petersburg. To be fully Russian, one had to be a citizen of the world. On the one hand, this meant that Russian intellectuals of the nineteenth century "had the broadest and most universal culture to be found in any European nation. But it also meant that Russian elite culture and learning were more cut off from both the church and the ordinary people than elsewhere in Europe" (Hosking 290).

According to the critic Vladimir Stasov, who undertook a survey of the arts in 1882-83 during the reign of Alexander III, Russian architecture was a "Janus-like art with two faces, one of which looked backward with an eye to the saleable potential of past civilizations" (quoted in Buckler 34). Stasov emphasized the relationship between eclecticism and the nineteenth-century search for a national identity. Russian Slavophiles and nationalists made use of eclecticism to forge a modern Russian identity out of Eastern cultural referents from Byzantium and old Russia. The second face of architecture, in Stasov's view, was the new "Russian" style used for churches, museums, theaters, apartment housing, and administrative buildings, which he heartily endorsed. The nationalists believed that "Western-style eclecticism was the logical extension of a classicism that had excluded Russia's own cultural legacy" (Ibid.).

The modern city, especially such a Westernized locus as St. Petersburg, the Russian capital during the imperial era, was a dangerous place: "As the site of commerce and exchange, it was governed by desire, driven by psychological and material need and selfish interests. Like the marketplace, the city challenged established social hierarchies with new and transient relations of wealth" (Engelstein 359). Nabokov has always been fascinated by urban spaces and explored their metapoetic nature in fiction (Leving 18-20). Like a litmus test, Petersburg underscores the raging debates that are associated with the status of the contemporary European city.

The question of national identity was an important one in both political and cultural life in the sprawling multinational empire of the nineteenth century. Jeffrey Brooks maintains that educated Russians influenced by Western ideas and culture sought new ideas to define Russianness: the spread of education and secular thinking influenced all classes, as did social and geographic mobility. Contact with new groups led to expanded aspirations and stimulated curiosity—a quest for the definition of Russianness was shared by Russians of all cultural levels (Brooks 214).

Nabokov's Anglophone family illustrates this intensive search for a new and revitalized Russian idea. If we look at the portrayal of the Russian people in *The Gift*, they appear to be a collection of ignorant outsiders, mostly servants, who are totally out of place in the special world inhabited by the main character. When they are described gawking uncomprehendingly at the mysterious rites of the elite Entomological Society, whose members are huddled together studying a rare species in the woods, Fyodor comments: "To this day I am wondering what the coachmen waiting on the road made of all this" (G108), a remark that constitutes at least a muted recognition of the gulf separating the classes. But, as David Rampton observes, instead of developing this insight, Nabokov proceeds to exploit the comic consequences of such a gap (96). One may get the distinct sense that we are reading about the self-satisfied snobbery of callow youth which the author is about to expose and condemn, but Nabokov's aims are quite different: he concludes with a sarcastic "The Russian common people know and love their country's nature" (G108). As a matter of fact, it is even more complex than that. As the narrator embarks on the mental travels either to the bygone Russia of Chernyshevski or to the distant Asian steppes of Godunov-Cherdyntsev,

Nabokov—a displaced citizen with a Jewish wife, a writer who rejected all forms of political affiliation and detested pathos in letters—quietly continues his own search for an answer to the core questions of his people's origins and future destiny.

The Myth of the City

By 1918 St. Petersburg no longer existed either in name or, according to Katerina Clark's poetic remark, "as those circles around a dot on the map which proclaim it to be the capital. Yet it has persisted in Russian culture to this day as an idea, an ethos, an ideal, and above all as a language of clichés that Russians have deployed in debating the country's way forward" (6). The myth of Petersburg continued to captivate the imagination while Russian writers found many of their "Petersburg" tropes among those that Balzac, Hugo, and others applied to Paris. This semi-real Petersburg of the turn of the century serves in *The Gift* as an anti-city and counter-space vis-à-vis Berlin of the 1920s.

It is not by chance that Osip Mandelstam's name appears in *The Gift* (first as an unnamed allusion in the Russian original, then stated explicitly in the translation). It was Mandelstam who pronounced in 1920, "We shall gather again in Petersburg," suggesting that, though a dark cloud had obscured the sun of the Great Tradition, "we," its torchbearers in the Soviet night, might yet triumph. As Clark states, "Petersburg became the locus, actual or symbolic, of certain segments of the intelligentsia who saw themselves as not implicated in the [Soviet] regime's culture and who declared themselves bards of Petersburg. The clichés of the myth had become so standardized that they could be used as a code" (7). Nabokov appeals to the very same code shared by the disciples of the Symbolist and Acmeist poetic schools who were contributing to the creation of the so-called "Petersburg text" of Russian literature based on the myths and cult of the city.

For Fyodor (and his creator) the remembrance of childhood in Russia also evokes images of the family estate, Leshino, not far from Petersburg ("the dusty road to the village; the strip of short, pastel-green grass, with bald patches of sandy soil, between the road and the lilac bushes behind which walleyed, mossy log cabins stood in a rickety row"; *Speak, Memory* 30). In fiction of the early twentieth century the modern industrial city was often juxtaposed with the symbolic terrain of rural space embodied in dachas and villages: "metaphor as much as memory shaped this pastoral nostalgia" (Steinberg 170). Nostalgia for the lost countryside was sometimes explicit even in the writings of Soviet workers "longing for the village they left behind...for country pleasures, and for the beauties of nature" (Ibid.). To avoid unabashed sentimentality Fyodor's/Nabokov's memories are frequently tinted with sarcasm (as in the episode describing Fyodor's encounter with a peasant who "had taken out a box from his gaunt breast and given it to him unsmilingly, but the wind was blowing, match after match went out before it had hardly flared and after every one he grew more ashamed, while the man watched with a kind of detached curiosity the impatient fingers of the wasteful young squire"; G78). In Soviet poetry, "hard labor in the fields was left in the darkness" of things that would best be forgotten; Marxist contributors to "proletarian" anthologies and periodicals offered memories of bucolic peasant life as part of a deliberate commentary on the aesthetic and ethical meanings of modern industrial life (Steinberg 170). Nabokov employs a similar device, but in *The Gift* he contrasts the Russian landscapes of Fyodor's youth with noisy Berlin of the late 1920s.

St. Petersburg — Petrograd — Leningrad

Nabokov lived in St. Petersburg during the period that would later be called the "Silver Age" of Russian arts, presuming that their "Golden Age" is associated with the epoch of Pushkin and his contemporaries. Symbolism emerged as the first dominant style during this period of cultural renaissance. It embodied a protest against the positivism and materialism prevalent in Russian art, and above all it challenged the hegemony of socially oriented and utilitarian civic art associated with the generations of Belinsky and Chernyshevski.

In the private Tenishev School the Futurist poet Vladimir Mayakovsky and the Acmeist poet Osip Mandelstam (who graduated from the same school a few years before Nabokov) gave public readings; the Symbolist Andrey Bely was writing his novel "Petersburg," devoted to the city, and poets and painters frequently met and held debates in the artsy downtown cabaret "The Stray Dog." Nabokov's own mansion became the hub of activities for progressive liberal politicians of the time, but culture had a strong presence there alongside politics — the hospitable Vladimir Dmitrievich Nabokov attracted musicians, artists and critics alike. The walls of the house on Morskaya Street were decorated with fine paintings by Alexander Benois and Leon Bakst, important members of the *Mir iskusstva* (*World of Art*), an artistic movement that helped revolutionize Russian and European art during the first decade of the twentieth century. Young Vladimir's teacher of painting was Mstislav Dobuzhinsky, an active member of the World of Art circle.

Nabokov was born at the turn of the century. The fin de siècle was both a thrilling and a troublesome period for Russia. It started with the grand coronation of Nicholas II in Moscow in 1896, resulting in a disaster at Khodynka Field with thousands of casualties when innocent participants in the festivities tried to take advantage of the free food, drink, and souvenirs offered to commemorate the occasion. St. Petersburg was not short of celebrations during the early 1900s. The year 1902 marked the hundredth anniversary of the government reform in which

Chapter Two. HISTORICAL CONTEXT

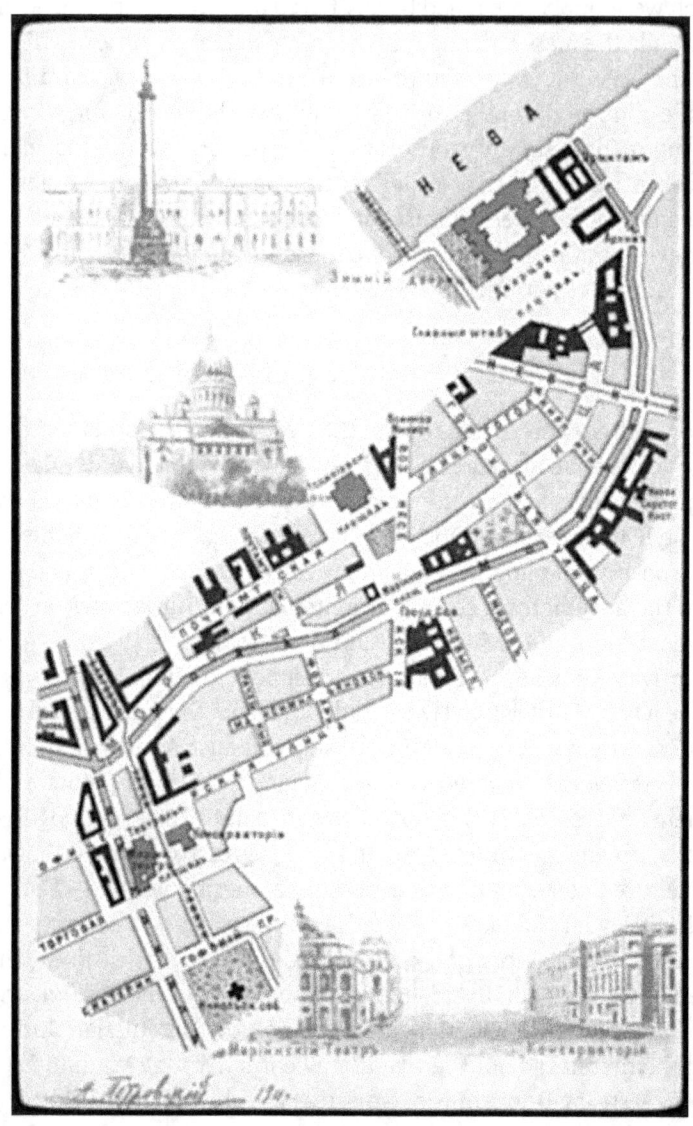

[Ill. 2-10] The 1911 postcard depicting Morskaya Street, where the Nabokovs lived

Alexander I established the ministries. In May 1903 the Russian capital founded by Peter the Great celebrated its 200th anniversary. The new Trinity Bridge was officially unveiled in the presence of the Tsar, and then a church service took place at Senate Square next to the "Bronze Horseman," the monument to the city's creator that acquired an almost mythological status due to Pushkin's poetic masterpiece of the same name.

Serious trouble arrived in 1905 as the war against Japan became more and more of a disaster. In what became known as "Bloody Sunday," on January 9, 1905, a peaceful demonstration of workers was fired on by troops at the Palace Square. This led to public outrage and the start of the revolution. The new phenomenon that dominated the entire period was the emergence of the popular masses into the political arena. This action infused the whole opposition movement with a special energy that made it seem a genuine threat.

Despite the apparent quelling of the revolution at the end of 1905, Nicholas II and his government "kept their promise to hold elections for the lower house (the State Duma), to grant broader (though by no means unrestricted) rights of free speech and assembly, to allow workers to form unions, and to confer various other rights. The old State Council, formerly appointed by the tsar, was transformed into an upper house; one half was still appointed by the supreme ruler, the balance elected from mostly conservative institutions on a very restricted and undemocratic franchise" (Zelnik 220). Vladimir Dmitrievich Nabokov, the writer's father, became a member of the parliament representing the party of Constitutional Democrats (or the *Kadets*, as they called themselves). Hopes for liberal democratic reforms were short-lived during the so-called Constitutional Experiment associated with the Third (1907-12) and Fourth (1912-17) Dumas, since the tsarist government soon curtailed many of the freedoms and often blocked the Duma's initiatives.

Everything ended with the cruelest of wars that humankind had known to that point—World War I. When it broke out in August 1914, it was decided to change the name of the Russian capital from St. Petersburg to Petrograd. Germany was now the enemy of Russia and the old name sounded too German. Most of the city's industry was diverted to support for the war effort and many of Petrograd's buildings, including a large portion of the Winter Palace, were turned into hospitals. Most construction work in the city was halted.

The Tsar's government became largely discredited and political tensions started rising. To make matters worse, the food supply of the Russian capital deteriorated significantly towards the end of 1916. Petrograd entered the New Year with its inhabitants infuriated by the long lines in front of food shops. To prevent the Soviet (workers' councils) from overwhelming Petrograd, moderate and conservative members of the Duma demanded Nicholas' abdication and struggled to form a Provisional Government. On March 2, 1917 Nicholas "bowed to the inevitable and signed a manifesto of abdication. Petrograd's workers cheered the tsar's abdication... For a few days, the palaces and townhouses of the well-to-do became fair game, as 'searches' inevitably ended in pillaging and looting" (Lincoln 231). Just a few blocks away from the Nabokovs' residence, a huge red flag replaced the imperial banner above the Winter Palace, and cheering crowds stripped the two-headed imperial eagles from government buildings and threw them onto bonfires.

For the next eight months, the revolution gripped Petrograd. Command of democratic Russia passed formally to the Provisional Government on the day after Nicholas abdicated, but the reality was "Dual Power" (*dvoevlastie*) with the Petrograd Soviet of Workers' and Soldiers' Deputies controlling the munitions plants, railroads, army, postal service, and telegraph, so that it alone commanded the masses and had real power (Ibid.). The political and economic crisis continued through 1917 and in the fall the Bolshevik party led by Lenin captured political power. When on October 25, 1917 (based on the Julian calendar used in Russia until 1918), a blank shot from the cruiser "Aurora" gave workers and soldiers the signal to storm the Winter Palace (there is some question whether this actually occurred), the future author of *The Gift* and *Lolita* had already escaped the city for his lifelong exile.

In 1924 the name of the city was changed to Leningrad, which symbolized its final transition to a socialist city. A gradual recovery began under the New Economic Policy (NEP) in 1921 immediately following the Civil War that consolidated the Bolshevik coup. But expunging the symbolic evidence of the old order did not satisfy the revolutionary nihilists who wanted to clear the ground for a new cultural order. Naming streets and hauling down statues was only the beginning, as Richard Stites explains it: "The entire corpus of pre-revolutionary culture had to be emphatically and enthusiastically repudiated. The roots of cultural nihilism go deep into the traditions of the nineteenth century intelligentsia—especially the 'nihilism' of the 1860s, an outlook that [Nikolai] Berdiaev once defined as a secular version of religious asceticism that held art, thought, and religion in utter revulsion" (68). The earlier nihilists preferred science over faith, artifacts over art ('a pair of boots is worth all of Pushkin'), and realism over romanticism. Although the milieu for nihilism in 1917 was different from that of the 1860s and 1870s, the cultural nihilists of the revolution inherited much from this lingering tradition. In his "The Life of Chernyshevski" Nabokov attempts to settle accounts with this entire legacy at its grass roots. History had made a full turn, and the circle was closed.

BERLIN: THE RUSSIAN ÉMIGRÉ COMMUNITY BETWEEN THE TWO WORLD WARS

Culture in Berlin: A Parallel World

By the middle of the nineteenth century Berlin's cultural life, permeated with the Romantic spirit, was pushed into the background by economic development. An important center of industry and commerce, Berlin was attracting the best technicians and economists from all over Germany (Baedeker 41). Within a few years of the foundation of the Reich in 1871 Berlin attained worldwide importance as the capital of the German Empire and the residence of the Emperors. At the turn of the century Berlin numbered about two million inhabitants, and the great period of the increasingly large metropolis began. Attracted by the cosmopolitan spirit of the capital, poets, artists, musicians, actors, scholars, and scientists gave Berlin a special atmosphere of its own, and in most cases they found a permanent home here. The early years of the new century brought the first taxis, buses, and underground trains. With the absorption of neighboring towns and rural parishes after World War I came another great leap forward.

If the 1820-30s are considered Russia's Golden Age, then the 1920s certainly were the Golden Age of Berlin. The period begins at about 1910 and ends very abruptly on the night of the January 30th 1933, with Hitler's accession to power:

> The twenties were a period of violence, creative anarchy, a Renaissance age of gangsters and aesthetes, in short—an extraordinary decade. The arts flourished on German soil in the 1920s as they had not since the age of Goethe. During this short period of artistic freedom in Weimar, Gropius founded his legendary Bauhaus with Mies van der Rohe, Vassily Kandinsky, Paul Klee, and Moholy Nagy. Einstein and Max Planck were at work in Berlin, where relativity in the world of physics seemed to find an echo in the despondent relativism of other disciplines, and soon enough in public and private morals. The twenties saw the great age of the silent film in Berlin: *The Cabinet of Dr. Caligari, Faust, The Golem, The Blue Angel*; and the short spectacular triumph of Expressionism in literature, music, and painting. (Mander 119)

Refugees poured into Berlin from Russia after the revolution and were compelled to continue their trek in the company of the largely Jewish-led Berlin avant-garde to Paris, London and New York after Hitler took power. One should not forget that although the action of *The Gift* unfolds during the late 1920s, the fact that Nabokov recreates it a decade later, when Hitler's thugs had rid Germany of the arts for a generation, strongly colors his and the readers' perception.

German intellectuals, especially artists, probably never felt at home in the German Reich either, being strangers in their own land: "From the time that Bismarck's Second Reich gave physical, materialist, and military forces precedence over the life of the intellect, when the character of the drill sergeant was proposed and recognized by the world as the typical representative of Germany, from that time German writers have felt they were living in moral banishment and exile. Behind the sergeant stood the engineer who supplied him with weapons, the chemist who brewed poison gas to destroy the human brain, and at the same time formulated the drug to relieve his migraine" (Roth 209). It is no wonder that before biding farewell to its readers *The Gift* also encapsulates a comic image of the police sergeant: the protagonist is stopped by a policeman on a rainy Berlin evening in the final pages of the novel ("'Standing in the nude is also impossible,' said the policeman. 'I'll take off my trunks and imitate a statue,' suggested Fyodor. The policeman took out his notebook and so fiercely tore the pencil out of the pencil-hold that he dropped it on the sidewalk"; G347).

The State of Russian Émigré Art

The abstract painter and art theorist Vasily Kandinsky's move to Germany was only one of thousands of such emigrations from Russia in the early 1920s. Refugees from Russia flocked into Berlin, and by 1922 the Russian population alone was estimated at 100,000. In addition to the permanent émigrés, there were a large number of privileged transients and temporary visitors such as artists Natan Altman, Iosif Chaikov, and El Lissitzky, "who traveled on Soviet passports and who did not intend to settle outside the Soviet Union" (Bowlt 217). Marc Chagall said of those days: "After the war, Berlin had become a kind of caravansary where everyone traveling between Moscow and the West came together.... In the apartments round the Bayrische Platz there were as many samovars and theosophical and Tolstoyan countesses as there had been in Moscow.... In my whole life I've never seen so many wonderful rabbis or so many Constructivists as in Berlin in 1922" (Roditi 27).

In spite of the large colony of émigrés, the new Soviet state paradoxically "enjoyed the sympathy of the new Weimar Republic. On both an ideological and a cultural level the two nations shared common ground" (Bowlt 218). Dadaism began in Zurich and Berlin; a painter like Max Ernst was hailed as a 'Surrealist' on migrating to Paris in 1923. Both Germany and the Soviet Union wished to establish a relationship between the working classes and art, and "both felt that radical politics and radical art made a reasonable combination" (Ibid.). Hence, the most important artistic developments in the Berlin of the early 1920s were the ideas of the nonobjective avant-garde who had developed a new world view of art from the Suprematism (nonobjective Cubism) of Kazimir Malevich (Neumann 21). The experimental works by the painter Vsevolod Romanov in *The Gift* seem to reflect these and other contemporary trends in the realm of visual arts.

Young Nabokov, on the contrary, contributed to an elegant Russian art journal published in Berlin, *Zhar-ptitsa (Fire-Bird)*, which "concerned itself with the national traditions of Old Russia and sought to uphold the concept of good taste" (Bowlt 218). Many of the old members of the "World of Art," such as Léon Bakst and Vasily Shukhaev, were associated with *Fire-Bird*. Also containing articles on Russian ballet and poetry, this popular journal appealed to those who nostalgically yearned for a bygone Russia.

Nabokov recalls that one of the striking features of émigré life, in keeping with its itinerant and dramatic character, was "the abnormal frequency of the literary readings in private houses or hired halls" (*Speak, Memory* 281). In addition to diverse exhibitions and cultural events regularly held in Berlin in the 1920s, there was a flourishing theatre scene, including dramatic cabarets such as *Der Blauf Vogel* and Alexander Tairov's Chamber Theatre in 1923. Between the World Wars, actors and companies that had emigrated together made efforts to establish permanent repertory theaters. Most of those were in fact carrying on the dramatic genres and styles that had developed and achieved popularity in Russia on the eve of the revolution (Raeff 407), but this is not to say that contemporary themes were dismissed altogether. For example, a number of Nabokov's plays were successfully staged at that time. Eventually the difficulties in setting up permanent theaters drove most émigré actors and directors from Germany to other centers of the Diaspora or back to their homeland.

The Vanished World of Russians in Germany in the 1920–30s

When asked to explain why he would never write another novel in Russian, Nabokov gave this detailed account of "the great, and still unsung, era of Russian intellectual expatriation": "Roughly between 1920 and 1940—books written in Russian by émigré Russians and published by émigré firms abroad were eagerly bought or borrowed by émigré readers but were absolutely banned in Soviet Russia...An émigré novel, published, say, in Paris and sold over all free Europe, might have, in those years, a total sale of 1,000 or 2,000 copies—that would be a best seller—but every copy would also pass from hand to hand and be read by at least 20 persons, and at least 50 annually if stocked by Russian lending libraries, of which there were hundreds in West Europe alone" (*Strong Opinions* 36-37). Nabokov's Berlin of White-Russian refugees generated a contemporary joke that "to cross the Tiergarten from the city centre to Charlottenburg one had to apply for a Russian visa" (Mander 125). Another popular anecdote of the time is about the German who, hearing only Russian spoken on the Kurfürstendamm, returns to his apartment and hangs himself because he is homesick (Struve 25). The effect of these refugees is discernible in the artistic life of the time—in the second-hand theatrical influence of Constantin Stanislavsky and Alexander Tairov on producers like Piscator, and in films like *Peter the Great*, which the Russian producer Buchovetsky made with Emil Jannings. However, the era of expatriation ended during World War II. Old writers died, Russian publishers also vanished, and the general atmosphere of exile culture inevitably faded.

Like James Joyce, for whom the suggestive potential of minor details in describing Dublin of 1904 was enormously fascinating, Nabokov tried to be meticulously exact in recreating the reality of Berlin in *The Gift*. The precision of his use of minor detail is among the most important aspects of his literary technique. Alexander Goldenweizer, a lawyer, publisher and family friend, wrote to Nabokov from the United States on 29 July 1938, sharing with the author his impressions of the recently published portion of the novel:

> A day before our departure, the latest issue of *Sovremennye zapiski* arrived, full of interesting stuff. The present excerpt from *The Gift* is especially good [Volume 66 contained Chapter Three of the novel. — Y.L.]. During my Berlin years I visited the barrister's firm of Traum, Baum, and Käsebier frequently, and I can testify that you have depicted the live and dead furnishings of this office perfectly well. Like your heroine, I was always astonished by the striking contrast of the exterior appearance of the staircase and the office, which reminded me of the cells of our lay magistrates, and comparatively luxurious furniture of the chiefs' offices... I am waiting for the next instalment impatiently — maybe I will meet more acquaintances there. (Glushanok 121)

In *The Gift* we read about the firm to which Goldenweizer refers: "It began with a dark, steep, incredibly dilapidated staircase which was fully matched by the sinister decrepitude of the office premises, a state of affairs not true only of the chief barrister's office with its over-stuffed armchairs and giant glass-topped-table furnishings" (G189).

The three names — Traum, Baum, and Käsebier — comprise a meaningful triad ("a complete German idyll, with little tables amid the greenery and a wonderful view" [G190]); in German *Traum* means a "dream," *Baum* = "tree," *Käse* + *Bier* = "cheese" + "beer." For Nabokov, in addition to the realia in the background, the names and toponyms hold a special place if they can be reinforced by identifiable literary references. The reader is prompted here by an earlier remark that the atmosphere of Zina's office reminds Fyodor "somehow of Dickens" (G189). The clue is not misleading; the required answer is indeed available from Charles Dickens himself: the London law firm of "Chizzle, Mizzle, Drizzle" is featured in *Bleak House* (1853), his ninth novel, which was viewed as an assault on the flaws of the British judiciary system. What is more, Nabokov then draws special attention to this play with the owners' "emblematic names" in his *Lectures on Literature* (72; noted in Dolinin, *Kommentarii* 695). The actual

[Ill. 2-11, 2-12] Haus Vaterland (Berlin, 1920s)

firm was then called Weil, Gans & Dieckmann. In the novel Nabokov has the lead partner writing popular biographies of figures like Sarah Bernhardt in his desire to cozy up to his French clientele. Like his fictional counterpart, Weil wrote on Dreyfus, to the same end (Schiff 64).

Details drawn from reality are abundant in *The Gift*, and the background against which the main plot unfolds produces a strong impression that the novel has an almost documentary quality. Chapter Three of this book, entitled "Setting," provides a more detailed analysis of this tendency; I will offer here only a typical example of the novel's dense Berlin texture: "The Shchyogolevs had finished their packing; Zina had gone off to work and at one o'clock was due to meet her mother for lunch at the Vaterland. Luckily they had not suggested that Fyodor join them—on the contrary, Marianna Nikolavna, as she warmed up some coffee for him in the kitchen where he sat in his dressing gown, disconcerted by the bivouac-like atmosphere in the apartment, warned him that a little Italian salad and some ham had been left" (G355). The Vaterland, where Zina is to meet her mother for lunch, was a restaurant located at Potsdam Square (Potsdamer Platz), in the heart of Berlin. It was identifiable by a traffic tower with a clock in the very center of the square; from the top of this tower a policeman (and later Germany's first traffic lights, installed in 1924) controlled the flow of traffic. Together with Leipziger Platz on its eastern edge the square formed the main road link between the east and west of the city (in 1925, close to the fictional time frame of *The Gift*, 600 trams passed through the square every hour). Numerous hotels and cafés attracted people to Potsdam Square, but a true magnet for tourists was the "Haus Vaterland" (*House of the Fatherland*), a restaurant and a variety theater. It could seat two thousand after a major renovation in 1927–28 by architect Carl Stahl-Urach, making it the largest restaurant in Europe. For Marianna Nikolavna, therefore, inviting her daughter to such a fashionable place before her impending departure is a symbolically generous gesture; Fyodor does not earn the same invitation because Marianna is not intending to waste money for a lunch on her dubious tenant whom she, presumably, will never see again.

Russian Literature in Exile

Nabokov's first Russian novel, *Mary*, was written in Berlin in 1926 (a German translation was published by Ullstein in 1928); his next seven novels were also written in Berlin and all of them were set at least partly in Berlin. This period, when Nabokov's first book was published, serves for two main reasons as a watershed in the development of Russian literary modernism emerging out of the political cataclysms of World War I and the Bolshevik revolution. The first reason, as Evelyn Bristol recapitulates, is that in 1925 the Central Committee of the Communist Party of the Soviet Union passed a resolution enunciating a comprehensive position on questions of literature and art (although it did not actually exert its control, it asserted its right to do so in the future, and eventually did so). The second reason is that this was the time in which many literary émigrés realized that their exile was not a short-term condition, and they began in a serious way to create a branch of Russian culture in emigration. Vladislav Khodasevich, one of the marshals of émigré Russian culture and Nabokov's mentor, settled in Paris in 1926 and helped make it the leading center of émigré literature until World War II (Bristol 387). It was Khodasevich who called Berlin the "Stepmother of Russian Cities" in his 1923 poem.

Upon moving to Berlin as a young émigré Nabokov feared he might lose the beauty and richness of his Russian by learning to speak German fluently. The task of linguistic occlusion was made easier by the fact that Nabokov, like many of his compatriots, lived in a closed émigré circle of Russian friends and read exclusively Russian newspapers, magazines, and books (if we are to believe Nabokov, his "only forays into the local language were the civilities exchanged with [his] successive landlords or landladies and the routine necessities of shopping"; *Strong Opinions* 189). Indeed, the emigration restored to writers an audience, a literary institution and a style of communication that had not existed in Russian literature since the salons of the 1820s: "That wonderful semipermeable membrane between reality and literature, which allowed readers to anticipate that they might find themselves or their Petersburg friends wandering into the pages of *Eugene Onegin* or frequenting the milieu from which it had arisen, had disappeared with the formation of a literary relation between author and public that was on a much larger, more anonymous scale" (Greenleaf 141). Enjoying absolute freedom of thought was not without certain disadvantages though, and many émigré artists experienced a sense that they were working in an absolute void: "True, there was among émigrés a sufficient number of good readers to warrant the publication, in Berlin, Paris, and other towns, of Russian books and periodicals on a comparatively large scale; but since none of those writings could circulate within the Soviet Union, the whole thing acquired a certain air of fragile unreality" (*Speak, Memory* 280).

Images of the city created by Russian authors in exile usually contrast with and defy the canonical myth of dazzling, sparkling, flashing Berlin. Instead of the multicolored, kaleidoscopic urban festival, they portray a dull, monotonous, and monochrome cityscape. Oswald Spengler's concept of the modern city as a demonic megalopolis—or, better, a necropolis—where Western civilization is coming to its imminent end served as a model for many Russian writers to conceptualize their Berlin experience (Dolinin, "The Stepmother of Russian Cities" 230; 234). Nabokov, however, was able both to preserve the charm of a thriving urban space and to stay in line with the émigré artistic tradition (as, for instance, in his short stories "The Reunion" and "A Guide to Berlin").

Russian literary forces in Europe were grouped around several "thick" journals, the most important of which, *Sovremennye zapiski*, was published in Paris. Other periodicals and almanacs, such as *Chisla* (*Numbers*) and *Krug* (*Circle*), were almost exclusively devoted to the works of the younger generation. Several publishing houses in Paris, Berlin, and even Harbin, China, published Russian prose and poetry; the Russian branch of the American YMCA press in Paris did much to promote Russian literature abroad. "Notwithstanding the encouragement and aid offered by various cultural organizations, the Russian literary emigration experienced great hardships"; it is greatly to the credit of the émigré literary community that it "continued its creative work in spite of these difficulties and remained true to its calling, instead of seeking a more lucrative occupation or letting itself be overwhelmed by [its] misfortunes" (Iswolsky 61). While the younger generation of writers and poets had inevitably submitted to the influence of Western literature, especially to that of the modern French and English masters, the memory of Russia formed the leitmotif of the works produced by the older generation headed by Ivan Bunin (winner of the Nobel Prize in Literature in 1933). Its representatives cherished memories of their native land and feared lest its image should be dimmed or forgotten. Poet Boris Poplavsky, a kind of Russian Rimbaud, "with the face of a soccer player rather than a poet" (Terapiano 112), living the life of the Montparnasse literary bohemian before dying allegedly by suicide, was one of the promising members of the younger generation. Nabokov's kaleidoscopic *The Gift* reserved a generous space for all of them, some more recognizable and others less, within the confines of a carefully reconstructed theatre of literary players.

REFERENCES

Andrew, Joe. *Writers and Society during the Rise of Russian Realism*. Atlantic Highlands, N.J.: Humanities Press, 1980.

Baedeker, Karl. *Berlin. Handbook for Travellers*. 7th edition. Freiburg: Karl Baedeker, London: George Allen, 1965.

Boyd, Brian. *Vladimir Nabokov: The Russian Years*. Princeton: Princeton University Press, 1990.

Bristol, Evelyn. "Turn of a century: Modernism, 1895–1925," *The Cambridge History of Russian Literature*. Ed. Charles A. Moser. Cambridge: Cambridge University Press, 1992.

Brooks, Jeffrey. *When Russia Learned to Read: Literacy and Popular Literature, 1861-1917*. Evanston: Northwestern University Press, 2003.

Brown, Edward J. "So Much Depends...Russian Critics in Search of 'Reality'," *Russian Review*, Vol. 48, No. 4. (Oct., 1989): 353-381.

_____ "Pisarev and the Transformation of Two Russian Novels," *Literature and Society in Imperial Russia, 1800-1914*. Ed. by William Mills Todd III. Stanford: Stanford University Press, 1978.

Bowlt, John E. "Art in Exile: The Russian Avant-Garde and the Emigration," *Art Journal*, Vol. 41, No. 3, The Russian Avant-Garde. (Autumn, 1981), pp. 215-221.

Buckler, Julie A. *Mapping St. Petersburg: Imperial Text and Cityshape*. Princeton: Princeton University Press, 2005.

Clark, Katerina. *Petersburg: Crucible of Cultural Revolution*. Harvard: Harvard University Press, 1998.

Connolly, Julian. "The Major Russian Novels." *The Cambridge Companion to Nabokov*. Ed. by Julian W. Connolly. Cambridge: Cambridge University Press, 2005: 135-150.

Dolinin, Alexander. *Kommentarii k romanu* Dar, in: V. Nabokov. *Sobranie sochinenii russkogo perioda*. 5 tt. St. Petersburg: Simpozium, 1999–2000. Vol. 4: 634-768.

_____ "The Stepmother of Russian Cities: Berlin of the 1920s through the Eyes of Russian Writers," *Cold Fusion: Aspects of the German Cultural Presence in Russia*, Ed. by G. Barabtarlo. New York: Berghahn Press, 2000: 225-240.

Drozd, Andrew M. *Chernyshevskii's* What is to be done?: *A Reevaluation*. Evanston, IL: Northwestern University Press, 2001.

_____ "Chernyshevski and Pushkin," *Russian Literature* LXII (2007) III: 271-92.

Engelstein, Laura. *The Keys to Happiness: Sex and the Search for Modernity in Fin-de-Siècle Russia*. Ithaca: Cornell University Press, 1994.

Goldfrank, David, Lindsey Hughes, Catherine Evtuhov, and Richard Stites. *A History of Russia: Peoples, Legends, Events, Forces*. New York: Houghton Mifflin, 2004.

Florinsky, Michael T. *Russia: A Short History*. New York: The Macmillan Company, 1964.

Freeborn, Richard. "The Nineteenth Century: The Age of Realism, 1855-80," *The Cambridge History of Russian Literature*. Edited by Charles A. Moser. Cambridge: Cambridge University Press, 1989.

_____ *The Rise of the Russian Novel: Studies in the Russian novel from* Eugene Onegin *to* War and Peace. Cambridge: Cambridge University Press, 1973.

Herzen, Alexander. "Bazarov Once Again," in: Ivan Turgenev, *Fathers and Sons*. Trans. by Michael Katz. New York: W. W. Norton & Company, 1996: 218-223.

Hunczak, Taras, Ed., *Russian Imperialism from Ivan the Great to the Revolution*. With an introduction by Hans Kohn. New Brunswick, New Jersey: Rutgers University Press, 1974.

Hosking, Geoffrey. *Russia: People and Empire*. London: Harper Collins Publishers, 1997.

Iswolsky, Helen. "Twenty-Five Years of Russian Émigré Literature," *Russian Review*, Vol. 1, No. 2 (April, 1942).

Jelavich, Peter. *Berlin Alexanderplatz: Radio, Film, and the Death of Weimar Culture*. Berkeley: University of California Press, 2006.

Gasparov, Boris. "Pushkin and Romanticism," in *The Pushkin handbook*. Ed. by David M. Bethea. Madison, Wisconsin: The University of Wisconsin Press, 2005.

Glushanok, G. "A. A. Goldenweizer i Nabokovy (Po materialam arkhiva A. A. Goldenweizera)." Publikatsiia, vstupit. statia i kommentarii G. Glushanok, in *Russkie evrei v Amerike*. Kn. 2. Ed. by Ernst Zaltsberg. Jerusalem—Toronto—St. Petersburg: Russian Jewry Abroad, Akademicheskii proekt, 2007.

Greenleaf, Monika. "Fathers, Sons and Impostors: Pushkin's Trace in *The Gift*." *Slavic Review: American Quarterly of Russian, Eurasian and East European Studies*, 1994 Spring; 53 (1): 140-58.

Katz, Michael and William G. Wagner. "Chernyshevsky, *What Is to Be Done?* and the Russian Intelligentsia," in Nikolai Chernyshevsky, *What Is to Be Done?* Transl. by M. R. Katz. Ithaca: Cornell University Press, 1989: 1-36.

Leving, Yuri. *Train Station—Garage—Hangar (Vladimir Nabokov and Poetics of Russian Urbanism)* [*Vokzal—Garazh—Angar. V. Nabokov i poetika russkogo urbanizma*]. St. Petersburg: Ivan Limbakh Publishing House, 2004.

Liatskii, E. A. *Chernyshevski v Sibiri*. Vol. II. St. Petersburg, 1913.

Lincoln, Bruce W. *Sunlight at Midnight: St. Petersburg and the Rise of Modern Russia*. New York: Basic Books, 2001.

References

MacKenzie, David and Michael W. Curran. *A History of Russia, the Soviet Union, and Beyond*. 6th Ed. Belmont, CA: Wadsworth, 2001.

Malia, Martin E., *Alexander Herzen and the Birth of Russian Socialism, 1812-1855*. Cambridge, Mass: Harvard University press, 1961.

Mander, John. *Berlin: The Eagle and the Bear*. London: Barrie and Rockliff, 1959.

Meyer, Priscilla. Review of *Vladimir Nabokov*, by David Rampton. *Slavic Review* 53 (2), 1994: 571-573.

Miliukov, Paul, Charles Seignobos and L. Eisenmann. *History of Russia: Informs, Reaction, Revolutions (1855-1932)*. Transl. by Charles Markmann. Vol. 3. New York: Funk & Wagnalls, 1969.

Milner-Gulland, R. with Nikolai Dejevsky. *Cultural atlas of Russia and the former Soviet Union*. Oxford: Checkmark Books, 1989.

Mirsky, D. S. *Russia: A Social History*, London: The Cresset Press, 1931.

Morson, Gary Saul. *The Boundaries of Genre; Dostoevsky's Diary of a Writer and the Traditions of Literary Utopia* (Texas, 1981).

Moser, Charles. *Esthetics as Nightmare: Russian Literary Theory, 1855–1870*. Princeton: Princeton University Press, 1989.

Moynahan, Julian. *Vladimir Nabokov*. Minnesota: University of Minnesota Press, 1971.

Nabokov, Vladimir. *Lectures on Literature*. Ed. by Fredson Bowers; introd. by John Updike. New York: Harcourt Brace Jovanovich, 1980.

_____ *Lectures on Russian literature*. Ed. by Fredson Bowers. New York: Harcourt Brace Jovanovich, 1981.

_____ *Speak, Memory. An Autobiography Revisited*. New York: G.P. Putnam's Sons, 1966.

_____ *Strong Opinions*. New York: McGraw-Hill, 1973.

Naiman, Eric. *Nabokov, Perversely*. Ithaca: Cornell University Press, 2010.

Neumann, Eckhard. "Russia's 'Leftist Art' in Berlin, 1922," *Art Journal*, Vol. 27, No. 1. (Autumn, 1967).

Paperno, Irina. *Chernyshevsky and the Age of Realism: A Study in the Semiotics of Behavior*. Stanford: Stanford University Press, 1988.

Pereira, N.G.O. *The Thought and Teachings of N. G. Cernysevskij*. The Hague: Mouton, 1975.

Priestland, David. *The Red Flag: A History of Communism*. New York: Grove Press, 2009.

Raeff, Mark. *Das russische Theater in Berlin, 1919-1931* by Michaela Bohmig, *Slavic Review*, Vol. 52, No. 2 (Summer, 1993).

Rampton, David. *Vladimir Nabokov: A Critical Study of the Novels*. Cambridge: Cambridge University Press, 1984.

Randall, Francis. *N. G. Chernyshevskii*. New York: Twayne Publishers, 1967.

Riasanovsky, Nicholas V. *A History of Russia*, 7th Edition. Oxford: Oxford University Press, 1993.

Roditi, E. "Entretien avec Marc Chagall," *Preuves* (Paris), No. 84, February, 1958.

Roth, Joseph. *What I Saw. Reports from Berlin: 1920-1933*. Tarns. with an introduction by Michael Hofinann. New York: W. W. Norton & Company, 2004.

Schiff, Stacy. *Véra (Mrs. Vladimir Nabokov)*. New York: Random House, 1999.

Sheldon, Richard. "Shklovsky's 'Zoo' and Russian Berlin." *Russian Review*, Vol. 29, No. 3 (Jul., 1970).

Slonim, Marc. *An Outline of Russian Literature*. London: Oxford University Press, 1958.

Stacy, R. H. *Russian Literary Criticism: A Short History*. Syracuse: Syracuse University Press, 1974.

Steinberg, Mark D. *Proletarian Imagination. Self, Modernity, and the Sacred in Russia, 1910-1925*. Ithaca: Cornell University Press, 2002.

Stites, Richard. *Revolutionary Dreams: Utopian Vision and Experimental Life in the Russian Revolution*. New York: Oxford University Press, 1991.

Struve, Gleb. *Russkaia literatura v izgnanii* (Russian Literature in Exile), New York: Izdatel'stvo imeni Chekhova, 1956.

Sumner, B. H. *A Short History of Russia*. New York: Harcourt, Brace & World, 1962.

Terapiano, Iurii. *Vstrechi*. New York: Izdatel'stvo imeni Chekhova, 1953.

Terras, Victor. *Handbook of Russian Literature*. New Haven: Yale University Press 1985.

Tertz, Abram (Andrei Sinyavsky). *Strolls With Pushkin*. Transl. by Catharine Thornier Nepomnyashchy and Slava I. Yastremski. New Haven: Yale University Press, 1993.

Tolstoy, Leo. *War and Peace*. Transl. by Louise and Aylmer Maude. In Three Volumes. The World's Classics, Read Books [electronic edition], 2006.

Tumarkin, Nina. *Lenin lives!: the Lenin Cult in Soviet Russia*. Harvard: Harvard University Press, 1997.

Woehrlin, William F. *Chernyshevskii: The Man and the Journalist*. Harvard: Harvard University Press, 1971.

Wren, Melvin C. *The Course of Russian History*. New York: The Macmillan Company, 1958.

Yarmolinsky, Avrahm. *Road to Revolution: A Century of Russian Radicalism*. London: Cassell & Co., 1957.

Zelnik, Reginald E. "Revolutionary Russia, 1890-1914," *Russia: A History*. Ed. Gregory L. Freeze. Oxford: Oxford University Press, 1997.

Chapter Three
STRUCTURE

Title

Encoded in the Cityscape

One of *The Gift*'s key scenes is disguised in the description of a mundane Berlin night, but the portrayal of the cityscape is deceptively laconic:

> Behind the brightly painted pumps a radio was singing in a gas station, while above its pavilion vertical yellow letters stood against the light blue of the sky—the name of a car firm—and on the second letter, on the 'E' (a pity that it was not on the first, on the 'B'—would have made an alphabetic vignette) sat a live blackbird, with a yellow—for economy's sake—beak, singing louder than the radio. (G174)

It is not accidental at all that, in the Russian version, the second letter on which the blackbird perches is "A," while the first letter turns out to be "D". The automobile brand remains the same in both versions of the text (Daimler-Benz), but the Russian version stresses the unfinished title of the novel, DA—*Dar*.

In fact it was Nabokov's original intent to entitle his novel with the life-affirming statement "*Da*" meaning "Yes" in Russian, according to two letters written by the author to Zinaida Shakhovskoy and sent in the first half of 1936, in which he confessed that the title of the novel he was currently working on had gathered an additional letter:

> I am afraid that my next novel (its title has been extended by one letter: not "Da" but "Dar," transforming the initial statement in to something flourishing, pagan, even priapic), will disappoint you. In my acquittal I wish to repeat that the only thing of importance is the question of whether the book is written well or badly—as for the author being either a rascal or a well-wishing sweetie, this is absolutely uninteresting. (Undated letter from 1936; see also the postcard dated July 6, 1935; Zinaida Shakhovskoy folder, Nabokov Collection, Library of Congress)

Chapter Three. STRUCTURE

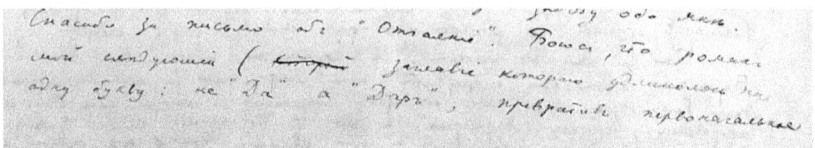

[Ill. 3-1] From *Yes* to *Gift*: the fragment of the 1936 letter: "Da" transforms into "Dar"

The new title includes a vital and universal acceptance (embodied in the positive "Da"), and also signifies the celebration of the gifts of life, epiphany of creation, literary bliss, powers of memory, and abstract metaphysics blended into the pleasures of the physical world. Despite his superficial similarities to Yasha and Hamlet, Fyodor resists the temptation of non-being: his life-affirming philosophy helps him to decipher the "correct" answer to Hamlet's famous question "to be or not to be?" (Barskova 205). The two letters illuminated in the name of the car company in the English translation supply an answer that is hidden in plain view in *The Gift*: BE!

Alexander Dolinin has compiled an impressive compendium of poems by Russian romanticists, symbolists and modernists alike that Nabokov may have been aware of and taking into consideration—all unified by one major theme which is a *thanksgiving* (*Istinnaia zhizn'* 231-238). Among these poets are Gavrila Derzhavin ("Life is a heavenly momentary gift"), Alexander Blok ("I became rich as I've accepted this world like a resonant gift, like a handful of gold"), Vladislav Khodasevich ("How could one not love this whole world, This incredible gift?.."), and Gleb Struve ("Your incredible gift—/Maybe life, maybe, death"). Each of the celebratory poems acknowledging divine favors includes the word *gift* or *present* in them.

The Gifts of Life and Creativity

The theme of the gift in the title refers to Russian literature in its entirety. Russian literature is as much the hero of *The Gift* as is Fyodor himself, for the novel is Nabokov's homage to his native literary heritage. Fyodor sees himself as an heir to that tradition, and two of his own works are inspired by Pushkin and Gogol, the seminal figures of modern Russian literature: "*The Gift* itself does not stand in the shadow of any single Russian literary voice but rather is a compendium deliberately redoing the voices of Russian writers from Pushkin to Pilnyak all set within a stylistic context that is purely that of Nabokov" (Johnson 94).

Like Proust's *In Search of Lost Time* tackles the philosophical problem of retaining lost things, the desire to save what can vanish forever is the impetus for Fyodor's decision to write an autobiography and is inscribed in the title of the book. Martin Hägglund reminds us that the gift of the title signifies Fyodor's life (and especially his relationship with Zina) but also his artistic talent. This other "gift" will possibly result in the book we are reading and includes some of Fyodor's preliminary efforts — among them a biography of his father and love poems to Zina after their nightly meetings (Hägglund 451). The act of writing as an attempt to remember something "is reinforced when, at the end of the novel, Fyodor tells Zina about his idea to write a sort of autobiography. *The Gift* shall commemorate the history of their love, Fyodor promises" (Ibid. 452). In making this pledge, he must position the promise as a memory for the future: "One day we shall recall all this," Fyodor reflects on the last page of the book, as he and Zina leave a restaurant and wander out into the summer night (Ibid.).

In what was supposed to be the end of the second addendum, "Father's Butterflies," we learn about one particular recollection from Fyodor's boyhood. Its lack of clarity is intentional and presents an enigmatic puzzle — an allusion to an unspoken source in which lurks a self-referential hint:

> Here I recall, with no connection to this eternal hurt or, at least, no rational connection, how, one warm summer night, a boy of fourteen, I sat on the veranda bench with some book — whose title, too, I shall surely recall in a moment, when it all comes into focus — and my mother, smiling as in a dream, was laying out on the illumined table cards that were particularly glossy against the thick, velvet heliotrope-soaked chasm into which the veranda glided. I had difficulty understanding what I read, for the book was difficult and strange, and the pages seemed out of order, and my father, with someone — with a guest, or with his brother, I cannot make out clearly — was walking across the lawn, slowly, judging by their softly moving voices. At a certain moment, as he passed beneath an open window, his voice drew nearer. Almost as if he were reciting a monologue, for, in the darkness of the fragrant black past, I have lost track of his chance interlocutor, my father declared emphatically and cheerfully, "Yes, of course it was in vain that [he] said 'accidental,' and accidental that [he] said 'in vain,' for here I agree with the clergy, especially since, for all the plants and animals I have had occasion to encounter, it is an unquestionable and authentic..." The awaited final stress did not come. Laughing, the voice receded into the darkness — and now I have suddenly remembered the title of the book. (*Nabokov's Butterflies* 234; with A. Dolinin's correction)

Two scholars, Brian Boyd and Alexander Dolinin, have offered their answers to the riddle of the unnamed book that title Fyodor tries to recall. The work, most certainly, is the very *Dar* (*The Gift*), and the quoted words "accidental" and "in vain" allude to Pushkin's well-known lyric, "Dar naprasnyi" ("Vain gift"). It starts with the following line: "Vain gift, chance gift, / life, why have you been given to me." In early January 1830, Pushkin's friend Elizaveta Khitrovo, an admirer of

Metropolitan Philaret,[20] sent to Pushkin the Metropolitan's rejoinder to his poem, which began with the exact opposite statement:

> Not in vain, not by chance
> Was life given me by God,
> And not without God's mysterious will
> Is it condemned to death...
>
> Ne naprasno, ne sluchaino
> Zhizn' ot Boga mne dana,
> Ne bez voli Boga tainoy
> I na kazn' osuzhdena...

Despite his unconditional love for Pushkin, Count Godunov senior takes the side of the prominent hierarch of the Russian Church (hence his words: "here I agree with the clergy"). As if the Pushkin echo is still not enough, the reader who knows Russian is prompted: "*Ozhidaemogo udareniia ne posledovalo*," literally "The expected lexical stress did not follow." The word "gift" is withheld, but the genetive case noun, "ud*ar*eniia" ("stress"), includes in itself the word *dar* (*gift*) (Boyd, "The Expected Stress" 24; Dolinin, "*Dar*: Dobavleniia"). The concept of the gift thus becomes a piece in a much larger metaphysical puzzle.

Also evident here becomes the link between the title theme and paternal legacy—the father literally vanishes in darkness leaving only a key word as his last testament. Nabokov's own father's tragic death by political assassination had a profound effect on his son. Writers of obituaries and eulogies recalled Vladimir Dmitrievich Nabokov's nervous, "poetic" voice as being "at odds with his correct, prim image and impeccable manners" (Malikova 17). This quality of his father's voice must have been ingrained in Nabokov's memory. Maria Malikova notes that strikingly similar descriptions of imaginary death and imaginary resurrection of the father character occur in the short story "Orache," and in *The Gift* and *Speak, Memory*. In each of these works the son cannot look at his father's face; "he can only hear the father's voice or feel his touch" (Ibid.). In the poem "Evening in a Vacant Lot" (1932) the same motif of the father's disembodied voice surfaces in the context of an obituary: "But in the distance sounds / insistently and tenderly a whistling, / and in the twilight towards me a man / comes, calls").

In another of Nabokov's poems, "Hexameters" (1923), dedicated to V. D. Nabokov, the angelic paternal figure bending over the sleeping narrator causes him to whisper: "*imia otchizny*" ("the name of the fatherland"): "Fyodor, imagining

---

[20] Metropolitan Philaret (Drozdov) of Moscow (1782–67) was the most influential figure in the Russian Orthodox Church for more than four decades, from 1821 till his death.

an otherworldly meeting with his father, at first hears the father's voice uttering words he can not make out" (Malikova 18). When the father begins speaking again, the son understands that "this was the true resurrection, that it could not be otherwise. *The Gift* lays bare the formation of a motif that is recurrent in Nabokov's artistic world: the merging of two real-life circumstances—V. D. Nabokov's distinctive voice prounouncing words (often Pushkin's) which are taken up by his son, and the word 'resurrection' pronounced by the priest during the Easter service and taken up by the parishioners (V. D. Nabokov died the day before Easter Sunday)" (Ibid.). All of the aforementioned examples follow the same pattern: intense painful anticipation, silence and the impossibility of making out what is being said, combined with a growing sense of joy that peaks in the cathartic Easter cry: "He is Risen." Godunov-Cherdyntsev senior, in some sense, endows his son with the gift of the word. The phrase "with Pushkin's voice merged the voice of his father" (G94) explicates one of the father's functions in the novel—that of donor, bestower of a gift (*daritel'*) (Ibid. 19).

Another possibility is that the word missing from Fyodor's father's speech and the title of the novel that he reads as a child may be two different words. Considering the thematic cluster that we have seen, the title in question might be that of Leo Tolstoy's last novel, *Resurrection*, published in the year of Nabokov's birth—1899, which among other issues critiqued the hypocrisy of institutionalized church. Nabokov's poem "Tolstoy" (1928) blends the same motifs of death and posthumously revived voice:

> A phonograph recording still preserves
> the cadence of his voice: he reads aloud,
> monotonously, hastily, opaquely,
> and mumbling when he comes to the word "God,"
> repeating "God," and then continuing—
> a slightly husky, almost senseless sound,
> like someone coughing in the next compartment
> when, in the old days, at a nighttime station,
> your railroad car would make a sighing stop.
> [...]
> One day, from a chance railroad station, he
> turned off toward the unknown and left for good;
> beyond lies night, silence, and mystery...
>
> (*Transl. from Russian by Dmitri Nabokov.*
> *Nabokov Online Journal 3, 2009*)

Although it seems that the passage from *The Gift* refers only to the unnamed *title* of the book, Gene Barabtarlo offers two likely candidates for the authorship of mysterious book: "Since the word 'dar' is a mnemo-homo-phonic trigger...it can launch an association indirectly, e.g. through the author's name. I suggested Darskii's *Wonderous Fantasies* of 1914, but would not a DARWin [a gift, a win] suit the subject of this addendum better? For instance, *The Origin of Species*..." (Barabtarlo 34).

The Interlinguistic Pun

Nabokov is famous for his multilingual games, and with *The Gift* one cannot rule out the possibility of a pun based on the German meaning of the word *Gift* (in English, "poison"). To illuminate the semantic plausibility of this connection Sergei Davydov reminds us that the real poet Vladislav Khodasevich allegedly served as a model for the poet Koncheyev, who plays a crucial role in Fyodor's artistic development. Two imaginary conversations that Fyodor has with him (Chapters One and Five) symmetrically frame the narrative. In the first chapter Fyodor considers Koncheyev his only true rival, is envious of Koncheyev's gift, and thinks of him as a "man whose mysteriously growing talent could have been checked only by a ringful of poison in a glass of wine" (G64) ("*tainstvenno razrastavshiisia talant kotorogo tol'ko dar Izory mog by presech'*"); in the Russian original the reference is clearer, as the entire phrase, "ringful of poison in a glass of wine," was added in translation as an equivalent of the two words, "*dar Izory*" (literally, *gift of Izora*); this is a quote from Pushkin's drama *Mozart and Salieri* (1830): "Here is the poison, the last gift of my Izora." Dmitri Nabokov and Michael Scammell jettisoned the opaque allusion because the English-language readers of *The Gift* would fail to recognize the subtext (each of Pushkin's four "little tragedies" succinctly deals with a philosophical problem; this particular work, based on a legend that Salieri poisoned Mozart, meditates on the nature of creativity).

Returning to the Fyodor–Koncheyev controversy: there is "no doubt that such a 'gift' is beneath the dignity of the hero of *The Gift*. As Fyodor matures, the Salieri–Mozart syndrome gives way to a rather symbiotic relationship between the two poets. By the time of their second imaginary conversation it becomes clear that their spiritual union is that of Virgil and Dante, with Koncheyev leading Fyodor through the labyrinth of exile" (Davydov, "Weighing Nabokov's *Gift*" 418).

The Title as a Reference

Nabokov's original title for *The Gift*—*Yes*, addressed to the world and its creator—has a literary precursor from Western fiction. For Brian Boyd, who considers the novel, in both subject and scale, a kind of reply and homage to

James Joyce's *Ulysses*, the resonant affirmation seems also to echo Molly Bloom's great "and yes I said yes I will Yes" at the end of *Ulysses* (Boyd, "The Expected Stress" 28). It is worth noting that in 1933, the same year he began *The Gift*, Nabokov had made an offer to Joyce to translate *Ulysses* into Russian. Nabokov quotes this finale with an apparent delight and comments in his lectures on *Ulysses*: "Yes: Bloom next morning will get his breakfast in bed" (*Lectures on Literature* 370).

Finally, there is an alliteration between the Russian title, *Dar*, and the second syllable of the protagonist's name, Fyodor (the Russian equivalent of Theodore, "*gift* of God"); in the Russian pronunciation, the vowel in the second syllable of the name is reduced to sound somewhat similar to the title: Fyo*dar*.

Plot

The novel's theme is developed in the unfolding of two major plot lines: the more obvious is "the gradual coming together of Fyodor and his beloved, Zina Mertz, in a protracted pattern of approaches and withdrawals ending in their final union. The second and more fundamental line of development is the ripening of Fyodor's artistic talent, which leads to the creation of *The Gift*" (Johnson 93), or at least some text almost coinciding with it. Both of the plot lines, as Donald B. Johnson formulates the issue, are structured in terms of a chess problem.

Contemporary Summary

The plot summary below is taken from an unpublished internal review by Alexander Nazaroff (see more on him in Chapter Seven, "Contemporary critics: 1937–39"). Though it is slightly biased in its description of the fourth chapter (to the point of suggesting another, more proper, writer for Chernyshevski's biography!), it nonetheless presents the plot of *The Gift* in a concise and accurate manner. The report, entitled "A Novel by V. Nabokoff (Sirin)," originally submitted for Bobbs-Merrill Company in 1938, is now a part of the Vladimir Nabokov Collection at the Library of Congress, Washington, D.C.:

> It is a novel about a young poet, Godunov-Cherdyntsev, a Russian émigré living in Berlin, about the two books he was writing, and about the two he didn't write.
>
> The novel is divided into five chapters.
>
> In the first chapter, the young hero who had just published his first book of poems, had also just moved into a new boarding house. The poems are about his childhood. By reading them over and quoting from about twenty, he tells us of his life in Russia, his mother, his sister, his scarlet fever, the old country estate

Chapter Three. STRUCTURE

and the snowy streets of St. Petersburg. Then he goes to see his friends who are very fond of him because he reminds them of their son, Yasha, who recently committed suicide. These friends of his want him to write a book about Yasha, who also was a poet. Yasha had fallen desperately in love with a boy, who was in love with a girl who was in love with Yasha. The three of them were friends; there was no way out of the fatal triangle but for all to commit suicide. All three of them went to the woods. Yasha's turn was first. He killed himself. The other two lost their nerve and remained alive. The poet muses over the subject, but decides not to write the book.

In the second chapter his mother comes to see him from Paris where she and his sister live. He and his mother talk and think about Russia and the old days and about his father. His father, the famous Russian naturalist, a noble and courageous (and rather ruthless) figure, had collected beautiful butterflies in the mountains of Tibet and written learned works about their life and habits. He seemed to know something which nobody else knew, but what that something was the reader does not find out. He never returned from his last expedition which took place in the early days of the revolution. Later his family received indirect reports of his death, but the poet and his mother believed that he was still alive and would some day suddenly return. His mother wants him to write a book about his father. And he begins to write. He writes about his father, and again about their old country estate, and about the expeditions and the butterflies and some butterflies and some more expeditions. At the end he finds himself inadequate to the task. He throws the whole thing into the waste basket and moves into a new room.

The third chapter is about his new room and his life in it. It is also about Russian poetry and what meter is the most suitable to it. It is also about his Russian landlord and landlady, and about her daughter by her first marriage, Zina, with whom he falls in love. Their romance consists of daily meetings in some unfrequented cafe, or quiet park, or street, because Zina despises her mother and her stepfather and does not want them to know of her love. In the course of this chapter the poet hits upon the idea of writing a biography of Nikolai Chernyshevski, one of the biggest figures in the development of Russian social thought. He writes the book. When the book is finished he takes it to the editor of a Russian paper who had promised to publish it. But when he comes back for an answer the indignant editor almost throws the book in his face. He declares it a cheap and low attack on one of the noblest and best loved characters of the Russian past. But the book gets published just the same, by an obscure publisher.

Chapter four is the biography of Chernyshevski written by our poet. It is far the best chapter of the book. It is interesting and vivid even if it is really a nasty, very nasty, attack on the character of Chernyshevski—the most outstanding of Russian critics of the last seventy-five years, the man who left the imprint of his thought on contemporary and subsequent revolutionary generations; a favorite of Lenin. The chapter is full of sordid and disagreeable details, of which the author is a real master. It left me with an unpleasant feeling, but also gave me an idea that a book on Chernyshevski would be a good one to publish if you could get someone like E. H. Carr, the author of a recent brilliantly interesting life of Bakunin, to write it.[21]

The fifth and last chapter contains several reviews from the Russian émigré press almost unanimously panning the book on Chernyshevski, and it contains the finale of our hero's romance. Zina's parents are leaving for Denmark. Zina and Fyodor are going to be alone and together at last. They'll have the apartment to themselves. But the reader never sees them there. They stop on the way home at a restaurant for supper. They are slightly embarrassed. They talk, and Zina discovers that all through the period covered by this book fate was unsuccessfully trying to bring them together—which immediately starts a new train of creative thoughts in our hero's head. Now he is going to write about this in his next book. The only intimation we have of the outcome of the romance lies in the fact that neither of them has a key to their apartment.

There the book ends.

NARRATIVE

Fabula and Siuzhet

The terms *Fabula* and *Siuzhet* originate in Russian Formalism (mainly Vladimir Propp and Victor Shklovsky's theoretical works) and are employed in narratology to describe narrative structures. The Russian formalist school defines the *fabula* as the objective series of events in the story, as distinct from the *siuzhet*, which is the story as reported in the narrative (an example of the former is Véra Nabokov's summary cited in Appendix II). According to the poststructuralist Jonathan Culler, *fabula* and *siuzhet* constitute a so-called double move. The first move is to set narrative in hierarchical domination over story. Story becomes relegated in the first move to a mere chronology of events. In the second move, narrative self-deconstructs its initial duality, in order to double back to efface the order of events (Culler 189). Other theorists propose different formulations, but there is always a basic distinction between a sequence of events and a discourse that orders and presents events.

Nabokov elaborately fuses both structures by telling the life of his heroes through flashbacks and hallucinatory episodes interspersed with his present-time investigations into the lives of other fictional and historical figures.

It has often been noted that the novel begins and ends with the same images of clouds, but it should also be remarked that Chapter One has its own repetitive

---

[21] Edward Hallett Carr (1892–1982), the author of *Michael Bakunin* (1937). Carr was a prolific writer and wrote dozens of books, including *Dostoevsky: A New Biography* (1931); *The Romantic Exiles: A Nineteenth-century Portrait Gallery* (1933); *Karl Marx: A Study in Fanaticism* (1934), and *A History of Soviet Russia* (1950).

pattern forming a thematic circle: it begins with an epigraph from a textbook and ends with the metaphor of "a self-teaching handbook of literary inspiration" (G76), thus presenting the idea of the novel as an insight into the nature of artistic gift, a kind of manual for Nabokov's own rules of conduct in the remaining four chapters. The plot movement and transitions (*fabula*) will be registered here chapter by chapter.

Development of Themes

Chapter One

The first chapter of *The Gift* consists of 73 pages (70 in Russian)
Place: Berlin
Time: 1926

I. Fyodor arrives at his new house and observes the neighbors (G1). He checks the shops in the vicinity (4-6). The first gift (that of *sight*) is mentioned. When Fyodor is back home, he receives a call from Alexander Yakovlevich Chernyshevski, who quotes to him the beginning of a (non-existent) review of Fyodor's recently published collection of poetry (8).

II. Intrigued by this news, Fyodor embarks on a mental re-reading of his book entitled *Poems*, which is primarily devoted to his own childhood in Russia on the eve of the revolution. Occasional quotes from poems alternate with excerpts from reviews of the volume; all reviews, it turns out, are actually imagined by Fyodor, who is impatiently trying to kill time before stepping into Chernyshevski's lodging. This long digression occupies twenty pages (9-29).

III. Back in his Berlin reality, Fyodor finally enters the Chernyshevskis' dwelling, only to discover that he has been the victim of an April Fool's prank (30-32). A literary party with guests is in progress and various Russian expatriates are introduced (33-36).

IV. The Chernyshevskis' transformation after their son's untimely death. The couple is strangely attracted to Fyodor, who reminds them of deceased Yasha (37-40). Yasha's story is told — an unlucky love triangle leading to his suicide (41-48). The death produced a painful effect on Yasha's father, Alexander Yakovlevich Chernyshevski, who has gradually slipped into mental illness (49-50).

V. Cut to the literary party at the Chernyshevskis' (begun in the section III) (51-53). Fyodor leaves the gathering and walks to his newly rented apartment and realizes at this point that he has left his key inside (54-55).

VI. Finally at home and still in his poetic mood, Fyodor muses upon a fresh verse (56-57).

Development of Themes

VII. After painstakingly describing the first day at a slow pace, Nabokov zooms out and recounts Fyodor's daily routine in Berlin following his move to Tannenberg Street. This includes observing his neighbors and old acquaintances (58-59), performing odd jobs—from private language lessons to commercial translations (60-61), and contributing to the local émigré newspaper *Gazeta* (57-63).

VIII. Another literary event is organized by Mme. Chernyshevski (64-69), where Fyodor meets a talented poet, Koncheyev. After the party a lengthy intellectual dialogue unfolds between the two poets, who discuss Russian literature since Pushkin. However, in the denouement (which coincides with the end of the first chapter) it turns out that the entire tête-à-tête had been nothing but a soliloquy—a product of Fyodor's fevered imagination (70-76).

Chapter Two

The second chapter consists of 68 pages (66 in Russian)
Places: Berlin, Russia, Tibet, China
Time: December 1926—April 1928; early 1900s

I. In a lyrical opening Fyodor recalls the Russia of his youth, his father, and the family estate in the rural suburbs of St. Petersburg (77-79).

II. Suddenly Fyodor regains consciousness in the middle of a Berlin street heading towards a private pupil's home (80). During a trip in the tramcar he ponders the nature of local citizens and Russian expatriates, which strikes him as irrevocably philistine (81-84). Fyodor changes his mind and decides to return home (84). The rest of the chapter will form a digression to Fyodor's parental theme only to reemerge as a Berlin reality of two years later, in April of 1928 [see sections X–XI] (138-45).

III. A brisk switch to Fyodor's Russian childhood, a time filled with warm memories of Tanya, his sister, and their parents (85). A quick shift is needed to gain momentum for the later "fatherhood" theme. Nabokov frequently uses this narrative technique: a seemingly insignificant and brief announcement of what is yet to emerge as a major topic shortly before it is to be explored in full.

IV. Fyodor's mother, Elizaveta Pavlovna, visits her son in Berlin after a three-year separation. Both plunge into lovingly cherished memories of the past, inseparable from the haunting images of Godunov-Cherdyntsev senior, who had never returned from his last scientific expedition (86-90). Fyodor introduces his mother to Mme. Chernyshevski (90), and then an account of Fyodor's visitation to Alexander Yakovlevich Chernyshevski in a psychiatric clinic follows (91-92). Shortly before his mother leaves for Paris, she and Fyodor go together to a Russian literary reading (92-94); Elizaveta Pavlovna's departure (95).

---Chapter Three. STRUCTURE---

v. Encouraged by conversations with his mother and deeply immersed in Pushkin's prose (96-98), Fyodor begins preparations for writing a biography of his vanished father. This requires months of preparatory research (January-June, 1927).

vi. Another example of an inserted "literary document": an excerpt from memoirs by A. N. Sukhoshchokov about Fyodor's grandfather, Kirill Ilyich Godunov-Cherdyntsev, and his innocent prank regarding Pushkin's alleged comeback (98-101).

vii. This section contains a surviving draft of the never-completed biographic sketch of Konstantin Kirillovich Godunov-Cherdyntsev by his son Fyodor, who portrays him as a prominent scientist (102-03). There is another long quasi-quotation, this time from Elizaveta Pavlovna's correspondence, in reply to her son's inquiry concerning her late husband's habits in the context of his family (104-105). Fyodor recollects meetings with his father which took place during the breaks between Konstantin Kirillovich's long voyages (106-15).

viii. The semi-biography slips into a first-person account of Fyodor's own journey to the mountains of Tyan-Shan, Tibet, and the desert of Lob; Fyodor the protagonist fantasizes that he accompanies his father on a scientific mission to the unexplored regions of central Asia (116-25).

ix. The Godunov-Cherdyntsev family is reunited shortly before World War I. Fyodor's father prepares for his next journey and writes a scientific volume on butterflies of the Russian empire. In June 1916, the father sets out on his last expedition (116-12). After that, no reliable information concerning Godunov-Cherdyntsev senior is available, and all attempts to verify his fate seem futile (133-37).

x. Fyodor has finally collected all the materials necessary for writing his father's life story, although the task proves to be insurmountable. Elizaveta Pavlovna reacts sympathetically to this news (138-39).

xi. Fyodor bids farewell to his old quarters and is ready to move into his next temporary lodging on 15 Agamemnonstrasse (140-45).

Chapter Three

The third chapter consists of 65 pages (63 in Russian)
Place: Berlin
Time: Friday, summer 1928—winter 1929

i. Fyodor Godunov-Cherdyntsev's routine in his new apartment is described (146-47).

ii. Writing poetry in his spare time causes Fyodor to explore his Russian youth again; he recalls the father's literary tastes (147-49) and his own first love

(149). The nature and process of versification is scrutinized (150-54); Fyodor is now able to assess his work more objectively. Two years passed since his debut, and his attitude toward his earlier poetic experiments has cooled compared to Chapter One of the novel (155).

III. Back to Berlin in the present. Fyodor observes the life of his new landlords and Russian compatriots, the Shchyogolev family, from within (155-61).

IV. Fyodor leaves the apartment to give a language lesson. The streets of contemporary Berlin, its inhabitants, and various means of transportation are introduced (161-66).

V. Fyodor is lured into the Russian bookshop at Wittenberg Square (167), where he peruses the latest magazines and books (168-69); he purchases the Soviet chess journal containing an article "Chernyshevski and Chess" (170-71).

VI. Fyodor pays a visit to Vasiliev, the editor of the Berlin émigré daily (172-73). On the way back home, engrossed in his reading of the chess journal, he misses his stop (174-75).

VII. Fyodor's Muse, Zina Mertz, enters. She turns out to be his current landlord's stepdaughter. The history of Fyodor's and Zina's clandestine affair is related (176-84); so are Zina's family background (185-87) as well as her present day working habits (188-93). Jokingly Fyodor suggests to Zina that he will write a biography of Chernyshevski, partly prompted by the earlier article in the chess magazine (194).

VIII. A week later: Fyodor is invited to a literary gathering at the Chernyshevskis where his ideas for the planned research take further shape (195-99).

IX. Fyodor scrupulously studies the subject of the future biography, and by winter of 1929 he is ready to start the actual writing (200-04). This is followed by a leap in time (the work itself will be reproduced in the next chapter of *The Gift*): Fyodor is now shown already completing his book about N. Chernyshevski. On the night when he completes the work, Fyodor skips the formal Saturday ball where he is supposed to be together with Zina (205-06).

X. Vasiliev reads Fyodor's manuscript and rejects it (207). Fyodor and Zina consider publishing the book privately but all their plans are to no avail (208). By chance Fyodor meets a fellow writer named Busch who arranges the publication of the Chernyshevski biography with his publisher (209-11).

Chapter Four

Chapter Four is the longest of all in *The Gift*, and consists of 88 pages (83 in Russian)
Place: Imperial Russia
Time: 1860s–1880s

Transitions between the plot segments differ here from the previous chapters, primarily because they are not motivated by characters' physical actions but governed instead by rapidly changing themes. The storyteller (presumably, Fyodor) traces these themes in the life his character, indexes and re-shuffles them; his voice frequently interrupts the fabric of the narrative with comments and achronological digressions, reminding the reader of his constant authorial presence.

I. The chapter opens as an imitation of the *literary biography* genre, introducing young Nikolai Chernyshevski at his home and then in the Saratov seminary (212-13). Notably, the main hero's full name won't be announced until p. 217.

II. The narrative proceeds by shifting through various *themes*—of "writing exercises" and "nearsightedness" (214); "angelic clarity" (215); "traveling," which the author calls his third theme when in fact it is the fourth one (216); "perpetual motion" and unsuccessful inventions (217-18),—all of which reveal the psychological depth of an otherwise rather unsympathetic character.

III. Chernyshevski moves to St. Petersburg and enters the philological faculty; his life in the capital (218-20) is introduced mainly through private correspondence and the diary that he keeps, description of his courtship of a close friend's wife (221-24) and his everyday habits (225); the segment ends with "the theme of pastry shops" (226).

IV. Chernyshevski is back to Saratov (228), where he meets his future wife, Olga Sokratovna Vasiliev (228-30); the *"petits-jeux"* theme (231), and teaching in the gymnasium (232).

V. Transfer to St. Petersburg. Chernyshevski teaches in the Cadet Corps and becomes active in journalism (233-34). Olga Sokratovna gives birth to Chernyshevski's three sons (234-35), which does not prevent her from being unfaithful to her husband (236).

VI. Chernyshevski defends his dissertation, "The Relations of Art to Reality," at the University of St. Petersburg (237). The thesis and its author's general aesthetic, literary, and philosophical views are discussed (238-54), with particular emphasis on Chernyshevski's attitude to Pushkin (255-58). Chernyshevski establishes an ideological alliance with radical revolutionary contemporaries, Dobrolyubov, Pisarev, and Herzen, resulting in surveillance by the government (259-68).

VII. Chernyshevski is arrested for engaging in antistate political activity and is held in the Peter-and-Paul Fortress (269-274). The captive writes a novel, *What to Do?* Eventually published in the journal *The Contemporary* (274-277), the work creates a public and critical sensation (278-79).

VIII. Chernyshevski is subjected to a mock execution (280-81) and banished to Siberia (281-85). In exile the author writes his new novel, *The Prologue*, and pursues other literary projects with little success (286-92). After years of banishment Chernyshevski is finally permitted to settle in Astrakhan, where he leads a lonely, dull life as a forgotten translator (293-95). His family falls apart, and his son Sasha becomes mentally unstable (296-98).

IX. Chernyshevski returns to Saratov and soon after that dies at the age of sixty-one (298-300).

Chapter Five

The fifth chapter consists of 65 pages (also 65 pages in Russian)
Place: Berlin
Time: Spring—Summer, 1929

I. If the previous chapter opened as an imitation of a *literary biography*, the last chapter of the novel starts as a pastiche of the genre of *literary criticism*. Different reviewers respond to Fyodor's recently published biography of Chernyshevski and, thus, the plot logically continues from the point where section X of Chapter Three was interrupted. Samples of reviews follow (Linyov's: 301-02; Mortus's: 302-04; Anuchin's: 305-08; Levchenko's: 308; unsigned quotations from the newspaper *Up!*; and the unprinted comments by Vasiliev, the editor of *Gazeta*, are summed up; 308-09).

II. Death of Alexander Yakovlevich Chernyshevski (309). Chernyshevski's passing triggers Fyodor's meditation over the nature of death and the other world (309-10); Chernyshevski's last days in a state of delirium are described (311-12); Chernyshevski's cremation (312-14).

III. On his way back from the crematorium, Fyodor stumbles across a fellow writer, Shirin (315). Both walk down to the park and converse about the state of contemporary émigré literature and its administrative organization (316-18).

IV. A month later: a general meeting of the Committee of the Society of Russian Writers in Germany takes place in a large café (319). Fyodor does not show interest either in the turbulent election of its officials or various factions' power games (320-325), and rides home through the Berlin night consumed by his passion for Zina (326).

V. Shchyogolev gets a job offer and will be leaving for Denmark soon, thus unexpectedly settling Fyodor and Zina's secret romance (326). In anticipation of the Shchyogolevs' departure, Fyodor, with his artistic gift maturing and personal happiness nearly achieved, spends extremely hot days in Grunewald (327-36).

VI. The last scenes of the book are precisely timed: this section starts on 28 June, at 3 pm (337). After swimming across the lake, Fyodor meets Koncheyev at the opposite shore and they have a lengthy dialogue centered on literary themes (338-42). At the end of the dialogue the reader (and Fyodor himself) realizes that "Koncheyev" was just an imaginary interlocutor (343).

VII. Returning to the other side of the lake Fyodor discovers that his belongings have been stolen; he has no choice but to retreat home half-naked (344-45). In the city Fyodor is stopped by a German policeman who interrogates him about his odd appearance under heavy rain (346-47).

VIII. Finally Fyodor is at home; this is the evening before the Shchyogolevs' departure from Berlin (347-48). The rest of the evening Fyodor spends writing (or imagining that he is writing) a letter to his mother (349-51), then he begins mumbling fragmentary verses (352).

IX. Frau Stoboy, Fyodor's former landlady, calls at night. She suddenly invites Fyodor to see someone special but doesn't specify whom. Fyodor rushes to his old apartment and meets his father there. But, after a few emotionally charged pages, the nocturnal rendezvous turns out to be a dream, just like his earlier fictitious conversations with Koncheyev (352-55).

X. The Shchyogolevs finally leave (355-59). Fyodor and Zina walk home together and celebrate their long-awaited union in an inexpensive restaurant: they try to discern in retrospect the patterns of fate that brought them together and to imagine what lies ahead (360-66).

Narrative "Gaps" or a Jigsaw Puzzle?

Despite the fact that the listing above presents a simple way of grasping the main movements in this complex narrative, the novel as a whole remains elusive. Many early reviewers complained about this strange quality of Nabokov's book, which they tended to interpret as its lack of coherence. Indeed, *The Gift* contains numerous samples of Fyodor's work in various states of incompleteness. But what some perceived as a weakness is in fact a literary device, which we might call *the poetics of incompleteness*.

Leona Toker offers a summary of the various levels of fragmentation in *The Gift* and claims that all the pieces are firmly held together by recurrent motifs, images, allusions, traces of "influence," hallucinations, and dreams (Toker 150). What are these representations of incompleteness? Fyodor's weak poems about childhood, his unwritten story about Yasha Chernyshevski, the monograph on his own father's life that remains in a fragmentary state, and the notorious biography of Nikolai Chernyshevski taking up the entire Chapter Four of the novel, which at one point is referred to as "firing practice" (G196). Further, Toker shows how fragments of the writings of several other people are incorporated into the text of the novel—from Fyodor's correspondence with his mother merging with the surrounding discourse to excerpts "from a boring philosophical play amusingly interpolated in the first chapter" (Toker 149). The very story of Godunov-Cherdyntsev senior's travels consists of bits and pieces of notes, sketches, letters, memoirs, thoughts, and reveries, while the biography of Chernyshevski incorporates "archival documents, diaries, memoirs, and both actual and spurious monographs" (Ibid.). Likewise Fyodor's existence is "deliberately presented in a fragmentary fashion: long periods are elided; nested texts blend with the master text"; and dreams are at times allowed to eclipse reality so the sense of incompleteness permeates both structure and subject matter (Ibid. 149-50).

But this "incompleteness" ultimately differs from the incompleteness of *The Original of Laura*, Nabokov's last unfinished novel. While the latter text represents a kind of void, *The Gift* does not fit the definitions of narrative "gaps" as usually described in literary theory (a missing link in a series of events, an absent motive, a contradiction that challenges the audience's understanding of the narrative, or an unexplained departure from standard form and structure). The novel, instead, can be compared to a jigsaw puzzle, or a "do-it-yourself" manual. What may look, upon the first and even second reading, like a chaotic mass of episodes, after meditation or with careful guidance starts making harmonious sense. When the pieces of jigsaw puzzle begin coming together, suddenly the links that had seemed separate move to form a chain, an anchor to which the novel is tied. When at the end of the novel Fyodor recapitulates the circumstances of his drab existence, he is able to recognize the work of fate and even a divine intervention of someone who made all these beautiful patterns possible:

> Use them immediately for a practical handbook: *How to Be Happy?* Or getting deeper, to the bottom of things: understand what is concealed behind all this, behind the play, the sparkle, the thick, green greasepaint of the foliage? For there really is something, there is something! And one wants to offer thanks but there is no one to thank. The list of donations already made: 10,000 days—from Person Unknown. (G328)

The quixotic Fyodor realizes that simple logic turns out to be wrong, and through sets of links he comprehends a revelation of the higher authority—the Author himself, or maybe the Creator of both of them (the figure of ten thousand days equals Godunov-Cherdyntsev's present age—he is 27 years old). In the Megillah, G-d's name does not appear, but when all is done, His presence is recognized everywhere. Every piece fits, His jigsaw puzzle is perfect.

Calendar

Time in *The Gift* is exact but not self-evident. Nabokov left a number of direct references and numerological clues allowing the reader to reconstruct the novel's chronology. An important recent find was Nabokov's own sketch of the timeline in *The Gift*, which largely confirms the earlier suppositions of scholars.

Chapter Three. STRUCTURE

Evidence in the Text

To arrive at a coherent timeline for the novel, the early scholars of *The Gift* isolated all specific mentions of the passage of time and either added or subtracted the dates to suit the thesis. According to Ronald Peterson's interpretation, the novel opens at 4 pm on April 1, 1925, and closes precisely three years and three months later at 3 pm on June 29, 1928 (Peterson). However, as will be shown later, the scholar miscalculated, and the real time frame is 1926–29. For Nabokov, time does not proceed in a neat linear fashion, but meanders circuitously between past, present and future.

Peterson's argument concerning the opening date of the novel relies on his establishing the closing date, which, he argues, is the centenary of Chernyshevski's birth in 1828. The scholar claims that, despite some incongruities and uncertain references, we should trust Nabokov's comment inserted near the end of the third chapter that shifts the narrative back to the original time frame.

These are the calendar reference points in the novel: Fyodor meets an untalented but helpful fellow writer named Busch, whom he recalls seeing "two and a half years ago" (G209), at a literary gathering shortly before his mother's Christmas visit. Further references in the fifth chapter make it obvious that the final events reported in the novel take place one year and three months—exactly "four hundred and fifty-five days" (G362)—after Fyodor had met Zina. Fyodor's last conversation with Zina's stepfather, Shchyogolev, also emphasizes that he and they "had one year and a half of cohabitation" (G348). To make it even clearer, Zina and Fyodor are shown retracing the twists of fate that began to bring them together (though they did not actually meet at that time) "three and a half odd years" earlier (G363), i.e. at the beginning of the book (Peterson 38). The penultimate day of the story is also known: "on the twenty-eighth of June, around three p.m." (G336), Fyodor finishes a swim in Grunewald Lake. On that day, before the Shchyogolevs leave by train for Copenhagen, Fyodor contemplates the "beginning (tomorrow night!) of his full life with Zina" (G345). The actual day of the departure, June 29, is "some kind of national holiday" in Berlin (G358), with parades and flags everywhere.

The Twisted Logic of Artistic Timing

Alexander Dolinin rightly disputes the straightforward logic that is solely based on the internal evidence and proposes a more complex understanding of the novel's intricate timetable. He takes into account Nabokov's overall treatment of time in fiction and claims that within the historical frame, in the world created by the author's imagination, chronology is usually "based on a sense of artistic timing" (*Lectures on Russian Literature* 190). For example, Nabokov was able to use historical data to determine the particular day on which Tolstoy set the action of *Anna Karenina*: February 23 (11, Old Style), 1872. Nabokov explains to his students the nature of an artist's interest in such details: "Some of you may still wonder why I and Tolstoy mention such trifles. To make his magic, fiction, look *real* the artist sometimes places it, as Tolstoy does, within a definite, specific historical frame, citing facts that can be checked in a library—that citadel of illusion" (*Lectures on Russian Literature* 213). Nabokov considers Tolstoy's referring to a specific historical fact, which places the beginning of the narration into the framework of calendar time, to be nothing more than a literary device aimed at mimicry, the camouflaging of fiction as empirical reality. In *The Gift* the reader is confronted with "an incessant change of planes and a sliding back and forth along the temporal axis" (Dolinin, "Nabokov's time doubling" 7). As Iurii Levin has demonstrated, the temporal positions of the text's narrator and its observer constantly shift: the narrator keeps returning from some indefinite future discourse into the present of the narration, and the protagonist/observer makes leaps from his present into the future, into the past, into historical time and into the time of recollections, as well as into the time of fiction and dreams. Moreover, Nabokov introduces into the narration a series of metatexts which substantiate "the equal validity of objective reality and recollection, of what really happened and what was imagined, of historical time and time as experienced by the character" (Levin, "Ob osobennostiakh" 201).

The main weakness of Peterson's argument based on tenuous historical connections, maintains Dolinin, is his assumption that pseudo-documentary references are "real" regardless of their mode of narration and their position in the space-time of the novel. Peterson correctly identifies the general time span of the novel as lasting three years; however, one can ascertain that some of the "historical allusions in the novel referring to specific events of the 1920s are intentionally misleading" and produce "the effect of temporal uncertainty" (Dolinin, "Nabokov's time doubling" 8). Here is an example of how Nabokov introduces several obvious anachronisms in a collage of sensational newspaper headlines, thus making it impossible to consider the narrative to be a chronicle of a specific year (1924, according to Peterson):

> In Russia one observed the spread of abortions and the revival of summer houses; in England there were strikes of some kind or other; Lenin met a sloppy end; Duse, Puccini and Anatole France died; Mallory and Irvine perished near the summit of Everest; and old Prince Dolgorukiy, in shoes of plaited leather thong, secretly visited Russia to see again the buckwheat in bloom; while in Berlin three-wheeled taxis appeared, only to disappear again shortly afterwards, and the first dirigible slowly stepped across the ocean and papers spoke a great deal about Coué, Chang Tso-lin and Tutankhamen... (G50)

While the deaths of Lenin, Duse, Puccini and France, as well as the ill-fated British expedition up Mount Everest, did in fact occur in the year 1924, all other datable allusions did not. Alexander Dolinin sets the record straight: the major strikes in England took place in 1925-26, the same years in which Prince Dolgorukov, the oldest member of the Cadet Party, twice crossed the Soviet border illegally; the first dirigible had allegedly flown over the Atlantic in 1919, and another traversed the Arctic Ocean in May of 1926 (Roald Amundsen's legendary flight from Europe to America via the North Pole); the death of the French psychiatrist Coué, much publicized in the newspapers, occurred in 1926; Tutenkhamen's tomb had been excavated in 1922, and the Chinese general Chang Tso-lin did not come to power until five years later. Considering this a parody of the "newspaper mentality" so alien to the protagonist, Dolinin believes that we are obviously dealing with a quasi-chronicle, the narrator's ironic glance back at the twenties from an uncertain future (Dolinin, "Nabokov's time doubling" 8-9).

Debut: The First Day

The reason for Nabokov's choice of April 1 as the beginning of his novel becomes apparent from the internal logic of the novel: on this day an April Fool's joke will be played on Fyodor.

In the 1962 introduction to *The Gift*, Nabokov states that its "heroine" is "not Zina, but Russian literature." While Zina makes her first appearance some 200 pages into the novel, Nabokov introduces his "true heroine" in the very first sentence: "One cloudy but luminous day, toward four in the afternoon on April the first, 192- (a foreign critic once remarked that while many novels, most German ones for example, begin with a date, it is only Russian authors who, in keeping with the honesty peculiar to *our literature*, omit the final digit)..." (Italics added). Indeed, some Russian novelists used the device (for instance, in the openings of Pushkin's *The Captain's Daughter* and Tolstoy's *Childhood*), but these examples are not as frequent as we are led to believe by Nabokov's generalization. The omission of the final digit is "only a small token in comparison with the overdose of honesty contained in the April Fools' date" (Davydov, "Nabokov's Aesthetic Exorcism" 360). As a matter of professional ethics, it is employed by the author at the outset of his novel in order to undermine any trust in the reality that lies beyond the text, possibly following the example of Pushkin, who starts his *Novel at a Caucasian Spa* (1831) with the sentence: "On one of the first days of April 181..," and places the birth of the "late" Ivan Belkin (his fictional narrator in *The Tales of Belkin*) on April 1st. Chernyshevski's novel does not pass this "test of honesty": *What To Do?* begins "On the morning of the eleventh of July, 1856" (Ibid.). Apart from the purely Russian subtexts (Turgenev's *Dnevnik lishnego cheloveka* [*Diary of a Superfluous Man*, 1850] also closes with an entry dated April 1), Nabokov's debut might parody Joyce (the entry for April 1 occurs close to the end of *A Portrait of the Artist as a Young Man* [1916]).

April Fool's Day was also the day of Nabokov's father's funeral—the end marks a new beginning in a typically Nabokovian fashion. In the definitive English version of his autobiography Nabokov determines the year of his father's birth as 1870 and the date as July 20 (*Speak, Memory* 173). In Old Style this would be July 8 (= 20-12), which turns out to be the birthday of Fyodor's father in *The Gift* (G103), albeit a decade earlier (1860, see G102). This, again, would be July 21 (= 8 + 13) in New Style in the twentieth century (Tammi 104). The conversion from Julian to Gregorian dates requires adding an additional day every century, thus the difference between the calendars in the nineteenth and twentieth centuries was 12 and 13 days respectively; the Gregorian calendar was introduced in Soviet Russia shortly after the Bolshevik Revolution.

The Last Year of the Novel

Fyodor's biography comes out about two months before the factual end of the narrative, therefore it seems reasonable to subtract the subtotal of dates and reconstruct the overall time frame retroactively. What, then, is the final year of *The Gift*?

Among the clues about the precise year that point to 1928 is the mention of a leap year (which 1928 was). Another hint is the statement that the writer Vladimirov, who Nabokov claims in the Foreword represents himself, was twenty-nine years old that year, as was Nabokov in April, 1928 (Peterson 39). As one of the reviews of Fyodor's book makes clear, the biography appeared almost exactly one hundred years after Nikolai Chernyshevski's birth on July 12, 1828 (Old Style). Pekka Tammi confirms that if one were to strictly follow the "internal evidence," the final year of the novel should indeed be 1928 (Tammi 98). Fyodor's embedded biography of Chernyshevski concludes with a joint mention of the writer's funeral and the year of his birth: "Sixty-one years had passed since that year of 1828 when [...] a Saratov priest had noted down in his prayer book: July 12th, in the third hour of morning, a son born, Nikolai..." (G300). It is also stated that a pro-Communist émigré newspaper reviewing Fyodor's book devotes an article "to the celebration of the centenary of Chernyshevski's birth" (G308), which would be 1928. Therefore, if the action of *The Gift* does conclude in 1928, the one-hundred-year figure marking the centennial of Chernyshevski's birth would indeed add up. At the same time, it is indicated that none other than Lenin had already once managed to mix up the last digits of Chernyshevski's birth and death years ("Lenin considered Chernyshevski to be 'the one true great writer who managed to remain on a level of unbroken philosophical materialism from the fifties right up until 1888' (he knocked one year off)" (G245). So it is also possible that the celebration mentioned was to mark the anniversary of his death.

On the other hand, there is just as much evidence for the year 1929, as this turns out to be the correct forty-year anniversary of the writer's death (1828 +

61 = 1889) (Tammi 99). The problem, in fact, may not be solvable because the contradictory clues inserted in the text intentionally maintain the ambivalence. Tammi wonders: Does anyone in the novel really know what year it is? Contrary to this view, Alexander Dolinin believes that in relation to objective historical time the mention of Chernyshevski's centennial, found in the author's rendering of reviews of Godunov-Cherdyntsev's book, is equally vague: "both the introductory phrase and the ensuing quotation are ambiguous, since it is not clear what is meant: a preparation for the anniversary or its actual celebration in the USSR. The latter version is more probable, since most of the materials used by Godunov-Cherdyntsev for his book were published only in 1928-30" (Dolinin, "Nabokov's time doubling" 9).

Endspiel: The Last Day

No commentary has yet satisfactorily explained the meaning behind the book's last day, 29 June. I will suggest that this requires taking into consideration the 13-day difference between Gregorian and Julian calendars. Deducting this amount from the date of Fyodor and Zina's first day of their life together, we get 16 June, the day when the narration in *Ulysses* takes place (*cf.* Moynahan, "Nabokov and Joyce" 438). The last day of the novel marks the culmination of Fyodor's learning how to say 'Yes' to the world and finding happiness in love with Zina Mertz, his ideal bride, reader and Muse (Dolinin, "*The Gift*" 135).

One might experiment with adding as well as subtracting in both directions: 16 June, according to the Julian calendar, must have been July 3, 1929 in Russia. However, Dublin is not in Russia, so we face the same insoluble problem again. Another possibility is that June 29 + 13 days = the birthday of both Godunov-Cherdyntsev and Chernyshevski: July 12. According to our fantastic calendar, July 12 in Russia would correspond to July 25 in Europe. If we accept the standard rules, the logic problem has no key, unless we admit that the fictional calendar has its own parameters (Omry Ronen to the author, private communication; see also Tammi 148, 21n).

In other words, the chronological world of *The Gift* does not fit any calendar at all—this becomes obvious from those few instances in the novel that include both the date and the day of the week (Tuesday, April 1, 1926; Thursday, April 18, 1923). Alexander Dolinin corroborates that they are *all* factually inaccurate: April 1, 1926 was a Thursday, and April 18—the day of Yasha's suicide—never fell on a Thursday in the period from 1920 to 1928! Dolinin also notes that the final day of the novel, June 29, 1929, was in reality a Saturday, which conflicts with Zina's words: "I get my wages only tomorrow" (G360). This is yet another indication that we are dealing with a "second reality," a "deceit" that is the result of Fyodor's artistic design ("Nabokov's time doubling" 10).

Calendar

Inside Nabokov's Creative Laboratory

In private notes that he made for one of the later reprints of the English-language edition, Nabokov added a few dates that were missing in the text and that had not been available to the scholars until that point. For example, the day when Fyodor's sister, Tanya, gives birth to her daughter is clarified—June 25, 1929. Adjusting Dolinin's estimate in accordance with Nabokov's notes, Yasha Chernyshevski's suicide would have happened on April 18, 1924—not 1923 ("Nabokov's time doubling" 10, 22n), but this still falls on Friday not Thursday, as in the text of *The Gift*:

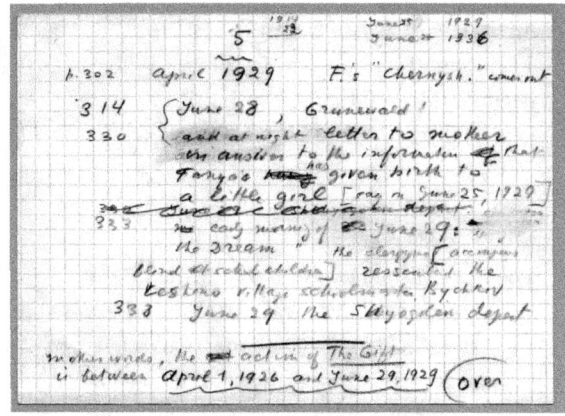

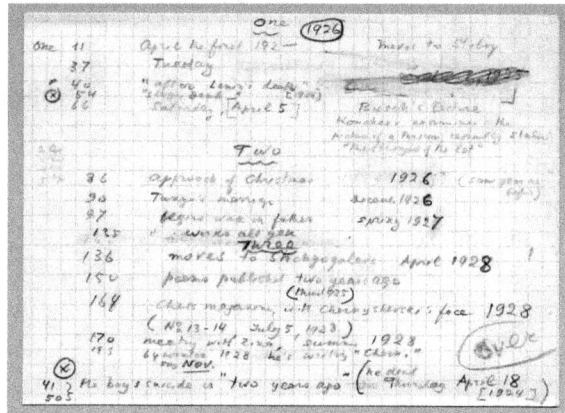

[Ill. 3-2, 3-3] A copy of the front and back of the index card found in the copy of *The Gift*. Cornell University acquired three author-owned copies of this title, both Russian and English editions, with notes, corrections, and inserts. Courtesy of Division of Rare and Manuscript Collections, Cornell University

Here is the transcription of the information in Nabokov's hand from the index card (page numbers from the Vintage edition are included in square brackets)

—149—

———————————— Chapter Three. STRUCTURE ————————————

ONE
1926

One 11	April the first 192–	moves to Stoboy
37		Tuesday
40 [35]	"after Lenin's death"	
x 54 [50]	"sloppy end" [1924]	
66 [63]	Saturday, [April 5]	Busch's lecture

    Koncheyev examines the picture of a Persian, resembling Stalin (G71) "the strongest of the lot"

TWO

86 [85]	Approach of Christmas	1926 (same year as before)
90 [89]	Tanya's marriage	December 1926
97 [95]	begins work on father	spring 1927
135 [144]	works all year	

THREE

136 [143]	Moves to Shchyogolevs	April 1928
150 [155]	Poems published two years ago (thus 1925)	

    [VN seems to have meant 1926 here, because under p. 136 he first wrote "April 1927," then corrected it to "1928" leaving the corresponding date beneath intact—Y.L.]

164 [170]	Chess magazine, with Chernyshevski's piece	1928

    (№ 13-14, July 5, 1928)

170 [176]	meeting with Zina, summer 1928
195 [199]	by winter 1928 he's writing "Chern.[yshevski's biography]"

say NOV.[ember]
x 41 [36]
50   the boy's suicide is "two years ago"
        (he died Thursday, April 18 [1924])

                OVER

FIVE

1914	June 25, 1929	
22	June 25, 1936	
302	April 1929	F.'s "Chernysh[evski]" comes out
314 [327]	June 28, Grunewald	
330 [348]	and at night letter to mother	

    in answer to the information that Tanya has given birth to a little girl [say in June 25, 1929]

332		[June 29, 1929 Shchyogolevs depart] *Crossed out by Nabokov*
333 [353]		early morning of June 29:
		the dream—the clergyman [accompanies blind school children] resembled the Leshino village schoolmaster Bychkov
338 [355]		June 29 The Shchyogolevs depart
		In other words, the action of *The Gift* is between April 1, 1926 and June 29, 1929

OVER

Remarkably, even many years later Nabokov supplies the exact date and full bibliographic entry for the Soviet chess magazine that featured a piece on Chernyshevski and chess. The article, described in *The Gift*, has recently been rediscovered: it was authored by A.A. Novikov, although the title of the real magazine turns out to be not "8 x 8" but "64: Chess and Checkers in the Workers' Clubs" (Zubarev).

Nabokov did not record the chronology of Chapter Four in his marginal notes, although evidently it was also a product of elaborate planning and readjustments. Let us take the example of the wedding date of the Lobodovskis, friends of Nikolai Chernyshevski: May 19, 1848. It is, notes the narrator of

 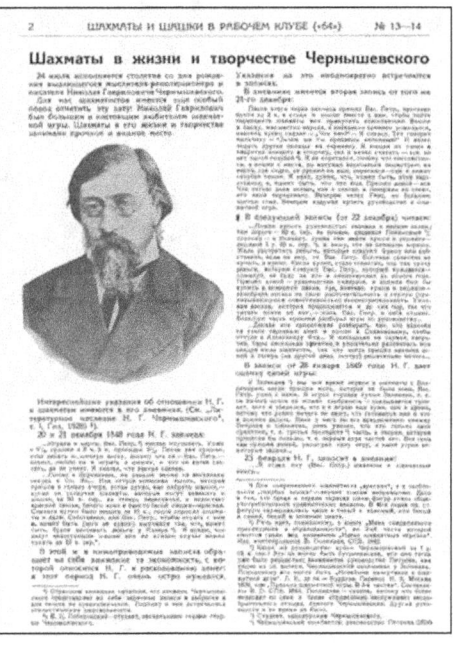

[Ill. 3-4, 3-5] Cover of the magazine, "64: Chess and Checkers in the Workers' Clubs" (1928), and the article about Chernyshevski and chess that served an impetus to Fyodor's writing the controversial biography.

The Gift, the same day of Chernyshevksi's execution sixteen years later (G220). In fact, Nabokov slightly retrofits chronology here in order to maintain the "patterns of Fate." According to the 1933 *Letopis'*, the actual wedding took place on 18 May (Chernyshevski describes it in his diary entry of May 19 as having taken place the day before); however, Chernyshevski made a slip—the correct date should be May 16 (Chernyshevskaia 27).

Whatever the case may be, as Alexander Dolinin demonstrates convincingly, one thing is evident: "when historical time in *The Gift* is not rethought and relived by the narrator or the character, it turns into fiction, and therefore lacks a coherent calendar. In this respect Nabokov's ironic remark about the peculiar honesty of Russian writers who 'omit the final digit' in the dates that open their novels fully applies to Nabokov himself: in terms of historical reality, the novel indeed begins and ends in 192-" (Dolinin, "Nabokov's time doubling" 9). In other words, Dolinin's novel discovery concerns a different, internally coherent chronology in *The Gift*, which holds to a different time: a time that is subjective and therefore, in Nabokov's world, more real. In this sense, fictional time is connected "not with newspaper headlines, but with major events in the protagonist's life" (Ibid.). Its calendar is based on the turning points of Fyodor's destiny: "the loss and death of his first love; the fatal day when he received the news of his father's passing, associated in Godunov-Cherdyntsev's mind with the loss of his homeland; the first encounter with Zina; and the history of his creative projects" (Ibid. 10).

Setting

> At the age of twelve my fondest dream was a visit to the Karakorum Range in search of butterflies. Twenty-five years later I successfully sent myself, in the part of my hero's father (see my novel *The Gift*) to explore, net in hand, the mountains of Central Asia. At fifteen I visualized myself as a world-famous author of seventy with a mane of wavy white hair. Today I am practically bald.
>
> From an interview with *The New York Times* (April 23, 1973; *Strong Opinions* 178)

The material world of *The Gift* is rooted in Nabokov's own actual experience in Russia (St. Petersburg and vicinity) and in Europe. What Nabokov did not see personally—be it the distant Asian steppes or imaginary historical excursions into the nineteenth century—he reconstructed with the power of his vision. This vision was constantly enhanced by meticulous study of secondary sources, which Nabokov reproduces with scientific precision and filters through the prism of high art.

―――――― Setting ――――――

In Search of Fyodor's Berlin

Nabokov's places in Berlin are numerous and are well documented (present data is based on Zimmer, *Nabokovs Berlin*; Boyd, *Russian Years*; and Urban, *Blaue Abende in Berlin*). His first literary engagement in the German capital took place in April 4, 1923 (a public reading at Schubertsaal, Bülowstrasse), just three years before a similar gathering was to happen in the novel.

Vladimir met Véra Evseevna Slonim at an émigré charity ball in Berlin-Halensee on 8 May of the same year. From January 31, 1924, he lodged in the Helene Andersen pension (Lutherstrasse 21, Berlin-Charlottenburg), and from late August at Pension Elisabeth Schmidt (Trautenaustrasse 9). On April 15 Nabokov married Véra at the town hall in Berlin-Wilmersdorf, and from April to late July 1925, they lived in two rooms at Luitpoldstrasse 13 (c/o canned goods merchant Erich Rölke). In late August the newlyweds embarked on a hiking tour of the Schwarzwald, and after spending the first half of September at Constance, Pension Zeiss, they moved into two rooms at Motzstrasse 31 (c/o a major's widow, Frau M. v. Lepel). From autumn 1926 the Nabokovs found themselves in yet another place, on Passauer Strasse 12 (Berlin-Charlottenburg), renting two rooms from merchant Horst von Dallwitz. From July 1929 Vladimir and Véra spent the remainder of the summer in the postman's hut in the village of Kolberg (Nabokov is working on *The Defense*), about 35 miles SE of Berlin, after they had purchased a modest lot on a nearby lake in the hope of building a sort of dacha (after some time, the land reverted to the seller due to lack of payment). From late August of 1929 to early 1932 the writer and his wife lived in the "vast and gloomy" apartment (parlor and bedroom) of Oberstleutnant Albrecht v. Bardeleben (Luitpoldstrasse 27), but then switched to a single room at Westfälische Strasse 29 (c/o Cohn family).

Between July 31, 1932, and January 18, 1937, the Nabokovs occupied two rooms on the third floor at Nestorstrasse 22, in Berlin-Wilmersdorf. Nabokov's only son, Dmitri (born in Dr. Friedrich Grambow's private clinic, Berchtesgadener Straße 25, on May 10, 1934), was also raised here. After their numerous relocations, this period provided some stability, but the Nabokovs' wanderings were clearly reflected on the pages of *The Gift*.

Fyodor's third address in the course of the novel is Agamemnonstrasse 15, where he lives with the Shchyogolev family. Although there is no street by that name in Berlin, the descriptions of Agamemnonstrasse in the novel seem to match Nestorstrasse. Both streets are named after Greek kings from the Trojan War (Zimmer "Nabokovs Berlin"). Real landmarks are interspersed in the narrative with the fictional names: Agamemnonstrasse is adjacent to Hohenzollerdamm and Wittenberg Square (Wittenbergplatz): "Crossing Wittenberg Square where, as in a color film, roses were quivering in the breeze around an antique flight of stairs..." (G166). This large square in western Berlin at the end of Tauentzienstrasse was created between 1889 and 1892 and named after the town of Wittenberg in Saxony-Anhalt to commemorate its liberation from Napoleon's army in 1814.

Is it possible to find the exact building where Nabokov lived for five years, longer than in any other Berlin building, and where he had "registered" his alter-ego, Fyodor? In a thrilling story from his research for *Nabokovs Berlin*, Dieter Zimmer writes that at first glance the location seemed to present no problem: the building at Nestorstrasse 22 still exists in Halensee (now part of the district of Charlottenburg-Wilmersdorf), near the far end of Kurfürstendamm. It is just behind the block that was the site of the roller skating rink that had witnessed Nabokov's first crush at the age of eleven and where he had later given tennis lessons. In the 1930s, there was a large cinema ("Universum") which was finally transformed into a theater. Nabokov scholars, Zimmer including, have visited the site and taken photographs. In 1999 a plaque was placed by the front door commemorating Nabokov's residence there.

Yet a few doubts remained: in 1943 the entire building at the corner of Nestorstrasse and Paulsborner Strasse was destroyed by bombs down to the second floor (Nabokov and Véra had lived on the third story). It had been rebuilt quite early, in 1952, which might account for its present plain look. But Zimmer persists: had Fyodor's third address in the course of the novel, where it is called "Agamemnonstrasse," been rebuilt as it was before? Drawing the perimeter of the area is a simple task due to the evidence given by Fyodor, who gives the following description in *The Gift*:

> A multitude of streets diverging in all directions, jumping out from behind corners and skirting the above-mentioned places of prayer and refreshment, turned it all into one of those schematic little pictures on which are depicted for the edification of beginning motorists all the elements of the city, all the possibilities for them to collide. To the right one saw the gates of a tram depot with three beautiful birches standing out against its cement background... (G161)

An old map of Hochmeisterplatz in Halensee, with the streetcar depot on the lower right, helped Zimmer identifying the place in question ("Nabokovs Berlin"): "There is only one square in Berlin where all these elements can be found in combination: an irregular intersection of various streets, a red brick church, a public garden (with a sandpit for children and an abandoned soccer field behind), a pissoir, a pharmacy, a tram depot. This is Hochmeisterplatz in Halensee, which intersects with Nestorstrasse. As a matter of fact, 'left' and 'right' in the above description are as they would appear from Nestorstrasse 22" (Zimmer, "Nabokovs Berlin"). In other words, Nabokov had not invented Fyodor's place of residence: "He had not even placed him somewhere else in the city, as he easily might have done. He had simply lodged him exactly where he himself was living during the time of writing (but not in the mid-twenties when the novel is set), only changing Nestor into Agamemnon, one Greek king of the Trojan War into another. There is no Agamemnonstrasse in Berlin but a Hektorstrasse close by" (Ibid.).

The importance that Nabokov places on maintaining some resemblance to reality, be it topographic markers or Fyodor's émigré counterparts, is a question that has been addressed by Monika Greenleaf. She notes that, while Nabokov may treat émigré society "with undisguised disdain and mockery, he is still addressing readers who can recognize the street names and shops, the rented rooms and shabby *culturedness* of émigré Berlin" (Greenleaf 141). Moreover, "exile introduces duality into time and space: what is real is what is absent, recoverable only by means of linguistic signs" (Ibid. 142). Nabokov and his readers also share unspoken values and attitudes: "intensely elegiac, yet intolerant of others' vulgar sentiments and memories; adversarial toward both 'them'—the lowly native 'host' culture—and the surviving Soviet citizens, Russian by geographical misnomer only" (Ibid. 141), convinced that they have brought the real Russia, using Nabokov's own words, like contraband into exile with them. Participation in literature becomes for Fyodor an act of communion with a spiritualized Russia, but Nabokov always makes sure that the reality of everyday émigré existence would shine through a thin fabric of fiction.

Buildings Larger than Edifices

In addition to the recurring biographical details taking place at fictitious addresses, there are in the novel numerous recognizable objects and architectural landmarks from everyday Berlin settings. The reader of *The Gift* should be made aware of their function: Nabokov is not interested in reconstructing merely a contemporary city, but rather its urban legends—discernible like a tender lining underneath a tawdry canvas. Although *The Gift* at times demonstrates the purely documentary quality of the prose, it remains highly ambiguous, as in the case of images related to "house-building" standing for "metaliterary metaphors describing the very process of writing a text" (Dolinin, *"The Gift"* 156). Gerard de Vries analyzes the metaphors marking the process of building or restoring houses. Numerous buildings in the text of *The Gift* are seen through scaffolding (Vries, "The Fourth Chapter" 28). Nabokov develops this metaphorical meaning in the following passage:

> As [Fyodor] read the sentence over, he wondered—should he leave it intact after all, made an insertion mark, wrote in an additional adjective, froze over it—and swiftly crossed out the whole sentence. But to leave the paragraph in that condition, i.e., *its construction hanging over a precipice with a boarded window and a crumbling porch*, was a physical impossibility. He examined his notes for this part and suddenly—his pen stirred and started to fly. (G206)

Rooms and apartments in *The Gift* have connotations comparable to those of buildings: "my exertions over the book, and all those little storms of thought, those cares of the pen—and now I am completely empty, clean, and *ready to receive new lodgers*" (G349). "Keys" are required to enter these lodgings and they form a dominant motif in *The Gift* (*misplaced keys* have symbolic relevance to three thematic dimensions of Fyodor's existence—exile, art, and love).

Nabokov's choices for locale are not random. Gerard de Vries points out the persistence of the building-related images in the novel that include theologically marked locations. Nikolai Chernyshevski is mentioned as living near the St. Isaac's church as well as "near the church of St. Vladimir"; later his "Astrakhan addresses were also defined by their proximity to this or that holy building" (G269; one may add that Nabokov's family mansion on 47 B. Morskaya St. in Petersburg was also located close to St. Isaac's cathedral). The same holds for Fyodor, whose rooms at 7 Tannenberg Street and 15 Agamemnonstrasse are quite close to a church. Rudolf grew up near "a cathedral-like sideboard" and Vasiliev's room has a window looking out over a "building, with repairs going on so high in the sky that it seemed as though they might as well do something about the ragged rent in the grey cloud bank" (G62). Churches, which are, after all, buildings designed for contemplating the hereafter, thus point to two of Nabokov's most important themes: art and the afterlife (Vries, "The Fourth Chapter" 28).

Berlin Landmarks and Everyday Life

The characters live and breathe in the atmosphere of contemporary Berlin. When Shirin arranges to meet Lishnevski about some business in the Zoological Garden and when, after an hour's conversation, Lishnevski casually directs his attention to a hyena in its cage, "it transpired that Shirin had hardly realized that one keeps animals in a zoological garden, and glancing briefly at the cage had remarked automatically: 'Yes, the likes of us don't know much about the animal world,' and immediately continued discussing that which particularly disturbed him in life: the activities and composition of the Committee of the Society of Russian Writers in Germany" (G316). The famous Zoological Gardens, known as the "Zoo," were the first of their kind in Germany, created in 1841–44 by Heinrich Lichtenstein, an explorer of Africa, with the assistance of the geographer Alexander von Humboldt. King Friedrich Wilhelm IV of Prussia donated his pheasantry and his menagerie, and up until World War II its stock of animals was one of the largest in the world; restaurants and banquet rooms in the Zoo were a centre of Berlin social life. Victor Shklovsky's novel *Zoo, or Letters Not About Love* (1922–23), written and published in Berlin, reshapes the traditional epistolary novel in metafictional style and revitalizes it by blurring the borders between documentary and poetic epistolarity.

Nabokov's statement that the first throb of *Lolita* was prompted by a story of a gorilla drawing the bars of its cage needs no introduction. Scholars have attempted to locate the exact publication and found a few similar reports in the media. In addition, one should also remember that one of the most famous animals of the Berlin Zoo and a favourite of the Berliners was the gorilla 'Bobby' (a great stone figure of Bobby still stands at the Budapester Strasse entrance of the park). He arrived at the zoo in 1918 when several months old and was the first gorilla to have produced offspring in captivity in any of the world's zoos. Bobby died in 1935, without leaving, to our knowledge, samples of any "artistic pursuits."

The Brandenburg Gate is another symbol of the German capital mentioned in the finale of *The Gift*. "The *defile* of the Brandenburg Gate" (G361) possibly alludes to the narrow pass from the New Tastement ("Because strait is the gate, and narrow is the way," Matthew, 7:13-14; Dolinin, *Kommentarii* 768). The Gate formed what was once the triumphal entrance to the city from the West. The rise of Prussia found its most striking expression in this monument, which soon became the hallmark of Berlin. The architect Carl Gotthard Langhans built the gate in 1788–91, basing his design on the Propylaea in Athens and thereby introducing Berlin architects to classicism. The gate is 215 ft wide, 36 ft deep, and 85 ft high (to the top of the quadriga) with five passage-ways between the massive walls.

After Fyodor and Zina dine at the restaurant in the last scene of the novel, it is stated that "they walked down the street... and the air, the darkness and the *honeyed scent of blooming lindens* caused a sucking ache at the base of the chest. This scent evanesced in the stretch *from linden to linden*, being replaced there by a black freshness" (G365). The unnamed street is, of course, Unter den Linden (meaning "under the linden trees") and it was constructed by the Great Elector in 1647 to connect his palace with the Tiergarten. It was made the show-piece of the capital mainly by Frederick the Great, who linked the former Schlossbrücke (Palace Bridge) with the Brandenburg Gate and had four rows of linden trees planted along the avenue. As Berliners claim, every stone there reflects the history of Berlin. The old Russian Embassy was also on the southern side of the Linden (in 1840 Tsar Nicholas I purchased the site of the former palace of Princess Amalie).

When Fyodor's mother presents her son with seventy marks in order to improve his eating habits, the son gladly accepts the gift, "instantly envisioning a year's *pass to the state library*, milk chocolate and some mercenary young German girl whom, in his baser moments, he kept planning to get for himself" (G96). We will note the systems of priorities here, as well as recall that a hundred pages later in the narrative, once Fyodor finds himself immersed deeply in the life of the nineteenth-century revolutionary writer, he signs out "the complete works of Chernyshevski from the state library. And as he read, his astonishment grew, and this feeling contained a peculiar kind of bliss" (G195). Indeed, there were many treasures

Chapter Three. STRUCTURE

in that building housing the University Library (900,000 volumes), founded in 1831, and the Library of the Academy of Sciences (100,000 volumes). At the time that Nabokov was among its patrons, the German State Library contained over 2,000,000 volumes, departments for manuscripts, autographs, incunabula, oriental books, maps, and musical manuscripts (part of the stock was inherited from the Prussian State Library founded in 1661). The sandstone facades show restrained baroque forms and are adorned with allegorical figures. Beyond the court of honor a broad flight of steps in the central block leads to a large octagonal reading room with a high ceiling and dome, where Fyodor spends almost a year while researching and writing "The Life of Chernyshevski."

Not far away from it is the famous corner of the Linden and Friedrichstrasse, which boasted the first traffic control (1902 by whistle, 1903 by trumpet) and the first moving illuminated advertisement in Berlin. Fyodor-the-writer navigates through Berlin by routes that are largely determined by his unquenchable passion for books. Lined by restaurants, offices and shops, Wittenbergplatz Station is located in the center of the square that Fyodor crosses on his way to the Russian bookshop (G166). Curiously, this was the real site of the Russian bookstore and library "Des Westens" which operated in Berlin during the 1920-30s. It was located on Passauerstrasse 3, next to a department store of the same name (abbreviated as KDW and mentioned in *The Gift* as "a huge department store that sold all forms of local bad taste" [G166]; the protagonist of Nabokov's 1928 Russian novel set entirely in Berlin, *King, Queen, Knave*, works at a big department store, whose title is playfully embedded in the abbreviation of its Russian title, KDV).

Nabokov loved the urban poetry of the Berlin streets despite the city's technocratic mess ("straight from the hothouse paradise of the past, [Fyodor] stepped onto a Berlin tramcar"; G80). Fyodor observes the tram-riding routine as a picture of nearly epic scale: "The tram came out on the square and, braking excruciatingly, stopped, but it was only a preliminary stop, because in front, by the stone island crowded with people standing by to board, two other trams had got stuck, both with cars coupled on, and this inert agglomeration was also evidence somehow of the disastrous imperfection of the world in which Fyodor still continued to reside" (G84). Similarly, Joseph Roth describes the city's main artery in his essay "The Kurfürstendamm" (1929): "I envy the streetcars, which are allowed to glide coolly and briskly over the strips of lawn that have been laid in the middle of the thoroughfare. They have been laid expressly for them, as if they were wild animals brought to Berlin from their lush green homes and, like the animals in the Zoologischer Garten, had to be offered a pathetic suggestion of their habitat... Strips of asphalt run parallel to the streetcar lines and lawns, and down these omnibuses and cars clatter, causing traffic jams. Often they enlist help of traffic lights, which alternate automatically among red, yellow, and green without any visible cause" (Roth 147).

Fyodor walks around the German capital as frequently as he uses the streetcars. The poetics of the urban myths transpires in twilight: "with a magic tinkling, by the light of crimson lanterns, *dim beings were repairing the pavement at the corner of the square,* and Fyodor, who did not have money for the streetcar, was walking home" (G52; here and henceforth in this paragraph italics are mine); "He scrambled over boards, boxes and a toy grenadier in curls, and caught sight of the familiar house, and there *the workmen had already stretched a red strip of carpet across the sidewalk from door to curb,* as it used to be done in front of their house on the Neva Embankment on ball nights" (G353). Roth, who like Nabokov was not a native Berliner, notes that "worst of all [in Berlin] are the slow roadworks": "I know of no other city where the streets are patched as glacially slowly as they are in Berlin. There are *some corners where the paving stones are carefully lifted out every night and put back in the morning. Around midnight ten or twelve workmen start to lever out the paving stones and lay them by the side of the road*" (Roth 101). Because the streets had to be smooth again before the first tram came through in the morning, men had to cover the unfinished repairs. "It's like replacing bandages every day after an operation. And there are too few men. Sometimes you see a sorry little bunch—three or four fellows—standing on a corner lifting stones either with some rudimentary equipment or even with their bare hands, pouring tar, eerily and garishly lit by bright darting flames, *looking like bizarre seekers after treasure, lonely, mysterious, and contemplative*" (Ibid.).

This aspect of constant construction in modern Berlin is summarized in Walter Benjamin's review of Döblin's novel: "What is the Alexanderplatz in Berlin? That is the place where for two years the most violent changes are taking place, bulldozers and drills operate continuously, the ground quakes from their blows and from the streams of buses and subways, where deeper than elsewhere the guts of the big city have been laid bare" ("The crisis of the novel," 1930). Readers of Nabokov should treat similar passages in *The Gift* with special care: as we know from his other writings, whenever the text shows some "work" in progress, it often signals the metatextual dimension of the narrative itself or, in Shklovsky's famous term, "baring the device" (*cf.* the short story "A Guide to Berlin"; Ronen, "Puti Shklovskogo").

Fyodor's Asia

In the closing years of the reign of Nicholas I, Russia had pushed her Siberian frontier farther south. Conquering the nomadic Kazakh tribes, which roamed the steppe between the northern end of the Caspian Sea and Lake Balkhash, was the trigger that set off a chain reaction of Russian conquests in Central Asia that continued through and beyond the reign of Alexander II. The wild mountain tribes of the eastern Caucasus were subdued as the Russian boundary moved down the west coast of the Caspian Sea to meet the Persian border. East of that sea the Russian frontier bordered the Moslem khanates of Khiva, Bokhara, and Kokand, from which raiders were wont to seize Russian traders or attack the Kazakh tribesmen recently brought under the Tsar's protection (Wren 432). The foreign minister, Prince Gorchakov, claimed that Russia could gain security on its Central Asian border only by subduing the khanates that constantly pressed against it; he reminded the other great powers that their own colonial histories had followed a similar course. He argued that until Russia established common boundaries with other civilized states in the area—Persia, Afghanistan, and China—the nation could not feel secure (Ibid.).

These historical developments soon gave rise to intense curiosity on the part of the Russian scientists and intellectuals wishing to explore the newly conquered regions. In her study of Pushkin and the travelogue tradition, Susan Layton asserts that the manner of producing travelogues and the motivations for consuming them are often difficult, if not impossible, to distinguish from the writing and reading of a piece of imaginative literature. The division between fact and fiction can also become imperceptible in the traveler's account itself. Since travel literature exists almost exclusively in prose, it is usually related to fiction alone (Layton 22).

The tale of Konstantin Godunov-Cherdyntsev's travel to Central Asia is told through the eyes of the man's son. On the other hand, Nabokov bases his portrait of the fictional Godunov-Cherdyntsev in large part on the celebrated Nikolai Przhevalsky (1839–88), a real geographer, explorer, and naturalist. Nabokov outfits Count Godunov with "an impressive and authentic list of publications and career of travels, and, using his own thorough knowledge of natural history, plants his fictional creation firmly in the real world of Lepidoptera" (Johnson, Coates 294). On the other hand, as an exile in Berlin, Fyodor dreams up his father's journey very much in line with the Russian travelogue tradition prefigured by Pushkin's poetic foray abroad, as something that served the dual functions of entertainment and learning. Even before Pushkin, Karamzin's *Letters of a Russian Traveler* (1789–90), a typical example of this hybrid genre, combined factual reportage with literary invention. Although inspired by an actual trip, the book was researched and written in the author's study after he returned to Russia (Layton 22). Pushkin's writings shared with travel literature a fundamental impulse to bring a foreign territory into a mutually illuminating relationship with the homeland. Like imaginative writing about a fictional trip, a real-life traveler's narrative clarifies the character of the native land by contrasting it to a different country. In the eyes of the readership of the 1820s, Pushkin's *The Prisoner of the Caucasus* coincided primarily with the semi-fictional informative genre of the travelogue. Just as Pushkin was never destined to receive the Emperor's permission to go abroad (as he expressed his wanderlust in a letter to Prince Pyotr Vyazemsky in 1820: "Petersburg is stifling for a poet. I long for foreign lands"), so Nabokov at the time of writing *The Gift* was tied to Western Europe by historical circumstances and his own financial limitations.

Firmly rooted in the sentimental era prior to the conquest of the Caucasus, the zeal for actual and armchair traveling was enormously intensified in young Pushkin's time by Byronism (Layton 24). The context of the letter written to Fyodor by his mother, on which she plots his father's life-story, is thoroughly Pushkinian: it is triggered by a confession that he is reading *Journey to Arzrum* (Pushkin's oriental essay of 1836) and hearkening to "the purest sound from Pushkin's tuning fork—and he already knew exactly what this sound required of him" (G96). The travelogue, Fyodor says, possesses a "transparent rhythm," and after receiving his mother's advice he "fed on Pushkin, inhaled Pushkin (the reader of Pushkin has the capacity of his lungs enlarged)" (G97).

Obviously, armchair traveling is not without its limitations. Thus in his treatment of the landscape in *The Prisoner of the Caucasus* Pushkin approximated the territory more to the Alps than the orient. Layton believes that authors can read whatever they like into nature, so that Russian literature would later "Islamize" the Caucasian peaks in the 1830s when war against the local tribes had escalated. Pushkin passed most of his time in the Caucasus around Besh-Tau ("five mountains" in Persian) and the other four peaks which gave Piatigorsk its name (a Russian calque of "Besh-Tau"). The southern-most destination on the poet's trip, this area of mineral springs is situated in the central range, about 80 kilometers north of the magnificent twin peaks of Elbrus (5,633 meters, by comparison to Mt. Blanc, 4,807 meters) (Layton 36). But, as opposed to Romantic authors who were concerned with things other than reality, Nabokov painstakingly tries to assimilate facts into his fictional geography. Along with his brilliant discoveries, he also had his failures. For instance, in the realm of Nabokov's literary imagination (and Fyodor's) the place called Tatsienlu was transformed into a locus where shaven-headed lamas in narrow streets suspected that the Westerners were stealing children rather than collecting butterflies. But it is "one of history's tricks (Nabokov would have appreciated the slip of the scribal hand) that Tatsienlu was not in Tibet," as Kurt Johnson and Steve Coates explain (Johnson, Coates 314). The village, today called Kangding, lies four hundred miles from the Tibetan border on the Yunnan Plateau, on the border between Sichuan and Yunnan Provinces in western China. The plateau is known to biologists as "one of the most hospitable climates in the world, famous for its mild temperatures and brilliant blue skies dotted for a great part of the year with fair-weather cumulus clouds. The village sits at an altitude of about 9000 feet, and its site is a far cry from the high-altitude Tibetan plateau, barren and snow-covered, upon which Nabokov's fiction placed it" (Ibid.). Nabokov had celebrated the small village in *The Gift* and in the short story "The Aurelian" (1930), repeating the error that somehow crept into history when dealers processed Pratt's collection—until Kurt Johnson discovered the error in 1991 and pointed out the correct location.

So how then could this confusion have come about? Most probably it resulted from an error in reproduction: the old typeset labels in museums and among dealers' stocks were copied from the original handwritten ink labels made by those who bought the specimens from their native collectors. Common labels in the old Asiatic collections began with regional names typifying nineteenth-century geography, like Tibet and Tashkent, and the famous mountain ranges that were the haunts of the early dealer-collectors—Altai, Nan-shan, and Tyan-shan, all mentioned in *The Gift*. Occasionally the labels also bore the names of specific towns or villages, like Tatsienlu, which is also cited in Nabokov's novel. "The old European collections were full of unusual, and often unnamed, butterflies bearing that label" (Ibid. 313), among them specimens acquired from local collectors by the British explorer-dealer A. E. Pratt. Pratt was "responsible for much of the exotic Asian material that reached the dealers' markets in the late nineteenth century, destined for the big aristocratic collections and, subsequently, the various national museums" (Ibid.). In science Tatsienlu was the type locality for large numbers of exotic species, including seven lycaenid butterflies. Many of these were made famous by John Henry Leech in his classic work *Butterflies from Japan, China, and Corea* (1893-94). This book was clearly familiar to Nabokov, who mentions Leech several times in *The Gift*.

CHARACTERS

The Fictional World of *The Gift*

An early reviewer of *The Gift* complained that Nabokov "moves fictional and historical characters [in his novel] about like chessmen" (Allsop 16). Indeed, there are over 620 episodic personages mentioned in *The Gift*. Compare this number with the list of characters for Nabokov's *Pnin*, prepared by Gene Barabtarlo, which includes all persons in that novel, acting or merely mentioned, named or anonymous, real or invented, and encompasses 318 entries (*Phantom of Fact* 291).

The names in *The Gift* can be identified both as references to real historical figures from a variety of fields—culture, literature, politics, and science—and as made-up characters; in a peculiarly Nabokovian way, sometimes both categories appear mixed together.

The characters in the novel belong to three major layers of time and space: the Chernyshevski milieu (1860-80s), the Asian journey (1900s, 1910s), and the Berlin milieu, contemporaneous to the implicit author of *The Gift* (late 1920s). In this section I will provide information on major and minor personages and their prototypes, some literary allusions carried by and attached to particular characters, as well as their principal functions in the novel. The aim here is to give a schematic guide, although some episodic personages with a meaningful literary genealogy (like the émigré Kern or the painter Romanov) are deemed important as well and will be given more extended commentary. The complete list of *dramatis personae* can be found in the online database.

Principal Characters

Fyodor Konstantinovich Godunov-Cherdyntsev

Fyodor is the protagonist of the novel—poet, critic, biographer of Nikolai Chernyshevski and, possibly, author of the very novel *The Gift*. He was born on July 12, 1900, and died no later than 1940. It is of course no mere chance that Fyodor's birthday falls on the same date as Nikolai Chernyshevski's, 12 July; but the fact that Chernyshevski's is based on the Julian calendar, while Fyodor's is probably based on the Gregorian calendar, makes the relationship between them a *parodic* one (Alexandrov, *Nabokov's Otherworld* 245, 7n). The most cogent summary of Fyodor's purpose in the novel formulated to date was that presented by Leona Toker, who maintains that the main character of *The Gift* has two problems to solve: "what sort of works he wants to write, and what sort of life he must lead. [Fyodor] solves the first by mobilizing the powers of his intellect and imagination and going through a strenuous apprenticeship. The second solves itself through his daily ethical choices" (145).

Origins and Etymology of Fyodor's Name

Fyodor's first name is of Greek origin, and its meaning is "God's gift." The early Christian and saint's name Θεοδωρος (Theodoros) in fact derives from two separate words, θεος (theos) "god" and δωρον (doron) "gift."

In the early 1934, Nabokov wrote with a special request to his old acquaintance, Nikolai Yakovlev, who had now moved from Berlin to Riga. Nabokov hoped that Yakovlev, an expert in Russian history, literature, and etymology, would help him to find the right last name for the protagonist of his future novel. The ideal name the writer is looking for should match the first half of the name that was already in place (Godunov) and should belong to some noble but forgotten aristocratic family. This last name, Nabokov specified, should meet the following two requirements: it must contain a hissing consonant and consist of three syllables, preferably with an amphibrachic stress, as in a metrical foot when a long or stressed syllable is located between two short or unstressed syllables (for example, the word *romantic* is an accentual amphibrach because a stressed syllable is inside of two unstressed ones). This could mean, as Alexander Dolinin implies, that by the time of the request Nabokov had already formed in his mind the image of the main hero of *The Gift* along with the semantic aura of his name (Dolinin, "K istorii sozdaniia i tisneniia romana Dar" 341). On January 18 and 27, 1934, Yakovlev supplies a list of names of extinct Russian noble families: Barbashin, Cherdyntsev, Kachurin, Ryovshin, Sineusov, Sukhoshchekov (spelled as "Suhoshchokov" in *The Gift*), and Koncheyev among others. Nabokov chooses Cherdyntsev, but most of them he will later bestow on invented characters in later short stories, novels, plays, and even verse (Boyd, *Russian Years* 255).

Historical Context

The first part of his surname, *Godunov*, implies the protagonist's royal descent (Johnson 109). Boris Godunov (1551–1605) was the famous member of an ancient Russian family of Tatar origin, as were a number of eminent Russian families, including the Nabokovs (whose lineage is traced back to the Tatar prince Nabok). Boris, the *de facto* regent of Russia from 1584, was ambitious and confident in his ability to rule, but he had never shown signs of being a usurper. In 1594 Boris began to bring forward his own son, Fyodor Godunov, as joint ruler: "The boy received envoys with his father and sometimes alone, and his name was included with that of Boris in official documents. Indeed, it seemed that, looking ahead to the succession of his son and to the firm foundation of a new Godunov dynasty, Boris was starting the training of his son early" (Grey 133). While Tsar Fyodor was alive, the boyars accepted him as a ruler, but many of them were hostile to his election as Tsar:

> With vivid memories of their complete subjugation to the throne during the reign of Tsar Ivan the Terrible, they were eager now to limit the power of the throne by some formal deed which would also secure their own powers and privileges, but Boris did not want the throne on such terms. (Ibid.)

Fyodor was said to be learned in the sciences; a map of Russia remains an interesting memorial of his interests. Fyodor commissioned it personally, and it was published in his name in 1614 by the German cartographer Gerard (Ibid. 154).

Cultural Ramifications

Fyodor Godunov-Cherndyntsev recreates a geographical fantasy in which he joins his father in travels across southwest Asia. The second chapter of *The Gift* is in turn modeled after Pushkin's prose. Alexander Pushkin's historical play, *Boris Godunov*, is devoted to Tsar Boris and the period referred in the Russian history to as the Time of Troubles. Although written in 1825, it was published only in 1831 and then was not approved for performance by the state censors until 1866, almost thirty years after the author's death. Production was finally permitted on the condition that certain scenes be cut—a demand which later haunted the story of Nabokov and his Godunov-Cherdyntsev.

In a diary entry written on the night of Vladimir Dmitrievich's murder, Nabokov's effort to recover his father's "last words" led him to Pushkin's *Boris Godunov*, which he apparently conflated with Glinka's opera *Life for the Tsar* (later renamed *Ivan Susanin*). Pushkin's Godunov passionately wants "to bequeath his kingdom to his son Fyodor; he feels that his legacy of good government has justified his son's claim to the title. By the middle of the play, however, Boris finds himself hounded from all sides by the power of an empty name, a shade, a 'threatening adversary': an impostor bearing the name of the dead Prince Dmitrii" (Greenleaf 147).

Nabokov's choice of the name "Godunov" may have been brought about by another opera based on Pushkin's original work, the eponymous work by Mussorgsky. In *Boris Godunov*, both in Pushkin's play and Mussorgsky's opera, there is a scene in which Fyodor is studying geography. Charles Nicol believes that Mussorgsky's "peculiar talent for children's songs probably makes this operatic scene more memorable than the original" (Nicol 29). Indeed, Fyodor Godunov-Cherdyntsev's imaginary travel and his namesake's pastime are profoundly related, and probably initially through Mussorgsky's opera rather than Pushkin's play. Pushkin's dramas have inspired many operas, which reinforced Nabokov's lifelong relationship with Russia's Bard (Leving, "Singing *The Bells* and *The Covetous Knight*").

Highlighting the artistic strategies in *The Gift*, David Bethea registers Fyodor's connection to Pushkin through his father and through his own study and contemplation of the poet ("Pushkin entered his blood. With Pushkin's voice merged the voice of his father"; G98). The notions of poetry, love, mortality, and chance are linked through different "bloodlines" (one hereditary, the other cultural), but "Fyodor is the living example—the phenotype as it were—attesting to each bloodline's reality" (Bethea 138). The "Godunov" of the double surname could be attributed to the family's place in Russian history, but it could also hark back to Pushkin's play about dynastic succession and impostorship—a more likely scenario given the context, according to David Bethea: "Indeed, by analogy to earlier aristocratic families, like the Musin-Pushkins, Nabokov has placed his hero in a genealogical force field between Pushkin on the one hand [Godunov], and the non-poetic Chernyshevski [Cherdyntsev], on the other. What Fyodor's father calls 'nature's rhymes' and what Fyodor himself is searching for when he comes down with rhyming fever early in the book belong to a common weave" (Ibid.).

Literary Allusions in the Name

When Yakovlev sent Nabokov the list of the surnames he prepared from genealogical and heraldic sources, he clarified that Cherdyntsev's name derives from *Cherdyn*, a small town on the Kama River in Urals.

It seems like an ominous coincidence that Osip Mandelstam, one of Fyodor's possible prototypes, was arrested on May 14, 1934, and sentenced to three years of exile in remote Cherdyn; when the Mandelstams arrived there in early June of that year, the poet attempted to commit suicide by jumping out of the window, very much like Nabokov's Luzhin. On June 28, 1934, Nabokov published a poem about a drowned woman ("L'Inconnue De La Seine") in *Poslednie novosti* under the cryptic memo: "From F. G.-Ch." — meaning "From poems by Fyodor Godunov-Cherdyntsev," the first time Nabokov ever used this invented name in print.

Thanks to the intercessions of Akhmatova and Pasternak, as well as Nikolai Bukharin's letter to Stalin, Mandelstam was transferred to the larger provincial city of Voronezh. Nabokov may have heard about the poet's troubles from fellow émigré intellectuals who closely followed Mandelstam's fate before and after he perished in the Stalinist Gulag (Timenchik, "O mandel'shtamovskoi nekrologii" 550-66). This is how in 1927 the contemporary émigré critic, Prince Dmitri Mirsky, described Mandelstam's poetic prose, which inspired some of the best passages in Nabokov's *The Gift* (Leving, "Tenishev Students" 141-62):

> If I were asked to name the book that was most representative of young Russian literature I should recommend [Victor Shklovsky's] *A Sentimental Journey*. Mandelstam's book, *The Noise of Time,* though less central and representative, is artistically a more significant book. It is an admirable example of a poet's prose, free from all adulterous poeticalness, but saturated with the poet's sense of the value of words, and his power of evoking images. It is also full of the sense of history, of the individual flavor and taste of its every moment. The Petersburg of the 'nineties and early nineteen-hundreds, the pre-Revolutionary suspense of a decaying regime, is crystallized into images of gem-like color and hardness. It is a book apart, and one of our generation's greatest contributions to the nation's literature. (Mirsky 256)

With minor changes, the same could actually have been said of Nabokov's novel itself, were Mirsky to have read it a decade later — but he could not. After

Mirsky's repatriation to the USSR (Nabokov, by the way, was "a great admirer of Mirsky's work"; *Selected Letters* 91; *cf.* Efimov), the independent critic soon found himself in the same place as the object of his glowing review: Mirsky was arrested in 1937, and remained a prisoner until his death in the Far East in January of 1939.

We do not have any evidence as to whether Nabokov was aware of the Cherdyn episode in Mandelstam's biography while he was writing the novel and whether it could have played any decisive role in choosing the name *Cherdyn*tsev for his exiled hero, but later in the English translation of *The Gift* the author did honor the memory of the banished Soviet poet by attaching his name to a previously disguised quote from his poetry ("the powder snow upon the wooden paving blocks of Mandelstam's neoclassicism, and the Neva's granite parapet on which one can scarcely discern today the imprint of Pushkin's elbow"; G38).

Prototypes for the Main Character

Nina Berberova, who knew Nabokov well in the mid-1930s, firmly believed that her husband, the influential Russian poet and literary critic Vladislav Khodasevich (1886–1939), provided the bulk of the material for the image of Fyodor. Berberova was even convinced that she overheard some historical conversations between the two poets that later served as a core of the famous dialogues between Godunov-Cherdyntsev and Koncheyev:

> The two visits to Khodasevich's place (which six months ago had been my place as well, but was no longer), in clouds of cigarette smoke, tea drinking, cat petting, proved a projection of Godunov-Cherdyntsev's dialogue with Koncheyev, that dialogue that later found its way into *The Gift*. I was (and still am) the only person who witnessed this strange phenomenon: the reality of an event (October 23 and 30, 1932, rue des Quatre Cheminées, Billancourt, Seine, France, from 4 to 6 pm) which was to become a fantasy—never wholly realized in the pages of the novel, only imagined, and consumed in its dreamy depth—a result of Godunov-Cherdyntsev's solitary insomnia.
>
> I had already heard of Nabokov in Berlin in 1922. Yuly Aikhenvald, literary critic of the Russian newspaper *Rudder*, spoke to Khodasevich of him as of a talented young poet. But his verse of that time did not interest Khodasevich: it was a pale and at the same time self-assured scanning of verse, as was written in Russia by cultured amateurs, sounding nice and imitative, recalling no one in particular and at the same time everyone. (Berberova 222)

Nabokov himself denied that Khodasevich served as a prototype either for Fyodor or Koncheyev.

Chapter Three. STRUCTURE

[Ill. 3-6] Vladislav Khodasevich

Nabokov was obviously fond of this last name, as evident from the fact that he employed it in passing later in *Pnin*—though in an ironic context—when he alluded to the "so-called Godunov Drawing-of-an-Animal Test" (*Pnin* 65). Gene Barabtarlo discovered a meticulous description of this "Drawing-a-Person Test," introduced in 1926 and originally "used as a measure of intelligence with children," in the first volume of a monumental work, *Comprehensive Textbook of Psychiatry* (ed. by Dr. Benjamin Sadock et al., 3rd ed., Baltimore-London, 1980, p. 954). The "incontestably Nabokovian touch: the real inventor's name is not Godunov (pronounced in Russian 'Gud-oon-off'), but, oddly enough, W. H. Goodenough" (Barabtarlo, *Phantom of Fact* 159).

THE GODUNOV-CHERDYNTSEV FAMILY

The Godunov-Cherdyntsev Family Tree

Kirill Ilyich is Fyodor's grandfather, mentioned in Suhoshchokov's *Memoirs of the Past*. Konstantin Kirillovich, his son and the protagonist's father, is the hero of the unfinished book: Fyodor reconstructs his scientific trip to Asia in Chapter Two of *The Gift*. Oleg Kirillovich, the brother of Konstantin Kirillovich, is living in Philadelphia (Shchyogolev, who happened to know Oleg Kirillovich, recognizes Fyodor's last name when he first meets him in Berlin; G143). The life of Fyodor's sister, Tanya, is described in a more detailed manner in the short story "The Circle," which Nabokov called a "satellite" of the novel.

Konstantin Kirillovich

Konstantin Kirillovich Godunov-Cherdyntsev is a puzzling figure: his presence in the story is tangible but he nonetheless remains elusive both for the readers and for the main character. The accursed question of *The Gift* is *where* is Fyodor's father—did he perish in the last expedition or has he miraculously escaped first the Asian dangers and then the Soviet persecutors on his way, presumably, back home; will he return to the lives of Fyodor and the rest of his loved ones

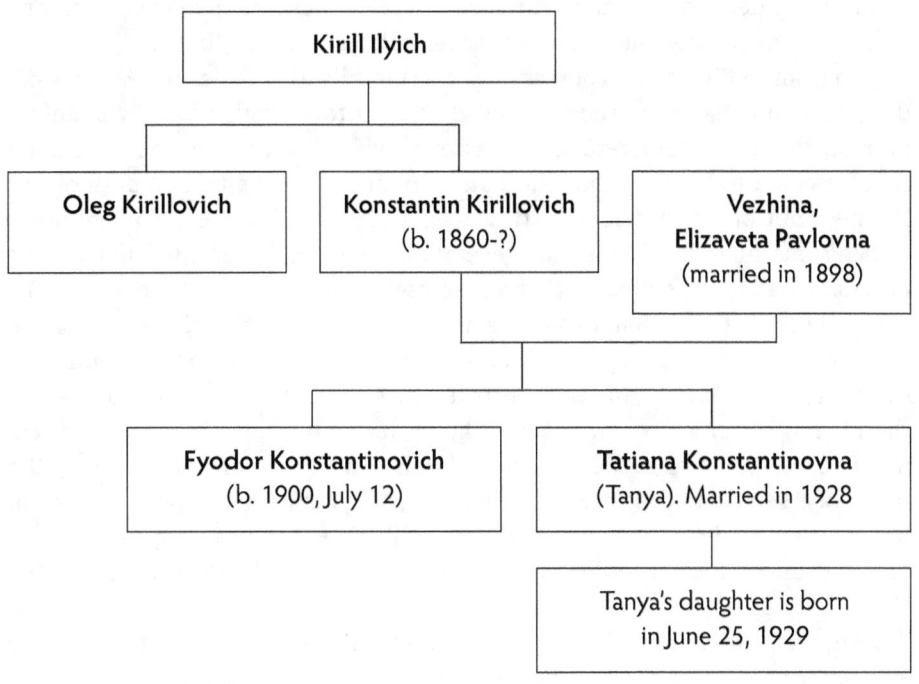

The Godunov-Cherdyntsev Family Tree

as unexpectedly as he used to do in the past? The clues are numerous, but not conclusive.

Analyzing an associative network of "invisible links" connecting the death of Konstantin Godunov—the town of Tatsienlu, the village of Chetu, French missionaries, and a mysterious butterfly named Thecla bieti—Dieter Zimmer proposes that this network be called "the Tatsienlu complex in *The Gift*." It seems that one of Fyodor's more or less subconscious fancies had been that his father had survived and stayed on in Tibet or China, "just like the two American bikers mentioned in *The Gift* whom his father had met in the Gobi desert and who had become a Chinese mandarin. That may be the reason why Fyodor's dream strangely vested his father 'with a gold embroidered skullcap' [G354], that is, with a mandarin's cap" (Zimmer, "Chinese Rhubarb" 16). Yet Nabokov's principal intent, Johnson and Coates caution us, was not to teach the reader about butterflies: "Rather, behind the mask of the lepidoptery, his deeper theme is the elder Godunov-Cherdyntsev's obsession and its cruel consequences for Fyodor" (Johnson, Coates 295). To advance his research, Godunov-Cherdyntsev leaves his wife and son on their own much of the time, "instilling in each an emptiness that could not ultimately be filled (in a crucial scene the father's interminable absences and his refusal to take Fyodor on one of his journeys causes the son to burst into helpless tears)" (Ibid.).

Konstantin Kirillovich's obsession seems literally to have destroyed him — he disappears on his last journey and Fyodor is left to struggle with the phantom hope of his miraculous return: it was only when Fyodor reached adulthood that he came to suspect that the elder Godunov-Cherdyntsev undertook his journeys out of a mysterious restlessness, 'not so much to seek something as to flee something' (G115). Fyodor eventually realizes "what a toll his father's obsession had taken on his mother and himself," but part of the splendor of *The Gift* is "how thoroughly an expansive and majestic treatment of the golden age of lepidoptery is made to serve Nabokov's larger artistic purposes" (Johnson, Coates 295). An interesting point is taken by Anat Ben-Amos, who remarks on the idea of *the presence of absence*: "the father who in his absence has a real influence on the artistic development of his son, may represent the way the fictional is central to the novel. The qualities that later enable Fyodor to develop his artistic abilities and to create effective illusions begin to appear when he uses his imagination in order to have his father near him" throughout his life (Ben-Amos 130).

Another aspect linked to Fyodor's father is Nabokov's use of this figure as a mouthpiece for articulating his own scientific ideas, mainly related to his perceived problems with the Darwinian theory of natural selection as the core explanation for the mechanism of evolution. Writing in 1939, Nabokov shows Konstantin Godunov-Cherdyntsev in 1917 as hostile to genitalic dissection, but by 1943, after two years at the microscope in Harvard, he was himself extending the scope of genitalic and alar description. In the opinion of Nabokov's biographer, there is no reason to think that had the writer returned to the laboratory in the 1950s or later he would not again have welcomed and extended new taxonomic tools (Boyd, "A Guide to Nabokov's Butterflies" 219). Only after Nabokov left the laboratory was the new synthesis of Darwinian natural selection and Mendelian genetics begun in the 1940s and consolidated in the 1950s.

Elizaveta Pavlovna

Elizaveta Pavlovna Vezhina, Fyodor's mother (married to Konstantin Kirillovich in 1898), lives in Paris and occasionally visits her son in Germany. She writes him relatively long letters, which Nabokov partially reproduces in the narrative. *The Gift* opens with a street that is described as "beginning with a post office and ending with a church, like an epistolary novel" (G4). This is not a mere simile, as Maya Minao maintains; although *The Gift* is not what we traditionally call an "epistolary novel," it is replete with "epistolary" motifs: the separated family members are linked through correspondence and Nabokov often presents this as samples of the respective characters' writings (Minao 6). In his commentary on *Eugene Onegin*, Nabokov points out the significance of this literary device, noting that in the course of the novel in verse Pushkin quotes writings by all three main characters: Onegin, Tatiana, and Lensky (*Eugene Onegin*, II:384). In *The Gift* Nabokov offers the writing styles of both the protagonist and his mother through their letters, which is especially poignant because it is Elizaveta Pavlovna who encourages Fyodor to write his early prose. Their written exchange thus forms a part of the father's biography in progress. Minao draws our attention to the fact that "there is no gap between each fragment of their letters: Fyodor's question is immediately followed by his mother's answer, which ignores and resolves the actual space and time separating mother and son. At least in the text, a long blank in which one waits for the other's letter mercifully disappears. The flow of the correspondence creates the impression of a dialogue unfolding in a single place and time, its continuity uninterrupted. Moreover, these fragments of their letters are all undated (except for the one Fyodor writes on his father's birthday), which encourages us to ignore the entire space/time lag" (Minao 7). The ideal correspondence marked by the bliss of sharing memories between two soul mates acts as the catalyst in launching Fyodor's initial experiment in fiction.

Zina Mertz

For Fyodor "the name of his beloved combines a direct appeal to memory as the ultimate source of artistic inspiration with a suggestive image for memory's status as a diminished yet persistent reflection of experience" (Foster 152). Fyodor exclaims: "What shall I call you? Half-Mnemo*syne*? There's a half-shim*mer* in your surname too" (G157). Both parts of Zina's name are included in this invocation, where they appear as the last half of *Mnemozina* (Mnemosyne in English) and the first half of the Russian word *mertsan'e* ("shimmer"), thereby forming a play on words that the English version approximates in the suffix "mer." Mnemosyne was one of the twelve Titans from Greek mythology, the mother of the Muses and the goddess of memory. In *The Gift* "her role is limited to a relatively modest allusion; for this writer, recollections of actual experience are just as inspiring as the imaginative invention stressed elsewhere in the poem" (Foster 151). "Mertsan'e," meanwhile, introduces the image of faint reflected light, the "pale fire" of a much later Nabokov novel. Linked to the idea of memory, the very name of Zina Mertz acquires a pointedly Proustian resonance, according to John Foster, who believes that she "epitomizes the largely camouflaged presence of European modernism" in the novel (155).

———————————— Chapter Three. STRUCTURE ————————————

That Zina is herself the key to Fyodor's third artistic phase is suggested not only by her producing the sound of the key outside at the very moment when Fyodor finishes his work on Chernyshevski, but by her wielding keys earlier in Chapter Three in the scene in which Fyodor's and Zina's romantic feelings for one another receive their first overt expression (Waite 64). As the tenant and the landlords' daughter pause in the half-light of the front hallway in a "prismatic rainbow" cast by the glass of the door (G183), Zina plays with her keys, and Fyodor gravitates toward Zina. Although it is difficult to agree with Waite that the key here may be understood as a phallic symbol or—a bit more plausible—as "the key to a heart," the attraction includes the growing impatience of passion as well as Fyodor's subconscious gravitation toward his inspiring Muse.

But in spite of the fact that the love between Fyodor and Zina springs from literature and is always related to it (Zina comes to know Fyodor through his poetry and sees him for the first time at an evening of poetry reading), there are subtle hints at a somewhat disturbing pattern: literature in Fyodor's life is not always a source of harmony in love (for instance, while finishing his biography of Chernyshevski, Godunov-Cherdyntsev stands Zina up at a ball despite his earlier commitment to meet her there; Ben-Amos 134). Thus Zina understands toward the end of the novel: "You know at times I shall probably be *wildly unhappy with you*" (G365; emphasis added).

Killing Zina

For those few who have read the projected continuation of *The Gift* (1939–40), the fate of Fyodor's beloved, however, is difficult to absorb. What started as a great romance in the main novel was destined to come to a tragic end in the never written second volume. To explain this paradox we will have to make a brief digression.

Irina Guadanini was an amateur poet whose texts have occasionally appeared in Russian émigré literary magazines, resulting in a small book of poetry, *Pis'ma* ([*Letters*], Munich, 1962). Although her Russian verses are no better than those of Fyodor's apprenticeship (critics pointed out both their charm and weakness; see Strakhovskii 75), some of these texts are of interest to Nabokov scholars since they might bear factual traces of Guadanini's relationship with Nabokov. The poems contain not an objective reflection of what happened but rather a personal point of view on their author's experience.

One of the thirty-six poems in Guadanini's book is entitled "Dar" (*Gift*) (*Pis'ma* 35). The poem is a reflection on the gift of oneself to another person. The main themes of *The Gift*—inspiration, mirrors, otherworldly shadows, and transparent dreams—are amalgamated in this disturbing declaration and expression of eternal love:

Zina Mertz

"THE GIFT"

Like a glimmer of past life,
An echo of highest empyrean inspiration,
Only a feeling remains...
My hands—for you, dear.

In the glint of the eyes, mirror-like, beckoning
—A cup full of unearthly reflection—
Eyes full of the shadow of embodiment...
My eyes—for you, dear.

By rare and flashing dreams of clarity,
And babbling reams of lovely words, and plain,
The soul, imbued in rapturous of admiration...
My heart—for you, dear.

"DAR"

Kak otblesk zhizni predydushchei
i ekho samykh vysshikh vdokhnovenii,
ostalos' razve tol'ko oshchushchen'e...
Ruki moi—tebe.

I otrazhen'em glaz, kak v zerkale zovushchikh,
—kak chashei polnoiu nezdeshnikh otrazhenii-
glaza polny lish' ten'iu voploshchen'ia...
Ochi moi—tebe...

Mel'kan'em snov, prozrachnykh, neobychnykh,
Struen'em slov, liubimykh slov privychnykh,
dusha napoena v vostorge voskhishchen'ia...
Serdtse moe—tebe.

The triple repetition of the words *otrazhenie* (reflection) and *otblesk* (reflection; gleam, sheen, vestige) deliberately evoke the synonymous *mertsanie* (twinkling, glimmer, flicker), which is also, as noticed earlier, the semantic root of the character Zina Mertz's last name. Guadanini plays with both notions imbedded in *mertsanie*—irrevocable memories and shining events of the past constitute the major motif of her poem.

[Ill. 3-7] The cover of Irina Guadanini's book of poetry, *Letters* (Munich, 1962)

[Ill. 3-8] The opening page of Irina Guadanini's short story, "The Tunnel" (1961), published under the pseudonym *Aletrus*, with an epigraph from V. Sirin's poem

Алетрус

ТУННЕЛЬ

На закате у той же скамьи,
Как во дни молодые мои...

В. Сирин

Несколько лет тому назад приехал я в небольшой городок на итальянской Ривьере, где случилось мне жить когда то раньше. Я занимал этаж виллы, расположенной в нескольких минутах ходьбы от моря. Знакомых у меня не было и много времени я проводил в одиночестве.

Хозяева виллы, — немолодой итальянец и его жена, — однажды пригласили меня к себе. Людьми они оказались приятными и я иногда стал заходить к ним по вечерам. Сидя в их небольшом благоуханном саду, окруженном каменной стеной, мы проводили время в оживленных разговорах.

Фамилия у меня интернациональная, я давно живу за границей и мало кто знает что я русский по рождению, духу и воспитанию. Не знали этого и мои хозяева.

Guadanini never forgot her liaison with Nabokov and cherished the memory of it until her death. As Zina Mertz did with Fyodor's poems (or Véra Slonim with Sirin's), the emotional blonde religiously copied and cut out all of Nabokov's published works–both before they met and long after they had separated. A quarter of a century after their initial encounter, Guadanini quotes generously from Nabokov's letters to her in her short story, "The Tunnel." The story appeared in the Canadian Russian-language émigré journal *Sovremennik* (1961) under the pseudonym *Aletrus* (which might be either an English pun on the phrase "Alert us," or a Russian address "Ale, trus"—i.e. "Hello, coward" [the latter interpretation belongs to A. Dolinin; private communication]). The title refers to the "accidental young lady reading a Russian translation of Kellerman's *The Tunnel*" in the émigré bookstore in *The Gift* (G167).

Guadanini's short story presents a slightly camouflaged history of the narrator's romance, and focuses on the lovers' dramatic last meetings in Cannes. As they stroll toward the port, the hero explains to his female companion that "he loves her but cannot bring himself to slam the door on the rest of his life" (Schiff 91). At nightfall the heroine passes by his house, but the sight of a woman's shadow in the window deters her from intruding. "At the entrance to the train tunnel she throws herself on the tracks" (Ibid.).

The aesthetic quality of Guadanini's prose is questionable, but it is significant that she integrates both identified quotations from Sirin's poetry (epigraphs to sections of this short story) and non-attributed citations from Nabokov's personal letters to her. Just one example of such use: "You always keep coming out of every corner of my thought with your puppy-like gait!"/"*Ty vsegda vykhodish' iz-za kazhdogo ugla moei mysli svoei shcheniachei pokhodkoi*!" ("The Tunnel" 8). Irina made her living in emigration by working as a dog groomer.

Some biographical background and unpublished works preserved in the writer's archive help to illuminate the juxtaposition of Guadanini's poem, "The Gift," with her short story, "The Tunnel." According to Boyd and Schiff, Nabokov first met Irina in Paris in January of 1937, during a public reading of two excerpts from *The Gift*. The fact that Nabokov had a tormenting forbidden liaison while working on *The Gift* should not be overlooked, inasmuch as Nabokov was at work on Chapters three and five of *The Gift*, a novel that has been described as his ode to fidelity, during the latter half of 1937. Stacy Schiff writes: "Vladimir appears to have been perfectly aware of the chasm that separated the reality of his fiction from the fiction of his reality. [...] Véra was battling a figure who was dangerously, splendidly flesh and blood, but Irina was playing a far more arduous game, having to run competition with a rival who existed partly in prose" (Schiff 91). The same technique of blending reality and fiction to a point beyond recognition is used in Nabokov's depiction of Fyodor's love affair with a prostitute, Yvonne, in the unrealized second volume of *The Gift*. Fyodor is "using art to preserve the erotic intensity of sensation and keep 'moral revulsion' at bay. Finally, when he has succeeded in transforming Yvonne from an object of desire into a subject of aesthetic contemplation her actual presence becomes unnecessary, superfluous" (Grayson 37). Vladimir confessed to Irina that he had had a series of fleeting affairs—including a moment of infidelity with a student, who possibly made it into the text of the novel ("a schoolgirl in a black jumper, whom he sometimes felt like kissing on her bent yellowish nape" [G60]). Véra's biographer believes that Nabokov "listed these to prove to Irina that she was in a category of her own. He does not appear to have mentioned the earlier transgressions to Véra" (Schiff 92).

As we learn from the draft of the unpublished sequel to *The Gift* (dated 1939), in a section under the working title, "The Last Chapter" [Posledniaia glava], Zina Mertz was to be run over by a car and killed:

> He left the building with Zina, parted company with her at the corner ... returned home, saw the landlady's back heading out into the street, found a note by the telephone: the police had just called (from such-and-such a street) and asked him to present himself forthwith ... There, on a leather sofa, wrapped in a sheet (where did they get that sheet?) lay Zina, dead. *In those ten minutes she had managed to alight from a bus and tumble straight under a car.* And there too was a vaguely familiar lady, who had chanced to be on that same bus, now playing the vulgar role of comforter. He shook her off at the corner. Wandered around, sat in square after square. (Translation is mine; quoted in Dolinin, "Zagadka nedopisannogo romana" 218)

The theme of "fate's methods" (G362) provides the novel with a hidden framework. The role of fate's envoy is assigned to the driver of the car. Shchyogolev's idea for a story involving a pubescent stepdaughter has often been cited as a glimpse of the future *Lolita*. Here is yet another preliminary sketch that will later materialize in the car accident scene in *Lolita*: "the laprobe on the sidewalk ... concealed the mangled remains of Charlotte Humbert who had been knocked down and dragged several feet by the Beale car as she was hurrying across the street ..." (103). The same accessories accompany the scene: the note, the telephone call in which a man is asked to come and identify the body of his wife, importunate comforters, etc. The driver in *Lolita* relieves Humbert of his nymphet's mother, but it becomes the reader's (and the character's) hermeneutic metatask to try to orient himself in the text, to detect correctly the "agent of fate" amid the "intricacies of the pattern," something Nabokov had probed earlier in his unrealized continuation of *The Gift*.

The *topos* of the traffic accident becomes the Nabokovian variant of the will of happenstance, which has perplexed every writer from ancient times to the present. It serves as a banal method of killing off a character without fuss or muss, a kind of narrative euthanasia (Leving, "Filming Nabokov"). The writer had experimented with the same device earlier with the death of Nina, the frivolous protagonist of the short story "Spring in Fialta" (1936), and uses it again with Zina.

The Z-*ina*/N-*ina*/Ir-*ina* combination shares the same sound pattern; what is more, Véra's name definitely fails to fit the triad. Mrs. Nabokov always made sure to distance herself from Mertz ("Of course I am not Zina, she would say dismissively"; Schiff 91). *The Gift* is the single major piece that Nabokov did not originally dedicate to his wife, but instead to his late mother.

As he was finishing the book, Nabokov wrote to Irina asking her to return his letters. He claimed that the letters contained mostly fictions. The last chapter of *The Gift* was written in January 1938; a letter went out to Irina in February (Ibid, 94). Thus life and fiction overlapped.

But why, after all, was Zina doomed to perish under the wheels of the automobile? This is a question that should trouble readers of the never-published second part of *The Gift*. She is not Mrs. Humbert; on the contrary, Zina is one of the most touching, kind-hearted, selfless female characters Nabokov ever created. Apparently Guadanini, who had a lively sense of humor and took great joy in playing with words, had certain grounds to recognize herself in Zina Mertz. On the other hand, she was known as a femme fatale, while Zina and Fyodor are quite chaste; Irina was aggressive, while Zina is stern and aloof. To reconcile this discrepancy would be tantamount to finding the beginning or the end of the Möbius strip associated with *The Gift*'s deep structure.

The clue is not in Nabokov's cruelty: any traces of Guadanini had to vanish in order to keep Vladimir and Véra, Nabokov's true Muse, together. Tender Zina had no choice but to die along with some inconvenient memories.

Koncheyev

The relationship of the characters in *The Gift* may not, in Clarence Brown's opinion, have the paradigmatic clarity of that in *The Real Life of Sebastian Knight*, but it is nevertheless there in an analogous way. Like most of the characters in the foreground of Nabokov's works, Fyodor Godunov-Cherdyntsev is not especially admirable; he is only moderately good as a poet, but he is improving and shows great promise (Brown 287). Contrary to Fyodor, Koncheyev is a versatile poet in the émigré colony in Berlin—and he serves, along with the heroine named in the foreword (i.e. *Russian literature*), as the magnet in the center of Fyodor's centripetal movements. Of course the real conversations that Fyodor occasionally manages to have with the admired poet named Koncheyev "are utterly banal, but the imagined conversations are miraculously urbane and wise" (Ibid.).

Mysterious poet-critic Koncheyev appears and disappears recurrently. In rapid, allusive dialogue Fyodor and this imaginary alter ego (they are linked even phonetically: кoncheyev = кonstantinovich; Koncнeyev = cнerdyntsev) "work out their aesthetic credo and dismiss from contention all those mystics, progressives, and poetasters who, in their arrogantly youthful view, appear as excrescences on the brilliant surface of Russian literature" (Moynahan 38). Fyodor and Koncheyev are always "in essential agreement about artistic values" (ibid.), largely because they have no dispute concerning the very foundation of their literary tradition.

In Pushkin's Shadow

According to Vera Proskurina, Nabokov's "pro-Pushkinian" novel *The Gift* serves as a counterpoint to the author's complex attitude toward different (often controversial) modern approaches to Pushkin's legacy (Proskurina 35). Moreover, the image of Koncheyev is deeply bound up with Nabokov's concept of Pushkin's poem *"Pamiatnik"* (translated by Nabokov into English as "Exegi Monumentum"). In the second conversation with Fyodor, Koncheyev conveys his pessimistic views on fame and the immortality of the poet as he seamlessly incorporates quotations from Pushkin's programmatic text:

> "Fame?" interrupted Koncheyev. "Don't make me laugh. Who knows my poems? A thousand, a thousand five hundred, at the very outside two thousand intelligent expatriates, of whom again ninety percent don't understand them. Two thousand out of three million refugees! That's provincial success, but not fame. In the future, perhaps, I shall recoup, but a great deal of time will have to elapse before the Tungus and the Kalmuk of Pushkin's *Exegi monumentum* begin to tear out of each other's hands my 'Communication,' with the Finn looking enviously on." (G341)

Compare this excerpt with the stanza that Koncheyev alludes to in Nabokov's 1941-43 translation:

> Throughout great Rus' my echoes will extend,
> and all will name me, all tongues in her use:
> the Slav's proud heir, the Finn, the Kalmuk, friend
>   of steppes, the yet untamed Tunguz.
>
>   (*Verses and Versions* 213)

The connection between Nabokov and Pushkin (Fyodor/Koncheyev) is complex because it involves yet another link in the chain of reminiscences, or a "figure of concealment" (Senderovich). *The Gift* presupposes a correspondence between Pushkin's "Exegi Monumentum" and its interpretation by Mikhail

Gershenzon, "with Khodasevich playing the role of mediator" (Proskurina 36). M.O. Gershenzon (1869–1925), a well-known writer, historian and thinker, author of many studies on Russian intellectual life, wrote a seminal book entitled *Mudrost' Pushkina* (*Pushkin's Wisdom*, 1919) with a chapter entitled "Monument." Nabokov took Gershenzon's concept of Pushkin as someone who broke with his readers and his time and gave additional emphasis to this fissure. Gershenzon's name probably appears in *The Gift* in the guise of one of "the best doctors," who treats Fyodor's Uncle Oleg after he is wounded (G130).

Proskurina provides evidence that Gershenzon's theory, the above-mentioned chapter in particular, produced a storm of discussion in the Soviet press. It became a topic of debate in practically all works about Pushkin in the 1920s and the beginning of the 1930s. Most controversial of all was Gershenzon's interpretation of "Monument," which irritated critics with its provocative image of a disillusioned poet ridiculing his readers (Proskurina 31). The nature of Nabokov's self-encoding and self-presentation through Pushkin's "Exegi Monumentum" ("An émigré novel... might have, in those years, a total sale of 1,000 or 2,000 copies—that would be a best seller," as he would later bitterly admit, repeating Koncheyev's lament almost verbatim; *Strong Opinions* 36) was linked with the concept of Pushkin's "autobiographism," developed by Khodasevich in his Pushkin study, which had in turn been strongly influenced by Gershenzon.

An Ideal Synthesis of Modern Poets

If, as critics have long assumed, the figure of the poet Koncheyev was modeled at least in part on Khodasevich, it is precisely in his capacity as Russia's last poet, the one who ends the tradition (*konchaet*; in Russian "konchat'" means "to end"). The more obvious phonetic association of Koncheyev's name is with the word "conch" (from Latin *concha*: pearl-oyster or trumpet), suggesting, on the contrary, the glorious continuation of Russian poetry (Greenleaf 143-44).

Although the origin of the rumor about Khodasevich as Koncheyev's prototype appears to be Berberova's *The Italics Are Mine*, it is clear, Alexander Dolinin contends, that Nabokov did not try to model the "real" Koncheyev either on himself or on Khodasevich. In contrast to the latter, Koncheyev is very young, even a year younger than Godunov-Cherdyntsev, and therefore, in spite of his name he does not end the great poetic tradition but renews and continues it, or, to play once more upon his name, becomes the keeper of the sacred *conch* which is a symbol of eternity, as in Osip Mandelstam's famous poem "Rakovina" ("A Conch") (Dolinin "*The Gift*" 150; 168, 56n). Koncheyev, this "legitimate heir to the throne of Russian poetry," as Dolinin calls him, incorporates in his poetry certain features of several of the most auspicious talents among the author's generation—Vladimir Korvin-Piotrovsky, Antonin Ladinsky, Boris Poplavsky, and Boris Pasternak (Ibid.). Therefore, although Koncheyev is rooted in the Russian poetic tradition as firmly as Fyodor, or Nabokov for that matter, he is also an exemplary contemporary poet.

Boris Maslov treats this character as the sum total of his excerpted texts (four fragments), noting that the longest of them in Chapter Three —

> Days of ripening vines! In the avenues, blue-shaded statues.
> The fair heavens that lean on the motherland's shoulders of snow. (G170)
>
> (*Vinograd sozreval, izvaian'ia v alleiakh sineli.*
> *Nebesa opiralis' na snezhnye plechi otchizny.*)

– recalls the fifth stanza of Mandelstam's *The Slate Ode* (1923), beginning with the line "The fruit was swelling. The vines ripening..." ("*Plod naryval. Zrel vinograd...*"). The ode was widely discussed in the émigré press, including articles by Georgii Ivanov and Iurii Terapiano (Maslov 179). A leading poet of her generation, Marina Tsvetaeva (1892–1941), whom Nabokov met in person in 1924, contributes another component to Koncheyev's lyrical universe. His major work, "Beginning of a Long Poem" (G65), possibly alludes in its title to Tsvetaeva's "Poem of the End." As Maslov points out, the literary meeting at which the magazine containing Koncheyev's poem was brought in takes place in the fall of 1926 (according to the novel's chronology); in other words, it happens right after the real publication of Tsvetaeva's long poem in the first issue of the Prague journal *Kovcheg* (*The Ark*) in the same year (Maslov 181). Does this mean that Koncheyev emulates Mandelstam or that he functions as the male embodiment of Marina Tsvetaeva? Of course not, asserts Maslov, but his "textual persona," even if on a subconscious level only, absorbs the poetic phenomena that Nabokov was himself attracted to as a poet.

Nikolai Chernyshevski

In a 1969 interview with the Associate Editor of *Vogue* (New York), Nabokov admitted that he loathes Gogol's moralistic slant and suggested that Gogol "would have been appalled by [Nabokov's] novels and denounced as vicious the innocent, and rather superficial, little sketch of his life" that he produced twenty-five years earlier. Nonetheless, Nabokov was keen on defending the principles of writing "vicious biographies," hurrying to draw a comparison with his similarly controversial experience:

> Much more successful, because based on longer and deeper research, was the life of Chernyshevski (in my novel *The Gift*), whose works I found risible, but whose fate moved me more strongly than did Gogol's. What Chernyshevski would have

thought of it is another question—but at least the plain truth of documents is on my side. That, and only that, is what I would ask of my biographer—plain facts, no symbol-searching, no jumping at attractive but preposterous conclusions, no Marxist bunkum, no Freudian rot. (*Strong Opinions* 156)

One should clearly distinguish between the fictional and historical Chernyshevski—something that many of Nabokov's émigré contemporaries and later critics failed to do. For more on the biographical sketch of Nikolai Gavrilovich Chernyshevski (1828–89), highly influential leftist political writer, subsequently very popular with the Soviets, see the second chapter of this book ("Historical Context"). The Chernyshevski of *The Gift* is based on the real person, but the fictional image and the true persona correlate with one another no more precisely than a silhouette corresponds to its original.

To understand the correlation between these shifting stencils that fail to coincide, one may take into consideration the flexibility and general potency of the very character's name (splitting itself in the novel into additional personages under the same last name): CHERnyshevsky shares its attribute with CHERdyntsev, the title hero of *The Gift*. CHERNYI in Russian means "black" and, in this sense, Nabokov's character duplicates Dostoevsky's Karamazov in *The Brothers Karamazov* (1880). In Turkic languages *kara* means "black" (the root, *maz*, in Russian conveys the idea of "paint" or "smear"). So, Karamazov means *black smear*, as in sin, or the stain of original sin. "CHERnila" is the Russian word for "ink," the primary tool of both Godunov-Cherdyntsev and Chernyshevski. However, Andrea Tompa notes, they apply it differently: Fyodor "began very slowly to unstopper his bottle of ink—although at other times, when he wanted to write, the cork would pop out as that in a bottle of champagne" (G179); compare: "Ink, indeed, was the natural element of Chernyshevski (he literally bathed in it), who used to smear with it the cracks in his shoes when he was out of shoe polish" (G225). This double functioning of ink in the actions of respective writers unveils their different approaches in corresponding concepts of life and creativity, aesthetics and existential pursuits (Tompa 173).

Minor Characters

Alexander Yakovlevich and Alexandra Yakovlevna Chernyshevski

Alexandra Yakovlevna's image is partially based on Amalia Osipovna Fondaminsky (1883?–1935), the wife of Ilya Fondaminsky, the editor closest to Nabokov among the editorial board of *Sovremennye zapiski* (Belodubrovsky 9; Khazan 732). Nabokov met her in 1932 in Paris, and she immediately began taking care of him as Mme. Chernyshevski did of young Fyodor (though Amalia Osipovna's role as patron appeared to be less obtrusive and much more subtle). Nabokov later recalled the benefactress's "wise smile" and her "attentive eyes": "there was something infinitely touching in her dark dress, low stature, and light step" (Nabokov, "Pamiati Amalii" 7).

The name and patronymic of Alexandra Yakovlevna are the feminine forms of the name and patronymic of her husband, Alexander Yakovlevich. An identical combination of names for a married couple, as Leona Toker observes, occurs also in Ilf and Petrov's *Twelve Chairs* (1928), a work that Nabokov admired (Toker 146). Nabokov's bestowing on the Chernyshevskis the names of the couple from the Soviet novel must be considered in conjunction with his conferring the name of Luzhin from Dostoevsky's *Crime and Punishment* on the protagonist of *The Defense*. Nabokov reclaims, as it were, the names marred by previous novels; he attempts to obliterate "their old connotations and endows them with new ones" (Ibid.). Toker traces a number of transformations that the images of both spouses undergo in *The Gift*: Alexander Yakovlevich—

> from a man who plays a crude practical joke on Fyodor to one who contritely apologizes for having caused pain; from a deeply suffering bereaved father to a spokesman of tritely elevated conventional liberalism; from a man who seems to be in contact with the other world to a skeptic who denies the hereafter out of sheer self-discipline. The character of his wife turns out to be an even more subtle study of the relationship between conventionality of thought and authenticity of intuition combined with an unflinching personal loyalty... (Toker 146)

Alexandra Yakovlevna is, to some extent, "a cautionary example for Fyodor," as Leona Toker believes, and not everything in this woman's soul is "alien" to him (G36). The death of Yasha awakens the indolent forty-five-year-old woman; by way of compensation, the shattering grief grants her a certain distinction, and reveals a fine literary taste (Ibid. 147).

Important in Fyodor's relationship with the Chernyshevskis is that it was Alexander Yakovlevich who gave him the initial impetus for the future mock biography of his own revolutionary namesake: "Look, you ought to write a little book in the form of a *biographie romancée* about our great man of the sixties" (G40). Somewhat naively, Alexander Yakovlevich even hints at his willingness to provide assistance, should Fyodor decide to describe the life of the "great man."

Yasha Chernyshevski

When Yasha Chernyshevski's tragic fate is proposed by his grieving mother as an appropriate subject for an elegy, Fyodor refuses, yet rehearses the story in his imagination. His first task is to differentiate himself from his "semblable" double, the sensitive young elegiac poet Yasha Chernyshevski, whom he resembles typologically in every detail, and yet, he insists with an allergic repulsion, not at all in essence. Monika Greenleaf believes that the plot of *Eugene Onegin* is chosen by Nabokov as the means of exorcism. "Yasha is to Fyodor precisely what Lensky is in relation to the 'I,' or Pushkin-the-narrator, in *Eugene Onegin*": the commonplace image of a young poet—the close-cropped haircut of the twentieth century poet instead of black curls to the shoulders (Greenleaf 150).

To situate the Yasha episode within Russian intellectual life at the turn of the century, Anna Brodsky claims that Yasha's story is Nabokov's way of debunking Silver Age philosophies that linked homosexuality, genius, and artistic/sexual communities. It also enables Nabokov "to make some critical observations about turn of the century ideals of the modern woman and sexuality" (Brodsky 97). Yasha's high-flown sentiments and vocabulary seem characteristic of poets of the preceding generation such as Viacheslav Ivanov, Briusov, or Bal'mont, with whom Yasha shares his excitement over Schopenhauer (and which is not shared by the narrator) (Ibid. 98).

Yasha is an outcast: a displaced citizen, an assimilated Jew, an artist with obsolete aesthetic tastes, and a sexual deviant in a society that does not tolerate the Other. Before the Nazis enforced their policies of intolerance, many regarded the Weimar Republic's acceptance of homosexuals as a sign of Germany's decadence. The so-called "Golden Twenties" in Germany were for some "a time of carefree entertainment and cutting loose. Homosexuality was a visible part of Berlin as well as of other major cities in the Republic. Clubs, organizations, and dances all catered to homosexuals" (Jones 31). Indeed, some of the bars and cafes serving lesbian and gay subcultures were listed in tourist guides to Berlin's risqué night life (McCormick 56). Educated people openly discussed the cause of homosexuality and various medical theories, and there were overt political campaigns in favor of homosexual rights. Nabokov portrays a young contemporary who is a product of this atmosphere that encouraged public awareness of homosexuality in Weimar Germany, and although the phenomenon itself was not welcome on Weimar screens, it became a recurrent motif of Döblin's *Berlin Alexanderplatz*. Opposition to article 175 of the Penal Code (the law against male homosexual practices, essentially an antisodomy law) was permissible, but all of the indirect reasons for suppressing other political viewpoints could be applied to depictions of gay activity (Jelavich 134).

As for his literary pursuits, Yasha is "an aspiring but mediocre" poet. He is intense, as befits a romantic poet, "but these qualities are congealed in a kind of preset mold: Yasha is conventionally passionate, and his intensity is all too predictable" (Brodsky 96). Ultimately, Yasha's most urgent feelings have nothing satisfying to connect with, since he has only hackneyed concepts to enthuse about and stale ways of expressing that enthusiasm:

He is associated with two other mediocrities, Rudolf (a young Berliner) and Olia (a fellow expatriate). Olia is in love with Yasha, Yasha is in love with Rudolf, and Rudolf is in love with Olia. In despair, the three of them decide to commit suicide. Yasha, however, is the only one who follows through with the plan. (Ibid. 96-97)

Yasha's "tragic triangle" and the idea of unearthly or "communal" love are also embodied in Nikolai Chernyshevski's perverse love triangles. Uniting the men of the Sixties with their Decadent and Symbolist successors, Nabokov approaches the views of controversial Russian critic Vasily Rozanov (1856–1919) and his portrait of Chernyshevski (Skonechnaia 43). The poets Leonid Kannegiser (1898–1918) and Boris Poplavsky (1903–35) are also among the possible candidates for a composite literary portrait of Nabokov's protagonist.

Yasha, as his very name (a diminutive from Yakov/Jacob) implies, is a child, not a mature artist (it has been suggested by a non-native scholar that Yasha, whose name can be read as the Russian pronoun 'ia' [I] with a hypocoristic suffix, is "a mockingly accurate simulacrum of [Fyodor] — the elegiac subject — minus the genius"; Greenleaf 150). Yasha's "tragedy is not that of a frustrated lover, as he ineptly believes, but of a victimized boy, mourned by his kind and gentle parents" (Brodsky 106). His suicidal note contains nothing but the desperate cry of a horrified child: *"Mummy, Daddy, I am still alive, I am very scared, forgive me"* (G48).

The Shchyogolevs

Fyodor rents a room from the Shchyogolevs at 15 Agamemnonstrasse. Marianna Nikolavna is Zina's mother; Boris Ivanovich Shchyogolev is her husband, "a bulky, chubby man whose outline reminded one of a carp, about fifty years old, with one of those open Russian faces whose openness is almost indecent" (G142-43). Shchyogolev is the manifestation of *poshlost'* (platitude, or the mental essence that emanates from a "smug philistine"; *Lectures on Russian Literature* 309). Shchyogolev's direct literary precursor is Peredonov, the main hero of Fyodor Sologub's popular Symbolist novel *The Petty Demon* (1907) (Leving, "Rakovinnyi gul" 502-509).

The name *Shchyogolev* evokes parallels with Petr Shchyogolev, a well-known historian and Pushkin scholar in Leningrad of the 1930s (Hughes 226; Dolinin, *Kommentarii* 683-84). Arkady Bliumbaum further elucidates this link by delving into a discussion of Shchyogolev's alleged profession in *The Gift* ("in Russia he was a public prosecutor, a very, very cultured and pleasant gentleman"; G174), and the extent to which it may hint at the prosecutor-like tone and argumentation style in Petr Shchyogolev's polemics with Vladislav Khodasevich concerning Pushkin's unfinished long poem *The Water-Nymph* (on the connections between this poem and the projected second volume of *The Gift*, see Chapter One of this book). In his response to his Soviet opponent, Khodasevich ridicules references to specific sections of the contemporary Russian Federation Criminal Code used by the real Shchyogolev in his studies and their straightforward application to literary criticism (*Sovremennye zapiski* 37, 1928; Bliumbaum 598-600).

Oscar Grigorievich Mertz, Zina's natural father, is the exact opposite of Shchyogolev. Adored by his daughter Zina, he "had died of angina pectoris in Berlin four years ago, and immediately after his death Marianna Nikolavna [his wife] had married a man whom Mertz would not have allowed over his threshold" (G185). According to Polina Barskova, this "hasty misalliance may remind the reader of what happened in another, much more famous family, in which the heir of a deceased father was disturbed by his dissolute mother's rapid remarriage to a totally unworthy man" (Barskova 193-94):

> But two months dead — nay, not so much, not two —
> So excellent a king, that was to this
> Hyperion to a satyr...
> ...frailty, thy name is woman!
>   (*Hamlet*, 1.2, 140–46)

Besides this parallel, the Shchyogolev episode includes several grotesque Shakespearean hints. Mertz died of angina pectoris, a disease called *grudnaya zhaba* ("a toad in the chest") in the Russian language of that time. Only a few lines after Nabokov mentions this cause of death, he describes Mertz's widow, Marianna Nikolavna, as "an elderly, fleshy woman with a toad's face" (G197). "At this moment, the reader might begin to suspect that the 'toad,' i.e., Mertz's wife, might have been the actual cause of his death, just as Gertrude was the cause of her husband's death" (Barskova 194). Nabokov's wordplay, as Polina Barskova implies, is even more complicated here: in *Hamlet*, the prince calls his stepfather, the murderer of his father, "a paddock" (3.4, 190) — which is a Middle English synonym for "toad." "Thus, the death-bringing toad of Nabokov's novel is embodied by the alliance of Marianna Nikolavna and Shchyogolev that symbolizes *poshlost'* in the flesh, just as does the matrimonial alliance of Claudius and Gertrude in Hamlet" (Barskova 194).

Obviously, Nabokov reassigns the part of prince in his version of the Elsinore dynasty to Zina, the only child of the hapless Mertz; Barskova explains such a "gender switch" by the peculiarities of Elizabethan theatre (in which sex roles were interchangeable) and by having Shchyogolev call Zina "a princess" (G360) — an indication of her status as a feminine version of the Prince of Denmark (Barskova 194). The story of the Shchyogolev-Mertz family not only provides a provocative use of *Hamlet* motifs in *The Gift*, but allows Nabokov "to transform Shakespearian heroes into their travesty doubles, and this projects the episode's double meaning" (Ibid. 195).

Finally, of all places in Europe, his new position will take Boris Shchyogolev to Copenhagen (G326), the locus linked in literature with the idea of madness thanks to the Bard's immortal play. Although not mentioned by Barskova, the following allusion in Chapter One is also meant to lead the reader to Ophelia's story and lay the groundwork for the Shchyogolevs' job relocation later in the narrative: "From Denmark the papers reported that as a result of a heat wave there, numerous cases of insanity were being observed: people were tearing off their clothes and jumping into the canals" (G60).

The Circle of Émigré Writers and Critics

Naturally for such a fiction-oriented, metadescriptive work as *The Gift*, the narrative incorporates many recognizable images of contemporary literati and critics. In the scene of the bacchanal at the Writers' Union, names of characters from different works and centuries of Russian literature mingle with their suddenly diminutive and distorted authors, such as the "repulsively small, almost portable lawyer, Poshkin" (G322) in whose "unlikely figure the two fathers of *The Gift*, the lyrical poet and the elided lawyer, are elliptically and festively fused" (Greenleaf 158). Poshkin is a debunked version of Pushkin; Charsky is a parody taken directly from Pushkin's *Egyptian Nights* featuring a hero of that very same name.

Poshkin and Charsky happen to come across the writer Vladimirov (G332-33), an Anglophile rival of Godunov-Cherdyntsev. Nabokov's preface to *The Gift* identifies this character as a partial representative of himself in the 1920s, soon after his graduation from Cambridge. It is evident that the autobiographical material in the novel has been "very carefully selected and filtered in order to bar readers from essential secrets of the author's private life. Giving his visage, his sweater, and his shortened curriculum vitae as of spring 1929 (twenty-nine years old, an English university graduate, the author of two novels), not to the protagonist but to the incidental character Vladimirov, who makes his fleeting appearance in a single scene of *The Gift* immediately after references to three characters from Vladimir Sirin's previous books, Podtyagin (*Mary*), Ivan Luzhin (*The Defense*) and Zilanov (*Glory*), the writer separates his factual biography from that of his hero and emphasizes its irrelevance in the world of his fiction" (Dolinin, "*The Gift*" 151).

Christopher Mortus

The critic's pseudonym derives from Latin *mortus* ("death," "the dead"), which, according to Dahl's Dictionary of the Russian Language, is defined as "a follower of plague victims, doomed or condemned to attend to plague-ridden corpses."

The title of Mortus's article, "The Voice of Mary in Contemporary Poetry," correlates with Pushkin's "Mary's Song" in his drama *A Feast During the Plague* (*Little Tragedies*, 1830).

John Malmstad suggests that Nabokov's lifelong nemesis, Grigorii Adamovich, might have served as a prototype for the critic Mortus (286). "Christopher Mortus" and Adamovich are blended in an entomological reference to the Adam's Head butterfly, also known as Death's Head moth (*Acherontia atropos* Linnaeus). This species of moth is so called because of the pattern on its back resembling a human skull ("the mouselike squeak of our Death's Head moth"; G110).

To resort to a metaphor, Nabokov's caustic parodies often function akin to a multi-target surface-to-air missile. Another possible target of the lampoon here is the Paris critic and influential Russian Symbolist poet Zinaida Gippius (1869–1945). As it turns out, the author hiding behind the alias "Christopher Mortus" in *The Gift* is "a woman of middle age, the mother of a family" in private life (G169). Gippius also often wrote under masculine pseudonyms (Anton Krainii, Comrade Herman, etc.), and had, according to Nina Berberova, "not the slightest comprehension of normal love" and "barely condoned other people's ordinary love" (*Kursiv moi* 282). In Olga Skonechnaia's view, this utterance should be viewed in the context of the novel's erotic theme: "In her 1931 article 'The Arithmetic of Love' which appeared in *Chisla*, a journal hostile to Nabokov, [Gippius] returns to the idea, so beloved by the Symbolists, of man's androgynous essence. The love of 'women-men' (*zhenmuzhchiny*) for 'men-women' (*muzhezhenshchiny*) is an attempt to surmount the division of the sexes and win the battle with death" (Skonechnaia 44).

Valentin Linyov

The name of another unsympathetic critic, Valentin Linyov, comes from the surname of the protagonist of a Soviet propaganda novel, *Grass and Blood (Linyov)* (1926), authored by Aleksandr Tarasov-Rodionov (1885–1938); the dilettante artist I. L. Linyov, best known for his 1836 portrait of Pushkin, also comes to mind (Dolinin, *Kommentarii* 692, with a misprint in the patronymic). Curiously enough, an article about Linyov's Pushkin drawings was published in the same issue of *Contemporary Annals* (p. 177) that contained the first chapter of *The Gift* (Linyov will make his appearance in the third chapter of the novel; G169; 301).

Troika

Another triumvirate of writers presents itself to Fyodor in the figures of Lishnevski, Shahmatov and Shirin (G312). All three names share a common denominator: the fricative letter "sh" (ш) (which is next to a letter "ch" (ч) in

Russian alphabetical order). These gentlemens' portraits parody a flattened version of an émigré author as epitomized by Cherdyntsev himself.

In the Society meeting episode, Shahmatov insists that Shirin be heard out without interruption and supports his request to see the Society funds; the two writers, evidently like-minded, their names recurrently appearing next to each other, evoke the poet Prince Sergei Shirinskii-Shikhmatov (1783–1837), in turn calling to mind Pushkin's scornful epigram (1815) (Dolinin, "Tri zametki o romane Dar"; Shapiro, "Nabokov's Allusions" 332):

> There is a gloomy troika of bards —
> Shihmatov, Shahovskoi, Shishkov,
> There is a troika of intellect's foes —
> Our Shishkov, Shahovskoi, Shihmatov,
> But who is more foolish in this evil troika?
> Shishkov, Shihmatov, Shahovskoi!
>
> (Translation is mine — Y.L.)

Nabokov purposefully plays with the epigram, teasing the informed reader of *The Gift* (especially of the book edition), who would recall that both names, S(h)irin and Shishkov, have been used by the author as pseudonyms during his Russian period. Sirin (a mythic bird) transforms into "Shirin" (from the adjective *shirokii*, meaning "wide"), who is said to be "blind like Milton, deaf like Beethoven, and a blockhead to boot" (G315). Likewise, the aristocratic family name "Shihmatov" undergoes a metamorphosis, becoming "Shahmatov" (from the Russian noun *shakhmaty* for "chess," Nabokov's and Nikolai Chernyshevski's favorite intellectual game), while "Shahovskoi" coincides with Nabokov's confidant at the time he composed *The Gift*—Countess Zinaida Shakhovskoy (Shakhovskaya, in a more faithful transliteration of the Russian).

Engineer Kern

Satirical use of literary detritus does not stop here: the image of the civil engineer Kern, who flashes the lenses of his pince-nez impassively several times in the novel, brings with him a host of literary associations. Kern prides himself on having been a close acquaintance of the late celebrated poet Alexander Blok, while his uncle "was thrown out of school for reading *What to Do?*" (G197). Kern agrees to deliver a talk at the Saturday literary meeting under the title "Alexander Blok in the War." When Alexandra Yakovlevna erroneously puts "Blok and War" on the announcement instead, he protests that this "certainly does make a difference," with a smile on his "thin lips, but with murder behind his thick eyeglasses, without unclasping his hands which were joined on his abdomen. 'Blok in the War' conveys the proper meaning—the personal nature of the speaker's own observations, while 'Blok and War,' if you will excuse me, is philosophy" (G52). Indeed, Alexander Blok served in the engineering construction unit in 1916, however, no records of anyone named "Kern" in his surroundings have been found. The name Kern, in fact, immediately evokes Pushkinian associations: Anna Petrovna Kern (1800–79) was a Russian socialite and the addressee of "*Ia pomnyu chudnoe mgnoven'e...*" ("I Remember a Wondrous Moment..."). Arguably the best love poem in the Russian language, written by Pushkin in 1825, it has been memorized by every educated Russian for generations. Blok metamorphosed Pushkin's poem into his own "*O podvigakh, o doblestyakh, o slave...*" ("Of feats, of braveries, of fame..."), while the composer Mikhail Glinka put the poem to music and dedicated it to Kern's daughter Catherine. A. Dolinin notes that from Blok's letters to his relatives, which were printed at the time Nabokov was working on *The Gift*, one could learn that among the poet's associates in the same regiment was K. A. Glinka, the composer's descendant. Thus adding to the real Glinka from Pushkin's circles an invented Kern, Nabokov surrounds "Blok in the War" with shadows from the life of Pushkin (Dolinin, "Tsena odnoi bukvy" 88).

Stockschmeisser

> Rudolf and Olya dragged [Yasha] through the bushes to the reeds and there desperately sprinkled him and rubbed him, so that he was all smudged with earth, blood and silt when the police later found the body. Then the two began calling for help, but nobody came: architect Ferdinand Stockschmeisser had long since left with his wet setter. (G48)

In translation from the German, this episodic character's surname means "thrower of sticks" which exactly corresponds with what the architect is doing. Boris Maslov asks, "what is the source of our knowledge of the name and occupation of this passing figure seen twice?" (the second appearance will be in the novel's last chapter). There are several possible answers. First, the architect Stockschmeisser is just a casual passerby who walks his dog in the park regularly; Fyodor observes him playing there with the setter. Thus the name is conditioned by the description of his actions (*Stock*, stick + *schmeissen*, to throw) plus a characteristic German first name, Ferdinand. Fyodor bestows the profession of architect on him possibly out of the acoustic semblance with the name of the Russian court architect, Stackensneider, who designed the imperial Mariinsky Palace (1839–44) not far from the Godunov-Cherdyntsevs' (and the Nabokovs') mansion in St. Petersburg on the south side of St. Isaac's Square (Maslov 176). We may add that in the eighteenth century, the plot of land under the future palace belonged to a man named Chernyshov (*cf. Chernyshe*vski) and in 1825–39 his mansion housed a military school, where the poet Mikhail Lermontov studied for two years. Nevertheless, the question of our knowledge remains open because Fyodor the narrator cannot be held responsible for the naming of a character in the Yasha episode: his Grunewald walks begin much later, when he moves in to the Shchyogolevs apartment. This means that Nabokov, as the omnipotent narrator, is always present in the text one level above Fyodor's cognition.

Scientists

Konstantin Godunov-Cherdyntsev collects butterflies and enjoys having close collegial ties with the international scientific community. Those mentioned as peers of Fyodor's father are, for the most part, real contemporary explorers and collectors: Charles Oberthür (1845–1924), a French entomologist; and John Henry Leech (1862–1900), British entomologist, explorer of the lepidoptera of Asia, an author of *Butterflies from China, Japan, and Corea* (London, 1892-94), and a member of the Entomological Society of London. One of Godunov's friends in *The Gift*, he discovered a deciduous woodland species, *Hemaris Staudingeri* Leech, in 1890. Adalbert Seitz (1860–1938), a German entomologist, was the editor of *Gross-Schmetterlinge der Erde* (*The Macrolepidoptera of the World; The Butterflies of the World*), a comprehensive work of a proposed sixteen volumes which he began in 1906. Seitz planned to complete his undertaking in 1912, but this proved to be unfeasible and publication came to a halt (Seitz's name will reappear in *Speak, Memory* and then in *Ada*). Otto Staudinger (1830–1900), also mentioned in the novel, was an influential owner of a German entomological store and the author of a catalogue, *Lepidoptera of Europe and Asia*, scorned by experienced scholars and explorers like Grumm-Grzhimaylo for its lack of scientific precision.

When Elizaveta Pavlovna learns that her son has decided to compose the elder Godunov-Cherdyntsev's biography, she offers a piece of advice:

> Write to Avinov, to Verity, write to that German who used to visit us before the war, Benhaas? Banhaas? Write to Stuttgart, to London, to Tring, in Oxford, everywhere, *debrouille-toi* because I know nothing of these matters and all these names merely sing in my ears, but how certain I am that you will manage, my darling. (G97)

First Dieter Zimmer in his splendid study, *A Guide to Nabokov's Butterflies and Moths* (Hamburg: Selbstverlag, 1996/1998), and then Kurt Johnson and Steve Coates vividly explicated the significance of the place names and personal names belonging to real lepidopterists in *The Gift*. Nabokov's texture is so rich that the novel "could in some ways serve as a commentary on the history of lepidoptery" (Johnson, Coates 295). "Avinov" is Andrey Avinoff (1884–1949), like Nabokov an aristocratic Russian who lost his extensive collection in 1917. He was a painter and an expert on Central Asian butterflies (an apt connection for Godunov-Cherdyntsev), and eventually became director of the Carnegie Museum of Natural history in Pittsburgh. When Nabokov himself moved to the United States in 1941, Avinoff was among the first people he contacted. "Verity" in the passage above is Ruggero Verity (1844–1926), an Italian physician and lepidopterist who in the early 1940s wrote *Le Farfalle diurne d'Italia* (*The Diurnal Butterflies of Italy*), a book that Nabokov called "the greatest work on butterflies published in the last thirty years ... Owing to that sumptuous and exhaustive work the Italian butterflies are remarkably well known" (Berg Collection, typescript, 1969 [?]). Fyodor's mother could not quite come up with the name of Andreas Bang-Haas, a senior partner in the renowned firm of insect dealers, Staudinger & Bang-Haas, Dresden-Blasewitz (Johnson, Coates 294-95).

Alongside these well-known figures, whose names are easily found in encyclopedias and dictionaries, Nabokov incorporates more obscure personages (*cf.*: "the Cossack corporal Semyon Zharkoy, for example, or the Buryat Buyantuyev"; G117). Nabokov plucks out these names, Zharkoy and Buyantuyev, from Vsevolod Roborovski's (1856–1910) memoir: Cossack Gantyp Buyantuyev accompanied the explorer on his 1893–95 expedition from Karakol, while S. Zharkoy was a member of Przhevalsky's team during his last trip (Dolinin, *Kommentarii* 672).

Nabokov frequently overdoses his readers to such a degree that it seems impossible to follow the narrator and to distinguish between facts and figments. The uniqueness of *The Gift*, however, is its maniacal persistence with documentary information. Compare this cascade of names next to Fyodor's father: "he was still a young man when his name occupied one of the first places in the study of the Russo-Asiatic fauna, side by side with the names of its pioneers, Fischer von Waldheim, Menetries, Eversmann" (G102). Johann Gotthelf Fischer von Waldheim (1771–1853) was a German anatomist, entomologist and paleontologist. In 1804 Waldheim became the Director of the Natural History Museum at the Moscow University. In August 1805 he founded the Société Impériale des Naturalistes de Moscou (Imperial Moscow Naturalist Society).

Another German biologist and explorer, Alexander Eduard Friedrich Eversmann (1794–1860), is considered the pioneer of research into Russo-Asiatic flora and fauna. His name is commemorated in the butterfly *Eversmann's Parnassian* and the moth *Eversmann's Rustic*.

Eduard Menetriés (1801–61) is probably the most engaging figure of all three scientists mentioned by Fyodor as his father's lepidopterist contemporaries. Since his biography and scientific interests recall those of Godunov-Cherdyntsev père, I will dwell on this figure at greater length. According to O.L. Kryzhanovsky, Menetriés was "the first professional entomologist in Russia who earned his salary by research work" (Kryzhanovsky), as opposed to other university professors who were paid for teaching. The Paris born Menetriés in his youth was a student of the great Cuvier and the "father of entomology" P. Latreille. On their recommendation he participated in 1821–25 in the expedition of the Russian Academician G. I. Langsdorff to Brazil where he acquired vast experience in field research and wrote a number of papers on zoology. After returning from Brazil he was invited to St. Petersburg, where he arrived in 1826 and became part of the staff of the Kunstkammer as the curator of the zoological collections. Menetriés was provided with an apartment at government expense and a salary 2500 roubles per year. In 1831 Menetriés published *The Annotated Catalogue of Zoological Objects Collected during the Journey to the Caucasus to the Boundaries with Persia*, a valuable resource devoted to Caucasian insects:

> This first large scientific work dealing with Caucasian fauna contained descriptions of several hundreds of species of Caucasian insects, mainly beetles and butterflies. In St. Petersburg Menetriés began his work as curator by reorganizing the collections. Before him the method of arranging collections in the Kunstkammer had been totally unscientific: the collections were exhibited in cases with glass covers grouped in such a way that a large and colorful insect, a butterfly or a beetle was placed in the centre and different species were arranged around it radially, symmetrically where possible. The center of each radius began with a small insect, which was followed by larger insects until the case was filled completely. No labels identifying the insects were applied; data on their origin were rarely present. Menetriés divided the collection by order, identified the material where possible and arranged the collection systematically. A large amount of material that was unlabeled and had been damaged by pests or mold was disposed of. When the Zoological Museum of the Academy of Sciences officially opened its doors in 1832, Menetriés was designated Curator of its entomological collections and held that position up to the end of his life. (Kryzhanovsky)

Another covert literary connection that Nabokov might well have enjoyed is the fact that Menetriés published one of the first works on the fauna of Kazakhstan based on the collections of the famous traveler S. Karelin, great grandfather of the poet Alexander Blok (Kryzhanovsky).

Stylization

The cases described above demonstrate Nabokov's careful handling of documentary sources. But even when his characters and their names are entirely or partically fabricated he weaves in the fictitious imagery in accordance with artistic principles, as in this opening of Chapter Four:

Afterwards (in the quiet of their poor and distant parishes) priests with names derived from Cypress, Paradise, and Golden Fleece recalled his bashful beauty with some surprise: the cherub, alas, proved to be pasted on tough gingerbread which was too hard for many to bite into. (G212)

Irina Paperno invites us to scrutinize the list of Chernyshevski's childhood friends (the Russian original simply lists their names; these are presented here in parentheses): "Cypress" (*Kiparisov*), "Paradise" (*Paradizov*), and "Golden Fleece" (*Zlatorunnyi*). At first glance these might seem to be merely typical last names of seminary students (the three names follow a well-known pattern of surnames traditionally assigned to Orthodox clergy), stylized by Nabokov to help create a picture of the "paradise" of Chernyshevski's serene childhood. Nevertheless, as established by Paperno, Kiparisov and Zlatorunnyi were actual family names of two of Chernyshevski's seminary friends; both are mentioned in his diary from the period. Paradizov is a plain translation of the surname of Chernyshevski's boyhood friend Raev (*rai* = paradise), whose memoirs Nabokov uses in creating this very scene (Paperno 305).

The sentence may in fact serve to illustrate the general structural principle lying at the heart of "The Life of Chernyshevski." To use Shklovsky's concepts, the narrative is constructed by means of an interrelation of "material" and "style." Textual elements that appear to be stylistic devices are actually based on original material: while Kiparisov and Zlatorunnyi are surnames belonging to real people, the third name in this group turns out to be a stylization! This is an element of form, which, in Shklovsky's terms, "de-materializes" the material. To quote Shklovsky, "what was assumed to be a 'reflection' [*otrazhenie*] actually turns out to be a stylistic device" (Shklovsky, *Mater'al* 220; "Pis'mo Tynianovu" 99; Paperno 305).

The Gift is saturated with literariness through and through. Often Nabokov simply borrows the characters' profiles or names from his predecessors; *cf.*: "a postmaster who resembled Simeon Vyrin...was lighting his pipe" (G97), alluding to a character from Pushkin's short story "The Station Master" (1825).

Artists

Painting is the art form that, after literature, interested Nabokov most, and discussions of it figure prominently in *The Gift*. Isaac Levitan (1860–1900) belonged to the *Itinerant Art Movement*, formed by a group of Russian realist artists in protest against the restrictions imposed by the Imperial Academy of Arts (G89). The group founded a new artistic code, influenced by the public and aesthetic views of Vissarion Belinsky and Nikolai Chernyshevski.

Belinsky and Chernyshevski based their social and political critique on an opposition to pure aestheticism in an effort to make art useful to society (see Chapter Two of this book). The group evolved into the *Society for Traveling Art*

Exhibitions in 1870, and between 1871 and 1923 it arranged close to fifty mobile exhibitions. As a true Itinerant, Levitan emphasized his subject matter in order to illustrate the multi-faceted social life of Russia. He is known for his extremely realistic techniques and his advancements in the genre of mood landscape.

Gerard de Vries and Donald B. Johnson have compiled a list of the identifiable paintings mentioned in Nabokov's works (Vries and Johnson). In *The Gift* they highlight the sample, "Vereshchagin's picture of the Moscow Fire" (G13), commenting that Vasily Vereshchagin's (1835–1904) work is actually titled "The Kremlin Burns" and belongs to a cycle of paintings based on Napoleon's invasion of Moscow in 1812 (Roman Timenchik was the first to point this out in his "Voprosy k teksty" 418).

Apart from the Russian paintings, *The Gift* features a few works of Asian and Western European art: "Persian miniatures...from the collection of the St. Petersburg Public Library—done, I think, by Riza Abbasi, say about three hundred years ago: that man kneeling, struggling with baby dragons, big-nosed, mustachioed—Stalin!" (G71). Nabokov might have seen the print in Kühnel's book, published some thirteen years earlier than *The Gift*, which shows a big-nosed shepherd with a heavy beard and moustache (*The Shepherd*) in a work by the Persian artist Riza-i'Abbasi (1587–1635).

Nabokov's mention of "'The Removal from the Cross'—by Rembrandt" (G215), clearly refers to Rembrandt van Rijn's (1620–69) canvas "The Descent from the Cross," dated 1633 (Alte Pinakothek, Munich). On the other hand, as the authors of *Nabokov and the Art of Painting* explain, it is hard to establish the specific painting Nabokov had in mind in the following brief description: "On her knees in a cave, Mary Magdalene was praying before a skull and cross, and of course her face in the light of the lampad was very sweet" (G223). There are various versions of paintings of Mary Magdalene by Italian Guido Reni (1575–1642) and the French artist Georges de la Tour (1593–1652). Reni painted several Mary Magdalenes, in one of which (located at the Galleria Nazionale di Arte Antica di Palozzo Barberini, Roma) she is sitting in a grotto, with a skull and a cross but no lamp. Georges de la Tour painted a number of pictures of the repenting Magdalene. In one she is sitting with her hand resting on a skull, gazing at a wooden cross, her face illuminated by an oil lamp. One version, *Magdalena with the Nightlight*, is in the Louvre and another, *Magdalena in a Flickering Light*, is exhibited at the Los Angeles County Art Museum (Vries and Johnson 170).

Hide Romanov—Seek Tchelitchew

Gerard de Vries, Donald B. Johnson, and Gavriel Shapiro, in their fine studies of art in Nabokov's writings, mostly deal with the historical artists and their authentic works, but there are quite a few invented artists and masked styles in his prose that require special attention as well. The artist Vsevolod Romanov presents quite a peculiar case to readers of *The Gift* for two reasons: the descriptions of his paintings look tantalizingly palpable, but no plausible prototypes for these have been identified so far. What is more, the compositional principles of Romanov's pictures are strikingly reminiscent of Nabokov's own devices, as articulated in the famous last sentence of *Speak, Memory* referring to a puzzle ("Find what the sailor has hidden"; 310). And although the very worldview of Romanov conflicts with Fyodor's aesthetic choices, one cannot deny that the artist possesses a *gift*—something that gives him a paradoxical kinship with the protagonist:

> "Countess d'X, stark naked with corset marks on her stomach, holding her own self diminished to one-third life-size..."

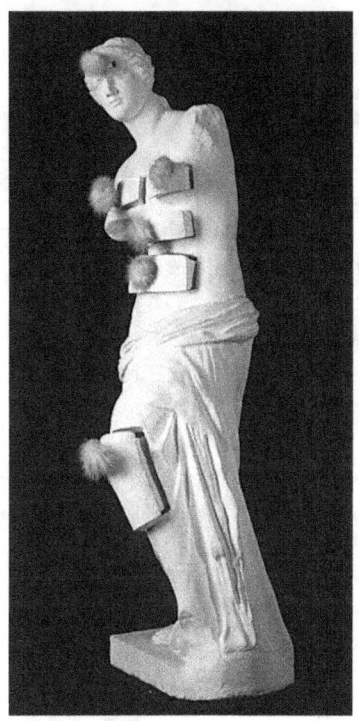

[Ill. 3-9] Salvador Dalí. *Venus de Milo with Drawers* (1936).
Original plaster of 1936 with metal knobs on the drawers and white fur tuft covers. 98 × 32.5 × 34 cm. Private collection

[Ill. 3-10] René Magritte. *Dangerous Liaisons* (1926).
Oil on canvas. Private collection

> This Romanov was of quite a different cut. Lorentz developed a sullen attachment to him, but since the day of Romanov's first exhibition (in which he showed his portrait of Countess d'X, stark naked with corset marks on her stomach, holding her own self diminished to one-third life-size) had considered him a madman and a swindler. Many, however, were captivated by the young artist's bold and original gift; extraordinary successes were predicted for him and some even saw in him the originator of a neonaturalist school: after passing through all the trials of so-called modernism, he was said to have arrived at a renovated, interesting and somewhat cold narrative art. (G58)

It is Romanov who invites Fyodor to a party where there is to be a young woman whom he has never met by the name of Zina Mertz. Naturally, Fyodor declines the invitation, but the odd link between the false Muse and Fyodor's true future Muse should not be overlooked. The English word "gift" and the German noun "Gift" (poison) have the common Germanic ancestor "geban" = "to give"; the homophone word for "to poison" used to be "vergeben." Romanov's "venomous" gift is deeply ambiguous, very much like that of the writer Ferdinand in Nabokov's short story "Spring in Fialta" (1936). Notably, Romanov's last name contains the Russian root *"roman,"* meaning a "novel," making its bearer a kind of a counterpart to Fyodor's endeavors, but in the realm of visual arts.

Simon Karlinsky, it seems, was correct in his early comment regarding the origins of Romanov, although this hypothesis has not been developed further. Karlinsky asserted that Nabokov enjoys devising and describing imaginary paintings which he then ascribes to his fictional painters in the same way as Thomas Mann devised and described the musical compositions of his hero in *Doctor Faustus*. The personality and the artistic development of the painter Vsevolod Romanov in *The Gift*, Karlinsky suggests, may contain a few remote references to the career of Nabokov's fellow émigré, Pavel Tchelitchew. It is also true that Romanov's paintings, as described in the novel, evoke the works of Henri Rousseau, Salvador Dalí, or René Magritte (the paintings in the stage directions and discussed in several of Magritte's speeches recall the work of Tchelitchew himself and so, incidentally, does the imaginary portrait of Sebastian Knight, with its reflecting pool and aquatic spider; Karlinsky 1967). Osbert Sitwell compares Tchelitchew's contribution to Western art with the impact of Russian literary expansionism in the nineteenth century, "when the first Russian novelists became engaged in the writing of the European novel": "He is, in fact, the first Russian painter of western power and originality, and counts, in the same way as does El Greco as a painter, or Dostoevsky as a novelist, as a European" (Sitwell 115).

After Karlinsky made his passing suggestion public, Alfred Appel asked Nabokov in a 1970 interview: "What of Tchelitchew, whose 'Hide and Seek'... in part describes the experience of reading one of your novels?" Nabokov's short, categorical answer is remarkable in that, for anyone who knows the master's habits, it only invites further inquiry: "I know Tchelitchew's work very little" (*Strong Opinions* 171).

Tchelitchew's life and artistic success in the West, nevertheless, resemble that of Nabokov himself (including the frequent accusations by émigré critics that Nabokov's prose exemplifies a "cold narrative art"). The son of a Russian landowner who lost everything in the 1917 Bolshevik Revolution, Pavel Tchelitchew (1898–1957) first gained artistic recognition in Berlin, where he developed a predilection for outrageous blues and pinks. Gertrude Stein noticed Tchelitchew's entry in the 1925 Salon D'Automne, *Basket of Strawberries* (1925), and bought the entire contents of his studio. In addition to becoming an accomplished painter, Tchelitchew also turned out to be one of the most innovative stage designers of the period: he designed sets for Rimsky-Korsakov's *The Wedding Feast of the Boyar* (1922) and met Sergei Diaghilev, director of Paris's *Ballets Russes*. The painter then settled in Paris, where he joined the circle of Gertrude Stein, who hailed him as the next Picasso (see Tyler for a more detailed account of Tchelitchew's biography).

Let us examine Nabokov's statement from the Appel interview a little more closely. In fact, he does not deny being familiar with Tchelitchew at all, admitting rather that his knowledge of Tchelitchew's art was limited ("very little"). Nabokov learned of Tchelitchew's works in Berlin and Paris, and most probably met him in person when he collaborated with the *Bluebird*, the famous Russian cabaret in Berlin (Brian Boyd does not claim that Nabokov and Tchelitchew crossed paths, but he does mention that both worked for the same theater in late 1923 and early 1924; *Russian Years* 227). Nabokov may also have kept track of the painter's work through his cousin, the composer Nicolas. Along with Diaghilev, the latter had closely collaborated with the émigré artist on the French production of his ballet, *Ode*, during 1928. Tchelitchew was responsible for the stage decorations (N. Nabokov, *Bagázh* 188-94). Besides this, Tchelitchew's paintings were frequently exhibited in Europe (Galerie Flechtcheim, Berlin, 1923; Galerie Henri, 1924; Salon d'Automne, 1925; Neo-Romantics, Galerie Druet, 1926, all three held in Paris).

It is hard to know whether Fyodor's creator was aware of the artist's patronymic ("Fyodorovich," meaning "son of Fyodor"), but his strange last name, Tchelitchew, (pronounced "Che'-lee-shchef"), must certainly have caught Nabokov's refined ear and drawn his attention. In fact, it is pretty close to the parameters that the author of *The Gift* had outlined for himself while looking for the second part of Fyodor Godunov's last name: it had to be made up of three syllables and to contain at least one hissing sound!

Tchelitchew left Russia in 1920 and moved to Paris in 1923, at which point his style changed dramatically, moving away from Constructivist and Cubo-

Futurist influences to his familiar representational works involving symbolic eggs, constellations, and so on, and from there to figures, such as in *The Juggler* (1931). In Paris he became the ideological leader of a group of artists practicing what was known in France as Néo-Humanisme (compare this with "the originator of a neonaturalist school" in *The Gift*); these artists "specialized in dream-like landscapes and figures in somber, usually blue, tonalities" (Prokopoff). Here is how Nabokov describes the early stages of Romanov's development as an artist:

> In his early works a certain trace of the cartoonist's style was still evident—for example, in that thing of his called "Coincidence," where, on an advertising post, among the vivid, remarkably harmonious colors of playbills, astral names of cinemas and other transparent motley, one could read a notice about a lost diamond necklace (with a reward to the finder), which necklace lay right there on the sidewalk, at the very foot of the post, its innocent fire sparkling. (G58)

While this plot point bears some resemblance to Maupassant's short story, "The Necklace" (1881), it is Tchelitchew's method of concealing images within images that is central here. Quite typical for Tchelitchew's works, this approach can be traced back to the late 1920s, when in his appealing landscapes (blue hills, autumnal foliage, streaming clouds) a leafless tree may, for instance, render up a figure standing with its back to us, its contours coinciding with those of the tree limbs; clouds become hair and distant cliffs in the sea can actually form heads with faces, as in his set for Balanchine's ballet, *Apollon Musagète* (1928).

[Ill. 3-11] Pavel Tchelitchew. The set design for ballet *Apollon Musagète* (1928)

The process of discovering a hidden image turns observers of Tchelitchew's pictures into the players in a challenging game. The "hide and seek" principle is also Romanov's core artistic device as described by Nabokov. Of course, it would be difficult to match any specific works by Tchelitchew with those ascribed to a fictional artist, but distant echoes and clear parallels in methods are evident: "In [Romanov's] 'Autumn,' though, the black tailor's dummy with its ripped side, dumped in a ditch among magnificent maple leaves, was already expressiveness of a purer quality; connoisseurs found in it an abyss of sadness" (G58); compare this to Tchelitchew's "Autumn leaves" (1939; gouache, watercolor, pen and ink). What matters, most likely, is not an exact replication but the parallelism in principles of artistic composition.

Despite the fact that he moved to the United States in 1934, Tchelitchew continued to spend his summers in Europe until the outbreak of the war. His artistic development at that time was marked by metamorphic works, followed by 'interior landscapes' of the human body and finally by stellar compositions. Tchelitchew sought to define an imagery of the soul's journey to immortality. A visitor to Tchelitchew's studio in 1937 described a huge canvas: "Small in the center was the face of an old woman, a tormented, wrinkled face—as if under a lens; above that a tennis court with naked figures on it below a glacier prospect made of ice-heads, infants packed in as though they were rounded ice cubes in a modern refrigerator... Siamese twins, women with six breasts, acephalic monsters, three-legged children, double-headed monsters, sexual freaks, dwarfs, giants, achondroplastic midgets, Mongolian idiots and the starved, bloated, misshapen by idea and social accident—of all the walks of life" (Williams 398). This work is usually characterized as an offshoot of Surrealism, but was also greatly indebted to Russian Symbolist painting from the turn of the century. Tchelitchew never abandoned his fondness for "the macabre Romanticism in the style of Mikhail Vrubel" (Alley 716). Incidentally, *The Gift* also features a fictional painter, Vrublyov (G39), a hybrid of Vrubel and Rublyov. The best-known Russian icon painter, Andrei Rublyov (1360?–1430), used a palette of pure and bright colors. Vrubel (1856–1910), one of the major artists in the Russian Art Nouveau movement, went mad towards the end of his life because he failed to convey his imagery on canvas, which was simply too limited for his richly apocalyptic visions.

The description above of a work in progress most certainly refers to Tchelitchew's *Phenomena* (1936–38). Basing his model of Hell, Purgatory and Paradise on the cosmic vision of Renaissance Neo-Platonists, Tchelitchew developed a complex iconography in a lengthy sequence of allegorical pictures, left unfinished at the time of his death. As preparation for the first element of his allegory, Hell, Tchelitchew completed several series of paintings containing sleeping figures, figures composed of found objects, freaks, bullfights and tennis

[Ill. 3-12] Pavel Tchelitchew. *Phenomena* (1936–38). Moscow, Tret'yakov Gallery

[Ill. 3-13] Pavel Tchelitchew. *Hide-and-Seek* (1940–42). Oil on canvas. Mrs. Simon Guggenheim Fund. The Museum of Modern Art, New York

matches. As in the narrative of *The Gift*, Tchelitchew embeds himself into the picture: the artist appears in this desperate environment of a modern Hell in the role of a trapped visitor (Prokopoff). Also featuring lesbian Gertrude Stein and nude male figures, the canvas aroused violent reactions on the part of reviewers. Tchelitchew himself was a homosexual; what is more, according to one source, Nabokov's own brother, Sergei, who perished in the Nazi concentration camp, at one time allegedly belonged to the Tchelitchew gay community in Paris (Sternweiler 189).

The Gift had already been completed when Tchelitchew painted the large composition for which he is best known, *Hide and Seek* (1940-42; New York, MOMA), although numerous studies for this large painting are dated by the late 1930s. In this treatment of Purgatory, Tchelitchew related nature to procreation and growth, showing plant and human forms to be similar in their physical structures and purposes: "One child's face resolves at closer inspection into mushrooms, dandelions, dew into vine tendrils, and these in turn can be identified as veins and arteries, tissues and muscles, and down among these are elfin children still. Organizing all this we can make out a cycle of the seasons, the ages of man, sexual organs human and vegetable, life as a game and biological process, a lyric and informed affirmation of the synthesis of flesh and spirit, and a network of allusions concerning the Tree of Life, innocence and vitality, natural design, fate" (Davenport 260). The idea for the painting seems to have germinated from some studies of an ancient tree in Sussex made as early as in 1934, a tree in which the painter saw a likeness to a large, gnarled, open hand, with its fingers about to close into a grasp; its root system looked to him like a foot. Romanov's painting also has a tree at its center:

> But his best work to date remained one that had been acquired by a discerning tycoon and had already been extensively reproduced, called "Four Citizens Catching a Canary"; all four were in black, broad-shouldered, tophatted (although for some reason one of them was barefoot), and placed in odd, exultant and at the same time wary poses beneath the strikingly sunny foliage of a squarely trimmed linden tree in which hid the bird, perhaps the one that had escaped from my shoemaker's cage. I was obscurely thrilled by Romanov's strange, beautiful, yet venomous art; I perceived in it both a forestalling and a forewarning: having far outdistanced my own art, it simultaneously illuminated for it the dangers of the way. As for the man himself, I found him boring to the point of revulsion. (G59)

Even if Tchelitchew, the "only living painter who can rival Picasso, [who] continually experiments and passes on to new modes of expression" (Sitwell 115), did serve as a partial inspiration for the image of Romanov, it is more plausible that the descriptions of his works in *The Gift* represent a mosaic of many paintings typical for the European Expressionist movement that was fashionable during the early decades of the twentieth century. Gavriel Shapiro suggests

Chapter Three. STRUCTURE

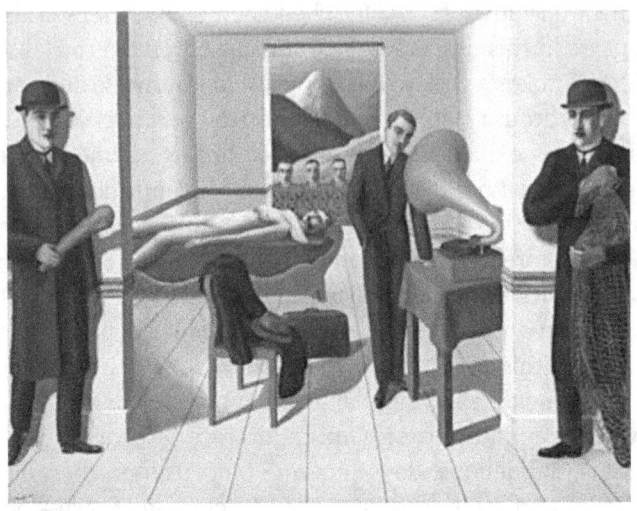

[Ill. 3-14] "All four were in black, broad-shouldered, tophatted..."
René Magritte. *The Menaced Assassin* (1927).
Oil on canvas. Museum of Modern Art, New York

[Ill. 3-15] "the bird, perhaps the one that had escaped from my shoemaker's cage"
René Magritte. *Elective Affinities* (1933).
Oil on canvas. Private collection

that Nabokov became more familiar with German Expressionist art after his emigration to Western Europe, and later when he settled in the German capital after graduation. Nabokov could certainly have seen a great deal of this art in German periodicals such as *Der Sturm* (1910-32), which reproduced many works of German Expressionism along with those of Russian-born painters—Marc Chagall, Natalia Goncharova, and Vasily Kandinsky (Shapiro 166). Although the writer nowhere directly voiced an opinion on German Expressionist art, Shapiro believes that Nabokov must have had an aversion to its perception of the world because of the focus on the sociopolitical; on the contrary, the aesthete Nabokov claims that a real work of art carries no "message" and "has no importance whatever to society" (*Strong Opinions* 33).

Nonetheless, as with Tchelitchew and his use of certain attractive compositional techniques, Nabokov and Expressionists had shared interests in the depiction of such subjects as urban life, sports, crime, prostitution, mannequins, war cripples, and resorts. German painters such as George Grosz, along with their Soviet counterparts (Alexander Deineka, Alexander Samokhvalov, and others), occasionally politicized sports and saw in them a means for creating a "new man." Regardless of their ideological affiliation, as Gavriel Shapiro remarks, the painters who depicted athletic activities by and large appear to have been captivated by the dynamism of sports' fierce physical encounters and by the competitive spirit of the events. This is evident in Henri Rousseau's *The Football Players* (1908), Max Beckmann's *Football Players* (1929) (Shapiro 169), Alexander Deineka's *Football* (1924; there was a sketch for the Soviet journal *Krasnaia Niva* under the same title in 1927), and others.

Soccer, hockey, and boxing, along with tennis, were among Nabokov's favorites too. It is likely no coincidence that the last Romanov canvas mentioned in the novel is also devoted to soccer:

You know his "Footballer"? There's a reproduction in this magazine, here it is. The pale, sweaty, tensely distorted face of a player depicted from top to toe preparing at full speed to shoot with terrible force at the goal. (G181)

As an artist Tchelitchew was fascinated by the vitality of sports, and the quotation above can easily be applied to his painting *Boxers* (1925). Even more fascinating is that the reverse side of the canvas, akin to a *Matryoshka* or a box-within-a-box composition, has a faceless self-portrait of an artist holding a frame, thus making the entire construct a triple frame within a frame within a picture. Since childhood, boxing was a hobby of Nabokov's. He sang its praises in his early poetry and prose (especially in *Glory*), and once even reported on a match between professional boxers, Breitensträter and Paolino, in December 1925 (published in the newspaper *Slovo*; reprinted in *Sobranie sochinenii* I: 749-54).

According to Nabokov, "every creator is a plotter; and all the pieces impersonating his ideas on the board were here as conspirators and sorcerers. Only in the final instant was their secret spectacularly revealed" (G172). A possible parallel to Nabokov's and Andrey Bely's metaphysical aesthetics of deception in art is found in this passage from *Zapiski chudaka* (*Notes of an Eccentric*): "Thus every novel is *a game of hide and seek* with the reader; and the aim of the architectonics, the phrase is exclusively—to lead the reader's eye away from the sacred point, the birth of myth" (Vol. 1, 63; italics added). The praxis of both writers is to conceal or complicate that which is most important (Alexandrov, "Nabokov and Bely" 362). Interestingly, Guy Davenport, who could not stand Nabokov but adored Tchelitchew, juxtaposed the writer and the artist in the same breath: "Like Nabokov,

Chapter Three. STRUCTURE

[Ill. 3-16] Henri Rousseau. *The Football Players* (1908), Solomon R. Guggenheim Museum, New York

[Ill. 3-17] Alexander Deineka. *Football* (1924)

[Ill. 3-19] Pavel Tchelitchew. "Boxers" (recto); "Study of Artist" (verso), 1925 Gouache on paper (32.3 × 23.8 cm)

[Ill. 3-18] Max Beckmann. *Football Players* (1929)

and Stravinsky, and Chagall, [Tchelitchew] took with him into his lifetime's exile a Russian childhood that became mythological over the years and served him as the Greek and Roman myths served Ovid in his exile in the Caucasus" (Davenport 323).

Structure

Novel as an Elegant Colonnade

Nabokov praised the structure of Pushkin's *Eugene Onegin* as a "model of unity" (*Onegin*, I: 16). He compared its eight chapters to an elegant colonnade, showing how they are linked by a system of subthemes responding to each other "in a pleasing interplay of built-in echoes" (Ibid.). The same definition can be applied to Nabokov's own novel: *The Gift* is divided into chapters of almost equal length (the entire corpus of the Russian original counts for 105,630 words; English text amounts to 145,400). With the exception of a part of Chapter Two and all of Chapter Four, the *fabula* unfolds within a precise period of time and is set in the same location. All actions are motivated by Fyodor's physical movements within the topographical space of Berlin while his spiritual rambling reflects his evolution as a maturing artist. As the detailed schematics have outlined earlier, all five chapters of *The Gift* consist of a comparable number of plot units, or "thematic movements" (they fluctuate from 9 to 11 in each chapter).

The poems devoted to Zina (composed by Fyodor in Chapter Three) or the broken sonnet ringing Chapter Four anticipate the greater structure of *The Gift* itself, which "depends on the same effect of commemorative distance" (Foster 152). Many readers wonder whether the book we are reading is, in fact, a fictional autobiography written by an older Fyodor (who adds the crucial proviso that it will take "a long time preparing it, years perhaps"; G364), but there is no evidence that such a book, after all, has been written or that *The Gift is* such a book. To continue the architectonic metaphor, the variety of possibilities takes scholars into an infinite enfilade of crossing corridors.

Novel as a Bach Fugue

A comparison from the realm of music seems almost as apt as that from the world of architecture. Simon Karlinsky in his groundbreaking 1963 analysis compares the structure of *The Gift* with "a complex double fugue" (285). He describes the novel as a structure based on symmetry and recapitulation (the loss of a key in Chapters One and Five, an imaginary conversation with the poet Koncheyev in the same chapters, the research for the Chernyshevski biography preceding Chapter Four and a review of the book following).

Chapter Three. STRUCTURE

Karlinsky breaks the action in *The Gift* into three interconnected levels: the basic level of the hero's daily life, his peregrinations through the streets and parks of Berlin, his relationships with fellow exiles, landlords, and the editor of the local émigré newspaper and his alienation from the local German populace, which is usually represented as a grotesque mob. The daily experiences of the hero provide the fundamental layer of the narrative, which is related to two subordinate themes: the hero's love affair with Zina and his friendship with an elderly intellectual Russian couple (the Chernyshevskis). Like in a fugue, the principal theme and the two subordinate ones have their "mirror inversions in the form of retrospective openings into the past, showing events occurring prior to the action of the novel" (Karlinsky 285). Observing his or her own past, each major character in the novel experiences an epiphany: for Godunov-Cherdyntsev the retrospective sections embrace his pre-revolutionary childhood and the travels of his father; Zina's flashbacks deal with her mother's past and with her own experiences as a typist in a depressing Berlin law office; for the Chernyshevskis, there is an account of the suicide of their son, Yasha, etc. (Ibid.).

The material in these first two planes of the novel is arranged symmetrically. "The Life of Chernyshevski" serves as the center which separates events and episodes from their mirror-image counterparts. It is framed by the author-protagonist's research and by a series of critical reviews. Fyodor's first imaginary meeting with the poet Koncheyev in Chapter One is counterbalanced by the second imaginary conversation in Chapter Five. All this leads Karlinsky to draw a natural comparison of the structure based on equilibrium and repetition of motifs to a musical composition. For Karlinsky it is a "measure of Nabokov's skill that the carefully concealed artifice of his form is made an occasion for art and that it can...be as much a source of intellectual pleasure as a Bach fugue" (Ibid. 286).

Equally reminiscent of musical technique, Karlinsky observes, is Nabokov's "method of imperceptibly introducing some of the principal themes and characters in the novel by oblique or casual references inserted long before their supposed appearance in the narrative" (Ibid.). Readers of Nabokov's novel more often than not fail to notice upon first reading that both Zina and Nikolai Chernyshevski appear quite early in the text, to say nothing of predicting their respective roles in the plot development. Similarly, Stephen Blackwell reflects on the reader-response process so typical for our comprehension of the novel:

> After a few readings, or after too much familiarity with Nabokov's works, it is easy to forget that *The Gift*'s plot is largely invisible in a first reading, that characters appear and disappear who seem purely incidental, that there is no obvious "problem," other than the lack of a problem, that unfolding events do not really relate to events gone by, as far as any of these textual moments can be called events at all; as Georgii Adamovich observed in a tepid review, "Sirin's *Gift* drags on, and through a reader's crystal, not a magic one, it is still unclear

where it is heading, and why." In brief, the novel resists a particular pattern of communication that assumes the quickest, most efficient passage of ideas from teller to listener (the "message" is stated and emphasized not in "plain language" but through rhetorical and stylistic devices). (Blackwell 61)

Normative readers face a common set of challenges in the obscured novel; according to Blackwell, they should: 1) identify a narrative perspective (first or third person, omniscient or limited, "subjective" or "objective" recounting); 2) grasp a plot, or a problem to be solved or thought about; 3) keep in perspective a location; 4) categorize main and minor characters (note: the loop patterns only complicate the task: *Alexander Yakovlevich—Alexandra Yakovlevna—Yakov Alexandrovich*); 5) relate unfolding events, new characters and preceding descriptions. What is more, "some ideas in *The Gift* do not withstand direct representation or translation into language: they must be hinted at or acted out, but they do not conform to precise...words" (Ibid. 61).

Novel as a Chess Problem

Fyodor, like Nabokov himself, is passionately interested in the game of chess and even more so—in composing chess problems. Likewise, the historical Chernyshevski is supposed to have shared this hobby. Although an obvious motif in the case of the author of *The Defense* (Nabokov's 1930 novel entirely devoted to the game), chess in *The Gift* might be something more than a passing topic—it constitutes a structural pattern. Donald B. Johnson aptly notes that in a classical chess problem "the solver's initial effort is directed toward finding the uniquely possible opening move for White that will force mate on Black in a specified number of moves. This critical opening play, ascertainable by the determination of the *theme* of the problem, is called the 'key' move or, more often, simply the 'key'" (102).

When Fyodor plans the plot of the novel, which in its imagined shape would presumably be nearly identical to that of *The Gift*, it strikes the reader as another foray into the art of composing chess problems using the lexicon and concepts of chess strategy. As Johnson notes, the critical act in the solution of a chess problem lies in finding the unique "key," and "this is precisely the process which Fyodor is going through in retrospectively seeking out the moves in his life which will provide the structural turning points in the plotting of his projected novel. As in solving a chess problem Fyodor attempts and rejects two of the false tries proffered by fate, the composer of the problem, before finally hitting upon the uniquely possible key which will produce mate and win Zina" (Ibid. 104; noteworthy is that the first structurally important chess allusion comes at a juncture in the plot arising from Fyodor and Zina's growing impatience to be alone).

The evolution of Fyodor's relationship with Zina, however, is not the only aspect of his life that is structured in terms of a chess problem; the development of his literary gift proceeds along the same lines. Johnson believes that, as a consequence, the "key" motif pattern "involves a contextual shift to the world of chess" and serves as "the basis for fate's plotting of the biographical moves which in turn provide the raw material for the plotting of *The Gift* itself" (Ibid. 106). The ending of the novel, an integral element in a chess problem, "entails the mating of Zina and the composition of *The Gift*, which is Fyodor's gift to Russian literature" (Ibid.). In a biography published after Johnson's study, Brian Boyd presents data corroborating these findings: Nabokov was intensely engaged in composing chess problems as he was completing his work on *The Gift* (Boyd, *Russian Years* 515). No wonder the writer repeatedly insisted on an analogy between the inspiration, composition, and design of *chess problems*—not chess games—and the inspiration, composition, and design of the novels (Gezari 47).

Novel with Nesting Dolls

Fyodor's text and that of the author are virtually indistinguishable in *The Gift*. To describe the prototypical Nabokovian fictional narrative, Sergei Davydov posits this complete merging of hero and author as the *"text-matreshka"* (Davydov "*Teksty-matreški*"). The analogy is based on the popular Russian stylized dolls that pull apart to reveal smaller versions of a similar brightly painted woman figure: Nabokov's text represents the outer doll while the inner text of the fictional hero corresponds to the inner doll, or dolls, of the *matreshka*. This textual form is consistent throughout Nabokov's career, although Davydov acknowledges that this structure involving a central character's narrative joined by intricate connections to a controlling authorial text has a literary pedigree dating back to Homer. Although the so-called "text-matreshka" principle may appear to be a rather banal and mechanical image to account for the complexity of viewpoints in Nabokov's prose fiction, Davydov's analysis "goes beyond the constriction of his own formulation and clearly shows that Nabokov does more than simply pull an ever repeated literary rabbit out of the same verbal top hat" (Katsell 495). How these "dolls" are interrelated is the question that we will try to approach next.

Novel as a Möbius Strip

The Gift closes with a striking structural device: the protagonist-author Fyodor conceives the idea of writing a "classical" autobiographical novel, the art of which is to resemble the work of destiny in his life; the novel he plans to write appears, in fact, to be the very novel (or close to it) of which he has been the protagonist. Much attention has been paid to this final twist. The structure of the novel has been compared to a circle, a Möbius strip, or a spiral. Omry and Irena Ronen were among the first to use the Möbius strip image as a way of metaphoric description of the novel's structure (Ronen 1981).

Novel in a "Figure-Eight Pattern"

Similar to the motif of the Möbius strip is that of the "miracle of the lemniscate" mentioned in *Pale Fire*. It seems as though Nabokov himself was keen to draw certain parallels between the two novels as he specifically told an interviewer: "I devoted as much honest labor to the task of gathering the material for the Chernyshevski chapter as I did to the composing of Shade's poem in *Pale Fire*" (*Strong Opinions* 65). According to Leona Toker, the *lemniscate*, a figure eight on its side, the mathematical symbol of infinity, could serve as a two-dimensional graphical symbol of the shape proposed by Omry and Irena Ronen (Toker 159). In *The Gift*, as in *Pale Fire*, it is traced by the tire of a bicycle. Fyodor's early poem about learning to ride a bicycle mentions the "wavers and weavers" in an alley (G26). The same lemniscate shape recurs at the end of the evening at the Chernyshevskis' (the departure of the tired guests is depicted as the waning of their faces in one's memory—"their outlines, weaving in figure-eight patterns, were evaporating"; G52).

The number eight soon reappears in a seemingly unrelated context: Fyodor buys himself a pair of shoes after the salesgirl brings him an *eighth* pair to try on (G64). The X-ray view of his foot in the shoe store gives him an impulse to start composing a poem about stepping ashore ("with this": that is, with his skeleton foot) from Charon's ferry (G64). The river, he notes, "is not the Lethe but rather the Styx" (G75): eternity can be free from oblivion, therefore, this "wish to arrest the infinite within the finite is also obvious in one of the main structural peculiarities of the novel: namely, the subversion of the ending" (Toker 159-60). As convincing as this simplified two-dimensional projection of the Möbius strip seems Toker herself doubts that it can offer an exhaustive interpretation of Nabokov's work. Primarily, the text itself does not quite support this analogy because:

> the novel that Fyodor is going to write will not contain an exact account of his experience as recounted in the master text. And if what we have just read is in fact Fyodor's novel, then the experience it describes has already been 'shuffled, twisted, and mixed' (G364). In other words, not only does the story of *The Gift* differ from the supposed 'real' experience of the narrator, but the novel that the narrator is planning to write must also differ from his experience. And if in the end the hero of that projected novel likewise decides to write a novel, it will likewise have shuffled, twisted, and mixed the loop that preceded it. (Toker 161)

Another figure representing this emerging relationship is that of a *receding spiral*. Such a spiral, Leona Toker suggests, may continue ad infinitum; it may be "imagined as a wedge that is stuck through the familiar material universe" wherein one, upon passing the twist of a Möbius strip, "repeats one's previous trajectory yet has, in fact, a new experience because the path is a continuation rather than a repetition of the surface covered before" (Ibid.). The repetitive nature of the spiral echoes the basic quality of Nabokov's art as noted by Clarence Brown: "This writer—one of the most Protean and entertaining masters of modern prose—is extremely repetitious" (Brown 285). Nabokov, Brown says, has been writing in book after book about the same thing; in *The Defense, The Eye, The Real Life of Sebastian Knight, Pale Fire,* and, of course, *The Gift*, Nabokov is offering his readership a remarkable consistency and unvarying unity.

On the other hand, all poets have their favorite themes and images, and even their favorite words. These recurrent themes and images form inner cycles in the work of a given writer, cycles which very often cannot be placed within exact chronological limits. Such recurrent themes and images may be characteristic of several poets, often independent of both the so-called poetic schools and even of historical periods (Taranovsky 6). Brown projects this "almost monomaniacal persistence" onto Nabokov's four-volume translation of and commentary on Pushkin's great novel in verse, *Eugene Onegin*. The relationship between Nabokov's translation of *Eugene Onegin* and his commentary on it recalls the relationship we have seen in other cases. The translation itself does not seem sufficient cause for the commentary. Pushkin's original masterpiece is "superior to all conceivable commentaries upon it, including Nabokov's, [but] Nabokov's translation of it is not" (Brown 291). The interpolated poetry of Godunov-Cherdyntsev is quite flat in *The Gift*, and in this respect it is in need of special elucidation. In the same manner, Godunov-Cherdyntsev's long embedded work, "The Life of Chernyshevski," is followed by the reviews of it, and these then constitute in effect a kind of commentary upon it, but since most of the émigré critics are "densely incapable" of understanding the opus, their responses result in a *parody of a commentary* (and here John Shade's long poem in *Pale Fire* comes to mind again) (Ibid. 290). Clarence Brown concludes that in every case the *included poem*, the base or source work, in this peculiarly Nabokovian structure is inferior to the commentary. But whatever the hierarchy is, the relationship between the elements of the narrative construct will be presented as a progression of plot advancing in a cyclical way.

Novel as an Apple Peel

Based on Fyodor's conception of the Chernyshevski biography as "a single uninterrupted progression of thought [which Fyodor] must peel [like an] apple in a single strip" (G200), Leonid Livak introduces yet another metaphorical description of the novel's structure, in the same category as the "Möbius strip" and "lemniscate." At first it seems that the circular structure of Fyodor's quasi-biography, which opens with the two tercets and closes with the two quatrains of a sonnet, encouraging readers to return to its beginning, is in keeping with Fyodor's artistic intent. But this is not quite what he longs for, asserts Livak: "Instead of following the never-ending spiral of an apple peel, the story is delimited by its closed circularity and is therefore finite, only caricaturing Fyodor's ideal of narrative infinity. This camouflaged compositional discrepancy is mirrored in the deceptive similarity of Fyodor's and Chernyshevski's quests. Chernyshevski dreams of a *perpetuum mobile*—utilitarian 'infinity with a minus sign' (G218), which distorts and caricatures Fyodor's idea of infinity as otherworldly transcendence" (Livak 174). The scholar believes that Fyodor/Nabokov borrows this conception from Gide's novel *The Counterfeiters*, along with the devices that help realize it (a sonnet as a marker of infinity haunts the work, whose narrator sees his own novel as a sonnet). However, in the context of Gide's work, the conception of Chernyshevski's story as a spiral apple peel and its realization as a circle appears to be a trap for the reader. Misled by the distorting mirror relationship of the text which incorporates and that which is icorporated, as Livak explains, one projects the circular narrative of the story upon *The Gift*, which also ends with a poem that suggests narrative infinity (Ibid. 176).

A Way out of the Spiral

This series of structural models offered for cracking the code of *The Gift* reflects the readers' desire to capture the infiniteness of circular motion without the finiteness or at least the essential limitedness implied by the repetition of circular motion. Sarah Tiffany Waite proposes yet another concept to encompass the novel's complicated structure: "When we consider, instead of the progression of chapters in *The Gift*, the progression of the hero's physical movements, literary accomplishments, and changes in artistic perspective, there emerges a tripartite linear structure which may provide 'a way out' of the circular structure" (Waite 55). According to Waite, "neither the structure of the 'double fugue' revolving around Fyodor's biography nor the structure of attempted biographies culminating in 'The Life of Chernyshevski' is the most comprehensive in *The Gift*. *The Gift* is a novel incorporating structures within structures, and perhaps even structures overlying or overlapping structures" (Ibid. 59). Her argument can be outlined as follows: the progressive tripartite structure (as opposed to a repetitive circular structure) indicated in the novel by reference to three different completed literary works on three different time planes is emphasized by accompanying patterns of three. As Fyodor's works increase in size and scope, their presentation becomes increasingly self-contained; whereas the poems are stirred into another narrative, and the biography is compartmentalized within another narrative, the novel is the narrative, encompassing all, free from intrusions or even contiguous distractions. The genres of Fyodor's three *completed* literary works (the first is his *Poems*, the second is his "The Life of Chernyshevski," and the third his novel *Dar*) are "entirely different and reflect both the Russian literary history to which he is heir and his steady growth as an artist in his own right" (Ibid. 60). Therefore, with his *Poems* and the biography of Chernyshevski, Godunov-Cherdyntsev progresses through his own artistic "ages" toward the modernism of *The Gift*.

Novel about an Artist's Growth to Maturity

The Gift is also a *Künstlerroman* covering three years of Fyodor's aesthetic education (albeit scarcely a traditional one from the structural point of view; Johnson 94). Moreover, Fyodor's own development as an artist loosely parallels the path of the history of Russian literature in the nineteenth century. Sergei Davydov charts a very convincing route for the basic moves in Fyodor's development as they correspond to the historical evolution of modern Russian literature. Chapter One, which covers the years of Fyodor's poetic apprenticeship and contains his juvenile verse, corresponds to the Golden Age of Russian poetry (the early 1820s); Chapter Two may be called Fyodor's "Pushkin period," during which he performs a transition from poetry to prose (following Pushkin's similar progress in the 1830s), with *Journey to Arzrum* serving as inspiration for his imaginary exotic journey to Central Asia. At the end of the chapter, Fyodor informs readers that the distance from his old residence in Chapter Two to the new one in Chapter Three "was about the same as, somewhere in Russia, that from Pushkin Avenue to Gogol Street" (G143). Chapter Three brings us to the 1840s, Fyodor's "Gogol period." Reading *Dead Souls*, Davydov observes, is a perfect exercise in detecting *poshlust* (Nabokov's attempt at a semantically meaningful transliteration of the Russian word *poshlost'*"), while Gogol's art of the grotesque sets a stylistic example of how *poshlust* should be mocked. Fyodor applies this new skill in his biography of Chernyshevski in Chapter Four, where he reenacts the literary polemics of the 1860s. Chapter Five is a recapitulation of all the previous motifs, leading to the eternal themes, death, religion, and immortality (Davydov, "Nabokov's Aesthetic Exorcism" 359).

David Bethea attempts to demonstrate that Nabokov challenges us to understand *The Gift* as both "open" and "closed" in structure, resembling an optical illusion *a la* Escher, modeling space as "outside" and "inside" at the same time (memetics). Bethea questions the spirals and spheres that imbed themselves in Nabokov's speculations "about sudden bursts of creativity and the very structure of *The Gift*, with its blurring and out of the 'I' and 'he' narrators and its tying-up of the plot by an Onegin stanza, itself a pseudo-genetic map for creating infinite meanings out of a single string (rhyme scheme)" (Bethea 139). In search of the most apt image to describe Nabokov's novelistic structure, Bethea resorts to an ancient deep-seated psychic trace, the visual reproduction of the double helix of chemically paired on-off switches whose codes and mappings cannot transcend themselves, but stops short of a conclusive statement, remarking: or "is it some time-in-a-bottle encapsulation of the two?" (Ibid.).

THEMES

Recurrent Motifs

The Gift serves as a focal point for many of Nabokov's leitmotifs that we recognize from his other writings. Simon Karlinsky recapitulates some of the most basic ones: butterflies, chess, European literatures, *audition colorée*, distant expeditions, and, of course, the solitary, creative individual facing a repulsive, conformist mob (Karlinsky 289). It is hard to call *The Gift* a gateway for a novice into the writer's oeuvre, but for an experienced Nabokophile this last of his Russian novels presents, in a sense, an *Encyclopaedia Nabokoviana*. Among Nabokov's later novels written in English, the one that has the closest ties with *The Gift* is *Pale Fire* (1962). The similarities, according to Karlinsky, include "the use of literary commentary and research as a subject for fiction; the profusion of verse and its importance in both novels; and, oddest of all, the occasional echoes of Chernyshevski's patterns of thought in the mentality of the Communist-inspired assassin Gradus" (for a fine summary see Vries 35).

As always, Nabokov gives his faithful readers hints as to the principles for reading *The Gift* in the very text of the novel. Just as Fyodor focuses on the fateful patterning of his own life, he pays particular attention to identifying it in Chernyshevski's, and lists several recurring themes he has discovered—"writing exercises," "nearsightedness" and spectacles, "traveling," "angelic clarity," and Chernyshevski's Christ-like pose. Vladimir Alexandrov charts parallels in the fates of the two characters that ultimately carry metatextual significance as well: the discovery that the radical's father had once advised his son to write a light little "tale" ("skazochka"), and that years later Chernyshevski informed his wife that he wanted to compose a "good little tale," prompts Fyodor to note that this is "one of those rare correlations that constitute the researcher's pride" (G288). Elsewhere, Fyodor claims that "fate sorts" dates "in anticipation of the researcher's needs" (G220; Alexandrov, *Nabokov's Otherworld* 133).

To encompass all the motifs in *The Gift* would require a separate comprehensive study—a task that will remain for future Nabokov scholarship. Since this is beyond the scope of the present work, I will list only some of the topics and then highlight those few that are worthy of being considered "superconcepts." Some important steps have already been undertaken in the direction of consolidating the data. Nassim Berdjis's carefully compiled book examines the imagery in Nabokov's *The Gift* and his prose of the 1930s through the following themes: metamorphoses; language games; the development of artistic talent; the power of vision; art and nature; numbers; forms and ideology; and religion. The themes cover sets of anywhere from three to twelve topics, which are followed through Nabokov's works in chronological order (see Berdjis).

Other motifs, presented in alphabetical order, are as follows: advertisement; architecture; art; Asia; beginnings/endings/thresholds (doors, windows, exits, etc.); biology; butterflies; certainty/uncertainty; clarity/ambiguity; communication; crossings (i.e. intersections, past with present, streets/paths, with people, etc.); death; dreams; emigration; embedded literature (i.e. poems, letter from mother, father's biography/journal, "The Life of Chernyshevski," reviews or references to literary figures and their works); family (fatherhood/motherhood); games (chess, sports); homosexuality; keys; light/dark/shadows; literature (poetry, prose, memoir, biography, media, literary criticism); love (Zina, Mother, Father, Russia); madness; mathematics/geometry (circles/circularity/continuity); metatext, mimicry; mirrors; music; nature; puzzles; reality/truth, reflections, reflective surfaces (puddles/eyes/glasses); time; travel/journey/moving; opening/closing; philosophy; telephone, trade, transportation (automobile/tram/train). The catalog is still far from being exhaustive, but many of these motifs have already been studied separately.

Life, Art and Literature

Art for Fyodor is an escape from life's linearity. In the words of Brian Boyd, *The Gift* was Nabokov's "tribute to the whole Russian literary heritage, which he saw as oscillating between tribulation and triumph" (*Russian Years* 466). Nabokov praises the genius of writers like Pushkin, Gogol, Tolstoy, and Chekhov, challenges Chernyshevski's clumsy concepts of literary labor, and actively engages contemporary émigré and Soviet peers. The novel allowed Nabokov not only to pay tribute to the Russian literary tradition, but also "to exorcise its grim shadow of censorship" from the right and the left; it provided "a chance to expose the philosophical flaws of utilitarian materialism and to advance an alternative metaphysic; the gleeful debunking and its tragic notes...offset the celebratory tones of Fyodor's account of his father and his own" life in *The Gift* (Boyd, *Russian Years* 399).

For Nabokov the attitude of Russian critics and writers toward Pushkin was the litmus test of their intelligence and talent, and he applied these same standards to his fictional characters as well. Fyodor, Nabokov's most autobiographical creation, is a beginning poet on his way to becoming a major writer. As *The Gift* traces three years of Fyodor's aesthetic education, each of his artistic accomplishments is weighed on Pushkin's scales (Davydov, "Weighing Nabokov's *Gift* 417). The central pillar of Nabokov's universe in this novel is Pushkin and his legacy. Chapter Two, consisting of Fyodor's fictional reconstructions of his father's journeys, is written under Pushkin's stylistic influence—filled with exotic yet scientifically exact descriptions of the plants, butterflies, and landscapes encountered en route, it "form[s] one of Nabokov's most marvelous achievements in prose" (Moynahan, *Vladimir Nabokov* 38). The venerable tradition begins for Nabokov and his central character with Pushkin: this legacy is passed down through a select few poets and prose writers "whose social views, radical or conservative," are of no importance whatsoever—it is "a tradition and dialogue of artists constituting the supreme gift the Russian literary genius and language have to offer, a gift which Fyodor aspires to receive" (Ibid. 37).

The Gift presents the "odyssey of an émigré writer, who, not unlike Nabokov, migrates from poetry to prose" (Scherr 113). The work's final lines, though recorded as prose, accurately follow the meter and rhyme of the Onegin stanza (Pushkin's *Eugene Onegin* consists of fourteen-line stanzas with the rhyme scheme AAbccbDDeeFgFg): "The bulk of the poetry in the novel is ostensibly written by Fyodor, including some eighteen poems from his first collection of poetry, presented either in their entirety or in part" (Ibid.). This body of verse is sufficient for its own analysis, but whether these poems differ from the rest of Nabokov's verse in terms of their rhythm and overall structural qualities remains debatable. Like early Sirin's poetry, Fyodor's verses are devoted to his memories of childhood in Russia before the revolution. His commentary deals with the relationship between childhood experience, memories of youth, and the eventual reworking of memory in poetry. Fyodor asserts that his juvenile lyrics "may succeed in representing the unmediated, 'authentic' experience of childhood perceptions" (White 274), calling to mind a more generalized universal experience of a maturing artist.

A Parody of Literary Biography

Literary biography has always been a mixture of fact, fiction, and myth. As Michael Benton writes in his survey of the genre, the main feature of any literary biography is the combination of its concern to document facts with a strong narrative impulse (18). Dr. Johnson and James Boswell are usually seen as the fathers of modern literary biography, though their approaches to biography were sharply different:

Chapter Three. STRUCTURE

> Johnson's style was to assimilate what information he could find about his subjects, to order it, interpret it, and weigh its significance and to produce a series of 'Lives' of generally modest proportions... Boswell's view of biography was to let his subject speak for himself by quoting *verbatim* letters, conversations, stories and words of wit and wisdom, thus creating a 'baggy', loosely formed 'Life' of elephantic size. (Benton 5)

Nineteenth-century biography generally favored the Boswellian type; in the early twentieth century, however, as with poetry and fiction, biography underwent its own modernist revolution (see, for instance, Virginia Woolf's preoccupation with biography in her writings during the 1920s and 1930s). The Soviet Formalist School followed suit with a few literary biographies, combining both the Johnson and Boswell models, but also enriching the genre with a distinctly formalistic dimension. In 1928, the publishing house Priboi issued the first installment of Boris Eikhenbaum's literary biography of Leo Tolstoy, which Nabokov, most probably, read and took into account while composing his mock biography of Chernyshevski. In *The Gift* Nabokov reflects on a concrete literary conception aimed at defining the parameters and principles of the novel as a genre itself. Edward Brown believes that Nabokov's text gives "a working model of the characteristic literary procedures identified and studied by the Formalists: estrangement, baring of the device, contrast of poetic and ordinary language, and especially and above all, parody" (Brown, "Nabokov, Chernyshevsky, Olesha" 282). Marina Kostalevsky examines Nabokov's novel in the context of the problems of the biographical genre posed by the Formalists and finds that Fyodor's work is written as a parody of *academic biography*. The story of Godunov-Cherdyntsev's life "in fact meets the requirements that the Formalists set forth with respect to the genre of biography; that is, the writer's life is a subject of interest only to the extent that it is related to his literary career" (Kostalevsky 285).

But how far does Nabokov go in his parody? Our image of Chernyshevski as constructed in *The Gift*, according to Andrew Drozd, is in need of revision. For example, Chernyshevski's alleged derogatory statements about Pushkin contradict the historical evidence. As a matter of fact, when the new edition of Pushkin's collected works by Annenkov appeared in 1855, Chernyshevski praised Annenkov's accomplishment and argued that it was of great service to the Russian public (Chernyshevski II: 428, 450, 477). He was so excited about the appearance of the collection that, grouping it together with the celebration of the anniversary of Moscow University, he stated, "what triumphs for Russian science and literature!" (II: 424). Elsewhere, he states regarding the collection: "Byron himself was not the object of such pride, such love, for the Englishman as Pushkin is for us" (III: 306).

Sometimes Chernyshevski's life is treated by Godunov as a kind of a hagiography, but with a clear implication that this is a false savior figure. At the beginning of "The Life of Chernyshevski," Fyodor condenses the socialist biographers' propensity towards religious imagery into a version of the revolutionary's life analogous to stages of Christ's life (Berdjis 350). Fyodor calls Chernyshevski "Christ the Second" and describes his mission as fulfilling everybody's material needs, implying that his creed excludes spiritual goals. Chernyshevski's actual life loses importance, and his image takes over. Even his dead body resembles that of Christ in Rembrandt's painting *The Removal from the Cross* (G215). Although Chernyshevski's "materialism cannot be reconciled with church doctrines, his own behavior echoes his Christian education" (Berdjis 351).

In this context, Chernyshevski's manner of reading utilitarian poetry "in the monotone of a Psalter lector" (G230) turns his literary recitals into church ceremonies; similarly, Chernyshevski's audience reads his novel *What to Do?* "the way liturgical books are read" (G277). Fyodor is not really concerned with the "easy irony of demolishing the romantic legend of the chief spokesman of realism. His task, rather, is the more difficult, subtle, and significant one of finding heroic possibility in Chernyshevski's obsessions, comic absurdities, and various misadventures" (Salomon 195). One important dimension of Fyodor's aesthetic discovery is his growing awareness of the instability of language and imagination as authentic instruments of power and truth. Even when he was writing poetry Fyodor had become aware of this problem. As a result he abandons earlier prose projects, in which "the verbal creation of proximate worlds can not literally be offered as a substitute for reality"; neither is Fyodor willing to become a naïve parodist of his father's life and career (Ibid. 192-93).

It seems that Nabokov must have admired Chernyshevski in several respects after all. Any discussion of the Nabokov—Fyodor—Chernyshevski dynamic would be incomplete without the fourth point (a triangle within a square, to adopt Nabokov's readily available metaphor of "a triangle inscribed in a circle"; G42), paradoxically represented by none other than Fyodor's father. A number of sober observations in this regard are offered by Gerard de Vries who addresses the discrepancy between facts and the assessment of them in the biographical sketch of Konstantin Godunov-Cherdyntsev: "Fyodor's love for his father is presented as very profound and sincere and rivaled only by his love for Zina" (Vries 31). The frequently noted resemblances of the relationship of Fyodor and Nabokov with their respective fathers also "concern the great affection and esteem both sons have for their respective parent. But one can hardly recognize in Fyodor's father the warm and loving personality from *Speak, Memory*" or Brian Boyd's biography of Nabokov (Ibid.). The main source of Fyodor's love for his father, according to his own sketch, is "the sweetness of [his] lessons" (G109) upon which Fyodor dwells. But it is difficult to see, admits de Vries, "how such lessons can generate more than the affection one feels for a popular biology teacher" (Vries 31). Fyodor is frequently seen suffering from a sense that he was the victim of neglect on the part of his father: at his final return, Fyodor observes the father checking his watch, which, as Gerard de Vries puts it, "is apparently of more importance to him than taking notice of his son." Konstantin Kirillovich goes back on his promise to take Fyodor with him on his next journey. The same uncaring attitude is obvious in Konstantin Godunov-Cherdyntsev's treatment of "his wife, whom he abandoned during their honeymoon trip for a whole day to pursue a butterfly hunt, leaving her to panic" (Ibid. 32).

A revived interest in literary biography within the Russian émigré milieu was, in part, triggered by the Soviet trend (five or six different life stories of Chernyshevski were produced there, including one tailored for children, along with many others devoted to prominent "heroes" of the new regime). However, the works that were written in exile had often featured some twist, as in Ivan Bunin's semi-autobiographical novel, *The Life of Arseniev* (1927-29), or Vladislav Khodasevich's brilliant spoof devoted to an invented poet named Vasilii Travnikov, an alleged contemporary of Pushkin. The author presented his hoax at a public reading in Paris on February 8, 1936; during the same literary event Nabokov read his short stories.

A Parody of a Fairy Tale

Another genre that is carefully hidden in the novel's depths is the Russian fairy tale. When Fyodor walks home in the Berlin night, he passes the square and the tall brick church and "the still quite transparent poplar, resembling the nervous system of a giant," as in the paintings of Pavel Filonov or Pavel Tchelitchew, but there, also, "is the public toilet, reminiscent of Baba Yaga's gingerbread cottage" (G53). The fairy-tale theme in *The Gift* is touched on in passing by Maria Malikova, who notes that Fyodor is a typical magical hero undertaking a journey. The beginning of Fyodor's journey follows the fairy-tale formula identified by Vladimir Propp, containing "a misfortune and the hero's exile from home. Sometimes exile from home is in itself a misfortune... This misfortune needs to be overcome, and usually the hero encounters some magical means of doing so. This, actually, determines the outcome" (Propp 146). In *The Gift* the "magical means" and the outcome are one and the same: Fyodor's artistic gift or, in a narrow sense, his novel (Malikova 25). On his journey the fairy-tale hero meets different donors (*dariteli*), the most important among them being his dead father. Frau Stoboy plays the role of "Baba-Yaga," a witch-like character in Slavic folklore. Characteristically, Stoboy is associated with the telephone, a mundane *memento mori*, one of the symbols of death and a motif used again by Nabokov in his English story "Signs and Symbols" (1948). Frau Stoboy's first name, Klara, derives from Latin (*clear, transparent*) and reflects Nabokov's idea of the relation between the "real" and the "otherworld," the first being only the dim, defective copy of the latter. Koncheyev, according to

Malikova, is another donor in *The Gift*: "In fairy-tales all donors are connected with the realm of the dead and this is made literal in the Grunewald scene. Here Fyodor crosses the water barrier (his swimming across the Grunewald lake is the ironic equivalent of crossing the Styx)" to meet Koncheyev dressed all in black. It is as if Fyodor returns from the country of the dead born anew, emerging naked as a baby (his clothes stolen) (Ibid.).

A Parody of the Roman à Clef

Roman à clef is French for "novel with a key," normally describing real life behind a façade of fiction. In the Soviet Union a few works of this kind appeared shortly before Nabokov started his work on *The Gift*: Konstantin Vaginov's novel, *Kozlinaya Pesn'* (*Goat Song*, 1926-28), and Olga Forsh's *Sumasshedshii korabl'* (*The Crazy Ship*, 1930), about an artistic commune in Leningrad of the early 1920s, inhabited by thinly veiled versions of Viktor Shklovsky, Mikhail Zoshchenko, Alexander Blok, and other identifiable literati.

Nabokov's *The Gift* is a novel with many keys, or codes, although many of them are lost or misplaced in the story. But while the physical keys as objects may be temporarily missing (*cf.*: Fyodor "located his front door... and pulled out his keys. None of them would open the door"; G53), the true meaning of a "key" in the narratological context means a chart one can use to swap out the names and concepts of *roman à clef*. As such, Nabokov's novel opens its hidden gateways to every attentive reader, and repeated attempts have been made to identify the real people behind masks. Everyone recognized the literary critic Adamovich portrayed as the episodic character Mortus; Berberova noted in her copy of the novel, next to the description of the émigré poet Busch: "Ilya Britan" (who had moved to France in the early 1930s; he authored several books, among them *To God*, and a mystery in verse, *Maria*, vaguely reminiscent of Busch's metaphysical mumblings).

Keys as a leitmotif appear in earlier chapters of the novel, but in Chapter Five this theme takes on a life of its own. Simon Karlinsky makes an instructive comparison between the fate of the servant Firs in the last act of Chekhov's play *The Cherry Orchard* and the leitmotif of the misplaced keys in Nabokov's *The Gift* (Karlinsky, "Nabokov and Chekhov" 36-37). Fyodor's set of house keys is stolen, together with his clothes, while he is swimming. On the next day, Zina's family is moving away, which should allow Fyodor and Zina to consummate their by now passionate affair. But in the eventful last pages of the novel, information is casually slipped in that Zina's and her mother's keys are locked in the apartment, that the janitor will not be able to unlock the door for them and that Zina is counting on Fyodor's keys, now stolen, to reach the place where their happiness will be achieved. A reader who is accustomed to simply skimming "may miss all this and be quite sure that the novel ends on the tonic chord of a familiar happy end" (Ibid. 36-37).

Chapter Three. STRUCTURE

The dominant motif of Fyodor's keys echoes and augments the book's theme of art and the artist. According to Donald Barton Johnson's eloquent rendering, just as the multi-faceted gift concept, the keys motif functions on several levels: "Keys not only play a pivotal role in the novel's plot but serve as the basis of an extended set of thematic allusions echoing different aspects of the novel's theme" (Johnson 95). Johnson first examines the plot role of the keys and then turns to their three thematic dimensions. The first aspect is represented by the dominant feature of Fyodor's "existence—exile. Exile has become a metaphor (as well as a reality) bespeaking the condition of the artist in the twentieth century. Generally the writer, and especially the young, unknown writer, is perhaps the most severely handicapped kind of exile, for his work is uniquely dependent on language and culture" (Ibid. 96). The second thematic dimension is related to the chess problem as discussed earlier. The third and final element will become evident if one considers the semantic potential of the word "key" in the Russian language. Key in Russian is *kliuch*, also meaning a *spring* or a *source* (of water), which brings to mind Pushkin's 1827 lyric "The Three Springs" about the Castalian spring of inspiration. The poem serves as an encoded subtext behind the surface of the novel (Johnson 100; Toker 158).

Keys are threaded through the verbal fabric of *The Gift* until the thematic link between *The Gift* and Pushkin's poem becomes established. Pekka Tammi adds that each of Pushkin's three springs finds its counterpart in the motifs associated with Fyodor's life: the Spring of Youth—"the Castalian Spring nourishing with its swell of inspiration the exiles of the world"; "the Spring of Oblivion that subdues the ardor of the heart"; and the third reference perfectly matches "Fyodor's own forgetfulness about his keys" (*kliuchi*) which effects the unrealized zeal for Zina at the end of the novel (Tammi, "The Three Springs" 37).

Memory, Loss and Recovery

Fyodor complains that he forgets the dynamic relations between things in his memory and admits that this destroys their authentic reality: "Already I am beginning to forget relationships and connections between objects that still thrive in my memory, objects I thereby condemn to extinction" (G18). Memory distorts authentic experience by isolating and replaying pictures that are static because they are isolated and trite because they are repeated, but "as a poet, Fyodor knows that the dynamic, harmonic principles of poetry may substitute themselves for partially lapsed memory, filling the lacunae" (White 276). Fyodor Godunov-Cherdyntsev's art is itself a compensatory mechanism against oblivion and non-existence.

Fyodor's forgetfulness and penchant for losing things are rewarded subtly but amply. Julian Connolly scrutinizes the compensatory power of art and the pattern of recovery in the novel and notes that one of Fyodor's "central concerns as an artist is the preservation of the fleeting experiences of mortal life" (Connolly 144). So

Fyodor's life, according to Connolly, has been marked by a series of losses—the loss of Russia and the loss of his father, as well as numerous minor annoyances; the theft of the keys to his apartment is just one of them. "Nabokov's novel asserts, however, that one does not have to be plunged into despair by such losses. For every frustration, life (or fate) provides some compensation, perhaps not on the material plane, but certainly in the realm of the mind and the spirit" (Ibid.). Art, therefore, fulfils for Fyodor a certain balancing function. This is the reason why much of the writing that Godunov-Cherdyntsev undertakes in the novel has autobiographical significance: recording the story of one's life is an attempt "to recapture and preserve the evanescent experiences," and Nabokov's exploration of the life of another (or stories about one's own life) "casts a patina of fiction over that life" (Ibid.).

Gifts, Money and Dividends

In 1925, the French sociologist Marcel Mauss wrote a short book entitled *The Gift*. In this now classic work, Mauss argued that gifts are never "free." The question that drove his inquiry into the anthropology of the gift was: "What power resides in the object given that causes its recipient to pay it back?" (Mauss 3). Mauss suggests that the gift is a "total prestation," imbued with "spiritual mechanisms." Every gift "produces a return gift in a chain of events that accomplishes many things all at once: goods are exchanged and redistributed in societies that do not have distinct commercial markets; peace is maintained and sometimes solidarity and friendship; and status is confirmed or competed for" (Davis 4). Above all, Mauss sees gift exchange as contracting over time. In a "total" gift economy, many functions were compressed into the exchange of presents between groups: markets, credit, contracts, arbitrations, marriage alliance, appeals to the gods, and more:

> The gift mode exists along with two other relational modes: the mode of sales—of market buying-and-selling—and the mode of coercion, that is, theft, punitive seizure, and forced payment. The gift mode may sometimes be in competition with the sales mode or the coercive mode; they may also cluster around each other, be in close interaction, or overlap. (Ibid. 9)

Prior to entering the Berlin shop, Fyodor reflects on the coercive nature of sales: "God, how I hate all this—the things in the shop windows, the obtuse face of merchandise, and, above all, the ceremonial of transaction, the exchange of cloying compliments before and after! And those lowered lashes of modest price...the nobility of the discount...the altruism of advertisements...all of this nasty imitation of good, which has a strange way of drawing in good people" (G5). Since it does not carry the Russian tipped cigarettes that he prefers, Fyodor leaves the shop almost "empty-handed" but suddenly notices the tobacconist's "speckled vest with mother-of-pearl buttons and his pumpkin-colored bald spot," which in turn reminds him of a literary reference to a Gogol character. The episode introduces one of the central motifs of Nabokov's novel—compensation for the losses that Fyodor incurs throughout his life (Ivleva 284).

Gregory Freidin takes this a step further and applies Mauss's theory to cultural studies, stating that it is a "unique feature of Russian and European modernism that the view of poetry as a charismatic calling—a gift that obligates—was inseparable from a great scholarly and popular interest in comparative mythology and religion" (Freidin xi). In this respect, the theoretical framework of Mauss offers "an important supplement to literary-rhetorical analysis proper, because its application makes possible an integral view of literary exchange—as genre, theme, device, and ritual" (Ibid.). Acmeist poetry based its poetics on the principles of simultaneity in successive stages of the poetic tradition and obligatory creative exchange (for instance, "the particular gift of poetry and the poetry of gift-giving produced by Tsvetaeva and Mandelstam relied on allusions to other poets and poetry, most obviously the classical Russian authors Derzhavin and Pushkin and their reworkings of Horace's *Exegi monumentum*"; Freidin 119).

Indeed, the "pocket money," to which the bulk of the novel's text is devoted, pertains to "the motif of insufficiency and incompleteness, whereas the 'dividends,' which are interspersed throughout the novel and have to be patiently collected, are tokens of the presence—ever receding—of the infinite. This quaint bookkeeping, the tension between the incomplete and the infinite, is reflected both in the major themes of *The Gift* and in the three main constituents of the novel's structure: the recurrent motifs, the features of perspective, and the self-referential games. The boundary between these techniques is often indistinguishable, as is the difference between structure and thematic content" (Toker 148). Alexander Dolinin outlines those "dividends" of faith, or the unexpected rewards for losses generated by an invisible "spiritual mechanism" (in Mauss's theory), that Fyodor receives in *The Gift*: the loss of temporary lodgings leads him to a meeting with Zina—his ideal love, reader, and Muse; disappointment in the Soviet chess magazine bought on credit lays the foundation of the future Chernyshevski biography; the theft of his clothes and keys augurs a new reciprocal gift—the main book which the hero plans to compose (Dolinin, *Istinnaia zhizn'* 128-30).

The concept of "money" concentrates the very utilitarian type of thinking that the hero of *The Gift* debunks through his ironic biography of Chernyshevski. Towards the finale of the novel the asymmetry of poverty and wealth, material losses and intellectual and artistic gratification fulfils the purpose of critiquing nineteenth century Russian literature: the power of money as well as its frequent rejection was its dominant motif (Kissel 24). *The Gift* needs money as a theme, and Nabokov uses it in order to realize all the miraculous metamorphoses that turn absence into presence, incompleteness into wholeness, robbery into endowment. A creator who multiplies literary works (and, should they be commercially successful, also accumulates financial gains) executes the right of choice by endowing his characters with gifts, bestowing upon them long fictional lives (Kissel 35).

― Themes ―

Authorship and Divine Creation:
Decoding Delirium, Or Who Will Help Chernyshevski?

In the scene involving the deathbed delirium of Alexander Yakovlevich Chernyshevski there is an aside that at first glance seems to be of little significance: "Boria will help—but then he might not" (*Dar* 486). The basic questions that will spring to mind for the attentive reader are as follows: who is this Boria, and how exactly might he be able to help the dying character (or his family)? For those reading the work in the original Russian, the name itself might go unnoticed due to the presence of various Borises throughout the text (Shchyogolev, Barski, and, in the imagination of the critic Linyov, Boris Cherdyntsev). When we examine it a bit closer, however, it becomes clear that Alexander Chernyshevski could not have known any of these Borises, and he does not encounter any of them within the confines of *The Gift*. The line must refer to some character that does not appear in the text either before or after this scene. In the opinion of Alexander Dolinin, the presence of a specific name for a person that Fyodor Godunov-Cherdyntsev does not and could not know indicates that Chernyshevski's stream of consciousness is located beyond Fyodor's cognitive horizon, and is being constructed by the author of the text (A. Dolinin to the author, private communication). Thus Nabokov's riddle is addressed directly to the reader, and the key to solving it must lie somewhere within the space of the novel.

Nabokov himself stated that he made minimal changes when editing Michael Scammell's English translation of *The Gift*, wishing to avoid the temptation to start rewriting whole chunks of the novel (Scammell 58). Although this objective was certainly achieved, there nevertheless remained a desire to apply a touchup here and there. And in this instance we have one of those rare revisions that is not simply a matter of style, but of meaning.

In the English version, the sentence takes the following form: "*David might help—but then he might not*" (G311). As evident from Scammell's typescript (NYPL, Berg Collection, p. 368) the translator had faithfully suggested "Boris" first. This change calls for an explanation: what was it about this unknown "Boria" that bothered the author, and why did he choose to replace him with the name "David," which has even less meaning in the context of the novel? An understanding of the logic behind this metamorphosis should serve as a structural component of the deeper model that constitutes the supporting frame of the scene containing Chernyshevski's deathbed delirium.

Alexander Dolinin has compiled a list of works on the theme of the poet's gratitude to his creator, all of which contribute to the atmosphere surrounding the title of *The Gift* (*Istinnaia zhizn'* 231-239). To his all but exhaustive catalog of anthems embracing the gift of life, we should add one important line from Apollon Maikov's poem "Byvalo, ulovit' iz zhizni mig sluchainyi..." ("There was a time when to catch a chance moment of life...") (1854):

> I thank Thou, Creator, I thank Thou,
> That we are not shackled by confining false wisdom,
> That I can say to all with pride, I am Russian,
> That I burn with Russia as one flame.

It has been noted that Maikov was among Sirin's early poetic teachers—for example, in an incisive observation made by Gleb Struve that was, however, not developed further (Struve 297). Maikov is also the author of a long poem, *Mashen'ka* (*Mary*, as in the title of Nabokov's first novel). It would seem that Maikov emerges here as the opposite national pole to the "Blagodarnost'" ("Gratitude") of Dovid (*David*) Knut, whose "slightly affected biblical inelegance" was commented on by Nabokov himself in his review of Knut's *Vtoraia kniga stikhov* (*Second Book of Poems*) (*Sobranie* 2:655). Godunov-Cherdyntsev's verse grows, and the dying Chernyshevski thrashes about, in the stress field between self-identification as a Russian poet and as a Jewish poet. Further evidence that these lines by Maikov were perceived as marked in Russian émigré culture is provided by the fact that years later they were used as the permanent epigraph to the literary "thick journal" *Sovremennik* (*The Contemporary*), published in Toronto and edited by Leonid Ivanovich Strakhovskii (the first issue with the stanza from Maikov's poem was published in March 1960).

When comparing the original of *The Gift* with its English translation, one notices a clear tendency to shed light on the novel's "dark places": Nabokov tried to make it easier for Anglophone readers to understand certain scenes and allusions. Given this tendency, we can assume that Boria was turned into David in order to make the passage more understandable,[22] but still we are left to establish the internal logic of the name change itself.

The name David is mentioned only once in the Russian original of the novel, in Chapter Four, in the description of Nikolai Chernyshevski's forays into poetry:

---

[22] In a private communication with the author, Alexander Dolinin suggested the following interpretation: the dying Chernyshevski is thinking about how his wife will get money to live on, and he hopes that, after his own resources have run out, she will be helped out by some well-off relative named Boria, who is not mentioned before or after this in the novel. This Boria might be the same person as the unnamed Svidrigailov-like "prim gentleman with a blond little beard and unusually red lips (a cousin, it seemed, of the dead man)" (G313), whom Godunov-Cherdyntsev notices at the funeral. Dolinin believes that Nabokov changed Boria to David in the translation in order to avoid confusion with Boris Shchyogolev, Boris Barski, and (in Linyov's review) Boris Cherdyntsev (in Russian the diminutive form "Boria" clearly indicates a close familial relationship, but this shade of meaning would be lost in English), while at the same time reminding the reader of Chernyshevski's Jewish roots.

He also wrote poems. In texture they are no different from those versificatory tasks which he had once been given in the seminary, when he had reset a psalm of David in the following manner:

> Upon me lay one duty only—
> To mind my father's flock of sheep,
> And hymns I early started singing
> For to extol the Lord withal.
>
> (G290)

The central themes of this Psalm are meditations on the greatness of man and gratitude to his Maker; indeed the entire Book of Psalms, which is traditionally ascribed to King David, embodies a continual hymn of thankfulness to the creator. It is precisely this word—*creator*—that seems to be the key to understanding the connection between the two names. One of the commonly used names for God in ancient Hebrew sounds like "Borye"—literally "creator," "he who creates" (בּוֹרֵא = borei), which paronomastically coincides with the diminutive form (Boria) of the Russian name Boris.[23] As if giving us a hint, Nabokov in the previous paragraph mentions a certain book written in *Aramaic* (G311). This bilingual pun is based in part on the definition for the word "God" given in Dahl's Russian Dictionary; the first sense of the word that Dahl lists is the same semantic unit as that of the Hebrew etymology: "*Maker, Creator,* the Almighty, the Highest One, the Omnipotent, the Eternal, the Eternally Existing, the Lord; Eternal Being, Creator of the universe. Glory to God, *thanks* be to God: an exclamation of *thankfulness* used in response to an inquiry after one's health... God will provide, *thank you.*" Dahl also lists several well-known sayings on the theme of "God help us" or "God will help." All these turns of phrase in the end lead us back to the phrase "*Boria will help.*" It is interesting that the combination of words in question also appears in Pushkin's *Boris Godunov* in the context of the cohesion of generations and the assumption of the throne by an heir: "But if *God help* us take / The throne of our *fathers.*" There is another example of paronomasia in *The Gift*, based on a biblical calque, in the phrase "Bedlam turned back into Bethlehem" (*Dar* 257/G72). The pun comes from the similarity of the Hebrew "Beit-Lehem" (literally: "House of Bread") to the word "bedlam."[24] Incidentally, one of the common names used to

---

[23] This corresponds to the present tense verb form "borei"; *cf.* the past tense form: "bara" (he created), as in the second word of the Torah (בָּרָא בְּרֵאשִׁית). For the two to coincide completely, the name Boria would need to be in the dative case (Borye), but then the stress would fall on the first syllable (which is allowable in the Ashkenazi oral tradition).

[24] Bedlam (a shortened form of Bethlehem) was (the name of a London priory which, 300 years after its founding in 1247, became a lunatic asylum; see Brewer). The Russian reader will be familiar with this story from commentary to the scene from *King Lear*, in which Edmund, the son of Lord Gloucester, compares himself to Tom o' Bedlam.

refer to Bethlehem in Old Testament times is the "city of David" (Luke 2:4), as it was the birthplace of the second King of Israel and the place where King Solomon was anointed to the throne (I Samuel 16:4-13).

Though the scene of Chernyshevski's deathbed delirium is disguised as an "uncontrollable" stream of consciousness, it is clearly among the most carefully orchestrated passages in the narrative. The aphorisms of the philosopher Delalande most likely have no concrete intertextual source—they flow smoothly into Chernyshevski's own discourse, and in this respect they represent a single unit of meaning. It would be mistaken and useless to search for a specific Psalm that corresponds precisely to the content of the deathbed delirium, which constitutes a collage of images and phrases taken from Holy Scripture. In order to demonstrate the general origin of these motifs and this topos, we will juxtapose one Psalm (№ 139) with excerpts from Chernyshevski's rants. Although there exist translations that are closer to the Ancient Hebrew original, we will use the generally accepted King James Version or English adaptations of the Russian Synodal Translation, which Nabokov would have had access to (138, according to the Eastern Orthodox Church).

David	Chernyshevski
1 O Lord, you have searched me and known me. 2 You know my sitting down and my arising, and you understand my thoughts from afar. 3 When I am going or when I rest—you encompass me, and all of my journeys are known to you. 4 Before a word is on my tongue, O Lord, you know it perfectly.	And then again: the unfortunate image of a "road" to which the human mind has become accustomed (life as a kind of journey) is a stupid illusion: we are not going anywhere, we are sitting at home. The other world surrounds us always and is not at all at the end of some pilgrimage.
5 You surround me from behind and from ahead, and lay Your hand on me. 6 Such knowledge is too wondrous for me—it is high, and I cannot attain it. 7 Where will I go from Your Spirit, and where will I run from Your presence?	Of course I am dying. These pincers behind and this steely pain are quite comprehensible. Death steals up from behind and grasps you by the sides.
8 If I ascend into heaven, You are there, and if I descend into the nether regions, You are there.	[For Fyodor Konstantinovich] it was somewhat disgusting to enter a real crematorium, where from beneath laurels in tubs a real coffin with a real body was lowered to the sounds of heavyweight organ music into exemplary nether regions, right into the incinerator.

―――――――――――――――――――――――― Themes ――――――――――――――――――――――――

David	Chernyshevski
9 If I assume the wings of dawn and dwell at the edge of the sea— 10 There also Your hand will lead me and Your right hand will hold me. 11 If I say: "Perhaps the darkness will conceal me and the light around me become night," 12 Even the darkness does not hide from You, and the night is bright like day: darkness and light are the same.	Fear gives birth to sacred awe, sacred awe erects a sacrificial altar, its smoke ascends to the sky, there assumes the shape of wings, and bowing fear addresses a prayer to it.
13 For You created what is inside of me, and You wove together in my mother's womb. 14 I will praise You, because I am wondrously created. Wondrous are Your works, and my soul knows this full well. 15 My bones were not hidden from You when I was created in secret and formed in the depths of the womb. 16 Your eyes saw my embryo; in Your book were written all of the days allotted to me, when none of them yet were.	It is terribly painful to leave life's womb. The deathly horror of birth. L'enfant qui nait ressent les affres de sa mere.
17 How precious also are Your thoughts to me, O God! How great is the sum of them! 18 If I should count them, they are more in number that the sand: when I awake, I am still with You.	Father, headmaster, rector, president of the board, tsar, God. Numbers, numbers—and one wants so much to find the biggest number...
19 O God, if You would only smite the wicked! Bloody men, depart from me! 20 They speak wickedly against You, and Your enemies take Your name in vain. 21 Am I not to hate those who hate you, O Lord, and despise those who rise up against You? 22 I hate them with complete hatred: they are enemies to me. 23 Search me, O God, and know my heart; search me and know my thoughts; 24 And see whether I be on a dangerous path, and set me on the path everlasting.	If the poor in spirit enter the heavenly kingdom I can imagine how gay it is there. I have seen enough of them on earth. Who else makes up the population of heaven? Swarms of screaming revivalists, grubby monks, lots of rosy, shortsighted souls of more or less Protestant manufacture—what deathly boredom!

Chapter Three. STRUCTURE

Many of the Psalms of David open with dedications such as "For the Chief Musician," "For the Director," etc. Nabokov ironically distorts this form of address into a series of synonyms: "Somehow simpler. Somehow simpler. Somehow at once! One effort—and I'll understand all. The search for God: the longing of any hound for a *master*; give me a *boss* and I shall kneel at his enormous feet. All this is earthly. *Father, headmaster, rector, president of the board, tsar, God*" (G310; italics added). The last sentence, consisting of a series of nouns in the nominative case, is comparable in its internal dynamics to the novel's epigraph (a sudden shift in scope; a metaphysical "zoom out"), and is in this respect a symmetrical statement. The theme of following the mission of one's father runs through the binary structure of *The Gift* like a red thread: David—Solomon (house of Peretz)/Boris—Fyodor (Godunov)/Konstantin—Fyodor (Godunov-Cherdyntsev). The common denominator shared by these pairs is that all of the names in the onomasticon belong to people with the title of King or Tsar. David, Constantine, and Boris are all historical rulers famous in Hebrew, Roman, and Slavic history respectively. King David founded Jerusalem (c. 1000 BCE) and prepared for the construction of the First Temple; Constantine is famous as the first Christian Emperor of Rome (313 CE); Boris (a shortened form of Borislav, from the Tatar *Bogoris*, meaning "glory in war") was the ruler of Bulgaria, who Christianized his people in the ninth century CE. In part, Nabokov is reacting to contemporary fashion: Russian émigré literature of the 1930s had a great interest in mythology, and many authors wrote biographical fiction with biblical and mythological heroes as the main characters.[25]

And finally, the name of the street where the funeral home is located in *The Gift* ("Kaiserallee," from Latin Caesar; the Slavic version is tsar) is also connected with the fatherhood-kingship-heredity theme with which Nabokov carefully saturates various levels of the narrative.

In the short story "Signs and Symbols," written several years after *The Gift* was completed, there appears a "Prince Isaac" on whom the elderly Jewish parents of an unstable son will also rely for help. The insane father in *The Gift*, having already lost his son, relies on the help of God, King David, or on the mercy of the Author himself (cf. the endings of the story "Cloud, Castle, Lake" and the novel *Bend Sinister*). Both the "Prince Isaac" figure and the "Boria-David" figure are shadowy, behind-the-scenes characters—they are mentioned in the third person, but they never manage to materialize in the events of the story.

---

[25] For example, King David in the novel by Ia. Donets, Samson the Nazarite in V. Jabotinsky, King Herod in the novel by L. Teplitsky, Count Cagliostro in I. Lukash, Father Fedor Kuz'mich in P. Krupensky, Prince Voronetsky in the novel *V strane nevoli* (*In the Land of Captivity*) by V. Shul'gin, and Princess Tarakanova in D. Dmitriev's *Avantiuristka* (*The Adventuress*). Also cf. the works of biographical history by Aldanov and Merezhkovsky (see Glushakov 72-73).

Before his death, Chernyshevski undergoes a stark religious identity crisis verging on a kind of agnosticism: "For religion subsumes a suspicious facility of general access that destroys the value of its revelations" (G310). His entire deathbed discourse is contained within the microgenre of the nighttime meditation involving a search for the meaning of life and an awareness of impending death. Such contemplations, dating back to the natural philosophy of antiquity, regarding the construction of the universe and the presence of a God-Creator were introduced into the Russian poetic tradition by Lomonosov ("Evening Meditation on God's Greatness"). Their echo is clearly discernible in canonical texts by Pushkin ("Verses Composed at Night during Insomnia"), Tyutchev ("Insomnia"), and many other poems that continue the tradition of evening services (vespers and compline) with Psalms (particularly Psalms 101 and 30) on the themes of death and Judgment Day (Mazur 250-260).

The metatextual frame around the episode is constructed as a metaphor of visually skimming a book in an unknown language. The character's inability to understand the meaning of life and his spiritual purpose is compared to marginal notes in a text whose "context is absolutely unknown" (G311) to him. The theme of the Creator is presented here more in a quasi-literary sense than a religious one—the author withdraws his character from the action and, in the Russian original of the phrase "Death…grasps you by the sides…" ("*Smert' beret za boka*") leaves an anagrammatic seal resembling his own name. On the other hand, the bilingual riddle with *Boria/beret/borei* (based on the same kind of phonetic calque that Roman Timenchik described with regard to a poem by Boris Pasternak[26]) makes it possible to assume that in this case Nabokov comes out on par with the omnipotent author—the creator of the text's creator.

We see a similar metaphysical tone in Nabokov's "Parizhskaia poema" ("The Paris Poem") which was written at almost the same time as *The Gift*, and not, as is commonly thought, several years later.[27] The speaker in the poem shifts his gaze from the black water to the evening sky:

---

[26] In Boris Pasternak's poem "Step" ["The Steppe"], the monotonous forced rhymes of "razreshit…zaporoshit…parashiut" ["will permit…will powder…parachute"], and so on, mimic the sound of the liturgical incantation of the Hebrew "bereshit" (בראשית— "In the beginning"). As the scholar demonstrated, these words were commonly heard among both Jews and non-Jews from Mikhail Tsetlin to Vasilii Rozanov (Timenchik, "Raspisan'e" 70).

[27] "Cambridge, 1943," the date for the poem that is commonly used today (which comes from Nabokov himself), is not accurate. His letters show that Nabokov had already begun working on the "Paris Poem" in 1937 (when he cites lines from the poem in unpublished correspondence with Irina Guadanini).

> And on high there are only unimportant things.
> Endlessly. Endlessly. Just a blur.
> The moon looms dead in a vortex.
> *Can it be the same with me? Forget.*
> *Death is still distant* (after tomorrow I
> Will rethink this), but sometimes
> *The heart wants "Author, Author."*
> Gentlemen, the author is not in the hall.
>
> (Nabokov, *Stikhotvoreniia* 213).[28]

The question and answer here coincide quite literally with the mumblings of the fading Chernyshevski: "Will all my friends go through it? Incredible!" (G311). It must be remembered, however, that Nabokov in no way shares his character's lack of religious sensibilities, and therefore diminishes his death throes and his hint at an epiphany ("Of course there is nothing afterwards"; G312) with parodic blindness and deafness. Chernyshevski is quite certain that it is raining outside, when in reality someone is just watering the plants while the sun shines.

It is no accident that the Russian name ("*Bytie*," or "*Bytiia*" in the genitive case form) for the first book of the Bible appears in the final line of the novel, in the pseudo-Onegin stanza, transitioning back to *the beginning*: "*prodlennyi prizrak bytiia sineet za chertoi stranitsy*" ("the extended shadow of existence/Genesis lies blue beyond the outline of the page"). The novel's biblical fabric shows throughout the text, which proves to be a testament in poetry and prose left by Sirin to Russian literature, before the author's transition to the world of another language.

A curious parallel arises between the fictitious Alexander Chernyshevski and his revolutionary namesake whose deathbed delirium had also produced a puzzling reference. Chernyshevski's last words, said in delirium (they were transcribed by a secretary), were: "Strange: in this book there is no mention of God." "It remains unknown," commented Chernyshevski's son Mikhail, who published the record, "which book he meant."

A copy of the Bible (one of the few books Chernyshevski took with him to Petersburg in 1846) was in his library during the last years of his life. God

---

[28] What follows is the idea, typical for Nabokov, of a "life rich with patterns," which can be laid out like a "wondrous rug." It is possible that this is a hidden rejoinder to Vadim Rudnev, who, though he was initially delighted by *The Gift*, later flatly refused to publish Chapter Four of the novel. Upon reading Chapter Three, he wrote: "I cannot convey to you how delighted I am with this chapter of the novel—as well as the previous one!" Later, in connection with Nabokov's play *The Event*, which was being prepared for performance, he wrote: "it would be outrageous to deny the audience the satisfaction of crying 'Author! Author!' after the first act. But you will come in, take a bow, and pretend to be embarrassed" (November 26, 1937. Berg Collection, NYPL).

is indeed mentioned in *What to Do?* and a rich network of allusions to the Bible and Christian tradition permeates the novel alerting the reader "that it is a text aimed at global solutions to the problems of human existence and the organization of human spiritual and earthly life. The very title of the novel, *Chto delat'?*, recalls the episode of the baptism in Luke (3: 10-14) and the question that 'the multitude that came forth to be baptized of him' asked of John: 'What shall we do?' (*Chto zhe nam delat'?*)" (Paperno, *Chernyshevsky and the Age of Realism* 206-7).

The finale of *The Gift* imitates Russian literature's Book of Books: Pushkin's immortal novel of creation and creativity, while the novel's main character bears a resemblance to Adam, who in his "primeval paradise" names the animals and primal phenomena ("I felt myself an athlete, a Tarzan, an Adam"; G333).

Both Boria and David are emanations from the author, masks worn by the author-Creator, who is able to help his character at the point where the story's final line ends.

Suicide

In the late nineteenth-century Russia several suicides of prominent literary figures shook the reading public. Count Aleksei Konstantinovich Tolstoy (1817-75), a talented satirist and dramatist, became addicted to morphine and died after emptying an entire phial. A decade after him the master of a short story form, prose writer Vsevolod Garshin (1855-88), jumped down a stairwell to his death in a fit of insanity. Famous literary suicides of the Silver Age of Russian poetry included the case of Victor Gofman (1884-1911)—a neurasthenic who shot himself in Paris—and several widely discussed deaths of female poets. Valery Briusov, the major early twentieth-century Russian poetic trendsetter and experimenter, presented his young lover, the aspiring poet, Nadezhda L'vova (1891-1913), with a Browning pistol, which she used to shoot herself in a moment of despair. Another female poet, Nina Petrovskaya (1879-1928), who was the friend and Muse at various points for such leading Symbolist writers as Bal'mont, Bely, and Briusov, poisoned herself by gas in a Paris hotel. The writer Ivan Boldyrev (aka Shkott; 1903-33) did the almost impossible—after being arrested as an anti-Bolshevik and exiled to Siberia, he was able to escape from prison; he lived in terrible destitution in the French capital, and killed himself by taking an overdose of barbiturates. Boris Poplavsky was probably the most promising among the many gifted young poets in the Russian Diaspora: at the age of thirty-two, he either overdosed accidentally or committed suicide by poison. The suicide of Poplavsky in 1935 garnered a great deal of attention in the émigré community, including Khodasevich's passionate obituary, and forced Vladimir Nabokov to reconsider his skeptical attitude toward this poet's legacy.

---- Chapter Three. STRUCTURE ----

As Anne Nesbet has found, the story of Yasha's suicide provoked by an unhappy *ménage à trois* had an actual basis in fact. On April 18, 1928, newspapers in Berlin circulated reports of a lovers' drama in the Grunewald involving young Russian émigrés (Nesbet 829). Indeed, in the 1920s the problem of suicide was understood to be typical of a certain kind of society. According to Nesbet, suicide works as an awkward joint not only between life and death, but between life and text (*cf.* Alfred Döblin's novel *Berlin Alexanderplatz* published in 1929). In addition to real life sources, Monika Greenleaf asserts that Yasha's story also has a background in fiction. The scholar suggests that Nabokov borrows certain features from the plot of Pushkin's *Eugene Onegin*. The three young students—Yasha, the Germanophile Russian student; Rudolph, the man-about-town; and the contemporary feminine cliché, Olga—"recreate a modernistic decadent version of the Lensky-Onegin-Olga triangle," with its culmination in the inertia of the duel on the one hand and "the 'fatality' of the suicide pact on the other. In both cases it is as if the fashionable automatism of their elegiac poetry has spawned a violent nemesis that is equally typical of the 'spirit of the times'" (Greenleaf 151). The suicide motif was neither unique nor ubiquitous in émigré writing: its peak in Russian literature came between 1905 and 1917 (in works by Gippius, Gorodetsky, Artsybashev, Kuprin and Andreev, whose fiction explored the experience of profound hopelessness and insurmountable loneliness) (Brodsky 98). In St. Petersburg in 1905, there were an average of 29.5 attempted suicides and actual suicides per month; by 1908, this figure had risen to 121; and in 1909 there were 199 suicides monthly, five times the number for 1908 (Prokopov 11-12).

The fact that suicide became an alarming social concern in Russia during the period between two revolutions—which coincides with Nabokov's development as an adolescent prior to his emigration—should not be overlooked when contemplating Yasha's terrible act.

Cremation

To close the existential cycle in *The Gift*, a novel that ranges from a life-asserting title and abundant descriptions of the birth of poetry out of the chaos of mundane reality to the physical demise of its several principle characters, let us turn to Yasha's father's posthumous fate.

Upon his death, Alexander Chernyshevski's body is committed to the flames in a crematorium on the corner of Kaiserallee, and the very choice of the procedure is another fashionable mark of the epoch (Fyodor is amused by the "German seductivity" of a miniature model crematorium in the mortician's window; G312). About one-fifth of the obituaries published in Berlin newspapers in 1926 announced that the bodies of the deceased would be cremated. A large majority of these bodies were male and obituaries published in the newspapers referred almost exclusively to members of the upper middle class. Analyzing this new European trend, historian Hans Ulrich Gumbrecht observes that to have oneself cremated was "an act of sobriety and worldliness":

> Whoever supports cremation seems an independent thinker and an ethically responsible person trying to live up to the demands of the Kantian categorical imperative...Most important, perhaps, choosing cremation presupposes the courage to face the fact of one's own death before this death occurs. (Gumbrecht 64)

The most frequently cited reasons for this decision were the "considerably lower cost" of the new method in comparison with "traditional burial, a concern for public hygiene," and an attempt to reduce "the expansion of cemeteries" (Ibid. 63).

Gumbrecht also notes that, judging by the names in the obituaries, a number of German Jews chose the option despite the fact that most Jewish communities continued to resist this practice as representing the logical conclusion of "emancipation," of abandoning their cultural roots, and of integration into lay society. The case of the converted Protestant A. Y. Chernyshevski belongs to the same category. Nabokov, the husband of a Jewish-Russian émigré, however, seems to be deeply skeptical regarding the prospective results of such emancipation. Yasha Chernyshevski is in love with a German youth, Rudolph; his attempted conversion through cultural and religious renunciation is doomed, and ultimately brings destruction upon his whole family. History would later prove that Nabokov's skepticism about the "emancipation" of Jews had been quite prescient.

Life after Death

On the other hand, Nabokov is not pessimistic or fatalistic. Behind the outer lining of cruel reality his philosophy always hides a tender lining of hope. The episode of Alexander Chernyshevski's cremation does not produce a disturbing effect; on the contrary, there is something soothing and peaceful about it (as he exits the crematorium and the bright and harmonious cityscape greets him, Fyodor reflects on this sensation). Life after death *is* possible, at least in literature, and Nabokov saturates the episode with literary allusions that speak to this theme.

Dostoevsky

In putting together the cremation scene, Nabokov seems to have found a source in Fyodor Dostoevsky's novel, *The Possessed* (Russian *Besy*, also translated as *The Devils* and *Demons*). Boris Maslov, who discovered this literary subtext for the episode, points to a character named von Lembke who has a passion for miniature models (Maslov 183-84). First von Lembke glues together a paper theatre ("The curtain drew up, the actors came in, and gesticulated with their arms. There were spectators in the boxes, the orchestra moved their bows across their fiddles by machinery..."), and then "...he suddenly began making a toy church: the pastor came out to preach the sermon, the congregation listened with their hands before them, one lady was drying her tears with her handkerchief, one old gentleman was blowing his nose; finally the organ pealed forth. It had been ordered from Switzerland, and made expressly in spite of all expense" (Dostoevsky 282). The description of a model is "relocated" to the Berlin mortician's window in the episode of Alexander Yakovlevich's burial. Nabokov claimed not to like Dostoevsky all that much, but there is another evident reference in the cremation scene to an author with whom he felt a much stronger kinship.

Tolstoy

The final farewell sequence prior to the cremation of Alexander Chernyshevski's body continues to serve the connection between life and death/life and text. In this scene the intertextual links lead to Leo Tolstoy's "The Death of Ivan Ilych" (1886). Nabokov included this short story in his analyses of Russian prose when he taught university courses. The descriptions of both deceased male characters and their widows are similar. In Tolstoy, the dead man's "yellow waxen brow with bald patches over his *sunken temples* was thrust up in the way peculiar to the dead, the protruding nose seeming to press on the upper lip" (Tolstoy 96). In *The Gift* Fyodor "forever remembered the white bristle on [Chernyshevski's] *sunken cheeks*, the dull shade of his bald head" (G312). This is Nabokov's description of the widow: "*Mme. Chernyshevski did not hold a handkerchief but sat motionless and straight, her eyes shimmering through the black crepe veil.*" Here is Tolstoy's widow:

> Praskovya Fyodorovna[,] a short, fat woman...dressed all *in black, her head covered with lace*...on her way to the sofa *the lace of the widow's black shawl* caught on the carved edge of the table...When this was all over she *took out a clean cambric handkerchief and began to weep.* (Tolstoy 98)

Nabokov follows Tolstoy in accentuating the estrangement and inner discord in the mood of the guests at the funeral ceremony. This is conveyed mainly by the liveliness of their eyes in contrast to their visibly constrained body language. Compare the descriptions:

> The faces of friends and acquaintances bore the guarded expressions usual in such cases: *a mobility of the pupils* accompanied by a certain tension in the muscles of the neck...the ladies who had used to visit the Chernyshevskis

all sat together...there were many people whom *Fyodor did not know*—for instance, a prim gentleman with a *blond little beard* and *unusually red lips*. (G312-13)

Two ladies *in black* were taking off their fur cloaks. Peter Ivanovich recognized one of them as Ivan Ilych's sister, but the other was *unknown* to him. His colleague...Schwartz's face,[29] with his *Piccadilly whiskers*...The ladies went upstairs to the widow's room, and Schwartz with seriously *compressed lips but a playful look in his eyes*, indicated by a twist of his eyebrows the room to the right where the body lay. (Tolstoy 95-96)

The Tolstoy source is carefully refracted through other fictional allusions (including those from Dostoevsky's *The Possessed*) and Fyodor's peculiar *modus operandi* of filtering his reality through a fixation on literary phenomena. Fyodor the character is not completely aware of the complex literary background of the scene with its intertextual references. It is up to a reader to reactivate the hidden relationships in *The Gift* with the traditions upon which it is constructed.

---

[29] There are possible mirroring connections here as well: the Russian meaning of Schwartz = Black = Chernyshevski (Nabokov played a similar verbal game in his short story "Breaking the News," composed around the same time as *The Gift*); additionally, the patronymic of Ivan Ilyich's widow, Praskovya *Fyodorovna*, coincides with Fyodor's name.

References

Alexandrov, Vladimir. *Nabokov's Otherworld*. Princeton: Princeton University Press, 1991.

_____ "Nabokov and Bely," in *The Garland Companion to Vladimir Nabokov*. Ed. by V. Alexandrov. New York: Garland, 1995: 358-366.

Alley, Ronald. *Catalogue of the Tate Gallery's Collection of Modern Art other than Works by British Artists*. London: Tate Gallery and Sotheby Parke-Bernet, 1981.

Allsop, Kenneth. "Nabokov…Long Before Lolita," *London Daily Mail*, November 7, 1963.

Barabtarlo, Gene. *Phantom of Fact: A Guide to Nabokov's* Pnin. Ann Arbor: Ardis, 1989.

_____ "'He said—I said': An Afternote," *The Nabokovian* 45, 2000: 29-36.

Belodubrovsky, Evgeny. V. Nabokov. "Pamiati Amalii Osipovny Fondaminskoi" (Publication, afterword, and commentary). *Literaturnoe obozrenie* 2, 1999: 8-9.

Ben-Amos, Anat. "The role of literature in *The Gift*," *Nabokov Studies* 4, 1997: 117-149.

Benjamin, Walter. "The Crisis of the Novel," in *Selected Writings: 1927–1930*. Ed. by Michael William Jennings et al. Vol. 2, pt. 1. Harvard: Harvard University Press, 2005: 299-304.

Benton, Michael. *Literary Biography: An Introduction*. Oxford: Wiley-Blackwell, 2009.

Berberova, Nina. *Nabokov: Criticism, Reminiscences, Translations and Tributes* (eds. Alfred Appel, Jr., Charles Newman), Evanston, IL: Northwestern University Press, 1970.

_____ *Kursiv moi. Avtobiografiia*. 2-e izdanie, isp. i dop. 2 vols. New York: Russica, 1983.

Berdjis, Nassim Winnie. *Imagery in Vladimir Nabokov's Last Russian Novel* (Dar), *Its English Translation* (The Gift), *and Other Prose Works*. Frankfurt am Main: Peter Lang, 1995.

Bethea, David M. *The Superstitious Muse: Mythopoetic Thinking and Russian Literature*. Boston: Academic Studies Press, 2009.

Blackwell, Stephen H. *Zina's Paradox: The Figured Reader in Nabokov's* Gift. New York: Peter Lang, 2000.

Bliumbaum, Arkady. "Marginaliia k *Daru*: Prokuror Shchyogolev," in *The Real Life of Pierre Delalande: Studies in Russian and Comparative Literature to Honor Alexander Dolinin*, ed. by David M. Bethea, Lazar Fleishman, and Alexander Ospovat. Stanford: Berkeley Slavic Specialties, 2007; Stanford Slavic Studies, vols 33–34. Vol. 2: 597-606.

Boyd, Brian. "The Expected Stress Did Not Come': A Note on "Father's Butterflies," *The Nabokovian* 45, 2000: 22-29.

_____ [Review of] Dieter E. Zimmer. *A Guide to Nabokov's Butterflies and Moths*. Hamburg: privately printed, 2001. *Nabokov Studies* 6, 2000/2001: 215-220.

_____ *Vladimir Nabokov: The Russian Years*. Princeton: Princeton University Press, 1990.

Brewer, E. Cobham. *Dictionary of Phrase and Fable*. Philadelphia: Henry Altemus, 1898.

Brodsky, Anna. "Homosexuality and the aesthetic of Nabokov's *Dar*," *Nabokov Studies* 4, 1997: 95-115.

Brown, Clarence. "Nabokov's Pushkin and Nabokov's Nabokov," *Wisconsin Studies in Contemporary Literature* 8 (2), 1967: 280-293.

Brown, Edward. "Nabokov, Chernyshevsky, Olesha and the Gift of Sight," in *Literature, Culture and Society in the Modern Age*, pt. 2, *In Honor of Joseph Frank*, ed. Edward J. Brown et al. Stanford, 1992.

Chernyshevskaia, N. M. *Letopis' zhizni i deiatel'nosti N.G. Chernyshevskogo*. Moskva, 1953.

Chernyshevski, N.G. *Polnoe sobranie sochinenii* in 16 Vols. Moscow, 1939-1953.

Connolly, Julian. "The Major Russian Novels," in *The Cambridge Companion to Nabokov*. Ed. by Julian W. Connolly. Cambridge: Cambridge University Press, 2005: 135-150.

Culler, Jonathan. *The Pursuit of Signs: Semiotics, literature, deconstruction*. London: Taylor & Francis, 2001.

Davenport, Guy. *The Geography of the Imagination: Forty Essays*. Jaffrey, New Hampshire: Nonpareil Book, 1997.

Davis, Natalie Zemon. *The Gift in Sixteenth-century France*. Madison: University of Wisconsin Press, 2000.

Davydov, Sergei. *"Teksty-matreški" Vladimira Nabokova*. Munich, 1982.

_____ "*The Gift*: Nabokov's Aesthetic Exorcism of Chernyshevskii," *Canadian-American Slavic Studies* 19 (3), 1985: 357-374.

_____ "Weighing Nabokov's *Gift* on Pushkin's Scales." *Cultural Mythologies of Russian Modernism from the Golden Age to the Silver Age*. Ed. Boris Gasparov, Robert P. Hughes, and Irina Paperno. Berkeley: University of California Press, 1992: 415-28.

Dolinin, Alexander. "Nabokov's time doubling: from *The Gift* to *Lolita*," *Nabokov Studies* 2, 1995: 3-40.

_____ "*The Gift*," in *The Garland Companion to Vladimir Nabokov*. Ed. by V. Alexandrov. New York: Garland, 1995: 135-169.

_____ "Tri zametki o romane Vladimira Nabokova Dar," *V.V. Nabokov: Pro et Contra*. Vol. 1. St. Petersburg: RKhGI, 1997: 697-740.

_____ *Istinnaia zhizn' pisatelia Sirina*. St. Petersburg: Akademicheskii proekt, 2004.

_____ *Kommentarii k romanu* Dar, in: V. Nabokov. *Sobranie sochinenii russkogo perioda*. 5 tt. St. Petersburg: Simpozium, 1999–2000. Vol. 4: 634-768.

_____ "K istorii sozdaniia i tisneniia romana 'Dar'," *Indiana Slavic Studies* 11, 2000: 339-47.

_____ "Zagadka nedopisannogo romana," *Zvezda* 12, 1997.

_____ "Tsena odnoi bukvy," in *Shipovnik. Festschrift in Honor of Professor Roman Timenchik's 60th Birthday*. Ed. by Yuri Leving, Alexander Ospovat, and Yuri Tsivian. Moscow: Vodolei Publishers, 2005: 82-90.

_____ "*Dar*: Dobavleniia k kommentariam," Part I. *Nabokov Online Journal* I, 2007: <http://etc.dal.ca/noj/articles/volume1/DOLININ.pdf> Accessed July 19, 2010.

Dostoevsky, Fyodor. *The Possessed*. Trans. from the Russian by Constance Garnett. Maryland: Wildside Press, 2009.

Drozd, Andrew M. "Chernyshevski and Pushkin," *Russian Literature* LXII (2007) III: 271-92.

Efimov, Mikhail. "Nabokov and Prince D. S. Mirsky," *The Goalkeeper: The Nabokov Almanac*. Ed. Yuri Leving. Boston: Academic Studies Press, 2010.

Foster, John Burt Jr. *Nabokov's Art of Memory and European Modernism*. Princeton: Princeton University Press, 1993.

Freidin, Gregory. *A Coat of Many Colors. Osip Mandelstam and His Mythologies of Self-Presentation*. Berkeley, Los Angeles: University of California Press, 1987.

Gezari, Janet. "Chess and Chess Problems," in *The Garland Companion to Vladimir Nabokov*. Ed. by V. Alexandrov. New York: Garland, 1995: 44-53.

Glushakov, P. S. "Problemy tipologii i funktsionirovaniia istoriko-biograficheskogo zhanra v literature russkogo zarubezh'ia." *Filologiia i chelovek* 1, 2006: 72-73.

Grayson, Jane. "Washington's Gift: Materials Pertaining to Nabokov's *Gift* in the Library of Congress," *Nabokov Studies* 1, 1994: 21-67.

Greenleaf, Monika. "Fathers, Sons and Impostors: Pushkin's Trace in *The Gift*," *Slavic Review* 53 (1), 1994: 140-58.

Grey, Ian. *Boris Godunov: The Tragic Tsar*. London: Hodder and Stoughton, 1973.

Guadanini, Irina. *Pis'ma*. Munich, 1962.

_____ [aka *Aletrus*]. "Tunnel," *Sovremennik* 3, 1961: 6-23.

Gumbrecht, Hans Ulrich. *In 1926: Living at the Edge of Time*, Cambridge: Harvard University Press, 1997.

Hägglund, Martin. "Chronophilia: Nabokov and the Time of Desire," *New Literary History* 37.2, 2006: 447-467.

Hughes, Robert. "V. F. Khodasevich. Pis'ma k M.A. Tsiavlovskomu," Publikatsiia Roberta H'iuza. *Russkaia literatura* 2, 1999.

Ivleva, Victoria. "A Vest Reinvested in *The Gift*," *The Russian Review* 68 (2), 2009: 283-301.

Jelavich, Peter. *Berlin Alexanderplatz: Radio, Film, and the Death of Weimar Culture*. Berkeley: University of California Press, 2006.

Johnson, Donald Barton. *Worlds in Regression: Some Novels of Vladimir Nabokov*. Ann Arbor: Ardis, 1985.

References

Johnson, Kurt and Steve Coates. *Nabokov's Blues: The Scientific Odyssey of a Literary Genius*. New York: McGraw-Hill, 2001.

Jones, Sonya L. and John P. De Cecco. *A Sea of Stories: The Shaping Power of Narrative in Gay and Lesbian Cultures*. New York: Haworth Press, 2000.

Karlinsky, Simon. "Vladimir Nabokov's Novel *Dar* as a Work of Literary Criticism: A Structural Analysis," *The Slavic and East European Journal* 7 (3), 1963: 284-290.

_____ "Illusion, Reality, and Parody in Nabokov's Plays." *Wisconsin Studies in Contemporary Literature* 8 (2). A Special Number Devoted to Vladimir Nabokov, 1967: 268-279.

_____ "Nabokov and Chekhov: Affinities, Parallels, Structures," *Cycnos* 10.1, 1993: 33-37.

Katsell, Jerome H. [Review of] *"Teksty-Matreški" Vladimira Nabokova* by Sergej Davydov. *The Slavic and East European Journal* 27 (4), 1983: 494-496.

Khazan, Vladimir. *Pinkhas Rutenberg: Ot terrorista k sionistu*. Moscow, Jerusalem: Mosty kul'tury/Gesharim, 2008.

Kissel, V.S. "O nemetskikh pfennigakh i russkom zolotom fonde: Tema deneg v romane V. Nabokova *Dar*," *Russkaia literatura* 4, 2008: 23-36.

Kostalevsky, Marina. "The Young Godunov-Cherdyntsev or How to Write a Literary Biography," *Russian Literature* 43 (3), 1998: 283-95.

Kryzhanovsky, Oleg. "Eduard Menetriés." Publication on the web site of the Zoological Institute of the Russian Academy of Sciences: <http://www.zin.ru/animalia/Coleoptera/eng/menetrie.htm> Accessed July 19, 2010.

Layton, Susan. *Russian Literature and Empire: Conquest of the Caucasus from Pushkin to Tolstoy*. New York: Cambridge University Press, 1994.

Levin, Iu. I. "Ob osobennostiakh povestvovatel'noi struktury i obraznogo stroia romana V. Nabokova *Dar*," *Russian Literature* 9 (2), 1981.

Leving, Yuri. "Tenishev Students Vladimir Nabokov, Osip Mandel'shtam and Samuil Rozov: Intersections." *Russian Jewry Abroad: Articles, Publications, Memoirs and Essays*. Parkhomovsky, M., Ed. Jerusalem, Israel. I (VI), 1998: 141-62.

_____ "Rakovinnyi gul nebytiia (V. Nabokov and F. Sologub)," *V.V. Nabokov: Pro et contra*, Vol. 2. St. Petersburg, Russian Christian State Institute, 2001: 499-519.

_____ "Filming Nabokov: On Visual Poetics of the Text," *Russian Studies in Literature* 40.3, 2004: 6-31.

_____ "Singing *The Bells* and *The Covetous Knight*: Nabokov and Rachmaninoff's Operatic Translations of Poe and Pushkin," *Transitional Nabokov*. Ed. by Duncan White and Will Norman. New York: Peter Lang Publishing Group, 2009: 205-228.

Livak, Leonid. *How It was Done in Paris: Russian Émigré Literature and French Modernism*. Madison: The University of Wisconsin Press, 2003.

Malikova, Maria. "V.V. Nabokov and V.D. Nabokov: His Father's Voice," *Nabokov's World*, ed. Jane Grayson, Arnold McMillin and Priscilla Meyer. Vol. 2. London: Palgrave, 2002.

Malmstad, John. "Iz perepiski V.F. Khodasevicha (1925-1938)," *Minuvshee* 2 (1987): 262-91.

Maslov, Boris. "Poet Koncheev: Opyt tekstologii personazha," *Novoe Literaturnoe Obozrenie* 47, 2001: 172-86.

Mauss, Marcel. *The Gift: The Form and Reason for Exchange in Archaic Societies*. New York: W. W. Norton, 2000.

Mazur, Natalia. "O myshinoi begotne, Pushkine, Marke Avrelie i ob uslovno-funktsional'nykh kontekstakh." in *Shipovnik. Festschrift in Honor of Professor Roman Timenchik's 60th Birthday*. Ed. by Yuri Leving, Alexander Ospovat, and Yuri Tsivian. Moscow: Vodolei Publishers, 2005.

McCormick, Richard W. *Gender and Sexuality in Weimar Modernity: Film, Literature, And "New Objectivity."* New York: Palgrave, 2001.

Minao, Maya. "In Search of a Mailbox—Letters in *The Gift*," *Nabokov Online Journal* I (2007). <http://etc.dal.ca/noj/articles/volume1/MINAO_Search_Mailbox.pdf> Accessed July 19, 2010.

Mirsky, Dmitri. "The Present State of Russian Letters" [*The London Mercury* XVI, 93 (1927): 275-86] in D. S. Mirsky, *Uncollected Writings on Russian Literature*. Ed. by G. S. Smith. Berkeley: Berkeley Slavic Specialties, 1989.

Moynahan, Julian. *Vladimir Nabokov*. Minneapolis: University of Minnesota Press, 1971.

_____ "Nabokov and Joyce," in *The Garland Companion to Vladimir Nabokov*. Ed. by V. Alexandrov. New York: Garland, 1995: 433-444.

Nabokov, Nicolas. *Bagázh* [Russian trans.: *Bagazh. Memuary russkogo kosmopolita*]. St. Petersburg: Zvezda, 2003.

Nabokov, Vladimir. *Dar* in *Sobranie sochinenii russkogo perioda*. 5 vols. St. Petersburg: Simpozium, 1999-2000. Vol. 4.

_____ *Eugene Onegin. A Novel in Verse* by Alexander Pushkin / Trans. with commentary by Vladimir Nabokov, in 4 vols. New York: Bollingen, 1964.

_____ *Lectures on Literature*. Ed. by Fredson Bowers. New York: Harcourt, Brace, Jovanovich, 1980.

_____ *Lectures on Russian Literature*. New York: Harcourt, Brace, Jovanovich, 1981.

_____ *Nabokov's Butterflies: Unpublished and Uncollected writings*. Edited and annotated by Brian Boyd and Robert Michael Pyle; new translations from the Russian by Dmitri Nabokov. Boston: Beacon Press, 2000.

_____ "Pamiati Amalii Osipovny Fondaminskoi," *Literaturnoe obozrenie* 2, 1999: 7-9.

_____ *Pnin*. New York: Alfreed A. Knopf, 2004.

_____ *Selected Letters: 1940-1977*. Ed. by Dmitri Nabokov, Matthew Joseph Bruccoli. New York: Harcourt, Brace, Jovanovich, 1989.

_____ *Sobranie sochinenii russkogo perioda*. 5 vols. St. Petersburg: Simpozium, 1999–2000.

_____ *Strong Opinions*. New York: McGraw Hill, 1973.

_____ *Speak, Memory. An Autobiography Revisited*. New York: G.P. Putnam's Sons, 1966.

_____ *Stikhotvoreniia. Novaia biblioteka poeta*. Ed. M. E. Malikovaia. St. Petersburg: Akademicheskii proekt, 2002.

_____ *Verses and Versions: Three Centuries of Russian Poetry*, selected and translated by Vladimir Nabokov. Edited by B. Boyd and S. Shvabrin. New York: Houghton Mifflin Harcourt, 2008.

References

Nesbet, Anne. "Suicide as Literary Fact in the 1920s," *Slavic Review* 50 (4), 1991: 827-35.

Nicol, Charles. "Music and the Theater of the Mind: Opera and Vladimir Nabokov," *Nabokov at the Limits: Redrawing Critical Boundaries*. Ed. by L. Zunshine. New York: Taylor and Francis, 1999.

Paperno, Irina. *Chernyshevsky and the Age of Realism: A Study in the Semiotics of Behavior*. Stanford: Stanford University Press, 1988.

Peterson, Ronald E. "Time in *The Gift*," *The Vladimir Nabokov Research Newsletter*. Fall 1982: 36-40.

Prokopoff, Stephen S. *Tchelitchew*. *Grove Art Online*. Oxford: Oxford University Press, 2009: <http://www.moma.org/collection/browse_results.php?criteria=O:AD:E:5821&page_number=&template_id=6&sort_order=1> Accessed July 19, 2010.

Prokopov, Timofei. "Zhizni i smerti Mikhaila Artsybasheva," in Mikhail Artsybashev. *Sobranie Sochinenii v dvukh tomakh*. Vol. 1. Moscow: Terra, 1994.

Propp, Vladimir. *Morfologiia skazki. Istoricheskie korni volshebnoi skazki (Sobranie trudov V. Ia. Proppa)*. Moscow, 1998.

Proskurina, Vera. V. Nabokov's *Exegi monumentum*: Immortality in Quotation Marks (Nabokov, Pushkin and Mikhail Gershenzon) // Nabokov's World / Ed. by J. Grayson. Vol. 2. New York: Palgrave, 2002.

Ronen, Irena and Omry. "'Diabolically Evocative': An Inquiry into the Meaning of a Metaphor," *Slavica Hierosolymitana* V-VI, 1981: 371-386.

Ronen, Omry. "Puti Shklovskogo v 'Putevoditele po Berlinu.'" *Zvezda* 4, 1999: 164–72.

Roth, Joseph. *What I Saw: Reports from Berlin 1920-1933*. New York: W. W. Norton & Company, 2004.

Salomon, Roger B. "*The Gift*. Nabokov's Portrait of the Artist," in *Critical Essays on Vladimir Nabokov*. Ed. Phyllis A. Roth. Boston: G. K. Hall and Co., 1984: 185-201.

Scammell, Michael. "The Servile Path. Translating Nabokov by epistle." *Harper's Magazine*. May 1, 2001: 52-60.

Scherr, Barry P. "Nabokov as Poet." *The Cambridge Companion to Nabokov*. Ed. by Julian W. Connolly. Cambridge: Cambridge University Press, 2005: 103-118.

Schiff, Stacy. *Véra (Mrs. Vladimir Nabokov)*. New York: Random House, 1999.

Senderovich, Savely. "Pushkin v 'Dare' V. Nabokova: figura sokrytiia," *Pushkinskii sbornik*. Vypusk 1. Jerusalem, 1997.

Shakespeare, William. *Hamlet*. Oxford: Oxford University Press, 1987.

Shapiro, Gavriel. "Nabokov's Allusions: Dividedness and Polysemy," *Russian Literature* [Holland] XLIII (1998): 329-338.

_____ *The Sublime Artist's Studio: Nabokov and Painting*. Evanston: Northwestern University Press, 2009.

Shklovskii, Victor. *Tret'ia fabrika*. Moscow, 1926.

_____ *Mater'al i stil' v romane L'va Tolstogo 'Voina i mir'*. Moscow, 1928.

Sitwell, Osbert. *Sing High! Sing Low!: A Book of Essays*. New York: Plainview, 1971.

Skonechnaia, Olga. "'People of the moonlight': Silver Age parodies in Nabokov's *The Eye* and *The Gift*," *Nabokov Studies* 3, 1996: 33-52.

Sternweiler, Andreas. *Goodbye to Berlin? 100 Jahre Schwulenbewegung.* Schwules Museum and Akademie der Künste. Berlin: Verlag rosa Winkel, 1997.

Strakhovskii, Leonid. "Novye knigi stikhov," *Sovremennik* 6, 1962.

Struve, Gleb. "Pis'ma o russkoi poezii. II." *Russkaia mysl'* 1-2, 1923.

Tammi, Pekka. "The Three Springs," *The Nabokovian* 24, 1990: 36-39.

_____ "Nabokov's Poetics of Dates" in *Russian Subtexts in Nabokov's Fiction: Four Essays.* Tampere: Tampere University Press, 1999.

Taranovsky, Kiril. *Essays on Mandel'shtam.* Cambridge: Harvard University Press, 1976.

Timenchik, Roman. "Raspisan'e i Pisan'e." *Themes and Variations. In Honor of Lazar Fleishman.* Stanford: Stanford University Press, 1994.

_____ "Voprosy k teksty," *Tynianovskii sbornik.* 6-7-8-ye tynianovskie chteniia. Moscow, 1998.

_____ "O mandel'shtamovskoi nekrologii," *Chto vdrug? Stat'i o russkoi literature proshlogo veka.* Jerusalem, Moscow: Mosty kul'tury / Gesharim, 2009: 550-66.

Toker, Leona. *Nabokov: The Mystery of Literary Structures.* Ithaca: Cornell University Press, 1989.

Tolstoy, Leo. *The Death of Ivan Ilych and Other Stories.* Chicago: Signet Classics, 2003.

Tompa, Andrea. "Kak 'sdelany' imena Nabokova? (Ob imenakh v romane Nabokova *Dar*)," *Studia Slavica Academiae Scientiarum Hungaricae* 46, 2001: 171-183.

Tyler, Parker. *The Divine Comedy of Pavel Tchelitchew: A Biography.* New York: Fleet, 1967.

Vries, Gerard de. "The Fourth Chapter of *The Gift*: Inserted or Concerted?," *The Nabokovian* 40, 1998: 26-36.

Vries, Gerard de and Donald Barton Johnson, Liana Ashenden. *Nabokov and the Art of Painting.* Amsterdam: Amsterdam University Press, 2006.

Urban, Thomas. *Vladimir Nabokov: Blaue Abende in Berlin.* Berlin: Propyläen, 1999.

Waite, Sarah Tiffany. "On the Linear Structure of Nabokov's *Dar*: Three Keys, Six Chapters," *Slavic and East European Journal* 39 (1), 1995: 54-72.

White, Duffield. "Radical Aestheticism and Metaphysical Realism in Nabokov's *The Gift.*" *Russian Literature and American Critics: In Honor of Deming Brown.* Ed: Kenneth N. Brostrom. Ann Arbor: University of Michigan, 1984: 273-291.

Williams, William Carlos. *The William Carlos Williams Reader.* New York: New Directions, 1966.

Wren, Melvin C. *The Course of Russian History.* New York: The Macmillan Company, 1958.

Zimmer, Dieter E. *Nabokovs Berlin.* Berlin: Nicolaische Verlagsbuchhandlung, 2001.

_____ "Nabokovs Berlin" [Presentation at the International Vladimir Nabokov Symposium, St. Petersburg, July 15, 2002] <http://www.d-e-zimmer.de/Root/nabberlin2002.htm> Accessed July 19, 2010.

Zubarev, Dmitrii. "«8 × 8», ili Chernyshevskii i shakhmaty. (Iz kommentariev k nabokovskomu *Daru*. 1—2)," *Philologica* 6 (1999/2000).

Chapter Four
STYLE

Method

The Gift as a Synthetic Work

Nabokov's ninth Russian novel, *The Gift*, is "the longest and most difficult in every respect," and it is also the most challenging of all "to fathom, unless you are steeped in knowledge and love (and, to some extent, linguistic comprehension) of much nineteenth-century Russian literature" (Levy 109). Being a story of creation (or a portrait of an artist at labor), *The Gift* has a style that mimics the texture of literary work in progress. In so doing, as one of the early English critics stated, it obliges one to "recognize the fact that a strong and highly personal literary gift is apt to present itself not as a glib talent to be exploited but as a difficult literary problem to be solved" (Malcolm).

The Gift contains multiple types of narrative—pseudo-biographical, quasi-documentary travelogues, imitations, pastiches, parodies, samples of literary criticism, and purely "artistic" discourses—in which these terms intersect and become relative (Kostalevsky 285). By Nabokov's own admission, the main protagonist in *The Gift* is Russian literature, hence the variety of styles that Nabokov employs in this highly stylized work of fiction.

The forte of Nabokov's style is "the utter concentration of attention, masquerading as the utter dispersion of attention" (Brown, "Nabokov's Pushkin" 286). One of the principal ideas in the formation of Nabokov's style, the old tautology of art for art's sake, is nevertheless inadequate to describe the phenomenon: in *The Gift* we find in one paragraph the entire plot of *Lolita* and then, a few pages later, the remark by the writer-hero which retroactively explains the method of his creator ("It's queer, I seem to remember my future works"; G194). Nabokov's working habits were surprisingly consistent and they are well documented.

Chapter Four. STYLE

Working Methods

When asked once about his working methods, Nabokov described them to Philip Oakes of *The Sunday Times* as follows: "Quite banal. Thirty years ago I used to write in bed, dipping my pen into a bedside inkwell, or else I would compose mentally at any time of the day or night. I would fall asleep when the sparrows woke up. Nowadays I write my stuff on index cards, in pencil, at a lectern, in the forenoon; but I still tend to do a lot of work in my head during long walks in the country on dull days when butterflies do not interfere" (*Strong Opinions* 139-40). This description evokes Fyodor's composing in bed, late night forays of inspiration and his countless strolls in Berlin and through Grunewald while mumbling verses.

A fairly accurate autobiographical description of Nabokov's working method is found in Fyodor's assessment of the insurmountable task—his attempt at writing his father's biography: of "swarms of drafts, long manuscript extracts from books, indecipherable jottings on miscellaneous sheets of paper, penciled remarks straggling over the margins of other writings of mine; out of half-crossed-out sentences, unfinished words, and improvidently abbreviated, already forgotten names, hiding from full view among my papers; out of the fragile staticism of irredeemable information, already destroyed in places by a too swift movement of thought, which in turn dissolved into nothingness; out of all this I must now make a lucid, orderly book" (G138). Although Fyodor cannot perform this task that seems to him bigger than life, Nabokov will take up the challenge of relieving his protagonist and himself of the incredible burden of memory.

Among the main methods that Nabokov used over the course of studying and processing the documentary sources for *The Gift* (especially for the Asian journey and Chernyshevski's biography), Irina Paperno points out the montage of texts, the addition of "color" and "sound" to original documentary "black and white" descriptions with missing dialogue, the realization of metaphor and metaphoricization of life (Paperno). In this, Nabokov's practice is strikingly close to that of the Soviet Formalist School. Fyodor reworks the travelers' notes and memoirs about Chernyshevski in precisely the same way that Shklovsky's Tolstoy and Tynyanov's Pushkin were shown to have assembled "montages" of historical sources in *War and Peace* and *Journey to Arzrum*. In some aspects, however, Nabokov consciously departs from the Formalist theoretical premise. As Boris Eikhenbaum noted in a letter to Shklovsky, the first volume of his monograph on Tolstoy was written "in a style that's half memoir, half novel" (Kostalevsky 285). To combine Fyodor's style with Chernyshevski's idiosyncrasies, Nabokov takes excerpts from real diaries by the revolutionary writer. While Eikhenbaum in his quest for scholarly objectivity "makes a distinction between 'psychological' and 'literary' analysis of the diaries," Nabokov in practice "substitutes a psychological

[Ill. 4-1] Page from *The Gift's* second chapter as printed in *Sovremennye zapiski*, with Nabokov's corrections (Library of Congress, Washington, D.C.)

analysis for a literary one. Under Nabokov's pen — or rather, Godunov-Cherdyntsev's — the idiom of Chernyshevski's diaries becomes a mirror reflecting the psychology of his personality" (Ibid. 287).

Fundamentally, the evolution of Nabokov's method throughout his career was extremely logical. It was based on a rational blending of literature with an ordinary landscape of everyday reality by weaving the documentary sources into refined fabric of prose. The key in *The Gift* is the multi-dimensionality — Nabokov always maintains a profusion of multiple planes (reality, fantasy, fiction) and bifurcate visions (in both the physical and the transcendental sense). Nabokov's *alter ego* reflects this constant duality of existence: there is a Fyodor "who lives in quotidian reality and a Fyodor who has access to another realm of inspiration and vision" (Connolly 143). The account of Fyodor composing a poem supports this formula: "He was somnambulistically talking to himself as he paced a nonexistent sidewalk; his feet were guided by local consciousness, while the principal Fyodor Konstantinovich, and in fact the only Fyodor Konstantinovich that mattered, was already peering into the next shadowy strophe" (G55).

Nabokov left clues for future readers willing to explore his methods, mainly through the descriptions of his protagonist's own research practices. This is how Fyodor's preparatory work is described: he "collected material, read until dawn, studied maps, wrote letters and met with the necessary people. From Pushkin's prose he had passed to his life, so that in the beginning the rhythm of Pushkin's era commingled with the rhythm of his father's life. Scientific books (with the Berlin library's stamp always on the ninety-ninth page), such as the familiar volumes of the travels of a naturalist in unfamiliar black and green bindings, lay side by side with the old Russian journals in which he sought Pushkin's reflected light" (G98). Through Fyodor, the author portrays here how he himself had composed Godunov's Central Asian voyages. When D. Zimmer was reconstructing Nabokov's potential sources for this part of *The Gift*, precedence in the search was given to books available at the State and University Libraries in Berlin in the 1920s and 1930s (Zimmer 39). Paperno, who also notes that Nabokov directly mentions the Berlin State Library as the main supplier of Fyodor's primary readings, focuses on the following quote: "I took the trouble to confront one or two passages in your book with the context in the complete edition of Chernyshevski's works, same copy you must have used: I found your cigarette ash between the pages" (G339). This is Nabokov's methodological hint to his critics — in a lapidary manner it describes the basic approach of Fyodor's "reworking of the sources." Boris Gasparov actually looked up the titles in question, which were probably used by Nabokov in the Berlin State Library, and he found that the copies of N. G. Chernyshevski, *Literaturnoe nasledie* [*Literary Heritage*], vol. 1 (diaries) and 2 (letters), contain notes in pencil (sharp, thin lines mark certain words and passages). Similar notes have been found in Steklov's *Eshche raz o Chernyshevskom*

([*More on Chernyshevski*]. Moscow-Leningrad, 1930). Only two words are marked in Steklov's book: "*bog*" (God) and "*bozhii [svet]*" (God's [light]). The marked passages are indeed among those Nabokov used in "The Life of Chernyshevski" (Paperno 317, 19n).

Some critics approach these parallels skeptically and point out that collating paragraphs from the dazzling array of travel and memoir sources available to Nabokov for assembling Fyodor's texts indicates that we are merely following Nabokov's instructions — "a chain of indicators carefully prepared for the reader-investigator" (Greenleaf 145). Monika Greenleaf raises doubts by asking whether Paperno "has not suppressed the ambivalence that Nabokov critics must feel on having 'cracked the code': aren't they just picking up the trail of crumbs Nabokov left especially for them — formalist-structuralist, device-minded readers?" (Ibid.). Pros and cons notwithstanding, reinforced by later discoveries, Paperno's findings still remain relevant.

FORM

The Problems of Form

Critic's Nightmare: "Perfect Cameos in a Poor Mosaic"

What now seems so obvious in scholarship on *The Gift* was still a mystery to bibliophiles half a century ago. The critical reception of the novel will be discussed in greater detail in Chapter Seven; now I would like to cite only a few examples demonstrating that the astounding stylistic beauty of Nabokov's novel actually attracted readers despite its unwelcoming façade of intellectual prose.

The Gift initially overwhelmed readers of both the original and the translation as a verbal barrage of references. Donald Malcolm complained in *New Yorker* that *The Gift* "resembles nothing so much as a mosaic whose every tile is itself a perfect cameo. There simply is no proper distance from which to view it. If one relishes each fragment, the larger patterns are lost. If one attempts to grasp the picture in its entirety, then one finds its manifold glimmering components a great hindrance to the larger vision" (Malcolm 202). The critic compared *The Gift* with *Pale Fire*, finding the former less elegant in its compound narrative structure:

> "In *Pale Fire* Mr. Nabokov strikes off a more formal solution to the problem of fitting a multitude of vivid miniatures into a single composition. Here he frankly offers the reader an intricate puzzle for solution and thereby induces him to sift and sort, to juggle and fit each vivid fragment into its proper place, in order to view the final portrait whole. The brief, bright visions of *Pale Fire*, which are embedded in the scholarly and totally insane notes of the narrator, serve the

purpose that is more coarsely served in the ordinary detective story by hidden clues and extravagant deceptions. Once the reader's interest is engaged by them, he is willing to riffle pages forward and back, pursue connections, and generally expend the intellectual effort necessary to solve the mystery and to bind the disparate elements into literary unity. For those readers who decline to make the mental effort, it remains—if one may judge by reviews of the novel—a mere aggravating jumble of components" (Ibid. 203).

Despite this accommodating approach, having no ability to put *The Gift* side by side with its Russian half-brother, the early American and British critics of the translated version still maintained that the novel inflicts "the boredom of surfeit." According to Malcolm, "in the instance of Fyodor Godunov-Cherdyntsev (and of Vladimir Nabokov), the afflictive gift is an almost preternatural acuity of the senses—chiefly of vision—coupled with the power to render each sensation dazzlingly manifest in words"; Malcolm quotes a sample sentence from *The Gift* as an illustration: "A crow will settle on a boulder, settle and straighten a wing that has folded wrong" (G25). Nabokov, Malcolm comments, "brings down his crow with a single shot and fixes him forever. But when each neighboring sentence similarly preserves in its amber a row of telegraph poles, the slant of a steering wheel, dust, stillness, a skylark, and a hay wagon, and when each succeeding paragraph further compounds the profusion of separate visions, then the reader is likely to run out of mental accommodations for them all" (Malcolm 201). The problem here, essentially, is one of proportion and scale.

Another reviewer casts serious doubts as to whether the novel can be understood without being properly armed with knowledge of Russian literature and history, again noting that this deficiency is amply compensated by the richness of style: "As always with Nabokov, the *word-play shimmers like the colors on a butterfly's wing*, and the novel is a series of perfectly executed intricate formal patterns. 'The participation of so many Russian muses within the orchestra,' as he puts it, makes the translation a stunning achievement—the verbal acrobatics are brilliantly emended, as it were, into English. But it is an essentially literary novel, and for English readers without a wide knowledge of Russian literature much is inevitably lost. Yet an enormous amount remains. Nabokov is one of the most original novelists alive, whatever language he's writing in, and *The Gift* has all the energy of youth, is wonderfully funny, and gives constant delight, phrase by dazzling phrase" (Mitchell 38; italics added). Nancy Sandrof, in the *Books* section edited by Ivan Sandrof (the name of the first president of the National Book Critics Circle sounded uncannily Russian), also praises the quality of Nabokov's language: "Nabokov's prose *flows along like silk* with almost no reminder that it is a translation. If there are finer examples of the modern Russian novel, they have not crossed our path" (Sandrof 16E; italics added). In short, the perceived opaqueness of the novel in the eyes of contemporaries was redeemed by its style.

Form

Translator's Nightmare: "A Glorious Puzzle, a Box of Tricks"

The "verbal acrobatics" were maintained due to the efforts of the translator of the novel, followed by Nabokov's careful editing of the English typescript. How, then, can we explain the relative lack of success of *The Gift* (compared to other translations such as *Laughter in the Dark* and *The Defense*) among the non-Russian audience even today, fifty years after acquiring its English exterior? Nabokov's translator Michael Scammell admits that the reasons are quite obvious: the novel is "very complex and self-referential. It has very little plot, in the conventional sense of the word, and its action is scattered among a largish number of important characters" (Scammell). It is not surprising then that some critics believed that *The Gift* worked better on the level of individual chapters than as a whole. Secondly, the Chernyshevski chapter depends for its resonance on a knowledge not only of Russian literary and political history, but also of the politics of the first wave of Russian emigration. Thirdly, the 'love interest,' such as it is, in the form of the central relationship between Fyodor and Zina Mertz is extraordinarily subtle and refined—"at the opposite pole from the love interest in, say, *Lolita*," as Scammell put it. For those who recognize the fact that the "difficulty" of *The Gift* is an inherent feature of its narrative, the book turns out to be of great interest. Even the non-Russian readership, not sufficiently familiar with the intricacies of Russia's history and culture, admit that "what was left—and it still was plenty—was the novel as a glorious puzzle, a box of tricks that the enchanted reader makes his way through as he opens more and more compartments" (Scammell).

In some ways, the "box of tricks" is a metaphor for the very act of translation that Michael Scammell was engaged in, because every text presents itself to the translator as a succession of obstacles to be overcome. In the case of *The Gift*, whose narrative landscape was deliberately strewn with elaborate traps and decoys, the challenge was doubled, and there were moments when the young translator seriously doubted his ability to cope: "Your husband's text is so crammed with nuances, so rich in diminutives, augmentatives, archaisms, slang, rare words, etc.," Scammell wrote to Véra Nabokov early on in his work, "that I despair of ever rendering even a tenth part of it into English. A pale copy seems to be about the best I can produce." But the battle of wits against the text strongly appealed to Scammell's competitive instincts, and he did improve with practice.

Reader's Nightmare: Experiencing and Immersing

In recent years, with the development of a body of research on *The Gift* and Nabokov's canonization in both Russian literature and American literature, there has emerged an interesting compromise in terms of the reader-response discourse;

at its core is neither a flat rejection of the novel as an incomprehensible mass of fragments nor an unconditional awe, but rather an approach to the novel as a rational problem. *The Gift* is opaque but penetrable; it is difficult but engaging; it is controversial but intellectually rewarding, etc. Peter-John Thomas recreates the typical experience of a reader immersing himself in the novel: "Like the room Fyodor moves into, *The Gift* is a place, not a space. What it does—for Fyodor, for the plot, for the reader—is less important than what it is" (Thomas 224). According to Thomas's phenomenological rendition, *The Gift* is "a thing unto itself, and as such it is to be experienced, not seen through. The intensity of the reading and the density of the description are the depth of the novel. At issue here is the actuality of Nabokov's words, not their meaning" (Ibid.). The outcome of such a philosophical approach is inevitable acceptance of the world beyond the end of the novel as the novel is reread; the proponents of such an interpretation would say that this is not a vicious circle, since the choice to reread the novel or not is a free one—it is an act of curiosity, not necessity.

STYLE

Inventing the Style: "Like a Snake Rendered Sluggish"

In *The Gift* Nabokov creates a special style for Fyodor, where almost every long sinuous sentence, as Brian Boyd metaphorically describes, "bulges with parentheses, like a snake rendered sluggish after swallowing too many plump, irresistible mice. Sentences stretch to accommodate their ample prey, the unruliness and the stray beauty of an inexhaustible world" (Boyd, *Russian Years* 452). Nabokov tames this snake, the beast of the Russian language, by searching for a place among his literary predecessors and the nature of his relationship with them through the lens of Fyodor's probing style.

During Fyodor's apprenticeship he absorbs many styles and confronts challenging questions: what do we find when we look at the literary works of those who believe that writers have a social responsibility, as compared to the works of those who view their tasks as first and foremost aesthetic? And what happens when we read the whole of Russian literature as something other than a commentary on contemporary affairs? David Rampton believes that the answers are found in the many passages devoted to literary matters in *The Gift*: the remarks on the formal aspects of literary art alone—Pushkin's prose style, narrative transitions in different novelists, Andrey Bely's scansion of Russian verse, the extraordinarily rich account of how a poem actually comes to be written—are enough to justify the claims made for the novel as an important study of Russian literature: "The parodies and the evocative details chosen from the works of various authors (and here Nabokov cuts across party lines) show us what a sensitive reader its author was. But it is the evaluations which effectively rewrite Russian literary history and form the centre of the argument...about committed and uncommitted art" (Rampton 89). Creating literature about literature is a particularly demanding task that requires special stylistic accommodations. Nabokov resolves this problem by arranging a panoptic survey of different styles and genres in *The Gift*, and it is through an empirical exploration of them all that Fyodor's talent is tempered.

Stylistic Evolution

In Chapter One of *The Gift* Nabokov experiments with mixing poetry and critical commentary. Poetry in *The Gift* plays a more prominent role than in any other Nabokov novels (Scherr 622), and Fyodor resembles his author in many ways, not the least of which is his own movement from poetry to prose. As another character says to Fyodor, his poems "are but the models of your future novels" (G71). The first chapter contains entire works from what is supposed to be his first collection of poetry, and other poems are scattered throughout, including one, "Lastochka" ("The Swallow") that Nabokov later cited as his favorite among all his Russian poems (*Strong Opinions* 14). Long passages in Chapter One are devoted to analysis of poetry, to questions of poetic influence, to descriptions of the poetic process and to the development of a youthful poet. Nabokov regarded the poetry in *The Gift* as an independent accomplishment, which is evidenced by his decision to include it in the book *Stikhi* (*Poems*). This collection was meant to be the definitive edition of Nabokov's verse, and Fyodor's poems occupy more than a dozen pages of it (Scherr 622). Nabokov himself translated the poetry in many of his novels, including *The Gift*.

In Chapter Two Fyodor abandons lyric poetry for narrative prose. This chapter is composed of two interwoven narratives: the first recounts Fyodor's crossing of Berlin on foot and by tram to teach the private lessons which support him in his writing habit; the second narrates Fyodor's fantasies of following his naturalist father on field journeys through Siberia, Central Asia, and China, observing the flora and fauna, and writing down his observations. The salient features of this style, as summed up by Duffield White, are its "continuous, step-by-step, 'navigational' attention to geographical orientation, its objective detachment (the narrator does not intrude), and its microscopic zeroing-in on the concrete details which are at the surface of sensory experience—revealing color and design to the observer's eye, sounds to the ear, smells to the nose, texture to the touch" (White 278). Fyodor exercises his power of microscopic observation as he passes on the observations and analyses of his father's entomological discoveries. Though most of the protagonist's entomological observations are visual, he opens his writing to all the senses. He demonstrates a finely tuned *sense of smell* when noting the "musk and vanilla" odors of butterflies, and demonstrates an acute *auditory awareness* in detecting the "mouselike squeak of the Death's Head moth" (G110).

Continuous evolutionary adaptation and metamorphosis are the reality that the trained naturalist's eye sees in nature. Fyodor values the narrative of nature because of the "stunning" intensity of perception. And although he comments ironically on how the language of naturalist prose may seem exaggerated insofar as it reflects the hyperbole that nature sometimes produces in evolution, Nabokov cites the following instructive apocryphal story in *The Gift*: later in his life Marco Polo was advised by his publishers to "water down" the miracles which he had observed during his travels (he rejected) (G124). The same quality of observation and overpowering visual acuity attracts contemporary readers of *The Gift*, especially of its entomological and naturalist descriptions. David Bethea compares this experience with the viewer "wearing special magnifying glasses" (341). The moths and butterflies in the second chapter are expertly named and their activities are minutely described; their colors, sizes, and shapes are lingered over "as in a finely drawn illustration for a scientific journal. Their tactile characteristics are brought to life, as though on the reader's own skin, through references to temperature and habitat" (Ibid. 342). White believes that the world described by Fyodor in the style of a naturalist's travel notes, with its continuous state of flux, is similar, essentially, to the authentic childhood experience that he attempts to recreate in his lyric poetry in Chapter One (White 279). Regardless of whether he writes about the hero's youth or his father's explorations, these crucial stylistic features give Nabokov's novel its magical, transformative quality.

In Chapter Three Fyodor changes apartments (and prose styles) "from Pushkin Street to Gogol Street." His method as satirical biographer in Chapter Four is to narrate Chernyshevski's myopic bumbling in a detailed Gogolian style, focusing his narrative on the concrete, material relationships between Chernyshevski and "the things themselves" that surround him in his milieu. Roger Salomon defines the narrative style of the novel in terms close to Joycean stream of consciousness:

> In various ingenious forms, *The Gift* offers what is essentially internal dialogue, and this dialogue, in turn, constitutes the most important formal expression of the fundamental duality of the parodic or mock-heroic self: its life in two "time zones" (Fyodor dates his present experience from the "Year Seven," i.e. time passed since his involuntary exile); its split into ideal hero and clownish ghost; its self-consciousness (direct or through surrogate voice) of its own duality, one avatar mocking the other, the irony generated by disparity. Sometimes Fyodor denigrates memory; at other moments, however, he affirms its enduring power; somehow it will determine the shape of the future or, rather, it *is* the future. (Salomon 188)

Style

The Chernyshevski biography in Chapter Four is written in a style that Nabokov had polished earlier in his own literary criticism, mostly reviews and essays that appeared in the Russian émigré periodicals (still not translated into English, they are available in the five-volume Symposium edition of Nabokov's Russian writings). This was a precise and imaginative non-fiction with deadly irony that subversively challenged dull samples of contemporary literature, be they works of Socialist Realism or those produced by his fellow compatriots in Berlin, Paris, or Prague. Chapter Five is a hodgepodge of all of the styles employed in the previous chapters.

Stylistic Peculiarities

Nabokov's prose is abundant with subtle stylistic connotations, neologisms, cross-lingual homonyms, and compound modifiers formed from English models. The following classification of Nabokov's style based on the linguistically relevant properties of the word was adopted by Alexander Nakhimovsky: 1) phonetic shape; 2) morphological structure; 3) typical syntactic and semantic environment; 4) lexical environment: stable combinations, clichés, idioms; 5) stylistic connotations. For Nabokov, the scholar insists, a sixth category is necessary: words in other languages associated with the original through phonetic shape and/or meaning (78). Nakhimovsky collects striking examples from many novels, but I will address only those paradigmatic instances that are relevant to *The Gift* and that derive from the text of this novel.

Nabokov's vocabulary is conspicuously rich, comprising words of widely differing origins. Neologisms formed by compounding are not typical, and the Russian language for the most part resorts to affixation; so does Nabokov, as in the phrase "ankle-high mirror" = "*shchikolodnoe zerkalo*" (G64). Nabokov's borrowings from English extend beyond the reworking of an occasional word. In English, it is possible to take an entire phrase and place it in front of a noun, thereby creating a compound modifier. Surprisingly enough, Nabokov does the same thing in Russian: "for cruelty in everything, self-satisfied, taken for granted" (G81; in Russian: "za zhestokost' vo vsem, samodovol'nuiu, *kak-zhe-inachnuiu*"); the modifier translated as "taken for granted" is formed from the Russian phrase "*Kak zhe inache?*" (literally "Of course, how else?") (Nakhimovsky 80).

Godunov-Cherdyntsev notes an ambiguity in a phrase from Lermontov: "Has it ever occurred to you that in Lermontov's most famous short poem the 'familiar corpse' ["*znakomyi trup*"] at the end is extremely funny? What he really wanted to say was 'corpse of the man she once knew.' The posthumous acquaintance is unjustified and meaningless" (G73). As Nakhimovsky justly acknowledges, "in the context of the poem only one meaning is permissible, and the extra possibility appears accidental and comic. In Nabokov ambiguity is a conscious device, multiplying associations and helping to break tradition" (Ibid. 81). Another illustration of such a multiplication is Nabokov's description of the editor Vasiliev's daughter, who makes a living in Paris as an actress, as a "cinema failure" (*"fil'movaia neudachnitsa"*). Here Nabokov combines two images — the unfortunate heroine and the unsuccessful actress; in the English translation this is simply reduced to "an unsuccessful actress" (G62).

Nabokov's urge to overcome flat prose includes what Nakhimovsky calls an *animation of style*, "reminding the reader that adjective-noun pairs are more complicated and richer than they may seem at first glance" (Ibid. 81). Initially, one might take *telefonnaia poza* ("telephone pose") for the positioning of the instrument itself, but it turns out to be the pose of Aleksandra Yakovlevna sitting next to the telephone receiver. The English text removes any duality ("As soon as she put the receiver to her ear her body assumed its usual *telephone posture* on the sofa"; G140).

Words that for various reasons do not belong together sometimes clash not only with another word, but with the syntactic construction in which they are placed. For example, in the use of the adnominal genitive case, which Nabokov employs for an unusual purpose ("a long dotted line of beautiful days, interrupted from time to time by the interjection of a thunderstorm," G339; "the globes of breasts," G336; "the hot silk of her body," G335; all cited in Nakhimovsky 82). Adding to Nakhimovsky's excellent thesis, one should also take into consideration the rhythmic organization of words within the syntactic units. Nabokov's prosaic sentences often read like a poetic construct profuse with inner-rhymes: "He broke crockery, soiled and spoiled everything" (G225); the mirroring elements here are *broke — crock* and *soiled — spoiled*.

Sometimes in *The Gift* the same verb will have different meanings in different semantic environments. For instance, the verb *to communicate* requires uniting animation and spatial proximity in a single context. Therefore, of the barefoot Godunov-Cherdyntsev Nabokov says: "moss, turf, sand, each in its own way, communicated with the soles of his bare feet" (G335). Here "communicated" (*soobshchalsia*) means physical contact. But there is also a sense of communication and a hint of *soobshchestvo* ("complicity"), a shared secret — all because of the introduction of "each in its own way," which turns the moss, grass, and sand into the animated characters of the sentence (Nakhimovsky 83). Note also the metaphysical dimension of the word in the title of Koncheyev's book "Communication." Even a subtle difference between the active and passive voices of the verbs in Nabokov's fiction can acquire semantic importance. Thus, for instance, Chernyshevski's arrival in Siberia brings about neither the end of his travels nor any improvement in his habits of observation: the convict is subjected to frequent resettlement within the region, and he no longer has a permanent place to call home, becoming a prisoner who has no control over his movements or destination. This situation, according to Hana Pichova, is underscored by Fyodor's literary style. At this point of his biography, Fyodor chooses passive verb constructions, such as "He had been removed to Siberia" (G281); "Chernyshevski was transferred to Alexandrovski Zavod" (G285); "He was taken to Krasnoyarsk, from there to Orenburg" (G293). Since throughout the rest of his sketch Fyodor "uses active verb constructions, the passivity on the stylistic level underlines and mirrors here the thematic level—Chernyshevski's own inertia" (Pichova 81). Inertia prevents the doomed hero from making anything out of his condition and it is because of this passivity that Chernyshevski remains unproductive in Siberia.

To sum up the stylistic arsenal of Nabokov: the writer employs the entire linguistic and cultural context of the word. Moreover, he never uses a stylistic device in isolation: "neologism appears in a metaphor, a metaphor is supported by an alliteration, an alliteration leads into a bold grammatical construction. Nabokov tests the strength of grammatical barriers for the sake of maximal expressiveness, which he achieves through the artful disregard of generally accepted norms" (Nakhimovsky 84).

TRANSITIONS

From Prose to Prose

Despite being a patchwork of pieces, narrated in different voices and from multiple perspectives, *The Gift* does not produce the effect of an amalgam of texts chaotically or arbitrarily sewn together. The joints between narrative planes are exceptionally subtle and often remain invisible at the first reading. Let us study just two examples of Nabokov's skilful transitions within the discourse. The first is when Fyodor suddenly regains consciousness in the middle of a Berlin street while heading towards his pupil's home:

> ...in Grandfather's time and past some shortish fir trees which used to become quite round in winter under their burden of snow: the snow used to fall straight and slow, it could fall like that for three days, five months, nine years—and already, ahead, in a clear space traversed by white specks, one glimpsed *a dim yellow blotch approaching, which suddenly came into focus, shuddered, thickened and turned into a tramcar*, and the wet snow drifted slantingly, plastering over the left face of a pillar of glass, the tram stop, while the asphalt remained black and bare, as if incapable by nature of accepting anything white, and among the signs over chemists' shops, stationers' and grocers', which swam before the eyes and, at first, were even incomprehensible, only one could still appear to be written in Russian: Kakao. (G80)

―――――――――――――― Chapter Four. STYLE ――――――――――――――

The techniques used here by Nabokov are striking: like an experienced cinematographer or stage designer he first erects the "noise screen" to obstruct the visual field ("snow used to fall straight and slow"); then he accelerates the temporal dimension ("for three days, five months, nine years") until the perception is literally blurred, and next—in a purely cinematic technique—he starts adjusting the lenses ("suddenly came into focus"). The result of this visual transition is a spatial movement to a new terrain, from Russia to Germany, with sophisticated reinforcement by an interlinguistic joke: the word "Kakao" (meaning "hot chocolate" as in the cacao tree: *Theobroma cacao*) is written the same way in both Russian and German fonts.

A slightly different device is employed in another transition between the narrative planes just a few pages later. As with the first example, I will highlight the exact juncture with italics. Crossing the square and turning into a side street, Fyodor

> walked toward the tram stop through a small, at first glance, thicket of fir trees, gathered here for sale on account of the approach of Christmas; they formed between them a kind of small avenue; *swinging his arms as he walked he brushed his fingertips against the wet needles*; but soon the tiny avenue broadened out, the sun burst forth and he emerged onto a garden terrace where on the soft red sand one could make out the sigla of a summer day: the imprints of a dog's paws, the beaded tracks of a wagtail, the Dunlop stripe left by Tanya's bicycle, dividing into two waves at the turn, and a heel dent where with a light, mute movement containing perhaps a quarter of a pirouette she had slid off it to one side and started walking, keeping hold of the handlebars. (G85)

The shift point here is compressed to the narrator's "fingertips" and it concentrates on a tactile rather than a visual experience. Nabokov communicates the feeling of touch ("thick," "wet," "imprints," "tracks") with the utmost care and approaches a three-dimensional effect. The experiential corridor, however, serves the same function and leads the reader through a spatial-temporal vortex ("a kind of small avenue") into another realm—the protagonist's past materialized in a complex discursive model made out of the *sigla*. Sigla (pl. of *siglum*, Lat.) is the list of symbols used in a book, often collected together as part of the front matter; in the Russian original Nabokov has *"pometki"* instead (usually meaning "scribbles," "notes," or "remarks" on the margins of the text). Thus the whole transitive experience is ultimately bookish but seamlessly vivid in its experiential sensibility.

From Prose to Blank Verse

Nabokov constantly shifts styles in *The Gift*, but while at times these transitions verge on invisible, in other instances they might be expressed rather abruptly, as in the bold case of the Marxist quote arranged in verses and recapitulated with an infamous statement ("I have put it into blank verse so it would be less boring"; G245). The idea was probably borrowed from Vladimir (Ze'ev) Jabotinsky's (1880–1940) comic drama, *Chuzhbina* (*Strange Land*) (Vaiskopf 9). Jabotinsky is mainly known today for his leadership of the international Zionist movement; less remembered is the fact that he was a frequent contributor to Russian émigré periodicals. His brilliant essays, originally composed in passionate and beautiful Russian language, were even published simultaneously with the serial installments *The Gift* (see his "Bunt starikov" ["The Elders' Revolt"]. *Sovremennye zapiski* 63, 1937: 390-97).

To a certain degree, the fate of Nabokov's novel repeated that of Jabotinsky's biting satire: the play was first printed in 1908, and immediately confiscated by the Russian authorities. Extended parts of it were published by the Russian-Jewish journal *Rassvet* (*Daybreak*) in 1910, although publication of the complete text of the drama in a separate edition became possible only in 1922, in Berlin. In *Strange Land*, Comrade Makar parodies the Marxist synopsis in the following comic verses:

> Transition
> From semi-natural economy
> To commodity-exchange opened wide
> Before the young Russian capital
> Broad ways for development. But next to it,
> At the very same time, there already grew another
> Force, refuting its essence —
> It was growing, powered by its juices,
> In order to outgrow it one day
> And to overthrow. The name of this force —
> The Great Russian Proletariat.

Jabotinsky's *Strange Land* appeared in the same year as the satirical magazine *Satirikon* started its publication. Sasha Chernyi, Nabokov's future teacher and friend in Berlin, had developed ideas close to those that were expressed in *Strange Land*. As Chernyi mentored the maturing Sirin, Jabotinsky had introduced Kornei Chukovsky, the future children's author and literary critic, to the Russian cultural establishment a few decades earlier.

Nabokov's penchant for ironic rendering of Marx's work on the pages of *Sovremennye zapiski* could also be triggered by the articles that had appeared in the issues preceding the appearance of *The Gift* (*cf.*: V. Voitinsky. "Planned Economy and Contemporary Workers' Movement"; V. Rudnev. "Communism and Nationalism" [both in 1935, Vol. 57]; E. Maksimovich. "Historical Science in the USSR and Marxism-Leninism" [1936, Vol. 62]).

From Blank Verse to Rhymed Verse

Several layers of reality operate together in the description of Fyodor's re-reading of his own poems. While imagining the unpublished review, he contemplates the first poem of his book *Stikhi* (*Poems*), "The Lost Ball," and recreates the feeling of the moment depicted in it. The texts relate the theme of memory and the close link between fiction and non-fiction in Fyodor's consciousness. On a broader level, the entire novel emphasizes "the continuity between poetic experience and the reading of its product," so that fiction in *The Gift* "seems to influence non-fiction" (Ben-Amos 121).

The iamb is the dominant metric foot in Nabokov's poetic repertoire, and within it, iambic tetrameter occupies an unusually prominent place. Nabokov did not accept the less strictly regulated measures that were giving Russian verse such diversity during his time (nor did he adopt any of the typographical experiments that modified the physical appearance of the poetry on the page); Fyodor's father had also been reluctant to recognize these developments: "As to avant-garde verse, he considered it rubbish" (G148). For Nabokov and other émigré poets of the inter-war period, "verse form was an ideologically semanticized area: formal innovation was characteristic of those poets who stood politically to the left, who accepted the Revolution of 1917 and remained in Russia or soon returned to it. For Nabokov, this rendered them unacceptable; the formal choices that he made indicated his nostalgia for a time before the spirit of innovation had changed Russian poetry and Russian society" (Smith 302). Childhood experience as recreated by Fyodor's memory belongs to this early era.

Poetry in Prose and Prose in Poetry

In spite of what might be understood as conservatism in his poetic tastes, Nabokov was well aware of the developments in modern Russian verse. He made intense use of some common innovations of his time for satirical purposes; although remaining largely content with pre-Symbolist conventions, Nabokov did adopt some of the least radical new devices. Godunov-Cherdyntsev's poetry in many respects differs from that of Nabokov—not only architectonically and structurally but also stylistically and thematically. Mikhail Lotman, for instance, believes that the formal and emotional austerity of Fyodor's poetics, and his preoccupation with description of material surroundings, put his poems in close proximity with Osip Mandelstam's first book, *Stone* (1913) (Lotman 65). Maria Malikova specifies that Godunov-Cherdyntsev's poetry should not be evaluated in terms of direct connections to specific authors, but rather with reverberations and imitations of Acmeist poetics in general. This adaptive technique is personified in the writings of Mandelstam's émigré epigone, Antonin Ladinsky, whose collection *Black and*

Blue (1931) Nabokov reviewed and praised. Another young émigré poet, Boris Bozhnev, produced a book of poems, *Fountain* (1927), consisting entirely of eight-line iambic stanzas containing variations on the same topic (Malikova 33).

Nabokov permeates *The Gift* with either complete poems or poetic bits using different motifs and techniques. Yuri Orlitsky elaborates on the "over-saturation" of Nabokov's prose with poetry: his count yields 1889 fragments in *The Gift* that might be formally considered examples of syllabo-tonic verse, including all major meters (Orlitsky 510):

> (1) The first and most evident group consists of simple quotations which appear in indented columns as poetry, as well as those disguised in regular prosaic lines.
>
> (2) The second group encompasses the poems composed by Fyodor and included in cited reviews (ten poems, 8-12 lines each, plus a few fragments written in iambic tetrameter). A cluster of newer poems being composed by Fyodor before the reader's eyes, which are not part of the book under review, form a subcategory in this group. In his "conservative" metrical repertoire, Nabokov may be seen as a follower of Khodasevich. In Nabokov's poetry as a whole, as with many Russian poets of the nineteenth century, iambic tetrameter "forms a thematically neutral, all-purpose formal resource, a regularly recurring background against which rarer measures are thrown into relief" (Smith 281).
>
> (3) Two additional poems in the novel belong to the final cluster: a sonnet split in two parts and framing Chapter Four, and Fyodor's "translation" of the passage from Karl Marx's *Holy Family* presented in a free iambic pentameter.

Analysis of the various poetic insertions in the text of *The Gift* is inherently difficult because these fragments often glide into a metric prose. This process is emphasized by the author—his rhythmic prose is characterized by irregular meter and occasional inner-rhymes and the shifts between prose and poetry appear to be semantically motivated. Even more interesting are the instances when Nabokov "suddenly" destroys the metric anticipation: a reader, prepared by the cadence of a sentence or a whole paragraph, is waiting for the rhyme or meter to realize itself, but it never does so. In building up these false expectations, Nabokov does not imitate verse within prose, but sets a trap. One of the inherent rules of his artistic game is that a phantom of verse should be obliterated *prior* to its shaping into "the cabbage dactylics of the author of *Moscow*" (G157) (Orlitsky 515). The unnamed author of the novel *Moscow* (1926) is Andrey Bely (1880–1934), famous for inventing the diagrammatic system of notation of poetic meter in which he calculated and graphically traced the patterns of unrealized metric stresses, or "half stresses" in works of Russian poetry.

Nabokov thus emerges in his novel not merely as a poet or critic, but also as a scholar of prosody who advances the findings of his indirect mentor ("When I was a boy, I was greatly fascinated by Bely's admirable work," Nabokov would confess in 1964 in his *Notes on Prosody* 14). Bely's shadow also comes across in Fyodor's description of his work on systematization of Russian rhymes:

> There were also certain treasured freaks, rhymes to which, like rare stamps in an album, were represented by blanks. Thus it took me a long time to discover that *ametistovyy* (amethystine) could be rhymed with *perelistyvay* (turn the pages), with *neistovyy* (furioso), and with the genitive case of an **utterly unsuitable** *pristav* (police constable). In short, it was a beautifully labeled collection that I had always close to hand. (G53)

The "utterly unsuitable" image is found in Bely's poem "Here he is again, among the fighting men lines..." (*"Opiat' on zdes', v riadakh boytsov..."*):

> They will call and break open the door.
> In blind effort, *furioso*,
> Like a beast, he will bark a command,—
> And will enter with his squad, the ferocious *police constable*.
>
> *Vot pozvoniat, vzlomaiut dver'.*
> *V slepom userdii neistov,*
> *Komandu riavknet, budto zver',—*
> *Voidet s otriadom liutyi pristav.*
>   (Bely 453; noted in Lavrov 551, n. 6. Translation is mine)

Poetic Motifs and Patterns

Poems in the novel are associated with otherworldly motifs, leading back to the two central plot lines of the book. A rich and structurally complex novel, *The Gift* develops thematically along two fundamental plot lines: the more prominent of the two concerns the development of the artistic gift of a young writer; the second deals with the romance of Fyodor and Zina, the embodiment of his muse (Johnson 93). The representation of poetry is of prime importance in the elaboration of both of these plots, hence it occupies a substantial part of Chapter One in the form of Fyodor reciting poems from his recently published collection. This act of re-reading, which shifts in voice from the author to an imagined sympathetic reviewer, allows us to access the poet's creative consciousness, to understand why Fyodor wrote the poems and what he accomplished with them (Morris, "Nabokov's Poetic Gift" 461). For Fyodor, these poems are the keys to his past. In another context, the hero refers to the Russian language and memory as his *keys to Russia*. Poems cannot transport Fyodor to his native land, a place physically separated from him by distance and exile; nonetheless they take the protagonist to the childhood from which he is removed only by time (Ibid. 462). As Pichova argues, Fyodor is "not mentally trying to escape his rented room or Berlin in general; rather, he is in the process of learning how imaginatively to convert an uninviting and unfamiliar environment into a place of creative activity" (Pichova 31).

As already mentioned, Nabokov appears rather conservative in his poetic tastes and verse form compared to other émigré poets and, especially, his Soviet counterparts. His texts do not look as fresh as Mayakovsky's or Khlebnikov's verbal experiments, but Nabokov "was not merely dismissed or ignored"—his poetry had been subjected to rigorous critical review, and all but the most hostile commentators "conceded Nabokov's skill...as a poet" (Morris, "Vladimir Nabokov's Poetry" 310). When Nabokov's status as a major prose writer became established, criticism of his poetry alone became more problematic for observers: discussion of it gradually became a function of the perception of Nabokov the prose writer. This state of affairs, Paul D. Morris explains, "reflects as much on the ability of critics to assimilate the poetry of a prose writer as on the poetry itself" (Ibid.).

A survey of émigré responses reveals that the majority of critics assessed Nabokov's poetry primarily in terms of its formal characteristics, in particular his use of language and imagery: "The thematic concerns which were to occupy the attention of a later generation of critics were almost totally absent from the early émigré criticism of Nabokov's poetry. Given Nabokov's celebrated independence as a writer, both formally and thematically, this absence may reflect the inability of early viewers to discern the thematic trends and motifs visible to later critics who enjoyed the perspective of time and an expanding volume of critical response" (Ibid.). Curiously, in this vacuum Nabokov steps forward as his own impartial critic and offers rather harsh assessment of Fyodor's (and, to a certain extent, his own) juvenile poetry.

The Camouflaged Ending

The novel ends, appropriately enough, with a paragraph written out in such a way as to undermine our typographical conventions:

> Good-by, my book! Like mortal eyes, imagined ones must close some day. Onegin from his knees will rise—but his creator strolls away. And yet the ear cannot right now part with the music and allow the tale to fade; the chords of fate itself continue to vibrate; and no obstruction for the sage exists where I have put The End: the shadows of my world extend beyond the skyline of the page, blue as tomorrow's morning haze—nor does this terminate the phrase. (G366)

It is immediately clear that the language of this final *paragraph* of the novel "is not what we are accustomed to expect of written prose—fiction or otherwise" (Scott 153). Indeed, the apparent rhyme sets and iambic meter, particularly of the beginning and concluding lines of the paragraph, suggest that the discourse might better be interpreted as one of verse, rather than one of prose. Conventional publication of poetry "has established a certain cultural bias in our understanding of the *poetic line*," but the example of *The Gift*'s finale demonstrates that the typographical practice associated with *paragraphs* cannot disguise the real identification of the discourse as a *poem* (Ibid. 158).

Arranging the passage in the following way shows that it is, in fact, a poem:

Good-by my book! Like mortal eyes,	a
imagined ones must close some day.	B
Onegin from his knees will rise—	a
but his creator strolls away.	B
And yet the ear cannot right now	c
part with the music and allow	c
the tale to fade; the chords of fate	D
itself continue to vibrate;	D
and no obstruction for the sage	e
exists where I have put The End:	F
the shadows of my world extend	F
beyond the skyline of the page,	e
blue as tomorrow's morning haze—	G
nor does this terminate the phrase.	G

Printed in such a manner, the verse is identical to the rhyme scheme known as the "Onegin stanza," conforming to strict rhyming pattern: aBaBccDDeFFeGG (the lowercase letters represent feminine rhymes and the uppercase—masculine rhymes, i.e. on the final syllable). The name of this form derives from Pushkin's *Eugene Onegin*, which is composed in fourteen-line stanzas following this standard structure with consistent rhyme, rhythm, and cadence. Unlike other traditional forms of prosody, the Petrarchan or Shakespearean sonnets, the Onegin stanza is not divided into quatrains or couplets. Additionally, it is written in iambic *tetrameter*, rather than in iambic *pentameter* as in traditional sonnets, which gives Pushkin's stanza a sense of gliding reinforced by the dynamic transitions from sonnet to sonnet.

Through Pushkin's invented stanza the reader is invited to enter the poetry of the novel and simultaneously look both beyond the confines of the artifice and back to the beginning of the novel. This structural closed circle is reminiscent of Fyodor's poetry; the protagonist concludes his published collection of poetry with a poem which refers back to the first work in the collection, and his book about Chernyshevski begins and ends with a sonnet (Morris, "Nabokov's Poetic Gift" 467). In *The Gift*, a novel about art, as Nabokov says in the Foreword, lyricism and parody are characteristically held in suspension in the final paragraph: "lyricism creates emotional heightening, proper to the conclusion of a novel, until the rhyme's jangle obtrudes, suffusing lyricism with parody" (Williams 254).

Leona Toker notes that the final words "The End," which Nabokov "revised into" the English version, suggest an almost cinematic device (Toker 152). One should also be aware of the fact that this phrase — absent in the Russian original — is conditioned by the translation itself: instead of "*tam, gde postavil tochku ia*" [in Russian, literally: "where I have put the dot," referring to the period at the end of a sentence], which could be unclear to the English-language reader, Nabokov opts for a clearer analogy.

The anticlimactic ending, which might remind a contemporary reader more of the Coen Brothers' enigmatic finales, will not hinder the readers from picturing it to themselves. Fyodor's keys have been stolen, Zina's keys were left inside the apartment, but the lovers, finally alone together, have attained the code that will let them into a whole new world. Whether the readers will be allowed to follow the heroes along their route is merely an epistemological problem.

The fact that Nabokov's novel functions like a "self-teaching handbook of literary inspiration" (G76) is obvious on many levels; although it has been frequently cited that the circular structure of the last paragraph leads back to the novel's opening exposition, it has not been noted that the sentence concluding Chapter One of *The Gift*, which contains the words "self-teaching handbook," in fact sends the attentive reader straight to the epigraph from the *Textbook of Russian Grammar* preceding that chapter and indeed the whole book.

POINTS OF VIEW

Shifting of Narration: I — He — We

What gives Nabokov's novel its specific quality as a work that both discusses and reproduces literary creativity, presenting literature as a main component in the reality of its characters and its readers, is the "double identity of Godunov-Cherdyntsev" (Ben-Amos 118). Godunov-Cherdyntsev "imagines the inner life of others and assumes their identities": in the imaginary review of his poetry the main character "speaks of himself in third person; he conducts imaginary dialogues with Koncheyev, invents inner monologues for Yasha's father, and assumes the 'I' of his own father" (Livak 180). This duality is made possible by the constant shifting of narration, initially outlined by Iurii Levin as three modes of narration: first person narration at the time of the action described, first person narration from a distance of time and third person authorial omniscient narration.

The narrator of *The Gift* blurs the lines between narrative voices, mixing "I" and "we," as in the description of Fyodor's trip home: "He was walking along streets...Here at last is the square where we dined" (G53). Prepared by previous alternation in narrative voices, one initially understands that it is Fyodor who says "we." This assumption is broken several lines later. At the intersection of chronological time and narrative time in *The Gift*, "the protagonist turns into the author and the reader has to return to the beginning of the book to read it as a novel by Godunov-Cherdyntsev" (Dolinin, "Nabokov's time doubling" 40). The fictional biography constituting the plot of the novel, according to Anat Ben-Amos, "is presented as generated together with the experiences it is based on, so that fiction and non-fiction are intertwined rather than hierarchically measured; none is more important than the other as they are parts of a whole in the world of the novel" (119).

Pekka Tammi tackles the problem of narrative voices in *The Gift* as follows: the first assumption is that all voices in the novel belong to Fyodor, who relates the story of his artistic maturation from the distanced position of a mature artist, in which case *The Gift* is his creation; the second assumption is that the voices are divided between the author-narrator and Fyodor, in which case Fyodor's novel cannot coincide with *The Gift*; the third and final assumption postulates that all voices belong to Fyodor but he does not control them, for they constitute his "stream of consciousness" (a view elaborated by Levin). Initially, these problems can be illustrated with the following catalogue of narrative forms (Tammi 82-83):

> 1st person + past tense referring to the hero's past
> 1st person + past tense referring to the hero's present
> 1st person + present tense referring to the hero's present
> 3rd person + past tense referring to the hero's past
> 3rd person + past tense referring to the hero's present
>
> (Example: "Did I take the keys? Fyodor suddenly thought, stopping and thrusting his hand into his raincoat pocket"; G29)

According to Julian Connolly, "although Fyodor's initial descriptions of one of his father's expeditions are conveyed from the position of external chronicler" (Connolly 145) ("I now imagine the outfitting of my father's caravan"; G116), the gradual involvement in the imaginary reconstruction of Konstantin Godunov-Cherdyntsev's expedition forces him to slip into the scene. Thus Fyodor begins using the first-person plural pronoun 'we' ('*our* caravan moved east'; '*We saw*' [G117])" (Connolly 145), and, finally, he "seems to take on his father's personal perspective" resorting to the first-person singular pronoun as if he speaks from his father's position (Ibid.):

> In Tatsien-Lu shaven-headed lamas roamed about the...streets spreading the rumor that I was catching children in order to brew their eyes into a potion for the belly of my Kodak. (G122-23)

Eventually, as Connolly suggests, the character "recognizes the problem with this approach" (145). Fyodor tries to explain to his mother the inability to continue the biography: "If you like I'll admit it: I myself am a mere seeker of verbal adventures..." (G139).

Stephen Blackwell thoughtfully describes this problematic aspect of the novel and its effects on the experience of reading *The Gift*:

> Considering that a book's beginning is the place where a reader becomes situated in its context, the first chapter of *The Gift* makes for an inauspicious start. The chapter comprises at least sixty narrative segments representing five or more points of view, some "real" (the narrator, Fyodor old and young), some imagined (reviewers, Alexander Chernyshevski, Koncheyev). Making matters still more complex is the tendency of these fragments to bleed seamlessly into each other. As a result, it is a common experience in a first reading of *The Gift* to imagine the continued presence of a narrator who "faded out" several paragraphs earlier, and finally to be shocked by the unexpected "new" voice that suddenly announces "I...." (Blackwell 61)

Blackwell singles out in Nabokov's novel the following six primary unmarked transition types, in order of complexity:

• Unmarked shift between third and first person narration;
• Unmarked insertion of a character's discourse into the context of third person narration;
• Unmarked transition to an inserted prose text (article, letter, or novel);
• Unmarked transition to verse forms;
• Unmarked shift between different levels of first or third person narrators (imagined or real sources, various time frames);
• Unmarked shift to "imaginary" events, dialogues, texts (Ibid. 60).

The "Hidden" Author

The problem of "narrative voices" leads us to the notion of narrative "points of view" and to the ultimate question: who is *the author* of the novel we read? This has become perhaps the single most debated issue in scholarship on *The Gift*;

Chapter Four. STYLE

I will try to give an overview of the different theories after an appropriate literary-historical introduction. Paul Debreczeny's analysis of Pushkin's semi-fictitious family chronicle *The Blackamoor of Peter the Great* can be applied to our analysis of Nabokov's experiments with narrative modes; as Debreczeny maintains, when Pushkin sought a new manner of writing, what mattered most to him "was not just the question of whether the author was hidden from the reader or revealed to him, of whether he spoke in the first person or the third, but the question of whether he would be courageous enough to write as an intelligent chronicler, whose attitudes would be subtle and implicit, without clownish masks and false assumptions" (31). Pushkin's effort to find an omniscient mode of narration was a ground-breaking endeavor, "but it involved—because of its very novelty—enormous technical difficulties" (Ibid. 33). These complexities may well have caused Pushkin's decision to abandon this novel, yet Nabokov, a hundred years later, was ready to take up the mantle.

Alexander Dolinin posits three possible readings of the novel: the first involves "the status of the text being indefinite"; the second assumes the book to be Fyodor's creation; and the third occurs "when the reader can finally detect the persona of the omniscient author who has hidden behind the mask of the protagonist" (Dolinin, "*The Gift*" 161). The various types of "authorial omniscient narration that encompass and transcend the linear time of the text" represent the super-temporal position of creative consciousness (Ibid.). In his "The Life of Chernyshevski" Fyodor "again uses a first-person narration combined with 'quotes' from a fictitious source (Strannolyubski), but [he] constructs his 'I-mask' in a new way" (Ibid.), different from the one he had used in the unfinished book about his father.

Pekka Tammi suggests that an extrinsic and controlling "author-figure" (the implied author, "Nabokov") has left clues to his own transcendent existence outside the narrative, and at least a portion of the "first-person" references in the novel (i.e. the conclusion: "Good-by, my book!") are assigned to "the author," with no regard for the protagonist's own control over the narrative (84). The scholar states that "there is no sufficient textual evidence to support the view that Fyodor actually 'narrates' his own history, in the proper sense of uttering—and even less *writing*—the totality of the discourses that we encounter in the novel" (Ibid. 86). Rather, one should maintain that Fyodor is "an agent who is struggling to overstep the limitations imposed by his status, consciously aspiring towards the controlling position" of the omnipotent Author (Ibid. 86).

Stephen Blackwell disagrees with this analysis and argues that Tammi has ignored the crucial next step: asking the question, could a "future" Fyodor be that "omnipotent Author" figure? (9). According to Blackwell, this is a possible scenario, and accepting Fyodor's later authorship would resolve questions of his limited awareness and of passages beyond his purview: "a later Fyodor would have access to all such information and more and would be in a position to recombine it artistically" (Ibid.). Therefore, Blackwell concludes, "Fyodor's authorship is the key to the novel's deepest probing of selfhood and otherness, past and present, 'art' and 'reality,' in addition to bringing with it Zina's transformative participation" (Ibid.). Blackwell falls in with those who call Fyodor the novel's "author"; he is convinced that "that the entire novel can be consistently understood as Fyodor's discourse (albeit from several of his perspectives). However, the anomaly in Chapter Three, combined with the fact of Zina's creative participation in the Chernyshevski project, force us to consider that the novel *we* read may indeed represent Fyodor's reading of his novel *The Gift,* perhaps aloud to Zina, thus occasioning the enigmatic half-dialogue about Fyodor's first love" (84).

Still, this interpretation falls short of explaining several gaps in the text, including some very basic questions: for instance, Fyodor's initial failure to notice the April Fool's Day joke behind Alexander Chernyshevski's prank in the first chapter, or more subtle discrepancies related to the descriptions of the protagonist's appearance. Iurii Levin, who asserts that *The Gift* contains "no explicit author, nor...any other figure who would be writing the text of the novel" (Levin 196), has also claimed that we see Fyodor exclusively through his own eyes (Ibid. 205). Pekka Tammi in *Problems of Nabokov's Poetics*, and then Boris Maslov, raise an objection to this view: in the portrayal of Fyodor's appearance, as captured by Zina who has just returned from a fancy-dress ball, the narrator clearly separates himself from the character ("His door was ajar, and as she passed by it through the hall, Zina caught sight of him, pale, with mouth wide open, in an unbuttoned starched shirt with suspenders trailing on the floor, pen in hand and the half-mask on his desk showing black against the whiteness of paper," G206; Maslov 174, 7n). The protagonist of *The Gift* does not have unlimited powers of observation; he cannot be the possessor of an all-embracing consciousness in relation to his own identity.

And what did Nabokov himself think of this? In her letter to Walter Minton of June 15, 1960 Véra Nabokov wrote: "DAR consists of five chapters, four of these are written by the author (as 'invisible observer'), the fifth (No. 4 in the sequence) purports to be the work of the main protagonist" (*Letters to G. P. Putnam's sons*, Berg Collection, NYPL). Véra Nabokov's letters written on behalf of her husband were usually authorized by Nabokov himself. Citing this fact, Marina Grishakova asserts that the correspondence "serves as evidence, which settles the question of the relationship between the auctorial narrator and the protagonist of *The Gift* in favor of advocates of the auctorial presence" (Grishakova 242). However, both sides agree that the protagonist participates in the authorial function and is "more" than a character: the novel is wrapped up in itself, it is both the "cover" and the "content." Although the narrator as the external consciousness retains control over the narrative, the protagonist takes part in the authorial function. Thus there is every reason to speak of *The Gift* as the anticipation of the experimental post-modernist prose of the 1950-1990s (Robbe-Grillet, Pynchon, etc.). On the other hand, Grishakova continues, metafictional recentering is not at all rare in modernist fiction, as seen in prose of Gide in France, and in the Serapion Brothers or Konstantin Vaginov's novel *Goat Song* in the early Soviet Union (243).

I concur with Leona Toker and Alexander Dolinin who argue in their studies that *The Gift* is not entirely a product of Fyodor's artistic labor. The corpus is written instead by an external, invisible author figure whose point of view occasionally coincides with Godunov-Cherdyntsev's cognitive horizon and, at times, is crucially distanced from the main character.

Sources

Where Was Nabokov Borrowing From?

For such a literary-minded author as Vladimir Nabokov the most obvious source for subject matter would be literature itself. Nabokov freely operates within the realms of various cultural traditions and never felt constrained to any particular time frames or languages.

Among Nabokov's often innovative Russian novels of the 1930s, even this "most Russian of Nabokov's later Russian novels" (Foster 146) does reveal its author's multicultural identity. It bears certain English, French and German elements. Postwar German neo-romanticism and contemporary fiction like Alfred Döblin's *Berlin Alexanderplatz* (1929) colors the self-contained story of Yasha Chernyshevski's suicide pact, especially the portrait of Yasha's German friend Rudolf. More significant, however, is the French undercurrent that marks several key discussions and scenes in *The Gift*. While reassessing the Russian literary tradition in his imaginary conversations with the poet Koncheyev in chapters One and Five of *The Gift*, on two occasions Fyodor and Koncheyev depart from their overwhelmingly Russian agenda, and each of these departures highlights Fyodor's modernity as a writer by referring to major figures from nineteenth-century French literature. Fyodor speaks in Chapter One of Rimbaud's sonnet "Voyelles" (G74), which seems to influence his own colored hearing (*audition colorée*). Rimbaud thus, as Foster suggests, becomes a crucial model for Fyodor's authorship, yet only in a special, limited sense: on the one hand, Rimbaud epitomized radical innovation for many early twentieth-century European modernists, but on the other, the poet failed to see the full novelty of what he discovered. Rimbaud's experiments thus correspond to Nabokov's doubts about what he called the "super-modern" or "ultramodern" side of modern literature, now known as the avant-garde. The second imagined dialogue, in *The Gift*'s fifth and final chapter, develops a contrasting view of the modernity of French literature (Foster 147).

The Method of Processing Historical Sources

"Art Based in Fact"

Alfred Appel's *Annotated* Lolita, Carl Proffer's *Keys to* Lolita, Gene Barabtarlo's *Phantom of Fact* on *Pnin*, Brian Boyd's annotations to *Ada*, as well as Dolinin's meticulous notes on the Russian edition of *The Gift*, have advanced Nabokov research greatly by focusing on literary commentary and the historical background of the respective texts. Some of Nabokov's specific methods for working with documentary sources for *The Gift* have been detailed in major studies that researched the "inserted" texts of the novel—Dieter Zimmer's and Sabine Hartmann's analysis of the Asian journey, and Paperno's dissection of the Chernyshevski biography by Fyodor. According to the German scholars, the reconstruction of Central Asia from travel reports presents Nabokov's systematic effort at visualization, rivaling only his efforts to capture childhood and youth from memory: Nabokov "thoroughly studied the literature available to him, carefully lifted from it the kind of facts he wanted (sometimes just one or two from a book of several hundred pages), homogenizing, blending, paraphrasing, embellishing, condensing, summarizing, expanding, and intensifying the material until it became an artifact of his own: art based in fact" (Zimmer and Hartmann 35).

Like Joyce's Dublin, daily existence in Berlin often supplied Nabokov with facts that he utilized in his fiction. The misfortunate ménage a trios of the Yasha episode in Chapter One turns out to be such a reflection of reality in the novel. The émigré newspaper *Rul'* (with which Nabokov, as a frequent contributor and son of its former editor, was associated) carried a story entitled "The Russian Drama" in the April 19, 1928 issue:

> In Grunewald a Russian student, the medic Aleksei Frenkel', 21 years old, shot and killed his girlfriend, student at an art school, Vera Kaminskaia, 22 years old, after which he shot himself. A second young girl, Tat'iana Zanftleben, who was also supposed to do away with herself, changed her mind at the last minute and, leaving both of her friends lying on the floor, ran out onto the street and meeting a police patrol, informed them of the catastrophe. A doctor in attendance found Frenkel' still among the living but, brought to the hospital, he soon died. Frenkel', a native of Odessa, worked as a secretary for one of the Russian doctors in Berlin. Vera Kaminskaia had lived earlier in Munich and came to Berlin to study the applied arts. Frenkel' and Kaminskaia planned to marry, but material circumstances hindered their plans. This in turn led them to thoughts of suicide.

Their friend Zanftleben, serving as a governess in a Russian family, having discovered the intention of Frenkel' and Kaminskaia, had also announced her intention to do away with herself. (*Rul'* 2248, April 19, 1928: 4; Quoted in Nesbet 828)

The initial report, as it turns out, substantially altered many of the original details of this anecdote. In a follow-up article in *Rul'* the next day, the editors explained that Vera's real name was "Valeria"; that Aleksei Frenkel' had come to Berlin to study medicine and "that, in fact, Tat'iana Zanftleben had had no idea suicide was in the offing until too late—that is, until the three of them were on their way to the banks of the lake in Grunewald" (Ibid. 829; the scene has even moved outdoors—"a rather romantic change" in the process of literary deformation, as Nesbet remarks). What is clear, though, is that Nabokov takes note of this event and further "blends, paraphrases, embellishes" (or, in Fyodor's words, "shuffles, twists, mixes, rechews, and rebelches"; G364) it, guided solely by his own sense of creative function.

Times Nabokov Missed: Reconstruction of a Historical Milieu

In reconstructing Chernyshevski's life Nabokov did not limit himself to the available biographies (specifically, the one authored by Steklov); he also reached directly to the original editions of memoirs by Chernyshevski's contemporaries quoted in Steklov's book. Let us examine this opening paragraph of Fyodor's story:

> The soul sinks into a momentary dream—and now, with the *peculiar theatrical vividness* of those risen from the dead they come out to meet us: *Father Gavriil*, a long staff in his hand, wearing a silk, garnet-red chasuble, with an embroidered sash across his big stomach; and with him, already illuminated by the sun, an extremely attractive little boy—*pink*, awkward, *delicate*. They draw near. Take off your hat, Nikolya. Hair with *a russet glint, freckles on his little forehead*, and in *his eyes the angelic clarity* characteristic of nearsighted children. (G212)

Most of the scenes in Chapter Four are based on "collaging of 'deformed' material from several documentary sources" (Irina Paperno's term). The appearance of the hero in "The Life of Chernyshevski" is no exception: it is a montage from several different real accounts of Chernyshevski's childhood. Memoirs of Chernyshevski's childhood friend, I. U. Palimpsestov, present the main source:

> I often saw *Gavriil Ivanovich leading his little boy by the hand*, on their way from church, or sitting with him on the banks of the wide Volga, listening to the lapping

of the waves. The facial features of the boy, whom people called invariably *the little cherub*, were engraved in my memory: *a clean, white little face, with a slight rosy glow*, and barely *noticeable freckles*; a bare little forehead; humble, *inquisitive eyes*; a tiny, *delicately* outlined mouth with *pink lips*; silky *reddish curls*; a friendly smile for acquaintances; a quiet voice, just like his father's,—such are the traits that *have stayed in my memory*... (Steklov, Vol. I: 5; quoted in Paperno 304)

Many details from this description, slightly "deformed," as Paperno notes, were transferred to Nabokov's text: the "reddish curls" were turned into "hair with a russet glint"; the two-neighboring phrases, "[a] little face, with... barely noticeable freckles; a bare little forehead..." were combined into one image, "freckles on his little forehead"; the attribute "pink" was separated from its object and applied to the boy's overall complexion; the nickname "little cherub" was borrowed, but in addition to being transformed into simply "cherub," it became more than a mere description of external appearance. The image in Nabokov's phrase, "and in his eyes the angelic clarity characteristic of nearsighted children" is a combination of Palimpsestov's "humble, inquisitive eyes" and a detail taken from another source—the memoirs of A. I. Rozanov. In describing the "delicate" face of the little boy (*cf.* Nabokov's "delicate little boy"), Rozanov makes the following observation: "to his great misfortune, he was extremely nearsighted" (Rozanov's memoirs are cited in Steklov, Vol. I: 6).

Places Nabokov Never Visited: Reconstruction of Geography

Quasi-memoirs

Konstantin Godunov-Cherdyntsev had presumably disappeared in Central Asia around 1917. For his son, Fyodor, writing the father's biography a decade later turns into a series of verbal adventures in an "inky jungle" (G138)—a dark and chaotic world of writing rough drafts and reading notes and recollections. Fyodor slowly projects himself into the story and seamlessly changes pronouns (from neutral "he" to a plural "we"), thus usurping the father's place. Monica Manolescu, who has studied the metamorphosis of the narrative outsider into an autodiegetic storyteller at the center of the plot, observes that this is a "classical scenario in a biographer's life, since every biographer is a divided character, both a submissive servant and a rebellious subject" (4). A different understanding of the pronominal fluctuations in *The Gift* can possibly be traced back to Marco Polo's *The Description of the World*, a major intertext, overtly mentioned several times in the novel. A miniature of Marco Polo leaving Venice decorates Fyodor's father's desk:

Chapter Four. STYLE

> Among the old, tranquil, velvet-framed family photographs in my father's study there hung a copy of the picture: Marco Polo leaving Venice. She was rosy, this Venice, and the water of her lagoon was azure, with swans twice the size of the boats, into one of which tiny violet men were descending by way of a plank, in order to board a ship which was waiting a little way off with sails furled — and I cannot tear myself away from this mysterious beauty... (G113-14)

The picture described here is an anonymous English miniature from the Bodleian Library, Oxford (Codex Bodley 264, fol. 218r, c. 1400), which appears at the beginning of a manuscript of Marco Polo's voyages, in French, entitled *Li Livres du Graunt Caam*. The miniatures from this book have been reproduced with several modern editions of Marco Polo's book (Vries and Johnson 170), and its description in *The Gift* functions "as a magical visual stimulus provoking Fyodor's vision of his father's travels, the emergence of his visionary voice following closely the progress of the paternal caravans" (Manolescu 4). When taking a close look at Marco Polo's *The Description of the World*, one is struck by pronominal inconsistencies reminiscent of those in *The Gift*, inconsistencies which, in the case of *The Description*, stem from the double paternity of the text. As a matter of fact, Manolescu emphasizes, Marco Polo's famous book was not written by the Venetian merchant himself. In 1298, in a prison in Genoa, he "dictated the story of his travels to a professional scribe, an Italian writer Rustichello of Pisa" (Ibid. 6). Despite this technical bifurcation, the book is defined as "our book," in which Marco Polo and Rustichello, a narrator and a hired pen, share textual space. Moreover, due to the shifts between the first-person singular and plural pronouns it is sometimes difficult to distinguish between the two figures. "Gradually, the space of the voyage itself and the space of the narrative with its forward and backward movements from one topic to the other are superimposed, with the effect of a total blurring of boundaries between the act of traveling and the act of telling" (Ibid. 6-7). Fyodor certainly does not go so far as to construct a complete explorer identity ("In this desert are preserved traces of an ancient road along which Marco Polo passed six centuries before I did"; G124). He quickly dissipates the illusion of his personal participation in an Asian expedition and, at the end of Chapter Two, abandons his text.

Travellers' Accounts

While Marco Polo's medieval memoirs, with their dual authorship, may have served Nabokov as a model narrative text, other sources he relied upon in the intertextual construction of the explorer's biography mostly included recent accounts of journeys to Central Asia, Tibet and China. The beauty and the complexity of Chapter Two of *The Gift* lie "precisely in the ambiguous encounter between skilful, lucid documentation and ardent subjectivity, between a yearning for influence and the birth of an original, insolent voice" (Manolescu 5). Dieter Zimmer has made a significant breakthrough in identifying the explorer A. E. Pratt's rare book, *To the Snows of Tibet through China* (1892), which contains illustrations of the species Nabokov had in mind when he was writing of mimicry and crypsis, as well as photographs of Tatsienlu (the farthest point Pratt reached on his trip to Tibet). This source played a major role in the composition of Godunov-Cherdyntsev's travels, and is responsible for the accuracy of *The Gift*'s depiction of Tatsienlu and local geography.

Zimmer writes of his circuitous route in identifying the sources for obscure passages related to Fyodor's father in *The Gift*. In Chapter Five, for example, Fyodor is dreaming of his return to the old Berlin lodging where he meets his (presumably dead) father. The explorer had last been seen alive by a French missionary in the "mountains of Tibet," near a village named Chetu. Fyodor's dream transforms the bluish tulips on the yellow wallpaper of the modest rented room into swans and lilies, and its ceiling becomes "wonderfully ornamented with Tibetan butterflies (there, for example, was *Thecla bieti*)" (G354). How reliable are these projections on the ceiling? They actually are, although one is tempted to read "bieti" as a near anagram of "Tibet" (Boyd, *Russian Years* 470). The butterfly, *Thecla bieti*, whose modern scientific name is *Esakiozephyrus bieti*, turns out to be "a small hairstreak, first described by the French lithographer, publisher and entomologist Charles Oberthür in 1886" (Zimmer, "Chinese Rhubarb" 3). "The specimens Oberthür examined had been sent to him from Tatsienlu by a French missionary, Bishop Félix Biet" (1838–1901) (thus the butterfly's name), who spent nearly three decades in Tatsienlu and vicinity (Ibid.).

Once the real people behind the mysterious names are established, Zimmer inquires further: where was Chetu? Scanning the maps of Tibet in search of the village does not provide "any place whose name even remotely resembles it" (Ibid. 2). Yet another clue comes from Pratt's book about his voyage from Shanghai to Tatsienlu: it describes "a little Tibetan hamlet of some four wooden huts and a kun-quan, a sort of primitive hostel for traveling Chinese mandarins, ten miles west of Tatsienlu. It is on the old trade road called 'Tea-Horse'—the main trade was brick tea going west and horses going east" (Ibid. 4). The name of this place was Chetu (Zheduo in Hanyu Pinyin spelling), and Pratt claims he had caught there with his forceps as many as three hundred *Thecla bieti* in one morning. Although it never found its way onto any map, Zimmer finds a picture of Chetu dated before the 1880s, from the Austrian geographer Gustav Ritter von Kreitner's monograph about Count Béla Széchenyi's expedition to Central Asia. Thus, what first looks like a fictitious place is matched with a real but little-known location. Nabokov knew the book and "had borrowed more than a dozen details from it...including two sentences and one whole paragraph," when imagining Konstantin Godunov's Central Asian voyages (Ibid. 5; see more such examples in the "Intertexts" section in this chapter).

How Did Nabokov Borrow?

On October 15, 1929, a few weeks after his butterfly hunting trip to the Pyrenees, Nabokov and Véra visited the German Entomological Museum in Berlin, in the company of an entomologist friend, Nikolai Kardakoff (1885–1973). Nabokov's name is recorded on the guest list ("V. Nabokoff mit Frau") along with Kardakoff's. Between their signatures is one *A. Kricheldorff*. Zimmer establishes with certainty that this refers to "the Berlin naturalist and some-time insect dealer Adolf Kricheldorff" who had happened to be in Tatsienlu with Pratt! Nabokov may have heard about their joint expedition to western China directly from Kricheldorff and, as a result of the meeting, gone to look "soon after" for Pratt's obscure book in the Prussian State Library (Zimmer, "Chinese Rhubarb" 8). Nabokov did borrow scientific literature from this repository, though it is doubtful that he did this right away (the work on what will form the nucleus of Chapter Two of *The Gift* would not start until 1935).

There are numerous commendable findings with regard to sources for Nabokov's novel, but before moving on to more detailed examinations of allusion and intertext as common techniques in *The Gift*, I will conclude by pointing out the main principle at work here. Gérard Genette, in *Palimpsests*, makes a distinction between intertextuality, defined as co-presence—text A is present in text B—and hypertextuality, defined as derivation—text A is not effectively present in text B, but B is derived from A (Genette 8-13). *The Gift* is a brilliant constellation of veiled hypotexts (the earlier text upon which the hypertext is based) embodying different narrative and pronominal strategies. Nevertheless Nabokov would not be the writer we all know without his distinctive sense of irony, an artist who simultaneously employs his own tools and undermines them with an occasional subtle touch. Robert Hughes suggests that the name of one of the authors whose memoirs Nabokov uses in his "The Life of Chernyshevski," Palimpsestov, can be read as a meta-description of the device—the principle of *palimpsest*, i.e. a text written upon previous texts that are still visible (Paperno 318, 24n). Indeed, Nabokov never completely erases the previous layer, leaving some faintly visible traces for the attentive reader and interpreter. Following Zimmer ("Chinese Rhubarb" 8), it is tempting to believe that the copy of Pratt's 1892 edition which survived the war bombings and that still bears a light pencil mark in the margin next to Chong Cao, the caterpillar fungus, was the one that Nabokov himself leafed through.

Allusions

Nabokov's allusions usually follow the standard definition of this term—a reference in a literary work to a person, place, or event in history, or another work of literature. Allusions are often indirect or brief and are used to summarize broad, complex ideas or emotions in one quick, powerful image. Nabokov often appeals to multiple sources as either overt or encoded subtexts. Needless to say, he was not an imitator—disguised reminiscences and direct quotations in *The Gift* acquire a new dimension, the same quality that was noted by Taranovsky with respect to Mandelstam's poetry (3).

Roses and Samovars

Borrowing from scientific sources was for Nabokov a pleasant necessity, while appealing to the collective memory of an imaginary refined reader was a kind of game. In Chapter Three the unperceptive critic Linyov reviewed Koncheyev's book and "inadvertently," as Nabokov puts it, "extricated something more or less whole." Nabokov follows with a two-line fragment, which begins "Days of ripening vines!" (G170). Alexander Dolinin recognizes this as a quasi-quotation from Boris Poplavsky (*Kommentarii* 692), and Boris Maslov attributes it to Osip Mandelstam (172-86). Mandelstam's line containing the image of a grape: "I was a letter, I was a grape line of verse" ("*Ia bukvoi byl, byl vinogradnoi strochkoi*") is explained in his 1932 poem dedicated to the nineteenth-century poet Batiushkov, where it is an allegory for genuine freshness in poetry: "The grape flesh of verses / Has accidentally refreshed my mouth" ("*Tol'ko stikhov vinogradnoe miaso / Mne osvezhilo sluchaino iazyk*"), in line with the earlier metaphor of the grape as poetic nourishment in *The Slate Ode* (1923), Mandelstam's celebrated long poem about the creative poetic process (Taranovsky 2).

However, Nabokov does not stop with this metapoetic reminiscence and continues: "– and it was as if the voice of a violin had suddenly drowned the hum of a patriarchal cretin."

Nabokov's commentary to this passage on the margins of the typescript of the English translation of his novel (Berg Collection, New York Public Library) elucidates an unidentified reference: *Allusion to Turgenev's (samovar)*. The note obviously concerns an excerpt from Ivan Turgenev's poem in prose, "*Kak khoroshi, kak svezhi byli rozy...*" ("How beautiful, how fresh were those roses..."): "and Laner's waltz cannot deafen the grumbling of a patriarchal samovar..." Composer and conductor Joseph Franz Karl Laner (1800–43) became famous for the composition of dance music, waltzes in particular, in which the leading themes were typically delivered by violins.

―――――――――――――――― Chapter Four. STYLE ――――――――――――――――

Beneath the Blot: Why Was Danzas at the Dentist's Office?

"... [she] managed to push her spitting pen between la Princesse Toumanoff, with a blot at the end, and Monsieur Danzas, with a blot at the beginning..." (G18)

In the first chapter of *The Gift*, a Monsieur Danzas has an appointment with the dentist immediately after those of Fyodor Godunov-Cherdyntsev and his sister Tanya. The last name Danzas evokes Konstantin Karlovich Danzas (1801–70), a Russian officer and friend of Alexander Pushkin, notorious for his role as second in the poet's duel with Baron Georges d'Anthès (1812–95), adopted son of the Dutch ambassador in Russia, Jacob van Heeckeren. But what does the name Danzas have to do with the dentist's office in *The Gift*?

The answer is in Danzas' memoir (first printed in 1863), which Nabokov must have read, since he was interested in his own family's relationship to him. Danzas was a distant relative of the Nabokovs, as we see from this description of a member of the Danzas family: "Ekaterina Dmitrievna Danzas (my father's first cousin and a grandniece of Colonel K. K. Danzas, Pushkin's second in his fatal duel)" (*Speak, Memory* 256). The memoirist describes in detail the circumstances leading to the fatal duel between Pushkin and Lieutenant d'Anthès:

> Concerning d'Anthès' assuming of Heeckeren's last name someone, as a joke, set a rumor afloat in town that the Cavalry regiment soldiers allegedly mangling the names of d'Anthès and Heeckeren were saying: 'What happened to our lieutenant, he used to be a *dentist*, and now all of a sudden turned *healer*.' (Danzas 395; italics in the original)

The pun in Russian based on the auditory similarity of the names and medical professions is less obvious but still discernable in English–*dentist* (d'Anthès) and *healer* (Heeckeren) ("Chto eto sdelalos' s nashim poruchikom, byl *dantist*, a teper' vdrug stal *lekarem*"). It was speculated that Heeckeren and d'Anthès were lovers. In *The Gift*, the rumor that surrounded d'Anthès' marriage to the sister of Pushkin's wife Natalya Goncharova is exploited in reference to Dobrolyubov's intrigue with Nikolai Chernyshevksi's spouse. Dobroblyubov similarly wanted to marry Olga Sokratovna's sister (who had a fiancé) to conceal his affair (G260).

Another less probable candidate for a possible namesake of the character (though considering *The Gift*'s abundant transportation and travel motifs, not absolutely meaningless) could be the entrepreneur, Louis Danzas. He fought for Napoleon at Waterloo before starting a world famous freight company in the mid nineteenth century; the firm had numerous branches across Europe at the time Nabokov was composing *The Gift*, and it still bears Danzas' name today.

The iconic embodiment of the transportation motif is set in motion on the first page of the novel, which features a peculiar van with the inscription *Max Lux* painted in blue letters and shaded in black ("a dishonest attempt to climb into the next dimension"), that Fyodor observes in front of his new apartment on 7 Tannenberg Street. Stephen Blackwell notes that moving to a new dwelling, or motion generally, is one of the novel's chief concerns for a variety of reasons: emigration, the father's adventurous travels across Asia, Nikolai Chernyshevski's exile in Yakutsk: "Everything is in motion, and when characters do sit still, it is with the purpose of contemplating the motion around them, or imagining still greater departures and arrivals" (Blackwell, *The Quill and the Scalpel* 147). According to Blackwell, if one treats a Cyrillic reading of the first word as another kind of "next dimension," *Max* would be pronounced "makh," pointing to Ernst Mach, Einstein's revered predecessor (ibid.). To Blackwell's shrewd suggestion we might add that both "Maks" and "Luks," if read in reverse, conceal perfectly homophonous "scam" and "school," with Nabokov winking at the reader in between. One needs to be especially cautious with these absorbing word games, as they seem to continue ad infinitum.

Based on the description of the printed letters along the moving van's entire side — "the name of the moving company in yard-high blue letters, each of which (including a square dot) was shaded laterally with blue paint" (G3) — Dieter E. Zimmer suggests that it could belong to the A. Schäfer moving company. The ad that Zimmer reproduces is convincing indeed ("Nabokovs Berlin"). First of all, it comes from the illustrated Russian art magazine *Firebird* (*Zhar Ptitsa*), to which Nabokov himself contributed in the mid-1920s, so it is obvious that the company was catering to the Berlin émigré community. By coincidence, Zimmer adds, ten years later the company's head office was in the "Universum" cinema that Nabokov passed every time he walked from Nestorstrasse to Kurfürstendamm. Secondly, and even more importantly, the way A. Schäfer is inscribed on the van as seen in the ad matches the description on the opening page of *The Gift* — the title letters are shaded on the left side to give a three-dimensional effect.

All of these suppositions are close, but still fall short of hitting the center of the target. It has recently been established that the moving company's name is not fictitious at all — it did in fact exist in early twentieth-century Berlin (Shapiro 146). In addition to duplicating a photograph of an advertisement for the Max Lux firm, Shapiro picks up the visual thread and proposes that, by way of the conspicuous Roman letters in the moving company's name, Nabokov evokes the mystical painter Gabriel von Max (1840–1915). Max's painting *Light* depicts a blind girl garbed in a light-colored dress; she proffers a lit oil lamp to a person clad in black. Nabokov purportedly alludes to this artwork in order to underline the perspicacity of blind Fate, whose "attempts" the protagonist was able to appreciate only toward the end of the novel (Shapiro 148). This is in line with the earlier suggestion that the idea of light in Max Lux hints at inspiration, which for Fyodor is connected to earthly delights like travel, exploration, sunbathing, or even gardening. Furthermore, the name of Fyodor's father's biology professor in Cambridge is "Brait" in the Russian version of *Dar*, translated by M. Scammell as "Bright" in *The Gift* (G98) and endorsed, as seen in the typescript, by Nabokov (Ben-Amos 123).

Real as it was, Nabokov was still able to use the Max Lux firm's name as a playful reference to the final words of Johann Wolfgang von Goethe, whose alleged dying utterance in 1832 was "*Mehr Licht!*" (More Light!). In one of only two fleeting appearances in *The Gift*, the German poet-philosopher is tellingly cited in connection with flickering empyreal light: "remember how Goethe said, pointing with his cane at the starry sky: 'There is my conscience!'" (G178).

Motifs of mechanized motion and dental surgery would seem to be distant from Pushkin, but they are tied together in a poem which Fyodor, one tooth now missing, composes on his way home from the dentist's office. The blot of ink (an iconic representation of a blood stain as, for example, in Eisenstein's *Strike* [1924]; Fyodor watches this film with his mother in the Berlin theater) and the means of transportation evoke Pushkin's tragic death: after being mortally wounded, Pushkin was brought from the duel scene on Chernaia rechka (the Black Stream) to his Petersburg apartment in his adversary's coach. The fact appears to be reflected in an unintended parody when Fyodor half-consciously imagines himself as a reduced version of the great wounded poet:

> What will it be like to be sitting
> Half an hour from now in this brougham?
> With what eyes shall I look at these snowflakes
> And black branches of trees?

The often-quoted passage in *The Gift* states: "Pushkin entered [Fyodor's] blood" (G98). Via Danzas, Pushkin's blood was metaphorically infused into Nabokov's creative circulatory system.

Browning in "Seven Shots"

> A Browning had once been fired at [a birch-lyre] by his English tutor—also Browning—and then Father had taken the pistol, swiftly and dexterously ramming bullets into the clip, and knocked out a smooth *K* with seven shots. (G79)

John Moses Browning (1855–1926) was an American firearms designer who developed varieties of firearms, cartridges, and gun mechanisms, and is considered a key figure in the advancement of modern automatic firearms (his first patent was granted in 1879). The seven shots necessary to make a smooth K require the maximum capacity of the *Browning M1903* pistol (7 rounds, 9mm, Belgium). In Europe, the M1903 became a favorite police pistol, and was adopted by several armies, as well as by the Imperial Russian security forces (about 700,000 of them were produced from 1900–11). The previous model of this semi-automatic pistol, reliable, accurate, and comfortable to carry and fire, was used by Eugen Schauman in his 1904 assassination of the Russian Governor-General of Finland at the time, Nikolai Ivanovich Bobrikov.

There is a self-referential layer in this passage: the theme of firearms in *The Gift* is connected to Yasha Chernyshevski's suicide, and Fyodor's mother is also the owner of "a little mother-of-pearl revolver" (G105). Nabokov was always extremely attentive to minute technical details. In a 1944 letter to Edmund Wilson he quotes from Richard Connell's detective fiction: "'What about your other pistol?' 'That is an ordinary five-shot automatic of a well-known American make.'" (*Nabokov–Wilson Letters* 144). In his preparatory notes to *Lolita*, Nabokov would later painstakingly draw Humbert's 1940 model *Colt* automatic 32 caliber pistol, checking the exact capacity of the deadly weapon's cartridge (The index card with the pistol sketch is reproduced in Boyd, *The American Years* 226-27).

Yet what is more intriguing here is a literary allusion: Nabokov's doubling of the English tutor's last name evokes a poem by Robert Browning (1812–1889), "Incident of the French Camp" (1842), also dealing with the motif of a fatal shooting:

> You looked twice ere you saw his breast
> Was all but shot in two. […]
>
> "You're wounded!" "Nay," the soldier's pride
> Touched to the quick, he said:
> "I'm killed, Sire!" And his chief beside
> Smiling the boy fell dead.
>
> (Browning 66)

The poem is written in iambic meter (five stanzas, eight lines each), as are most of the poetic segments in *The Gift* itself (ten of them vary from eight to twelve lines in length). Nabokov names Browning among the poets whom he enjoyed mostly in his teens (*Strong Opinions* 42). Browning's wife, Elizabeth, was also a well-known poet who died on June 29, 1861; *The Gift* ends on June 29. Vladimir Dmitrievich Nabokov (1870–1922) was shot twice and died instantly in Berlin while defending the politician, historian, and his former ally, Pavel Miliukov.

Chapter Four. STYLE

Literary Deformation of Primary Sources

The Gift is deliberately constructed such that additional layers of meaning are uncovered in the process of scholarly investigation; as Irina Paperno has shown, this in turn reveals the sources of the text and the devices Nabokov used to assemble it. The structural devices themselves carry a message, and Formalist devices in the artistic world of Nabokov's novel express his conception of the relationship between literature and reality, with its metaphysical projections (312). By applying such devices as "coloring," "vocalizing," naming, and the realization of metaphors, the novel's very construction realizes the metaphor of art as a "resurrection of the word" (Shklovsky's term). Nabokov employs his own particular variety of this literary phenomenon, a shade pattern or a shadow effect, as in the inscription bearing the Max Lux company brand ("blue letters, each of which (including a square dot) was *shaded laterally* with blue paint: *a dishonest attempt to climb into the next dimension*"; G3). It is not by chance that the same "shadow effect" recurs when Fyodor ponders his own verses through the lens of an imaginary critic: "Now he read *in three dimensions*, as it were, carefully exploring each poem, lifted out like a cube from among the rest..." (G9). The allusion functions in a similar way in the following series of examples representing the various ways in which Nabokov processes literary sources and incorporates them in the texture of *The Gift*.

Direct Poetic Allusion

FOR THE BABY A MEAL, FOR THE FATHER A COFFIN (G208)

Source: A line from Nikolai Nekrasov's poem, *"Edu li noch'iu po ulitse temnoi..."* ("If I ride at night along the dark street..."; 1847). When Nekrasov printed this text in the Russian magazine *Sovremennik*, N. G. Chernyshevski praised the poem in a letter to his wife sent from Viluisk on March 15, 1878. Fyodor quotes the line to Zina when attempting to acquire funds to publish his novel.

Indirect Poetic Allusion

BEYOND THAT GATE LIES BAGHDAD'S CROOKED SHADE, AND YON STAR SHEDS ON PULKOVO ITS BEAM (G156)

Allusion: Nabokov alludes to Osip Mandelstam's poetics of exoticism in mundane reality:

> "Not far to Smyrna and Baghdad,
> But it's hard to drift, and the stars are everywhere the same"

> *"Nedaleko do Smirny i Bagdada,*
> *No trudno plyt', a zvezdy vsiudu te zhe"*
> (Lotman 221)

Historical commentary: *Pulkovo* is the principle astronomical observatory of the Russian Academy of Sciences (G135), opened in 1839 on Pulkovo Heights, 19 km south of St. Petersburg. As noted earlier, Nabokov adds the clarifying phrase—"the wooden paving blocks of Mandelshtam's neoclassicism" (G38)—to the English translation of *The Gift*.

THE DOOR OF HIS DAMP CELL WAS LINED WITH BLACK OILCLOTH; THE TWO WINDOWS...WERE BARRED UP (G288)

Source: The description of Chernyshevski in jail paraphrases Pushkin's famous line: "Sizhu za *reshetkoi* v temnitse *syroi*" ("I am sitting behind the bars in a damp cell") from "*Uznik*" ("A Prisoner," 1822). The echo is especially evident in the Russian original (dver' *syroi kamery* byla obita chernoi kleenkoi; dva okna...byli zabrany *reshetkami*).

Motif: Nabokov associated the captivity motif with Pushkin and his long path in exile. The reference to "A Prisoner" has also a double parodic function: if we extend the Pushkin analogy, it becomes apparent that Chernyshevski plays the role of the "young eagle" (Pushkin's phrase describing the prisoner in the same poem). However, when applied to the fate of Chernyshevski, Pushkin's elevated style turns out to be a trivial mockery. Strannolyubski's remark makes this subversive message abundantly clear: "Once an eagle appeared in his yard... 'it had come to peck at his liver, but did not recognize Prometheus in him'" (G289).

THEIR EVENING MEETINGS HAD SINCE SPRING GONE BEYOND THE SHORES OF THEIR INITIAL STREET (LAMP, LIME, FENCE), AND NOW THEIR RESTLESS WANDERINGS CARRIED THEM IN EVER WIDENING CIRCLES INTO DISTANT AND EVER NEW CORNERS OF THE CITY. NOW IT WAS A BRIDGE OVER A CANAL, THEN A TRELLISED BOSKET IN A PARK... (G327)

Source: Fyodor and Zina's evening strolls in Berlin Nabokov evoke Alexander Blok's famous short poem "Night, street, lamp, drugstore..." ("*Noch', ulitsa, fonar', apteka...*," 1912):

> Night, street, lamp, drugstore,
> A dull and meaningless light.

Go on and live another quarter century —
Nothing will change. There's no way out.

You'll die, then start from the beginning,
It will repeat, just like before:
Night, icy ripples on a canal,
Drugstore, street, lamp.
        (Trans. by A. Wachtel, I. Kutik and M. Denner)

Not only the objects are the same here (except for the drugstore, which appeared earlier in the novel in "the most frequent arrangement... for the streets of a given city, for example: tobacco shop, pharmacy, greengrocery"; G5), but also the very syntactic structure — a triple cadence of nouns, all in nominative case in the Russian original, and separated by commas.

For more on Blok's presence in *The Gift*, see the note on the character Kern in the previous chapter; here I will just mention another playful reference to a group of mysterious poets whose names start with the letter B ("the five poets whose names began with 'B' — the five senses of the new Russian poetry"; G74). Though Blok is surely one of the five, a long list of candidates for the other four positions has been suggested: Balmont, Baltrushaitis, Batiushkov, Bely, Briusov, Bunin, and so on.

The relationship of Valery Briusov (1873–1924) to *The Gift* is a curious case. In volumes Two and Three of *The Russian Symbolists*, which this founder of Russian Symbolism edited, published, and largely composed on his own during the 1890s, a number of poems were published under the pseudonym "Vladimir Darov" (literally, *Vladimir Gifted*). Among the fictitious female authors (whose texts Briusov had also devised himself in an attempt to lend some ornamentation to the movement he headed) was a certain lady, *Zinaida Fuks*, who specialized in writing sonnets. Nabokov was well aware of Briusov's made-up undertaking, and not only because of the prominent cultural position that Briusov had secured by the 1910s, but also through his Tenishev school teacher of literature, also a Symbolist poet, Vladimir Gippius (see Ledenev).

Emulation and Parody

AT THE SECOND STOP A LEAN MAN IN A SHORT COAT WITH A FOX-FUR COLLAR, WEARING A GREEN HAT AND FRAYED SPATS, SAT DOWN IN FRONT OF FYODOR [WHO] INSTANTLY CONCENTRATED ON HIM ALL HIS SINFUL HATRED (FOR THIS POOR, PITIFUL, EXPIRING NATION) AND KNEW PRECISELY WHY HE HATED HIM... (G81)

Allusions

Source: The object of emulation is Pushkin's famous record of his encountering Wilhelm von Küchelbecker, his school friend, a poet who had been convicted for his participation in the Decembrist uprising. Pushkin, traveling in an irritable mood after playing cards and losing badly, saw a group of Poles being transported from Shlisselburg to some other place of incarceration. Among them there was "a tall, pale, thin young man with a black beard, in a baize greatcoat, a real Jew by appearance, so I took him for a Jew, and the inseparable notions of a Jew and a spy produced in me their usual effect; I showed them my back [...] As he noticed me, he gave me an animated glance. Involuntarily I turned round toward him. We looked at each other closely—and I recognized K. We embraced each other. The gendarmes pulled us apart." As Omry Ronen writes, Jews in this episode are replacing Germans as an object of scornful hatred ("Emulation, Anti-Parody" 67). Fyodor's "sinful hatred" of the degenerating German nation lasts until the moment when the man in the streetcar unfolds a Russian newspaper and clears his throat "with a Russian intonation." Note that Küchelbecker (1797–1846) himself was a Russian of German origin who later became the subject of the Formalist scholar Yuri Tynyanov's novel "Kukhlia" (1925), which Nabokov almost certainly read (see on Nabokov and Tynyanov: Mondri).

THIS SHOP DID NOT CARRY THE RUSSIAN TIPPED CIGARETTES THAT HE PREFERRED, AND HE WOULD HAVE LEFT EMPTY-HANDED IF IT HAD NOT BEEN FOR THE TOBACCONIST'S SPECKLED VEST WITH MOTHER-OF-PEARL BUTTONS AND HIS PUMPKIN-COLORED BALD SPOT. YES, ALL MY LIFE I SHALL BE GETTING THAT EXTRA LITTLE PAYMENT IN KIND TO COMPENSATE MY REGULAR OVERPAYMENT FOR MERCHANDISE FOISTED ON ME. (G6)

Allusion: In this scene, Edward Brown suggests, Nabokov may have rehashed the nacre button of the sausage-maker which Kavalerov describes in Iurii Olesha's novel *Envy (1927)*: "He is stripped to the waist and wearing jersey underpants fastened by a single button in the middle of his stomach. The blue and pink world of the room spins round in the mother-of-pearl lens of the button" (Brown 284).

Theme: The image of the shopkeeper's vest, which the protagonist of Nabokov's *The Gift* encounters in the tobacconist's shop, stimulates Fyodor's artistic sensibility and gives impulse to his imagination. Leaving the shop without the cigarettes and feeling nostalgic about his homeland, Fyodor nevertheless acquires a small sartorial compensation which he reworks in his writings. Thus, the vest becomes associated with the theme of artistic reflection and transformation (Ivleva 288).

―――――――――――――― Chapter Four. STYLE ――――――――――――――

Double Allusion to a Prosaic Source

A BLINDINGLY WHITE PARALLELOGRAM OF SKY BEING UNLOADED FROM THE VAN—A DRESSER WITH MIRROR ACROSS WHICH, AS ACROSS A CINEMA SCREEN, PASSED A FLAWLESSLY CLEAR REFLECTION OF BOUGHS SLIDING AND SWAYING NOT ARBOREALLY, BUT WITH A HUMAN VACILLATION, PRODUCED BY THE NATURE OF THOSE WHO WERE CARRYING THIS SKY, THESE BOUGHS, THIS GLIDING FAÇADE. (G18)

Allusion: Here Nabokov reconstructs Stendhal's famous saying, "*Un roman: c'est un miroir qu'on promène le long d'un chemin*" ("A novel: It is a mirror you take for a walk down the road"; Stendhal 94; Livak 173). Nabokov employs the same image in his poem "Mirror" from the collection *The Aerial Path*: "A bright, sleek mirror was carried in the morning down the long street, / like a holy relic" ("*Iasnoe, gladkoe zerkalo, utrom, po ulitse dlinnoi, / budto sviatyniu vezli*"; *Sobranie sochinenii* 1, 553). Similar to the poem, the image of a mirror reflecting the gliding sky serves as a self-reflexive trope. Nabokov makes this traditional trope even more dynamic and complex (*cf.* Fyodor Sologub's manifesto in his preface to the second edition of *The Petty Demon*: "This novel is a mirror, skillfully polished. I polished it for a long while..."; (Sologub 27; noted in Dolinin, "'Dar': Dobavleniia").

Theme: Reflection, cinematography, life versus art.

INTERTEXTUALITY

"A Widening Spiral, Not a Narrowing Vortex"

Kiril Taranovsky defines the notion of context as a set of texts which contain the same or a similar image; "subtext" may be defined as an already existing text (or texts) reflected in a new one. There are four kinds of subtexts: (1) that which serves as a simple impulse for the creation of an image; (2) borrowing of a metric structure and the sounds contained therein (mainly in poetry); (3) a text that supports or reveals the poetic message of a later text; (4) a text that is treated polemically by the author. These types may be combined and blended, and it is self-evident that the concepts of context and subtext may overlap in cases of self-quotations and self-references (Taranovsky 18). Nabokov uses all four kinds of subtexts and incorporates them into what Alexander Dolinin has called the "three-tier" intertextual strategy of this most literary-minded Russian prose writer of the twentieth century ("Nabokov as a Russian writer" 62). The layers of this edifice include *continuation* (of classical and neoclassical poetic idiom), *amelioration* (of the nineteenth-century realist novel), and *mocking parody* (of influential contemporary trends). To Taranovsky's and Dolinin's definitions we should add one more type of subtext: the outside, non-artistic text whose function is transformed by virtue of its insertion into a larger fictional context.

Better understanding of various types of intertexts and their interaction in Nabokov's writing has allowed a gradual shift in the way scientific models describing Nabokov's artistic principles are presented. Priscilla Meyer notes that "early critics of Nabokov's work mistakenly viewed his fictional worlds as hermetic, arcane self-referential systems designed as metaliterary manifestos" (Meyer 327). Interpretation founded on annotation can show a way out of a hermetic reading to the world beyond the text. Annotation, Meyer insists, is an essential component of literary scholarship: "Nabokov points to a widening spiral, not a narrowing vortex, through intertextuality, which has itself been misread as a closed system" (Ibid.). "Studies that fail to trace Nabokov's system of references," she warns, "often remain trapped among truisms about patterning, fate, and the otherworld" (Ibid.).

Two types of intertexts should be distinguished: covert artistic allusion and direct borrowing from documentary sources for the purpose of reconstructing the required historical reality or geographical space. The first group has been treated earlier as allusions; the second, less substantial, has been the subject of several meticulous studies in scholarship on *The Gift*.

Russian Intertexts

Turgenev

Nabokov's "widening spiral" covers dozens of sources, but not all of them are equally worthy from the aesthetic point of view, even by his characters' admission. However, the kind of dismissal that Fyodor (and Nabokov) employs in *The Gift*, especially in his conversations with Koncheyev, when they discuss the writing of other authors, might be misleading. Moreover, David Rampton insists, "it threatens to obscure the very real resemblances between Nabokov and the writers he characterizes so arbitrarily" (90). For example, the pointed criticism of Turgenev can distract readers "from more significant matters":

> Accusing the author of *Rudin* and *Smoke* of appeasing the radicals, or dismissing *Fathers and Sons* for its "inept tête-à-têtes in acacia arbors" (G73) — these claims are so unusual that they may have the desired effect and actually make us reconsider Turgenev's work. But when we hear his descriptions of nature being ridiculed for their "howlers" ("My father used to find all lands of howlers in Turgenev's... hunting scenes and descriptions of nature..."; G73), we may well begin to feel that Turgenev, the "novelist's novelist," is being deliberately misrepresented by one of his old admirers, now overly anxious to assert his independence. (Rampton 91)

Rampton draws our attention to the following example of an obvious intertextual moment in a passage from Chapter Five of *The Gift*. Fyodor is lying on his back in a forest, looking upward:

> And still higher above my upturned face, the summits and trunks of the trees participated in a complex exchange of shadows, and their leafage reminded me of algae swaying in transparent water. And if I tilted my head back even farther, so that the grass behind (inexpressibly, primevally green from this point of upturned vision) seemed to be growing downward into empty transparent light, I experienced something similar to what must strike a man who has flown to another planet. (G332)

Now compare this with a passage from Turgenev's *A Sportsman's Sketches*:

> It is an extremely agreeable occupation to lie on your back in the woods and look upwards! It seems that you are looking into a bottomless sea, that it is spreading itself out far and wide *beneath* you, that the trees are not rising from the ground, but, like the roots of huge plants, dropping perpendicularly down into those glass-clear waves; and the leaves on the trees are now transparent as emeralds, now condensed to a goldish, almost blackish green.

A coincidence perhaps, admits Rampton, "but a more promising field of inquiry for someone interested in Nabokov and his relations with Russian novelists of the mid nineteenth century than the territory so zealously fenced off in *The Gift*" (91). Omry Ronen adds another source from Turgenev, the tale "*Neshchastnaia*" ("The Unhappy One"), containing an antecedent for Zina Mertz's character treated by Nabokov in the spirit of polemical emulation: "I don't think our Zinaida Oscarovna will look after you too well. Eh, princess?" (G348). In Turgenev's original, an illegitimate daughter of a Russian nobleman and a Jewish mother (a musician) is cruelly abused and eventually driven to suicide by her Bohemian stepfather, who has had designs on her. The stepfather addresses her ironically with the same vulgar Russian interrogative interjection "*As'*?" (Ch. vIII): "*Vse zhidy, tak zhe kak i chekhi, urozhdennye muzykanty! Osobenno zhidy. Ne pravda li' Susanna Ivanovna? As'? Kha-kha-kha-kha!*" ("All yids, just as Czechs, are born musicians! Particularly the yids. Is this not true, Susanna Ivanovna? Eh? Ha-ha-ha-ha!"; Ronen, "Nine Notes" 26).

Gogol

One of Fyodor's poems read at the literary evening in Chapter Two (G91) begins with the stanza:

———————————— Intertextuality ————————————

> Things here are in a sorry state;
> Even the moon is much too rough
> Though it is rumored to come straight
> From Hamburg where they make the stuff.

This image of the moon is an allusion to Nikolai Gogol's short story "The Diary of a Madman" (1835), in which the entry for "February 13" contains the following: "The moon, as everyone knows, is usually made in Hamburg, and they make a complete hash of it" (Gogol, *Diary* 38). Alexander Papapulo adds a possible contemporary source to this allusion: an article in the Soviet *Literary Gazette*, entitled "The Moon is Made in Hamburg" ("Lunu delayut v Gamburge"; February 17, 1933), that may have come to Nabokov's attention (Papapulo). The author of that article, G. Korabelnikov, was reacting to an essay by Victor Shklovsky, published in the same newspaper six weeks earlier under the title "South-West" (devoted to the Odessa group of Soviet writers). As Nabokov was working on *The Gift* at the time, it may well be true that this title had reminded him of the quotation from Gogol, but by no means is this context necessary to explain the Gogol quotation. Ben-Amos believes that Gogol's story is famous enough not to need a reference in a literary journal directed toward a Russian educated and literature-oriented audience. Whether prompted by this article or not, the reference in Godunov-Cherdyntsev's poem anticipates the place of Gogol in Fyodor's next work, "The Life of Chernyshevski," which is being created as Chapter Three transpires (Ben-Amos 134).

The "Asian" Intertexts

Examples that illustrate Nabokov's method for importing documentary subtexts into his fiction are found mainly in Chapter Two of *The Gift* and concern Fyodor's unfinished biography of his father. Dolinin, Zimmer, Hartmann, and Ronen consider Nabokov's established sources to be those subtexts that might supply conclusive evidence, such as highly specific details, unique occurrences, singular combinations, and in some cases whole phrases and sentences that are quoted verbatim.

HIS COSSACKS WENT ROUND THE NEIGHBORING VILLAGES BUYING HORSES, MULES AND CAMELS (G116)

Intertext: [At Przhevalsk] "Cossack officer Bainov was sent with a horseman to the surrounding Kyrgyz villages to buy camels that were to carry the caravan's baggage. Cossack officer Shestakov was sent with a horseman to buy horses as mounts" (Roborovskii 38; Hartmann 42).

Chapter Four. STYLE

WHAT WAS THERE NOT IN THESE SARTISH YAGTANS AND LEATHER BAGS TRIED BY CENTURIES, FROM COGNAC TO PULVERIZED PEAS, FROM INGOTS OF SILVER TO NAILS FOR HORSESHOES (G116)

Intertext: "Best are the Sartish yagtans or boxes constructed like yagtans, i.e., made of very thin three-layered wood, cardboard or very tough cloth the corners of which are reinforced by leather. We avoided boxes made completely of wood, as they are less elastic and can easily hurt the animals' backs. Things like cartridges, ingots of silver, horseshoes, nails, etc. were stowed in special leather pouches.... In rarer cases the fodder for the horses consisted in barley or sorghum; usually they were fed pulverized peas that are very nourishing and important as they kept the animals filled up for a longer time" (Grumm-Grzhimailo *Opisanie* Vol. III (1907) 443-45; Hartmann 42-43). Practically all explorers of Central Asia, as Zimmer and Hartmann demonstrate, described the outfitting and organization of their caravans, and the Russian expeditions were accompanied by Cossacks with Berdan rifles. Przhevalsky, on his first and third expeditions, also mentions taking along a box of cognac, which Hedin emphatically refused to do (*Cf.* Przhevalskii 4; DEZ in Zimmer and Hartmann 43).

AFTER THAT I SEE THE CARAVAN, BEFORE IT GETS DRAWN INTO THE MOUNTAINS, WINDING AMONG HILLS OF A PARADISEAN GREEN SHADE, DEPENDING BOTH ON THEIR GRASSY RAIMENT AND ON THE APPLE-BRIGHT EPIDOTIC ROCK, OF WHICH THEY ARE COMPOSED (G116)

Intertext: [In Dzungaria] "Climbing the plateau I met with hills of green color, depending both on their grassy raiment (*Festuca ovina* L.) and on the underlying layer of rock—apple-bright epidotic slate prevailing on all of the plateau" (Grumm-Grzhimailo *Opisanie* Vol. III [1907] 239; Dolinin, *Kommentarii* 671-72). Dolinin points out that Nabokov alters only a few words in the original but adds the very important motif of "entering paradise."

THE COMPACT, STURDY KALMUK PONIES WALK IN SINGLE FILE FORMING ECHELONS: THE PAIRED PACKLOADS OF EQUAL WEIGHT ARE SEIZED TWICE WITH LARIATS SO THAT NOTHING CAN SHIFT AND A COSSACK LEADS EVERY ECHELON BY THE BRIDLE (G116)

Intertext: "In general the Kalmuk pony is a sturdy and strong animal....The packs were distributed pairwise...which was not difficult and facilitated loading; also the loads could be kept in balance by simply shifting some objects. Like the yagtans the different cases were tied by lariats by which they hung from the saddle.... an echelon of 10 to 12 horses was led by a Cossack holding the reins of the first one" (Grumm-Grzhimailo *Opisanie* Vol. III (1907) 441-45; Hartmann 43).

―――――――――――― Intertextuality ――――――――――――

THE BOOM OF WATER IN THE GORGE WAS ENOUGH TO STUN A MAN... SUDDENLY SWELLED OUT MONSTROUSLY AS IT REACHED THE RAPIDS, ITS VARICOLORED WAVES PILING UP AND FALLING OVER THE LUSTROUS BROWS OF THE STONES WITH A FURIOUS ROAR;... SEETHING, SMOKE-BLUE AND SNOWLIKE FROM THE FOAM, IT STRUCK FIRST ONE SIDE AND THEN THE OTHER OF THE CONGLOMERATIC CANYON IN SUCH A WAY THAT IT SEEMED THE REVERBERATING MOUNTAIN FASTNESS COULD NEVER WITHSTAND IT (G117)

Intertext: [Ulan River, Tian Shan] "The current was strong, the river struggling through the rocks it sprayed with wisps of foam and millions of splashes.... A little higher up,... powerful currents crashed against a wall some six feet high with a roar and a howl that filled all of the canyon so that two paces away you could not understand a word... And imagine our surprise when the trail leading to the waterfall turned sharply in this very direction and before our eyes disappeared under the surface of the water... The moisture, the din and the twilight... Yes, a gloomy, wild place!" (Grumm-Grzhimailo, *Opisanie* Vol. I [1896] 88; noted in Dolinin, *Kommentarii* 672; the actual quote is reproduced in Zimmer and Hartmann 45)

"BUSTLE DEVOID OF FEELING" THAT CONSISTED SOLELY OF SHOUTING WITHOUT THE SLIGHTEST HINT OF LAUGHTER... THAT SPECIAL AIR BELONGING TO ANY PLACE WHERE CHINESE DWELL — A RANCID MIXTURE OF KITCHEN FUMES, SMOKE FROM BURNED MANURE, OPIUM AND THE STABLE (G118)

Intertext: Omry Ronen restores this collage of quotations from Nabokov's well-known source, G. E. Grumm-Grzhimailo's *Puteshestvie v Zapadnyi Kitai* (Vol. III, 1907, pp. 319-320), which previous annotators have overlooked: "Much noise and shouting, but no laughter at all, which is characteristic of any Chinese gathering [...] As any other place where Chinese dwell, Gurtu is surrounded by a quite special atmosphere; but now, in consequence of a remarkably calm air and frost, all this disgusting and rancid mixture of kitchen fumes, smoke from burned manure, opium and the stable hovers, as it were, over the village" (Ronen, "Nine Notes" 22).

The World of Garments

Dress and Vest

In the opening of *The Gift* Fyodor observes a dresser with a huge mirror being carried along a Berlin street. Architectural and natural images that move with "a human vacillation" across its mirror (G6) give the dresser a metaliterary meaning in this novel with a mirror composition (Livak 173-74). The metaliterary significance of this image, however, should not diminish its primary function; as Victoria Ivleva cautions, "first and foremost, the dresser is a keeper of the novel's costumes" (284). The mention of the dresser immediately follows the appearance of the speckled vest in the shop of a tobacconist. Nabokov, a fan of bilingual puns, was aware of the semantic richness of the lexemes *vestis* and *vest,* which lead to such derivatives as *invest, investigation,* and *travesty*. Ivleva demonstrates how Nabokov "reinvests" the image "by revising its meanings in the works of his precursors—Pushkin, Gogol, and Lewis Carroll—and how the vest mirrors the design of the novel and reflects Nabokov's key aesthetic formulations on art" (Ibid. 285; *cf*.: G6). It turns out that "speckles, tobacco, and a simile in which the tobacconist's bald spot is compared with a pumpkin are slightly transformed images from Gogol's *Dead Souls* and Petersburg stories" (Ibid. 291).

The vest, Ivleva reminds us, is rare among garments in that its primary function is aesthetic. Fyodor will later appropriate the mother-of-pearl buttons from the tobacconist's vest (changing them into gaudy diamond ones) when he dresses Mr. Ch., who returns to Russia after being overseas for twenty years, in a "blue, lilac and pink waistcoat with diamond buttons" (G100). In the fourth chapter, Fyodor reinvents the second detail of the vest—its speckles—when he depicts Pisarev in a motley vest (Ivleva 289). Thus, Fyodor reworks the tobacconist's vest twice in a novel abundant with motifs of disguise, cloaking and uncloaking, parodic travesties, and symbolic dismantling of attire.

Mr. Ch.'s waistcoat and the tobacconist's vest do not exhaust the list of possible allusions in *The Gift*, and they are certainly not limited to Gogol's grotesque art. The image of the vest/waistcoat framing Nabokov's novel introduces an intertextual reference to Pushkin's writings as well. As Alexander Dolinin comments, the waistcoat image quoted in Fyodor's biography of Chernyshevski ("'To be a genius it is not enough to have manufactured *Eugene Onegin*' wrote the progressive Nadezhdin, comparing Pushkin to a tailor, an inventor of waistcoat patterns"; G256) revives the polemic between the keepers of the classic tradition like Fyodor or Nabokov and the 'progressively-minded' anti-Pushkinists. Obviously, the critic insinuates that Pushkin's works are merely beautiful knickknacks that have a pure aesthetic value but no utilitarian application (Dolinin, *Kommentarii* 734; Ivleva 289).

Shoes and Footsteps

The waistcoat is not the only garment that adorns the novel's rich texture. Suits, gloves, hats, glasses and canes appear so frequently in *The Gift* that they seem to fit into certain opaque patterns, notes Gerard de Vries, who also offers an original reading of the leitmotif of shoes in Nabokov's prose. In *The Gift*, at the end of the first chapter, Fyodor buys new shoes, with which, the hero fantasizes, he will step on the shore after crossing the Lethe, the river of oblivion, or the Styx, the obstacle to the afterlife. In the final analysis, however, everything material appears superficial to Fyodor, as hinted at in his visit to the shoe shop. There a young woman leads him to the X-ray gadget and when Fyodor looks down in the glass aperture, he sees, "against a luminous background, his own dark, neatly separated phalanges. With this, with this I'll step ashore" (G64).

At the end of the novel Fyodor is walking through Berlin "wearing bedroom slippers" (G358); he is involved in a peripatetic discourse, a monologue on life and art which culminates in a praise of death as a justification for celebrating. Then, "his left slipper falls off his heel," a possible reference to the Cinderella story; moreover, as Fyodor "keeps the other slipper, his right heel remains protected, a hint at Achilles, whose right heel was the only mortal part of his body" in the Greek myth (Vries, "Shoes" 44). The indication of an afterlife is also presented in the concluding poem that points to the novel's endlessness (Ibid.). The "plethora of feet, shoes, boots and slippers...which seems to cover many impenetrable patterns," concludes de Vries, also seems to underpin Nabokov's "main theme, the belief in an afterlife" (Ibid. 45).

Vladimir Alexandrov delineates the "footstep motif" in *The Gift*: in addition to the shoe-purchasing episode there are two more instances of the motif near the novel's end, the first when Fyodor is swimming in the lake in the Grunewald, the second in Fyodor's dream about his father's return (Alexandrov 112). Water continues to be associated with a non-quotidian realm of existence: what had presumably been a swim of some normal duration for the mundane Fyodor appears to be weeks long from another point of view ("He swam for a long time, half an hour, five hours, twenty-four, a week, another. Finally, on the twenty-eighth of June around three P.M., he came out on the other shore"; G336). Alexandrov also notes that it is no mere coincidence in Nabokov's world that "the shore onto which Fyodor steps is near the ravine where Yasha Chernyshevski had committed suicide. The association between crossing bodies of water and surviving death that has been established in the novel heretofore raises the possibility that Yasha's death may also not have been final" (Alexandrov 112).

The "footstep motif" acquires a supernatural significance in *The Gift*, although as elsewhere with Nabokov it is characteristically tinted with intertextuality. Before making the fateful move from "Pushkin Avenue" to "Gogol Street" at the end of the second chapter, Fyodor buys shoes which, as he admits, "pinch unbearably" (G72). This complaint, made during an imaginary conversation with Koncheyev right in the midst of references to Tolstoy, Puhskin, and Gogol, is not a mundane detail but a veiled reflection of "Gogol's shoe" as mentioned by the Formalist critic Boris Eikhenbaum. The Soviet author of the biographical study *Lev Tolstoy* (1928) quoted the critic Druzhinin: "Gogol's shoe pinches our foot because it is not our size—we do not want to know this and therefore we suffer" (Eikhenbaum 194). However, for Nabokov it is "clear that the differences between Pushkin and Gogol are not insurmountable if one repudiates the doctrines of Chernyshevski with his attempt to 'regulate' art" (Kostalevsky 290).

Crossing the physical and metaphysical barriers leads Fyodor/Nabokov back in time and history to his native land: "Perhaps one day, on *foreign-made soles*... I shall again come out of that station [...] When I reach the sites where I grew up and see this and that... because my eyes are, in the long run, made of the same stuff as the grayness, the clarity, the dampness [*serost', svetlost', syrost'*] of those sites..." (G31). The fantasy of returning home alludes to a similar phonetic-semantic series in Marina Tsvetaeva's poem "*Rassvet na rel'sakh*" ("Daybreak on the Rails," 1922; Translations of the poems are mine):

...*Rossiiu vosstanavlivaiu*...	...I am reconstructing Russia...
Iz syrosti—i svai,	from dampness—and from bearing piles,
Iz syrosti—i serosti [...]	from dampness—and grayness [...]
Iz syrosti—i shpal,	from dampness—and railway ties,
Iz syrosti—i sirosti...	from dampness—and shabbiness...

It has been suggested that Nabokov was deliberately drawing on Tsvetaeva's poem in *The Gift* (Dvyniatin 137). In fact, a year before Tsvetaeva, Nabokov had published his poem "On a Train" (*Rul'*, July 10, 1921): "*Vnimaia trepetu i pen'iu smolkaiushchikh koles,—ia ramu opustil: pakhnulo syrosti, siren'u!*" ["Harking to the shudder and whine / of the wheels decelerating into silence, I pulled down the window, / and the waft of lilacs and dampness (*syrost'iu, siren'iu*) rushed in!"]. Both poems describe a return to Russia, but Tsvetaeva adds the word *shabbiness* [*sirost'*]. Nabokov's poem appeared under his penname Sirin. The poets met on January 24, 1924 in Prague. In 1927 Nabokov developed the triad *syrost'—serost'—sirost'* as a euphemistic code for S-S-S-R (the USSR). He proposed a similar encoding for the abbreviation in the essay "*Iubilei*" ("Anniversary Celebration"), written on the anniversary of the Bolshevik coup: "These very days, when they celebrate their gray, s-s-erish [*seryi, esesernyi*] jubilee, we celebrate the decade of contempt, faithfulness, and freedom" (*Sobranie Sochinenii* II, 647). A year later he completes the lexical series that would reappear in *The Gift* in the poem "Lilac" ("*Siren'*"; *Rul'*, May 13, 1928): "The night...quavered with the lilac, gray [*siren'iu, seroi*] [...] My night is misty and light [*svetla*]" (Leving, "Six Notes" 39-40).

Intertextuality

Zina's Dress: Made in...

Although an entire book has been published on "Zina's paradox," up to now no scholars have commented on why Fyodor is in fact so mysteriously "hooked" by the charming dress of his landlord's daughter in the episode in which he rents the Berlin room in *The Gift* (Leving, "Five Notes" 8-9). This dress forces him to accept not only an exorbitant rental fee, but also the torturing presence of the repulsive philistine Shchyogolev. In fact, it is not only the aura of his future love that Fyodor senses in the gauze dress; the situation is additionally reinforced by a strong literary allusion, which Godunov-Cherdyntsev probably guesses while still failing to realize its true origin. The author, however, incorporates the hint, saying that such dresses were worn "then at [ballroom] dances" (*togda na balakh*). Here is the passage:

> "Here is my daughter's room, here is ours," [Shchyogolev] said, pointing to two doors on the left and right. "And here's the dining room," and *opening a door in the depths*, he held it in that position for several seconds, as if taking a time exposure. Fyodor passed his eyes over the table, a *bowl* of nuts, a *sideboard*...By the far window, near a small bamboo table, stood a high-backed armchair: *across its arms there lay in airy repose a gauze dress, pale bluish* and very short (as was worn then at dances), and on the little table gleamed a *silvery flower* and a pair of scissors. (G144; Italics added)

The perspective from lodger's view turns out to focus on the enfilade of a Petersburg mansion of the 1830s from Gogol's "The Diary of a Madman" (the optical comparison, tossed in as if in passing, by the unidentified camera, represents an eye smuggled into the text as contraband). Fyodor himself as it were only tries on the setting, prior to resolutely entering this cramped apartment inhabited by the Russian classics, with *The Gift* tucked under his arm, in order to occupy the space assigned him there by Nabokov's writ.

> I should like to peek into the drawing room into which one only sometimes sees the *open door*, and through the drawing room into another room. Oh! What sumptuous furniture! Such *mirrors and porcelain*! I'd love to get a peek in there, into that half where Her Excellency lives—that's the place for me! Into her boudoir: there are so many little jars standing there, and *little bottles*, such *flowers* that one is afraid to breathe on them; see how *her dress lies thrown, and looks more like air than a dress.* I'd like to get a glimpse inside her bedroom...what wonders, I feel, must be in there, such paradise, I feel, as doesn't even exist in heaven. (Gogol, *Arabesques* 244; Italics added)

And, no wonder, this page—which is the very end of the second chapter—concludes with: "The distance *from the old residence to the new* was about the same as, somewhere in Russia, that from Pushkin Avenue to *Gogol Street*" (G145). As Fyodor learns later, this dress does not even belong to Zina, who is by now his fiancée. Yet he is able to create a mysterious inhabitant of the room from a limited number of details, and the "gauze dress," or rather a misinterpretation of the object's aura, therefore, serves as a trick of fate.

The circulation of the images related to garments reveals a mechanism of literary evolution in *The Gift*. As Victoria Ivleva puts it, "literary images are either 'purchased' or stolen by different authors. (They can be considered purchased when a new author alludes to the previous writer, immortalizing him in his footnotes). However, in order to be recognized, the images need to receive public attention either in the form of criticism or in the form of a 'theatrical' performance on a real or metaphorical stage" (Ivleva 301). The images of the vest, shoes, and Zina's dress generate a number of "internal rhythms" in Nabokov's metapoetic novel abundant with distant echoes in historical and literary perspectives.

Western Intertexts

Shakespeare

The Gift contains one direct reference to *Hamlet*, an allusion to a few words from Gertrude's description of Ophelia's tragic death: "And [Fyodor] returned at once to that world [of fiction] which was as natural to him...as water to Ophelia" (G125). This allusion, as Polina Barskova shows, confirms Nabokov's detailed knowledge of the Shakespearian text (where Ophelia is described as being "Like a creature native and indued / Unto that element"; *Hamlet* 4.7, 155-56). This close familiarity is not surprising: Nabokov had been working on a translation of Hamlet at the beginning of the 1930s and published two fragments from it in the émigré newspaper *Rul'* in the fall of 1930. One of these fragments is the very description of Ophelia's death mentioned in the novel (October 19, 1930). "Nabokov's quotation of his own translation of *Hamlet*" demonstrates that the project "was still current for him, or at least that it was very much on his mind at the time when he was writing *The Gift*" (Barskova 192).

After the cremation of Alexander Chernyshevski, Fyodor exits to the street and repeats the irrevocable sentence: "The braked line from *King Lear,* consisting entirely of five 'nevers'—that was all he could think of" (G313). The source is the utterance with which King Lear parts from Cordelia: "Never, never, never, never, never." Although in its solemn immediate context this line looks more than apt, the true (and very Nabokovian, by the way) link between this passage in *The Gift* and Shakespeare's drama becomes apparent in the next line dealing with unbuttoning the attire (which was not included in the novel):

KING LEAR

And my poor fool is hang'd! No, no, no life!
Why should a dog, a horse, a rat, have life,
And thou no breath at all? Thou'lt come no more,
Never, never, never, never, never!
Pray you, undo this button: thank you, sir.
Do you see this? Look on her, look, her lips,
Look there, look there!

(Act 5, Scene III)

Compare this with the following scene glimpsed by Fyodor in the same episode right after his quote from *King Lear*: "through the window of a cleaning and pressing shop near the Orthodox church, a worker with devilish energy and an excess of steam, as if in hell, torturing a pair of flat trousers" (G314): yet another "internal rhyme" to the "world of garments" motif just described.

Proust

Early critics of *The Gift* rarely substantiated their claims of the novel's Proustian undercurrent, assuming that parallels with the semi-autobiographical novel in seven volumes focusing on the notion of involuntary memory were self-evident. There is even a direct reference to the saga when Nabokov states that in Zina's "version the image of her father took on something of Proust's Swann" (G187).

In a recent study, Martin Hägglund has introduced two terms, *chronophilia* and *chronophobia*, that fit well with Nabokov's novel seen as an elaborate response to Proust. The fear of time (chronophobia) does not stem from a metaphysical desire to transcend time; on the contrary, chronophobia and chronophilia are "two aspects of the same condition. It is because one desires temporal phenomena (chronophilia) that one fears losing them" (Hägglund 448). The inception of Fyodor's idea for his version of *The Gift* testifies that the character's chronophilia and chronophobia are in perfect harmony:

> Fyodor conceives the idea of writing the book when he spends a couple of early summer days sunbathing in the Grünewald. Pursuing memories of recent years, he is seized by a "panicky desire" to prevent these past events from fading indefinitely. This desire to keep what can be lost is the impetus for Fyodor's decision to write an autobiography and is inscribed in the title of the book... The common feature [of Fyodor's unfinished texts] concerns the act of writing as an endeavor to remember... *The Gift* shall commemorate the history of their love, Fyodor promises. In making this pledge, he must figure the presence of the promise as a memory for the future. "One day we shall recall all this," Fyodor reflects on the last page of the book, as he and Zina leave a restaurant and wander out into the summer night. (Hägglund 451-52)

Chapter Four. STYLE

This final scene, in Hägglund's opinion, is a version of Fyodor's future retrospections, "the anticipation of a memory to come" and a delicate balancing act "between the watery abyss of the past and the aerial abyss of the future" (G342). Fyodor's promise to narrate his life embraces the past and the present with regard to the future, constituting "both the possibility of remembering and the risk of forgetting" (Hägglund 452).

Gide

Although *The Gift* is filled with allusions to *In Search of Lost Time*, Nabokov in the novel was able to find a way out of a Proustian hermetic world, resisting many aesthetic notions commonly ascribed to Proust by his French and émigré readers. Leonid Livak argues that Nabokov uses André Gide's novel, *The Counterfeiters* (*Les Faux-Monnayeurs*, 1925) as a starting point for refining his novelistic aesthetics (Nabokov opposed his own writings to those of his Parisian émigré peers). Gide's work is comprised of numerous characters and interwoven plotlines, and its main theme is that of the original and the copy. Edouard, a character based on Gide's own experiences, endeavors to write a book entitled *Les Faux-Monnayeurs*, which lends its title to the metanarrative framework, also called *The Counterfeiters*. Livak contends that like his fellow émigré writers—Gazdanov, Fel'zen, Yanovsky, and Poplavsky—"Nabokov creatively reworked [the] French source, but unlike his esthetic rivals, he did not use it as a conspicuous textual marker" (Livak 166).

Livak, in justifying his claim against the accepted notion of the strong "Proustian" traces in *The Gift*, asserts that Nabokov "saw the issue of artistic borrowing as a bone of contention in his clash with the Paris School" (Ibid.). Nabokov's interest in Gide's work must have originated in the compositional, narrative, and thematic vistas that it opened up. Indeed, *The Gift* includes texts that function like Edouard's journal and diary: Fyodor's poems and the stories of Fyodor's father, Yasha, and Nikolai Chernyshevski punctuate the progress of the protagonist's artistic search: "For Edouard, narrative infinity is contingent on his ignorance of the novel's finale; his novel is a mystical undertaking and its realization is mostly intuitive. [...] Both writers think that fate will reveal the denouement of their novels: the role of fate in their lives is their novelistic material" (Livak 171). Thus, Livak concludes, Fyodor's "method of trial and error is consistent with Edouard's cult of process"; moreover, neither *The Counterfeiters* nor *The Gift* presents the end result of their fictitious writers' quests. "Instead, they offer experiments that mirror both the ideal and the incorporating novels" (Ibid.).

Döblin

In addition to French modernism we should consider contemporary German-language sources responsible for the rich fabric of *The Gift*. Berlin, with its department stores, cinemas, and hectic traffic, became the subject of Alfred Döblin's novel *Berlin Alexanderplatz* (1929), which was adapted for the screen shortly after publication (directed by Piel Jutzi in 1931). *Berlin Alexanderplatz* was written partly in colloquial German, from the viewpoints of many characters and with a narrative style reminiscent of James Joyce (Döblin, though, denied being familiar with *Ulysses* at this time). The construction of a north-south subway line in Berlin began in early 1926. The Alexanderplatz was drilled to allow the construction of a vast underground station in Berlin; the "process of demolition and excavation... plays a major symbolic role in Döblin's novel. When it finally opened in December 1930, the station offered not only passageways connecting subway lines, commuter trains, and long-distance trains on several levels but also a variety of brightly lit stores amid the profusion of shiny, pale blue tiles covering the underground corridors" (Jelavich xvi). The shooting of the film *Berlin Alexanderplatz* took place after the completion of the subway, but it was still able to show numerous scenes of the construction in process. On the other hand, "despite its increasing importance as a center of commerce and transportation, the Alexanderplatz could never shake its image as a somewhat suspect locale" (Ibid. 6) and in the popular imagination as well as in Döblin's novel, "its environs comprised a variety of contradictory images" (Ibid. 7). Yasha's story in *The Gift* is a remake of the same newspaper report about the Russia émigré student's suicide that made its way to Döblin's novel.

As Franz Hessel notes in *Walking in Berlin* (1929), the very fact that the square was in constant flux attracted transients and provoked accounts of the city from the perspective of a flâneur. Fyodor's position is close to Walter Benjamin's concept of the urban observer, an uninvolved but highly perceptive bourgeois dilettante. Fyodor lives in Berlin in a kind of a parallel reality—the hero is not lost, but his keys, literally and figuratively, do not match the city's locked doors.

Joyce

The motif of missing keys representing displacement also appears in a novel that Nabokov considered one of the best of the twentieth century, James Joyce's *Ulysses* (1922). Both *The Gift* and *Ulysses* are urban novels and in both works, as Anat Ben-Amos writes, "keys are a metaphor for home and the homeland" (Ben-Amos 142). In one sense *The Gift* was an homage to the Russian Diaspora and to what Nabokov and his fellow compatriots had abandoned in leaving their motherland. In another aspect, as Brian Boyd states, "it is a very European work, deliberately challenging Joyce's *A Portrait of the Artist as a Young Man* and *Ulysses*... on their own terms" (Boyd, "Nabokov's Butterflies" 55). The parallels are obvious: *The Gift* is also "a portrait of its young artist-hero, who matures as a writer in émigré Berlin. In *Ulysses*, Joyce ironized a son's search for his father in *The Odyssey*, because Stephen and Bloom are neither physical nor spiritual kin, and when Bloom offers him a place in his home, Stephen answers by walking away into the night. But in *The Gift*, Fyodor seeks tirelessly for his father, Count Konstantin Godunov-Cherdyntsev, a famous lepidopterist and explorer of Central Asia, who has never returned from a last expedition..." (Ibid.).

In *Ulysses*, keys are related to the main characters of the novel, Leopold Bloom and Stephen Dedalus (both Dedalus and Bloom are forced into abandoning their keys to their residences, Stephen by his resentment about his life in the Tower and Bloom by his refusal to return home where he suspects that his wife, Molly, intends to receive a lover). Alexander Dolinin even suggests that the name of the French writer whom Alexander Yakovlevich Chernyshevski mentions in his internal monologue before death, *Delalande*, contains a partial anagram of the name of Joyce's protagonist, *Dedalus*, thus implying a kinship between the protagonists of the two novels, especially in the context of artistic creation and their shared prototypical myth — the invention of wings to escape exile (Dolinin, "The Gift" 167, 50n). Stephen's attitude is shown in his reflections when he realizes the key is not in his hands: "Have you the key? a voice asked" (Joyce 10); "Stephen put the huge key in his inner pocket" (15); "He has the key. I will not sleep there when this night comes" (37).

Furthermore, Ben-Amos highlights Bloom's Jewish origins as providing a framework for the character's "alienation from his native town. Unlike in *The Gift*, the protagonists of *Ulysses* are exiled in the city in a metaphorical rather than a national-political sense, yet Bloom's Jewish origins serve as an objective correlative to his spiritual displacement, so that the motif of keys express also a more general, political, displacement" (144). In *The Gift* Fyodor despises Zina's anti-Semitic stepfather, Shchyogolev, but "finds a harmony between love and literary creation and thus establishes a metaphorical home" (Ibid. 145). The delay in entering the flat is another example of the way failure leads to success, undermining the polarization of opposites.

And a Thousand Male Writers...

Alfred Döblin asserts that "advertising is a good contemporary manner of speaking, form of speaking for today. Whoever does not take a close look at it, whoever does not employ it, will not be able to capture the big city of the present... I suggest: take note of advertising and leave Stefan George and Rilke behind" (quoted in Jelavich 21). Döblin regards advertising as an appropriate linguistic medium because it speaks directly to the average person in pithy and often witty slogans and verses. Indeed, the brevity of the messages matched the accelerated nature of life in the metropolis, while the humor and the rhymes served as mnemonic devices that lodged in consumers' minds. Nabokov muses over the same technique but turns it into a more complex instrument of literary allusion: "Fyodor climbed aboard, and the conductor, on the open top deck, smote its plated side with his palm to tell the driver he could move on. Along this side and along the *toothpaste advertisement upon it swished the tips of soft maple twigs*—and it would have been pleasant to look down from above on the gliding street ennobled by perspective..." (G163).

Nabokov almost forces his reader to pay heed to a conglomerate of literary quotations:

> *Down the helical stairs* of the bus that drew up came *a pair of charming silk legs*: we know of course that this has been worn threadbare by *the efforts of a thousand male writers*, but nevertheless down they came, these legs—and deceived: *the face was revolting*. (G157)

One of the "thousand male writers," probably the first to use the pattern, is Alexander Pushkin:

> The street was crowded *with vehicles*: one after another, carriages rolled up to the lighted entrance. F*rom them there emerged, now the shapely little foot of beautiful young woman,* now a rattling jack-boot, now *the striped stocking*... (Pushkin 286)

Another "male writer" is James Joyce, to whom Nabokov offered his services in 1933 to translate *Ulysses* into Russian:

> Watch! Watch! *Silk flash rich stockings white*. Watch!
> A heavy tramcar honking its gong slewed between.
> Lost it. *Curse your noisy pugnose.* (Joyce 61)

As I have stated above, *The Gift* was an homage to the Russian emigration and to what Nabokov and his fellow émigrés had lost in leaving their homeland. In another sense it looked in the other direction towards Europe, drawing on and challenging Joyce's *A Portrait of the Artist as a Young Man* and *Ulysses*, Proust's *In Search of Lost Time*, and other European masterpieces on their own terms.

Visual Intertexts

It has been suggested that Nabokov's main devices for processing documentary sources (for Godunov-Cherdyntsev's Asian journey and the Chernyshevski biography) in *The Gift*—montage, colorization, the addition of sound—are plausibly linked with the techniques used by the early Soviet film-makers. The device of adding color has a direct analogue in Eisenstein's *The Battleship Potemkin*. One scene of this otherwise black-and-white film features a red flag flying from the *Potemkin*'s mast. Victor Shklovsky wrote on this device in his *"Piat' fel'etonov ob Eizenshteine"* (in the fifth feuilleton, — which was first published in the magazine *Sovetskii ekran*, № 3, 1926) (Paperno 319, 30n; see also the chapter devoted to Nabokov and Russian Formalism in: Glynn 2007). Given Nabokov's study of Joyce's *Usessyl* during his work on *The Gift*, it is worth recalling that James Joyce was especially interested in *Potemkin* (1925). Ten years before a similar encounter between Joyce and Nabokov took place in 1939 (Noel 1970), the two famous innovators, Joyce and Eisenstein, met on November 30, 1929 in Paris (according to Eisenstein's account; as far as is known, the writer never documented this meeting; Werner 491-507).

The kinship between the technical elements used or implied in *Ulysses* and in Eisenstein's work, striving for a true synthesis of all major art forms — literature, painting, music, and motion pictures — underscores the paradigmatic interest that writers had in film in the 1920s and 1930s.

The Gift contains a tantalizingly brief description of a fragment from an unnamed contemporary film: accompanied by his mother, the hero, Fyodor Godunov-Cherdyntsev, goes to a Berlin movie theater "where a Russian film was being shown which conveyed with particular *brio* the globules of sweat rolling down the glistening faces of the factory workers — while the factory owner smoked a cigar all the time" (G90). Alexander Dolinin has suggested that this is "a textbook example of parallel montage" and close-up, taken from Sergei Eisenstein's *Strike* [*Stachka*] (Nabokov, *Dar* 4:662). Although *Strike* contains a montage sequence similar to the one described, some minor elements in this particular episode still depart from Nabokov's vivid rendition. Dolinin refers to scene № 7 ("The Workers' Demands"), featuring four fat factory owners smoking cigars; however, this *mise en scene* is inter-cut with long shots of the crowd of strikers and then the mounted police squadron. The close-up of the workers next to their lathes is found only at the beginning of Eisenstein's film.

However, I believe that this excerpt from Nabokov may represent a hybrid of *two* films directed by Eisenstein, combined here in a cross-cut montage: *Strike* (1924) and *The Battleship Potemkin* (1925). The effects of light and shadow projected onto the faces of the agitated rebelling sailors are emphatically presented in *Potemkin*. The latter film was shown on screens in Berlin in the spring of 1926, which is when the action of Nabokov's novel begins. In addition, the author could very well have been aware of the scandal that developed around the German release of the film.

The presence of *Potemkin* becomes obvious if one expands the passage under scrutiny to include the preceding sentence, which contains a fleeting portrayal of a Communist demonstration in the town: "Once, [Fyodor and his mother] saw a modest Communist procession walking through the slush—with wet flags—most of the marchers battered by life, some crookbacked, others lame or sickly, a lot of plain-looking women and several sedate petty-bourgeois" [*podbitye zhizniu, gorbatye, da khromye, da kvelye, mnogo nekrasivykh zhenshchin i neskol'ko solidnykh meshchan*] (G90/Nabokov, *Dar* 4: 273). It is this collision, parodying the flow of humanity consisting mainly of cripples, women, a sick child, and confused bourgeois from the now canonical Odessa steps sequence, that might have been reflected in *The Gift*.

It is impossible to say precisely which version of the film Nabokov watched in the Berlin movie theater. Peter Jelavich calls the editing of *The Battleship Potemkin* for German distribution "a process that turned into one of the most spectacular cases of film censorship" (Jelavich 131). Sergei Eisenstein's account of the naval mutiny during the Russian revolution of 1905 had not attracted much attention when it was released in the USSR in 1925, although it did receive a more enthusiastic response (at least by left-of-center members of the press and the public), when a leftist film distributor arranged for showings in Germany (Ibid.).

The right to screen the work, however, was not easy to win. *The Battleship Potemkin* was initially banned by the Berlin film board on March 24, 1926. The appellate board ruled on 10 April that the work could not be banned for its political slant, "nor was it likely to pose a threat to public order and security, as the lower film board had argued. Yet the appellate board further ruled that certain scenes had a 'brutalizing effect' and thus had to be cut—namely many of the shots of the mutiny aboard the ship as well as the massacre of civilians on the Odessa steps" (Jelavich 131). This is the likely explanation for why Nabokov focused his attention on the crowd rather than on the violent imagery of the oppression which he, in any case, would surely have considered a side effect of the ridiculously exaggerated Bolshevik propaganda.

The Weimar argument for censoring *The Battleship Potemkin* was that audiences would equate the conditions shown in the film with present-day Germany and thus be incited to violence. But after severe cuts (hundreds of meters!) were made, the Berlin film board declared that the "German people, even the workers... know exactly how to distinguish between the type of state and the governmental policies in tsarist Russia and those of the German Republic, between the tortured and oppressed soldiers of czarist Russia and the free, self-governing people of the German Republic" (Berlin film board report of July 12, 1926; quoted in Jelavich 132).

Nabokov mentioned Eisenstein twice in his correspondence with Edmund Wilson, and both times he distorted the name of the Soviet director as "Eisenstadt." The first instance dates to 1948, at which point Nabokov instructed his American friend as follows: "In fact a typical Russian intelligent would look askance at an avant-garde poet...But of course people who read Trotsky for information anent Russian culture cannot be expected to know all this. I have also a hunch that the general idea that avant-garde literature and art were having a wonderful time under Lenin and Trotsky is mainly due to Eisenstadt films—'montage'—things like that—and great big drops of sweat rolling down rough cheeks. The fact that pre-Revolution Futurists joined the party has also contributed to the kind of (quite false) avant-garde atmosphere which the American intellectual associates with the Bolshevik Revolution" (*Nabokov–Wilson Letters* 222).

It becomes clear when we compare this excerpt with the text of the novel that Nabokov is quoting the fragment from the same scene that he depicted earlier in *The Gift* ("great big drops of sweat rolling down rough cheeks" / "the globules of sweat rolling down the glistening faces of the factory workers"), first noticed by S. Karlinsky, who made no attempt to identify which Eisenstein film this referred to (*Nabokov–Wilson Letters* 224, 5n). This time Nabokov separates the two parallel scenes and does not mention the factory owner smoking a cigar.

References

Alexandrov, Vladimir. *Nabokov's Otherworld*. Princeton: Princeton University Press, 1991.

Barskova, Polina. "Filial Feelings and Paternal Patterns: Transformations of Hamlet in *The Gift*," Nabokov Studies 9.1 (2005): 191-208.

Bely, Andrey. *Stikhotvoreniia i poemy*. Vol. 2. St. Petersburg: Akademicheskii proekt [Novaia Biblioteka poeta], 2006.

Ben-Amos, Anat. "The Role of Literature in *The Gift*," Nabokov Studies 4, 1997: 117-149.

Bethea, David M. *The Superstitious Muse: Mythopoetic Thinking and Russian Literature*. Boston: Academic Studies Press, 2009.

Blackwell, Stephen. *Zina's Paradox: The Figured Reader in Nabokov's* Gift. New York, NY: Peter Lang; 2000.

____ *The Quill and the Scalpel: Nabokov's Art and the Worlds of Science*. Columbus: The Ohio State University Press, 2009.

Boyd, Brian. "Nabokov's Butterflies." Introduction by B. Boyd. *The Atlantic Monthly* 4 (Vol. 285), April 2000.

____ *V. Nabokov: The American Years*. Princeton: Princeton University Press, 1991.

____ *Vladimir Nabokov: The Russian Years*. Princeton: Princeton University Press, 1990.

Brown, Clarence. "Nabokov's Pushkin and Nabokov's Nabokov," *Wisconsin Studies in Contemporary Literature* 8 (2), 1967: 280-293.

Brown, Edward. "Nabokov, Chernyshevsky, Olesha and the Gift of Sight," in *Literature, Culture and Society in the Modern Age*, pt. 2, *In Honor of Joseph Frank*, ed. Edward J. Brown et al. Stanford, 1992.

Browning, Robert. *The Poetry of Robert Browning*. Indianapolis: Bobbs-Merrill, 1971.

Connolly, Julian. "The Major Russian Novels." *The Cambridge Companion to Nabokov*. Ed. by Julian W. Connolly. Cambridge: Cambridge University Press, 2005: 135-150.

Danzas, Konstantin. "Poslednie dni zhizni i konchina A. Pushkina v zapisi A. Ammosova," *Pushkin v vospominaniiakh sovremennikov* Vol. 2. St. Petersburg: Akademicheskii proekt, 1998.

Debreczeny, Paul. *The Other Pushkin: A Study of Alexander Pushkin's Prose Fiction*. Stanford: Stanford University Press, 1983.

Dolinin, Alexander. "Nabokov's Time Doubling: from *The Gift* to *Lolita*," *Nabokov Studies* 2, 1995: 3-40.

_____ "The Gift," in *The Garland Companion to Vladimir Nabokov*. Ed. by V. Alexandrov. New York: Garland, 1995: 135-169.

_____ "Kommentarii k romanu *Dar*," in V. V. Nabokov, *Sobranie sochinenii russkogo perioda* Vol. 4. St. Petersburg: Symposium, 2000.

_____ "Nabokov as a Russian writer," *The Cambridge Companion to Nabokov*. Ed. by Julian W. Connolly. Cambridge: Cambridge University Press, 2005.

_____ "'Dar': Dobavleniia k kommentariiam," *Nabokov Online Journal* I, 2007.

Dvyniatin, Fyodor. "Nabokov i futuristicheskaia traditsiia," *Vestnik filologicheskogo fakul'teta* 2/3, 1999.

Eikhenbaum, Boris. *Lev Tolstoy*: Kniga pervaia, 50-e gody. Leningrad, 1928.

Foster, John Burt. *Nabokov's Art of Memory and European Modernism*. Princeton: Princeton University Press, 1993.

Genette, Gérard. *Palimpsestes*. Paris: Seuil, 1982.

Glynn, Michael. *Vladimir Nabokov: Bergsonian and Russian Formalist Influences in His Novels*. New York: Palgrave Macmillan, 2007.

Gogol, Nikolai. *Diary of a Madman and Other Stories*. Trans. by Ronald Wilks. London: Penguin Books, 1972.

_____ *Arabesques*. Translated by A. Tulloch. Ann Arbor: Ardis, 1982.

Greenleaf, Monika. "Fathers, Sons and Impostors: Pushkin's Trace in *The Gift*," *Slavic Review* 53 (1), 1994: 140-58.

Grumm-Grzhimailo, Grigorii. *Opisanie puteshestviia v Zapadnyi Kitai* in 3 vols. St. Petersburg: Nikolaev, Kirshbaum, 1896–1907.

Hägglund, Martin. "Chronophilia: Nabokov and the Time of Desire." *New Literary History* 37.2 (2006): 447-467.

Hartmann, Sabine. See under "Zimmer, Dieter E. and Sabine Hartmann."

Ivleva, Victoria. "A Vest Reinvested in *The Gift*," *The Russian Review* 68 (2), 2009: 283-301.

Jelavich, Peter. *Berlin Alexanderplatz: Radio, Film, and the Death of Weimar Culture*. Berkeley: University of California Press, 2006.

Johnson, Donald Barton. *Worlds in Regression: Some Novels of Vladimir Nabokov*. Ann Arbor: Ardis, 1985.

Joyce, James. *Ulysses*. London: The Bodley Head, 1986.

Kostalevsky, Marina. "The Young Godunov-Cherdyntsev or How to Write a Literary Biography," *Russian Literature* 43 (3), 1998: 283-95.

Lavrov, Alexander. "Andrei Bely i 'kol'tso vozvrata' v *Zashchite Luzhina*," in *The Real Life of Pierre Delalande: Studies in Russian and Comparative Literature to Honor Alexander Dolinin*, ed. by David M. Bethea, Lazar Fleishman, and Alexander Ospovat. Stanford: Berkeley Slavic Specialties, 2007; Stanford Slavic Studies, vols 33–34. Vol. 2: 539-554.

References

Ledenev, A. V. "Ot Vladimira Darova—k *Daru* Vladimira: V. Briusov i V. Nabokov," in *Briusovskie chteniia 2002 goda*. Ed. S. Zolian et al. Erevan: Lingva, 2004: 189-210.

Levin, Iurii. "Ob osobennostiax povestvovatel'noi struktury i obraznogo stroia romana V. Nabokova *Dar*," *Russian Literature* 9.2, 1981: 191-229.

Leving, Yuri. "Six Notes to *The Gift*," *The Nabokovian* 45, 2000: 36-41.

_____ ["Five Notes"]. *The Nabokovian* 48, 2002: 8-14.

Levy, Alan. *Vladimir Nabokov: The Velvet Butterfly*. New York: Permanent Press, 1984.

Livak, Leonid. *How It was Done in Paris: Russian Émigré Literature and French Modernism*. Madison: The University of Wisconsin Press, 2003.

Lotman, Mikhail. "A ta zvezda nad Pulkovom...Zametki o poezii i stikhoslozhenii V. Nabokova," in *V. Nabokov: Pro et contra*. Vol. 2. St. Petersburg: RChGI, 2001: 213-226.

Malcolm, Donald. "A Retrospect," *The New Yorker*. April 25, 1964: 198-204.

Malikova, Maria. "Zabytyi poet," in V. V. Nabokov. *Stikhotvoreniia* [Novaia biblioteka poeta]. St. Petersburg: Akademicheskii proekt, 2002: 5-52.

Manolescu, Monica. "Verbal Adventures in the Inky Jungle: Marco Polo and John Mandeville in Vladimir Nabokov's *The Gift*," *Cycnos* 24 [special issue: "Vladimir Nabokov, Annotating vs Interpreting Nabokov"] (2007). <http://revel.unice.fr/cycnos/index.html?id=1060> Accessed July 19, 2010.

Maslov, Boris. "Poet Koncheyev: Opyt tekstologii personazha," *Novoe Literaturnoe Obozrenie* 47 (2001): 172-86.

Meyer, Priscilla. "Nabokov's Biographers, Annotators, and Interpreters," *Modern Philology* 91 (3), 1994: 326-338.

Mitchell, Julian. "Dazzling Energy," *London Sunday Times*, November 10, 1963.

Mondri, Henrietta. "O dvukh adresatakh literaturnoi parodii v 'Dare' V. Nabokova (Iu. Tynyanov i V. Rozanov)," *Rossiiskii literaturovedcheskii zhurnal* 4, 1994: 95-102.

Morris, Paul D. "Vladimir Nabokov's Poetry in Russian Émigré Criticism: A Partial Survey," *Canadian Slavonic Papers* XL (Nos. 3-4) 1998: 297-310.

_____ "Nabokov's Poetic Gift: The Poetry in and of *Dar*." *Russian Literature* 48 (4), 2000: 457-69.

Nabokov, Vladimir. *Notes on Prosody and Abram Gannibal*. Princeton: Princeton University Press, 1964.

_____ *The Nabokov–Wilson Letters: 1941-1971*, Ed. Simon Karlinsky, New York: Harper and Row, 1979.

_____ *Dar* in *Sobranie sochinenii russkogo perioda*. 5 vols. St. Petersburg: Symposium, 1999-2000. Vol. 4.

Nakhimovsky, Alexander. "A Linguistic Study of Nabokov's Russian Prose," *The Slavic and East European Journal* 21 (1), 1977: 78-87.

Nesbet, Anne. "Suicide as Literary Fact in the 1920s," *Slavic Review* 50 (4), 1991: 827-35.

Noel, Lucie Léon. "Playback," *Nabokov: Criticism, Reminiscences, Translations and Tributes*. Ed. by Alfred Appel, Jr., and Charles Newman. Evanston: Northwestern, 1970.

Orlitsky, Yuri. *Stikh i proza v russkoi literature*. Moscow: Rossiiskii gosudarstvennyi universitet, 2002.

Papapulo, Alexander. "Godunov-Cherdyntsev on the Moon," *The Nabokovian* 20, 1988: 20-22.

Paperno, Irina. "How Nabokov's *Gift* Is Made." *Festschrift in Honor of Joseph Frank*. Ed. by Edward J. Brown, Lazar Fleishman, Gregory Freidin and Richard Schupbach. Stanford: Stanford Slavic Studies, 1992: 295-322.

Pichova, Hana. *The Art of Memory in Exile: Vladimir Nabokov and Milan Kundera*. Carbondale: Southern Illinois University Press, 2001.

Przhevalskii, Nikolai. *Iz Zaisana cherez Khami v Tibet i na verkhove Zheltoi reki*. St. Petersburg: Balashev, 1883.

Pushkin, Aleksander. *The Complete Prose Tales of Alexandr Sergeyevitch Pushkin*. Trans. by Gillon R. Aitken. New York: W. W. Norton, 1996.

Rampton, David. *Vladimir Nabokov: A Critical Study of the Novels*. Cambridge: Cambridge University Press, 1984.

Roborovskii, Vsevolod Ivanovich. *Puteshestvie v Tian-Shan i v Nan-Shan*, [1893-95]. St. Petersburg: Stasyulevich, 1899/1900.

Ronen, Omry. "Emulation, Anti-Parody, Intertextuality, and Annotation," *Nabokov Studies* 5 (1998/1999): 63-70.

_____ "Nine Notes to *The Gift*," *The Nabokovian* 44, 2000: 20-26.

Salomon, Roger B. "*The Gift*. Nabokov's Portrait of the Artist," in *Critical Essays on Vladimir Nabokov*. Ed. Phyllis A. Roth. Boston: G. K. Hall and Co., 1984: 185-201.

Sandrof, Nancy. "Work of Uncanny Lucidity," *Worcester Telegram*, May 26, 1963.

Scammell, Michael. "Translation is a Bastard Form." An Interview with Michael Scammell by Yuri Leving. *Nabokov Online Journal* 1, 2007. <http://etc.dal.ca/noj/articles/volume1/Scammel_Interview_3.pdf> Accessed July 19, 2010.

Scherr, Barry P. "Poetry," in *The Garland Companion to Vladimir Nabokov*. Ed. by V. Alexandrov. New York: Garland, 1995: 608-625.

Scott, Charles T. "Typography, Poems, and the Poetic Line." *Linguistic and Literary Studies in Honor of Archibald A. Hill*. Mohammad Ali Jazayery et al eds. Trends in Linguistics; Studies and Monographs; Nos. 7-10, Vol. 4. Hague: Mouton, 1979: 153-160.

Shapiro, Gavriel. *The Sublime Artist's Studio: Nabokov and Painting*. Evanston: Northwestern University Press, 2009.

Smith, Gerald. "Nabokov and Russian Verse Form," *Russian Literature Triquarterly* 24. Ann Arbor: Ardis, 1991: 271-305.

Sologub, Fyodor. *The Petty Demon*. Trans. by Samuel David Cioran. Ann Arbor: Ardis, 1983.

Stendhal (Marie-Henri Beyle). *Le rouge et le noir*. Fribourg, Switzerland, 1973.

Tammi, Pekka. *Problems of Nabokov's Poetics: A Narratological Analysis.* Helsinki: Suomalainen Tiedeakatemia, 1985.

Taranovsky, Kiril. *Essays on Mandel'shtam.* Cambridge: Harvard University Press, 1976.

Thomas, Peter-John. *Beside the Point: Places in Nabokov's* The Gift [Ph.D. dissertation, AAT 3331154]. Evanston, Illinois: Northwestern University, 2008.

Vaiskopf, Mikhail. Introduction to Vladimir Jabotinsky. *Chuzhbina. P'esa. Komediia v piati deistviakh.* Jerusalem, Moscow: Gesharim, Mosty Kul'tury, 2000.

Vries, Gerard de. "Shoes," *The Nabokovian* 24, 1990: 42-45.

Vries, Gerard de and Donald Barton Johnson, Liana Ashenden. *Nabokov and the Art of Painting.* Amsterdam: Amsterdam University Press, 2006.

Werner, Gösta. "James Joyce and Sergej Eisenstein," *James Joyce Quarterly* 23.3, 1990: 491-507.

White, Duffield. "Radical Aestheticism and Metaphysical Realism in Nabokov's *The Gift*," in *Russian Literature and American Critics: In Honor of Deming Brown.* Ed: Kenneth N. Brostrom. Ann Arbor: University of Michigan, 1984: 273-291.

Williams, Carol. "Nabokov's Dialectical Structure," *Wisconsin Studies in Contemporary Literature* 8 (2), A Special Number Devoted to Vladimir Nabokov, 1967: 250-267. [Also in: *Nabokov: The Man and His Work.* Ed. L.S. Dembo. Madison, WI: University of Wisconsin Press, 1967]

Zimmer, Dieter E. "Nabokovs Berlin" [presentation at the International Vladimir Nabokov Symposium, St. Petersburg, July 15, 2002]: <http://www.d-e-zimmer.de/Root/nabberlin2002.htm> Accessed July 19, 2010.

_____ "Chinese Rhubarb and Caterpillars" [presentation at the International Vladimir Nabokov Symposium, St. Petersburg, July 18, 2002]: <http://www.d-e-zimmer.de/Root/rhubarb2002.htm> Accessed July 19, 2010.

Zimmer, Dieter E. and Sabine Hartmann. "'The Amazing Music of Truth': Nabokov's Sources for Godunov's Central Asian Travels in *The Gift*," *Nabokov Studies* 7, 2002-2003: 33-74.

Chapter Five
COMMENTARY

> Anyone who is going to read a somewhat sadistic author like Nabokov must keep encyclopedias, dictionaries, and handbooks handy if he wants to understand even half of what is going on... The reader must be a researcher.
>
> Carl Proffer, *Keys to Lolita*

THE GIFT AS HYPERTEXT: DIGITAL DATABASES

Though arguably the greatest Russian novel of the past century, *The Gift* is also Nabokov's most challenging work, especially for readers lacking familiarity with Russian and European culture and history of the late nineteenth and early twentieth centuries. In this book I have decided not to provide a page by page commentary to *The Gift* for several reasons: firstly, because it would expand the present edition considerably, and secondly because this effort has already been made by Alexander Dolinin in his exemplary commentary to the Russian edition of the novel, published in the fourth volume of Nabokov's *Collected Works* by Symposium (1999–2001). Since this publication a decade ago, Dolinin has been regularly updating his findings, and the expanded English translation of his work is due to appear soon.

Some additional important work aimed at providing essential explanatory commentary on the novel has been undertaken by the students in courses on Nabokov taught by the author of this book over the few past years at Dalhousie University in Canada. The project was established as a wiki and has allowed students to collaborate and to display their work both to their peers and to any interested readers worldwide through the creation of an original scholarly compendium with multimedia material and digital images. The main goal was to create a comprehensive concordance, along with some basic annotations, but without exploring the subtle literary allusions in the way that Alexander Dolinin has done so well.

This collaborative project has yielded a functioning computerized database devoted to the novel, where commentary is organized both page by page and alphabetically (hyperlinks lead to an extensive network of materials, and various articles are interconnected and provide a useful critical apparatus to Nabokov's novel). Paintings, photographs, and other works of visual art are linked on this site for identification and critical commentary, including images illustrative of a particular technique or school. The project showcases various covers and jacket designs for *The Gift*, including archival photographic reproduction of the original journal publication in 1937. The portal hosts basic entries under the headings: "Timeline in the novel," "Motifs," "Criticism," "*The Gift* Bibliography," and other categories. The interactive interface features elements of flash animation and complements the present print edition. It is available at www.keystogift.com.

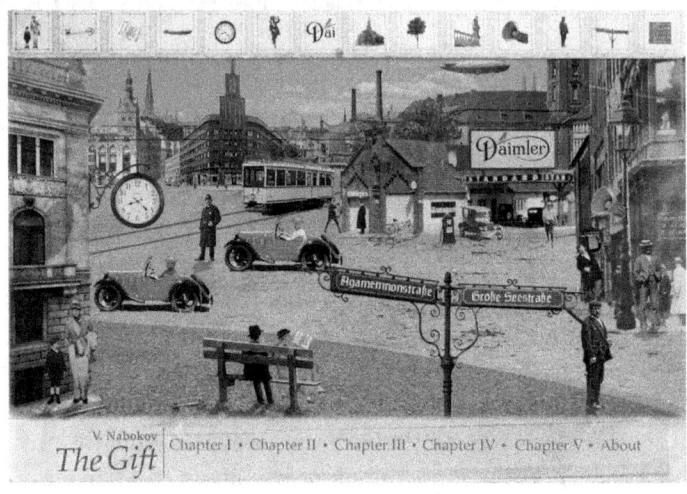

[Ill. **5-1**] Screenshot of the main page of the website.
Concept — Y. Leving; design and computer graphics — A. Bashkin, 2009

What Requires a Footnote?

Some general imperatives related to broader problems of commentary, as well as those peculiar to *The Gift*, should be touched upon. I will outline some rules of thumb which can be applied to studying and appreciating Nabokov's last novel of the Russian period, and provide some specific examples. A typical complaint about annotating literature in general and Nabokov in particular that has been raised again in the debates surrounding the recent publication of Nabokov's last unfinished English novel, *The Original of Laura* (Knopf, 2009), is that academic studies by nature concentrate their attention on detailed aspects of Nabokov's oeuvre and

> tend to establish that Nabokov knew an outlandish amount about almost everything... [T]hey establish clearly that Nabokov knew a surprising amount about, respectively, painting, especially Old Master painting, and science — and they establish that knowledge with sanity and energy, and no hint of the presence of Charles Kinbote, the crazy enthusiast who takes over the task of annotating John Shade's work in *Pale Fire*, and who presides over Nabokov studies like Banquo's ghost (Lanchester 16).

Indeed, one would not want to resemble Kinbote in his academic writing, and comments by critics and general readership such as the one above should not be simply dismissed, despite what might be interpreted as disdain towards serious scholarship. In a more sober context, an example of a *very close*, almost a "Kinbotian," reading of the opening pages of *The Gift* will be offered in the second part of this chapter.

A commentator's goals, to a certain extent, can be modeled on the literary-philosophical school of explication in Judaism. Wolfgang Iser maintains that "interpretation as we have come to understand it in the West arose out of the exegesis of the Torah in the Judaic tradition" (Iser 13). The oral tradition of the Torah distinguishes between four basic approaches in analyzing the Biblical text: *Pshat* (this level refers to the intended meaning of the text), *Remez* (alluded meaning, hint), *Drash* (interpretative or allegorical meaning that is not explicit in the text), and *Sod* (literary, secret; the mystical or esoteric meaning). The entire complex of the four levels is referred to as *Pardes*, an acronym formed from the first letters of each word, which also means 'orchard' in Hebrew (the English word "paradise" is derived from the same root). In the case of *The Gift* we are mainly concerned with *Pshat*, or the intended meaning of Nabokov's work. In my close reading, which I call a "total commentary," I will offer a near-molecular analysis, registering direct linguistic links between the words along with the thematic nodes and subtexts in the narrative itself.

What Constitutes a Footnote?

Names and Characters

I will start with what would seem to be the easiest method—by posing a series of empirical questions and possible answers.

What must be annotated in order to provide essential assistance to the reader when dealing with such a complicated work of art as *The Gift*? Obviously, the historical events, dates and real-life personae mentioned in the narrative should be glossed in notes. Thus we would have, for instance, for all the names occurring on just one page (G50): Italian composer Giacomo Puccini (1858–1924); French author Anatole France (1844–1924); Italian actress Eleonora Duse (1858–1924), known for her naturalistic and unique style as well as for her many love affairs, and British mountaineer George Mallory (1886–1924), who took part in the British expeditions to Mount Everest in the early 1920s. *The Gift* enlists real people from fields as diverse as science, the arts, and politics both contemporary and historical: from the "Westernizing" Russian Tsar Peter the Great (1672–1725), to the German revolutionary philosopher Karl Marx (1818–83); from the canonical John Milton (1608–74) and Ludwig van Beethoven (1770–1829) to the less recognized (in our time) German general and statesman Paul von Hindenberg (1847–1934) and French mathematician and politician Paul Painlevé (1863–1933).

How extensive should the encyclopedic information on each mentioned character be? Minimal biographic data would suffice; it is essential to indicate the era and occupation of a given historical figure. Briefly noting the relevance of each character to the narrative, whenever this makes practical sense, would add to the understanding of the larger context and the theme in question.

> Sample:
> *Sand, George*: "George Sand" was the pseudonym of the French novelist and feminist Amantine-Lucile-Aurore Dupin, later Baroness Dudevant (1804–76). Frau Stoboy is said to have "George-Sandesque regality" (G9). The possibility that "his restive spouse should take to it into her head to wear male dress — in the manner of George Sand" is one of Chernyshevski's points against marriage as he weighs the pros and cons in his "Diary of my Relations with Her Who now Constitutes my Happiness" (G9, 229).

The commentator will have to make choices based on assumptions about the *a priori* knowledge of the contemporary audience, presuming, for example, that some readers might be more familiar with the German philosophers Immanuel Kant and Georg Hegel than with the ancient Greek classics: page 67 features three of them — Pythagoras, Anaximenes, and Phales (also known as Thales the Milesian, c. 624 BC — c. 546 BC); if this is the case, then the fundamental theoretical doctrines can be sketched in a couple sentences for each. The same principle applies to politicians (Édouard Herriot [1872–1957], three times President of France's Third Republic, is virtually unknown today outside of his native country; G36) and eminent writers: the commentator should probably omit introductory information whenever Leo Tolstoy is mentioned in the text, but he will have to insert some explanations regarding less famous yet important Russian novelists appearing on the pages of *The Gift* — Nikolai Leskov (1831–95), Aleksey Pisemsky (1821–81), and Sergei Aksakov (1791–1859; remembered for his semi-autobiographical tales of a landlord's family life, hunting, and butterfly collecting). When Ivan Turgenev's (1818–83) name surfaces, the relevance of his programmatic novel *Fathers and Sons* (1861) to Fyodor's life and the text's central paradigm should be mentioned; in the same vein, Nabokov's far from reverent attitude to Fyodor Dostoevsky (1821–81) may be noted in connection with this writer. Nabokov's personal predilections color his prose, both in negative and positive contexts. This is true with respect to Mikhail Lermontov (1814–41), a romantic writer and poet, who died in a duel like Pushkin, and whose works

Nabokov admired and translated into English. In *The Gift*, the critic Christopher Mortus quotes Lermontov's poem "The Angel" in his critique of Fyodor's novel (the line from the poem reads: "And the sounds of heaven could not be replaced / With the dull songs of the earth"; G73, 203, 304).

The effect of "turning realia into *realiora* intensifies when the author injects into this world a dose of accurate references to authentic sources which can be checked by the reader" (Barabtarlo 17). One of Nabokov's challenges in writing *The Gift* was evidently the construction of Fyodor's father's persona. To bring this complex figure to life, Nabokov places him right next to some recognizable figures from the historical milieu: "I liked the fact that, in contradistinction to the majority of non-Russian travelers, Sven Hedin for example, [father] never changed his clothes for Chinese ones on his wanderings" (G113). Indeed, Sven Hedin explains that he never "renounced the prestige European garments confer" (Hedin, *Enfardgenom* 1:303). "However, in order to be allowed into Lhasa, Hedin disguised himself as a Lamaist pilgrim from Mongolia (Hedin, *Scoutliv* 293-5), wearing Mongol clothes, shaving his head, and dirtying his skin; on his later travels he liked to pose in various local costumes. The ploy was not successful; rain and sweat used to wash away the mud, and the Tibetan spies were never fooled as to the identity of this 'pilgrim'" (Zimmer 40). Like all compound descriptions in the novel, the continuation of the very same passage quoted above borrows from another source, this time Russian (Przheval'skii 8; noted by Dolinin, quoted in Zimmer): "In camp [father] practiced shooting, which served as an excellent precaution against any importuning" (G113). Nabokov not only connects the historical Hedin and the fictitious Godunov-Cherdyntsev, but also invents a dialogue between them:

> Sven Hedin, sitting next to my father, asked him how it had happened that, traveling with unprecedented freedom over the forbidden parts of Tibet, in the immediate vicinity of Lhasa, he had not gone to look at it, to which my father replied that he had not wanted to sacrifice even one hour's collecting for the sake of visiting "one more filthy little town"... (G113)

Dieter Zimmer is right to point out that the last Europeans to be allowed into Lhasa in the nineteenth century were the French missionaries Gabet and Huc in 1846: "All others who tried were turned back about 200 km away. The two who probably tried hardest were Przhevalsky (1879) and Sven Hedin (1901). Hedin [in his 1913 report] gives a detailed account of how he was complimented out of the country by Tibetan troops and officials" (Zimmer 41). Yet one more intertextual touch in Godunov-Cherdyntsev's uncomplimentary description of Lhasa ("one more filthy little town"; G113) has a documentary source that requires explication. Évariste-Régis Huc writes in *Souvenirs d'un voyage dans la Tartarie et le Thibet pendant les années 1844, 1845 et 1846* (Paris: Adrien le Clerc, 1850; Russian trans.: E. R. Huc. *Vospominaniia o puteshestvii po Tatarii.* St. Petersburg: Vol'f, 1866): "Lha-Sa is not a large town, its circuit being at the utmost two leagues [c. 10 km]... The principal streets of Lha-sa are broad, well laid out, and tolerably clean, at least when it does not rain: but the suburbs are revoltingly filthy" (Huc 2:170). Alexander Dolinin suggests that the remark may also have been prompted by the Russian Buriat G. Ts. Tsybikov, who visited Lhasa as a Buddhist pilgrim in 1899–1902 and in his book *Buddist-palomnik u sviatyn' Tibeta* (*A Buddhist Pilgrim among the Shrines of Tibet*; Petrograd, 1919: 94, 101) described Lhasa as an extremely filthy place where people relieved themselves in the streets (both quoted in Zimmer 41).

Playing with Readers

Cases of references to real people mixed with purely fictional characters are tricky by default; as Gene Barabtarlo points out in his discussion of the dramatis personae in *Pnin*, "a slight adjustment or merely a shift of familiar accent in presenting well-known persons produces a subtle but distinct 'not-quite-of-this-world' sensation" (Barabtarlo 17). There are quite a few such semi-fictitious characters in *The Gift*. The civil engineer named *Kern*, whom Fyodor Godunov-Cherdyntsev encounters at the Chernyshevskis' Berlin apartment, is a typical example: as noted earlier in the chapter entitled "Structure," the engineer's name bears easily recognizable Pushkinian associations (via Anna Kern), but he also shares his name with a prominent German linguist, Otto Kern (1863–1942). Nabokov's selection of a name with potential associations usually creates an array of resonating meanings—none of which, however, seems to be dominant; the reference instead ends up serving as a red herring.

The commentator's task is to point out Nabokov's such deliberate attempts to confuse, or "red herrings." An illustration of Nabokov's onomastic deceit is the character named X. B. Lambovski (G107). The narrator's remark, that "there was something paschal about him," requires explanation: the "Paschal" overtones hint at a quasi-religious connection. "X. B. Lambovski" is a literal translation from the Russian original (which the Anglophone reader could not possibly understand). The man's surname in Russian is Baranovski, which derives from *baran*, meaning "ram," whence the related, Paschal "lamb" in English (with the difference that "baran" also implies "dolt" in Russian). But hidden in this "translation" is the fact that the man's initials, if read as Cyrillic letters, are the traditional abbreviation for the Russian Orthodox Easter greeting in Old Church Slavonic: "Christ is risen" (*"Khristos voskrese,"* for which the Cyrillic abbreviation reads "X. B.")—commonly used on Russian postcards in Nabokov's youth (Alexandrov 136). Although the true prototype behind the ridiculed Lambovski-Baranovski remains unknown so far, to some of Nabokov's contemporaries his satirical approach seemed too cruel; the author of *The Gift* answered these charges in a letter to Mark Aldanov:

> I was guided not by an urge to laugh at this or that person (although there would be no crime in that—we are not in class or in church), but solely by a desire to show a certain order of literary ideas, typical at a given time—which is what the whole novel is about (its main heroine is literature). If in this case a style of criticism I feature corresponds to the style of particular figures and fops, that is natural and unavoidable. (Quoted in Boyd 480)

Nabokov ends his letter with a frank statement that seems prophetic today: "You say that *The Gift* can count on a very long life. If that's the case, then it's all the more obliging to take along for the ride, free of charge, some of my contemporaries who would otherwise have stayed at home forever" (Ibid.).

Who else had the opportunity to ride at Nabokov's expense? Mostly those whom Nabokov needed in order to propel his plot—multiple extras who form the novel's rich backdrop, everyone with his or her own engaging biography. From "a friend of my father" (G121), Grigory Grumm-Grzhimaylo (1860–1936), the author of *La pamir et sa faune lepidopterologique* (1890), who led an Imperial Russian Geographical Society expedition to the Pamirs and the Tyan-Shan, to Charlie Chaplin (1889–1977), the greatest silent comedy actor in film history (G314).

Establishing the Difference between Reality and Fiction

While some names mentioned by Nabokov are quite obvious and easy to explain, others pose a sort of riddle. For example: "In London, lords and ladies danced the Jimmie and imbibed cocktails" (G315). Unlike the common foxtrot or tango, "danc[ing] the Jimmie" is a mystery, and the commentator wishing to explicate it will have to confront a few possible scenarios: (1) Because Shirin speaks in a lisping voice, Jimmie may be a mispronunciation of the word "Shimmy," a popular fast dance from the 1920s; (2) "Jimmie" is British slang for the Charleston song and dance and could be a reference to the popular tune's creator, James P. Johnson (1894–1955) (this African-American composer, pianist, and jazz pioneer wrote the tune in 1923, and it became a hit throughout the 1920s); (3) Jimmie may not be a dance at all, but a reference to an African-American jazz alto saxophonist and bandleader named James Melvin "Jimmie" Lunceford (1902–47), who was noted for Big Band swing music. By 1935, his band, the Jimmy Lunceford Orchestra, had achieved national recognition. Nabokov is blurring the boundaries with the chronology of events and creates a rich and potent context, where an "actual person" meets a fictitious one, and the point of contact becomes what Barabtarlo calls "a light-emitting chink." As a source of contradiction, for it at once emanates credibility and incongruity, Nabokov "purposely and deftly sets up this antinomy. Fact and phantom tinge one another, and although in a good novel the fictitious always overcomes and absorbs the factual, the resulting environment is masterly colorable, *vraisemblable*" (Barabtarlo 17).

Literary characters, such as Shakespeare's Othello or Washington Irving's Rip Van Winkle, might require some basic explanation, though both have become a part of the cultural canon even for those who have never read the originals. With the greats of Russian literature, things get more complicated: when Nabokov mentions the "voice of Pushkin's Mary" (G65), the annotator must explain that Mary is the heroine of Pushkin's drama *A Feast During the Plague* (1830). But the simple mention of this source may not be enough: Nabokov specifically refers to her *voice*. Therefore, the commentator should consider the opera based on the Pushkin work. Indeed, Mary's part is performed by a mezzo-soprano in a one-act opera composed by César Cui in 1900. In the midst of a feast, a young man calls for everyone to raise a toast to one of their friends who recently died from the plague. Walsingham, however, asks for a moment of silence in order to request that Mary sing something sad—this particular part is known as "Mary's Song."

Fake Books, Real Societies

Konstantin Kirillovich Godunov-Cherdyntsev's scientific works concerning lepidoptera look deceptively real (take, for example, *Lepidoptera Asiatica*, a fictitious edition allegedly consisting of eight volumes published in parts from 1890 to 1917). Another of Konstantin Kirillovich's scientific works concerning lepidoptera is *The Butterflies and Moths of the Russian Empire*; the first four out of six proposed volumes came out in 1912–16 (G102).

Not only invented books, but whole organizations and institutions that appear in the novel sporadically cast their shadows in the imaginary world of the novel: their factual existence is delicately elusive, if not downright dubious.

Konstantin Kirillovich Godunov-Cherdyntsev is made a member of the "Imperial Russian Geographical Society" (G103), which, in fact, was established in 1845. The society organized and funded the systematic exploration of the Northern Urals, Kashgaria, Dzungaria, and Mongolia. However, frightened by the revolutionary movements of 1848 in Europe, Nicholas I squelched the formation of even scientific societies and meetings, so it was not until after his death that the motion to found the Russian Entomological Society passed. The society was re-launched during the reign of more liberal Alexander II, and the organizing meeting of the Russian Entomological Society took place on February 25, 1860 (the year Fyodor's father is born in *The Gift*) in the official apartment of Superintendent of the Peter-and-Paul Fortress—where Nikolai Chernyshevski will be placed just a few years later.

[Ill. 5-2] Library of the Russian Geographical Society in Saint Petersburg, a pre-revolutionary photograph

Unreal Becoming Real

Not surprisingly, some information found in *The Gift* is still in the process of verification. A character who might first appear to be entirely fictional later turns out to be a real person, as in the case of the American travelers Sachtleben and Allen: "[Fyodor's] Father loved to recall how once at such a sunset, in 1893, in the dead heart of the Gobi desert he had met with—taking them at first for phantoms projected by the prismatic rays—two cyclists in Chinese sandals and round felt hats, who turned out to be the Americans Sachtleben and Allen, riding all across Asia to Peking for fun" (G120). The Americans authored a memoir about their Asian adventures, but when Alexander Dolinin was preparing his commentary for the Russian edition, the two names were considered an unidentified reference ("Insofar as no biographical information can be found about these men, it is entirely possible that they are fictitious," Dolinin surmises; *Kommentarii* 674). Luckily, with the recent wave of digitization, some remarkably rare editions have begun surfacing in Google Books and are now available for research purpsoes. An electronically scanned original of *Across Asia on a Bicycle* (New York: Century, 1894) by Thomas Gaskell Allen and William Lewis Sachtleben is among them.

[Ill. 5-3] Across Asia on a Bicycle (New York: Century, 1894)

Types of Commentary

Commenting on Technique

Some passages in *The Gift* require more elaborate commentary than others. Unraveling meaningful subtexts and providing detailed explanations will assist in greater appreciation of the novel; for instance, the following sentence presents a number of questions at once: "Andrey Bely's monumental research on 'half stresses'...hypnotized me with its system of graphically marking off and calculating these scuds" (G151). Who is Bely, what was his research about, and what is the difference between "half stresses" and "scuds"? Andrey Bely is the pseudonym of Boris Nikolaevich Bugaev (1880–1934), a Russian novelist, poet, Symbolist theorist, and literary critic. Nabokov claimed that Bely's novel *Petersburg* (1916, 1922) was one of the four greatest works of twentieth-century prose, together with Joyce's *Ulysses*, the first half of Proust's *In Search of Lost Time*, and Kafka's "Metamorphosis" (*Strong Opinions* 57). On a number of occasions, Nabokov praised Bely's approach to Russian versification (presented in several essays in Bely's volume *Simvolizm* [*Symbolism*, 1910]). In a letter to Wilson from 1942, Nabokov refers to these writings as "probably the greatest work on verse in any language" (*Nabokov–Wilson Letters* 78). Further, in the commentary to his translation of *Eugene Onegin* (Vol. III, 459), Nabokov acknowledges that he was fascinated by Bely's essays during his youth. In a letter to his sister (1950) Nabokov reveals that the utility of Bely's ideas on versification has still not paled for him with the passing years, as he still uses in his teaching at Wellesley the tables based on Bely's system that were fashioned in the Crimea in 1919 (*Perepiska s sestroi* 62).

Commenting on Textual Parallels

Despite Nabokov's categorical judgment in 1966 that Joyce's *Portrait of the Artist as a Young Man* was "feeble and garrulous" (*Strong Opinions* 71), J. Foster maintains that certain external details surrounding Fyodor's poem about Zina Mertz, which he writes at the beginning of Chapter Three, recall Stephen Dedalus's villanelle of the temptress: "He lay and smoked, and gently composed, reveling in the womblike warmth of the bed" (G155). Both Fyodor and Stephen "lie in bed as they compose their poems, both have awakened in sordid rooms that clash with their mood of poetic exaltation, both are conscious of returning to a period a decade earlier in their lives, and—most strikingly—both use similar metaphors for the poetic state. Thus Stephen's triumphant conviction that 'in the virgin womb of the imagination the word was made flesh' is matched by Fyodor's sense of 'reveling in the womblike warmth of the bed' as he composes. And Stephen's notion that his inspiration radiates outward 'in cloud on cloud of vague circumstance' corresponds to Fyodor's euphoric experience of a 'pulsating mist'" (G156; Foster 150). If this example presupposes the annotator's exceptional familiarity with the literary sources that have presumably been used by Nabokov in his writing, the next case, in order to be rightly identified, would require a keen awareness of historical non-fiction:

> ...the unfortunate words which in his youth [Turgenev] had allegedly addressed to a sailor during a fire on board ship: "Save me, save me, I am my mother's only son." (G249-50)

This accident happened to the young Turgenev in May of 1838. It was described in *Pisania I. S. Turgeneva, ne vkliuchennye v sobraniia ego sochinenii* (*Works not included in his collections*. Vol. 3, Moscow, 1916), and reproduced in part in A. G. Ostrovsky's *Turgenev v zapisiakh sovremennikov* (*Turgenev in the Records of His Contemporaries*), Leningrad, 1929. The latter may have served as a starting point for Nabokov:

> Prince P. V. Dolgorukov thought it fit to unearth an old yarn concerning my crying on board of "Nicholas I," which burned down near Travemunde: "Save me,—I am my mother's only son!" (the sarcastic point here is supposed to consist in the fact that I called myself the only son, while I have a brother)...This is not my aim to persuade the reader that I was staring at [death] indifferently, yet I did not utter the aforesaid words. (Ostrovsky 40)

Chapter Five. COMMENTARY

Commenting on semantic nuances

An alternate name that Shchyogolev uses to address his stepdaughter, depending on his mood, is AIDA (G187). It is true that Giuseppe Verdi's (1813–1901) opera *Aida*, about an Ethiopian princess captured and brought into slavery in Egypt, has certain distant parallels with *The Gift* (the Pharaoh's military commander, Radames, struggles to choose between his love for Aida and loyalty to his superior; as with the love triangle in the Yasha episode of *The Gift*, to complicate the story further, Radames is loved by the Pharaoh's daughter Amneris but does not return her feelings). And yet the main target here is not the famous operatic heroine. A lover of flat puns, Shchyogolev here hints mainly at Zina's Jewishness [a-yid = Jew; cf. yid, Yiddish], in this abbreviated form of "Zin*aida*."

Commenting on Linguistic Obscurity: Puns, Onomatopoeia, Charades

In the phonetically playful Russian phrase "*polzalo po polu zaly, po kovru, poka vrem*" (translated into English as "crawling on all fours along the floor of the hall, along the parquet, along the quarpet"; G21) the last syllable changes in the final two phrases (*po kovru, poka vrem*), while the first two syllables are pronounced identically. Taken literally, as Nassim Berdjis points out, the phrase in Russian means "on the carpet, when we tell lies"; Nabokov plays with rhyming suffixes of verbs and nouns as in "I walk on the carpet, we walk when we tell lies" (Berdjis 167). This sentence includes a conjugated verb (*vrem*), but the ending of the adverbial phrase playfully sounds like it might be trying to use the preposition "*po*" incorrectly with the instrumental case ("*po kovrem*"); a hearer can easily perceive this as "*poka vrem*" (= "while we are lying"). In the English version, Nabokov replaces this play on words by rearranging the sounds from "parquet" into its phonetic anagram "carpet" (assuming an Anglicized pronunciation of "parquet"). A similar phrase is also uttered by one of the heroes in Chekhov's short story "Ionych" (1898): "Ia idu *po kovru, ty idesh', poka vresh'*,—Ivan Petrovich was saying while seating his daughter in the carriage,—*on idet, poka vret*...Well, now you can go! Good-bye!" (Chekhov 8: 330). The humor in Chekhov's phrase comes from a play on the two possible phonetic meanings of the first phrase (*Ia idu po kovru* = I am walking on the rug; *Ia idu poka vru* = I am walking while telling lies), which puts the following two statements in a state of limbo between being grammatically incorrect analogs to the first phrase (*Ty idesh po kovresh* = "You are walking on the rug," with rug having an impossible noun ending; the "*on idet*" phrase is the same thing with the pronoun "he") and being grammatically correct but not analogous to the first phrase (*Ty idesh poka vresh'* = you are walking while telling lies).

Other examples of the linguistic peculiarities in *The Gift* include specifically Russian references pertaining to foreign languages or areas of common knowledge that would otherwise be clear to a native Russian, German, or French readers or speakers, as with the "large, predatory German woman [with] a funny name: Klara Stoboy—which to a Russian's ear sounded with sentimental firmness as 'Klara is with thee' (*s toboy*)." The landlady who rents Fyodor Godunov-Cherdyntsev a room on 7 Tannenberg Street, Berlin, appears with a different first name in the Russian original. In the English variant Zina informs Fyodor: "Your former landlady, Frau Stoboy. She wants you to come over immediately. There's somebody waiting for you at her place. Hurry" (G352). Nabokov spares readers of the translation from what could be interpreted as unnecessary confusion, but the same phrase looks different in Russian: "Your former landlady, Egda Stoboy" continuing the pun initiated by the quasi-German last name (*S* + *toboi* = "with you"). *Egda* is formed by truncation of the adverb *Vsegda* (= "always"). An additional irony here is that the one who presupposes being "always with you" calls Fyodor for a meeting with his father's phantom. In a fictitious three-dimensional perspective one can also notice that the missing letters are those standing for the author's own initials—*V*ladimir *S*irin (noted by Mikhail Bezrodny, in Russian, in his personal blog).

Commenting on Theological Concepts

THE CONSTANT FEELING THAT OUR DAYS HERE ARE ONLY POCKET MONEY...AND THAT SOMEWHERE IS STOCKED THE REAL WEALTH FROM WHICH LIFE SHOULD KNOW HOW TO GET DIVIDENDS IN THE SHAPE OF DREAMS, TEARS OF HAPPINESS, DISTANT MOUNTAINS. (G164)

Nabokov mentions Bergson, awarded the Nobel Prize for literature in 1927, among the poets and novelists who were his "top favorites" between the two World Wars (*Strong Opinions* 43). Compare the quote above from *The Gift* with Henri Bergson's remarks in *The Two Sources of Morality and Religion* (first published in 1932) on writers who succeed in capturing "a unique emotion, an impulse, an impetus received from the very depths of things," perhaps at the expense of "strain[ing] the words" and "do[ing] violence to speech," and thereby enrich humanity "with a capital yielding ever-renewed dividends, and not just with a sum down to be spent at once" (Bergson 254; noted in Toker 369).

Pocket money, dividends, and economics in general, encapsulate mundane reality as a multiplication problem without any real solution (*cf.* Ecclesiastes 1:2: "Vanity of vanities, all is vanity"). Masataka Konishi has suggested that Alexander Chernyshevski's delirium "evokes thoughts on religion and mathematical theorems as two related mysterious paradoxes" (28): "Numbers, numbers—and one wants so much to find the biggest number, so that all the rest may mean something and climb somewhere. No, that way you end up in padded dead ends—and everything ceases to be interesting" (G310-311). According to Konishi, "the biggest number" alludes to ideas developed by the mathematician Georg Cantor (1845–1918). Cantor formulated the idea of "the transfinite number" in his famous article (published as a separate monograph), "*Grundlagen einer allgemeinen Mannigfaltigkeitslehre*" (*Foundations of a General Theory of Aggregates*) in 1883. He argues that transfinite numbers are cardinal or ordinal numbers that are larger than all finite numbers, yet not necessarily absolutely infinite. Cantor showed that transfinite numbers are a systematic extension of natural numbers, and defined procedures for their addition and multiplication.

Nabokov was interested in mathematical problems and they feature repeatedly in *The Gift*. The character in Herman Busch's play declares: "All is number. My bald Pythagoras cannot be wrong" (G67). In memories of his childhood Fyodor suggests:

> ...let us describe also the delirious state in which one feels huge numbers grow, inflating one's brain, accompanied by someone's incessant patter quite unrelated to you, as if in the dark garden adjoining the madhouse of the book-of-sums several of its characters, half out (or more precisely, fifty-seven one-hundred-and-elevenths out) of their terrible world of increasing interests, appeared in their stock parts of apple-woman, four ditchdiggers and a Certain Person who has bequeathed his children a caravan of fractions, and chatted... (G21)

The telling comparison of an arithmetical nightmare, "the madhouse of the book-of-sums," echoes in the scene prior to Chernyshevski's demise. On his deathbed, Alexander Yakovlevich is preoccupied with similar thoughts: "Religion has the same relation to man's heavenly condition that mathematics has to his earthly one; both the one and the other are merely the rules of the game. Belief in God and belief in numbers: local truth and truth of location" (G309).

There is a striking resemblance between the fates of Cantor and Chernyshevski, who loses his son Yasha and passes on, consumed by insanity. Cantor was born in St. Petersburg in an assimilated Jewish family and moved to Germany when he was 11. His mental illness was partially triggered by his own scientific discoveries of paradoxes that at the time seemed difficult to prove. Soon after his second hospitalization—which coincided with the year of Nabokov's birth—"while Cantor was delivering a special lecture on the Bacon–Shakespeare question in Leipzig, his youngest son [Rudolph] died suddenly" (Dauben 283). This tragedy devastated the mathematician and his passion for mathematics. Cantor was again hospitalized in 1903 and he was troubled by recurring attacks of severe depression for the rest of his life, being confined in asylums.

The reason why Nabokov was "attracted to strange mathematical conundrums," Konishi believes, "lies in the metafictional aspect of his novels and in his interest in the otherworld": Nabokov's "image of the otherworld is not important for the moment; rather, what matters here is how he attempted to verify its existence. Mathematically formalizing it, Nabokov considered the otherworld as something whose existence one cannot prove without falling into contradiction or paradox. To take a simple example, supposing it is true that the otherworld exists, the sentences 'I am dead' or 'The dead are alive' must be read in the literal sense of the words. In this case, it becomes impossible to decide whether those who say, 'I am dead' are in fact dead or alive. However, Nabokov never draws the conclusion that the existence of the otherworld is doubtful from paradoxes such as this. On the contrary, he believes that it exists through such paradoxes" (Konishi 28). Nabokov was not alone in his interest in mathematics — his peers, Russian writers such as Bely, Khlebnikov, and Evgeny Zamyatin (who "hailed Sirin as a dazzling talent" in 1932; Boyd 374), were all experimenting with mathematical laws as applied to contemporary prose and poetry. And before them European thinkers were absorbed in similar problems; it is more to them than to the Russian poets that Nabokov is indebted for the construction of Delalande's philosophy.

Commenting on Philosophical Concepts

Obviously Delalande's *Discours* incorporates various philosophical postulates, including Bertrand Russell's well known observation, as pointed out by Omry and Irena Ronen, that: "Physics is mathematical not because we know so much about the physical world, but because we know so little: it is only its mathematical properties that we can discover" (quoted in Ronen, "Diabolically Evocative" 379). The rules of the game are as general and accessible as mathematics, hence the dying Aleksandr Yakovlevich Chernyshevski disposes of religion because it "subsumes a suspicious facility of general access that destroys the value of its revelations" (G310).

Another thesis from Delalande's opus, namely his "free eye," recalls a famous passage in Ralph Waldo Emerson's proto-symbolistic essay "Nature" (1836). In *The Gift*: "Our transformation into one complete and free eye, which can simultaneously see in all directions, or to put it differently: a supersensory insight into the world accompanied by our inner participation" (G310). Compare this with Emerson describing the effect that immersion in nature has on him: "I become a transparent eyeball; I am nothing; I see all; the currents of the Universal Being circulate through me; I am part or parcel of God" (Alexandrov 245, 11n).

Chapter Five. COMMENTARY

Commenting on Philological Concepts

The scholar's goal is to uncover an intricate web of allusions, but it is the commentator's mission to demonstrate the synchronic layers of the novel and to point out the details that might be lost for the next generation of readers (this distinction between the scholar and commentator is, admittedly, an artificial one, because the two roles are seldom separable). Let us turn to this passage:

> But a few days later he happened to come across that same copy of 8 X 8 [...] he ran his eyes over the two-column extract from Chernyshevski's youthful diary; he glanced through it, smiled, and began to read it over with interest. [...] the drubbing-in, rubbing-in tone of each word, the knight-moves of sense in the trivial commentary on his minutest actions... (G194)

Brian Boyd observes that the chess magazine's title *(8 x 8)* is "a transparent allusion to the Soviet chess journal *64*" (*Russian Years* 456). The chess publication might also insinuate Victor Shklovsky's book, *Khod konia* (Moscow-Berlin, 1923), literally: *Knight's move*. The cover of Shklovsky's book pictured a chess board with a diagram showing the knight's move. As pointed out by John Malmstad, "it is possible that the idea of writing a biography of Chernyshevski came to Nabokov from the remarks on Chernyshevski's diary made by Vladislav Khodasevich. In the article 'Melochi' ('Trifles') (*Vozrozhdenie* 2963, July 13, 1933) Khodasevich quoted several passages from the young Chernyshevski's diary with the aim of showing that the 'half-ridiculous' 'half-pathetic' 'seeds' of the new phenomena of Soviet everyday life and literature were 'sown' long before the victory of the Soviet system" (quoted in Paperno 315, 5n).

Khodasevich disliked the Formalists, but he took their ideas seriously (Malmstad). Nabokov must have followed this debate closely: the expression "knight's move" not only appears in the novel in the description of Fyodor's purchase of the Soviet chess magazine, which helps Fyodor to conceive the plan for his biography of Chernyshevski, but refers to the core of the formalist method of "deformation of material" (Ronen, *"Putevoditel' po Berlinu"*). In their descriptions of literary development, the Formalists coined the metaphor of the "knight's move," another graphic term for the so-called *literary evolution*: "In opposition to the positivistic notion of a linear course of literary development (progress), the Formalists envisioned it as a curve with a regular pattern of displacement (*sdvig*), the 'knight's move'" (Paperno 297). In *The Gift* Nabokov presents the development of literature in a similar fashion, explaining in the foreword to the English edition "that the novel's subject is the creative evolution of its writer-hero, Fyodor Godunov-Cherdyntsev" (Ibid.).

Commenting on Self-references

Passing remarks on geographical locations are numerous in the novel (Kiev, Riga, or the Godunov-Cherdyntsevs' mansion on the banks of the Neva river), and it would suffice to annotate only those that are significant in the context of the work. Such is the case with *Leshino*, the country estate of the Godunov-Cherdyntsevs, Fyodor's presumed birth place (G12, 25, 131, 137, 156, 353). The estate lies "ten or so versts" from the nearest station and Fyodor imagines his return from exile, when he will once again walk this distance. Konstantin Kirillovich comes from town to Leshino to bid his family farewell before departing on his final trip to Asia. Literally *"Leshino"* derives from *"leshii"* which means "wood-goblin" or "wood-sprite"—according to popular myths, *Leshii* lives in the forest; he appears frequently as a folk character in nineteenth century art, including the opera by Ostrovsky and Rimsky-Korsakov. *Leshii* is also the hero of Nabokov's first prose work, the short story "The Wood-Sprite" (1921). In that story, as later in *The Gift*, the creature incarnates the idea of lost childhood and Russia destroyed by the Bolshevik revolution (Katz 516). Nabokov's family estates were in reality situated in places called Vyra and Rozhestveno.

[Ill. 5-4] "Leshino"—Rozhestveno: The Family Estate of the Nabokovs (2009)

Chapter Five. COMMENTARY

Less frequently, it becomes clear that segments of the fictional text contain self-references or replicate the author's own writings only if one has access to documentary sources, such as personal correspondence, diaries, and notes. Nabokov's long letter to his classmate (reproduced in the Appendix) is an excellent example of such a confluence between literature and historical documentation in *The Gift*. Let us take the example of the following excerpt from the novel:

> ...during the last days of March...in the classroom the large window was open...teachers let lessons go by, leaving in their stead squares of blue sky, with footballs falling down out of the blueness. (G106)

This is taken almost verbatim from a letter that Nabokov wrote on September 4th, 1937, to Samuil Rozov, his best friend at Tenishev School, who had moved to Palestine. This communication (now in a private collection) contains several autobiographical flashes from *The Gift*, which was being written at the time: "In spring, I remember, teachers let lessons go by leaving as it were squares of blue sky, with a football dropping down out of the blue."

The same type of autobiographical reference is "In den Zelten" street; this is not a mere place in Berlin where the Chernyshevskis once resided (G37), but also the location of an orthodontist whom Nabokov visited in 1910 (who possibly served as an inspiration for Dr. Lawson in *The Gift*).

Nabokov could hardly have expected his audience to be aware of all the personal intricacies related to one or another latent reference or context, but it is the commentator's task to provide the readers with such keys. The reconstructive efforts should result in a comprehensive annotated edition that will embrace all types of commentary.

The Flying Birds of Russian Literature, Or "On the Risks of the Overinterpretation"

In the previous chapter we have already noted some guiding principles for making Nabokov's subtexts and allusions more accessible. Here I would like to expand and apply the commentator's technique in order to demonstrate how knowledge of particular sources (or, speaking more broadly, the cultural memory to which Nabokov appeals) might elucidate our general understanding of *The Gift*.

As Omry Ronen points out, the phrase "*prozrachen, kak khrustal'noe iaitso*" ("as transparent as a cut-glass egg"; G22) bears "a distinct resemblance to the magic crystal in H. G. Wells' fantasy 'The Crystal Egg'" (Ronen, "Nine Notes"). However, there is one more subtext here, a Russian one that has not yet been commented on: in Ivan Goncharov's short story "The Month of May in St. Petersburg" ("*Mesiats mai v Peterburge*"), a certain character "bought an egg of such a monstrous size somewhere in Nevsky prospect in a foreign shop at Easter that everybody at home gasped. He filled the egg up to the top with candies and brought it to his young sisters for Easter salutation" ["*na Sviatoi nedele… kupil gde-to na Nevskom prospekte, v inostrannom magazine, iaitso takoi chudovishchnoi velichini, chto akhnul ves' dom. On doverkhu nabil iaitso konfetami i prines k sestram-devitsam, chtoby pokhristosovat'sa s nimi*" (Goncharov 262)]. The location of the shop is the same—Nevsky Prospekt—and in both cases it is "foreign" (*inostrannyi*), and the physical size of the purchase is emphasized in both ("a Faber pencil a yard long"; G23). One will notice as well that the trademark of the pencil turns out to be a reflection of the famous gold-and-enamel Easter eggs by Peter Carl Faberge (Leving, "Six Notes" 36).

[Ill. 5-5] The Faber pencil advertisement

Another illustration is the topoi, or the repository of common metaphors that Nabokov shares with his contemporaries and predecessors:

> The van had gone and… There remained next the sidewalk a rainbow of oil with the purple predominant and a plumelike twist. Asphalt's parakeet. (G29)

The flying birds of Russian literature make several stops before perching in *The Gift*. The passage from Vladimir Narbut's 1922 long poem "Alexandra Pavlovna" reads as follows:

> *Oranzhevye, raduzhnye peria*
> *i zhenshchin sudorozhnye glaza, —*
> *pavlinia neft'!*
>
> [Orange rainbow plumes
> and convulsive eyes of women, —
> peacock's petrol!]

That was taken up by Osip Mandelstam in his *Egyptian Stamp* (1925-28): "Thousands of eyes looked at the petrol-rainbow water, glistening with all the kerosene tints of the mother-of-pearl swill and a peacock's tail" (Mandelstam 33). There is no evidence that Nabokov borrowed this image from any of the aforementioned authors and, therefore, one should be especially cautious when deciding whether to make it a part of the commentary.

Overinterpretation is one of the biggest pitfalls for any commentator of fiction. Let us take the protagonist Fyodor's date of birth—July 12, 1900. Julius Caesar, Henry David Thoreau, and the French poet Max Jacob share the same date of birth. This is certainly a pure coincidence and, therefore, should be dismissed; but the fact that Nikolai Gavrilovich Chernyshevski (1828–89), the historical protagonist of *The Gift*, was born on July 12th, fulfils a structural function and has thematic significance in the narrative (see the "Calendar" section in Chapter Four). Certain information might appear to be superfluous and can easily be omitted, though some readers may want to know the meaning of rare and foreign words (for instance: *Yashmak* [G96], a face veil worn by Muslim women). But should one also gloss occurrences like "Fedya" (G12; a diminutive form of Russian name Fyodor), or specify that *"srazhenie"* (G14) in Russian means "battle" (Fyodor compares its sound to that of a spring-operated toy gun being loaded), or that "zwieback" (G10) in the protagonist's poem is the German word for "twice baked" sliced crisp bread?

Experience in teaching *The Gift* to undergraduate students in North America has shown that contemporary readers' erudition has decreased dramatically; still, the fact that a reference is not immediately recognizable in a modern context does not in itself mean that it should be included in a commentary. For instance, the word *"lividus,"* meaning lead-colored, or the term "magnesium oxide" (G72), a solid white mineral used medicinally to relieve heartburn and indigestion, can simply be looked up in a dictionary. The same can be said of terms like "typhus," "Styx," and "enjambment" (G75) belonging to the fields of medicine, mythology, and poetics respectively (all of the aforementioned examples have been looked up by students when asked to highlight the "difficult places"). Equally questionable is the explanation: "Spanish for 'an unknown woman'" in the case of "Incognita," a poem by Alexander Blok that is mentioned by Godunov-Cherdyntsev. On the other hand, a diligent annotator might provide a synopsis of the poem and the year of its composition, as well as note other instances when Nabokov alludes to the same text elsewhere (in fact, Nabokov cited Blok's poem a number of times during his Russian period and later in the novel *Ada*).

Visual Aids to Commentary

Most scholarly editions come without lavish illustrations, but for a work deeply rooted in a historical context, charts, maps and accompanying illustrations are particularly useful in understanding the material world of a given novel. I will offer here a few typical examples from the dense texture of Nabokov's novel where the visual aids can provide an additional commentary.

THE SHCHYOGOLEVS HAD FINISHED THEIR PACKING; ZINA HAD GONE OFF TO WORK AND AT ONE O'CLOCK WAS DUE TO MEET HER MOTHER FOR LUNCH AT THE VATERLAND. LUCKILY THEY HAD NOT SUGGESTED THAT FYODOR JOIN THEM... (G355)

As discussed in chapter 1, the Vaterland was a fashionable and expensive venue. Marianna Nikolavna's invitation to her daughter is a generous gesture; Fyodor, as an unrelated tenant, does not receive the same generosity.

While the average reader probably hardly questions (at least on the first reading) the origins of a restaurant, the multiple insects under mysterious names frequently mentioned in the text of *The Gift* will certainly puzzle someone who is not steeped in lepidoptera. There is detailed information and distinct image behind each species mentioned in passing. A butterfly appearing in Fyodor's poem ("Or those utterly battered Brimstones, / Through transparent woods flying"; G24) is the so-called *Brimstone Gonepteryx rhamni*. Godunov refers to this member of the Pieridae family as "battered" possibly referring to its wing shape with the orange spot often present on the ever-closed wings.

These descriptions in *The Gift* often contain the discoverers' names: "On the southern slopes we had already met our first interesting butterfly—Potanin's subspecies of Butler's pierid" (G121). Grigory Potanin (1835–1920), a Russian explorer of Inner Asia, led an expedition to northern China in 1884–86 and there collected various biological specimens. In addition, he was the first westerner to report on the West Yugur and East Yugur languages and ultimately published a book on *The Tangut-Tibetan Borderlands of China and Central Mongolia* in 1893.

Some other passages might remain vague without having a clear frame of reference, which Nabokov trusts his contemporary readers possessed. Thus we see Fyodor lying in his bed, seized by creative energy: "he again turned on the light, lit a cigarette, and lying supine, the sheet pulled up to his chin and his feet protruding, like Antokolski's Socrates" (G56). Nabokov refers here to a specific sculpture, "Death of Socrates" (1875, marble), and at the time of writing *The Gift* he may also have seen the Soviet postcard printed in 1938 (Photograph by A. S. Rochmilovich, edition of 20.000 copies) from the collection of the State Russian Museum in Leningrad.

[Ill. 5-6] *Brimstone Gonepteryx rhamni*

[Ill. 5-7] "Death of Socrates" (Postcard, 1938)

It is similarly important for readers to have in mind the visual prototype for the following description in Fyodor's reminiscence of his childhood in Russia: "We did have a puppet theater with cardboard trees and a crenellated castle with celluloid windows the color of raspberry jelly through which painted flames like those on Vereshchagin's picture of the Moscow Fire flickered when a candle was lighted inside—and it was this candle which, not without our participation, eventually caused the conflagration of the entire building" (G13). Vasily Vereshchagin (1842–1904) was a prominent Russian battle painter whose realistic canvases depicting dramatic plots were and still are quite popular in his homeland. "The Moscow Fire" refers to the 1812 burning of Moscow on September 16, shortly after Napoleon's troops entered the city following the Battle of Borodino, the decisive clash between the Russian and French armies. It is meaningful in the context of Nabokov's novel that Vereshchagin traveled to Central Asia (his journeys in Turkestan in 1869, the Himalayas, India and Tibet in 1873, yielded a number of paintaings, which Nabokov very likely knew).

[Ill. 5-8] V. Vereshchagin, "The Moscow Fire"

Like any work of art, even novels with broad appeal such as those of Nabokov or Joyce reflect their own times, and therefore certain aspects are subject to obsolescence. It is vital for a commentator to annotate the signs of everyday reality in the characters' surroundings that might become unclear to subsequent generations of readers. When Fyodor receives a giant display model from his mother ("a Faber pencil a yard long and of corresponding thickness"; G23), the commentator can clarify that pencils of the "A.W. Faber" brand were commercially successful in Russia, and the firm had stores in both St. Petersburg and Moscow (in fact, the best lead for Faber's products had been brought from Siberian mines beginning in the late nineteenth century). The brands of bicycles that Fyodor rides (mentioned in his poem) were also available in the Petersburg of Nabokov's youth—"*Pobeda*" ("victory" in Russian) and "*Dux*" ("to lead" in Latin).

In their literary conversation, Koncheyev and Fyodor compare Russian *belles-lettres* to a legendary stallion: "Don't forget that the whole of Russian literature is the literature of one century and, after the most lenient eliminations, takes up no more than three to three and a half thousand printed sheets, and scarcely one-half of this is worthy of the bookshelf, to say nothing of the bedside table. With such quantitative scantiness we

[Ill. 5-9] The advertisement for "*Dux*" bicycles (1912)

Chapter Five. COMMENTARY

[Ill. 5-10] The cover of *Iunaia Mysl'* (No. 6, 1916)

must resign ourselves to the fact that our Pegasus is piebald, that not everything about a bad writer is bad, and not all about a good one good" (G71). The origins of Pegasus are well-known (in Greek mythology, he is a winged horse born from Poseidon and the Gorgon Medusa); what the commentator should mention, in addition to this generally available information, is that Nabokov authored two early poems under this title (in 1917 and 1922), and that the Tenishev School journal, *Iunaia Mysl'* (*Youthful Thought*), to which young Nabokov regularly contributed, also featured an elegant drawing of Pegasus on its cover.

In general, knowledge of Nabokov's early creative output is essential for a better grasp of the character of Fyodor. Consider this ironic pseudo-critical review: "We have before us a thin volume entitled *Poems* (a plain swallow-tailed livery, which in recent years has become just as much *de rigueur* as the braiding of not long ago—from 'Lunar Reveries' to symbolic Latin), containing about fifty twelve-line poems all devoted to a single theme: childhood" (G9). "Lunar Reveries" is a take on Nabokov's own juvenile poem "*Lunnaia greza*" ("Lunar Reverie"), which appeared in journal *Vestnik Evropy* in 1916.

THE OPENING SCENE

Finally, any discussion of the type and amount of information to include in a commentary on *The Gift* will ultimately depend on the kind of edition that is pursued, as I touched on briefly in the first chapter of this book (see "Towards the variorum edition"). If it is designed for study at a college or university, then the samples that set the standard for presentation of world masterpieces to students and teachers should be employed: these editions usually include literary history commentary, backgrounds, sources, criticism, the author's chronology and a select bibliography. Existing editions for nineteenth century Russian literature include Tolstoy's *War and Peace* and *Anna Karenina*, Dostoevsky's *Crime and Punishment* and *The Brothers Karamazov*, Turgenev's *Fathers and Sons*, as well as works by Gogol and Chekhov. Considerably less attention has been devoted to the twentieth-century Russian masterworks, except an edition of short stories by Isaac Babel edited by Gregory Freidin in the Norton Critical Editions series (New York, 2009) and the growing number of companions to single literary works; see, for instance, the useful volume by Thomas Seifrid, *A Companion to Andrei Platonov's* The Foundation Pit (Boston, 2009), and Julian Connolly's *A Reader's Guide to Nabokov's* Lolita (Boston, 2009). Nabokov's *The Gift* is a quintessential Russian novel that perfectly bridges literary traditions of two centuries. Putting together a critical edition of the English version of *The Gift* would go a long way toward making its rich texture of literary echoes, allusions, and parodies apparent and accessible to non-Russian speaking audiences who are not conversant with the nuances of Nabokov's Russian background.

Reading as Strolling Versus Reading as Biking

The opening of *The Gift* plays a key role in introducing the reader into the world in which the rest of the work will take place. To a large extent, further understanding of both the sequencing and internal logic of Nabokov's work on the text, as well as the structural interplay between plot elements and the poetic mechanisms in the novel as a whole, is dependent on successfully applying the technique of *slow reading* in the first pages and on accurately reconstructing the manuscript variants. Customary reading speed obscures and blocks many of the author's intentions, while with a slow re-reading we can take into account all of the lexical meanings (both potential and *hapax legomenon* variants) of the words. Though this approach is often taken when analyzing poetry, it has unfortunately not reached any serious level of development in the Russian humanities tradition, although it has been around for a long time (there is, it would seem, one fortunate exception: a special branch of study in the tradition—Pushkin).

In *The Wisdom of Pushkin* (Moscow, 1919), Mikhail Gershenzon first proposed the method of *slow reading*. In his article entitled "Reading Pushkin" (1923), he lamented that "reading today resembles a quick ride on a bicycle, with pictures flashing past by the wayside, merging and fading out like a motley, undifferentiated procession," whereas "in bygone days people read more slowly and contemplatively, like pedestrians" (Gershenzon 13).

A dense analysis of the textology and semantics of the opening pages of a novel might, in light of a future academic edition, seem patently superfluous (and to a certain extent this is indeed the case). Although Nabokov's novel requires, I believe, just such a thorough scholarly apparatus (in terms of both concepts and interpretations) in addition to the generally accepted views, *The Gift* is still without such a publication and without such commentary.

Formatting Conventions Used

The methods listed below will be used to signify differences between the source being studied and the canonical text (the lifetime edition with author's corrections, published by Ardis, Ann Arbor, 1975; English translation in the Vintage edition). Capital letters represent the text of *The Gift* as published. *Italic type* in [square brackets] signifies words and marks that were crossed out in the manuscript. When there is more than one rejected variant, each subsequent version is represented by a subscript number 1, 2, and so on. Versions of lines are presented in sequence, from the initial layer to the final one. Plain text in [square brackets] indicates text that is in the final version in the archive copy but differs from the published version. Insertions written in above the line in the manuscript are presented in {curly brackets}. The corresponding notes are grouped into the following categories: *plot points, commentary, themes, motifs, methods, subtexts,* and *context*.

Author's Name, Dedication, Epigraph

The author's pseudonym is part of the semantics of the novel, as is the dedication. All of Nabokov's novels, with the exception of one that was dedicated to his mother, Elena Ivanovna Nabokova (1876–1939), were dedicated to his wife, Véra Evseevna Nabokova (Slonim). Elizaveta Pavlovna Godunova-Cherdyntseva, the

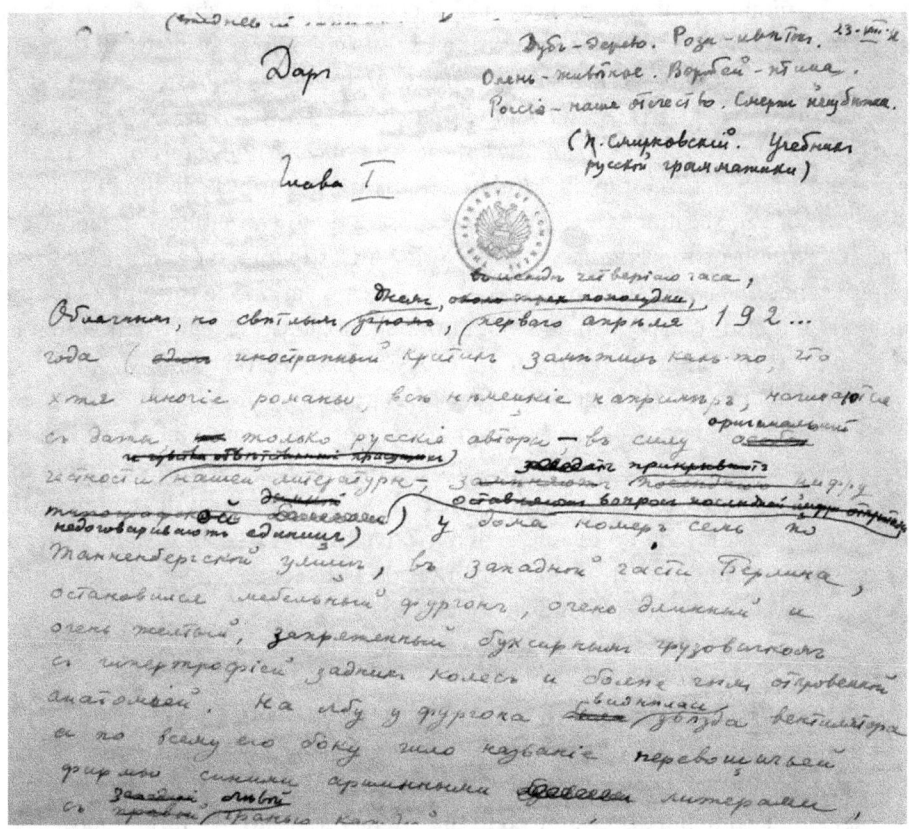

[Ill. 5-11] The opening page of the manuscript of *The Gift*. Courtesy of the Manuscript Division, Library of Congress, Washington, D.C.

mother of the main character, lives in the "real time" and the physical space of the novel, compensating for the absent father, who appears in the novel as a fictional player on the border between this world and the other world.

(0). AN OAK IS A TREE. A ROSE IS A FLOWER. A DEER IS AN ANIMAL A SPARROW IS A BIRD. RUSSIA IS OUR FATHERLAND. DEATH IS INEVITABLE.
P. SMIRNOVSKI. *A TEXTBOOK OF RUSSIAN GRAMMAR.*

Plot point. The epigraph constitutes both the *starting point* and the *design* for the novel's coming conflict.

Commentary: The dynamics of this short text-within-a-text are built on the increasing mobility of the nouns that are listed (from zero potential for movement to the maximum speed likely to be found in the natural world):

plant → animal → bird). The notion of a country includes the previous three species (categories of flora and fauna), and thus encompasses them all. Death, however, is a cessation—the absolute opposite of the idea of motion—and it stops the movement that had been developing, including on the syntactic level, with the presence of the root *beg* (*running*) in the word *neiz<u>bezh</u>na* (*inevitable*). Death also lends this set of seemingly unrelated phrases a metaphysical dimension.

Each of the six items in this chain corresponds to the biblical sequence in the description of the creation of the world. After dividing the light from the darkness and the water from dry land, the plants appear on the third day and the animals and birds on the fifth day; not until day six did God create man. And it is this link—man—that is missing in Smirnovski's inserted text.

The semantic series suggests the idea of a circle: the epigraph posits a closed cycle of life and energy. Taking this fragment out of its context, Nabokov exposes Smirnovski's "circle" and undermines it by giving it an ironic distance from its highlighted prototype. Instead of man there is an empty space; instead of birth there is death; instead of a teleological narrative there is a Möbius strip; instead of the Old Testament there is an elementary school reader; instead of an epic hero there is Chernyshevski; and so on, and so forth.

Theme 1. Fatherhood. Kin/Family.

The subjects associated with the notion of "tree" (here, an oak) include the categories of *roots* (the *father* theme) and *branches* (the continuation of the family). This theme is etymologically present in the word отeснestvo (from *otets*: "father"), and even more pronounced in the English translation: "fatherland." The logical progression in each of the first four items in the list is from *specific* to *general*. In *Invitation to a Beheading* (1935), Cincinnatus reads a novel by the name of *Quercus* (Latin for "oak"): "Its protagonist was an oak. The novel was a biography of that oak"; *Invitation* 122-23). What keeps Cincinnatus from enjoying the novel is "the inevitability of the author's physical death" (Ibid. 124).

Theme 2. The Textbook.

The theme of the textbook is introduced in the epigraph to *The Gift*. The selected excerpt from this textbook (the 17th edition, 1903: 78) by Petr Vladimirovich Smirnovski (1846–1904) is an example of a mute, dead text (it has no verbs in the Russian original because the copular "is" generally gets omitted in Russian). It is also important that Nikolai Chernyshevski himself was the author of a Russian grammar textbook written in the mid-1850s. At the time that Nabokov wrote *The Gift*, this textbook existed only in manuscripts under the simple title *Grammatika* (*Grammar*), but Nabokov did know of it from the book *Chronology of Chernyshevski's Life* (Chernyshevskaia-Bystrova 78); excerpts from the textbook were printed in the journal *Zven'ia* (No. 8, 1951: 506-7).

Grammar participates in the principles on which a given text is constructed. In the case of *The Gift*, we are taught that it is possible to take a patently non-artistic text (a travel account, an intellectual's diary, a political manifesto) and, without changing a single letter, make it into an artistic text. Transformation of an aesthetic skeleton is also an author's gift. The text of the novel has to consciously include parts that are repulsive and that one has no desire to reread. The gift of reading is the same gift that we acquire through this novel. The descriptive word that is sought after at the beginning of the novel—*immortal*—is only found by the reader at the end; the novel might justly have been called *The Immortal Gift*, and thus represent a response to the epigraph.

Theme 3. *Discovering the Gift of Speech.*

The Russian word *otrok* ("adolescent") etymologically means *non-speaking* (i.e., "not having the right to speak," from the roots *ot* + *reku*), much like the Latin *infans*. A text about the inability to speak is a topos of beginning (education), literally: "from the beginning of speech" (cf. the expository prolog scene depicting the curing of a stutter in Andrei Tarkovsky's film *Zerkalo* [*Mirror*, 1975]: "I can speak!"). Nabokov's novel—from beginning to end—is a novel about *the gift of speech*.

Motif.

The motif of "excusing oneself" is an obligatory rhetorical device in poetic speech: asking forgiveness for the length of the work, for digressions, for appeals to God, man, and so on. But along with all the disclaimers, there is also a desire to learn the language.

Methods.

An epigraph is, by definition, a fragment of something that is well formulated: *a poetically organized text* that stands out for its rhythm and striking syntax.

This excerpt mimics the structure of a syllogism but, unlike the classical form, this one is open-ended, because the first five premises in no way lead to a conclusion. However, the content of the Smirnovski epigraph unwittingly brings to mind the example of Pushkin's prose, with its synoptic nature and its abrupt shifts in content.

Examples from grammar books are what is usually learned by heart and then recited. In children's folklore, excerpts from textbooks become part of the workings of the oral tradition. Texts that stand out for their phonetic regularity tend to remain in the collective mnemonic tradition for a particularly long time. Nabokov's book begins with a triple stress (in the first version the title of the novel is *Da* [*Yes*]), which unfolds in the sound sequence: *Dar—Dub—Der* (*Dar* = [The] Gift, *Dub* = oak, *Der* = the first syllable of the word "*derevo*"—"tree"). If we go back even further, to the first word on the book's cover, we can also include the first syllable of the author's pseudonym, Sirin: *Sir—Dar—Dub—Der*.

Chapter Five. COMMENTARY

Readers of various levels perceive the strangeness of the text in the first two or three pages of the novel (the syntax seems artificial and the text seems forced). In terms of form, the opening of *The Gift* is constructed less according to the rules of prose than it is in accordance with verse techniques familiar since ancient times, becoming at times an unfinished anagram and at others a lipogrammatic text.

The epigraph is based on the alternation of nouns of contrasting grammatical genders in the original Russian. If we represent masculine nouns with 1, feminine nouns with 2, and neuter nouns with 3, the sequence is: 1-3, 2-1, 1-3, 1-2, 2-3, 2 + verb.

Subtexts.

DEATH IS INEVITABLE. The syllogistic tone of this closing assertion recalls the Book of Ecclesiastes and reproduces its rhetoric: "For that which befalleth the sons of men befalleth beasts; even one thing befalleth them: as the one dieth, so dieth the other; yea, they have all one breath; so that a man hath no preeminence above a beast: for all is vanity. All go unto one place; all are of the dust, and all turn to dust again" (Ecclesiastes 3:19-20). On the level of the plot, there is a possible reference to the dreams of Joseph (the movement from the world of plants through animals into space; see Genesis 37:6-10), which brings in the themes of exile (Egypt/Germany), the journey far from home, and, as a reward, the meeting with the beloved father, Jacob, after a long separation (though in *The Gift*, Fyodor's meeting with his father happens only *in a dream*). Motifs from the Bible, from mythology, and from the Homeric epics operate on an intertextual level as the author introduces them as "others" relative to his own system of artistic ideas. They are arranged hierarchically above all life events and literary situations and are fundamentally separated from these things in terms of chronology—they are either outside of time or at the beginning of time (Shcheglov 83).

Context.

Every textbook gravitates towards an alphabetic discourse, with its direct associations: a semiotic system of "signified" and "signifier." (*Oak* is a symbol of the resiliency of life. *Rose* is associated with innocence, but not without a shade of concealed aggression [and also with a woman's name]. *Birds* are agents of death, and so on.) Using this "alphabetic technique," however, does not deplete the tradition of multiple meanings, and to understand these meanings adequately we must still reestablish the point of view and the range of expectations held by a standard reader in 1934. For example, an oak coffin (for Pushkin, in the context of memory and death) would inevitably evoke in our hypothetical reader certain ceremonial associations representing the continuity of the tradition on the eve of celebrating the hundred year anniversary of the canonical author's death (*cf.* Pushkin's "Golden chain on that *oak*..." from *Ruslan and Liudmila*—Russian literature's ultimate beginning, and, ad hoc, a paradigmatic *children's text*). Certain readers at the end of the 1990s decoded the phrase *"An oak is a tree"* in part as a macaronic reference to the names of Nabokov's contemporaries: the father of Russian formalism Boris Eikhenbaum (Eiche = oak; Baum = tree; this was first suggested by M. Kostalevsky), and the pillar of Russian émigré literary criticism, Yuly Aikhenvald, who supported Sirin in his literary youth (Aikh = oak; Wald = forest; this was first suggested by S. Blackwell). And if we search for the deepest roots, we might recall that *Dub* (*oak*) is also the last name of a character from among a number of high school teachers, the lieutenant from Jaroslav Hašek's *The Good Soldier Švejk* (1921-22), who "was a teacher of Czech during peace time" ("a member of the 'troika' of abject idiots and asses. Besides him, this troika included the district superintendent and the headmaster"). In sum—the reader's feeling of *double encoding* leads to an understanding that other meanings shine out from behind the words presented to us in the text.

Close Reading

(1). ONE CLOUDY BUT LUMINOUS DAY [*MORNING*], TOWARDS FOUR IN THE AFTERNOON [*AROUND THREE IN THE AFTERNOON*] ON APRIL THE FIRST, 192- (A [*ONE*] FOREIGN CRITIC ONCE REMARKED THAT WHILE MANY NOVELS, MOST GERMAN ONES FOR EXAMPLE, BEGIN WITH A DATE, IT IS ONLY RUSSIAN AUTHORS WHO, IN KEEPING WITH THE [*SPECIAL*] HONESTY [*AND CHARACTERISTIC FEELING OF RESPONSIBILITY*] PECULIAR TO OUR LITERATURE, OMIT THE FINAL DIGIT [1][*REPLACE THE FINAL DIGIT WITH TYPOGRAPHICAL HAZE*] [2][*LEAVE OPEN THE ISSUE OF THE FINAL DIGIT*]) A MOVING VAN, VERY LONG AND VERY YELLOW, HITCHED TO A TRACTOR [*HAULING TRUCK*] THAT WAS ALSO YELLOW, WITH HYPERTROPHIED REAR WHEELS AND A SHAMELESSLY EXPOSED ANATOMY, PULLED UP IN FRONT OF NUMBER SEVEN TANNENBERG STREET, IN THE WEST PART OF BERLIN.

Plot point.
Starting point for narrating the plot. Expository scene establishing the time and place of the beginning of the action.

Commentary.
CLOUDY BUT. Because the adjective introduces a semantic catalyst in the reader—the question "a cloudy what?"—the WORD "but" is in this sense somewhat dubious. Every pause has a tendency to be filled in with meaning, and the reader immediately finds himself in the middle of some sort of action, *in media res*—and in the place to which he has been led by the *instrumental* case (in Russian the words for *cloudy, luminous,* and *day* are in the instrumental case, which is significantly called *tvoritel'nyi padezh*—literally the *creation case*).

---———————————————— Chapter Five. COMMENTARY ————————————————---

TOWARDS FOUR IN THE AFTERNOON. As we see from the manuscript, the exact time (3:50 pm, say?) is not of much importance for Nabokov. The Russian—*v iskhode chetvertogo chasa*—means something like "in the waning of the fourth hour." The usual rendering of this Russian expression would be <u>na</u> *iskhode* (~*at the waning*) rather than <u>v</u> *iskhode*. This slight stylistic distortion makes us look closely here at a microscopic semantic development. The word Iskhod is also the Russian word for the second book of the Torah—the Exodus—and as such it introduces a fundamental mythopoetic category. The captivity in Egypt is the prototype for all exiles, including the Russian diaspora in Europe between the two World Wars. The émigré community projected their exile from Russia onto the poetics of history complete with the meanings that this brought with it: (1) the destruction of the temple, i.e. Russia, and (2) the diaspora. These associations became part of the cultural aura that defined the fate of the Russian émigré settlement. The insertion of this deliberately chosen awkward pronoun, like a mnemonic device, is intended to arrest the reader's attention; later the context will clip off the meanings that do not work, but for the time being we are simply carving out the rough edges.

ON APRIL THE FIRST, 192- (A [ONE] FOREIGN CRITIC...). Despite the hyphen (in the Russian version an ellipsis), the reader internally continues the numbers in this passage—the question is raised and contemplated. As with all of Nabokov's riddles, this one has a definite answer: the exact digit is established later, not only in the text of the novel, but also by an intrinsic analysis of the expression itself. The truncated series of unknown digits is a variation on the Sophianic number, the mystical trinity: $[192\text{-}] = (1 + 9 + 2) = 3(1 + 2) + 3 + 3 + 3 + (9)$. Simple addition of the known items in the equation: the first day of the month, the fourth month of the year, and one critic $(1 + 4 + 1)$ yields the desired six in the place of the hyphen (in the manuscript Nabokov abandons the number "one" to modify the word critic because this information is self-evident). It should serve as confirmation for the reader at this point that the next digit mentioned in the text is seven—the street number of the house.

MOST GERMAN ONES. The English translation is less absolute than the Russian original, which says "all German ones" (*vse nemetskie*).

OMIT THE FINAL DIGIT. The Russian word for "digit" is *edinitsa*, which is etymologically related to the word "one" (*odin*) and can also mean "an entity," "a unity," or can substitute directly for the number one itself. Thus, the theme of categories and beginnings is once again "soldered in" with this *edinitsa*. The first of April is a carnival day, the end of a fast, and from the 1880s (seen in Chekhov, for example) these associations begin to be overtaken by the connotation of the April fool's joke. Within the plot of *The Gift*, this date will play a major role (Fyodor's less than successful visit to the Chernyshevskis).

TANNENBERG STREET. A real street in Berlin at the time of writing *The Gift*. This fictional place name—7 Tannenbergstrasse—would have evoked a painful association for a Russian reader in the first quarter of the twentieth century: the defeat of Russian troops in a battle with the German Army near Tannenberg in 1914 (though it is true that in 1410 the Russians defeated the Teutonic Knights in the same location at the Battle of Grunwald).

This historical thread is supplemented by the purely poetic reverberations from the root of the word (Tennenbaum = coniferous tree), which introduces the theme of Russian-German cultural interaction. Cf. Lermontov's translation ("In the wild north a pine tree / Stands alone on a bare peak...") of Heinrich Heine's poem "Ein Fichtenbaum steht einsam" from the collection *Buch der Lieder* (*Book of Songs*) (1827). The carol about the Christmas tree (*die Tanne*) ("O Tannenbaum, o Tannenbaum, / Wie treu sind deine Blätter. / Du grünst nicht nur zur Sommerzeit, / Nein, auch im Winter, wenn es schneit. / O Tannenbaum, o Tannenbaum, / Wie treu sind deine Blätter") might also be among the aural impressions of an urban Russian boy (one popular version of this song from 1824 is that of Ernst Anschütz). This connection also evokes associations with the New Year's holiday (and thus continues the theme of beginnings, crossing of thresholds, and cycles). In other words, it is not only the conflict that is important for Nabokov, but also the dialog between cultures.

A MOVING VAN, VERY LONG AND VERY YELLOW, HITCHED TO A TRACTOR THAT WAS ALSO YELLOW. Finally, the subject of the sentence appears ("van"). The adjective "yellow" denotes a relative characteristic rather than a qualitative one. Something can be *pale* yellow or *bright* yellow, but in no way can something be *very* yellow. In everyday conversational speech, if such a phrase were to appear, it would refer to the intensity or harshness of the color (the shade of a baby chicken). The color yellow generally has negative connotations (director Sergei Eisenstein gathered a special collection of "bad" quotes about the color yellow): in Russian, the expression "yellow house" refers to a mental institution, yellow is the color of infidelity, "yellow press" has a meaning similar to that in English, and so on. The repetition in this passage creates a certain tension or suspense.

In addition, the description of the moving van (a kind of centaur made up of a house and a vehicle) on the first page of *The Gift* not only functions as an imitation of a manuscript—with the inevitable repetitions, awkward alliteration, and clunky, seemingly unpolished style ("a mo_v_ing _v_an, _v_ery long and _v_ery yellow, hitched to a tractor that was also *yellow*; in Russian: "mebel'nyi *furgon, furgon* ochen' dlinnyi i ochen' _zh_eltyi, zapria_zh_ennyi _zh_eltym _zh_e traktorom) —but also concentrates the theme of the literary process as such.

HYPERTROPHIED REAR WHEELS. This is typical for vehicles designed for hauling (cf. a steamroller), on which the diameter of the rear wheels is greater than that of the front wheels.

The "rear" part of the sentence has by this time grown all out of proportion—the sense of imbalance and sickness conveyed by the adjective is supported by the word "anatomy." The Russian letter ZH (see Russian alliteration noted in the previous paragraph) is generally an impolite one (given its place at the beginning of the Russian colloquial word referring to one's "posterior," which is an approximate paronym of the word for yellow, *zheltyi*). If one were to study the design features of a tractor from 1926, one would very likely discover the presence of something resembling "reproductive organs" (a drain plug or shaft). Around the middle of the 1930s, the word "caterpillar" (after the US company, founded in 1925) was used in Russian as much as the word "tractor."

EXPOSED ANATOMY. The design of the moving van as it is described is a metaphor for the "exposed anatomy" of the creative text itself (it is symbolic that the manuscript theme is introduced through a dual allusion to Pushkin as early as the third sentence of the novel). The word "shamelessly" in the English translation, which is not stated explicitly in the Russian, strengthens the erotic component.

Theme 1. The Birth of Creativity.

In addition to foregrounding various types of literary craft that accompany the creation theme, Nabokov introduces the motif of cultural memory. The notion of intertextuality marks the opening of *The Gift* with a seemingly insignificant (but entirely Nabokovian) detail—a means of transportation.

Theme 2.
Juxtaposition of *native* vs. *foreign* (*our literature/foreign critics*).

Motif.
ON A CLOUDY...ANATOMY. The motif of creativity is meted out gradually on a syntactic level in this expository scene—in Russian the first and last noun phrases in this long sentence are in the instrumental case—literally, as noted above, the *creation case*.

Methods.

The structure borrowed from old Russian prose creates the feeling of comfort that comes with a traditional literary cliché. The hyphen/ellipsis and the omission are one of the stylized features of a classic novel, though the omitted date (1 April 1926) is easily calculated as one reads the novel. *The Gift* is a bridge that spans the classic nineteenth century Russian novel and the new literature of modernism, and the style of the first sentence can be compared with an elegant salon photograph.

The trajectory of the viewpoint on the text's subject (from high to low: cloud → house number → a moving van at eye level → wheels) echoes the composition of the text, which is built on multiple levels. The next phrase, as any skilful prose writer would have it do, will return the mental viewpoint of the reader back to its accustomed plane.

———————————————— Close Reading ————————————————

Subtext 1.

The opening sentence of Chernyshevski's *What to Do?*: "On the morning of July 11, 1856, the staff of one of the large hotels near the Moscow Railway Station in Petersburg was in a quandary, almost in a state of distress" (Chernyshevski 39).

Subtext 2.

In 1926, in the magazine *Russia Illustrated* (*Illiustrirovannaia Rossiia*, No. 26), a prominent writer and Nabokov's mentor, Sasha Chernyi, published a short story called "The Yellow Moving Van" ("Zheltyi furgon"). Its plot is exceedingly simple: the five-year-old daughter of Russian emigrants gets lost in Paris, and the only thing she can remember about the place where she is living is a big yellow moving van that was parked in front of her hotel in the morning. The focus of the narrative is Russian emigrants and their attempt to blend into the fabric of a foreign city. On a thematic level, the yellow van plays the role of an everyday ornament of émigré life. It is a minute detail and a sign of impermanence: "The van had gone..." (*The Gift*); "the large yellow van meant for moving furniture... had already left" (Chernyi 373). Chernyi's story was published in the same year in which the action of *The Gift* begins.

Subtext 3.

In Ilf and Petrov's novel *The Twelve Chairs* (1928), which we know Nabokov thought very highly of, Chapter XIII (entitled "Breathe Deeper: You're Excited!") is devoted to the opening of the Stargorod Street railway. The scene begins with the exact date on which the hero emerges from his house into the street (13 months later than in *The Gift*): "On the morning of May Day [1927], Victor Polesov, consumed by his usual thirst for activity, hurried out into the street and headed for the center" (Ilf and Petrov 108). In the following chapter, Polesov takes Ostap and Vorobyaninov to see Elena Stanislavovna, and when the locals assume that the partners and saviors of Russia have just arrived from Paris, Bender corrects her by saying: "My colleague and I have come from Berlin" (Ilf and Petrov 125). In chapter XIII, the streetcar is not the only means of transportation to play a role: there are also exotic mutant automobiles, including "a truck disguised as a green plyboard locomotive with the serial letter S [in the Russian Щ: Shch]" (Ilf and Petrov 108), a streetcar as depicted by the poet and feuilleton writer Fedia Kletchatyi (*My stallion is electric / Better than a filly*), Gavrilin's lilac Fiat, and finally the Ford station wagon (*polugruzovik*, literally—half-truck) of the film crew. In the episode depicting the ceremonial opening of the city's street rail system, there are also a number of less significant details scattered about that might also be associated with the beginning of *The Gift*: the effigy of Chamberlain carried by the demonstrators, which was "being beaten on the top hat with a cardboard hammer by a worker possessing a model anatomical physique" (Ilf and

Chapter Five. COMMENTARY

Petrov 109) and which had an inscription on the top hat with the words "League of Nations"—the key terms here: *anatomical* and *inscription* (the relationship between inside and outside); threes are emphasized in this chapter: the surname of the character *Tre*-ukhov, his "three-quarter turn"; three passengers ("this was followed by a truck carrying *three members* of the Communist youth league *in tails* and white gloves" [ibid.]), and the "three glasses of vodka" that Treukhov drinks (cf. the tribute to *The Twelve Chairs* in the form of the "three blue chairs" pulled from Nabokov's van in sentence 24 of the novel). After the three glasses of vodka, Treukhov "turned crimson" (cf. the color of the movers in *The Gift*) and launched into a tirade against the bourgeois press ("Those acrobats of the press, those hyenas of the pen! Those virtuosos of the rotary printing machine!"; Ilf and Petrov 123); cf. the *our literature / foreign critics* theme). Treukhov's efforts to establish the streetcar are a parody of literary labor ("The decision taken on the Friday was favorable. But that was when the trouble started" [literally—"the pains of creation began"]; Ilf and Petrov 113), which pales in comparison with the art of the Moscow film crew that jumps out of their truck (their appearance recalls the couple who had hired the movers in *The Gift*—one of the men has on an *elegant sleeveless leather coat,* and the other is the owner of a long scarf in the style that Bender calls "chic moderne" (Ilf and Petrov 122).

Context.
The novel is constructed as a cycle along the lines of the epigraph. The first word in the Russian text is CLOUDY and the last word is CLOUD (translated in the English as "haze") followed by a stage direction for the reader to return to the beginning ("nor does this terminate the phrase").

(2). THE VAN'S FOREHEAD BORE (lit.—*on the forehead of the van was seen*) [WAS] A STAR-SHAPED VENTILATOR. RUNNING ALONG ITS ENTIRE SIDE WAS THE NAME OF THE MOVING COMPANY IN YARD-HIGH BLUE LETTERS (lit.- *characters*) [LETTERS], EACH OF WHICH (INCLUDING A SQUARE DOT) WAS SHADED LATERALLY (lit.—*from the left*) [1][FROM THE RIGHT] [2][WITH THE WESTERN EDGE OF EACH SHADED] WITH BLUE PAINT: A DISHONEST ATTEMPT TO CLIMB INTO THE NEXT DIMENSION.

Plot point.
Scene one: the moving van containing furniture is parked across from the house.

Commentary.
BORE (lit.—WAS SEEN). In the fair copy Nabokov uses the word *vidnelas'* (*was seen*), with the root "*vid*," instead of the neutral auxiliary verb *byla* (*was*), thus reinforcing the motif of vision. This is further strengthened by an anagram of the

word for vision (*zrenie*) contained in the last word of the sentence, dimension (*izmerenie*).

STAR-SHAPED VENTILATOR. This is yet another *mechanical device* in the parade of technological advancements put forth by the author. This capacious image (a rotating star) anticipates what follows — a hole in space. In Russian, *ventiliator*, in addition to being a pretty word, also more or less rhymes with the word *traktor*.

(INCLUDING A SQUARE DOT). Nabokov's technique here is to announce a coming metaphor in the preceding phrase. Readers of Nabokov's prose must pay close attention to such junctures and these sorts of "announcements" (akin to the psychological effect produced by visual stimuli in some films of the 1960s, when shots from the end were spliced into the film at much earlier points). A dot turns into a circle, and the circle turns into a square. Turning a circle into a square is, in essence, a manifestation of the notorious "next dimension." The situation involving the unlawful attempt to reach the next dimension is directly demonstrated by this very parenthetical text with the phrase "including a square dot." A square dot (■), or a dot squared (■)^3, both graphically and mathematically illustrates the notion of a three-dimensional cube [X^3]: the dot squared, when combined with the shading, appears to be a dot cubed. We recall that on a child's alphabet blocks, the same letter is applied to all sides of a cube (the theme of grammar and learning to read).

ATTEMPT TO CLIMB INTO THE NEXT DIMENSION. Nabokov here formulates the overarching goal of his metanovel, and this statement thus serves as the creator's admission regarding his own composition.

The optical illusion of depth in a commercial design is usually created by shading the letters from the left (not from the right as the author initially wrote), that is — adding a dark area to the edge of the letters to create the illusion of three dimensions. As we see, in the English version Nabokov simply refuses to specify the side (*shaded laterally*). Nabokov had to abandon the use of the cardinal direction (western) because he had earlier used the phrase "WEST PART OF BERLIN"; however, this "west — shadow" connection concealed in the manuscript partially explains the societal nature of the area in which the emigrant Fyodor Godunov-Cherdyntsev first settles (in contrast to the light bourgeois downtown — this area is dark, marginal, and less prestigious).

Theme 1. Initiation.
The first chapter contains all the ur-phenomena of the narrative — it serves as an introduction to the grammar of *The Gift* and to Nabokov's own language.

Theme 2. Transportation.
In the introduction to his English translation of *Eugene Onegin*, Nabokov wrote: "Pushkin has likened translators to horses changed at the posthouses of

civilization. The greatest reward I can think of is that students may use my work as a pony" (Nabokov *Eugene Onegin* X). The art of literary translation—a type of literary process that makes it possible to transform and adapt the original (a moving van metamorphosed into a horse). Means of transportation in Nabokov often occur as an intertextual mechanism for carrying literary allusions and traditions (Leving, *Train Station—Garage—Hangar* 11-16).

Methods.
The prose narration of *The Gift* is packed with poetic techniques. Parallelism and contrast are used as procedures for deriving simple semantic figures from etymological meanings.

Subtext 1.
THE VAN'S FOREHEAD BORE A STAR-SHAPED VENTILATOR (lit.—*on the forehead of the van was seen the star of a ventilator*). *Cf.* Pushkin's "And on her forehead shines a star" (Pushkin, *Skazka* 456/*The Tale of Tsar Saltan*). Once again, Nabokov hooks the reader by using a different preposition than the one the Russian audience would be conditioned to expect from childhood: Nabokov has *na lbu* (on the forehead) while Pushkin has *vo lbu* (~in [her] forehead). The metaphor of a "van's forehead" describes the part of the cargo compartment that sticks out above the cab of the vehicle. For the untrained Anglophone reader who does not recognize the reference to Pushkin's canonical image, the trope is replaced by a relative construction using an adjective (*a star-shaped ventilator*).

Subtext 2.
Brian Boyd sees the moving van as a reference to Gogol's britzka from the opening of *Dead Souls*, where the muzhiks discuss how far it will get on those wheels: "From first page... *The Gift* also pays tribute to, takes issue with, or tries to transcend other literary works... The first page of *The Gift*—the hypertrophied rear wheels of the tractor... is Nabokov's tribute to one of the great moments in Russian literature" (Boyd 465-66).

Subtext 3.
YARD-HIGH BLUE LETTERS. Both Sasha Chernyi and Nabokov have a yellow moving van for carrying furniture. The name of the moving company in *The Gift* is on the side of the van, and for the time being the protagonist can read it but the reader of the novel cannot. The motif of letters that vanish and then reappear is an important one ("...in somewhat the same way as the jumbled letters find their places in a film commercial"), and it is also found in Chernyi's short story. When a policeman asks the lost girl her last name, she tells him: "Shcherbachenko.—Huh?—Shcher-ba-chen-ko.—What's the first letter? Shch

(Russian: Щ). Hmmm...*There's no such letter in the French alphabet*" (Chernyi 373). In his poem "Iubileinoe" ("Anniversary Poem"), the futurist Vladimir Mayakovsky suggested sending the lyrical poet Semyon Nadson, who barged into the alphabet between him and Pushkin, "somewhere out by Shch!" (Leving, "Nabokov i Sasha Chernyi" 52-57) (Щ, the 27th letter of the Russian alphabet, appears towards the end with a number of other little-used letters). The passage from Ilf and Petrov's novel is interesting in this regard: "a truck disguised as a green plyboard locomotive with the serial letter S [Russian: Shch] kept running into the music workers from behind, eliciting shouts from the bowels of the locomotive in the direction of the toilers of the oboe and flute" (Ilf and Petrov 108). The series Щ (sнсн) marking was used on locomotives designed by N. L. Shchukin (1848–1924). This series was manufactured beginning in 1905, and by the middle of the 1920s was already considered an obsolescent design and, therefore, discontinued.

Nabokov, it would seem, noticed the game his predecessors were playing with this letter, taking it to a level of pathos, which was in itself a manifestation of a "hypertrophied" technique of literary borrowing. The moving van travels from Paris to Berlin—or, if you will, from one capital of Russian émigré literature to another—and then from Berlin to the new Soviet Stargorod—and then back into the space of Nabokov's Berlin novel. This fantastic route, in and of itself, begins to demonstrate the *attempt to climb into the next dimension*.

In the big picture, this *text within a text* performs the same function as subtitles, and the fact that this parallel with cinematic text is not accidental is attested to by the ice cube-screen that appears in Nabokov's sentence 19 and, it seems, is also an isomorph of *The Twelve Chairs*, just like the tractor-van and the truck-locomotive. When the camera crew at the end of Chapter XIII finally makes it to Stargorod to shoot the opening of the streetcar line, the authors parody the birth of a cinematic text: "'Yes, yes, we are a little late. We came across some good nature shots. There was loads of work. A sunset! But, anyway, we'll manage. Nick, lights! Close-up of a turning wheel. Close-up of the feet of the moving crowd. Lyuda, Milochka, start walking! Nick, action! Off you go! Keep walking, keep walking!.. Comrade Treukhov? Would you mind, Comrade Treukhov? No, not like that. Three quarters. Like this, it's more original! Against a streetcar... Nick! Action! Say something!..' 'Aren't you going to film the street railway?' asked Treukhov shyly. 'You see,' lowed the leather producer, 'the lighting conditions make it difficult. We'll have to fill in the shots in Moscow. 'Bye-'bye!'" (Ilf and Petrov 122-23). The conveyance itself remains (literally) in the shadows.

(3) JUST IN FRONT OF THE BUILDING ([*WHERE I*] IN WHICH I MYSELF WILL BE LIVING), OBVIOUSLY HAVING COME OUTSIDE TO [WHERE] THEIR FURNITURE [WAS WAITING] (AND IN MY SUITCASE [(*WHICH WAS*) ONLY FOR A ZOLOTNIK *OF LAUNDRY*] THERE WERE MORE MANUSCRIPTS [*A POOD OF MANUSCRIPTS*] THAN LAUNDRY) STOOD TWO PERSONS.

Plot link.

The theretofore unnamed hero, Fyodor Godunov-Cherdyntsev, newly arrived to his new apartment, observes his future neighbors.

Commentary.

I MYSELF WILL BE LIVING. Up to this point, the narrative has used past tense--here, there is a jump into the future. This is the first time that the all-seeing omnipotent author appears in the frame of the text, painting himself into the periphery of the pictorial canvas (a compositional device familiar from the works of Velázquez and Van Eyck). The author has already been announced, but the reader has for some time been unaware that he, the author, will be the main character. Thus far, this is similar to the role of the narrator in Dostoevsky, with the usual "eavesdropper" characteristic of Russian novels, who is present in all scenes, as it were, but who, nevertheless, is never seen by anyone.

HAVING COME OUTSIDE TO [WHERE] THEIR FURNITURE [WAS WAITING] [*vyidia navstrechu svoei mebeli*]. In this phrase, with its German syntax, the reader should experience discomfort and uncertainty (the assumed questions being: Whose? What furniture?). In the dramatic space the first person appears, and two more are behind him. Against the background of the city landscape, a human triangle becomes visible. Dziga Vertov was studying the device of "life caught unawares" at about the same time (not only are bystanders shown that they are being photographed at the cinema, but their reactions are also imprinted onto the camera's film).

The furniture is a prop for the upcoming narrative (metaphor: the narrative is "furnished" with characters and becomes cluttered with connections). For the meantime, the quadrangular form (the van, building, dresser, and suitcase) predominates among the objects—these are all potential containers.

IN MY SUITCASE. The suitcase is yet another volumetric cube, setting forth the "boxiness" theme. Further along in the novel, there will be many kinds of *containers*, including the "Matryoshka doll composition" (the ironic image of the nameless "Russian thinker with a suitcase" will flash by momentarily in the novel's fifth chapter, not long before the end of the novel).

The little suitcase with its modest contents is not only a surface play on words (*bel'e* [laundry]—*chernovik* [manuscript—rough copy]—*belovik* [fair-copy manuscript]), but also forms an anagram with other objects in the scene (me*bel'* [furniture]—*bel'e* [laundry]), and is a slight phonetic provocation (*chem*odan [suitcase]/*chern*ovik). Via a network of references to a series of chrestomathic sources, this image constructs the central idea of a literary text (or of a book in general) in the form of a sort of travel bag/box—or a curious *depositary of texts* with free access. In the age of modernism, the space itself of Russian literature in its auto-meta-descriptive moments serves as a suitcase filled with manuscripts (an early example being Rozanov's literary reflections assembled into "boxes," and a later one, Sergei

Dovlatov's collection *Suitcase*, organized in such a fashion that each separate item in the author's suitcase functioned as a springboard to the next story in the cycle). All of the wordplay is completely lost in the English translation, but Nabokov uses italics in the phrase "in *my* suitcase," hinting at the existence of *other* suitcases.

MORE MANUSCRIPTS THAN LAUNDRY. As is seen in the rough-draft manuscript, Nabokov at one stage of working on the text rejects another play on words—"only for a *zolotnik* of laundry"—seemingly because of its obvious scabrousness. Among the definitions of *zolotnik* in Dahl' is "womb, uterus" (this meaning could successfully work for the image of the container and the theme of birth, as with the narrator of Ivan Bunin's "Story with a Suitcase" (1931) who hurried "as if to a lovers' meeting" toward his new purchase: "[the suitcase] stood before me in all its splendor: big, heavy, durable, well-made, with that amazing lustre of magnificent new leather.... You can easily imagine the feeling with which I *opened it, laid it flat, gazed on its virgin interior, the big pocket made of dark red morocco lining on the upper half!*" (Bunin 220); in his introduction to his memoirs, Nikolai Nabokov describes various kinds of traveling bags, trunks, and suitcases (noting the Tatar origin of *chemodan*--suitcase) that belonged to the Nabokov family, pointing out in particular his mother's *nécessaire*: "It was made of *dark-red saffian leather*... [Nécessaire] opened *like a ripe* fruit, like the loins of a goddess, the two halves of its cover falling gently apart and offering its enchantments to the gaze of the onlooker" (Nicolas Nabokov 6-7). In the classic dictionary definitions, *zolotnik* can mean either a brocade sarafan, or a unit of weight equal to "about 1/96th pound." The latter meaning leads Nabokov to play with categories of weight: "a *pood* of manuscripts" (compare the saying that Dahl' introduces with the definition: "Misfortune arrives by the *pood*, but leaves by the *zolotnik*"; a pood weighs about 36 English pounds; this is something like saying, "it comes in big buckets, but leaves only by drops"). However, having sacrificed the word *zolotnik*, he also discards *pood* as unnecessary. Let us note that, had the original intention held, this would have allowed Nabokov to conveniently introduce the theme of commerce via the seme 'gold' (*zoloto*) (and, in fact, both "underwater gold" and economics would soon appear, with the themes of cheating in weight, hired workers, and the like).

Theme. Three-dimensionality.
Suitcase/van/book—these are different incarnations of the cubic form, with which the theme of the third dimension is continued (in terms of the viewer's perception—stereoscopy).

Methods.
The phrase is constructed emphatically due to the grammatical contrast. The obvious delay of the subject until the end provides a concatenation to the following sentence, which "blurts out" the new subject: "The man...."

Chapter Five. COMMENTARY

Subtext 1.

In the foreword to the English translation of *A Hero of Our Time*, Nabokov points out the "involute structure" in Lermontov's narrative, which anticipates (and Nabokov passes over this in silence) the structure of *The Gift*, providing the attentive reader one of the keys to Fyodor's suitcase. In Lermontov's "Bela," we find:

> I was travelling post from Tiflis. The only luggage I had on my cart was *one small portmanteau half-filled with travel notes* on Georgia. Luckily for you most of them have been lost, but luckily for me the portmanteau and the rest of my things have survived. (Lermontov 5)

Following this is a description of a valley in the Caucasus — material and inspiration for the future descriptions of the travels of the elder Godunov-Cherdyntsev.

Subtext 2.

Dostoevsky writes about manuscripts and laundry in *The Insulted and Humiliated*. Although its hero is said to carry, in a pillowcase (owing to his lack of a briefcase), "papers" and not manuscripts, it is of course meant that they are manuscripts. This is not [in] the first chapter, but the ninth; nevertheless, the beginning of the story is in present tense, to which the narrator returns after a (nine-chapter-long) excursion into the past. The action occurs, as in *The Gift*, in springtime:

> All that morning I had been *busy with my papers, sorting and arranging them. For want of a portfolio I had packed them in a pillow-case. They were all crumpled and mixed up.* Then I sat down to write. I was still working at my big novel then; but I could not settle down to it. My mind was full of other things. (Dostoevsky 69)

Subtext 3.

Near the end in *Fathers and Sons,* Bazarov says portentously to his younger friend Arkady:

> You see what I'm doing: it turns out there's empty space in my suitcase and I'm stuffing hay into it. *That's just how it is in the suitcase of our lives; it doesn't matter what you stuff in,* as long as there's no empty space. (Turgenev 140)

The "metaphysics of the traveling bag" is a well-established motif in Russian literature. The layering of subtexts by Lermontov, Dostoevsky, and Turgenev allows one to suppose that they (and others, too) are the very "manuscripts" that fill the writer's briefcase of Nabokov's hero.

―――――――――――― Close Reading ――――――――――――

Context.
The pragmatics of communicating a preamble saturated with reminiscences consist of the following: the main character of the narrative is a *storyteller*. Fyodor Godunov-Cherdyntsev will write, in order, the story of his father's trip to Asia, and next the life of Chernyshevski; he will also apparently turn out to be the author of the novel, *The Gift*, that we are reading.

(4). THE MAN, ARRAYED IN A ROUGH GREENISH-BROWN [*WOOL*] OVERCOAT [*LODEN COAT*] TO WHICH THE WIND °[*AND THE HIGH POCKETS*] [1][*POCKETS THAT HAD SWALLOWED HIS HANDS*] [2][*IN WHOSE CUTOUTS*] [3][*INTO WHICH HE HAD TUCKED BOTH HANDS*] IMPARTED A RIPPLE OF LIFE, WAS TALL, BEETLE-BROWED AND OLD, WITH THE GRAY OF HIS WHISKERS TURNING TO RUSSET [*A YELLOWISH COLOR*] IN THE AREA OF THE MOUTH, IN WHICH HE INSENSITIVELY HELD A COLD, HALF-DEFOLIATED CIGAR BUTT.

Plot point.
As before, the plot is still at its starting point. The cameo role of the couple standing by the entrance to the house amounts to a narrative vignette, and these characters fulfill no plot function and do not enter into the novel again except as phantom neighbors or in Fyodor's reminiscence.

Commentary.
ARRAYED. The Russian original uses the adjective *oblachennyi*, which grammatically and semantically echoes the word *oblachnym* ("cloudy") from the first sentence. The overcoat behaves like a cloud (the man is not simply *dressed*; he is as if surrounded by the overcoat—"a cloud in a coat," so to speak). Another change was made based on the poetic principle of emphasizing sound patterns: *ob*lach*ennyi*—*ob*lach*nyi*—*voi*loch*noe* (Nabokov, as we see in the manuscript, abandoned the adjective "wool" (*sherstiannoe*) in favor of "felt" (*voilochnoe*), which is translated as "rough.").

GREENISH-BROWN. The next in a series of color strokes (*green* follows *yellow* in the spectrum; here it anticipates the GREEN PUPIL and the GREENGROCER from the 10th and 12th sentences of the novel. Yellow + gray + green + brown is a range of colors with slightly negative connotations (cf. "gray-brown-raspberry" [*sero-buro-malinovyi*]—a Russian expression for something having a nondescript color).

ROUGH...OVERCOAT [lit.—FELT OVERCOAT]. As we see, in the English translation Nabokov decided to convey the coat's texture instead of naming the material, and to this end chooses the ambiguous word *rough*, which may refer either to coarse, ragged, or unfinished cloth, or to a rough copy or rough draft of a manuscript. There is a similar play on words in the Russian title of Victor Shklovsky's *Mater'ial i stil' v romane L'va Tolstogo 'Voina i mir'* (Moscow: Federatsiia, 1928) (*Material and Style in Lev Tolstoi's novel 'War and Peace'*).

Chapter Five. COMMENTARY

THE WIND IMPARTED A RIPPLE OF LIFE. The key here is the "ripple of life" (in Russian, this is expressed by the adjective *ozhivliaemoe*—animated or enlivened). The static picture is gradually beginning to gather some internal kinetic energy.

CIGAR BUTT. The sentence develops by using close-ups of increasing size, like a nesting box or onion composition: cigar butt → mouth → beard → overcoat. The cigar butt is enlarged more than any other detail to this point. To see a "half-defoliated" cigar, one needs to change focus; thus we have here not a simple zooming in, but an *extreme close-up*.

INSENSITIVELY held the cigar butt. In a metonymic way, this adverb creates a tone of coolness relative to these two people, despite the fact that they are described quite objectively (BOWLEGS).

Theme 1. Betrayal, falseness, inconstancy.

In the European tradition of visual art, having reddish hair ("russet") is negatively marked: Judas is always red-haired in paintings and frescoes (the color was also adopted in the icon painting). The Russian word *ryzhevatost'* is clear, but in the translation Nabokov chooses the more neutral *russet*, presumably because this word can also refer to a coarse, homespun wool cloth of a russet color (and thus it echoes the overcoat and, by extension, the rough draft). Let us take note of Nabokov's technique here: when a pun or a subtext is muted or lost in one place, he tries to compensate for it in other places nearby, using whatever methods are available in the target language of the translation.

Theme 2. Cinematographer.

This sentence creates in the reader a sense of the type of movement associated with cinematographic techniques (if not exactly with modern computer graphics).

Theme 3. Palimpsest.

In Russian as in English, the word for *leaves* (*list'ia*) can also refer to *pages*—thus the fact that a cigar is rolled from *leaves* of tobacco points to the combination in *The Gift* of various types of texts, narrative points of view, chronological layers, geographical spaces, and narrative axels.

Motif.

The burning *cigar* is a symbol of urbaneness and also of the natural cycle. A "half-defoliated" cigar brings to mind autumn and the anticipation of an ending.

Methods.

Reduction: the gaze rests at the end on an object on its way out. The reader will later have to return to this "frame."

Grammatical overlap (in the Russian the words <u>obl</u>achennyi [arrayed] and pol<u>uobl</u>etevshii [half-defoliated] clearly echo each other), accompanied by parallel attributes (a man wrapped in an overcoat and a rolled cigar).

The metaphor of undressing: the striptease applies even to the cigar (in the following sentence the subject's gaze will be moved to a woman's legs). It is possible that Nabokov is playing with an omitted component of the saying about old men susceptible to seduction—the first half of the saying—"Gray in the beard, a beast in the bosom" (*Sedina v borodu, a bes v rebro*)—is clearly present in the phrase GRAY OF HIS WHISKERS (*sedina v borode*).

Subtext.
In Lermontov, right in a scene involving an author moving (!), a group of Ossetian movers appears with Maksim Maksimych: "He looked about fifty. His *swarthy complexion*...his prematurely *grey whiskers* accorded ill with his firm step and brisk appearance. I went up to him and bowed. He returned my bow in silence and puffed out an *enormous cloud of smoke*" (Lermontov 6). In *The Gift*, the coat of this man (with *gray in his whiskers* and a *cigar* in his mouth) seems to be a euphemistic description of an ordinary overcoat, while the "swarthiness" of Captain M. M. corresponds to the "pseudo-Chinese face" of the man's companion in *The Gift*.

(5). THE WOMAN, THICKSET AND NO LONGER YOUNG, {WITH BOWLEGS} AND A RATHER ATTRACTIVE [FALSELY-] PSEUDO-CHINESE FACE, WORE AN ASTRAKHAN JACKET; THE WIND, HAVING ROUNDED HER, BROUGHT A WHIFF OF [SHE SMELT OF] RATHER GOOD BUT [SOME SORT OF LONG-HELD] SLIGHTLY STALE [STALE] PERFUME.

Plot point.
The heroine (a figure in close-up—a cut from the previous scene; a montage splice) evokes a series of reactions in the narrator.

Commentary.
THE WOMAN. A contrast is introduced using the woman as an example: she has unfortunate legs but, on the other hand, a pleasant face.

ASTRAKHAN JACKET. The Russian adjective used here is *karakulevyi* which, like the English translation *astrakhan* is associated both with a fur cloth and with a place name: Karakul introduces the theme of Eurasia to the Russian ear (in the sixteenth and seventeenth centuries Astrakhan was a border city in the Muscovite Empire, which served as its gateway to the East). The texture of the jacket also conceals a meta-descriptive etymological pun on the Russian word *karakuli* (hieroglyphs, scribbles, etc.) and thus continues the theme of *manuscripts*.

WHIFF OF PERFUME. Smell becomes an additional dimension (the "next dimension"). The text begins to "emit an odor."

―――――――――――― Chapter Five. COMMENTARY ――――――――――――

Theme 1. Loss of individuality.
The image of this cameo pair and the breaking up of their features does not bode well. Any attempt to construct a composite picture of each of them individually would not prove successful.

Theme 2. Fluctuation of things; instability of matter.
The wind staggers the man and "rounds" the woman. Everything is flowing and changing—the cloud loses its shape, things disappear, and the half-defoliated cigar burns up; this is life itself.

Theme 3. Predicting a journey.
(A) The Chinese theme in a false, reversed, parodic variation; (b) something unreal, pseudo-authentic.

Motif.
The coldness and insensitivity of the man. The basic scheme: an "unequal marriage" (he is an old man, she is much younger). A caricature of German burghers in the style of the illustrated weekly *Simplicissimus* or the humor section of the émigré journal *Russia Illustrated* (*Illiustrirovannaia Rossiia*).

Methods.
The semantics in the sound play gradually instill in the reader a sense of uncertainty and caution about what is happening. In the Russian, the repetition of *kar* and similar sounds sets in: *korenastaia—krivymi—krasivym—karakulevyi* (the words translated as "thickset," "bow[legs]," "attractive," and "astrakhan" respectively). The Turkic lexeme *kara* means black (cf. *Karamazov*).

There is a second semantic dominant in this passage: *pakhnul—neplokhie—zatkhlovatye—dukhi* ("brought a whiff of," "rather good," "somewhat stale," and "perfume" respectively). The subjectivity of the text increases in the fifth sentence. The perspective still belongs to an outsider and not yet to the suggested observer, but his presence becomes more and more palpable as more evaluation gets introduced into the text (evaluation of appearances, the smell of the perfume, etc.).

(6). THEY BOTH STOOD MOTIONLESS AND WATCHED FIXEDLY, WITH SUCH ATTENTIVENESS THAT ONE MIGHT THINK THEY WERE ABOUT TO BE SHORTCHANGED, AS THREE RED-NECKED HUSKY FELLOWS IN BLUE APRONS WRESTLED WITH [1][SET ABOUT UNLOADING] [2][UNLOADED] THEIR FURNITURE.

Plot point.
The movers carry the furniture from the van into the house.

Commentary.

MOTIONLESS. The couple is frozen (a still frame), and against that background appear new protagonists with formulaic movements. Thus a conflict is laid out directly within a single sentence.

THREE RED-NECKED HUSKY FELLOWS. There is something butcher-like about these fellows from the service sector (partly because of the Russian verb *obvesit'*—literally "to hang," also, colloquially, to give a customer less of something than what they are paying for, here translated as "shortchanged"—and partly because of the color red).

RED-NECKED. The "stiff-necked" are a biblical trope (see Psalm 75:5). The word "red" (*krasnyi*) in Russian can be ambiguous: it is not always clear whether it means "beautiful" (the historical meaning of the word *krasnyi*), and when it simply refers to the color (in this scene it may refer to the color of the company shirts worn by the movers, sunburned skin, etc. The latter interpretation is clearly the most likely in the English, but this is not the case in the Russian). In light of the previously mentioned subtext from Ilf and Petrov (the "three members of the Communist Youth League in tails" in the car), the color red also carries the suggestion of an ideological meaning. There is typically a "beautiful maiden" (*krasna devitsa*), and so, in this amalgam of idioms, there are "beautiful fellows" (*krasny molodtsy*, close to the *krasnovyinye molodtsy* in the original Russian).

WRESTLED WITH. The Russian verb here is *odolevat'*—meaning something like "defeat" or "conquer." Thus we have the connotation of a military exploit, and the number of the movers (the archetypal number of *bogatyrs* in Russian folklore is three) reinforces the folk epic tone in the scene. The clean, primary colors (red, blue) presume a certain amount of caricature in this depiction and specifically seem to point to the *lubok*—a type of cheap woodblock print popular among Russia's lower and middle classes in the eighteenth and nineteenth centuries.

Theme 1. Construction.

The topos of building will gradually be developed over the course of the novel. In the text, as in mythology, we see the ritual of *building a human*. For now, the separate members—forehead, face, legs, neck—are being gathered up (cf., in Egyptian mythology, the dismemberment of Osiris' corpse, which is gathered together in pieces to conceive Horus. The infant then grows and gathers his forces in order to revenge himself on Set *for the death of his father*).

Theme 2. Settling in a house.

What happens is not simply the protagonists moving into a new home, but also the stage filling up with the dramatis personae; the extras help the author

Chapter Five. COMMENTARY

prepare that area for the unfolding of the plot. In this sense, in the sixth sentence of the novel Nabokov is already departing from classical tradition by revealing a little bit of the supporting structure.

Motif.
ONE MIGHT THINK THEY WERE ABOUT TO BE SHORTCHANGED. Here the theme of commercial interactions is introduced. The English translation uses the verb "short-change" (differing slightly from the Russian *obvesit'*—see note above); shortly after this, Fyodor will go shopping and get small change in return.

Methods.
The feelings of readers are produced by words—roots, morphemes, and prefixes. For now, the feeling is of that which is incomplete and illicit; all around there is either deceit (*short-changed*), or inferior and non-functional things (an *extinguished* cigar butt, *hypertrophied* wheels, *bow* legs).

Context.
Later in the first chapter, similar motifs will be repeated in one bundle of words—in the parody of an image from an advertisement: someone is "holding in his brawny hand, with a carnivorous grin, a sandwich containing something red ('eat more meat!') ... " (G13).

(7). SOME DAY, HE THOUGHT, I MUST USE SUCH A SCENE TO START A [NOVEL] GOOD, THICK OLD-FASHIONED THING [BOOK]. THE FLEETING THOUGHT WAS TOUCHED [HE THOUGHT] WITH A CARELESS IRONY; AN IRONY, HOWEVER, THAT WAS QUITE UNNECESSARY, BECAUSE [ALREADY] SOMEBODY WITHIN HIM, ON HIS BEHALF [ON BEHALF OF FYODOR KONSTANTINOVICH], INDEPENDENTLY FROM HIM [FROM FYODOR KONSTANTINOVICH], HAD ABSORBED ALL THIS, RECORDED IT, AND FILED IT AWAY.

Plot point.
The protagonist relates the observed developments in the outside world to a plan for an artistic work.

Commentary.
SOME DAY ... TO START. Despite the growing feeling that the novel has started to roll, we are continually withdrawn once again—this whole passage is written in subjunctive (in English, this is accomplished with the modal "must"; in Russian with a subjunctive construction using an infinitive: *vot tak by nachat'*).
THING. In Russian, the word *shtuka* (thing) is another archaizing element, a stylization based on nineteenth century classics. The "thing" remains untouched.

ON HIS BEHALF. The reader is meant to experience a small stylistic shock from this sudden and unpredicted switch from the first to the third person singular pronoun ["I" → "He"]; this is the first signal of the hero's future bifurcations reinforced in the next sentence by the use of an ordinal number ("for the *first time*..."). The English translation introduces Fyodor one sentence earlier than in the Russian original, where an impersonal verb is chosen (*"podumalos'"* instead of *"on podumal"*/"he thought").

[ON BEHALF OF FYODOR KONSTANTINOVICH]. Nabokov weighed the possibility of unmasking the main character at this early stage, but in the end refused to go through with this idea, and for now keeps his name hidden (postponing the moment at which the narrative "I" is personalized until the 45th sentence of the novel).

ABSORBED ALL THIS, RECORDED IT, AND FILED IT AWAY. The idea of accounting of things, thus dematerializing them (cf. Pliushkin, the pack rat in Gogol's *Dead Souls*).

Theme 1. Hide and seek.

A game with gradations of knowledge. The reader does not have all of the information (the protagonist looking at the moving van with the name of the company on it clearly sees more than the reader of the text, but much less than the creator of the text). In the fomentation of this secretive atmosphere there is a verbal catalyst: in other words, the reader must have a sneaking suspicion that there is, if not a solution to the riddle, then at least something important *hidden* in the phrase itself. We understand by looking at the manuscript how Nabokov achieves this effect — for example, by removing the personal pronoun in the phrase *"podumal on"* and replacing it with the impersonal construction *"podumalos'."*

Theme 2. Literature as Process.

The overture of *The Gift* is a sample text — *an exemplary manuscript*. A Russian formalist technique: concealing the discourse of the manuscript (see Boris Eikhenbaum's "How Gogol's Overcoat Is Made"). For Shklovsky and Tynianov, every text becomes automatized after repeated and quick readings, the shades of meaning are lost, and the rough edges and nicks are smoothed over. Nabokov's *The Gift* graphically illustrates the theme of literature as process, touching on matters of the overall procedure — the interactions among the literary text, the author's consciousness, the reader's reception, and reality.

Methods.

SOME DAY... A GOOD, THICK OLD-FASHIONED THING. The style has changed in this sentence as compared to the previous six. The forced stylistics that have been building up become particularly clear here in order to create the impression of something **old-fashioned**; there are many archaisms concentrated in the first paragraph (*arshin*—an old Russian unit of measurement translated in the English phrase "yard-high," *krasnovyinye molodtsy* [red-necked husky fellows], with its folk overtones as outlined above, the word *pud* [another archaic unit of measurement, a weight equivalent to 16 kg] that appears in the working draft, and so on).

(8). HE HIMSELF HAD ONLY MOVED IN TODAY [*HE HIMSELF HAD JUST MOVED HERE FROM A BOARDING HOUSE THREE BLOCKS AWAY*], AND NOW, FOR THE FIRST TIME, IN THE STILL UNACCUSTOMED STATE OF LOCAL RESIDENT [*DWELLER*], HE HAD RUN OUT TO BUY A FEW THINGS.

Plot point.
At the beginning of any epic plot, the hero *leaves his home*. This process is so banal that it almost does not register in the reader's consciousness. Nabokov (as instructed by the textbook!) focuses our attention on the ur-phenomenon of the narrative—on the starting point when the hero departs from his dwelling.

Commentary.
HIMSELF. The text is also old-fashioned in that each new sentence leads to a question that is then answered by the following one (which is indeed one of the features of antique narrative style). Here we ask: "And who is this 'he himself'?" The answer from VN (or the Almighty Author), is "HE" (in the Russian, the word "he"—*on*—does not first appear until the next sentence and is preceded by the word *sam*—himself). First of all, we already know that the protagonist is a man. Second, we know that he has just arrived. Third, in the Russian we are told that he left without any outer layers of clothing (though the word—*nalegke*—can also mean that he had nothing with him to carry). The English translation, unlike the original, hints at the protagonist being out of something (*run out*).

In the manuscript Nabokov marks out the phrase "three blocks" (*tri kvartala*), most likely in order to avoid overburdening the text with more numbers (a number expressing volume, "quarter," is present even in the Russian word *kvartal*, block).

FOR THE FIRST TIME. This is the first use in the text of the word "first," marking the consecrated *beginning of the text*. In *Eugene Onegin*, which Nabokov saw as akin to *The Gift* both in terms of structure and narrative style, the word "beginning" (*nachalo*) does not appear until Chapter V. In *The Gift*, we have a beginning, but an unusual one. The ambiguity and dualism of beginnings and ends (at first there

———————————— Close Reading ————————————

is an ending, and then there is not) will recur many times in the text, because this is a novel about perpetual creation, about making something out of the abyss of chaos (the idea of constancy is contained directly in the patronymic of the main character: Konstantinovich).

IN THE STILL UNACCUSTOMED STATE... For now the protagonist does not yet have a station in life (the word translated as "state" is the Russian *chin*—one's rank or status)—possibly even *nalegke* (see comments above on "HIMSELF"). The usage of the word *chin* here is not entirely correct from a linguistic standpoint, but it is necessary to introduce the theme of rank and hierarchy.

RESIDENT. Both the term and the event here may be associated by Nabokov with the corresponding entry in Dahl's Russian dictionary for the verb *obitat'* (to dwell, reside), which is the root of the Russian noun *obitatel'*, translated here as "resident." Dahl considers the debatable etymological root of this verb to be the Latin *vita*—to linger, to live (of an inhabitant), to settle in a place (*cf.* the epigraph from Smirnovski). As examples of usage, Dahl cites "Lord, who dwelleth in thy house" (Psalms) and "The Albazinians, descendents of Russians, live in *China* to this day." The origin of the "THICKSET WOMAN" is not so much Oriental as literary (*cf.* Pushkin's "The residents (*obitateli*) of Goriukhino were for the most part *of average height*").

HAD RUN OUT. The adverb *nalegke*, meaning "lightly dressed" or "with nothing to carry," follows this verb in the Russian and is not translated in the English. A properly structured wording here with the verb *vybezhal* ("ran out") would require answering the two questions "from where?" and "to where?" The word *nalegke*, beginning as it does with the syllable *na* (a preposition meaning *on, into* or *at*), purports to answer this question—this is how poetic diction is constructed (in Mandelstam, for example). The word that Nabokov had chosen initially—*zhilets* ("dweller"), judging by the manuscript, was unsatisfactory because the author did not want that sound repetition of *zh*; the repetition of this sound in *zhilets* and *vybezhal* would have obscured the effect created with *nalegke*. Nabokov uses all of the techniques in the author's arsenal—first pulling the reader in the direction of a certain euphony, then destroying any harmony that was about to develop. The horizon of the reader's expectations is filled with all the right valences for the appearance of a certain word in this context; but instead of the expected word, a different word appears that resembles the expectation in only one distant way—phonetically. In this case, the reader expects the phrase *vybezhal na ulitsu* ("had run outside" or "into the street") and instead gets *vybezhal nalegke* ("had run out lightly dressed").

TO BUY. The semantic emphasis is here at the end of the phrase in the words "to buy" (*kupit'*; in Russian it is the last word of the sentence). By the time we reach the end of the sentence, the stylistic register has sunk: we expect a word like "procure," but we are given the more colloquial "buy a few things" (*koe-chego kupit'*). We have already encountered the "buying-and-selling" theme in the text (service-related things have included the name of the company on the moving van, the furniture, and the movers, with their meat-market associations). To understand how "weighty" this theme is, we must return to the word *obvesit'* (translated as "short-change," more literally something like to "short-weight," i.e. to give a customer less weight than they are charged for). The protagonists are watching to make sure that they will be "weighed up" to the right amount.

Theme 1. Creation of the world/text.

The theme of the creation is introduced to the reader's consciousness by literally sticking it into the beginning of the novel ("to start a thing"—all novels begin some place at some time!).

Theme 2. The quest.

In creating his rules, the hero—by definition a demigod—also does not simply leave home for no reason. The traditional Russian fairy tale opening, *zhili-byli* ("there lived-there were") is exploded by the need to go outside. Humankind has not thought up any other narrative plot. In the *byliny* (Russian folk epics), the hero is obligated to get up from the traditional resting place, the stove, and abandon his native locale, because the death of someone close to him serves as an impulse for him to leave his home (Ershov's *The Humpbacked Horse*; *Puss in Boots*; *Ivan the Fool*). What is emphasized in this case is usually a set interval of time and a dwelling place (which might be reduced to a stove); but if the family is complete, then the hero has no justification for leaving home (there are various types of incompleteness: for example, the Russian tale of the old couple and their speckled hen simply involves a problem of *coloratura*). Propp divides the world of the folk tale into two areas: the home and the forest. Everything that is outside the home is *forest* (which can be disguised, as in the case of cultured forests: cities with vertical spires) (Propp 42). We still do not know Godunov-Cherdyntsev's motivation for leaving the house, but the function of this device is clear.

Motif: Absence, shortage.

Without fail, the classical hero has some sort of shortcoming, which he attempts to make up for over the course of the narrative. In a folk tale, the hero is presented with a condition that he is forbidden to violate. The hero does not adhere to this condition (a dual plot cycle: [1] *prohibition* and [2] *violation of the prohibition*), at which point magical helpers appear. Several times in the novel we glimpse the ghost of a fairy tale (upon returning home from the Chernyshevskis' in the first chapter, in the square the character passes by "the public toilet, reminiscent of Baba Yaga's gingerbread cottage" [G53]). Godunov-Cherdyntsev's position is an everyday shortage processed into literary forms from the travelogue genre to biography and saint's life (Sadko, a hero of the *byliny*, goes out to find a bride because *he is missing something*). The deep mythological layer of the novel reveals the absence of the *father*. We see here the old motif, common throughout European literature, of the absence of a physical father and of his spiritual substitute (from the Christian story of Jesus' reproach to the Father for forsaking him at that moment, all the way up to Raskolnikov).

Methods.

Before this we have already been presented with all of the dramatis personae in the first scene of the novel. Now we have a localization of the action in cultural space, but we still do not know the social status of the main character.

Context.

When did the move take place? The actual positioning in time (April first, before 4:00 pm) carries the reader of *The Gift* to *the beginning* of the novel's plot; cf. the shot of the room in the prologue to *Speak, Memory* (19-20) before the hero appears in this world. Both aesthetically and philosophically, this is the most interesting moment (it is always fascinating to be in a place where we are not, but especially to be transported to the eve of our own birth). The flashback is the first *tour de force* of this type in the novel; there will be many more to come in various places. The temporal shift is characteristic of Russian culture, in which it is customary to experience nostalgia for the epoch of one's fathers and older brothers.

Nabokov is making use of one of the most ancient plots in world literature: a young man awaiting his father—a soldier, traveler, *an accomplished man*. This is the field of meaning that comes about as the result of the main character running out without his coat on to buy something.

(9) HE KNEW THE STREET ¹[THIS STREET, HE HAD OFTEN WALKED ALONG IT;] ²[HE HAD OFTEN HAD OCCASION TO BE THERE] ³[TANNENBURG <STREET>], AS HE KNEW THE WHOLE DISTRICT [AREA]: THE BOARDINGHOUSE FROM WHICH HE HAD MOVED WAS NOT FAR; BUT UP UNTIL THEN, THIS STREET [IT HAD AS IF] HAD TURNED {AND SLIPPED}, [BUT STILL] NOT CONNECTED TO HIM IN ANY WAY, BUT THAT [VERY] DAY [JUST THEN], IT STOPPED SUDDENLY, ALREADY HAVING STARTED TO SOLIDIFY ¹[AND NOW HAVING ASSUMED THE ONLY FORM THAT IT COULD HAVE WITH RESPECT TO THE POINT ON IT WHERE *I* NOW LIVE] ²[(WITH ALL THE CHANGES OF CORNERS AND CURVES THAT FLOWED OUT FROM IT), WHICH PROJECTS FROM THE

───────────────── Chapter Five. COMMENTARY ─────────────────

POINT WHERE I NOW LIVE] ³[HAVING TEMPORARILY SOLIDIFIED] IN THE FORM OF A PROJECTION OF HIS NEW LODGINGS.

Plot link.
Orientation to the locale. Godunov-Cherdyntsev establishes a connection between his new lodgings and the surrounding topography.

Commentary.
STREET. The word *street*, concealed in the end of the preceding text, begins the ninth sentence (in the Russian, the syntax is *ulitsu on znal*). The artificial delay of this word (or name) to the beginning of a new syntactic construction is needed to reveal its second meaning, which is veiled by a sound pattern: *ulitsa* (street) = *Uliss* (Ulysses). The subject of Telemachus and Odysseus is key to the problems raised in *The Gift*: the hero waits for his father, searches for him, and does not recognize him. Nabokov read the epic in Vassily Zhukovsky's translation from the ancient Greek ("If you should hear your father lives yet, that homeward he will return..."). Typologically, *The Gift* has much similarity to Joyce's novel, which Nabokov had been seriously planning to translate into Russian in the mid-1930s (the correspondence between Nabokov and Joyce about this is preserved in the National Library of Ireland in Dublin).

HE KNEW. Repetition, stumbling over the word, rapid speech: STREET... THIS STREET; HE KNEW, AS HE *KNEW*. One can imagine a valid phrase without this twofold doubling. But the repeated verb, generally speaking, is one of the main words in the narrator's and reader's life.

DISTRICT... IN THE FORM OF A PROJECTION. There was a *square* at the beginning, and then the theme of the circle (the Russian word for district, *okrug*, is derived from the word *krug*, meaning 'circle'). It is telling that Nabokov crossed out the word "area" [Russ. *raion*] in the manuscript: in the etymological semantics of his vocabulary, this unsuccessful synonym does not resonate with its direct context, in which an oxymoronic geometry (squaring the circle) accumulates.

Theme. Creative work.
Writing (or composition) is in fact a form of *cognition/knowledge*. Nabokov's novel is about an initiation into a world of imagination, about approaching and then attaching oneself to higher levels of knowledge.

Methods.
The tautological nature of discourse, stuttering in the text. The text of *The Gift* is poetic, and everything in it is important—process, *duration*, the length of our experience of phrases and words. Nabokov takes into account a gap or

discrepancy of meaning between incomprehension of the first reading and the pleasure from understanding upon a repeated reading.

Subtext.
STREET TURNED. Throughout the phrase is, as it were, a picture of a revolving phonograph record. The comparison in Nabokov's sentence to a gramophone record requires further explanation—"turning and stopping"; we should recall that old records turned for a very short time. In the subtext, more than anything else, is the folkloric "Where is this street, where is this house?/Where the young lady, the one that I love?" from the song "The blue sphere turns and spins..." (a pre revolutionary text, revived in the 1934 Soviet film, "Maxim's Youth").

References

Alexandrov, Vladimir. *Nabokov's Otherworld*. Princeton: Princeton University Press, 1991.

Barabtarlo, Gene. *Phantom of Fact: A Guide to Nabokov's* Pnin. Ann Arbor: Ardis, 1989.

Ben-Amos, Anat. "The Role of Literature in *The Gift*," *Nabokov Studies* 4, 1997: 117-149.

Berdjis, Nassim Winnie. *Imagery in Vladimir Nabokov's Last Russian Novel (Dar), Its English Translation (The Gift), and Other Prose Works of the 1930s*. Frankfurt, Germany: Peter Lang; 1995.

Bergson, Henri. *The Two Sources of Morality and Religion*. New York: Doubleday Anchor Books, 1954.

Blackwell, Stephen H. *Zina's Paradox: The Figured Reader in Nabokov's* Gift. New York, New York: Peter Lang, 2000.

Boyd, Brian. *Vladimir Nabokov: The Russian Years*. Princeton: Princeton University Press, 1990.

Bunin, Ivan. *Sobranie sochinenii v 5 t.*, Vol. 4. Moscow: Pravda, 1956.

Chekhov, Anton. *Sobranie sochinenii v 12 t.*, Vol. 8. Moscow: Gosudarstvennoe izdatel'stvo khudozhestvennoi literatury, 1956.

Chernyshevskaia-Bystrova, N.M. *Letopis' zhizni i deiatel'nosti N.G. Chernyshevskogo*, Moscow: Academia, 1933.

Chernyshevsky, Nikolai. *What Is to Be Done?* Transl. by M. R. Katz. Ithaca: Cornell University Press, 1989.

Chernyi, Sasha. *Sobranie sochinenii v 5 t.* Moscow: Ellis Lak, 1999.

Dauben, Joseph W. *Georg Cantor: His Mathematics and Philosophy of the Infinite*. Boston: Harvard University Press, 1979.

Dolinin, Alexander. *Kommentarii k romanu* Dar, in: V. Nabokov. *Sobranie sochinenii russkogo perioda. 5 tt.* St. Petersburg: Simpozium, 1999–2000. Vol. 4: 634-768.

Dostoevsky, Fyodor. *The Insulted and Humiliated*. Moscow: Progress Publishers, 1976.

Foster, John Burt Jr. *Nabokov's Art of Memory and European Modernism*. Princeton: Princeton University Press, 1993.

Gershenzon, M. *Stat'i o Pushkine*. Vstup. Statia L. Grossmana. Leningrad: Academia, 1926.

Goncharov, Ivan. *Complete Collected Works* [*Polnoe sobranie sochinenii*]. Vol. 11. St. Petersburg, 1899.

Hedin, Sven. *Enfardgenom Asien 1893-97.* 2 vols. Stockholm: Bonnier, 1898.

_____ *Scoutliv i Tibet.* Stockholm: Bonnier, 1913.

Ilf, Ilya and Evgenii Petrov. *The Twelve Chairs*. Translated from the Russian by John H. Richardson. New York: Vintage Books, 1961.

Iser, Wolfgang. *The Range of Interpretation*. New York: Columbia University Press, 2000.

Katz, Boris. "Chto zhe sluchilos' s Martynom Edel'veisom?," *The Real Life of Pierre Delalande. Studies in Russian and Comparative Literature to Honor A. Dolinin.* Ed. by D. Bethea et al. Stanford, 2007. Vol. 2: 512-520.

Konishi, Masataka. "Nabokov's Paradox" in *Abstracts of papers delivered at The International Nabokov Conference in Kyoto*, Kyoto: The Nabokov Society of Japan, 2010: 28.

Kostalevsky, Marina. "The Young Godunov-Cherdyntsev or How to Write a Literary Biography," *Russian Literature* 43 (3), 1998: 283-95.

Lanchester, John. "Flashes of Flora," *The New York Review of Books*, Volume 56, Number 20, December 17, 2009.

Lermontov, Mikhail. *A Hero of Our Time*. Transl. by Paul Foote. London: Penguin Books, 2001.

Leving, Yuri. "V. Nabokov i Sasha Chernyi," *Literaturnoe obozrenie* 2, 1999: 52-56.

_____ "Six Notes to *The Gift*," *The Nabokovian* 45, 2000: 36-41.

_____ *Train Station—Garage—Hangar (Vladimir Nabokov and Poetics of Russian Urbanism)* [*Vokzal—Garazh—Angar. Nabokov i poetika russkogo urbanizma*]. St. Petersburg: Ivan Limbakh Publishing House, 2004.

Malmstad, John E. "Khodasevich and Formalism: A Poet's Dissent," in *Russian Formalism: A Retrospective Glance. A Festschrift in Honor of Victor Erlich.* Ed. by Robert L. Jackson and Stephen Rudy. New Haven: Yale Center for International and Area Studies, 1985.

Mandelstam, Osip. *Egipetskaia marka*. Leningrad: Priboi, 1928.

Nabokov, Nicolas. *Bagázh: Memoirs of a Russian Cosmopolitan*. New York: Atheneum, 1975.

Nabokov, Vladimir. *Invitation to a Beheading*. New York: Capricorn Books, 1965.

_____ *The Nabokov–Wilson Letters: 1941-1971*, Ed. Simon Karlinsky, New York: Harper and Row, 1979.

_____ *Eugene Onegin. A Novel in Verse* by Alexander Pushkin / Trans. with commentary by Vladimir Nabokov, in 4 vols. New York: Bollingen, 1964.

_____ *Perepiska s sestroi* [Correspondence between Nabokov and Helene Sikorski]. Ann Arbor: Ardis, 1984.

_____ *Strong Opinions*. New York: McGraw Hill, 1973.

_____ *Speak, Memory. An Autobiography Revisited*. New York: G.P. Putnam's Sons, 1966.

Ostrovsky, A. G. *Turgenev v zapisiakh sovremennikov*. Moscow: Agraf, 1999.

Propp, Vladimir. *Morphology of the Folk Tale*. Austin: University of Texas Press, 1968.

Przheval'skii, Nikolai Mikhailovich. *Iz Zaisana cherez Khami v Tibet i na verkhov'e Zheltoi reki*. St. Peterburg: Balashev, 1883.

Pushkin, Alexander. *The Tale of Tsar Saltan*. Transl. by Louis Zellikoff. Moscow: Progress Publishers, 1970.

_____ "Skazka o tsare Saltane" in *Polnoe sobranie sohinenii v 10 t*. Vol. 4. Moscow: Izdatel'stvo Akademii nauk SSSR, 1962-1966.

Ronen, Irena and Omry. "'Diabolically Evocative': An Inquiry into the Meaning of a Metaphor," *Slavica Hierosolymitana: Slavic Studies of the Hebrew University* 5-6, 1981: 371-86.

Ronen, Omry. "Nine Notes to *The Gift*," *The Nabokovian* 44, 2000: 20-26.

_____ "Puti Shklovskogo v 'Putevoditele po Berlinu'" *Zvezda* 4, 1999: 164-172.

Shapiro, Gavriel. *The Sublime Artist's Studio: Nabokov and Painting*. Evanston: Northwestern University Press, 2009.

Shcheglov, Iurii. *O romanakh I. Il'fa i E. Petrova*. Moscow: Panorama, 1995.

Toker, Leona. "Nabokov and Bergson," in *The Garland Companion to Vladimir Nabokov*. Ed. by V. Alexandrov. New York: Garland, 1995: 367-373.

Turgenev, Ivan. *Fathers and Sons*. Transl. by Michael Katz. New York: W. W. Norton & Company, 1996.

Zimmer, Dieter E. and Sabine Hartmann. "'The Amazing Music of Truth': Nabokov's Sources for Godunov's Central Asian Travels in *The Gift*," *Nabokov Studies* 7, 2002-2003: 33-74.

CHAPTER SIX
ENGLISH TRANSLATION

> The participation of so many Russian muses within the orchestration of the novel makes its translation especially hard.
>
> Foreword to *The Gift*, 1962

"I Am Still Looking For Somebody..."

Upon immigrating to the United States in 1940 Nabokov saw a translation of *The Gift* into English as one of his priorities. However, finding the right person for this difficult task was no simple matter. From the outset Nabokov stressed that whoever did the translation, the author would be closely monitoring the entire process. American publishers rejected several proposals for the English-language publication of the novel, but Nabokov continued pushing in spite of the external circumstances.

On July 25, 1941, Nabokov suggested that Peter Pertzoff, who had earlier translated his short stories from Russian to English, might do the same for *The Gift*. Nabokov wrote to Pertzoff from Palo Alto, California, offering him an exclusive option on the project until the fall of that year: "The book that I would like to publish is *The Gift*. It must be published in one edition of approximately 500 pages. This condition is of fundamental importance — the book cannot be broken into two volumes. I am hereby willing to give you the option that you ask for translating *The Gift* before November 1, 1941. Since the book is much longer than you estimated earlier, you should also probably adjust your own calculations. By the way, one folio equals 16 pages" (Shrayer 281; 556).[30]

In spite of the firm deadline that he had in mind, Nabokov hardly knew who could complete an English version of his novel. Ironically, it still remained unpublished as a separate edition even in its original language. When, apparently, he did not hear back from Pertzoff until the middle of November, Nabokov mentioned his "longest novel, the untranslated 'Dar' (*Gift*), which is the story of a great writer in the making (Nothing to do with Sebastian)" (*Selected Letters*

---

[30] The correspondence between Pertzoff and Nabokov was originally conducted in English; here I am translating it back from M. Shrayer's Russian study because the original is not available to me.

39) in a letter to James Laughlin, the editor and president of the New Directions publishing house. Attempting to pique Laughlin's interest in the project, Nabokov continued a few months later:

> A propos: I have made up my mind to get my best Russian novel (*The Gift*) translated and published. It is about 500 pages long. What I would like you to supply me with first of all is a good translator as I have no time to do the job myself. I need a man who knows English better than Russian—and a man, not a woman. I am frankly homosexual on the subject of translators. I would revise every sentence myself and keep in touch with him all the time, but *I must* have somebody to do the basic work and then to polish my corrections. *The Gift* was published serially in the *Annales Contemporaines* (the great Russian review that appeared in Paris during twenty years, since 1920), but the war, or rather the complete destruction of Russian intellectual life in Paris by the German invasion, has made its appearance in book form impossible—naturally. (July 16, 1942; *Selected Letters* 41; italics in the original)

In the hope that Laughlin would pursue the project, Nabokov suggested the name of a possible translator, Bernard Guilbert Guerney, who has translated Gogol's *Dead Souls*[31] shortly before ("apart from...the rather self-conscious slang occurring here and there in the translation—the latter is far better than anything that has been published before. True, it lacks the poetic and musical (and nightmarish!) qualities of the original, but it is fairly exact and is the work of an honest mind. In fact it might be a good idea to try and get him to translate my *Gift*—with my assistance"; *Selected Letters* 44). With no signs of real progress, especially once the translation issue turned out to be a stumbling block, Nabokov dropped the plan to publish *The Gift* through Laughlin. Guerney would remain a candidate for at least another year, but would never come to fruition. Pertzoff's translation was never completed either, and his correspondence with Nabokov ceased in 1944 due to his mental illness.

Three weeks after initially addressing Laughlin, Nabokov cunningly suggested to Edmund Wilson that he translate *The Gift*. Nabokov's friendship with the American critic could probably have ended even earlier than it had in reality, had Wilson agreed to undertake the translation of this masterpiece into English. Nabokov complained to Wilson about his publisher, reprimanding him for the delay in coming up with a suitable translator:

---

[31] It appeared under the title *Chichikov's Journeys; or Home Life in Old Russia* (the translation that Nabokov seemed to like). A prolific translator, B. G. Guerney (1894–1979), also translated into English modern Russian classics such as Alexander Kuprin's *The Pit*, Ivan Bunin's *The Dreams of Chang and Other Stories*, as well as *An Anthology of Russian literature in the Soviet period from Gorki to Pasternak*.

I am begging Laughlin to find me a translator for my *Gift*. Sex ♂, nationality American, knowledge of Russian good, vocabulary *richissime*, style his own. Laughlin asked Knopf, and Knopf suggested Yarmolinsky whose English is no better than mine and whose translations of Pushkin (with Babette D[eutsch]³²) are worse than mine. So I am still looking for somebody who might make a translation of that 500 page book, with myself only controlling the meaning and nuance. I know of one man who could do it if I helped him with his Russian. This is a roundabout way of putting it but I am afraid you have other dogs to beat whereas I have no illusions about the sums Laughlin can pay, — at least such sums as have come to me; they might come in bulkier form to others. (August 9, 1942; *Nabokov–Wilson Letters* 75-76)

In response Wilson cited a lack of time as well as his insufficient command of Russian: "If I had the leisure, I'd be glad to translate your book. I'd like to see you translated, and I'd probably learn a lot of Russian. But I've got so many things to do that I couldn't possibly. I'm working on a couple of books, and I think I'll have to take on a part-time job that has been offered me at Smith. The truth is, besides, that my Russian is so uncertain that going over my work would probably be nearly as much trouble for you as translating the book yourself" (August 20, 1942). As if compensating for his refusal, Wilson suggested: "How about Alexander Werth, who translated Ognyov's *Communist Schoolboy*?³³ You don't have to have an American, do you?" (*Nabokov–Wilson Letters* 78). Like Nabokov, Alexander Werth (1901–69) was a native of Russia, whose family fled to the United Kingdom in the wake of the Russian Revolution (Werth's father was a Tsarist politician), but here the similarities end. Apparently Nabokov was not overly inspired by his friend's suggestion to employ the services of a man who had not only translated a blatant piece of propaganda, but was currently residing in Stalin's Russia.³⁴

In the spring of 1943, Wilson brought in the name of another possible candidate. While lecturing at Smith College, he had met Helen Muchnic, who

---

32   Avraam Yarmolinsky's wife, who was a poet and who collaborated with him on translations of Pushkin.
33   Mikhail Grigor'evich Rozanov. *The Diary of a Communist Schoolboy [by] N. Ognyov.* [Original Title: *Kostia Riabtsev v vuze*]. Translated from the Russian by Alexander Werth (New York, Payson & Clarke, 1928). Werth also translated Sof'ia Tolstaia's *The Diary of Tolstoy's Wife* (New York, Payson and Clarke, 1929).
34   Nabokov's suspicions proved to be well founded: Werth, who spoke and wrote both Russian and English at the native level, spent World War II in the Soviet Union as the BBC's correspondent, and later as the Moscow correspondent for the *Guardian* newspaper (1946 to 1949). He was one of the first outsiders to be allowed into Stalingrad after the World War II battle. His other works include: *France 1940-1955: the de Gaulle Revolution*; *Moscow 41*; *The Last Days of Paris: a Journalist's Diary*; *Leningrad*; *The Year of Stalingrad*; and *Musical Uproar in Moscow*.

was now writing to him what seemed to be "a very appreciative and intelligent letter" about Nabokov's novel *Podvig* (later translated as *Glory*). Wilson found Muchnic's English skills perfect[35] and suggested Nabokov give her a chance to translate something of his (March 7, 1943; *Nabokov–Wilson Letters* 104). Despite his earlier insistence on the translator's gender as a *sine qua non*, Nabokov confided to Wilson: "I do want very much Miss Muchnic to translate my *Gift*, but I shall send her a short story first" (*Nabokov–Wilson Letters* 105). This test did not yield any results either, and the names of the novel's potential translators continued to shift like a kaleidoscope.

Just three months later Nabokov assured Wilson that "a translator called Guerney is going to do…Даръ [*The Gift*, spelled in Russian with pre-1918 orthography]" (June 11, 1943; *Nabokov–Wilson Letters* 112). Unfortunately, this announcement proved to be premature: Bernard Guilbert Guerney was soon given Nabokov's attention in a slashing review of his *A Treasury of Russian Literature*. It remains unclear whether there was any link between Guerney's unrealized translation project for Nabokov and the author's "bilious mood" (as Nabokov confessed on December 10, 1943) upon receipt of the book for the commissioned review (Ibid. 127). Nabokov's review appeared in *The New Republic* under the self-explanatory title, "Cabbage Soup and Caviar" (January 17, 1944).

In short, none of those whom Nabokov could or was advised to consider at various points as potential collaborators—Pertzoff, Yarmolinsky, Wilson, Werth, Muchnic, or Guerney—reported for duty.

Attempting to interest the Viking Press in the project a decade after the failed attempt with New Directions, Nabokov recounted the novel's plot to Viking's editor, Pascal Covici:

> The Chekhov Publishing House of the Ford Foundation has just published my novel DAR (*The Gift*). This book deals with the development of a writer of genius. It contains his early poetry, the material he assembles for his second book (which he does not write), his first great book which is the biography of a famous Russian critic of the sixties (this biography, for some reason, created something of a furor in the Russian émigré circles, though it was never published until the recent edition by the Ford Foundation), and a happy love story involving my young man and his half-Jewish fiancée. Would you be interested in publishing a translation? (May 16, 1952; *Selected Letters* 133-34)

---

[35] Helen Muchnic left Russia at about the age of 11, studied Russian literature in London with Dmitry Svyatopolk-Mirsky (a Russian political and literary historian who published *A History of Russian Literature: From Its Beginnings to 1900*, which Nabokov recommended to his students as the best history of Russian literature) and wrote a doctoral thesis on the influence of Dostoevsky in English (1939). In the late 1940s she briefly taught at Harvard University.

Mentioned as the fifth item in the list of various projects in the letter (translations of *Eugene Onegin*, *The Song of Igor's Campaign*, and a book of memoirs among them), *The Gift* interested the publisher least of all.

His frustration resulted in Nabokov's temporary decision to abandon the dream of translating *Dar* in the near future. He focused on his current English-language writing instead, leaving the problem to be resolved by a stroke of luck.

A Sheer Happenstance

Seven years passed, and Nabokov mentioned the possible publication of the translation of the novel—though it still existed only in Russian—in a letter to George Weidenfeld, calling the novel simply but elegantly: "a novel of love and literature" (January 12, 1959; *Selected Letters* 273). At this point Nabokov trusted that Dmitri would provide a rough draft. "How is the translation of my poor *Dar* coming along?" he inquires of his son from Los Angeles in late August 1959, while working on the screenplay of *Lolita* for Kubrick (*Selected Letters* 298).

Nothing came out of this project with Weidenfeld and Nicolson, and he was about to lose his potential translator, Dmitri, who was planning to travel to study opera in Rome. Despite all this, Nabokov could feel that the moment when the English-language edition of *The Gift* would see the light of the day was closer than ever.

Indeed, everything became clear within a year, in early 1960. A lucky opportunity, or a "sheer happenstance" as the translator himself called it, presented itself twenty-five years after the novel was written in its original language.

Having secured a contract with G. P. Putnam's Sons, Nabokov successfully approached a talented novice named Michael Scammell, born in 1935—the time of the composition of *The Gift*. Scammell turned out to be the right man in the right place to embark on the translation of Nabokov's most intricate and multilayered Russian novel. He had rented a room from a Russian émigré landlady, Anna Feigin, during his first year of graduate studies at Columbia University in New York. Unbeknownst to him, this courteous woman was Véra Nabokov's first cousin. In the course of occasional conversations in the kitchen (where Scammell "had privileges to go and cook his meals" [Leving—Scammell]) Anna learned that her tenant was working on his first professional translation—*Cities and Years* by the Soviet novelist Konstantin Fedin. Anna had nothing but disdain for the author and book, but was impressed by Scammell's diligence, his "monastic existence" (being British, the student had no family in America), his devotion to graduate studies, and his grasp of Russian. Feigin evidently communicated some of this to Véra (Ibid.).

Chapter Six. ENGLISH TRANSLATION

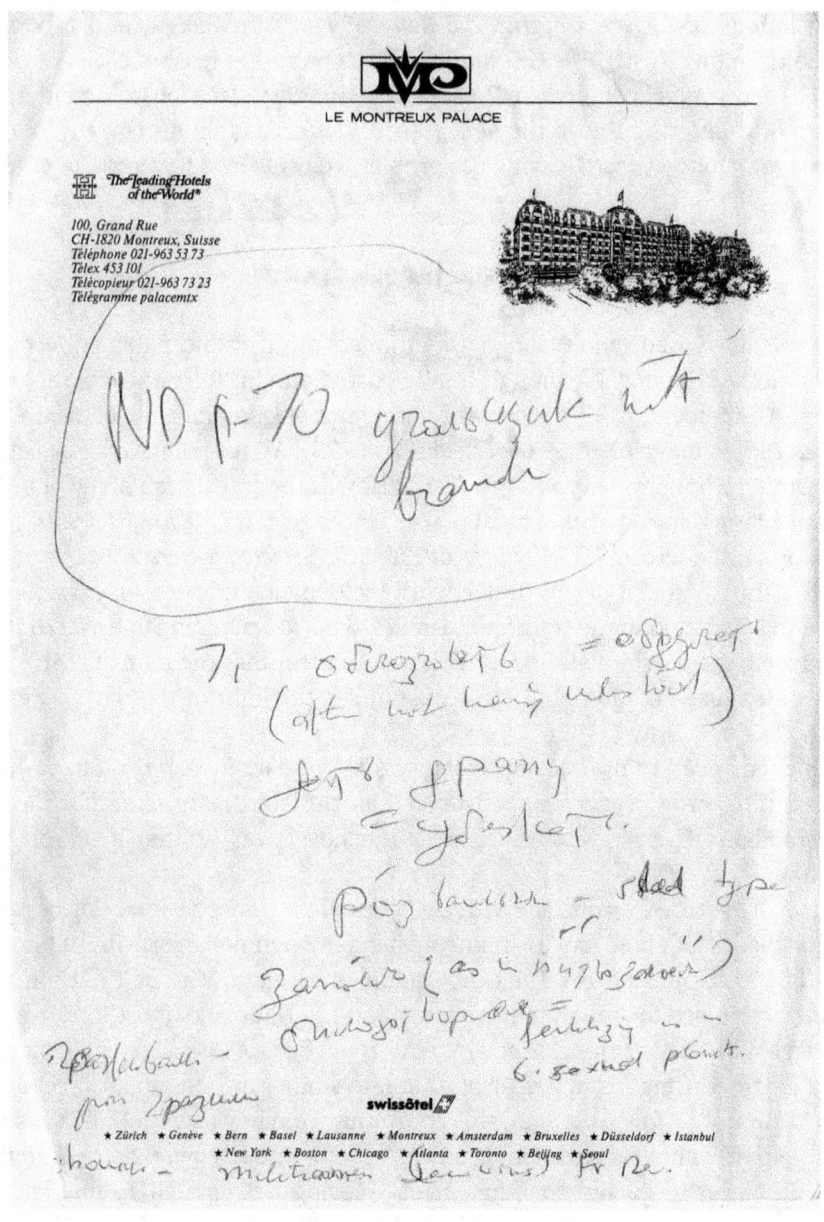

[Ill. 6-1] Dmitri Nabokov's notes for translation of *The Gift* on the letterhead of Le Montreux Palace (Courtesy of Division of Rare and Manuscript Collections, Cornell University)

Nabokov, who had just negotiated a contract with Putnam for several of his Russian novels to be published in English, "was clearly looking for someone young and malleable enough (like his son, presumably), who wouldn't object to the extensive rewriting that Nabokov proposed to do in revising the translation" (Ibid.).

Passing the Test

In February 1960, Anna unexpectedly invited Scammell to tea, which was a unique occasion. Despite their many friendly chats, the young tenant had never before been through the door that led to her parlor and private living quarters. On the winter night he:

> knocked on her door, entered, and was solemnly introduced to a tall avuncular gentleman with an Edwardian air, a plummy English lisp, and a firm handshake, and to a perfectly coiffed, petite, white-haired lady, who looked perfectly elegant in the perfect French manner—Mr. and Mrs. Vladimir Nabokov. An immensely tall young man, about my age, uncoiled himself from a low armchair and introduced himself as their son, Dmitri. (Scammell 52)

A short time after that meeting, Anna casually asked Scammell if he could give her one of his translations to send to Nabokov. Scammell handed her a short story, "Gusev," by Anton Chekhov. He received a letter back from Véra, now in Hollywood, to say that she and her husband had no copy of Chekhov in Russian to compare his work with, but would Michael care to translate three pages from Chapter Four of Nabokov's last Russian novel, *The Gift*? "My husband asks me to add that the passage in question is difficult"—"much more difficult," she herself added, "than Chekhov" (May 11, 1960; Berg Collection). Véra had covered herself by saying that Nabokov might suggest Scammell's name to publishers if he liked his translations. The publishers would pay six dollars a page, Véra added, a handsome price at the time.

It seems that it would have been more logical to assign Scammell the very beginning of *The Gift*, especially since it could be compared with Dmitri's already available draft translation. It is also possible that Nabokov saw some hidden traps in this particular fragment that might trip the potential translator up, but he never explained any such traps, and Scammell did not ask.

The three pages began with a poem, which Scammell was asked not to bother with, and a passage whose opening sentences he translated as follows:

> A sonnet, apparently barring the way, but perhaps, on the contrary, providing a secret link which would explain everything—if only man's mind could withstand that explanation. The soul sinks into a momentary dream—and now

with the peculiar theatrical vividness of those risen from the dead, they come out to meet us: father Gavriil, in a silk *pomegranate* chasuble, with a long staff, an embroidered sash across his *wide* stomach, and with him, already illumined by the sun, an extremely attractive little boy—pink, awkward, and delicate.

It took a month for Scammell to submit the three pages; not because they were so difficult (though they were certainly that, and certainly different from Chekhov) but because he had his graduate studies to attend to. Véra wrote to thank Anna's lodger for the translation: "My husband thinks it is perfectly wonderful." "Pomegranate," a literal translation, was amended by Nabokov to "cerise" and later to "garnet-red"; the "wide" stomach became a "big" one, and there were more changes further on, but the passage survives recognizably in the published version.

Véra asked if Scammell would be prepared to translate the rest of Chapter Four. Dmitri was still planning to translate most of the novel, but he had just won a scholarship to sing with La Scala in Milan and doubted that he could manage the whole book. She also added the small but meaningful stipulation that her husband always reserves the right to make any changes in the finished translation and wants from the translator as close an adherence to the original as possible.

Scammell had been covertly tested without knowing it, but he was "happy to have passed the test and had no problem with Nabokov's last stipulation" (Scammell 53). Although he hadn't then heard of Nabokov's notion of translators following "the servile path," he firmly believed that the translator's job was to come between author and reader as little as possible. As a translator, Scammell was "servile by instinct and therefore closer to Nabokov's ideal than [he] realized" (Ibid.).

COLLABORATION BY CORRESPONDENCE

The literary tastes of the man who was to impersonate Nabokov's English voice in *The Gift* were rather eclectic: he had grown up loving English realism—Fielding, Dickens, Thackeray, George Eliot, D.H. Lawrence, and Arnold Bennett, and he greatly admired the Americans, Steinbeck and Hemingway. Scammell, as he himself admits, preferred Tolstoy and Chekhov to Dostoevsky and Gogol, and Balzac to Flaubert. Yet he had developed a private passion for some of the great modernists—Sterne, Joyce, and Nabokov's own master, Andrei Bely, along with a couple of Nabokov's near contemporaries, Babel and Zamyatin. Despite the fact that he had some models before him, the future translator of *The Gift* knew very little of Nabokov's own work: *Pnin,* which he thought amusing but decidedly minor, and *Lolita,* which struck him "as being enormously clever, but cold as ice at its core," and which he had never finished. *The Gift* for him was a much warmer and more interesting novel than *Lolita* (Leving—Scammell).

Satisfied with the test results and without Dmitri in the immediate vicinity, Véra asked if Scammell could do Chapters Two through Five of *The Gift*. "Nabokov, it must be remembered, although an instant celebrity, was not yet a literary colossus," Scammell explained in retrospect years later, "*Lolita* had been a *succès de scandale* as much as it had been a literary event" (Scammell 53). Indeed, Nabokov's nine Russian novels, short stories, poems, and plays were completely unknown to the English-speaking world, while *Pale Fire* and *Ada* were still to come. Scammell admired what prose he had seen, but he was "far from falling in love with it"; nevertheless, he was "highly honored and flattered by Nabokov's attention, and the six dollars a page spoke loudly to an impoverished graduate student" (Ibid.). He undertook to deliver a complete translation of *The Gift* (except the first hundred pages, which had been completed by Dmitri) within one calendar year. The contract was signed in August 1960 (Leving—Scammell).

It was six more months before Michael Scammell could embark on the translation of *The Gift*, which, contrary to his hopes, turned out to be a long-distance collaboration with the author. He started it in New York, did most of the work in Southampton, England, completed the book in Paris and Milan, and mailed the final chapter from Ljubljana in the former Yugoslavia. The Nabokovs during this time moved from Los Angeles to Nice, then to Stresa, Italy, to Champex in the Swiss Alps, where Nabokov hunted butterflies, to Geneva, and finally to Montreux.

Nabokov and his translator did at one point discuss a meeting to go over the text together, but in the end it proved impossible, and the whole thing was done by correspondence: "correspondence, in this case, meant correspondence with Véra. As Stacy Schiff has shown in her biography of Véra, it was a convenient way for Nabokov not only to guard his time but to erect yet one more barrier between himself and the outside world" (Scammell 54). He annotated the letters and lists of questions Scammell sent to him, and Véra wrote the formal replies, often reproducing the exact phraseology he had used in his notes. In the three years of their distant collaboration, Scammell received only three letters signed by Vladimir Nabokov.

SOME GENERAL PRINCIPLES OF TRANSLATING *THE GIFT*

Faithful Translation

Nabokov entrusted the translation of several of his short stories and five novels to other translators, with the author playing the part of editor and reviser. Two novels (*Invitation to a Beheading*, 1959, and *Glory*, 1971) and one chapter of the third (*The Gift*, 1963) were translated by Dmitri Nabokov. Scammell translated

The Defense (1964) and most of the *The Gift*; Michael Glenny did *Mary* (1970). From his collaborators Nabokov "expected a faithful translation, leaving to himself the task of revising and embellishing it, linguistically and stylistically" (Struve 127).

Nabokov believed that a given work should be translated as precisely as possible into the target language. This literalist endeavor is perhaps flawed in some fundamental way, because even in his own practice as translator, according to Judson Rosengrant, for whatever reasons, Nabokov was not always able to sustain this approach at a consistently high level (Rosengrant 25). Nabokov's theory of translation does have "genuine sophistication and value, even if his own application of it was erratic, and even if that theory in its literalist mode may require more literary skill and scholarly insight than most translators are capable of providing" (Ibid.). Whatever the merits of this approach in theory, Nabokov required it from those who prepared drafts of translations for him to supervise and authorize.

A Magic Triangle

In her brief but very useful attempt at systematic analysis of Scammell's translation of *The Gift*, Marina Grishakova argues that in revising Scammell's draft Nabokov uses the so-called "springboard method" (313). The springboard metaphor had been introduced by the writer himself in *The Real Life of Sebastian Knight* where it was applied to the main hero's approach to writing prose: "As often was the way with Sebastian Knight he used parody as a kind of springboard leaping into the highest region of serious emotion" (*Sebastian Knight* 76). Michael Scammell suggested a similar figure of speech ("using the author as a springboard") in describing a silly type of reviewer embodied by the careless critic Linyov in *The Gift*. "Despite the cases being seemingly opposite," notes Grishakova, "both the enigmatic Sebastian and the uncontrollable Linyov share the same passion for deformation and 'rewriting' the texts that do not belong to them" (312; my translation).

Nabokov's use of the springboard method lies in departing from Scammell's English-language draft in order to redraw the semantics of the denotative and connotative meanings of the Russian master text: thus, "a triangle '*original text—text of translation—edited text of translation*' is established, and Nabokov is able to deform more or less significantly the former two elements [of the triangle]" (Grishakova 313).

In attempting to make certain shades of meaning more explicit, Nabokov revised not only the text of the translation, but also his own Russian original. One finds an example of such an approach in the draft of Chapter One prepared by Dmitri. In the imaginary conversation with Koncheyev, Fyodor discusses Leskov, who mentions "*Galileiskii prizrak, prokhladnyi i tikhii, v dlinnoi odezhde tsveta zreiushchei slivy*." Dmitri renders this as "the ghost of Galileo, cool and quiet." Nabokov's son obviously confuses here Christ (aka 'Jesus of Nazareth,' 'Judas the Galilean') with the Italian astronomer Galileo Galilei (1564–1642); Nabokov, alerted, makes everything plain: "how about his image of Jesus 'the ghostly Galilean, cool and gentle, in a robe the color of ripening plum'?" (G72).

Grishakova describes yet another illustration of Nabokov testing the opaqueness of his text while observing the reaction of his first English-language readers (Dmitri Nabokov and Michael Scammell, in this case). When Scammell translates "*gorshki s bal'zaminom*" ("pots with balsam flowers") as "jars of balsam" instead, Nabokov lightly edits the text and elucidates the allusion to Pushkin, which had not been made explicit in the Russian *Dar*:

> Toward him out of a Pushkin tale came Karolina Schmidt, "a girl heavily rouged, of meek and modest appearance," who acquired the bed in which Schoning died. Beyond Grunewald forest a postmaster who resembled Simeon Vyrin (from another tale) was lighting his pipe by the window, and there also stood pots with balsam flowers. (G97; Grishakova 312)

Revisions and elaborations have been prompted not only by translators; upon reading the text of the translation Nabokov sometimes realized that certain imagery requires a more precise definition or is in need of paraphrase. Scammell diligently translates from Russian: "one had to go at first in order to enter an only just laid-out garden, with Alpine flora along geometric paths" (*Gift* typescript 390), but Nabokov specifies and adds to the description something that is actually missing in the original. The garden is not green but made out of rocks similar to the Japanese style: "according to the scheme of the local Lenôtres—one had to go in order to enter at first a newly laid-out *rock* garden, with Alpine flora along geometric paths" (G330).

Explication and Adaptation

Apart from suggesting that Scammell omit the poems from his translation, Nabokov also instructed him as follows: "If you come upon some idiom you do not know and cannot find in the dictionary, give as close a translation as you can and put an interrogation mark against it, or leave it out altogether" (May 11, 1960; Berg Collection).

In line with his general principle of facilitating the Anglophone readers in their understanding of certain scenes and allusions that native Russians may have taken for granted, in the English translation Nabokov frequently includes the authors of popular sayings and puts cited passages in quotation marks (which were *not* included in the Russian original). In some cases Nabokov even visually sets off passages involving stream of consciousness or quoted speech. The letters from Fyodor's mother (G104-6) are indented and printed in small font in the English edition, while in the Russian they are printed as part of the regular text, making it difficult for the reader to make an immediate psychological adjustment in the interpretation of the passage: "Like the false review and the dialogue with Koncheyev, the perceived status of the text as first read is undermined as one reads further on; the magic carpet is pulled out from under the reader's feet" (Blackwell 37).

While in the Russian original Nabokov made little effort to ease his readers' process of comprehension, the English-language version of the novel was designed to smooth the rough terrain of *Dar* and to adapt it for a contemporary Western audience. This was not a unique compromise for *The Gift*, but in full compliance with Nabokov's long-term strategy: from the start of his career as an English author Nabokov assumed an American voice, consciously and deliberately introducing American idioms into his style (Grayson 190). Scammell obviously had to deal with the issue of idiomatic flavoring in *The Gift*, whose main heroine is, as defined by Nabokov, Russian Literature.

"The Zonal Commandments": British or American English?

The question of what kind of English to use for the translation—British English or American English—much worried Michael Scammell, an Englishman by origin, who labored very hard to keep things American (as he had done in his version of *Crime and Punishment*—billed as the "first American translation" of Dostoevsky's novel):

> I think I once asked Mr. Nabokov whether he wanted the novel translated into British English or American English, and he replied British English. I find, however, that the first chapter is written in a mixture of both, with the emphasis heavily on American (107 Americanisms as against 8 Anglicisms), although on occasion both terms for a single object have managed to creep to within a few lines of one another on the same page (*tram* and *streetcar*, *traveler* and *traveller*). I myself am quite agreeable to working in either dialect (my first book was done into American) and either spelling, but I must point out that chapter two was done, according to what I understood to be Mr. Nabokov's wishes, into British English. So now it is a question of either turning chapter one into British or chapter two into American—either way you prefer. Please let me know what you feel about this. (MS to Véra; June 24, 1961; Berg Collection)

Though a real concern for Scammell, it mattered less to Nabokov. Despite the fact that the translator assures Nabokov that he is comfortable with "either dialect," he later complains: "You have changed my Anglicisms to Americanisms and my Americanisms to Anglicisms—which way do you want to go?" It did not matter to Nabokov nearly as much as transliteration:

"American English, please, whenever there is an essential divergence between the two. On the whole, however, my husband thinks that the idiom should be more or less neutral. He does not mind if *'tram'* and *'streetcar'* appear on the same page," Véra reiterates. (July 5, 1961; Berg Collection)

This did not go unnoticed by certain hair-splitting critics, who later reproached the Nabokovs and Scammell for inconsistency: "The translators have added their own exiguously bizarre note by getting mixed up from time to time in British and American English, so that Berlin's *trams* are changing to *streetcars* and back again as if they were subject to the whim of contemporary zonal commandments" (Share 10).

CHALLENGES IN TRANSLATING

"If I Was the Band, He Was the Orchestra"

The agreement called for Scammell to work at considerable speed. On the level of syntax he found Nabokov unusually easy to translate: as Tolstoy's Russian was influenced by French, so was Nabokov's influenced by English, unlike that of Gogol or Bely. This made the sentences quite straightforward to construct in English. Scammell worked by making a first draft by hand, correcting it, and then typing it out on his small Olivetti portable. In doing the first draft, he would sometimes make a list of terms that he did not understand and send them to Nabokov, who would often, but not always, send him back answers, or annotate the typescript.

Obviously, Scammell's biggest challenge in translating *The Gift* was vocabulary:

> Nabokov was the master of a colossal range of synonyms for every conceivable action, object, thought, idea, appearance, sound, or smell, and he played the instrument of language like a virtuoso. I couldn't possibly match him for range of reference, or for nuance or exactitude, and was frequently left groping for equivalents. My translation must have sounded to him at times as if his symphony was being played by a brass band instead of a full-blown orchestra (if I was the band, he was the orchestra). (Leving—Scammell)

The explanatory lists that Véra attached to her letters to Scammell give an understanding of the minute details and challenges that the translator was facing in his craft. Amazingly, Scammell was able to overcome most of the difficulties by himself and left almost no blank spots. In Chapter Two he was puzzled, for example, by the following Russian words which Véra translated for him: "'lavatory humor' will do for *pipifaksoviy yumor*," she writes and goes on to explain other unclear points: *rovnitsa*—dandy roll (this is a machine used in the manufacture of paper); *bertoletovi'y sneg*—artificial snow is all right; *kvolie* – sickly; *barishnya-krest'yanka*—lady-cum-peasant is fine [an allusion to the title of Pushkin's short story—Y.L.]; *orlov* [liter. "eagles"]—"please delete the fourth word in line 13, the three last words in line 15, and all of the lines 16-25; *rampetka*—net." Other examples included *otverstie zenitsi*—wide-open eyes; *Step' Otchayaniya*—The Steppe of Despair ("I wonder if the 'The' needs being capitalized?," asks Véra); *rogatiy zhavoronok*—horned lark; *pishchuhi*—creepers (birds); *kosyak kiangov*—a herd of kiangs (wild asses); *ryazheniy zhuk*—beetle in fancy dress; *chubaraya yurga*—piebald pony, and so on.

In her letter Véra touches upon transliteration issues:

> "Tsar" is all right (instead of "Czar"). "Yvonne Ivanovna" may be turned into "Yvonna Ivanovna," although actually the name is French and is only Russified by the addition of the "a." If you write "Yvonna" with an "a" at the end, the initial "Y" becomes slightly unjustifiable. But this is not essential. My husband prefers "verst" to "vyorst" because 1) this is Webster's accepted rendering and 2) it is anyway "versta" (not "vyorsta") in nominative singular in Russian. (July 5, 1961; Berg Collection)

Véra's Input

Véra once helped Scammell translate an entire problematic passage consisting of a dialogue between Fyodor's father and Uncle Oleg. In the following chart, Scammell's original draft is compared with the same passage in its printed version of *The Gift* with Vladimir's alterations in bold (in the right column):

UNCLE OLEG (*playfully*): Tell me, Kostya, did you ever happen to see on the Wie reservation the little bird So-was? FATHER (*curtly*): I did not. UNCLE OLEG (*warming up*): And have you never seen, Kostya, Popovski's horse stung by Popov's fly? FATHER (*still more curt*): I have not. UNCLE OLEG (*in ecstasy*): And have you never chanced to observe the diagonal motion of entoptic swarms? FATHER (*looking him straight in the eye*): I have.	UNCLE OLEG (*in a bantering tone*): **Well**, tell me, Kostya, did you ever happen to see on the Wie reservation the little bird So-was? FATHER (*curtly*): **I'm afraid** I did not. UNCLE OLEG (*warming up*): And Kostya, **did you** never see Popovski's horse stung by Popov's fly? FATHER (*even more curtly*): Never. UNCLE OLEG (*completely ecstatic*): And have you never **had occasion, for example**, to observe the diagonal motion of entoptic swarms? FATHER (*looking him straight in the eye*): I have. (G130)

On July 8, 1961, Scammell reported: "I have now incorporated the corrections in Chapter Two and it is ready to be sent off. I was formerly under impression that you would be sending the poetry translations to me and that I would type them in, but since they have not come and since Chapter Two is already overdue, I am sending it to you as it is." There remained, however, just a few outstanding problems; for instance, Scammell was puzzled by two words, *chiy* and *kipets*. Guided by her own and her husband's experience in similar cases, Véra advises: "Please try to look up both *kipets* and *chiy* first in [the dictionary of] Dahl (he may have their Latin names); then, armed with the Latin names, try the Webster's new international dictionary." Among the dictionaries, both in English and Russian, that Scammell used during that project was a photo-reprint of Vladimir Dahl's pre-revolutionary four-volume dictionary, and a four-volume Soviet dictionary, though because of his travels he often made do with a one-volume Russian dictionary and a one-volume Russian-English dictionary. None of them would offer any meaningful clue this time and Scammell continued to seem frustrated:

> *Chiy* is in the latest Soviet dictionary but no Latin name is given. The only clue I could garner was that it is some kind of feather grass. *Kipets* remains a mystery. (I also checked these words in a botanical and in a general technical dictionary, by the way, and in neither were they given). (July 8, 1961)

Véra did not respond to another of Scammell's pleas ("I regret to say that I forgot to ask you about '*sartskiye yagtany*'"); the phrase later appeared as "Sartish yagtans" in the printed book. In any case, readers of Nabokov tend to value his prose for just this kind of occasional riddle, requiring a mental effort or a short consultation with an encyclopedia, so constant prompting might simply ruin the pleasure of little discoveries along the way.

Translating Lepidoptera, Idioms, and Dialects

More complicated issues eventually arose as well. The second chapter on Fyodor Godunov-Cherdyntsev's lepidopterist father and his expedition to Asia was the most difficult part of the novel to translate. Scammell checked the geographical names wherever possible in the Times Atlas and Gazetteer, and a few that were not listed he left for Nabokov to decide. Véra addressed further queries in her letter from July 16, 1961, advising that *Grobphilosophen* (in German) means "Grobianistic philosophers," or that "*Limitrophe* (adj. and n.)" will be found "in any large dictionary (e.g. Webster's New International), and the meaning is the same as in Russian. It was widely used to denote small countries along the Russian border, later swallowed by the USSR."

Typically Véra's explanations were succinct, ranging from a simple reference ("use the Russian word *muzhichok* [with the stress accent on—*chok*] which serves to illustrate Koltsov's anapaest. *Tryohdol'nik*—verse line in three-syllable feet"; "f3-g1 [this is a move of the knight in chess, according to the continental notation]") to a helpful idiomatic illustration: "'*prokatit' na voronyh*' [literal translation: 'to give someone a ride on black horses'] means in Russian 'to blackball,' in the sense of voting against by means of casting black balls. The next image is an allusion to the black balls hoisted on signal towers to indicate weather conditions" (August 12, 1961). Finding the right match for Russian proverbs usually proved to be tricky, especially when Nabokov deliberately twisted certain recognizable sayings, as in this case of: "*Nynche—pan, zavtra—papan.*" Véra comments: "the saying goes in reality '*libo pan libo propal*' [in Russian the phrase means 'sink or swim' or 'make or break' and reads literally: 'either master, or vanish']. My husband suggests here a distortion of another saying, put 'here today, goon tomorrow'."

Nabokov's wife revealed a great deal of knowledge of dialects and even of modern slang, although she warned at the same time that her suggestions should not be taken literally: "*Odnomu dazhe pustili 'gorokhovoe pal'to'*—and even the appellation 'plain clothes' was directed at one of them (I think, American slang for it is 'dick' but it could hardly be usable here"; "*Kanashechka*—'ducky'? 'piggy'? Derived from *kanal'ya* (Fr.: 'canaille'), a vulgar endearment of the time and set"; "No. The meaning goes something like that: 'So that is what it really amounts to, that vaunted freedom of yours!' (Perhaps you can make this more rustic in a corny way?) *yornicheskij*, incidentally, is 'corny'" (August 3, 1961).

In providing her answers Véra does not go into subtleties ("*Zhukovina*—not 'quid,' cigarettes. Of Zhukov tobacco is o.k."), but occasionally she would make an exception if she thought it might benefit the general reader. Here she explicates a particular poetic reminiscence: "Say: 'For the baby a meal, for the father a coffin,' he said, garbling Nekrasov,—and at any other time she would have taken offence, etc. (The line in Nekrasov goes: '*Grobik rebyonku i uzhin ottsu,*' which the wretched wife and mother brings home after prostituting herself)" (Ibid.).

At one point, Véra gave a mini-lecture on mythology in response to Scammell's questions concerning Chapter Four. In her appendix to the same letter dated August 3, 1961, she writes that "Phryna was a famous hetaera of the IV cent. B.C., a beauty who had served as model to many statues and pictures; Semiradski, a popular painter of the XIX cent., who specialized in 'pretty' pictures, made one of Phryna bathing." Resuming the lesson, she adds, however, that "if Phryna does not mean anything to the English reader, my husband suggests that you say 'fairies, hetaerae, fauns'; or, if this does not convey the meaning, put 'nymphs' for 'Phrynae'."

In the summer of 1962, when his relations with the Nabokovs were extremely cordial, Scammell had planned to meet the author in person to discuss the finished translation of *The Gift*. A year later, in the summer of 1963, Nabokov had still been intending to read the proofs of *The Gift*, but he wrote to say it would not be necessary (Scammell 60). In the foreword to the 1963 publication by G. P. Putnam's Sons (dated March 28, 1962) Nabokov asserts that he had "carefully revised the translation of all five chapters" at Montreux already "in the winter of 1961." Contrary to this statement, Brian Boyd demonstrates that Nabokov was still revising the last four-fifths of the translation between mid-January and mid-March of 1962, "spending up to seven hours a day on the task" (463). Considering the temporal discrepancy, it is possible that Nabokov had achieved his desired vision long before he let his young translator know about it. Nabokov thought it would be superfluous for Scammell to see the passages that had practically been rewritten, since this would further delay the already slow process.

I will proceed now to assess the nature and scope of Nabokov's revisions in the edited version of Scammell's manuscript, which was never shown to him; indeed, he had no idea of the thorough extent to which the final draft had been revised.

Nabokov's Revisions of Scammell

The novel had undergone at least two stages of linguistic metamorphosis: from the original to the first draft in English and from Scammell's advanced but still raw material to Nabokov's authorized version. Scammell's translation, totaling 435 pages, with Nabokov's heavy editing in red and black pencils over the typed text, has been preserved at the New York Public Library. The manuscript gives a clear picture of the techniques used and the stylistic choices made by Nabokov while polishing this titanic work.

Nabokov's revisions covered diversification of vocabulary; expanding and providing scientific terminology; adding stylistic effects and ensuring that the translated text was not flat and retained at least some of its original linguistic games; adjusting the alien context to his contemporary readership; and much more. In addition, Nabokov paid extraordinary attention to puns, translations of poetry, and neologisms which had to be either omitted as untranslatable word play or replicated as well as possible.

While Scammell was still advancing with the novel's translation, Nabokov answered various questions and solved minor linguistic issues occurring in the early chapters.

Diversification of Vocabulary

Nabokov's vocabulary in both Russian and English is astonishingly rich, and he expected his translator to mimic it masterfully. On the top of page 400 of Scammell's manuscript Nabokov supplies a long list of Russian synonyms for verbs depicting light, with their English equivalents: *glimmer, glow, gleam (small or interrupted), flash, shine, twinkle, sparkle, dazzle, coruscate*, and so on.

Chapter Six. ENGLISH TRANSLATION

p. 177.

sugar bowl I would pass my glass or a napkin ring. ~~In spite~~ Despite of my inexperienced desire to ~~translate~~ transpose into verse the ~~noise~~ murmur of love filling me (I would, I remember uncle Oleg saying ~~just that;~~ that if he were to publish a ~~collection~~ volume of poetry he would undoubtedly certainly call it "~~Noises of the Heart~~" Heart murmur ~~into verse~~, I was already building myself a had rigged up my own, albeit poor and primitive, wordsmithy ~~word workshop~~. Thus, in selecting adjectives I already was aware ~~innumerably~~ ~~intangible~~ knew that ones like "mysterious" or "meditative" would simply and C conveniently fill the yawning gap, which was longing to sing, word closing the line ("For we shall dream innumerable dreams") from the caesura to the final word; and again that for this last of only two syllables word one could take an additional adjective, ~~short, disyllabled~~, so so as to combine it with the long centerpiece ("Of loveliness intangible and tender") that I got, say, "mysterious and tender", a sound pattern, by the a melodic formula which, by the way, has had a quite disastrous effect on way, ~~which constitutes~~ a real disaster anent Russian poetry (and in Russian, as well as in French, poetry); ~~French too~~; I knew that handy adjectives of the amphibrachic type a trisyllable that one visualizes variety (~~i.e. those which one can imagine visually~~ in the shape the middle one dented of a sofa with three cushions - ~~with a dent in the middle one~~) in Russian enchanteds were legion, and how many such "dejecteds", "~~beloveds~~" and, rebellions ("tender") "~~defiants~~" I wasted; that ~~there were~~ we had also plenty of trochees; ("sorrowful") these somehow but far fewer dactyls, and ~~somehow they~~ all stood in profile; is adjectives that finally ~~anapestic~~ and iambs were on the rare side, and in rather dull incomplete forlorn addition always ~~tedious~~ and inflexible, like "~~discontent~~" or "~~intent~~". ones like I knew further that great long "incomprehensibles" and "infinitesimals" the bringing with them would come into tetrameters ~~complete with~~ their own orchestras, and unwanted and misunderstood that the combination "~~mysterious and discontent~~" gave a certain line moiré quality to the ~~tetrameter~~; look at it this way - it is an amphibrach, and that way - an iamb. A little later Andrey Byely's on "half-stresses" (the "comp" and the "ble" in the line "Incomprehensible desires") monumental research ~~on rhythm~~ hypnotised me with its system of "these scuds graphically marking off and calculating ~~secondary stresses~~, so that I immediately reread all my old tetrameters from this new point of Paucity of modulations. view and was terribly pained by the ~~predominance of the straight line~~,

[Ill. 6-2] Page 177 of the manuscript submitted to Nabokov by Michael Scammell (Berg Collection, New York Public Library)

—390—

Another distinctive mark of Nabokov's English is a "preference for precise terms" and specialized vocabulary. When revising an earlier English version, Grayson maintains, Nabokov "frequently replaces a simple English word with a more unfamiliar or specialized equivalent" (193). To establish an individual style and stamp it with difference and distinction, Nabokov was consciously "choosing to step out of the ordinary in his use of words and quite deliberately preferring the extraordinary" (Ibid). The words the author prefers are those of Latinate origin, technical terms, and custom-built or invented word forms. The subsequent list from *The Gift* is compiled based on Grayson's selections (194-95; once again, Nabokov's revisions follow the choices suggested by Scammell):

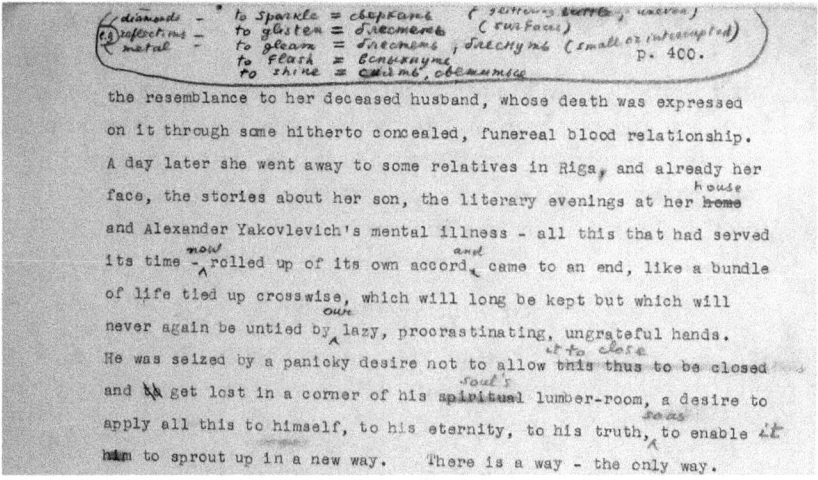

[Ill. 6-3] Page 400 of the manuscript submitted by Michael Scammell with Nabokov's revisions (Berg Collection, New York Public Library)

- "a pink pig-like paunch"/"pink *porcine* paunches" (G336);
- "Down the curved staircase"/"Down the *helical* stairs" (G163);
- "the intellectual life of a young dilettante member of the St. Petersburg literary set"/"the intellectual *habitus*" (G101);
- "then, coming right in"/"then, *ingressing* entirely" (G186);
- "The trellised touch of her salty lips through the veil"/"The *reticulate* touch of her salty lips through the veil" (G154).

To add to Grayson's examples, we have Nabokov's obvious preference for words with clear Latin origin: "incapable of expressing the marks of this kinship" (*Gift* typescript 390), which he substitutes for "incapable of formulating the *indicia* of this kinship" (G329) in the final version.

It was Edmund Wilson who cited the abundance of technical terms as an example of Nabokov's "addiction to rare and unfamiliar words" in his review of *Eugene Onegin* (1965). Nabokov countered this criticism in his "Reply to My Critics" (1966); since the English language "offers even greater resources of technical vocabulary than Russian, in his later writing Nabokov draws upon and exploits these resources" (Grayson 204). Here are several examples of how Nabokov substitutes rare words for more familiar ones in Scammell's draft:

- "showing the educated world the whole of his inside"/"showing the educated world all his *viscera*" (G247);
- "the size of a bent little finger"/"the size of a bent *auricular* finger" (G312);
- "spiritually progressive people understood that mere 'art' and the 'lyre' was not enough"/"spiritually progressive people understood that mere 'art' and the 'lyre' were not a sufficient *pabulum*" (G304);
- "Between the platform and foremost semicircle of the auditorium"/ "Between the platform and foremost *hemicycle* of the auditorium" (G258);
- "the specks of blood at their roots"/"the blood-red *maculation* at their roots" (G118); (all cited in Grayson 199).

Scientific Terminology

In Chapter Three, Scammell encountered a characteristic blizzard of butterfly names and was absolutely bewildered until Nabokov sent him a list of equivalents (the list is reproduced only partially):

Niobeya—Niobe Pritillary
Apollon—the small Black Apollo
Noclinitsa—moth
Krapivnitsa—Tortoiseshell
Golubyanka—a Blue (of a Blue)
Malayskiy sumerechnik—Malayan Hawkmoth
Arktidi—Arctidae
Pyadenitsa—Geometrid moth
Kavaler—Swallowtail
millioni belyanok—miriads of Pierids
Repeynitsa—the Painted Lady
Sovka—owlet
Satir—Satyrid
Boyarishnitsa—Black-veined White
Tsiganka—Burnet moth
Malen'kiy brazhnik—small hummingbird moth, etc., etc.
(July 5, 1961; Berg Collection)

Scammell was "determined to do better later with a long description of mushroom hunting" (Scammell 57), so he labored for several days and through several dictionaries to do the passage justice, but when the emended text came back Nabokov had simply erased the scene. "Mushroom hunting is a continental passion that means little to Anglo-Saxons" (Ibid.). If it did not refer to butterflies, the exact name was often not a priority for Nabokov; in one instance, Scammell was at a loss for the right English term for *podosinoviy grib* — and Véra responded: "put merely 'an edible mushroom'" (July 5, 1961). She might have known that the latter kind of a mushroom, in fact, is an orange-cap boletus (*Leccidium aurantiacum*), but apparently either no dictionary at that moment was available at her fingertips, or the reasons again were purely pragmatic.

There were miniature lessons on Russian verbs of motion and extensive instruction on botany, zoology, entomology, and every possible aspect of natural history. "A wild orchid" which "bloomed unceremoniously in a patch of marshy ground" (*Gift* typescript 89) Nabokov transforms into "a bog orchis," also known as *Platanthera dilatata* (G79).

Stylistic Effects

In her discussion of sound instrumentation and word-play in Nabokov's writings, Jane Grayson remarks that, when translating his own work, the author "quite often values the retention of the stylistic effect more highly than the retention of meaning. In [Nabokov's] translation of alliteration and onomatopoeia, he will often modify and change his meaning in order to give an equivalent auditive effect" (176-77). Although it is hard to agree with Grayson's assessment in this particular case (a thorough study of *The Gift* typescript shows Nabokov's diverse approaches in the aspects of rendering both stylistic and semantic effects), a few examples that she cites might help substantiate the observations. Scammell's literal translation precedes the one that Nabokov chooses in the final version:

- "twilight Siberian years"/"somber Siberian years" (G219);
- "with equally respectable seriousness"/"with equally stolid seriousness" (G239);
- "as if it had turned from a partition into a gap"/"as if it had turned from a partition into a pit" (G252).

Sometimes Nabokov succeeds "in rendering the sense as well as contriving a play on the same consonants," but more frequently, he "renders the sense and provides alliteration on *different* consonants":

- "kogda druzhba byla *vel*ikodushna i *vl*azhna"/"when friendship was generous and moist"/"when friendship was *m*agna*n*i*m*ous and *m*oist" (G220);

- "*rez*kost'iu *vz*gliadov i *raz*viaznost'iu maner"/"with the sharpness of his views and the undue familiarity of his manner"/"with the h*arshness* of his *views* and the b*rashness* of his *ways*" (G232) (Grayson 178).

More rarely, Nabokov makes a play on the same consonant: "dol*bia*shchii, *bub*niashchii zvuk slov"/"the battering and harping sound of the words"/"the dru*bb*ing-in, *rubb*ing-in tone of each word" (G194). In general Grayson's study corroborates Proffer's commentary in his analysis of *Lolita* upon the "sound-determined" quality of Nabokov's style (*Keys to Lolita* 82-97). The scholar develops Proffer's thesis further by showing this to be a prominent feature not only in Nabokov's original writing but also in translation (Grayson 179).

At the same time Nabokov did not intend to give the exact equivalents to the Russian sound orchestration for each individual case, and at times deliberately saved the original words—providing transcriptions in parenthesis. There was one passage in which Scammell tried to emulate Fyodor's Russian rhyme scheme in English. Preserving the original rhythm and wordplay was challenging:

> 'Crying' immediately suggested lying and dying under sighing pines on a silent night. 'Waterfall' prompted his muse to recall some long forgotten ball. 'Flowers' called for hours about bowers which were ours, and so on for the better part of a page.

Nabokov carefully read through Scammell's suggestions and resisted the temptation to convert the original into a series of "crying/lying/dying" rhymes, and sent back the following:

> "*Letuchiy* (flying) immediately grouped *tuchi* (clouds) over the *kruchi* (steeps) of the *zhguchey* (burning) desert and of *neminuchey* (inevitable) fate" (Scammell 56).

In accordance with the principle that Nabokov himself applied in his translation of *Eugene Onegin*, the collaborator was not to diverge from the servile path even for a moment.

Linguistic Games

Interlinguistic puns are numerous in *The Gift*. During the Émigré Writers' meeting Fyodor reflects on the fact that the pseudonym chosen by one of his colleagues—"Foma Mur"—contains "a complete French novel, a page of English literature, and a touch of Jewish skepticism" (G321). This associative leap is entirely characteristic of the "Joycean" manner (Tammi 87); in French the pseudonym can be understood as a combination of two words: femme (*lady*) and amour (*love*); besides this, it alludes to an Irish Romantic poet

Thomas Moore (1779–1852), whose Russified first name reads as "Foma," as well as to Thomas the Apostle, also called Doubting Thomas [Jn. 20:24-29] (Dolinin, *Kommentarii* 763). Scammell faithfully translated the name as "Thomas Moore," but Nabokov restores the ambiguity: *Fama Mour* (*Gift* typescript 386), and in the English translation adds all the missing information in brackets.

Discussing Nabokov's multilingual puns, Alexander Nakhimovsky observes that "sometimes Nabokov smuggles in a borrowing [from a foreign language], masking it as a native word. The result is a multilingual pun, a phenomenon well known to readers of Nabokov's English-language novels. Usually the characters remain innocent of the author's intentions; in other cases characters explain things to the reader. Godunov-Cherdyntsev compares the Russian *blago* "good" with the French *blague*" ["trick," "joke"] (Nakhimovsky 80).

Nabokov omits this particular pun (*blago/blague*) from the passage in question—it is, however, compensated for by a number of other dazzling equivalents (G352). Fyodor falls asleep but continues inventing senseless rhymed patterns in mind:

> Как всегда, на грани сознания и сна всякий словесный брак, блестя и звеня, вылез наружу: хрустальный хруст той ночи христианской под хризолитовой звездой...— и прислушавшаяся на мгновение мысль, в стремлении прибрать и использовать, от себя стала добавлять: и умер исполин яснополянский, и умер Пушкин молодой...— а так как это было ужасно, то побежала дальше рябь рифмы: и умер врач зубной Шполянский, астраханский, ханский, сломал наш Ганс кий...Ветер переменился, и пошло на зе: изобразили и бриз из Бразилии, изобразили и ризу грозы... тут был опять кончик, доделанный мыслью, которая опускалась все ниже в ад аллигаторских аллитераций, в адские кооперативы слов, не 'благо', а 'blague'. (Dar 527)

Scammell translates this tricky passage with erudition and tact (Nabokov's later interpolations are added in bold type and his omissions during the revision process are underlined in curly brackets):

> As always on the border between consciousness and sleep all sorts of verbal marriages [**rejects**], sparkling and tinkling, crept out [**broke in**]: "The crystal crunching of that Christian night beneath a chrysolitic star"...and his thought, listening for a moment, aspired to gather them {in} and use them and began to add of its own: and dead is the Yasnopolyanski mammoth, and dead is Pushkin in his youth... [**Extinguished, Yasnaya Polyana's light, and Pushkin dead, and Russia far...**] but since this was horrible the rippling of rhymes ran further [no good, the stipple of rhymes extended further]: and dead is the dentist Jan Shpoliansky, Astrahanski, you've broken that man's key [**NOTE: Scammell actually attempts to provide his own rhyme; the Russian text literally says here: "our Gans broke a billiard cue"**] ["A falling star, a cruising chrysolite,

an aviator's avatar..."] {The wind changed and it went to "zee": a zebra zat in the Zuider zoo and freezing breezes froze his toes... here was another ending reached by thought, which sank} [**His mind sank**] lower and lower into a hell of alligator alliterations, into hellish [**infernal**] cooperatives of words. (*Gift* typescript 418/G352)

Nabokov heavily edits Scammell's text, looking for the most apt equivalents for his own "infernal cooperatives of words"; among other things, he decides to let go an interesting "zee" experiment ("a zebra zat in the Zuider zoo") altogether.

Most of Nabokov's revisions, of course, bear the writer's genius, as in the following funny rendition of Shchyogolev's anti-Semitic rubbish, when he says, "for instance, to a guest who had left traces on the carpet: 'Oh, what a tracer you are!'" (*Gift* typescript 222); in Russian: "*govoria mokromu gostiu, nasledivshemu na kovre: 'oi, kakoi vy naslednik!*'" [the essence of the joke here is that "*naslednik*," i.e. "an heir," can be read as the distorted noun based on the similarly sounding verb "*nasledit',*" meaning "to leave traces"]. Nabokov coins a witty pun instead, joining the English "mud" and Yiddish "nudnik" plus imitating the "Jewish" accent ("vat" instead of "what"): "in imitation of a farcical Jewish accent as when he said, for instance, to a wet guest who had left traces on the carpet: 'Oy, vat a mudnik!'" (G188).

Puns

Even though in his adaptation of the original puns Nabokov often sacrifices the exact wording, he preserves the semantics and tonality of the message. For instance, in the phrase "From Pan to Simplicissimus" (*Dar* 510) Nabokov removes the title of the satirical German weekly magazine (published since 1896), which would have meant little to English-language readers, and changes it to the British equivalent: "From Pan to Punch" (G335), which works even more effectively due to the alliterative pattern.

In the scene of the Shchyogolevs' departure, Boris cries to Zina: "Sarotska, telegrafui!" (*Dar* 532; distorted name and ungrammatical verb literally mean: "Sarotska, send a telegram"). Since there is a clear anti-Semitic undercurrent embedded (a parody of a Yiddish-type pronunciation or, possibly, a direct quote from some Jewish anecdote of the period), Nabokov, who wants to retain some of the original meaning in the English address, chooses the following rhymed linguistic absurdity: "Sarotska, Sarotska, send us a telegramotska!" (G357).

Because puns in *The Gift* and Nabokov's other prose works of the late 1930s exploit the positions of single letters, similarities of sound, and ambiguous meanings of words, it becomes extremely difficult to render those qualities of the original in translation to any language. As Nassim Berdjis expertly demonstrates, Fyodor "disintegrates and recomposes" words by "mixing elements of an anagrammatic recombination of letters and of homophonic congruency" (167). There is an example of a word "*pas ta loque*" (*Dar* 524), which in translation becomes "ceiling" (G349). The chain of metamorphosis is as follows: Nabokov "replaces the first syllable by its homophone 'sea,' thus creating 'sealing' and 'sea-ling.' Further distance from the original term comes about by anagrammatic change of the first syllable ('ice-ling') and of the whole word ('inglice') (Nabokov's hand-written comment in pencil; *Gift* typescript 414). This method of distancing oneself from the original word works similarly in Russian. The Russian word '*potolok*' ('ceiling') turns into a translingual homophone, the French expression "pas ta loque.' Shifting the stress from the third to the second syllable produces a '*patolog*' [i.e. 'pathologist'] thus keeping the correct pronunciation of the first and the last vowel, but pronouncing the otherwise unstressed second 'o' (Berdjis 167).

Another example cited by Berdjis comes from the end of the novel, in the scene when Fyodor observes the banners displayed during a public festival in Berlin. One of the flags features the misspelled phrase: "Za Serb i Molt!" (*Dar* 533), literally: "For Serbs and Molts!" (Grammatically this can be read as two plural animate nouns in the accusative case; it is a misspelling of "*Za Serp i Molot*": "For the Hammer and Sickle"). Since the mistake is "obvious for a Russian native speaker, the original text lacks these explanations, but it adds Fyodor's reaction, [who] perceives '*serb*' as the Russian word for 'Serb' and wonders, where a '*molt*' lives" (Berdjis 167). In English the only way to retain the wordplay is through the addition of the appropriate clarifications in parenthesis: "*serb* instead of *serp* (sickle) and *molt* instead of *molot* (hammer)" (G358).

WHAT HAD TO BE COMPROMISED?

Adjustments to a Foreign Context

It was not only the English-speaking readership that lacked the necessary contextual frame of reference while navigating through the text of *The Gift*: Russian readers over the years were also becoming less conversant with the recent past. Realizing this, Nabokov deleted from the 1952 Russian version of *The Gift* a reference to Yasha Chernyshevski as "a blend of Lenskii and Kannegiser" ("*Smes' Lenskogo i Kannegisera*"). As Jane Grayson explains, it was evidently done because the mention of Kannegiser, the student who shot the Chief of the Petrograd Secret Police Moisei Uritsky in 1918, would not be as relevant to the Russian reader of the 1950s as it was in the 1930s (Grayson 308). Still, as Anat Ben-Amos suggests, "this comparison contains an emphasis on the cultural-symbolic nature" of Yasha's story; it reflects the Romantic-desperate nature of his suicide, which is reminiscent of Lensky's death in Pushkin's *Eugene Onegin*, and thus establishes "an intertextual bridge" (Ben-Amos 126).

In the English version of the novel Nabokov offers more contextual guidance to readers. One such case transpires in Fyodor's discussion with Koncheyev of the problem of the audience faced by the émigré writer: "Who knows my poems?" asks Koncheyev. The answer in the Russian version is:

> One hundred, one hundred and fifty, at most, at most, two hundred intelligent expatriates, of whom again ninety per cent don't understand them. That's provincial success, but not fame. (*Dar* 516)

David Rampton points out that "these figures increase by a factor of ten in the English translation, and Nabokov adds the sentence: 'Two thousand out of three million refugees!' (G341). He regularly helps the English reader out with bits of information of this kind, but only very rarely changes actual points of detail in a translation that is not a substantial reworking of the original" (Rampton 97). Most likely, as Rampton suggests, Nabokov made the adjustment because he thought the second set of figures more realistic, although "the point about a paucity of receptive readers is essentially the same in both versions" (Ibid.).

Omissions Due to Untranslatable Word Play

In many cases *Dar* cannot be adequately translated into any foreign language. Especially problematic are the phrases incorporating idiomatic speech or quoted material such as this: "*Ot stikhov ona trebovala tol'ko iamshchiknegoniloshadeinosti*" [ямщикнегонилошадейности] (*Dar* 260). The last monstrous noun is actually made up of four words in one, and it is a citation of an old song, allegedly part of the gypsy tradition. Nabokov does not even try to emulate his own Russian tour de force, communicating the idea in this statement: "Her taste in poetry was limited to fashionable gypsy lyrics" (G75). Alexander Nakhimovsky, nevertheless, offers a fairly interesting English translation that provides a more or less literal approximation of the Russian original: "From poetry she demanded only 'coachman-don't-chase-the-horses-ness'" (80).

Yet another example of untranslatability is found in the description of the émigré scribbler named Shirin. In Russian he is characterized in a beautiful acoustically and metaphorically orchestrated comparative tirade:

> "Slep kak Mil'ton, glukh kak Betkhoven, i glup kak beton" (Nabokov, *Dar* 490; literally: "blind as Milton, deaf as Beethoven, and stupid as concrete," with the wordplay stemming from the fact that the Russian word beton is a hybrid of the two artists' names)

Scammell suggested an interesting rendering:

> "He was as blind as Milton, deaf as Beethoven, and daft as a baton" (*Gift* typescript 373).

Nabokov disapproved this and proposed his alliterative version:

> "He was blind like Milton, deaf like Beethoven, and a blockhead to boot" (G315).

The reason Nabokov chooses the last phrase is not only phonetic (*Bee—blo—boo*), but most probably because it is actually a quote from Chapter XVI of his beloved *Don Quixote* (which he had taught about at Cornell University a few years earlier). While putting spurs to Rocinante, the hero cries:

> "You are a saucy publican and a *blockhead to boot*" (Cervantes 406).

Tobias Smollet's rollicking English translation of Miguel de Cervantes's novel first appeared in 1755; the same phrase was preserved in later editions.

The exclamation involving a dull-witted personage being compared to great historical figures (each with some famous physical deficiency), appears to be the only addition that Nabokov had made to the text of *The Gift* when preparing the 1952 Russian edition for the Chekhov Press. It might have been influenced by a somewhat similar formula found in Ilf and Petrov's satiric novel *Zolotoi telenok* (*The Little Golden Calf*, 1931). There Ostap Bender bursts forth with a rhetorical tirade: "There's another great blind man—Panikovsky! Homer, Milton and Panikovsky! What a bunch of rogues!.." (Chapter 12, "Homer, Milton and Panikovsky"; my translation).

Poetry Translations

When Dmitri tried his hand at translating the poems from Russian in Chapter One, Nabokov did not find the results adequate. Fyodor's versification in the original is not overly sophisticated; nonetheless Nabokov constructed it painstakingly—with all its inherent imperfections—at a point when he was already a mature poet himself. This, coupled with his son's early poor drafts, was the reason Nabokov decided to translate all the poetry in *The Gift* by himself. Let us examine just one sample poem ascribed to Fyodor:

> Мяч закатился мой под нянин
> комод, и на полу свеча
> тень за концы берет и тянет
> туда, сюда, — но нет мяча.

> Потом там кочерга кривая
> гуляет и грохочет зря —
> и пуговицу выбивает,
> а погодя полсухаря.
> Но вот выскакивает сам он
> в трепещущую темноту, —
> через всю комнату, и прямо
> под неприступную тахту.
>
> *(Dar 197-98)*

Compare this to Dmitri's version (on the left) and the revised, final poem:

My ball has rolled in back of Nurse's Commode; the candle's lowered flame Tugs at the shadow's ends, traversing This way and that—the ball remains. And, afterwards, the crooked poker Explores and clatters, all in vain— It yields a button with its stroke, and Later half a toast obtains. But look—the ball darts out, unaided, Into the palpitating night, Spans the whole room, and stops, blockaded For good beneath the sofa's might. *(Gift* typescript 13)	My ball has rolled under Nurse's commode. On the floor a candle Tugs at the ends of the shadows This way and that, but the ball is gone. Then comes the crooked poker. It potters and clatters in vain, Knocks out a button And then half a zwieback. Suddenly out darts the ball Into the quivering darkness, Crosses the whole room and promptly goes under The impregnable sofa. (G10)

It is not difficult to guess what Nabokov did not like in the first translation, especially in the light of his own theory of literal translation. First of all, to Dmitri's credit, his treatment of the verse is quite careful: he preserves the original structure, even an enjambment in the second line (postponing the word "commode" which Nabokov, for the sake of smoother reading, has restored to the first line in later revision). On the other hand, a few spots in the translation were obscure. The phrase "the ball remains" in place of the Russian "there is no ball" becomes in Nabokov's redaction "the ball is gone." "The sofa's might" sounds odd, whereas the Russian uses one adjective *nepristupnaia* (which can be translated as "unassailable," "unattackable," "inviolable," or "invulnerable"). Nabokov chooses the most appropriate word—*impregnable*—with connotations of a castle or fortress which one is unable to break into or take by force during a game.

Fyodor's poetic style is simple and straightforward and, therefore, Nabokov replaces Dmitri's elaborate vignettes with short active verbal constructs ("yields a button with its stroke" becomes "Knocks out a button"). At the same time, Nabokov finds the word *toast* too easy or too American, so he mercilessly replaces it with the German synonym, *zwieback*, though in the original text of the novel the word is, in fact, Russian (*polsukharia*).

Dmitri's attempt to maintain the rhyme scheme was largely successful (Nurse's // traversing; Flame // remains; remains // obtains, unaided // blockaded, night // might, etc.). As seen from the end result, Nabokov does not care about the "beauty" and eliminates most of the rhymes in favor of semantic accuracy.

When Scammell joined the project, the author had already made a categorical decision to keep their collaboration limited to translation of prose only.

Striving for Clarity of Expression

Nabokov seeks the utmost clarity, for direct and elegant prose rhythm: not only does he often cross out the patronymic *Konstantinovich*, which is long and difficult to pronounce for any average English-language reader, but he also ensures that the whole cadence of each sentence is clear and straightforward. In the description of Fyodor's quick morning routine (a three-second dressing) Scammell faithfully renders the Russian sentence structure: "he took a traveling rug under his arm, wrapping his swim-trunks inside it" (*Gift* typescript 388); Nabokov deletes "traveling rug" to insert a more accurate term, "lap robe"; he takes out "inside" and changes the grammatical form of the verb: "under his arm, with his swim-trunks *wrapped* in it" (G327). This example shows how Nabokov, by a slight paraphrase of what is already available in Scammell's rough draft, imparts dynamic sense to a fairly long sentence.

Here is another illustration of the same technique: "At that moment a black hearse, which yesterday had been standing outside a repair shop, came cautiously out of some neighboring gates..." (*Gift* typescript 388). Nabokov feels that the beginning slows down the scene; therefore he gets rid of "At that moment," starting with "A black hearse..." in order to emphasize the motion. He substitutes then the neutral verb "come out" with the more appropriate in this case "roll out"; an adjective "neighboring" provides unnecessary information cluttering the sentence which, otherwise, should completely focus on smooth motion. In a final redaction we get a simple and expressive phrase: "rolled cautiously out of a gate" (G328).

Contrary to what one might presume, Nabokov does not always "beautify" the translation with an eye towards its aesthetic dimensions: thus, he firmly revises Scammell's delicate "fresh dog's stool" (*Gift* typescript 388) to "fresh excrements of a dog" (G328).

With his virtually unsurpassed knowledge of the biological and zoological vocabulary, Nabokov carefully revisits Scammell's choices related to flora and fauna, and ensures that the species are named correctly: "thickets of acacia and osiers" (*Gift* typescript 388) becomes "a growth of locusts and sallows" (G328), etc.

Mistakes

As the translation of *The Gift* was advancing, some inevitable misprints in the Russian edition came to light. Véra pointed out a few such instances: "There is a bad misprint in the Russian text...It should be *zapah*, not *zapas* [*smell*, not *stock*]. For the rest your translation is correct. This smell reminds a Russian of the stench of a squashed bedbug (see further, '*klopovonyayushchiy*')"; "*Priznaki kalanchevykh ballov*—there is a misprint in Russian text: *priznaki* should be *prizraki* [i.e. *signs* should be *ghosts*]" (August 3, 1961; Berg Collection).

On a few occasions Scammell was not aware of an accepted term (Nabokov revises his awkward *Transactions of the Wise Men of Zion* into *Protocols of the Sages of Zion*; *Gift* typescript 220), or simply did not understand Nabokov's text. The author had carefully edited those few blunders (like a phrase "standing on tiptoe" [*na noskakh*], which Scammell confused with its homonym and delivered a comic phrase "standing in his socks"; Ibid. 386).

Speaking of socks and tiptoes, not every obscure passage should be treated as an error on the part of the writer or translator. Peter-John Thomas draws our attention to the episode of Fyodor's buying a pair of new shoes in the Berlin shop ("A young woman in a black dress [...] addressed Fyodor's large, shy, poorly darned foot"; G64). He complains that "no one notices—even during the process of translating this laboriously descriptive passage" that Fyodor's *foot* is poorly darned; "a foot may be large, and it may be shy, but even an anthropomorphized foot cannot be darned without having been wounded first" (Thomas 121). The scholar believes that this is one of those rare details that put "the Nabokov scholar in a quandary. Nabokov's texts are logically consistent and coherent. Everything has its place and function. This detail seems *not* to fit" (Ibid.). There is nothing extraordinary illogical in this image or in a poetic figure of speech akin to a simile, moreover this type of construction is quite typical for Nabokov's style (especially considering the fact that in one of the sequences Fyodor's mother is shown "easily and skillfully...darning and mending his pitiful things" (G94; noted by Thomas himself). Scammell's typescript reinforces this supposition: neither the translator nor the author found this place unusual—the only thing that Nabokov revised was an epithet—"poorly darned" instead of "badly" (*Gift* typescript 97).

The same Peter-John Thomas does, however, mention a much more curious parallel from Kozma Prutkov, the nineteenth-century fictional author of satirical verses, invented by Aleksei Konstantinovich Tolstoy and his cousins, who once stated: "The poet's imagination, dispirited by grief, is *like a foot confined in*

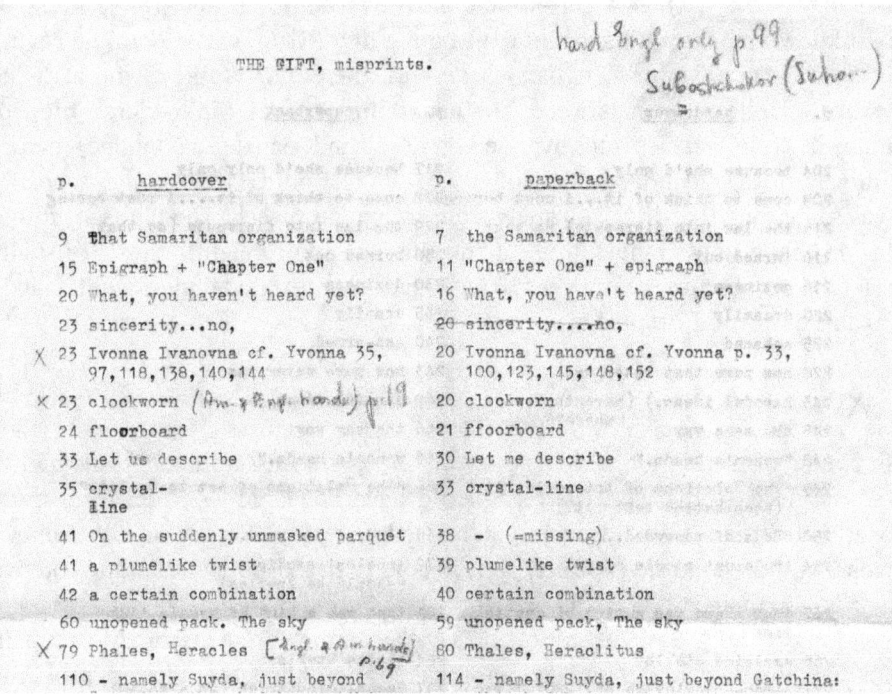

[Ill. 6-4] Vladimir Nabokov's list of misprints in the first English edition of *The Gift* (Courtesy of Division of Rare and Manuscript Collections, Cornell University)

a new boot" (Prutkov in Thomas's translation; Ibid.). Godunov-Cherdyntsev's imagination tries various subjects and styles, and often acquires surprising forms and exchanges distant echoes with variegated poetic traditions.

Another subtext possibly derives from Blaise Pascal's *Pensées*, a philosophical treatise that served as an important backdrop for *The Gift*, as will be shown later: "*Heel of a shoe*. How well shaped it is! How skilful that craftsman is!.. Here is the source of our inclinations and our choice of situations" (*Pensées and Other Writings* 15). Fyodor's choice is an ultimate one: "With this, with this I'll step ashore. From Charon's ferry" (G64).

On rare occasions, mistakes were added by Nabokov himself in the process of revising the translation. For example, when he tries to explicate the author of a quote, "God, let us not see a Russian riot / Senseless and merciless," unnamed for obvious reasons in the Russian original, the 1963 edition of *The Gift* has an insertion: "Pushkin's *History of the Pugachyov Rebellion*" (G97). This is, of course, a grave error, possibly caused by Nabokov's haste in the revisions: the real source is not the 1834 historical study by Pushkin, but his later novel, *The Captain's Daughter* (1836). The same slip happens when Nabokov relies on his memory and attributes a certain axiom to Ivan Krylov (1769–1844), Russia's best known fabulist: "this is a lion and not a dog (Krilov)" (G172). The saying is cited during Fyodor's English lesson with the editor Vasiliev, who asks the tutor for "a literal translation of the usual phrases found in leaders." Indeed, many of Krylov's fables (loosely based on Aesop and Jean de La Fontaine) feature animals, dogs, and indeed a lion, but this particular phrase ("*Se lev, a ne sobaka*") was something that Nabokov knew from colloquial speech. The phrase is found in M. Mikhelson's compendium of the Russian and foreign idioms: it usually refers to an obscure creative work that requires an explanation of what exactly its author meant to express.[36]

Neologisms

In course of translation, the majority of Nabokov's Russian neologisms had to be sacrificed—otherwise the text would have appeared to critics even more overloaded than it was ultimately perceived in reality. For instance, Nabokov's wonderful metaphoric product, *benzinopoy*, is based on the blending of two words—a modern *benzokolonka* for "gas station," and a classical *vodopoi* denoting "pond." "Say 'gas station' or 'service station,'" Véra instructs Scammell, thus eliminating the secondary poetic denotation altogether (letter from July 16, 1961).

Some contemporary Russian readers frowned upon Nabokov's neologisms in *The Gift*. Petr Pil'skii, who reviewed Chapter One, was one of them: "As are many writers, [Nabokov] is nauseated by customary, overused, tired words. He wants new ones—words and epithets" (Pil'skii 3; for complete text of this review see the next chapter). The critic cites: "They are not menacing but 'mean-aching' in the editorial office [*ne grozili razgromom, a grazhivali*]" (G61). "*Grazhivali razgromom*" literally means "threatened with rout." Even Dmitri Nabokov, as the papers preserved at the Cornell library archive testify, did not quite understand this word and had to consult with his father. Having received these clarifications, Dmitri listed them on a piece of hotel stationery from Le Montreux Palace: *grazhivali* derives from *grozili* ["to threaten," past tense]. (Other explanations from the same sheet: *zapoem* from *pit' zapoem* [be a heavy drinker]; *rozval'ni* = sled type; *dat' drapu* = "*ubezhat*" ["to run away," "to escape"]).

---

[36] See, *Russkaja mysl' i rech'. Svoe i chuzhoe. Opyt russkoi frazeologii. Sbornik obraznyh slov i inoskazanii*. Vol. 1-2. *Khodiachie i metkie slova. Sbornik russkikh i inostrannykh tsitat, poslovits, pogovorok, poslovichnykh vyrazhenii i otdel'nykh slov* (St. Petersburg: Tipographiia Akademii Nauk, 1896-1912). Both errors were spotted by Alexander Dolinin, to whom I am grateful for pointing them out to me. The future English-language text of *The Gift* in print should be edited accordingly.

Translation as a Form of Self-Commentary

Marina Grishakova believes that "Nabokov's revisions of the translation may be treated not only as a mere adaptation of the Russian text for American readers, but also serve as a form of self-commentary (both on the level of language and to the self *per se*)" (Grishakova 313). Keeping in mind this thesis, I will continue to examine the passage that so annoyed Petr Pil'skii. In it Nabokov presents the daily business of the Russian émigré newspaper and of its editorial office. Initially Dmitri Nabokov translates this passage almost literally (on the right):

…восьмой этаж, где в конце серого как пластелин коридора, в узкой комнатке, пахнувшей "разлагавшимся трупом злободневности" (как острил первый комик редакции), сидел секретарь, лунообразный флегматик, без возраста и словно без пола, не раз спасавший положение, когда граживаали разгромом недовольные той или другой заметкой,—какие-нибудь местные платные якобинцы или свой брат, шуан, здоровенный прохвост из мистиков. (*Dar* 247)	…the ninth floor [above the line DN types in a question: "in Europe 8th = 9th??"] where at the end of a corridor the color of gray modeling clay, in a narrow little room smelling "of the decaying corpse of actuality" (as the number-one comic in the office cracked), sat the secretary, a moonlike, phlegmatic man, ageless and virtually sexless, who had more than once saved the day when people angry about some article or other threatened annihilation—some local [professional?] hired Jacobins, or his own brother, a Chouan, a tremendous scoundrel and a mystic. (*Gift* typescript 93)

Nabokov substantially rewrote the ending of the scene. The final version is as follows:

> …the ninth floor, where at the end of a corridor the color of gray modeling clay, in a narrow little room smelling of "the decaying corpse of actuality" (as the number one office comic used to crack), sat the secretary, a moon-like, phlegmatic person, ageless and virtually sexless, who had more than once saved the day when, *angered by some item* in Vasiliev's *liberal* paper, *menacing rowdies would come, German Trotskyists hired locally, or some robust Russian Fascist, a rogue and a mystic*. (G61)

Replacing "man" with "person" in the description of the "sexless" creature or leaving the "ninth" instead of the "eighth" floor as unimportant detail is understandable; but then Nabokov decides that allusions to the French history might be less resonant with contemporary American readership. Hence he uproots this associative layer altogether and substitutes it with allusions to the recent past—the Stalinist terror and Nazi fascism. The original reference in Russian was aimed at the radical revolutionaries known as Jacobins; the Chouannerie was a royalist uprising against the French Revolution and the First French Republic (1794–1800). The namesake of the insurrection, Jean Chouan, was a counter-revolutionary and a staunch royalist, who led the revolt together with his brother (*cf.*: "his own brother, a Chouan" in *The Gift*). This rebellion is featured in the novels *Les Chouans* by Honoré de Balzac, and in Victor Hugo's *Ninety-Three* (*Quatrevingt-treize*).

In a characteristically Nabokovian way, this last *literary connection* seems to provide a possible link to the parallel set of associations unraveling in the English version: that Hugo's novel made a deep impression on Stalin was well known; in 1896, a young Georgian seminarian named Dzhugashvili was sentenced to a lengthy confinement for reading the forbidden book, *Ninety-Three* (Boobbyer 101). But the next step for Nabokov is to recode the French context to the Russian/German context. Hence he preserves the antinomy and specifies the political orientation of the émigré newspaper (adding an epithet: "Vasiliev's *liberal* paper") in order to contrast it with belligerent opposition represented by counter-revolutionaries (in Stalin's official rhetoric) of the Trotskyist movement in Imperial Germany. "Russian Fascists" would be the third party, an adversary of the previous two—liberal and communist: in 1933, after Hitler and the Nazis rose to power, the German Trotskyist group had been labeled an "illegal organization."

Some of Nabokov's comments on the margins of Scammell's typescript are helpful for interpretation of the novel in general; for example, next to the episode of Busch's reading of a metaphysical hodgepodge, Nabokov remarks: "Busch in his grotesque way expresses a deep and important theory, and its meaning should be brought out clearly, despite the ranting." Busch says that his

> "...novel is the tragedy of a philosopher who has discovered the absolute formula. He starts speaking and speaks thus [Busch, like a conjurer, plucked a notebook out of the air and began to read on the move]: 'One has to be a complete ass not to deduct from the fact of the atom the fact that the universe itself is merely an atom, or, it would be truer to say, some kind of trillionth of an atom. This was realized with his intuition already by that genius Blaise Pascal!..'" (G209)

Indeed, one can discern here a maxim from *Pensées* (*Thoughts*) by the French mathematician and Catholic philosopher Blaise Pascal (1623–62): "The whole visible world is only an imperceptible atom in the ample bosom of nature. No idea approaches it. We may enlarge our conceptions beyond all imaginable space; we only produce atoms in comparison with the reality of things. It is an infinite sphere, the centre of which is everywhere, the circumference nowhere" (Pascal 21; see Grishakova 313).

Divan vs. Sofa: The Power of Persuasion

When Scammell received the heavily edited Chapters Two and Three from Nabokov, he reviewed the manuscript and sent it back along with a detailed list of responses. Scammell advised the author on further embellishments and, in many instances, disagreed with Nabokov's alterations to the fruits of his labor. All in all, Nabokov accepted only four of Scammell's suggestions (from a total of 64!). This unequivocally demonstrates that in the matters of English language Nabokov did not recognize anyone's authority but his own, and trusted only his personal instincts.

One of the revisions that Nabokov did accept was the substitution of the word "sofa" for "divan" in the third chapter, in the scene describing Fyodor's poetic experiments: "I knew that handy adjectives of the amphibrachic type (a trisyllable that one visualizes in the shape of a *divan* with three cushions — the middle one dented) were legion in Russian — and how many such 'dejécted,' 'enchánted' and 'rebéllious' I wasted..." (G151). Scammell argued against Nabokov's revision passionately:

> "Divan" may mean any kind of couch in Russian, but in English it can mean only one thing: a flat bed without headboard or back, so that it can be completely covered up and used as a couch (I am looking at ours at this minute). A true "couch" is also flat, but with a half-back and head-end (usually an arm-rest), usually used for both sleeping and sitting (especially on the continent). We also have one of these. The only word in English that could possibly fit your (so apt) image of three cushions with an amphibrachic dent in the middle is a "sofa." A sofa has cushions (usually three), a high back and arm-rests at either end and is usually intended mainly for sitting, although it too (and again especially on the continent) can be used for sleeping. Thus although "divan" in Russian can he used to describe any one of these three things, you have to be careful to distinguish in English. In chapter one (*cf.* your notes) it is relatively unimportant, I assume, whether thing has a back to it or not, or whether it has cushions, so you can call it a divan and no-one will mind, but here the very image depends on the presence of cushions and it must be rendered by "sofa." (Incidentally, I personally visualize Fyodor as always sleeping on a sofa or couch in his various lodgings and cannot see him on a divan.) (April 19, 1962; Berg Collection, NYPL)

The young translator's reasoning had convinced his correspondent concerning "divan," but Nabokov remained unmoved with the other sixty cases, dismissing Scammell's at times mentoring tone and often equally demonstrative evidence.

                   evanesced in the stretch
chest. This scent ~~dwindled~~ from linden to linden, being replaced there
                                      the next canopy,
by a black freshness, and then again, beneath a ~~waiting tent, a~~
an oppressive and
heady, ~~intoxicating~~ cloud would accumulate, and Zina would say,
tensing
~~straining~~ her nostrils: "Ah, smell it," and again the darkness
    drained of savor   would be heavy with   Will it really happen
would be ~~fresh~~ and again ~~was bathed in~~ honey. ~~The leaden threat~~
to-night? Will it really happen now? The weight and the threat of bliss.
~~of happiness.~~ When I walk with you like this, ~~slowly-slowly, and~~
ever so slowly, and   my head hums
hold you by the shoulder, everything slightly sways, ~~there is a roar~~
                                                           falls
~~in my head~~ and I feel like dragging my feet; my left slipper ~~slips~~
                                                                                                                                  shall
off my heel, we crawl, dawdle, dwindle in a mist — now we are almost
all melted... And one day we ~~will~~ recall all this — the lindens and
                                                              a
the shadow on the wall, and ~~somebody's~~ poodle's unclipped claws
tapping over the flagstones of the night. And the star, the star.
       here   the   light of its
And ~~hear~~ is the square and the dark church with ~~its~~ yellow clock.

And here, on the corner, ~~↳~~ the house.

*Good-bye, my book! Like mortal eyes, imagined ones must
close some day. Onegin from his knees will rise — but his creator
strolls away. And yet the ear cannot right now part with the
music and allow the tale to fade; the chords of Fate itself
continue to vibrate; and no obstruction for the sage exists
where I have put The End: the shadows of my world
extend beyond the skyline of the page, blue as to-morrow's
morning haze — nor does this terminate the phrase.*

The End

[Ill. 6-5] The last page of M. Scammell's typescript of *The Gift* with the handwritten poem inserted by Nabokov (Courtesy of Division of Rare and Manuscript Collections, Cornell University)

Lost — and Gained — in Translation

When visiting the author in Los Angeles, Michael Scammell asked Nabokov why it was that he even needed a translator into English. After all, the author of *Bend Sinister, The Real Life of Sebastian Knight, Pnin,* and *Lolita* was hardly lacking in English prose style. He was given two reasons. The first was that Nabokov required the "precious time to go on writing original works in English" (he was already in his early sixties when he made his popular breakthrough, and he planned to do much more); the second reason, the writer said, was that "he wanted to spare himself the temptation of rewriting his early Russian books in English instead of simply translating them" (quoted in Scammell 57). Both reasons held largely true for Nabokov's *The Gift*, although the introduced changes were at times considerable.

The next chapter will be entirely devoted to the critical reception of *The Gift*, especially to its English-language release and, therefore, I will cite here only a few characteristic responses dealing with observations on the merits of the published translation. Some contemporary American and British critics questioned the faithfulness of the translation to its original, noting a certain "odd feeling of dislocation," a new subtlety under the proven *Nabokovian* brand: "The translation, we are told in the foreword, has been 'carefully revised' by the author, and while a monolingual reader cannot determine the extent of the verbal adjustments, he may be tempted to guess that they have been considerable. The ear repeatedly detects the accomplished, the assured, the very individual English voice of the contemporary Mr. Nabokov; at the same time, one's literary sense is perpetually reminded that the substance of *The Gift* belongs to an earlier period in the author's career. To the susceptible reader, this subtle discrepancy between matter and tone produces an odd feeling of dislocation in time" (Malcolm 198).

Particularly pedantic readers noticed a few imperfections: "The author tells us in his foreword that he himself has 'carefully revised' the translation. Not carefully enough: we are indebted to the translators for some howlers that would have delighted Fyodor if he had detected them in Chernyshevski. At one point the Thales and Heraclitus of the original appear farcically as Phales (the well-known Symbolist?) and Heracles; at another Apelles is transformed into Apuleius" ("Russian Romp" 901).

Despite these scattered provisos, the quality of this translation of *The Gift* was undeniable and critics frequently praised it. Scammell "is no doubt responsible for much of [the novel's] magical phrasing" (Perley 7); "The primary delight in the book arises from the way things are said: the sentences never sound like translation" (Thorpe B-5); "Nabokov's command of English is idiomatic as well as extensive. It is affected, in some degree by a persisting exoticism, but this quality derives from the originality of his mind and not from an unfamiliarity with the language" (Sherman 4C). Scammell's translation "must have been a most exacting job, for much of the book, while dealing with daily life in Berlin, deals also with the technicalities of Russian poetry and prose" (Ross 852).

In conclusion: Scammell's main mission was to turn Nabokov's Russian prose into more or less fluent English—"without either falling into the pit of literalism or sliding into the swamp of interpretation" (Scammell 57). He was adjured to reproduce the original as faithfully as he could but was expressly forbidden to be "creative," which was Nabokov's prerogative, as the author confirmed in one of his rare signed letters to Michael Scammell:

> Besides correcting direct mistakes I have dealt with a number of inaccuracies. In a few cases the changes are meant to simplify or clarify matters, or else they reflect my own predilections of style. I realize quite well that the odd turn of some of your sentences is owing to your desire to be faithful to every detail of the original, as I had asked you to be; but here and there you have been handicapped by not quite knowing the exact meaning of a Russian term, especially in the case of homonyms or words deceptively resembling one another. I have put an exclamation mark in the margin...merely in order to draw your attention to these shortcomings. (Quoted in Scammell 59)

Nonetheless, Nabokov graciously concluded that his book is "very hard to translate" and that Scammell "in many cases...found clever and elegant solutions" and, on the whole, did "a very good job" (Ibid.). The co-translation of the novel will serve as the only definitive basis for any future variorum edition of *The Gift* in English.

References

Ben-Amos, Anat. "The role of literature in *The Gift*," *Nabokov Studies* 4, 1997: 117-149.

Berdjis, Nassim Winnie. *Imagery in Vladimir Nabokov's Last Russian Novel* (Dar), *Its English Translation* (The Gift), *and Other Prose Works*. Frankfurt am Main: Peter Lang, 1995.

Blackwell, Stephen H. "Three Notes on *The Gift*: A Mutation, an Intertext, and a Puzzle Solved," *The Nabokovian* 40, 1998: 36-39.

Boobbyer, Philip. *The Stalin Era*. New York: Routledge, 2000

Boyd, Brian. *Vladimir Nabokov: The American Years*. Princeton: Princeton University Press, 1991.

Cervantes, Miguel de. Don Quixote, in *The Waldie's Select Circulating Library*, Vol. 11. Philadelphia: Adam Waldie, 1838.

Dolinin, Alexander. *Kommentarii k romanu Dar*, in: V. Nabokov. *Sobranie sochinenii russkogo perioda. 5 tt*. St. Petersburg: Simpozium, 1999–2000. Vol. 4: 634-768.

Grayson, Jane. *Nabokov Translated: A Comparison of Nabokov's Russian and English Prose*. Oxford University Press, 1977.

Grishakova, Marina. "Dar V. Nabokova: Opyt sovmestnogo perevoda," in *Perelomnye periody v russkoi literature i kul'ture*. Ed. by Arto Mustajoki, Pekka Pesonen, et al. Vol. VII. Helsinki: Helsinki University Press, 2000: 311-326.

Leving — Scammell: "Translation is a Bastard Form." An Interview with Michael Scammell by Yuri Leving. *Nabokov Online Journal* 1, 2007. <http://etc.dal.ca/noj/articles/volume1/Scammel_Interview_3.pdf >

Malcolm, Donald. "A Retrospect," *New Yorker*, XL (April 25, 1964).

Nabokov, Vladimir. *Dar* in *Sobranie sochinenii russkogo perioda*. 5 vols. St. Petersburg: Simpozium, 1999-2000. Vol. 4.

_____ *Gift* typescript: The typescript draft (partially carbon) submitted by M. Scammell with V. Nabokov's extensive revisions. Berg Collection, NYPL.

_____ *The Real Life of Sebastian Knight*. London: Penguin Books, 1964.

Nakhimovsky, Alexander. "A Linguistic Study of Nabokov's Russian Prose," *The Slavic and East European Journal* 21 (1), 1977: 78-87.

Pascal, Blaise. *Pensées and Other Writings*. Translated by Honor Levi, Ed. by Anthony Levi. Oxford: Oxford University Press, 1999.

____ *Pensées*. NuVision Publications: LLC [electronic edition], 2007.

Perley, Maie E. "The Book Scene—A Glowing Work By Nabokov," *Louisville Times*, July 29, 1963, Sec. 1.

Pil'skii, Petr. [Review of *Sovremennye zapiski*, Book 63], *Segodnia* 117 (April 29, 1937).

Proffer, Carl. *Keys to Lolita*. Bloomington: Indiana University Press, 1968.

Rampton, David. *Vladimir Nabokov: A Critical Study of the Novels*. Cambridge: Cambridge University Press, 1984.

Rosengrant, Judson. "Nabokov, Onegin, and the Theory of Translation," *The Slavic and East European Journal*, Vol. 38, No. 1 (Spring, 1994): 13-27.

Ross, Maggie. "New novels," *The Listener*, LXX (November 21, 1963): 852-853.

Scammell, Michael. "The Servile Path: Translating Nabokov by Epistle," *Harper's Magazine*. May 2001: 52-60.

Share, Bernard. "The Moth and the Candle," *Irish Times* (Dublin), November 16, 1963.

Sherman, Thomas B. "Nabokov Nets Another Mixed Literary Bag," *St. Louis Sunday Post-Dispatch*, September 22, 1963.

Shrayer, Maxim. *Nabokov: Temy i variatsii*. St. Petersburg: Akademicheskii proekt, 2000.

Struve, Gleb. Review of *Nabokov Translated: A Comparison of Nabokov's Russian and English Prose* by Jane Grayson, *Russian Review* 37 (1), 1978: 126-128.

Tammi, Pekka. *Problems of Nabokov's Poetics: A Narratological Analysis*. Helsinki: Suomalainen Tiedeakatemia, 1985.

The Nabokov–Wilson Letters: Correspondence Between Vladimir Nabokov and Edmund Wilson, 1941-1971. Revised and Expanded Edition. Ed. by Simon Karlinsky. Los Angeles: University of California Press, 2001.

Thomas, Peter-John. *Beside the Point: Places in Nabokov's* The Gift [Ph.D. dissertation, AAT 3331154]. Evanston, Illinois: Northwestern University, 2008.

Thorpe, Day. "Earlier Nabokov from the Russian," Washington (D.C.) *Sunday Star*, May 26, 1963.

[Unsigned]. "Russian Romp," *Times Literary Supplement*, November 7, 1963.

Chapter Seven
CRITICAL RECEPTION

Contemporary Critics: 1937–38

Essentially, *The Gift* did not receive any sort of developed, thorough analysis in émigré periodicals, which were hardly living through the best of times. Besides the sharp decrease in émigré publications, which had traditionally devoted a certain amount of attention to new literature, it was also significant that the novel was printed in relatively small parts over almost a year and a half, from May 1937 to November 1938 (Mel'nikov 149). The omission of Chapter Four also rendered it impossible for reviewers to develop a complete impression of the novel. This fact was mentioned repeatedly both by Georgii Adamovich and Vladislav Khodasevich: "There is an entire chapter omitted from the novella, and the publication of it has taken so long that it does not seem possible at this point for me to comment on the thing as a whole. I hope to devote a separate article to it when it appears in its entirety as a monograph" (Khodasevich 1938c, 9). Khodasevich wrote about the same thing in a letter to Nabokov himself on January 25, 1938: "I read the latest chunk of *The Gift* with the usual rapture. My one regret is that, apart from 'ooh' and 'ah' (and what's the use of that?) I don't know how to write anything about it. If only you knew how difficult and awkward it is to write about the chunks that were taken out of the middle!" (Khodasevich 1997, 532). Khodasevich's promise to continue his analysis of the novel remained unfulfilled: on July 14, 1939, after a failed operation, he died of cancer. His comments on the excerpts of *The Gift* from its serial publication are, by necessity, in a rough form.

Petr Pil'skii came out with a quite hostile response to Chapter One of *The Gift*. In his review of Book 63 of *Sovremennye zapiski*, he portrayed the author of the novel as a bitter and soulless "literary illusionist":

> The first part of the novel *The Gift*, which is printed in this Book of *Sovremennye zapiski*, raises the question of literature. I will venture to say that Sirin is in general writing not for any reader, but for literature and about literature. In this respect, he performs experiments, invents things, plays and juggles. His protagonist,

a poet, recommends the "pink flannel 'm'." He thinks the Russian letter 'y' is so grubby that words are ashamed to begin with it. "Ch" for him is a gutta-percha, and "s" is radiant. To describe the characteristics of Sirin himself, I would choose the letter "f"; at various times in his writings, he appears to be a dandy [*frant*], a fop [*fat*], an illusionist [*fokusnik*], and a fencer [*fekhtoval'shchik*.] As are many writers, he is nauseated by customary, overused, tired words. He wants new ones—words and epithets. Therefore in Sirin's prose "a stuffed tropical songbird...[is] about to take wing" [*vsporkhlivoe chuchelo tropicheskoi ptichki*] (G11), Yasha recites his poems "in an oblivious singsong" [*samozabvennym pevkom*] (G38). They are not menacing but "mean-aching" in the editorial office [*ne grozili razgromom, a grazhivali*] (G61). Then follow the epithets: "handsome—in a hard, sinewy way, remindful of a gundog" [*liagavaia krasota*] (G42), "flimsy weather" [*dyriavaia pogoda*; literally: "hole-ridden"] (G46), "unfruitful brow" [*nedokhodnyi lob*] (G68). One can say of Sirin the very same words that were mentioned in the reviews devoted to a young poet, the hero of *The Gift*. This is "the strategy of inspiration and the tactics of the mind, the flesh of poetry and the specter of translucent prose" (G9). The poet attends a literary evening, listens, observes, and, finally, admits: "I am unhappy, I am bored, nothing rings true here and I don't know why I keep sitting here, listening to nonsense" (G35). Sirin feels the same way. He is tired of all the old word forms—old ones, current ones, and especially Russian ones. Using his protagonist as a mouthpiece, he gently and, by the looks of it, softly flagellates Russian writers; he mockingly points out how in Goncharov's *The Precipice* the character Raiskii has pink moisture on his lips in moments of deep thought, how Pisemsky's characters massage their chests with their hands when they are anguished, how Leskov is peppered with amusing Anglicisms ('*eto byla durnaya veshch*' [this was a bad thing] instead of simply '*plokho delo*' [G72]), and how Dostoevsky is like "Bedlam turned back into Bethlehem" (ibid.). Turgenev has intolerable intonation, rows of dots, and maudlin endings of chapters; Fet was nothing but rational in his verse, and put stress on antitheses, and so on.

Sirin is ironic, and in his irony he is cruel and properly arrogant. All of his writings display this. Here is a "family" in one of the games—an impossible boy with the girl wearing laced red boots next to him, both are stringing beads on straw-like rods, "and, with similar enthusiasm, their half-witted parents take part in the same pastime" (G13). The editor Vasiliev is wearing "prewar socks" at the Chernyshevskis' party and he is accompanied by a "fragile, charmingly debilitated girl with pink eyelids" (G33). Rudolf is "the son of a respectable fool of a professor" and has "a certain propensity for obscure poetry, lame music, lopsided art" (G43). The painting "Autumn" depicts the black tailor's dummy with its ripped side, dumped in a ditch ("connoisseurs found in it an abyss of sadness") (G58). All of this takes the form of unkind assessments, jeering and pointed observations, and an unforgiving soul. Sirin is a caricaturist. He is in search of an outlet for the barbed sharpness of his mind. In order to appease this need, he turns people around to their ridiculous and repellent sides, cuts them down to size, puts makeup on them, makes masks out of their faces; he slaps them on the forehead and then rejoices because he has figured out how to construct things such that this slap on the forehead produces the sonorous sound of an empty pot.

Sirin resents, or perhaps simply hates, the work of the writer—the process, the professional technique. The protagonist of *The Gift*, the poet Godunov-Cherdyntsev, writes verse. Sirin presents some excerpts from this verse. They do not always show a lack of talent, but Sirin deforms them, inserts stupid lines, and deliberately makes the poems helpless and pitiful. In order to write poetry, one needs unceasingly to repeat to oneself the same combinations—this is the secret of creativity. For example: "And in these talks between tamtambles, tamtam my spirit hardly knows..." (G56). If one repeats such nonsense over and over, a sufficiently meaningful stanza will emerge.

Sirin loves plays on words and he believes that the mysterious power of word combinations verges on delirious ramblings ("along the parquet, along the quarpet" [G21]). He has a passion for doubles: a husband named Alexander Yakovlevich and a wife named Alexandra Yakovlevna. Frau Stoboy's room is covered in pale yellow wallpaper with bluish tulips, and she herself goes around in a pale yellow dress with bluish tulips. The 18th anniversary of the death of Olya's father happens on the 18th day of the month.

Doing battle with the usual tendency of writers to strive for clarity and facility of phrasing, Sirin draws out periods of time, lengthens phrases, rams them full of foreign words, overloads the meaning, disperses and diminishes the reader's attention with details, particulars, numerous parenthetical insertions, and one has to seek out their meaning in a thick cloud of parentheses. In one episode he describes the death of Yasha, his suicide, the relationships between three people—Olya, Rudolf, and this Yasha: "This was the banal triangle of tragedy, formed within an idyllic circle, and the mere presence of such a suspiciously neat structure, to say nothing of the fashionable counterpoint of its development" [G42-43], etc. I absolutely cannot imagine who will like such cant, as I do not see any sort of novel in *The Gift*, nor do I foresee one in the future. There would be no reason to speak of any of this were it not the case that Sirin will achieve some renown, and were it not the case that he has talent. But this is the talent of a literary illusionist; from the ceiling falls an artificial rain of words—not real at all.

There are some well-placed lines in the novel with respect to Riga—Russian Rigans. Herman Ivanovich Busch, an elderly, shy, solidly built, likable gentleman from Riga, with a head that looked like Beethoven's, reads his philosophical tragedy out loud. "From the very beginning it was apparent that the road led to disaster. The Rigan's farcical accent and bizarre solecisms were incompatible with the obscurity of his meaning" (G66). In the Prologue there appeared a "Lone Companion" (*odinokiy sputnik* instead of *odinokiy putnik,* lone wayfarer) walking along that road. The Chief of the Town Guard not admitting the traveler repeated several times that he "would not pass definitely" (rhyming with "nightly"). After that one of the heroines explains "lispering" (instead of "whispering") that someone is caressing her, and finally the dance of the Maskers, not masks begins. In conclusion Busch exclaimed, "*Zanaves* [curtain]," accenting the last syllable instead of the first (G69). And this last touch is not a fib… (Pil'skii 3)

In his review of the same issue of the journal, Vladislav Khodasevich gave a much more balanced assessment:

The recently published Book 63 of *Sovremennye zapiski* opens with the new novel by V. Sirin entitled *The Gift*. Already, upon reading the first chapter (rumor has it there will be five in all), there are some reflections on the novel that I would like to share with readers. But I will not yield to this temptation. Judging by the scale, the intensity, and the general "grasp" with which *The Gift* is begun, one may believe that it plays a vital role in the development of Sirin's work, that it will express much that the author has yet to say, but that is essential for a complete understanding of Sirin. Yet at this point, in the one chapter that has been printed, this is all only a matter of hints and promises; nothing is foretold, and it is unknown how it will all turn out and what meaning will eventually emerge. Presumably, Sirin is consciously "piquing" the reader, not revealing even such essential things as the relationship of the author to the main character—this relationship may turn out to be both positive and negative, which will lead to the novel taking on one meaning or another. We can expect that Sirin will continue for some time to tease the reader's curiosity. Thus, we must be armed with patience and, for the time being, remark only on the most general, but already doubtless, characteristics of the novel—first and foremost its great depth of imagery and style. Already lavish in general, in *The Gift* Sirin seems to have decided to display utter extravagance. There are times when he inserts as much diverse material into one phrase as might be sufficient for another writer, more economical or less talented, to fill an entire story. (Khodasevich 1937a, 9)

Khodasevich finishes his review, which differs from other printed responses to *The Gift* in its tone of good will, with a clear understanding that conditions at the time were not ripe for any serious investigation of Sirin's novel:

"However, it is hardly possible for the 'capacious reader,' or even the 'capacious writer' in our time to evaluate this remarkable (perhaps the most remarkable) side of Sirin's gift on its own merits. It is still too early to 'sum up' Sirin, to measure his 'value.' However, it is certainly clear that, unfortunately (for us, not for him), the complexity of his craftsmanship and the level of artistic culture in his work are not in step with our literary epoch. He is in equal measure alien both to Soviet literature, which is currently living in a sort of stone age, filling the air with wild cries of exultation whenever someone manages to craft a stone axe, and to émigré writing, which has replaced the tradition with epigones and fears innovation more than a chilly draft in the air" (*ibid.*).

Nabokov read Khodasevich's survey and shared his satisfaction with Véra the very same night: "Today there was an intelligent review of *Dar* by Khodasevich" (May 15, 1937; Nabokov *Selected Letters* 26).

Georgii Adamovich reacted to the next part of Nabokov's novel in a review of the following issue (№ 64) of *Sovremennye zapiski*:

> ...Ordinarily a critic will get away with a remark to the effect that 'we will reserve judgment until the novel is finished.' In most cases, this remark is, of course, entirely justified and correct! But with regard to this story about the protagonist's father, delightful in its craftsmanship, originality, and inspiration, and the no less delightful lines about Pushkin, it is already worth it, so to speak, *les saluer au passage*. Gazdanov, for example, is also stylistically gifted. But in Sirin's case nothing is quite right. Here it is not the style that amazes and captivates, nor is it the ability to write beautifully about this or that thing; instead it is the merging of the author with his subject, the ability to set a fire from all sides, the gift of finding his own theme—no one else's—and turn it inside out, pick it to the bone, and wring it out to the extent that nothing more can be gleaned from it. (Adamovich 1937, 3)

And here is what Khodasevich wrote about the same excerpt printed in issue № 64:

> Sirin's *The Gift* continues in this book, but it is only one half of the second chapter of this wide-ranging work, whose most remarkable characteristic is its structure, and whose meaning cannot be understood outside of its connection to that structure. The pages that we have read so far do not yet make it possible to puzzle out the structure. Consequently, the author's overall intention is also still completely hidden from us. Sirin, it must be said, is such an experienced and skilful 'builder' of novels that one has to believe that this time, as with *Invitation to a Beheading*, he will spend a great deal of time piquing the reader's interest and then reveal his cards only at the very last moment. However, the fragment we have before us does have great virtues in its own right. The story of the protagonist's father, his scholarly work, his family life, and the imagined journey that the main character undertakes with him—all of this is created with such animation and such rich inventiveness as concerns the development of the plot, that it could serve as most intriguing material for research on contemporary prose. The only trouble is that no one at present has the space, the time, or the readers for such research, and when speaking of a literary phenomenon as complicated as Sirin, we are forced to limit ourselves to the most aggravating general spaces." Nevertheless, Khodasevich expresses the hope that, when *The Gift* is published in its entirety, he "will be able to examine it more closely and carefully." (Khodasevich 1937b, 9)

In the meantime the critic continues his analysis as successive parts of the novel are published. In his review of issue № 65 of *Sovremennye zapiski*, Khodasevich specifically advises the editors as follows:

The reader would be no less satisfied if Aldanov and Ivannikov were sacrificed and the editors allocated that space to Sirin's *The Gift*. The arc of this novel, which is broad both in its conception and its dimensions, develops at a naturally slow pace, and thus these relatively small excerpts in a journal, particularly in this instance, spoil the integrity of the reader's impressions and understanding of the novel. Nevertheless—I tell you sincerely—*The Gift* is written so beautifully and with such virtuosity that, when reading it, one is so amazed and delighted at Sirin's inexhaustible inventiveness that it is frustrating to part with him so quickly every time. (Khodasevich 1938a, 9)

Khodasevich goes on to speak in more detail of the author's inventiveness and virtuosity: However wonderful they are in their own right, and however elegantly they demonstrate Sirin's remarkable talent, I still believe that the extravagance with which Sirin uses them will diminish somewhat over time as his talent matures and he begins to seek out more austere and "classical" forms. Here I am in no way contradicting myself: it is a good thing that Sirin's work is at this point still so turbulent—this is evidence of a strength that is abundant and still young, an excellent sign of a productive future... Sirin's unfortunate rivals were all but ready to bury him by respectfully acknowledging that 'yes, he undoubtedly has talent, but he has already exhausted it.' However, *The Gift*, as distinctly as anything possibly could, speaks to the contrary, and the partisan sorties against Sirin are beginning anew. Isn't it a funny thing? (Khodasevich 1938a, 9)

One of Khodasevich's last printed responses emerged in a review of Book 66 of *Sovremennye zapiski*: Sirin's *The Gift* is appearing in such small doses that I was ready to refuse altogether to comment on this remarkable novel until it appears in its entirety. However, I cannot deny myself the satisfaction of directing the reader's attention to the latest excerpt, which tells the story of the protagonist's work on a biography of Chernyshevski. This chapter, which, under the guise of a mischievous prank, says some very important and very sad things, will certainly bring the author a great deal of trouble. All the apprentices and admirers of the progressive thought police that has been overseeing Russian literature since the 1840s will now have to fly into a rage. Their prevalence has not yet completely passed, and now they will hover above the author of *The Gift* in a classic "journalistic swarm" of gadflies and mosquitoes. Incidentally, Sirin's entomological acumen led him to an amusing discovery. It turns out that Nekrasov, 'despite his country strolls,' mistakenly referred to a gadfly as a bumblebee (over a herd there was a 'swarm of restless bumblebees'), and ten lines later as a wasp (the horses 'took refuge from the wasps under the smoke of the campfire')... (Khodasevich 1938b, 9)

Many critics of the time struggled to react impartially and objectively to Nabokov's innovative composition, which summarized the development of an entire epoch of Russian literature. Moreover, many did not find the satirical nature of *The Gift* to their liking. Georgii Adamovich, perhaps recognizing himself in the fictional literary critic Christopher Mortus, was cautious, mostly limiting himself to terse comments such as the following: "Sirin's *The Gift* continues — and through the reader's 'crystal ball' (which does not have magical powers), it is still not clear where and towards what it is progressing" (Adamovich 1938a, 3; the allusion here is to a "crystal ball" of creative imagination evoked in Pushkin's *Eugene Onegin*, Chapter VIII). This is how Khodasevich interpreted the remark in a personal letter to the author of *The Gift*: "Incidentally, the parodies of the reviews are wonderful. Mortus, as you have no doubt noticed, was incensed, but this is useful. I don't know whether you were thinking of Tsetlin when composing the verse portion of Linyov's criticism, but you hit him right on the nose..." (Khodasevich 1997, 532). It is no coincidence that Mortus ultimately turns out to be a woman who signs with a man's name. In his commentary on the letters, John Malmstad notes that Nabokov, as he often does, combined the features of two hostile critics: Adamovich and Zinaida Gippius (Gippius's pen name was Anton Krainii).

Adamovich gave a more detailed response in his review of Book 67 of *Sovremennye zapiski*, which (for obvious reasons) devoted most of its attention to the element of parody in *The Gift*. Insulted, he remarked: "Parody is the easiest of literary genres":

> *The Gift* is finished and is, of course, worthy of a thorough analysis. Unfortunately, the hiatus of three or four months between issues of *Sovremennye zapiski* spoils the overall impression of the novel to the extent that it is hard to judge the novel without having read it. And what's more, it was published with omissions, all of which means that it will be best to read it once it is published as a separate edition. The latest chapters of *The Gift* open by reproducing several pieces of literary criticism, supposedly in response to *The Life of Chernyshevski*, which was written by Sirin's protagonist, Godunov-Cherdyntsev. As one might guess from previous clues, these reviews amount to parodic effigies.
>
> Parody is the easiest of literary genres and, we will say without bias, Sirin's 'reviews' are successful in this regard. If these pages of *The Gift* are still somehow uncomfortable and aggravating to read, it is because not only are they portraits of real people, but also self-portraits: it is clear that Linyov is so-and-so, Christopher Mortus is so-and-so, but it is still clearer and more apparent that Godunov-Cherdyntsev is Sirin himself!.. The shallow critics respond negatively to Godunov, while the discerning and perceptive ones respond favorably: it is an extremely simple formula. Some critics, the most penetrating, even maintain that "you will hardly find a dozen people abroad who are capable of appreciating the fire and wonder of this fabulously witty work."
>
> With regard to the wit, we can agree, though not with the 'fabulously.' Sirin really is an exceptionally witty writer, not in the sense of the mockery or scoffing

expressed in the parody, but in his ability to create the most unanticipated conclusions out of unexpected observations. But wit and intelligence are not at all the same thing; sometimes they are even mutually exclusive. As an example, I will just refer to the lines from *The Gift* that mention how Dostoevsky 'always brings to mind somehow a room in which a lamp burns during the day.' It is quite a nice image! But in the context of all of Sirin's writings, when juxtaposed to his own conception of people and of life, behind this 'lamp' there is nothing more than a gaping abyss of disarming naivety. The phrase has nothing to do with Dostoevsky, but with regard to Sirin it contains quite valuable commentary.

Of course, these observations in no way change our estimation of the author of *The Gift* as an artist. I have had to write more than once about his brilliant resume, about his amazing independence. In the published excerpt from the novel there are many pages that confirm our previous opinion: the scene in the forest, for example. We must accept a writer as he is, just as with anyone else. But Sirin, whatever his faults, is in any case a unique figure in our literature, and it would be stupid and petty to surrender to haphazard irritation, as in other cases it is stupid and petty to surrender to flattery. (Adamovich 1938b, 3)

But while Adamovich, who was himself the target of Nabokov's wit, continued to comport himself with dignity and did not give in to Nabokov's provocation, other critics did not exactly stand on ceremony with Nabokov. There were accusations of the nihilism and misanthropy supposedly displayed by the author of *The Gift* heard in the pro-fascist *Novoe slovo*: "Sirin's formula is extraordinarily simple: he thinks up some monsters and knocks them together; he himself creates these situations, and then he digs around in the situations he has invented as though this is how life really is, and not something he has invented." This is how a writer for that newspaper, Andrei Garf, expressed his indignation, upset at the satirical way in which Germany and its inhabitants were portrayed in *The Gift*. Certain episodes in the novel (for example, the description of the beach at Grunewald) caused him to burst forth with a feuilleton called "Literaturnye pelenki" ["Literary Diapers"], in which foul anti-Semitic statements mixed with coarse attacks on the "Paris swamp" of the Russian émigré community and on Sirin personally. Sirin, according to the vigilant Garf, was carrying out a certain type of social mandate in his novel:

Is Sirin talented? Talent on its own says nothing. One can be a talented swindler and also a counterfeiter. It is where the talent is directed that determines its relative weight. So Sirin's antics and contortions, his open mockery of both his characters and his readers, the unhealthy racket raised around him by those who are for some reason trying to inflict him on the reading public, and the herd mentality of that very public, which is ready to believe that this disgusting, hideous, naked king cynically parading around is dressed in the most fashionable suit—from a tailor 'of Paris and Berdichev'—all of this makes the 'case of Sirin' into the most typical and unsightly one in émigré literary life. All the streams of literary art, streams that are often clean and fresh, are flowing from all the countries of our diaspora into the swamp of Paris. But once they flow into the swamp, they get infected with the stench being spread by the literary clique that has settled there and that has an agenda having nothing in common with Russian literature or Russian thought—an agenda of antifascist, or really anti-German, propaganda.

It is a matter not of talent, but of where the art is directed. If the art is directed towards things Russian, then it doesn't matter how much talent is in it—it will not make it to the surface of the swamp. It will be drowned... All you need to do is carry on, whine and yearn, lose faith in oneself and in other people... And the main thing is that you need to curse Germany. You can curse anything you want about Germany—the climate, the soil, the people, the government, the dogs or the sausages, but it must be cursed.

Sirin was faithful to this formula when he 'described' the beach in Grunewald. In today's Germany, where sports have become a national cult, where the young people are training as nowhere else in the world—in Germany, which emerged victorious in practically all kinds of sports at the Olympic Games—Sirin saw nothing more than "hoarse-voiced adolescents; the globes of breasts; voluminous posteriors; flabby thighs; bluish varices; gooseflesh; the pimply shoulder blades of bandy-legged girls," etc. (G336). The author, without knowing it himself, presented a fairly accurate picture of Grunewald Beach, but it was not the Grunewald Beach of today's athletically toned Germany; it was that of inflation-period Germany, when the beaches were filled up with representatives of a race which has never been remarkable for its athleticism or its beauty of form, and which has now moved on to the banks of the Seine with "the globes of breasts" and "the pimply shoulder blades of bandy-legged girls" (G336). (Garf 6-7)

In Chapter 5 of *The Gift*, Nabokov made all sorts of criticism the subject of his parody, but he could hardly have foreseen the appearance of such a crudely brazen feuilleton bordering on libel (Mel'nikov 150). In more general terms and viewing the whole debate retrospectively, it becomes clear, however, that it was Khodasevich's series of insightful responses that ultimately set the tone for almost all subsequent critical reception of Nabokov's Russian-language novels, and of *The Gift* in particular. In his article "On Sirin" (1937), Khodasevich identified the formalist nucleus of each work, up to but not including *The Gift*, showing that devices "turn out to be its indispensably important characters" and that Nabokov's main intent is not to create a portrait of the artist as a young man, and certainly not of his "life and times," but "to show how devices live and work" (Khodasevich 1982, 61-64).

Chapter Seven. CRITICAL RECEPTION

CONTEMPORARY CRITICS: 1938–56

Behind the Scenes

In sharp contrast to the *succès de scandale* following the publication of Godunov-Cherdyntsev's *The Life of Chernyshevski*, this unparalleled instance of censorship in the most liberal Russian magazine attracted little attention in the émigré press and did not contribute to any immediate popularity for Nabokov's latest novel. The number of critical responses to the serialized publication of *The Gift* was small, but contemporaries' private utterances found in surviving correspondence reflect the prevailing mood. Ill-disposed opinions about *The Gift* appear constantly in correspondence of the older generation of the émigré writers, first and foremost between Ivan Bunin and Boris Zaitsev ("Pis'ma B. Zaitseva" 147-148; "Perepiska I. A. Bunina" 179). Even as years passed, upon rereading the old issues of *Sovremennye Zapiski*, the winner of the 1933 Nobel Prize in Literature Bunin confided to Mark Aldanov: "So much interesting stuff! And so many monstrosities! Take, for example, Sirin's *The Gift*! In some places it reminds one of Ippolit from *War and P[eace]*" (Prince Vassily's dull-witted son in Leo Tolstoy's novel tells pointless stories and his mystified interlocutors do not know whether to regard Ippolit as a clown or a wag; "Perepiska I. A. Bunina" 179). Later Bunin added in another letter to the same addressee that rereading the "wild, lecherous" novel *The Gift* had caused him to begin swearing dirty words ("*dikii, razvratnyi* Dar*, rugaias' materno*...") (February 14-15, 1946; "Perepiska I. A. Bunina" 159). Maxim Shrayer sees this as a clear case of rivalry between the defeated teacher and his more gifted younger disciple (Shrayer 170).

Pil'skii (who, unlike Adamovich, did not recognize himself in one of the ridiculed critics) maintained that Sirin's primary talent is in caricaturing: "Smiling and delighted, one gulps down pages filled with parodies of the critical reviews in *The Gift*" (*Novoe Russkoe Slovo*, December 15, 1938). Others believed they were more observant. Thus Mark Aldanov wrote to Nabokov indignantly that everybody in the *Poslednie Novosti* offices, even the typist, recognized Georgii Adamovich behind the mask of "Christopher Mortus." Rather than seeing this as a tribute to Nabokov's satiric precision, Aldanov felt only the indecorum of it all. Nabokov tried to explain to Aldanov that *The Gift* paints a picture of the whole complex life of a writer, and just as he had to endow Fyodor with certain literary traits akin to his own, he also had to render a whole socio-cultural milieu:

> I was guided not by an urge to laugh at this or that person (although there would be no crime in that—we are not in class or in church), but solely by a desire to show a certain order of literary ideas, typical at a given time—which is what the whole novel is about (its main heroine is literature). If in this case a style of criticism I feature corresponds to the style of particular figures and fops,

that is natural and unavoidable. My friends need not be offended. Smile, Mark Alexandrovich! You say that *The Gift* can count on a very long life. If that's the case, then it's all the more obliging to take along for the ride, free of charge, some of my contemporaries who would otherwise have stayed at home forever. (Quoted in Boyd 480)

In January 1938, while Nabokov was wintering in Menton, a new installment of *The Gift* appeared in *Sovremennye Zapiski*. Nabokov's friend Georgii Gessen wrote from Paris to tell him: "You're a genius. If your chess or tennis or football were remotely like your writing, you old scoundrel, you could concede Alekhine a pawn and Budge fifteen points and make Haydon a reserve goalkeeper on any professional team" (January 13, 1938; Boyd 479). The catchphrase "you old scoundrel" is most probably a conscious reference to "What a Pushkin, what a son of a bitch!" from Alexander Pushkin's 1825 letter to his friend, the poet Pyotr Vyazemsky. Since then the phrase become common to express the elation felt after finishing one's work, but even more curious is that this particular exclamation originally marked the finishing of Pushkin's drama *Boris Godunov*.

Putting his archive in order in 1967, Gleb Struve found a copy of a letter written to him on February 3, 1942, by Zinaida Shklovskaia. Shklovskaia was the widow of prominent publicist Isaak Vladimirovich Shklovsky (who had written under the pseudonym Dioneo), and was living alone in post-war Paris, suffering from a severe case of diabetes. Rereading the old issues of *Sovremennye Zapiski*, she had a chance to reevaluate Sirin's prose as well: "I rushed to read and, despite my nearsightedness (almost blindness), swallowed almost everything and was overjoyed, although I stumbled over *The Gift*. I have to admit that I don't understand a lot. I'll try to finish it and maybe I will get wiser. How witty he is, how original, lively, smart, and interesting! The mere thought of reading anything else makes you nauseous." She asked Struve whether he knew Sirin's current address:

> I would very much like to write to him, it would make things easier, because there is no one else with whom I can share. Everybody nowadays looks at him from the English point of view [sic], and you know very well what this means. It is like Vij [a character of Gogol's fantasy story of the same name] would translate *Invitation to a Beheading*—one cannot explain it, no one would understand. Sirin should be understood and read between the lines; one must feel, penetrate and breathe in that atmosphere in which he surrounds his works. You can't immerse the English into this ambience; they need something tangible and precise, rather than elusive. If this were a description of a spade with a price tag attached, something like 6/6, it would be much more comprehensible... (Malikova 223)

Zinaida Shklovskaia died three years later, on February 24, 1945, but Nabokov learned about her praise only in 1967 (On December 7, on behalf of her husband, Véra thanked Struve for this excerpt and told him that "V.V. was extremely touched"). What he probably never knew about, however, was Struve's own reserved attitude to *The Gift*. In a private letter between two professors of Russian literature, Gleb Struve and Vladimir Markov, the former wrote: "We were reading this last week Sirin's *The Gift* (out loud) as well [...] This is not Nabokov's finest achievement, but like everything else he has written, it shows extreme talent at times. Though there is something age-old wanton about it... I suspect that Nabokov gives a certain key to an equitable understanding of himself in *The Gift*, in the critique of Godunov-Cherdyntsev's book, and especially in the imaginary dialogues with Koncheyev" (July 29, 1952; see Martynov 1119). Struve preferred Nabokov's earlier writings to his last Russian novel. *The Defense*, he confided to Markov on April 12, 1953, was superior in both its structure and its humanity: "Although [this preference] may stem from the fact that I read it much earlier, and the sense of newness and freshness then struck me more strongly, *The Gift* is just a repetition, development, and refinement of the same flavoring, albeit headier." Nabokov's former friend concluded with rather ruthless remarks: Sirin's "single major theme is creativity; he is obsessed with it. This may be because somewhere in the depths of his soul he realizes his own creative impotence. In the end, his writing boils down to some fruitless combinations. In *The Defense* he had succeeded in elevating this theme to the height of tragedy, but in *The Gift*, which is composed probably better and with more maturity, all the sterility of his own creativity came out. Godunov-Cherdyntsev is, of course, Nabokov's alter ego, and this is also tragic in its own way; however, the tragedy here is not objectified but subjectively bared..." As a result of such disdain, Struve devoted just a few lines to the novel in his otherwise substantial chapter on Nabokov in his groundbreaking study of Russian literature in exile: "*The Gift* may occupy a central place in Nabokov-Sirin's writings. However, the novel turned out to be not exactly what Khodasevich had hoped for: the hero is hardly presented 'with merciless satire' and, on the other hand, the major role is given to Chernyshevski's biography which the protagonist satirically doctors. And yet nowhere else does Sirin's incomparable gift for parody, his arresting imitativeness show itself with such boldness" (Struve 289).

"How Inattentive People Are In Their Reading"

When the full Russian edition of *The Gift* was finally published by the Chekhov publishing house, a few close friends and colleagues privately shared with Nabokov their thoughts and feelings upon the appearance of the repackaged and seemingly long-forgotten novel. Elena Sikorski would often quote minute details from Nabokov's books in letters to her brother: "Do you remember writing about that 'grayish' [*o 'seren'kom'*] in *The Gift*? So I see it all the time; I am surrounded by it" (November 8, 1945; Nabokov, *Perepiska* 20). Still living in Europe, she exclaimed:

You have yet to give me an explanation of Kachurin [the hero of Nabokov's poem "To Count S. M. Kachurin"—Y.L.] and the others. I really want to know whom he had in mind and whether there was anyone at all. Many have read *The Gift*, many people liked it very, very much, but it is surprising how inattentive people are in their reading—a splendid story with the keys remaining unnoticed by *everyone*; "*polumnemozina*" and "*polumertsanie*" amused no one. I simply can't grasp, is it really because I read all this so, so differently? (September 29, 1952; Nabokov, *Perepiska* 72; italics in the original)

Although reaction to the publication was indeed sparse, if not virtually absent, the emphasis that Nabokov's younger sister places on the unreceptiveness of *all* readers of *The Gift* seems not entirely true. The inquisitive Avraam Yarmolinsky, translator of many Russian classics, tried to elicit additional information from the author in a similar way to Elena. In the year of the first Russian publication of the book, Yarmolinsky applauded it and shared with Nabokov some hidden traces which he was able to discover. He praised *The Gift* highly ("...This is indeed a gift to literature. While reading, I thanked my stars for being blessed with the knowledge of Russian language...") and asked a few questions with regard to the novel's sources (in a letter dated November 11, 1952). A few days later he added: "Just yesterday I accidentally came across the printed sources of Myshkin's aiguillettes and little boats made from the pages of *Kapital*. This is Steklov and 'Chernyshevski in Siberia' by Liatsky..." (November 15). Nabokov confirmed the reader's insightful comment in his reply on November 22, stating that "all the documentary information in Chernyshevski's biography was based on 'sources'." Yarmolinsky continued probing Nabokov later, noting certain incongruities between Nabokov's own interpretation of facts and the different explanation given by Steklov (December 21).

The émigré critic Marc Slonim reflected on the occasion of the publication of the first complete Russian edition of *The Gift* by calling it "a maliciously polemic novel" in which Chernyshevski is presented as "some half-idiot" (*Novoe Russkoe Slovo*, July 3, 1955). A couple years earlier the same Marc Slonim, who was well acquainted with Nabokov in Europe, opted to dissemble the existence of Nabokov's major work in his general introduction, *Modern Russian Literature from Chekhov to the Present* (New York, 1953). Although Slonim credited Nabokov with a unique place among the émigré prose writers due to his "stylistic pyrotechnics" and "sense of the bizarre," he noted at the same time that Nabokov "had gone from traditional realism toward Expressionism and Surrealism, and his stylistic experiments are scintillating. The verbal texture of his novels certainly shocked many readers—and this despite the fact that most of his writings consist of nostalgic reminiscences of old Russia." The last sentence, no doubt, accurately evoked the unnamed *Dar* (Slonim 401).

Soon thereafter another "shocked reader," Georgii Adamovich, accused Nabokov of depicting Chernyshevski as a "dullard hack" [*tupaia bezdarnost'*]: "All of Nabokov's ties are severed. He plays at life instead of living it through. He fails to test his scribbles against empirical truth, because for him there is no such thing as an empirical truth: everything that has been said on that subject was concocted by dullard hacks like Chernyshevski, whom he lambasted with such capricious flippancy in *The Gift!*" [*s takim kapriznym legkomysliem obrushilsia*].[37]

Vladimir Markov represented the younger generation of émigré literary scholars. His voice sounded surprisingly out of tune with the choir: "The chapter on Chernyshevski in Nabokov's *The Gift* is splendid! And despite that some of Nabokov's statements aren't fair, everyone had grown tired of waiting for a slap in the face of 'public' Russia [*zazhdalis' opleukhi 'obshchestvennoi' Rossii*]" (*Opyty*, No. 6, 1956: 65). This remark by Markov outraged a number of the émigré literati and public figures of the older generation. Mark Vishnyak attacked Markov for his connivance with Nabokov against the older generation and its values both publicly and in private correspondence (Dolinin 2007; Dolinin 2008).

"The Book Is Dazzlingly Brilliant...But"
Two Early Internal Reviews of *The Gift*

The first English-language review of *The Gift* appeared long before the novel became available to a non-Russian audience. The text of this internal review remained unpublished and buried in the Nabokov manuscript collection at the Library of Congress. It was written by Alexander I. Nazaroff (1898–1981), a Russian-American who lived in New York beginning in the 1920s. Nazaroff was an author of several insightful books on Russian history and literature,[38] and also served as a frequent reviewer and commentator on Russian cultural issues for *The New York Times*. Nazaroff had earlier published an article in *Novaya Zarya* [*The New Dawn*] (August 11, 1934, in Russian), entitled "Sirin—the New Star in Literature," in which he gave Nabokov an extremely high place among the leading new talents emerging in both émigré and Soviet literature. Nabokov read some of Nazaroff's reviews during the 1930s (Dolinin, "Pis'ma Nabokova k Struve. Chast' 2" 157).

In a letter accompanying his two-page review of *The Gift*, commissioned by the Bobbs-Merrill publishing house, Nazaroff tried to give a painstaking explanation of the pros and cons of its possible publication in the United

---

[37] G. Adamovich's *Odinochestvo i svoboda* [*Solitude and Freedom*] was originally published in 1955 (New York: Izdatel'stvo imeni Chekhova, 1955); reprinted: Adamovich 1996, 82-83.

[38] Among them, *Tolstoy the Inconstant Genius* (Fredrick A. Strokes, 1929) and *The Land of the Russian People* (Philadelphia: J. B. Lippincott, 1944).

States. Although unbiased, this appraisal, unfortunately, recommended against introducing the novel to American readers. As a keen observer, Nazaroff realized that contemporary audiences were not yet mature enough for such a complex work as *The Gift*. Essentially he was correct: it would take several decades, and the explosion of the *Lolita* "time-bomb" (in Nabokov's own words), before even the most perceptive critics would be ready to turn their attention to Nabokov's finest achievement in Russian.

"I always have regarded V. Nabokoff [sic] as by far the most talented, brilliant and original of the young Russian writers (no matter whether Soviet or émigré) and perhaps of the young European writers in general," Nazaroff began his letter, adding that he believes that a publishing firm which has taken upon itself the task of "establishing" Nabokov in the USA "sooner or later will be well rewarded for it, even if, in the beginning, the task appears to be ungrateful." Moreover, Nazaroff thought that Bobbs-Merrill made a good choice by introducing the writer to American readers with his *Laughter in the Dark*, though he refrained from advising them to add *The Gift* to that line-up: "But I am not at all sure that [this novel] would be the right selection for following up your effort." Nazaroff's doubts were due to the following considerations:

> 1. In its general type, *The Gift* sharply differs from that which hitherto was the common run of Nabokoff's novels. No matter how Nabokoff has always been fond of original (and often inimitably brilliant) tricks and artifices of composition and style, *Laughter in the Dark*, *Luzhin's Defense*, *The Exploit* [*Podvig*, later translated as *Glory* (1971) — Y.L.], and *Despair* are 'normal' novels; they either have a well-constructed and developed dramatic plot (*Laughter in the Dark*, *Despair*), or are built "biographically" around one central character which holds the reader's interest (*Luzhin's Defense*, *The Exploit*); withal, they all firmly stand on the ground of reality (although Nabokoff often "alleviates" that reality and fascinatingly plays with it).
>
> Now, in contradiction to this, *The Gift* is not a realistic novel. I even am not sure that it can be called a novel at all. It is an ultra-sophisticated and modernist piece of introspective, almost "non-subjective" writing which, in composition, may be likened to James Joyce's *Ulysses*.
>
> 2. The narrative is—very loosely—centralized around Godunov-Cherdyntsev,[39] a young Russian émigré poet living in Berlin. At moments the author completely identifies himself with his hero; at others, without warning, he dissociates himself from him and speaks of him "from outside." The book follows no factual narrative thread of any kind; from beginning to end, it is

---

[39] The reviewer writes "Cherdyntzev" and refers to the novel title without the definite article — changed here and elsewhere in quotes to conform to Nabokov's transliteration and the accepted norm.

a detailed disclosure of Godunov-Cherdyntsev's inner world, in which pictures of Berlin's streets or of the young poet's present life in a poor émigré's room, reminiscences of Cherdyntsev—the father's (who was an explorer) trips to Pamirs, the young man's reflections on life, poetry and literature and, above all, the constant watching of the intricacies of his own creative artistic process mingle in a succession which is determined not by any "outside logic" but by the free play of associations in his mind alone. The book thus is a crazy quilt of bits of reality drowning in the author's (or his hero's) "inner comment" on them. *The Gift*, no doubt, is a correct title for the work, for the unconquerable urge of Cherdyntsev's mind to digest artistically and transfigure by his imagination all things (including the most trivial ones) with which he comes in contact is the leitmotif of his narrative.

In the second half of the book, the author, to the reader's astonishment, inserts a comparatively very long biography of N.G. Chernyshevski, a famous Russian critic of the xix century, which, supposedly, has been written by his hero Cherdyntsev; the biography is followed by long quotations from the comment made on it by various Russian reviewers and by the author's reaction to that comment. It is only towards the end of the book that this strange deviation finishes and that the reader finds himself again in the crazy quilt of Cherdyntsev's introspection.

In the third section of his evaluation, Nazaroff displayed his profound understanding of Nabokov's text. In fact, the peer-reviewer presented one of the most favorable accounts ever produced by someone who was not among the writer's friends or sympathetic readers (as were Vladislav Khodasevich and Gleb Struve), a capability later to be found probably only in the lucid review of *Pale Fire* by Mary McCarthy, who described it as "a jack in the box, a Fabergé gem, a clockwork toy, a chess problem, an infernal machine":

> Now, one who accepts and likes that [introspective] type of literature can pronounce but one verdict on *The Gift*; with the exception of the deviation on Chernyshevski (which is decidedly weak), the book is dazzlingly brilliant—one is tempted to describe it as a work of genius. The author's unique gift to convey to the reader the most complicated characterization of human beings or implications of thought, emotion and humor by a gliding, imperceptible stroke of the pen; the nervous burning and palpitation in the light and precipitous flight of his phrases which often, with a truly miraculous grace and plasticity, embrace the whole universe in a few casual words; the abnormal keenness of his eye which notices every human gesture and immediately discloses a whole "inner panorama" behind it; and a colossal spiritual culture, erudition and amount of knowledge touched off by imagination and fantasy in whose divine flight there is something of madness—all this renders the very texture of his pages so fascinating that one cannot tear oneself away from them. But how many American readers will appreciate that fascination?

Among the amusing incidents surrounding the difficult publication history of *The Gift* were critics' attempts to provide Nabokov with some practical advice for improvement. The novel could be turned into a more readable piece, according to such well-wishers, either by revising the subject matter, or writing it out in a more accessible manner. Alexander Nazaroff, for example, went as far as suggesting to Bobbs-Merrill a more suitable author for the possible English-language biography of Nikolai Chernyshevski: "[Nabokov's Fourth Chapter] left me with an unpleasant feeling, but also gave me an idea that a book on Chernyshevski would be a good one to publish if you could get someone like E.H. Carr, the author of a recent brilliantly interesting life of Bakunin, to write it" (For complete text of Nazaroff's recommendation, see Chapter Three). Others were less radical, and did not go beyond offering "friendly" advice: "With only *The Gift* to judge by, a friendly reviewer might be tempted to urge Mr. Nabokov toward a style of broader strokes and coarser texture, as being more suited to the amplitudes of the novel. Such advice, however, would merely go to demonstrate that writers seldom can derive much benefit from their critics and ought never to attend to them" (Malcolm 198-204).

Despite the crescendo of positive remarks, Nazaroff, nonetheless, concluded with a decision unfavorable to Nabokov:

> Obviously, this type of a work can appeal only to a very limited group of not only exceptionally cultured, but also ultra-sophisticated readers. Worse still, since the chief source of interest lies not in *what* Nabokoff tells, but in *how* he tells it, that is to say, in his unsurpassed verbal mastery, the book is bound considerably to fade out in translation [Emphasis is in the original—Y.L.].
>
> I can see in advance how an American will shrug his shoulders in disappointed astonishment over some of the passages which hold a Russian reading the original literally spellbound. In a normal-type realistic novel that, of course, would not be an insurmountable obstacle—the dramatic or human interest would make up for it; but in a piece of introspective writing this is a serious thing indeed. Finally, the appearance of this book in this country, where Nabokoff is not known, may easily scare away from him numbers of readers who would thoroughly enjoy his earlier, 'normal' novels.

Nazaroff's verdict left no room for doubt: "All this leads me to believe that *The Gift* is not a thing to be published in America—or, at least, not a thing to be published at the present time, when Nabokoff's reputation has not yet been established. Besides *The Gift*, he has so many truly excellent and perfectly 'understandable' and 'normal' works, from *Luzhin's Defense* to *Despair*; I am of the opinion that, at the present moment, it would be much better both for the publisher and for the author to pick out one of them."

Altagracia de Jannelli, Nabokov's literary agent at the time, forwarded a copy of Nazaroff's detailed analysis to Europe where the writer read it with ardent

Chapter Seven. CRITICAL RECEPTION

interest. As a result, Nabokov entered into an argument with the publisher's internal reviewer via an intermediary—quite an unusual step for someone who publicly dismissed all kinds of critical opinions. Nabokov's staunch desire to publish the novel uncensored at all costs meant even the compromise of publishing it first in English translation. In the atmosphere of the disintegrating Russian émigré community and while the Russian critics were virtually silent, Nabokov made his choice. On July 14, 1938, Nabokov wrote to his agent from Hotel de la Poste, a small mountain resort in Moulinet, France:

> On the whole I rather liked N.'s description of *The Gift*, although it is very superficial—there is a lot more in my book both for the connoisseur and the lay reader. Here are some objections:
>
> *The Gift* is thoroughly realistic, as it tells the story of a definite person, showing his physical existence and the development of his inner self. As he is an author, I naturally show his literary progress. Moreover, the whole story is threaded on my hero's love-romance, with the underground work of fate revealed—an essential point which N. has entirely missed. My style and methods have nothing in common with Joyce (though I greatly appreciate *Ulysses*). The novel is not 'a crazy quilt of bits'; it is a logical sequence of psychological events: the movements of stars may seem crazy to the simpleton, but wise men know that the comets come back.
>
> I don't understand why the reader should be 'astonished' at the 'insertion' of my hero's work (Chernyshevski's biography). The preceding chapters lead up to it and, as samples are given of all my hero's literary production, it would have been an impossible omission to leave his chief book out. Moreover, at this point, my hero's interpretation of Chernyshevski's life (which, incidentally, took me four years to write) lifts my novel to a wider plane, lending it an epic note and, so to say, spreading my hero's individual butter over the bread of a whole epoch. In this work (Chernyshevski's life), the defeat of Marxism and materialism is not only made evident, but it is rounded out by my hero's artistic triumph.
>
> As to the interest which *The Gift* might represent to the foreign (American) reader, I want to repeat that I know how to translate the book in such a way as even to avoid the necessity of footnotes. 'Human interest' means Uncle Tom's cabin to me (or Galsworthy's drivel) and makes me sick, seasick.
>
> Your faith in my work is of the greatest value to me and I thank you warmly for your kind words. (Nabokov, *Selected Letters* 27-28)

Since Nabokov refers to the reviewer only as to "N.," it is likely that de Jannelli used only the first letter of Nazaroff's name when she was sending a typed copy of the original—her regular practice as evident from her correspondence with other publishers.

Most probably Alexander Nazaroff's identity remained unknown to Nabokov for a long time. In her letters to Nabokov, Altagracia de Jannelli referred to the anonymous critic consistently as "N." Dmitri Nabokov, who translated and published this communication in *Selected Letters*, listed "N" in a footnote as an "unidentified person." Upon reconstructing the entire polemic, it is now possible both to restore the real name and to correct the bibliographic note on the folder in the Library of Congress Nabokov archive. The latter dates Nazaroff's review as "1942" with a question mark; the accurate date should read "1938."

Nazaroff's comments should be viewed as a rare instance of critical acumen. Considering that the Chernyshevski chapter had not yet been published and that Nabokov's status as an intellectual celebrity was still far into the future, Nabokov would have especially appreciated the comparison of his novel with Joyce's *Ulysses*, and the characterization of *The Gift* as an "ultra-sophisticated," "modernist piece of introspective writing." Although Nabokov claimed in response that his style and methods have nothing in common with Joyce, this is true only in part. Perceptive as Nazaroff was, he pointed out not just "style and methods," but also the psychological depth of the protagonists' minds and the general similarity in the artistic universes of *The Gift* and of *Ulysses*.

In a last-ditch effort to override Nazaroff's external opinion, which so oddly blended ecstatic praise with cool, rational market considerations, de Jannelli forwarded a copy of Nabokov's letter to D. L. Chambers, the president of the Bobbs-Merrill company. In her note, dated August 2, 1938, she explained: "This was sent me in reply to my sending him a copy of Nazaroff's silly review. I know it will make no difference, but I am simply sending you this because I would like you to hear what the author himself has to say of his work." The agent was right in her assumption, as it did not bring about the desired change in the decision. Two days later Chambers politely thanked de Jannelli for her "courtesy in letting [him] see a copy of Mr. Nabokoff's very interesting comment on Mr. Nazaroff's review of *The Gift*" and wished him all success with adapting *Laughter in the Dark* to the stage or screen (another project that Nabokov was trying to pursue at that time with the help of his American agent).

Nazaroff's review was by no means "silly," as Altagracia de Jannelli hastily called it in her letter to the Bobbs-Merrill president. On the contrary, it remains one of the most vivid examples of shrewd critical feedback to Nabokov's novel.

"Like Rising Bread Forgotten by the Baker..."

Another early internal review that had survived in the archive was also written by a contemporary and former compatriot of the author. This second reader appears to have been a less sophisticated one than Alexander Nazaroff, although this in no way makes the document less distinctive, first and foremost as an illustration of 'naïve reading.' Charles Scribner's Sons Publishers commissioned this short review by a Russian émigré whose name was never mentioned in the correspondence between the publisher and Nabokov's literary agent.

Chapter Seven. CRITICAL RECEPTION

Charles Scribner's Sons, founded in 1846, was well known for publishing Ernest Hemingway, F. Scott Fitzgerald, and Thomas Wolfe, among others; several Scribner titles and authors garnered Pulitzer Prizes and National Book Awards. After the Bobbs-Merrill fiasco, it was decided to offer a possible translation of *The Gift* to this respected firm.

However, on September 16, 1938, John Hall Wheelock of Charles Scribner's Sons returned the manuscript of *The Gift* to Mme. de Jannelli. In accordance with the agent's request, Wheelock also enclosed his reader's report along with the cover letter to Mr. Perkins[40] (which was not copied to Nabokov). "When you have examined these, will you kindly return them to me? We don't usually do this, but perhaps it may help you in guiding Mr. Nabokoff," wrote the editor.

The unknown external reader opened his remarks with an apology that it had taken him so long to read the book — "it seems to take much longer to write about it. I am terribly sorry about the delay. It is not entirely my fault." Despite the cautious preamble it is clear that the reader made a genuine effort to work his way through the dense forest of modernist fiction, a category that he admits he was not particularly used to: "What the author sets out to do in this book is to give his reader the inside dope on the inner life of a person endowed or cursed with the gift of creative imagination. It is through the eyes of such person, in this instance a poet, Godunov-Cherdyntzev [sic!], or rather through his reactions, that we see the events and the characters of the book. The result is that we do not see them clearly, but as if we were looking through a double screen which makes their outlines not only vague, but also crooked. It is a stunt, and as such it is successful and amusing. Whether it is original or not, I cannot tell, because I do not read enough modernist literature."

The critic found it especially irritating that Nabokov uses various "stunts" that confuse the conservative reader and blur the line between reality and imagination. "Another favorite stunt of the author," the reviewer continued, "is to make his hero live in his imagination for ten or twelve pages and then suddenly, without warning, jerk both him and the reader back to reality, so that the reader never quite knows where either of them is. For instance, the hero would be looking at an old tree with the swing which he and his sister used to enjoy so much in their childhood; then he would walk away from that tree and take the reader with him over the paths and avenues of his old country estate, talking to his father, and smelling buckwheat fields and what not; and then it will all suddenly vanish and the bewildered reader will find himself in front of just any old tree in the crowded public park in Berlin."

---

[40] Maxwell Perkins (1884-1947) was the influential literary editor who worked with the writers such as Ernest Hemingway, F. Scott Fitzgerald, and Thomas Wolfe. Hemingway's *The Old Man and the Sea* (1952) was dedicated to Perkins' memory.

The reviewer was paticularly upset with what he believed to be unmotivated and confusing transitions within the narrative: "Or our hero will be holding a discussion with another poet, whom he meets in a park, about the respective merits of this or that Russian literary style, and after twenty pages of this discussion the other poet will suddenly break the flow of our poet's ideas by some trivial remark in German, because he really wasn't that other poet, but just a German unemployed resting on a bench, who happened to recall the image of this other poet to our poet's restlessly creative brain."

At a certain point the bleary-eyed critic felt that he had to defend his methodology, but instead just resorted to an expressive simile, almost foreshadowing the title of one of the American reviews which appeared twenty five years later:

> I am talking so much about these tricky stunts because they are the best thing about the book. The story itself, the characters and the events, do not have the amusing quality of these tricks. The book itself has no form; it sprawls around like rising bread forgotten by the baker. It seems that in making his hero a fellow writer the author thought he had provided himself sufficient excuse for stringing together all sorts of heterogeneous subjects, practically everything he had ever heard of or thought about, and trying to squeeze them into this book. Some of the subjects he had thought about might be interesting to people well acquainted with Russian poetry, Russian literature, and Russian literary criticism of the latter half of the last century. They would not be interesting to others, and even to me they fail to redeem a dull book. There is no real plot and no suspense whatever. The characters of the hero and his friends and acquaintances, Russian émigrés in Berlin, are drawn with indifferent disapproval rather than sympathy, with dull mockery rather than humor. (Iglehart 4F)

It was not only the novel's plot and subject matter that the reviewer found weak; the author's language also came under fire from the carping critic. Nabokov's colloquial Russian, he suggested, "seems to have suffered from his many years of absence from his native land." The dialogue, the evaluator continued, did not sound authentic to him, though he admitted parenthetically that he himself had also been away from Russia for a long time.

In what is generally a confused response, the anonymous reader stated that *The Gift* "was a real disappointment," and that it was not worth translating and publishing it because of its length, its contemplative nature, and the fact that it deals with subjects that would be accessible and interesting only to readers who are well acquainted with the nuances and ongoing polemics of Russian literature and criticism.

The critic's suggestions to the publisher appear to be in tune with what Nazaroff had independently expressed to Bobbs-Merrill earlier. In his opinion, novels like *The Defense* (which he briefly recounted, though omitting the title) were much more accessible and more suitable for the purpose of introducing the

Russian writer to the American public. "Several years ago I read another book by the same author built very much on the same idea—only there the hero was a chess-player. The reader was made to live in the same way in his head. The book was short and lively and interesting. I remember that I liked it and recommended it to Simon and Schuster, for whom I was doing the reading. And I think [that this novel] would be a much better book to translate. I met the author in Paris and liked him too..." One suspects that this final personal mention was meant to imply the opposite of what it stated explicitly.

A long pause followed after these two internal reviews, and it was not until twenty five years later that *The Gift* was once again exposed to the scrutiny of the English-speaking audience.

CONTEMPORARY CRITICS: 1962–77

The Gift after *Lolita*:
Responses to the English Publication

The appearance of another novel from the author of *Lolita* was much anticipated. Thus after the English translation of *The Gift* hit the bookstores it was—due to inertia and, ironically, wrong expectations on the part of the readers—reviewed extensively in the American and European press. More than a hundred responses were published in 1963 in English alone, immediately following its release in the USA, Canada, and Great Britain (Bryer, Bergin 353-358).

Although hailing *The Gift* as an indubitable achievement by Nabokov, most critics accepted it with reservations, calling it "disconcerting," "boring," and "irritating" (Malcolm), a novel that puts readers "in the dock" forcing them "to set [their] teeth on edge" (Davie), or even an "artifice" constructed by a "maniacal creator" (Hyman).

Along with many articles praising the author for his brilliant style, even more critics were wary of Nabokov's Trojan gift. The review headlines during the spring and fall of 1963 ran: "Early Nabokov Tale Wordy, Confusing" (*Toledo Blade*), "A Bizarre Tale By *Lolita*'s Creator" (*San Francisco Examiner*), "Strangest Prose-Poet Russia Ever Produced" (*Houston Chronicle*), "Nabokov's Merry Pranks Hard to Follow in *Gift*" (*Charlotte Observer*), "Scarey Sophistication" (*Newsweek*), "Early Nabokov Novel Charms But Befuddles" (*Newport News Daily Press*), "Early Nabokov Novel Paradoxical Wonder" (*Omaha Sunday World—Herald*), "Nabokov Nets Another Mixed Literary Bag" (*St. Louis Sunday Post-Dispatch*), "Early Nabokov Novel—*The Gift* Not Up to *Lolita*" (*Atlanta Journal and Constitution*), "Even the Mighty Can Fall" (*Toronto Telegram*), "Nabokov Makes It Difficult" (*Nottingham Guardian Journal*). It seems that the overall disappointment was expressed in the title of W.G. Rogers's piece, "Nabokov Novel Not a *Lolita*" (Gary *Post-Tribune*).

Contemporary Critics: 1962–77

After his Russian magnum opus was finally out and immortalized in English, Nabokov could not have cared less about the fuss it provoked. One can even imagine that in the meantime Nabokov was enjoying the oddly amusing titles such as "Soviet Writer Remembers Berlin Life" (*Miami Herald*), or "Samovars in Berlin" (*Milwaukee Journal*).

[Ill. 7-1] Collage of clippings: reviews of *The Gift* (1963) published in the American and British press

Chapter Seven. CRITICAL RECEPTION

A Trojan Gift: Defining the Context

When published in English for the first time in 1963, Nabokov's *The Gift* was read alongside and perceived against the background of the latest literary bestsellers. Reviews of the novel were placed among the critical evaluations of such book market novelties as Günter Grass's *The Tin Drum* and *Cat and Mouse*, Thomas Pynchon's *V.*, Iris Murdoch's *The Unicorn*, Kingsley Amis's *My Enemy's Enemy*, Uwe Johnson's *Speculations about Jacob,* and John Fowles's *The Collector.* It is essential to keep in mind the contemporary referential framework for *The Gift* at the time of its initial introduction to the English-language.

It is also instructive to see what novels were read and enjoyed most in the spring of 1963, during the same few weeks when *The Gift* was first being widely distributed. According to the sales reports, the following works of fiction were the top sellers in the Washington area bookstores:

1. *The Unicorn* — Iris Murdoch
2. *The Glass Blowers* — Daphne du Maurier
3. *A Favorite of the Gods* — Sybille Bedford
4. *The Tin Drum* — Günter Grass
5. *The Shoes of the Fisherman* — Morris L. West
6. *Raise High the Roof Beam, Carpenters* — J.D. Salinger

(*Washington Post Times Herald*; May 26, 1963)

Puzzled contemporary reviewers admitted, with rare exception, that the style of Nabokov's novel is a work of genius; the most inquisitive of them tried to find apt parallels in existing literary canons. For parallels critics tended to look first to the Russian classics, calling *The Gift* "a sad yet often hilarious account, told with the eye and ear of a Dickens or a Gogol, of the tight little world of the émigré" (Perlberg 10). Comparison to Nikolai Gogol's art was almost inevitable: "In his latest book, Nabokov has written of Gogol: 'The strangest prose-poet Russia ever produced.' Nabokov is too modest. He, himself, deserves that accolade, if it is one" (Abram 10). The Western writers, however, prevailed. One critic was genuinely surprised by Nabokov's cosmopolitanism as he discovered that in a quarter-century-old Russian novel, "already way back then Nabokov could drop in a reference to Edgar Allan Poe who gave him the form for *Lolita* [and] quote Mallarmé's 'L'Apres-midi d'un faune'" (Rogers 9).

Critics offered various concrete examples of possible influence on *The Gift*, ranging from Imagist poetry[41] and French Symbolism, namely Remy de

---

[41] The reviewer quoted a sequence that cuts from naturalist's accuracy to Pushkin, and then to wild yaks frozen solid in a Chinese river, claiming that this is a paragraph "wonderfully constructed like an imagist poem" (Davie 8). "Frozen yaks" as a strong image was singled out by a number of contemporary critics (W. Rogers also noted "yak heads caught in swiftly freezing water" [Rogers 9]).

Gourmont's (1858-1915) "Physique de l'Amour" (in D. Davie's review), to Rilke's only novel, *The Notebooks of Malte Laurids Brigge* (1910). For the latter work, as Steven Spender suspected, Nabokov would have had little sympathy (a work "woven of reminiscences, dreams, history and introspection," it functions similarly to *The Gift*, which is "essentially a novel about imaginative truth: the truth of fiction, and beyond this, the truth of poetry"; Spender 289).

Rilke and de Gourmont notwithstanding, the majority of reviewers, obviously, mentioned that Nabokov's novel evoked comparisons with the writing of James Joyce. Paraphrasing Kinbote from *Pale Fire*, Stanley Hyman declared that Nabokov "succeeded in producing the most ambiguous *apparatus criticus* imaginable... twisted and battered... into the finest comic novel since *Ulysses*."[42] Spender evoked Joyce's *Portrait of the Artist as a Young Man* as a comparable story of a young man's consciousness of his gift: "Nabokov has more irony, humor, richness of enjoyment, love of real flesh and blood than Rilke; but in merging the actual with the imagined, he makes the question of what is real, what unreal, fundamentally an esthetic one, whereas Joyce, with his Jesuit philosophic training, avoided this identification of different kinds of truth. In *The Gift*, Nabokov steers clear of the ghastly spiritual self-indulgence of Rilke, but he does not altogether avoid whimsy."[43] Renate Wolff suggested yet another distinction to be made between Nabokov and Joyce: "From the mass slaughter of acquaintances, the only characters emerging with any physical or mental grace, any intelligence, dignity, or decency, are Fyodor himself, his idealized father and mother (unlike, for instance, Joyce's artist-hero, Nabokov preserves a fierce family loyalty), Zina, and a brother poet—all, in varying senses, extensions of his own ego..." (Wolff 9-D). Nabokov, together with other European modernists, was seen as a direct descendant of the classics:

> Now Nabokov can believe in curved space, in a geometry without parallel lines—indeed, in all the intellectual play and imaginative dreaming of which man is capable. It is this capacity that distinguishes him from most 19th century writers—with the possible exception of Joyce, Beckett, and a few others—and that leads us back to metaphysical poets, and to Rabelais, Sterne, and Peacock for helpful comparisons. (Hayes 6)

---

[42] Hyman 21; cf.: "[*The Gift*] is as marvelous in its own way as *Pale Fire*, and it displays another variety of the same fantastic form: the novel as literary criticism and the spoof of literary criticism. One would have to know a great deal more than I do about Russian literature to get all the references and parodies in *The Gift*. (This neatly reverses *Pale Fire*, where poor Kinbote didn't know enough about America to realize that Chapman's Homer was a home run by Sam Chapman.)" (Ibid.).

[43] The same Joycean parallel was mentioned in Mitchell 38.

Along with Joyce and Beckett, Marcel Proust was another author frequently mentioned among the literary predecessors of *The Gift*. Nabokov admitted his strong fondness for Proust and Flaubert as far back as 1934, in an interview given to *Poslednie novosti*, during the early stages of writing *The Gift*.[44] Nabokov himself may have endorsed this association with Proust: some newspapers simply reprinted the cover letter which the publisher circulated along with two now-famous photographs of the author.[45] This synopsis included a phrase describing the novel as "comical and satirical, Proustian in its evocation of Fyodor's childhood." This was repeatedly either reproduced intact (Watkins 21; Williams P-17; P-25) or slightly paraphrased. Thus Nabokov "evoked his childhood with a Proustian exactness" (Hutchens 28); his "characterization of the poet [was] a fine reconstruction of a personage, done somewhat in the manner of Proust, shadows and nuances tinting the scene, thoughts and memories filling the lines, and over all a sadness that will not permit the sunlight of life to enter at any aperture" (Weissblatt 14); Nabokov was said to have presented "a Proustian picture of émigré Russians in Berlin of the early 1920s" (Butler 31); Nabokov with his "wonderful vision and insight [and] great richness of imagery" was praised for "the unforgettable Proustian quality of combining vivid reminiscences with well-nigh unbearable pathos" (ibid.); it was said that Fyodor's "love affair with Zena [sic] and his literary endeavors [were] a Proustian remembrance of childhood" (Griffin 1688); and, finally, Nabokov apparently digressed "magnificently at several points... like Marcel Proust, who abandons his characters to expatiate on literature, music and painting" (Mercier 4).

However flattering a comparison with the French virtuoso may seem today, not every critic at the time viewed it as a great asset: "It is a decadent, static, exquisite, utterly reflex art that results; and that, at its best, almost out-Prousts Proust. The author has magnificent equipment, and he does nothing with it... There is an enchanting glimpse of Fyodor's father entering the 'base of rainbow' and leaving it again in a single step. Nabokov's own sensibility never gets outside its own 'colored air.' That is why, for all its coruscating brilliance, *The Gift* must be finally adjudged a failure" (Brady B-10). Others disagreed with that verdict: "This seems to be a major novel—and while it can stand rough treatment, it does not deserve such" (Brown 9).

Among the prominent French and British modernists of the early 20th century juxtaposed with Nabokov in this critical discourse was Virginia Woolf.

---

[44] Interview conducted by Andrei Sedykh. Quoted in: Grayson 218. Also cf.: "Nabokov [of *The Gift*] is one of the finest writers, a worthy addition to the line of craftsmen that include Flaubert and James" (Sanders 32).

[45] The first portrait was by an artist named Horst Tappe—Nabokov in a raincoat hood; the second one was made by a Swiss photographer Guy de Belleval and it featured Nabokov in a relaxed pose with an arm stretching up and behind his head. Newspaper editors were mostly interested in the close-up of the author (who was at the time still not widely recognized), and often removed Nabokov's arm by retouching.

Her semi-biographical novel was first published in 1928: "*The Gift* is, in a very special sense, Nabokov's equivalent of Virginia Woolf's *Orlando* or of that strange chapter in *Ulysses* in which Joyce recapitulates the history of England's language and literature" (Crane 5). Certain elements in Woolf's stylistically intricate novel could support such a parallel (for example, "The Oak Tree," the poem written by Orlando in the novel), but the author of *The Gift* dismissed women's writing and gender issues as a whole. As early as the 1930s, Nabokov pronounced *Orlando* a "first-class example of *poshlost*'" (Boyd 402).

Several of Nabokov's Western contemporaries were called to take the stand in the search for his Anglophone literary double. The names ranged from the 1949 Nobel Prize laureate, William Faulkner (who passed away shortly before the *Dar* translation appeared),[46] to Thomas Pynchon, the front-runner of a young generation of promising novelists. The Cornell graduate's debut novel *V.* was published the same year as the English version of *The Gift*, bringing Pynchon a William Faulkner Foundation Award for best first novel of the year.

Robert Kirsch compared *The Gift* with Nikos Kazantzakis's (1883-1957) novels *The Rock Garden* and *The Saviors of God*, both composed in Europe decades earlier and published in English only in the 1960s.[47]

Prompted by the "balletic effect" of Nabokov's style, even composer Igor Stravinsky's name was unexpectedly mentioned in connection with *The Gift*: "I don't suppose it's particularly true to life in Berlin in 1922," said the *New Statesman* observer (mixing up the fictional date), "but it does have a larger truth to the art of the time: experimental and antiquarian, Russian and international, and above all dominated by style. It reminds one of Stravinsky. But in spite of the intoxicated, balletic effect, Nabokov is nearer the earth here than in his latest novels; it's odd that this was to lead to *Pale Fire*" (Taubman 654). Stravinsky became a U.S. citizen in 1945 and in 1962 went back to Russia for an eightieth-birthday tour (his first and last return).[48]

---

[46] Cf.: "One critic described Nabokov as 'digressive and wayward' and so he is. But so are the works of Faulkner, and so is the life of every man" (Page 6).

[47] *The Saviors of God* opens with the statement: "We come from a dark abyss, we end in a dark abyss, and we call the luminous interval life" that closely mimics the prologue to Nabokov's autobiography *Speak, Memory*). According to Kirsch, "despite the differences in approach and technique, the wide variance of setting and subject manner...these novels share [something] in common. First, and most important since it is the indispensable function of fiction, each writer recognizes that the attention, the absorption of the reader must be earned...There are elements of autobiography in Nabokov's story of the writer Fyodor Godunov-Cherdyntsev exploring his past and living his present in the absurd nostalgia of Berlin in the 1920s. There are also elements of autobiography in Kazantzakis's tale of a European's experience in China in the 1930s" (Kirsch 12).

[48] Curiously, in chapter fourteen of *V.*, V. is entranced with a young ballerina, Mélanie l'Heuremaudit. The story is built around a riotous ballet performance, almost certainly modeled in part on the premiere of Stravinsky's *Rite of Spring*. The performance centers

While most of the comparisons were favorable, others occasionally brought up the names of Soviet writers such as Pasternak or Voloshin, a long forgotten champion of Socialist Realist prose. This review might have caused something of a nervous tremor for Nabokov: "'Humane' and 'humanitarian' are different. Yet *The Gift* seems to me not just brilliant (Nabokov is always that), but also profound and persuasive, the only émigré novel to stand beside [Pasternak's] *Doctor Zhivago*. (In their militant aestheticism the two books have much in common.)" (Davie 8). Pasternak was indeed a rival much to be desired when compared to that chosen by a Canadian critic who reached all the way to Alexander Voloshin's *Kuznetsk Land*, an epic which was awarded the Stalin Prize:[49] "About ten years ago, to catch up on a modern Russian fiction, I read a mass of novels written under Stalinism. One, *Kuznetsk Land*, by Voloshin, typified them all: the greater glory of the industrial growth of the new territories was the theme. Try as one might, it was hard to be sympathetic when such a juggernaut was deliberately intended to dominate the story. Mr. Nabokov's novel is nearly as bad: this time it is the Russian émigrés in the Paris [sic] of the twenties who prevail" (Rowe u.16).

One of the most intriguing comparisons of *The Gift* to Soviet literature was between Nabokov and Abram Tertz (pseudonym of Andrei Sinyavsky, 1925-1997). Paul Levine wrote in his survey of contemporary fiction for *The Hudson Review*:

> Tertz's hero is always the artist as madman and criminal: petty thieves who want to be magicians, men whose power to predict the future ultimately destroys them, insane writers who never publish anything. Sometimes Tertz's surrealistic apparatus seems too literal but in a brilliant tale like 'Graphomaniacs' he creates an underground world of crazed writers which does indeed 'correspond best to the spirit of our time.'

---

on a virgin sacrifice by impalement. The young ballerina fails to wear her protective equipment, and actually dies by impalement during the performance; everyone assumes her death throes simply to be an extraordinarily emotional performance. Igor Stravinsky (1882–1971), like Nabokov, enjoyed remarkable fame in old age—'the Picasso of music,' he was approached for private commissions, Hollywood film scores, jazz collaborations, and even a commission involving the Ringling Bros. Circus. Similar to Nabokov, who was able to reintroduce his Russian oeuvre to the world during the 1960s and 1970s, the composer supervised a complete recording of his works, and a series of *Conversations*, books of memoirs in the form of engaging answers to his friend Robert Craft's questions.

[49] *Kuznetsk Land* ["Zemlia Kuznetskaia"] (Moscow, Foreign Languages Publishing House, 1953. First English Edition), published in 1948, was the first major work by the Soviet author Aleksandr Nikitich Voloshin (1912-1978). Its action unfolds against the background of life in the Soviet mining town Kuznetsk between 1945 and 1947. The Kuznetsk coal basin ("Kuzbas") was developed in Western Siberia during the first five-year plan and became an important iron and steel area and cultural center. The novel's hero, Rogov, a former captain of the guards and an engineer in civilian life, returns from the front to the Kuzbas to start life anew at one of the local mines.

> Tertz depicts the recurrent problem of artistic communication in a dehumanized world by exploiting the vein of grotesque Russian fantasy that Gogol, Dostoevsky, and Chagall also drew upon. Nabokov's last Russian novel, *The Gift*, now published for the first time in English, reminds us that fantasy and alienation are the dual artistic heritage in Russia. *The Gift* concerns a group of Russian exiles living in Berlin in the 1920s but Nabokov is less interested in 'the pale ghosts of innumerable foreigners flickering among those natives like a familiar but barely noticeable hallucination' than he is in the nature of the artistic imagination... In a central portion of the book Fyodor recounts the biography he has written of a revolutionary of the 1860s who was exiled by the Tzar. The ironic parallel between the writer and his subject is beautifully handled in this generally exquisite novel — and when put together with *Fantastic Tales* [Published as *Fantastic Stories* (New York: Pantheon Books, 1963) — Y.L.] one begins to feel that the problem of art in Russia is historical and not narrowly ideological. (Levine 461-462)

Another important point advanced in Levine's essay was that despite the visible failure of the protagonists, their creators demonstrate a defiant artistic triumph: "Nabokov's exiled poet and Tertz's frustrated graphomaniac, like [Sir Kingsley William] Amis's displaced intellectual and Pynchon's far-out jazz musician, are all reminders of the increasing difficulty of artistic communication in the modern world. But behind the failure of these heroes lies the success of their creators, reaffirming the power of art and teaching, as Tertz says, 'how to be truthful with the aid of the absurd fantastic.' The internationalism of the contemporary artistic vision — grotesque but human — recalls Melville's eloquent prophecy: 'For genius, all over the world, stands hand in hand, and one shock of recognition runs the whole circle round'."[50] In the end, it was this *shock of recognition* that Nabokov's fellow compatriots had difficulty tolerating and accepting.

It is just as instructive to look at which writers were contrasted to Nabokov by reviewers. The author of *The Gift* clearly had nothing in common with writers of the "Beat Generation," which came as quite a relief to one critic who was exasperated by modern English-language scribblers:

> Every time I begin to get depressed about the state of current fiction, something comes along to restore my spirits. In the present instance, a trio of books [including Nabokov's] have given me a respite from the outpourings of those novelists aptly described by Truman Capote in his description of Jack Kerouac. He said Kerouac doesn't write, he typewrites [...] In Nabokov's novel we see the pure and playful sense of the comic, the touch of parody, the remarkable

---

50   For more on A. Tertz's prose of the 1950-1960s and its affinities with and possible intertextual dialogue with Nabokov, see: Desyatov 214-224.

virtuoso performance of a writer who seems to be able to do anything with words and usually does. He is rooted in the 18th century, in that portion of the literature which rejected easy sentimentality and which made possible the handling of the complexities of human nature in terms of an external world. (Kirsch 12)

On the other hand, though Nabokov himself did not, his character Fyodor triggered certain curious associations with the Beat poets. According to Jim Dance, Fyodor "knows a group of intellectuals—Berlin's 'beatniks' of that era" (Dance 5), while the Russian exile reminded one of the young Beatnik theoreticians of David Benedictus: "Fyodor's debunking critical biography... is received with cold fury by the more established critics who regard the author as an upstart, and it achieves a scandalous success (shades of Colin Wilson, our scapegoat!)" (Benedictus 17). Colin H. Wilson, a British writer who left school and worked in factories while reading in his spare time, published *The Outsider* (1956) at the age of twenty-four.[51]

Nabokov's "new-old" Russian prose looked like it could have been written by virtually any great author, though not without one important reservation: no one could write it better than Nabokov himself. A typical critical stance while searching for Nabokov's nearest "Other" was concisely summarized in the following review:

> We can learn more about Berlin from Isherwood, more about Russia—although not its literature—from Pasternak, more about human nature under stress from any of the transcendental Russians, and more about a poem's particular form—well, not from anyone actually; here Nabokov is supreme. [...] If, like me, you are simpler in your tastes and less extravagant, you may be vastly impressed by the man's mind, but you will be intermittently bored and it will not be until the final section [of *The Gift*], which is as delicate and pleasing as a Jane Austen novel, or a chapter of Dickens, or a Max Beerbohm sentence, or an Oscar Wilde phrase or a word of advice from a true friend, that you will be either delighted or moved. (Benedictus 17)

With the appearance of *The Gift* in translation, Nabokov's much appreciated contribution to American fiction and the English language became manifest as never before: "It seems to me that this world [of émigré Russian literature]

---

[51] The study examined the role of the social "outsider" in seminal works of various key literary and cultural figures (Albert Camus, Jean-Paul Sartre, Ernest Hemingway, Hermann Hesse, Fyodor Dostoyevsky, and others). Wilson was labeled as an "Angry Young Man" and a chapter of *The Outsider* was excerpted in a popular paperback sampler, *Protest: The Beat Generation and the Angry Young Men*. This welcome by leading figures of their day was short-lived and Wilson was subsequently vilified.

was altogether too tight, too restrictive to contain such a free spirit as Vladimir Nabokov. A book like this which, in his own words, lies 'on a brink of parody,' is a sure sign that its author has come to the end of the street, that he must try something altogether new or simply stop writing. In Nabokov's case, the 'something new' was English; and in English, the 'something new' was Nabokov" (Cook 74-75). Nabokov's American success, it turned out, was not the whim of a couple of recent bestsellers, but the next stage in the long, complex evolution of a serious writer rooted in the traditions of the European literature and world culture.

Vodka and Samovars in Berlin

Terence Young's film "From Russia with Love" became the second James Bond movie after President John F. Kennedy listed the Ian Fleming book among his top ten favorite novels of all time (the list was published in *Life Magazine*); it was released in the same year as Nabokov's novel, essentially his declaration of love to all of Russian literature. David Benedictus of *The Sunday Telegraph* played with this coincidence in the opening of his review of *The Gift*: "Vladimir Nabokov is an international grand master. From Russia with love he brought the vision and method of a chess-player, an imposing knowledge of natural lore and a literary heritage that we can only envy" (Benedictus 17). The chess theme in the novel as well as Nabokov's own love for that game was relevant to the discussion.[52] Day Thorpe was similarly convinced that *The Gift* was "assured of at least partial immortality, for the pages that vivify the spirit of chess are the best ever written on the subject, and will grace anthologies forevermore" (Thorpe B-5).

The early English-language reviews of *The Gift* typically fell into a particular pattern. Most of the critics offered a summary of the plot (which most agreed was a fairly simple one[53]); usually they would quote from Nabokov's own foreword (more often than from the text of the novel itself) and then sum up their impressions. This last part is the most interesting in terms of the reader-response study as it shows the array of rhetorical devices employed in the attempt to cope with the perceived obscurity of Nabokov's Russian novel.

---

[52] Maggie Ross's review of *The Gift* was immediately followed by a "Chess Forum" which addressed the following question: "Why do players behind the Iron Curtain seem to do so well?" The article explained that the state support and the social and financial prestige of chess in the Soviet Union were the main reasons for their success, which really boomed when it became known that Lenin was an avid player and when card clubs were closed down by the communists (Ross 853).

[53] Cf.: "The plot is simple, though the treatment occasionally is maddeningly intricate" (Crane 5).

Chapter Seven. CRITICAL RECEPTION

Some reviewers, having fallen under Nabokov's spell, were obviously at pains to write "beautifully." It was felt as almost a must to find a particularly fresh metaphor or to resort to a bold comparison when assessing *The Gift*. As a rule, the results were banal.

Speaking of Fyodor and Zina's love one critic described it as "a romance as spectral and evocative as autumn mist" (Barrett 137). Another constructed his entire discourse based on the opposition of vodka and wine with their attributes representing the beverages' intrinsic characteristics accordingly (strong vs. delicate, bold vs. subtle, Russian vs. Western, etc.). "As a novel, this is a lot closer to vodka than it is to the author's later wine," asserted Miles Smith of the Ohio *Toledo Blade*. "It is very Russian and has a powerful kick: but the imbiber needs a strong constitution if he is to keep a clear head" (Smith 6). After recapitulating the plot, the author returned to his initial train of thought:

> Readers who are familiar with books that Nabokov has written in English—most recently, *Pale Fire*—are aware that he pours an exotic wine into his later books, and delights in playing tricky games with his audience. But they are easier to read than this one. *The Gift* is a wild cataract of words, rushing hither and yon, and it flashes with brilliant images and frequently dazzling observations—but it has a Slavic, mercurial garrulity. (Ibid.)

Smith objected to the "technical stunts" performed by Nabokov when he wrote "like several Russian authors"; Nabokov's sleight-of-hand in switching back and forth from the first to the third person, taking the reader inside and outside the character, was also questioned. In conclusion, this literary sommelier predicted: "Technically interesting, this volume doubtless will delight literary aficionados. As for the general reader, by the time he has finished the first chapter he may discover that the high-proof vodka has blurred his comprehension" (Smith 6).

The symbol of Russia's national hard drink was certainly in high fashion at that time. Walter Blum's film review, "Movie mayhem by James Bond," printed next to the review of *The Gift* in the *San Francisco Examiner* (May 26, 1963), quoted from the recently released sequel about the super spy: "Faced with imminent death from his arch-enemy, Dr. No, Bond's only request is for 'a medium vodka dry Martini—with a slice of lemon peel. Shaken and not stirred, please.'"

Nabokov did not like such brusque statements but there was little he could do—he had become, much like vodka, a part of the American pop culture mosaic. After seeing a magazine with a promotional blurb for *The Eye* that read, "A James Bond-type book by the author of *Lolita*!," he sent a short telegram to his New York publisher, Phaedra, all in capital letters: "FOR GOODNESS SAKE DON'T COMPARE ME IN ADS TO BOND OR [JOHN] LE CARRÉ WHOEVER THEY ARE."[54]

---

[54] 19 September, 1965; vn *Berg Collection*, New York Public Library.

Paradoxically, Nabokov's success as the English-language author of *Lolita* partly hampered any real engagement with the younger Sirin. The twisted logic of his apparent creative progress made it possible to declare that *The Gift*, "belong[ing] to the first period of Nabokov's career...of all his works now in English, is the one least worth anybody's attention...Most of the American readers will find it a heart-stopping bore, dulled by an excess of cleverness and a minimum of engaging materials" (Kostelanetz 7-8). What's more, some critics displayed an almost complete lack of understanding of Nabokov's literary career before switching to English, either stating that *The Gift* was his first and last Russian novel (Barrett 135), or reducing Nabokov to a Russian novelist who "wrote several inventive but essentially trivial comic novels" (Kostelanetz 7-8).

Most of the blind critics' blunders were anticipated and comically "pre-produced" by Nabokov himself at the beginning of the novel's fifth chapter. Nonetheless, time and again reviewers would launch into a summary of *The Gift*—muddling, misquoting, and inventing. It was not only small-town papers that sinned against the truth; even the reputable *Time* allowed itself an anonymous hodgepodge such as this:

> Count [sic!] Fyodor Godunov-Cherdyntsev is in his early 20s, living in exile in Berlin, struggling not to be crippled by memories of the ancient [sic!] family estate in Leshino, and trying to get his poetry and prose published in impoverished [sic!] émigré magazines. His sister marries and leaves for Paris; he meets and falls in love with Zina, a remotely fragile German girl [sic!]. All of this is simple, and corresponds roughly to the facts of Nabokov's own life. But from the first page, the reader is off fiction's flatlands into Nabokov's magic world. His aristocratic Fyodor is a lord of language, and this patrimony cannot be expropriated. ([Unsigned]. "Lord of Language" 102)

Endeavoring to demonstrate his expertise in Russian culture, another critic blended the name of Pushkin's fictional title character into a list of famous nineteenth-century authors, reminding one of the "Tolstoevsky" centaur once made up by Nabokov himself: "*The Gift* is only incidentally political, just as it is only incidentally a love story. Primarily it is a celebration of Russian literature, and its various sections quite consciously evoke Pushkin, Gogol, Onegin [!] and others—not in parody or imitation, but in reflecting the influences upon young Fyodor in his development as a writer" (Coffey 13).

Similar errors prevailed in critical discourse such as the following: "Godunov-Cherdyntsev, with slashing irony and occasional outright belly laughs, demolishes the pompous, awkward journalist (and his materialist metaphysics), who in his Siberian exile writes a lumpish novel, titled, *What Is to Be Done?*" (Perlberg 10). Chernyshevski, of course, wrote his novel while still under arrest in St. Petersburg and before he was transported under guard to Siberia (as Nabokov accurately describes in Chapter Four of *The Gift*). For most American critics Chernyshevski remained no more than "a liberal thinker and critic exactly contemporary with the great novelist Dostoevsky," and what really mattered was that "the resulting biography is written in a mood of sardonic despair and youthful debunking" (Rollow 5-C).

At the same time some critics were justifiably inquisitive: "It is surprising that Nabokov should have devoted so much vigor and fantasy to the demolition of a figure he considered so completely insignificant" (Sherman 4C). Admittedly, the Chernyshevski section revealed both Nabokov's strengths and weaknesses:

> His portrait of the great *narodnik* ... is perfectly consistent and convincing, so long as it is considered by itself. But when one thinks of the influence which this man exercised on his contemporaries and on succeeding generations of Russian intellectuals ... then one suspects that Mr. Nabokov has somehow overlooked the most important feature of his subject. The omission (if omission there is) stems from the central weakness of Mr. Nabokov's extraordinary talent—his inability to see man as a social animal. ([Unsigned] "Russian Romp" 901)

Only those unfamiliar with Nabokov's philosophy could cite the inability to regard "man as a social animal" as one of the writer's characteristics. Nabokov's arrogant attitude in *The Gift* toward critics in general was not a plus either. While the worlds of Chernyshevski and Russian expatriates in Germany seemed to be totally irrelevant to the Western audience, contemporary reviewers could not fail to notice Nabokov's consistent invectives against their colleagues, albeit nonexistent, the émigré critics of bygone days:

> There is a book within a book in *The Gift*, the last of Vladimir Nabokov's books to be written in Russian, and of this a reviewer writes: 'If this is a beginning it cannot be called a particularly reassuring one.' The same might be said of the whole book.
>
> Indeed, if it were not for a certain precocious bobby-soxer this novel, first published in 1937-38 and dealing with Russian émigrés in Berlin of the Twenties, would surely not have been translated, since most of the interest it may have had vanished with the period it describes. Who now has heard of Belinsky, Mikhailovsky and Fet or wishes to read pages of stilted dialogue about their literary merits? (Hinde 605)

A few others disagreed and enjoyed the fourth chapter despite not possessing an encyclopedic knowledge of the Russian historical context: "The most impressive thing in the novel is [Godunov-Cherdyntsev's] detailed study of the nineteenth-century literary-social critic, Chernyshevski" (Cook 74-75). What is more, not everyone flatly rejected the disjointed and eclectic method of blending Chernyshevski's biography with the hero's poems or a tribute to his scientist

[Ill. 7-2] Collage of clippings: reviews of *The Gift* (1963) published in the American and British press

father. According to one such defender of the novel's structure, "[c]ombined, these elements offer (despite the academic and extremely devious style and construction) a three-dimensional replica of a certain time, place, intellectual climate, mood and motivation; in short, a tangible 'atmosphere'" (Dwight 5-F). Even those who seemed to be scared away by early Sirin's excessive erudition still appreciated the gems of mature Nabokov:

> The publishers claim that this is the greatest Russian novel of the twentieth century, but for me its interest lies in the early rumblings it contains of later Nabokov. One can already detect the ornate style (here frequently out of control), the love of bizarre situations, the minute observation of female physical attributes. If, however, one were to predict a future for the author on the strength of *The Gift* one would see him not as a novelist but as an essayist. A couple of set pieces on advertising and butterflies, inserted amid pages of self-conscious stream of consciousness, are excellent. (Hinde 605)

The "certain precocious bobby-soxer" is, of course, Lolita, but it is unclear exactly what Hinde is referring to when he mentions Nabokov's minute observations of "female physical attributes" in *The Gift*. Glendy Culligan of the *Washington Post* had been equally assertive regarding the gloomy prospects that this Russian novel would have had if not for the recent scandalous success of its author: "[N]early twenty years before her time, we meet the embryonic Lolita, who, grown to mature nymphhood in 1955, would establish Nabokov's reputation, and make possible the rescue of this fascinating work, doomed otherwise to be read only by White Russians" (Culligan G8).

The "Purple Cow" in the "Surrounding Murk" (The Metaphors)

Nabokov's richly metaphoric language in *The Gift* mesmerized readers. Reviewers quoted various examples of what attracted their attention ("She was slowly mixing a white exclamation mark of sour cream into her borshch" [G159]—this phrase was called "brilliant...startlingly keen, with the observation of the naturalist"; Wolff 9-D). However, what is more interesting is that the very language of some reviews became metaphorically intensified as a result of their authors' attempt to convey their message through half-conscious imitation of the subject of their critique.

Particularly abundant were comparisons of Nabokov's language with fire: "It is a dazzling display of verbal pyrotechnics, crammed with thoughts, dreams, memories, and digressions into such far-flung fields as lepidoptery and poetry. As the reader makes his way through the dense maze of personal and literary reflections, his mind is filled with images and associations: it is stretched beyond ordinary limits and pushed into new realms of seeing, feeling, and believing" (Gilmore 25). W.G. Rogers, after quoting Fyodor revealing his love for words, colors, mental fireworks, and Russia, added: "All that is here, anecdotal but unified, brilliantly colored, not just ordinary fireworks but the grand finale set-piece itself, most dazzling, farthest spreading of all fireworks" (Rogers 9).

A number of readers shared the perception of the writer-reader relationship in *The Gift* as one akin to a totalitarian model in which Nabokov appears as a kind of magus, dictating his authorial will to the audience. Characteristically, the confused reader's experience was described as a blind journey arranged by an invisible guide: "This book can be read on many levels and in fact must be as the reader is moved like a puppet from one level to another and is never entirely sure on which level he is" (Hunter 8). This reader-as-puppet comparison was eventually supplemented by a harsher parallel—that of reader-as-trapped-mouse:

> – "Mr. Nobokov [sic] is a past master at playing cat and mouse tricks and seemingly takes an impish delight in obfuscation, sometimes permitting only occasional shafts of lucidity to penetrate the smog he has generated" (A. Brown 9);
> – Nabokov is "cunningly supercharged with wicked wiles. He plays cat and mouse with the reader. He moves fictional and historical characters about like chessmen" (Allsop 16);
> – "[*The Gift*] probably is a portrait of the novelist as a young poet. The arch tone of Nabokov's disclaimer in the foreword to this new edition leads us to assume that the subject of the portrait is none other than the author. Yet we are wary approaching Nabokov with assumptions, especially after reading *Pale Fire* which appeared last year. Who ever really trusts the prestidigitator? We have to watch him ever so closely—and still say, 'Do that again!'" (Idema 10)

Cats and mice were not the only animals implicated in the assessment of the novel; the search for the best descriptive model could take rather surprising turns: "This is one of the most eccentric yet in many ways one of the most beautiful novels in modern literature...Mr. Nabokov was 36 at the time [of writing *The Gift*] and hence this splendid, often exasperating purple cow of a book is a work of maturity" (Perlberg 10). "Why purple cow?"—asked the reviewer only to answer by himself: "Because the novel is a hybrid work, without parallel in form in my experience" (Ibid).

Donald Stanley explained the book's unusual form as one modeled on "classic Russian examples: Pushkin and Gogol, even Chernyshevski" (Stanley 18). But, without any familiarity with these literary predecessors, he added that the episodes "dangle like a team of acrobats who have missed a cue" (Ibid). The comparison functions here as a poetic device (much more convincing than the critic's claim to have firsthand knowledge of the structural complexities of the works by the three writers he mentioned).

"Yet what is most memorable in *The Gift*, or so it seems to me," insisted John Hutchens, "comes only in flashes cutting through the surrounding murk" (Hutchens 28). Anna Hunter compared the reader's experience with that of a traveler in a dark flood of words: "For our part it is enough to wade through endless torrents of words to come on gems which sparkle in the deluge. There is scarcely a page where one may not find some deliciously fresh expression, some striking idea" (Hunter 8).

And on the subject of "deliciously fresh expressions," many reviewers treated *The Gift* literally as a culinary product, and their reviews at times sounded like a recipe. Lloyd Weber started off his survey by describing the novel as "a rich, meaty book with a Slavic flavor," and finished cautiously: "For sophisticated palates and quality fiction collections" (Griffin 1688). *The Gift* reminded another critic of a delicious pot-pie full of plums: "[Th]is book is a magnificent pot-pie of metaphor, allusion, humor and factual dissertations, you can put in your thumb and pull out a plum almost everywhere" (Sherman 4C). (Most Anglophone readers will immediately recognize this food metaphor as a reference to the nursery rhyme "Little Jack Horner / sat in a corner / eating a Christmas pie / He stuck in his thumb / and pulled out a plum / and said 'What a good boy am I!'"). The same literary gourmand used Don Juan's phrase from Act III of George Bernard Shaw's *Man and Superman* (1903): "Nabokov — he of the pornographic eye, of the relentlessly epigrammatic style, is not everyone's dish. For devotees, *The Gift* is a rich hamper itself. For others, well — as Shaw says, 'A picture gallery is a dull place for a blind man'" (Abram 10).

At least everyone seemed to have agreed on one point — Nabokov's novel is far from stale: "Despite the almost three decades which have passed in the interim, the book has a freshness and flavor that contrive to make it of immediate interest" (A. Brown 9).

The "Dense Texture" of the "Missing Structure"

Evaluating *The Gift* as a standard narrative unavoidably meant that it was defined in an over-simplified way. It is understandable why critics "felt that this is a collection of memories and notes that didn't quite come off as a novel, and that if it is widely read it will be due to the success of *Lolita* and *Pale Fire*" (B., A.G. 11-C).

Stephen Spender, the co-editor of *Encounter*, called *The Gift* a "thickly woven, immensely rewarding novel," placing it on the readers' bookshelves right beside the stories of Tolstoy and Chekhov (Spender 289). This book that had never been allowed to become part of an active literary process in its original language and, as a result, lacked the usual contemporary readers' response, was granted canonical status thirty years later almost without any serious discussion. Ironically, once again this *recognition post factum* only served to prevent an unsullied look at the text itself. This is not to say that unbiased critics like Spender did not have the proper context or sufficient patience. On the contrary, the British poet read the book three times, and still confessed that he failed "to obtain an idea of the kind of novel it is":

> *The Gift* is extremely difficult to describe. How inadequate is the idea one gives of a book simply by saying it is a novel...It combines several levels of narrative on several levels (fiction, history and poetry) of truth. Here is autobiography thinly disguised, and repudiated (of course) by the author in his 1962 Foreword, the biography (fantastically and both accurately and inaccurately treated) of a famous Russian thinker and rebel, descriptive reportage of the Berlin of the nineteen-twenties, literary criticism and what it seems best simply to call poetry.
>
> On the top, the novel-reader's level, *The Gift* is the story of a Russian émigré, living among other émigrés, experiencing the life of White Russians in Berlin, evoking the Russia of his childhood, sustained and rescued from the pathos of his situation by the *deus ex machina* of his gift, which is to write poetry.
>
> All this is funny, sad, satiric, evocative. Fyodor Godunov-Cherdyntsev is a poet neglectfully supporting himself in the pre-Isherwood Berlin by giving lessons, translating and writing nostalgic patriotic poems 'composed in a kind of drunken trance,' which are published in the refugee magazine *Gazeta*. He woos Zina Mertz, whom Nabokov manages to make as real as life and whom he yet infuses with the qualities that make readers fall in love with Turgenev's heroines. (Ibid.)

Spender was convinced that Nabokov was willing to "demolish the illusory truth of fiction in order to assert another truth," namely the power of the writer to invent and destroy his fictitious situations: "The slowly developing love affair, the Berlin bed-sitting rooms, the literary groups meeting in upstairs rooms of cafes to hear poetic-philosophic readings of writers with absurd pretensions—all these are only the outer shell surrounding the development of Fyodor's creating and criticizing, reminiscing, observing and fantasy-weaving mind. Indeed, everything is subjective imagination here, and the narrator makes it clear that he is not responsible to the reader even to the extent of making him believe in the truth of his fiction" (Ibid.). But he is also willing to exercise the same powers—in which it is not the imagined situation but the imagining mind that reigns supreme—in dealing with real historical biography. James Page, who also contemplated all aspects of Nabokov's "poetic truth," said that Nabokov is notable for his "unexpected fillips" and that he invites readers on a difficult journey: the author "has made it before and will probably take the same path again. His point of view, his 'truth,' will once more be 'everywhere and nowhere'" (Page 6). (What is evoked here is Fyodor's monologue mentioning an "abyss of seriousness" above which he must make his way by the "narrow bridge between [his] own truth and caricature of it" [G200].)

Spender appears to have been confused regarding the "untrue ending" of Chernyshevski's biography in *The Gift*: "The untrue ending to the biography may be as true as the real one, and the illusion produced by the most solidly realized fiction, may be shattered to replace it with a more significant poetic truth. The dense texture of situations powerfully imagined may be more real than the threadbare texture of actuality" (Spender 289). In such context mistakes were pardonable to even less shrewd readers: Nabokov's "narrator-hero writes the life of Chernyshevski and gives it an ending other than the one it had in actuality. And why, indeed, should he not?" (Hutchens 28).

The same quest for poetic truth bothered Fred Holley, who called *The Gift* "an entire series of artful deceptions within an equally deceptive framework, which indeed may be not there at all [...] *The Gift* may well be an exposition of Pilate's question, what is truth?, and the answer, for which the jesting Pilate would not stay, that it is not. Young Fyodor refers to 'the hypnosis of error,' and he is certainly a victim of it himself [...] *The Gift*, which is also the title of Fyodor's projected novel, is man's talent for self-deception. In the rootless world of the Russian émigrés, and in the greater world in which we are all disinherited, we must deceive ourselves, beautifully and entertainingly if possible, and the most acceptable of these deceptions is Russian literature" (Holley B-6).

Spender's review concluded with an ambivalent and somewhat confusing message. On the one hand, he stated that Nabokov is "a writer of genius who is digressive, wayward and an imperfect artist," on the other hand, his books, "though written with immense care, do not seem architecturally planned" (Spender 289). The reviewer was right, but still he seems to have missed the main point. His architectural metaphor was also open to debate, as evident from Nicholas Sanders's ecstatic comment: "The architecture of *The Gift* is as delicately wrought as a fine piece of silver, the whole having the esthetic values of its parts. Taken individually, the sections of the novel are pieces of a grand construction, one that is unique in literature" (Sanders 32).

The trivial question of what kind of universe Nabokov created in his sophisticated novel—realistic or phantasmal—was hard to answer: "The problem is: we can't be interested in the phantasm. The émigrés are objects of private malicious fun—of gossip. And gossip isn't very important" (Malin 5). On the contrary, William Barrett argued:

> Technically, this is Mr. Nabokov's most realistic novel. Yet, in dealing with the vanished life of the Russian exiles, those wandering tribes dispersed over the earth, it creates a world as phantasmal as any in the author's other works. As always, Mr. Nabokov's sheer literary virtuosity is prodigious. When Fyodor writes, as part of his attempt to master his Russian past, a little book on Chernyshevski, a liberal hero of the nineteenth century, Mr. Nabokov not only tells us about the work but gives it to us entire in one long chapter, and it turns out to be a splendid

biographical sketch. However, it is not literary fireworks that hold us throughout but the finely sustained mood of tender nostalgia, a personal warmth never again so present in Mr. Nabokov's writings, after he had given up the love of his life, his 'beautiful Russian language.' (Barrett 137)

The review by English poet and critic Donald Davie in *The Guardian* bore a telling title—"Reader in the Dock" (probably out of respect to Nabokov this very title was omitted in the compilation featuring an excerpt from it, *Vladimir Nabokov: The Critical Heritage* 150-151). The observer began by announcing that the newly published translation of the thirty-year-old novel finally produced an answer to the tormenting question: how does the author of *Lolita* and *Pale Fire* connect these "bizarre, indirect, and seemingly heartless books" with the literary tradition they spring from, "the Russian tradition which we think of as direct, natural, and humane" (Davie 8). The hero of *The Gift*, continued Davie, is a young Russian émigré author living in Berlin, where he writes a "bizarre and cruelly debunking" book about Chernyshevski. The author cannot help but draw a parallel with Nabokov's infamous novel: "A hostile reviewer [in *The Gift*] declares that the book [on Chernyshevski] 'lies absolutely outside the humanitarian tradition of Russian literature'—which is what any one might be tempted to say of *Lolita*. Indeed it is what the present reviewer had said about the nonexistent book on Chernyshevski, since the substance of it is given as chapter Four, and it set his teeth on edge" (Ibid.). Davie remained perplexed:

> A foreword warns us against identifying Nabokov with his own author-hero, but since it invites us to identify him instead with a reviewer who applauds the Chernyshevski book we are back where we started—which is to say, in the dock. [...]
> As in *Lolita*, Nabokov sets our teeth on edge—but deliberately, to make a point that could be made so forcibly in no other way. The resolution he effects in his last chapter is the acceptance by the hero of the Imagist's world which impinges on the senses, for the case against the humanitarians is that characteristically, for all their materialism, they are blind to this world. But the resolution is also the acceptance, by the Russian writer, of the place where he finds himself, Berlin. Russian literature can and will be continued—but it may be written in other languages than Russian. Nabokov speaks of *The Gift* as 'the last novel I wrote, or ever shall write, in Russian'; and that too is part of what the novel movingly says about itself. (Ibid.)

One of the most elaborate responses to the English version of *The Gift* appeared in the intellectual magazine with which Nabokov collaborated most often during his career as an American writer. Writing for the *New Yorker*, Donald Malcolm admitted that he was a "friendly reviewer." Thus setting a tone of objectivity, he warned: "Admirers of Vladimir Nabokov are likely to find a reading of *The Gift* at once rewarding and disconcerting" (Malcolm 198-205). The main reason for this, the critic argued, is that the novel is a prolonged meditation upon the psychology of art. Its hero, whose consciousness is our window on literature and the world, is a young poet who sustains an existence that is far from rich in drama. The purchase of a new pair of shoes, a literary evening with his fellow exiles, moving from one boarding house to another—these are the inconclusive and modest happenings that make up the bulk of Fyodor's story. Many of these little occurrences scarcely impinge upon Godunov-Cherdyntsev's consciousness at all, "for he moves among them like a sleepwalker and is a great forgetter of latchkeys" (Ibid.).

Percy Rowe of *The Toronto Telegram* spared neither Nabokov nor Graham Greene, the man whose review had propelled *Lolita* to the top of world bestsellers. In a joint review of *The Gift* and Greene's new novel, *Sense of Reality*, the reviewer could not hide his disappointment: "When one has favorites, you are ready to stretch standards. This has really never been necessary for my favorites, Mr. Nabokov and Mr. Greene. My favoritism is purely the result of their very exceptional talents. It has never been required, for instance, that I say: 'Well, this latest book of N. (or G.) isn't as good as, but...' Each new book has been an exciting entity, a creative edition of their work. But now I have to say not only that neither *The Gift*, nor *Sense of Reality* are as good as etc., but that I didn't find them good at all" (Rowe u.16).

One of the main difficulties for American readers of *The Gift* was their inability to find common cultural ground with the alien world of the vanished Russian community in exile. Fyodor's life and writings were "seen against the *émigré* world, farcically funny and rootlessly sad" (Mitchell 38). "Unfortunately," wrote Sybil Weir, "the wit is an occasional flash rather than a sustained tone [in *The Gift*], and the five chapters never coalesce into a compelling unity. There are two causes of this failure to hold the reader's interest. Mr. Nabokov tells us in the introduction that the real heroine of the work is Russian Literature. Unless one has an intimate knowledge of the development of Russian literature, one cannot appreciate the unifying theme, the central joke—and the book remains nothing but five elusive chapters. The other defect of the novel is an artistic one. Not only Berlin but also Fyodor remains too shadowy; only Fyodor's father emerges fully as a memorable character in a brilliant, often lyrical chapter which is by far the best part of the book" (Weir EL2).

Even receptive professional readers did not feel at ease when analyzing *The Gift*. Milton Crane reasonably admitted that Nabokov's early novels, written and published in Russian during the years spent in Berlin, are "almost unimaginably remote from us. This is not to say that they are uninteresting, the one epithet that cannot be applied to any of Nabokov's writings, early or late, exotic or familiar, demure or shocking. But, as Nabokov himself says of this last work that he composed in the Russian language, 'The world of *The Gift* being at present as much of a phantasm as most of my other worlds, I can speak of this book with a certain degree of detachment'" (Crane 5). However, Crane insisted, the novel is still "oddly disappointing":

> What is unmistakably Nabokov's in this sensitive, intelligent, and yet oddly disappointing book is difficult to define yet highly characteristic of the mature writer — the delight in parody (compare *Pale Fire*), the moving evocation of the naturalist father (compare the exquisite *Conclusive Evidence*), the almost physical enjoyment of the Russian language (the epigraph, from a grammar, reads in part: 'Russia is our fatherland. Death is inevitable.'). But the perfection of form of which Nabokov is capable at his best — that still lies ahead of *The Gift*. (Ibid.)

The very American Nabokov impeded objective perception. The critics scrutinized the scarcely known Sirin through the prism of his latest American *tours de force*: "Unless the translation drastically falsified the text," flatly asserted Richard Kostelanetz, "the original *Dar* was not a good novel. Because he does not hold up the role Nabokov cuts for him, Fyodor is the weak plank on which the novel falls. Like all of Nabokov's narrators, he is supposed to be ironic; but in contrast to Kinbote of *Pale Fire*, Fyodor is never unquestionably stupid or dishonest, nor is he grossly deceived about his own importance" (Kostelanetz 7-8).

It was inevitable that Nabokov's *Lolita* and *Pale Fire* would provide the major points of comparison: "*The Gift* is an engaging early Nabokov, written in Russian before the war and now appropriated into his fully-fashioned English style — 'a monogram of light resembling an infusorian glided diagonally to the highest corner of his subpalpebral field of vision.' But this is no *Pale Fire* or *Lolita*: it's fairly simply a re-creation of Russian expatriate life in Berlin around 1922. The real heroine, he says, is Russian literature. The central figure is a young poet who lives mainly in dreams, imaginary conversations and the past with its endless impedimenta of Czarist nurseries" (Taubman 654). This remembrance of the distant past also prompted some devoted readers of Nabokov's fiction to recall the rich texture of his memoirs: "Nabokov expresses his love for Russia and Russian literature in a magnificent prestidigitation of words which transcend translation, and which reminded me a great deal of his autobiography *Speak, Memory*" (Pollock 829).

The Gift was regarded as the foundation on which Nabokov's ensuing career had been built. Julian Mitchell pointed out that it could be considered a precursor to *Lolita* (Nabokov's pre-war novella, *The Enchanter*, remained still unpublished): "[*The Gift*] is arrogant and deliberately self-conscious, it is full of lepidoptery and chess, it has a brief glimpse of a nymph, and the plot of *Lolita* is neatly summarized on page 179 [of the Weidenfeld and Nicolson edition] for the benefit of those writing theses on recurring themes in Nabokov's novels" (Mitchell 38;

the same noted in Holley B-6 and by others). A few others noticed this Ur-*Lolita* as well: "And somewhere in the book is an all-revealing paragraph that evidently marks the spot where *Lolita* was born" (Weissblatt 14). Ogden Dwight stated likewise that "[s]eparately, each part [of *The Gift*] is a demonstration of such acute and diverse scholarship and research that the reader is dumfounded—the same technique that, stretched to its absolute limits in *Pale Fire*, is positively flabbergasting. Further, *The Gift* contains the forecast and capsule plot of *Lolita*, and the same dissection of an author, by examination of his works and habits, that forms the fabric of *Sebastian Knight* and *Pale Fire*" (Dwight 5-F).

In short, with all their numerous blunders, the critics were still able to discern the continuity of Nabokov's oeuvre and find peculiar poetic birthmarks in *The Gift*—his recurrent "patterns," from butterflies and chess to the motif of keys: "There are long interludes—a loving account of [Fyodor's] father's Central Asian explorations, in the mood of Pushkin; and a spoof biography of a member of the old intelligentsia; Nabokov's special interests have their place—a chapter full of butterflies, and dissertations on scansion—and his own kind of realistic low comedy, involving lost keys or a shoe-fitting, holds the dreamy side of his hero in check" (Taubman 654).

Paradox, Riddle, Mystery

Donald Stanley began his review of *The Gift* in an entertaining manner: "Churchill once described Russian policy aims as 'a riddle wrapped in a mystery inside an enigma.' This seems an apt description of another product of Mother Russia, the 64 year old Vladimir Nabokov" (Stanley 18). Stanley admitted that the novel, "though its structure is formal, seems irritatingly complex":

> What it amounts to, in fact, is no less than a narrative depicting how the book itself came to be written. This is no mean feat and it must be said that the effect is what I imagine would feel watching a man reach down, grab his ankles, and lift himself off the ground.
>
> Unfortunately the feat is also impossible, laudable an act as it is in theory. The individual chapters are excellent, their amalgamation a failure. It's as if the episodes decided they might as well hang separately, since they surely could never hang together. [...]
>
> Those who somehow managed to scale the forbidding difficulties of *Pale Fire* ('a creation of perfect beauty, symmetry, strangeness, originality and moral truth' squealed the usually unsquealing Mary McCarthy) might find *The Gift* a mere Sunday stroll by comparison. (Ibid.)

By all accounts, the novel was a concoction made out of contrasts. Here are just a few typical responses voicing dissonant notes: "Like all of Mr. Nabokov's books, *The Gift* is a paradoxical wonder—cynical yet sentimental, tragic yet funny, nostalgic yet realistic" (Gilmore 25); "Committing as little surgery as possible, one can say that *The Gift* presents a fundamental contrast between splendor and meanness; the splendor of words, when dominated by an artist; the meanness of words, when used by a moralist" (Sylvester 8-F); "It is a most distinguished contribution to the fictional literature of our time" (Sandrof 16E). Alexander Brown summed up this Nabokovian polarity as follows: "Unquestionably Mr. Nabokov is an artist of very considerable talent. But he can both charm and annoy... I am left with a deflating sense of inferiority which, I suppose, naturally goes along with being awed" (A. Brown 9).

Being mostly put off by what they read, critics rarely made penetrating remarks, but William Sylvester belonged to the smaller category of astute reviewers. Besides stating that the felicity of *The Gift* is "playful and astonishing," he also provided examples of careful reading in a true Nabokovian sense, for instance, linking an episode from the last chapter of the novel with the charade featured in the first:

> Accused of blurring the lines between parody and reality, and accused of writing with an 'obscene sporty nudity,' Fyodor then discovers that his clothes have literally been stolen, and so he must appear, wearing only his trunks, before a bureaucratic German policeman in a hilarious scene, half-parody, half-real [...] Reality is ground down to dust, as Fyodor says about his own projected autobiography, 'but the kind of dust that makes the most orange of sunsets.' Orange? One recalls that in the beginning of the novel, a riddle left in French has the answer: orange. (Sylvester 8-F)

The ability to make connections, to see the hidden links throughout the entire corpus of the novel, was uncommon in early critical reception of *The Gift*. More often than not the reviewers limited themselves to random quotes, or simply picked from the opening paragraphs of *The Gift* ("Nabokov bathes his stories in a subtle poetry, writing of a woman 'with a rather attractive, pseudo-Chinese face' and 'a stale but good perfume,' the dreams of a sick child, the streets of Berlin at night..."; Mercier 4). Renate Wolff frankly admitted the sort of frustration common for readers of Nabokov's Russian masterpiece: "Perhaps the measure of [Nabokov's] artistic goals and limitations is taken by a remark put into the mouth of Koncheyev (or is it Fyodor himself? I refuse to retrace the entire conversation to its beginning) who considers a circular stain left on a table by a wine glass the only thing worth saving in *The Brothers Karamazov*" (Wolff 9-D).

Even those who admired the work's uncompromising quality repeatedly failed to grasp its basic meaning or to follow the ramified plot. Fyodor was never Yasha Chernyshevski's classmate, nor was the nineteenth century social democrat Chernyshevski Yasha's relative (as Day Thorpe of *Sunday Star* suggested). Mr.

Thorpe was uncertain whether the main character of Fyodor's biography had a historical prototype at all: "The central part of the novel is a biography of Chernyshevski, probably a man of Nabokov's imagination, but possibly a real man" (Thorpe B-5). His lack of knowledge did not prevent the same critic from reaching a clear-cut verdict: "*The Gift* lacks the unity of *Lolita* and *Pale Fire*, but it has the same sensuous appeal, it is as good a book as either. There may be three or four contemporary novels by three or four writers as brilliant as those of Nabokov, but no other modern novelist can boast of an *oeuvre* so extensive and of such quality" (Ibid.).

The bottom-line, as John Hutchens drew it, depicted Nabokov as "the astonishing virtuoso" who "can both dazzle and exasperate, entertain and bore": "Mr. Nabokov is an artist. An occasionally erratic and unsuccessful one, to be sure: still, an artist who remolds reality or lets it alone, as his judgment dictates, that being the business of artists" (Hutchens 28).

Advice

The advice given to Nabokov for improving *The Gift* ranged from shortening the text of the novel and simplifying its structure to adding action and suspense: "The monograph on Godunov-Cherdyntsev's father, despite the beauty of its language, ought to have been shortened, and this goes double for the little book about the journalist [i.e. Chernyshevski], despite the fact that it tells us much about the quality of Godunov-Cherdyntsev's mind. Still, it is an inside joke, studded with references to virtually every major Russian writer of the 19th century, and too long drawn out...Nevertheless, I would not part with this extraordinary book for a variety of reasons: for its descriptions of the natural world...for its madcap humor; for its beautifully touching love idyll; and finally because the book becomes a kind of rallying point for the transcendent importance of the solitary imagination" (Perlberg 10).

Complaints frequently had to do with the fact that "the plot is almost incidental in this book" (Hilgenstuhler K-5), and that Nabokov's "descriptions are often overwhelming and invariably complicated" (Hutchens 28). Both of these factors made *The Gift* "extremely difficult reading," in addition to its "elongated sentence structure and lack of action and suspense" (MacGillirray 123-124). In order to overcome these troubles columnists gave advice directly to the reader rather than to the author (which was clearly useless for a novel written a quarter century before): "In case the reader does decide to chance his luck in Nabokov's present hall of mirrors, he had better begin with *The Gift*'s fifth and final section" (Brady B-10). Wiser critics realized that any advice either to readers or to the creator would be futile: "With only *The Gift* to judge by, a friendly reviewer might be tempted to urge Mr. Nabokov toward a style of broader strokes and coarser texture, as being more suited to the amplitudes of the novel. Such advice, however, would merely go to demonstrate that writers seldom can derive much benefit from their critics and ought never to attend them" (Malcolm 198-205).

Thomas Sherman issued a warning statement against the "politically reactionary and verbally prolix" author: "[Nabokov's book] is a virtuoso performance. But I must add this warning: Readers who were charmed or shocked by *Lolita* should approach *The Gift* with different expectations. It is decidedly not that kind of book" (Sherman 4C). The majority of reviewers agreed that there was indeed a fundamental difference: "Anyone remembering the witty delicacies of *Lolita* or the scintillations of *Pale Fire* should take a deep breath before plunging into the exactitudes of Nabokov's *The Gift* and be prepared for a different world" (Ross 852). However, there were those who stated just the opposite: "It is as sure, deft, dense as *Lolita* or *Pale Fire*, and it is astonishing that, depending on the fitness of word-play as it does, it is so successful in translation" (Thorpe B-5).

In general, critics' recommendations to the reading public were not particularly cheerful: "The book is hard to evaluate, hard to follow, and hard to enjoy over long stretches...Nabokov's earlier *Invitation to a Beheading* is more successful...[and] the stories of *Pnin* are more wistful and more sympathetic to human foibles. Nabokov is facile, has both a keen eye and an acute ear, but his interest is off-beat...He is a lesser member of the literary generation that was 'so beautiful and so lost'" (Rollow 5-C).

The readership itself was not homogeneous enough and therefore, critics felt, it needed to be classified accordingly. "Summarily, the book will not appeal to the average reader who wants either relaxation or an imaginative experience," wrote Arthur MacGillirray, attempting to strike a balance. "Only the special reader who is vastly interested in words and the writing process will be attracted" (MacGillirray 123-124). As for the alleged lack of "imaginative experience" in *The Gift*, the critic teaching at Boston College was certainly wrong; his more attentive colleagues testified for the other side: "The subject of *The Gift* is that shaping power of imagination in whose light life can be transfigured" (Murray 5).

Maie Perley, the author of two books herself, also recommended Nabokov's novel to "the special reader," or rather—drawing on the vocabulary of travel so apt in the context of *The Gift*—"only to those lovers of literature who are willing to explore far and wide to discover rare passages of prose written by one of the great writers of our time" (Perley 7).

It was generally assumed that Nabokov had won over the discriminating common reader with the human warmth of *Pnin*, acquired a mass audience with the shock value of *Lolita*, and garnered the academic world's modulated applause with the hyper-elegant cryptogram *Pale Fire*. "It is hard to conceive of his attracting any sizable audience with *The Gift*," said Charles Brady in *Buffalo Evening News* (Brady B-10). Nonetheless, the potential target audience of *The Gift* was clear at least to critics like Leonard Brown, who shared this opinion with readers of the *Pasadena Independent Star News*: "Obviously this is a book for young writers. It is also a book for those who find no novel quite so filling as a Russian novel. But principally it is a book for Nabokovians, to whom there is a sort of spectator delight in watching this author hunt, capture and classify emotions and impressions, as he pursued and collected butterflies in his adolescence" (L. Brown 9).

All in all, it was considered hopeless for *The Gift* to win the hearts and minds of a wider audience longing for sensual plots, detectives, thrillers, and horror fiction. Thus Ted Hilgensthuler reacted with skepticism upon reading the book's blurb, which declared *The Gift* "to be the greatest Russian novel of the 20th century": "That may be. But it does not have one basic ingredient, which made *Lolita* such a fabulous success: Sex! And sex sells—as any American publisher can tell you" (Hilgenstuhler K-5). Lynwood Abram agreed: "Considering the pitiful shelf of good Russian novels written since 1900, [what the jacket proclaims] is a small boast. Russian literature, for all practical purposes, is a one-century affair—the 19th" (Abram 10). According to *Zest Magazine*, "[i]t is not easy reading. Disappointment is certain for fans of the artful pornography of *Lolita* and for admirers of the concise and brilliant *Real Life of Sebastian Knight*" (Ibid.). "Indeed, there is very little of the sexual in Nabokov; he exercises the classic Russian novelist's discreet approach to what is Topic A-Z in most contemporary novels" (Darack 10).

Genre Confusion, Tricks of Style

With rare exceptions, critics agreed that *The Gift* was a treatise on *how not to write a novel in a linear way*: "Labeled 'A Novel,' *The Gift* defies classification. A novel it certainly is not, at least according to our traditional ideas of what a novel is" (MacGillirray 123-124); "It is described as a novel, but is actually five separate chapters of writing strung together on loose threads" (Perley 7); "a novel, one calls it, because just offhand no more appropriate word for it comes to mind" (Hutchens 28). In attempting to come up with an appropriate description of the novel's structure a few observers employed the image of self-contained boxes (something that Sergei Davydov subsequently dubbed the "Matryoshka" [nesting doll] composition [Davydov 2004]): "*The Gift*...fits inside itself like a series of magic boxes, the narrative pronoun flickering like a warning dial between first and third person, the Berlin townscape at one moment hard and Germanic, the next softly rippling in a Russian transmogrification" (Share 10). David Benedictus echoed with a similar association: "*The Gift* is another quirk: we are in a world of Chinese boxes. [...] Underlying the whole work is an ironic detachment which leads the alert reader up tortuous but seductive garden-paths..." (Benedictus 17).

Standard theoretical approaches in the study of prose seemed quite unsuitable in Nabokov's case: "The novel by definition is a fictional work of certain length whose extensive canopy, thus spread, includes everything from *Les Misérables* to *Miss Lonelyhearts*. Despite the permissiveness of such a term, one may question its application to Vladimir Nabokov's book *The Gift*" (Sherman 4C). Especially objectionable to some critics were the inconsiderate disruptions in the course of the plot: "Mr. Nabokov eschews the usual manner of developing a novel. Instead of portraying the growth of his character by showing the young man in action, he twice interrupts the flow of the book and gives us the young writer's actions themselves — in the form of two long manuscripts written by Godunov-Cherdyntsev as he learns his craft" (Perlberg 10).

Due to its defiant nature, and its location at the juncture of several genres, Nabokov's novel seemed to be proving once again that neither the *novel* as a genre, nor the *author* himself were dead (as Roland Barthes proclaimed in the same year that *The Gift* was published in English):

> Amid the usual plaints about the decline of the novel coupled with strictures on the lack of originality displayed in that form, we are indeed presented with a gift in V. Nabokov's novel of that name... Nabokov is surely the most original novelist of our time as well as one of the most important, a genuinely comic writer (that rarest of breeds), who blithely and mockingly ignores our entire constellation of hallowed assumptions about 'art' and 'life' to produce one unique work after another. (Murray 5)

Though they were unable to judge the work as a synthetic whole, certain critics nonetheless were able to focus on the particulars. Mostly they praised the "brilliant, jeweled style" (Iremonger 17) of the novel, to the point that the author, ironically, was accused of the sin of "fine writing." "His writing is sometimes too rich," complained Thomas Sherman quoting as an example from among "hundreds of others" this sentence from *The Gift*: "The edge of a cloud suddenly caught fire and the sun slipped out. It emitted such hot blissful strength that, forgetting his vexation, Fyodor lay down on the moss and began to watch the next snowy colossus draw near, eating up the blue as it advanced" (G345). Sherman commented: "Well, this is Nabokov — but more often than not his trills, roulades and cadenzas are reinforced with the lining of interwoven ideas" (Sherman 4C). Donald Malcolm offered yet another sample of writing that was "too rich":

> Although Fyodor Godunov-Cherdyntsev does not achieve anything like the success of his more antic descendants, he does provide their joint creator with one sharp vision that might very well stand as Mr. Nabokov's rejoinder to Stendhal's view of the novel as an ambulatory and impartial mirror that 'now reflects the blue of the skies, now the mud puddles underfoot.' It will be seen that Nabokov's mirror, like his novels, does not merely reproduce the roadside but dazzles the gaze with new possibilities for wonder. (Malcolm 198-205)

Maggie Ross added that Nabokov's "minute attention to shades of meaning, cadences, stress, rhythms—some too delicate to transpose—shows us an earlier Nabokov and evokes great respect for his scholarship. But, unless you possess a wide knowledge of Russian literature, this Nabokov is less able than he is now to elicit applause" (Ross 852). Another critic claimed that "the book contains numerous aphorisms which are bound to turn up in advanced examination papers in front of the word 'Discuss'" ([Unsigned] "Russian Romp" 901). The novel's cognitive difficulty (perhaps a blessing in disguise) was especially noticeable: "Nabokov doesn't invite readers, he challenges them. His vocabulary alone requires, not a desk dictionary, but a whopping big one, for where else would we find *lampad*, for instance, or *stang*, or *sigla*?," asked W.G. Rogers in the Gary *Post-Tribune* (Rogers 9). Alexander Brown shared the same fear that a large number of ordinary would-be readers would never progress much beyond the first of the five chapters, "because, quite frankly, it is just too hard work. Countless trips to Webster's Unabridged do not make it any easier" (A. Brown 9).

Funny or Serious?

In terms of Nabokov's literary evolution, critics were tempted to define the novel as the work of an apprentice, which would later lead to his English masterpieces: "[*The Gift* is] a wonderfully fragrant evocation of youth [and] rich comedy. More than enough, in fact, to make up for the insolence and the swank... This novel, which is perhaps the best of Mr. Nabokov's first, Russian language, phase, makes it plain that in the principal faculty of the novelist, the ability to create a character, its author continued to develop: *Lolita* and *Pale Fire* are richer, solider novels than *The Gift*, even though they may lack its youthful charm" ([Unsigned] "Russian Romp" 901).

The "insolence and swank" highlighted by the critic above haunted the author of *The Gift*. Anthony Hern referred to its stylistic elegance as mere "linguistic jokes," although, judging by his synopsis of the novel (about "a young poet and his aristocratic but poor girl-friend, Zina"), it is hardly likely that he read the entire novel: "Fyodor teaches English [sic], scribbles verse (too typically Russian to be either true or good), and writes the biography of another Russian writer... The novel contains all those conscious literary grace-notes that tricked out *Lolita*. The author is clearly pleased with his little linguistic jokes. I wish I were. The man is clever, no doubt about it—but what a show off!" (Hern 19).

It should particularly be noted here that many critics had a soft spot for this special brand of Nabokovian humor. "This is a book of wry humor and wit, a conscious evocation of Pushkin and Gogol, and a rather loose orchestration of many tones," pronounced Lloyd Griffin (Griffin 1688). John Hutchens reinforced this view: "The Nabokov humor can grow windy and arch, as when long conversations turn out never to have taken place, and would not have been breathlessly interesting if they had" (Hutchens 28). In addition to the illusory conversations, certain situations in the novel elicited comic associations: "There are scenes of comic pandemonium that make one think of certain bits of Dostoevsky purged of the sinister undertones" ([Unsigned] "Russian Romp" 901). The critic elaborated and, in support of his argument, gave the example of the literary evening at which Herman Busch gives a reading of a philosophical tragedy in the Symbolist manner. In short, the novel was perceived as "a portrait" and "comic-sad courage and intrigue of the literary Russian émigrés of forty years ago; a mélange of satire, history and parody in tones ranging from the purely eloquent to the raucous laugh; a *roman a clef*, no doubt, for those capable of reading it as such" (Hutchens 28).

The Gift may have been far from a "magnetically readable comedy," as it was called, but it possessed an undeniable witty wisdom which made its readers smile: "But, change languages though he may, Nabokov remains always a fine comic writer, with a sense of the mischievously fantastic (or fantastically mischievous) few other authors can equal... [T]he conflict between illusion and everyday reality is projected with the usual Nabokov skill, in the form of a highly intellectual and magnetically readable comedy—vintage Nabokov, not to be missed" (Moore 10).

What kind of humor were the critics talking about? *The Gift* is hardly a slapstick comedy, but it contains provocative statements, satirical portrayals, and absurd situations, which caused some observers to admire its author's sharp wit, but forced others to deny even a hint of humor:

> Philosophy, politics, entomology, mathematics, human emotion, conflict, searching, slogging persistence, love, minute observations—all are there full flower, except the wheeling-dealing humor and literary practical joking that spice Nabokov's later novels. The reader who finishes and understands any one of them completely will have paid himself a high compliment. Contrary-wise, he may decide it is a waste of time. (Dwight 5-F)

Nelson Hayes called humor the feature of Nabokov's novel that baffled so many readers. He noted that the average readers "expect that a work of art be a serious treatment of a serious theme, while Nabokov often treats serious matters with high good humor. This is also to say that he is contemptuous of the ponderous and the pedantic, of the posturings of self-conscious and conceited intellectuals" (Hayes 6). Jim Dance, who also discerned a very serious tone behind the novel's frolicsome jokes, explored the crucial relationship between the reader and the author—in which both players are trapped in a haunting interdependency:

In *The Gift* Nabokov is seriously concerned with the author as communicator: and in this case the reader is not the butt of a practical joke but the engrossed listener to a self-revealing confidence. [...] The gift young Fyodor has is the ability to channel his own experiences, his imaginings, and his gleanings from literature into an original creative act. Learning to control this gift is a chore many lesser writers relinquish at the plateau where they become competent hacks. As the book ends, we hope Fyodor will go farther than this—and that Nabokov, now in his artistic maturity, will stop playing jokes [as in *Lolita* and *Pale Fire*] and recapture the essential serious communication of *The Gift* (Dance 5).

And yet, with all its occasional moments of satire, *The Gift* was recognized as "a major novel of unquestionable seriousness, more explicit than any of his later work in clarifying the meaning Nabokov puts to the phrase 'aesthetic bliss'" (Feinstein 152). Later Nabokov would continue to use humor effectively for extremely serious purposes. Humbert is acutely aware that humor is a potential means of manipulation and uses it in an attempt to deflect his readers' attention from his less attractive traits and from what he has done to Lolita. By analyzing Nabokov's humor, readers come to understand this rhetorical strategy and recognize the enormous power humor has to entice, create a collective empathy, and cause moral myopia (Grant 165).

The Politics of *The Gift*

American readers had only a rough idea of the man behind the name on the front cover of *The Gift*. To most he was still known only as someone, "who made them suddenly uncomfortable about their teen-age daughters" (Stanley 18). The same expert introduced the author in his sympathetic, but hardly error-free, introduction as follows: "Nabokov (born Vladimir Sirin [sic]) was a member of the Leningrad [sic] aristocracy" (Ibid.). A number of pensive attempts to comprehend *The Gift* on a deeper intellectual level resulted in examining the novel in the context of modern political history. "Ironically," maintained Jerry Coffey, "the book, dealing with effects of one flight from political tyranny, was written during the rise of another reign of oppression that eventually would drive the author even farther away from his homeland, to the considerable enrichment of American literature" (Coffey 13).

Elaine Feinstein assessed the English translation of the novel in *The Cambridge Review* "as brilliant in sensuous detail and as highly charged with the peculiar Nabokov atmosphere as any of the later books" (Feinstein 152). Rather like *The Real Life of Sebastian Knight*, this earlier novel, explained Feinstein, was about the ethic of dedicated talent, but in the context of those émigré Russian intellectuals who made their home in Berlin between the wars. In explaining the excitement of that dedication and the cold control it exacts, Nabokov intentionally resisted not only those who read literature in terms of politics, but also those critics who demanded, and did not find, an interest in the general welfare of humanity: "Nabokov himself is impatient with this kind of criticism, convinced that particularity and precision will be undervalued when critics read with their eye on general principles. Once this is seen, Nabokov's apparently heartless aestheticism seems less dangerously alien" (Ibid.).

Though she occasionally resorted to platitudes (the usual statements about Nabokov's books being filled with nostalgia for the old Russia and hatred for the revolutionaries who forced him into exile), the critic, nonetheless, showed a firm grasp of Nabokov's philosophy:

> His indifference extends rather to causes and ideologies. If he has at any time understood and rejected the temptations of those who desire to better the fate of human beings by political means he shows little sign of it. And whatever he may have observed of Berlin during the rise of Hitler, very few details of that dictatorship find their way into *The Gift*. He is not, however (and perhaps after fifteen years of chosen residence in Berlin of that time it does need saying) anything like a Nazi sympathizer. Nor is he callous about the horror of violence done to individual people (Ibid.).

Feinstein believed that Nabokov's sense of *human vulnerability* is part of the texture of all his books. At the same time, she noted that Nabokov was highly selective in his sympathies, wasting little time on the complacent, the "fat-faced" (who no doubt suffer as much as everyone else). And, like Gogol, she added, Nabokov had an irritable sensitivity to all the physical unpleasantness of the human body:

> Chernyshevski's every pimple, blotch, and unclean habit is mentioned. Of his economic theories, or his political courage, we hear little. For Fyodor, he is to be judged entirely by the way he responds to literature and the details of life around him. And he is offered for contempt as a symbol of a woolly, and inaccurate humanism.
>
> It is not difficult to see (from the quotations given) why Chernyshevski has been singled out for this anger. A short-sighted man, with little interest in the details of natural history, or any ability in distinguishing particular literary merit from general views held, some of his remarks make a natural target for Nabokov, to whom the catching of accurate detail is the only bulwark against total chaos. Chernyshevski becomes a symbol, a true and fitting opposite of the poet's father (that cold and dedicated searcher after Lepidoptera), of all those who prefer general ideas to particular facts; a man who cannot be trusted, in fact, since he lacks an elementary fastidiousness about accuracy. But in some ways it is a puzzling chapter. It is worth contrasting the affectionate permissiveness Nabokov accords a bungling academic like Pnin, with the severe attitude he takes up to Chernyshevski's physical clumsiness.

Nabokov's admiration is reserved for those with talent and solitary dedication (like the passionate explorer or the poet) who pursue the perfection of one particular skill with all the strength of their gift. The peculiar pains, excitements and isolations of this life he makes real to us as few other novelists have. (Ibid.)

While most Western critics did not particularly care for the Russian émigrés whose "rooming houses [were] dismal, their landladies stolid or stupid" (Mercier 4), the pictures of pre-Hitler Berlin could at times lead to controversy. Renate Wolff, a critic of German origin, seemed appalled: "I may add that, to a native Berliner, the unrelieved ugliness and pettiness of Nabokov's portrait [in *The Gift*] is not only offensive, but simply untrue. Of course, the difference is chiefly between the points of view of a native and an exile, and Fyodor himself is aware of his bias" (Wolff 9-D). Wolff settled the score with Nabokov by pronouncing in the closing paragraph of her lengthy article: "I would hardly have read [the novel] to the end but for my promise to review it."

The Gift as Discovery

The criticism that *The Gift* has no form and sprawls around like rising bread forgotten by the baker, as provocatively formulated by one of the earliest English-language critics, was almost repeated years later. Unintentionally and independently, L.T. Iglehart used the Scribner's Sons anonymous internal reviewer's pioneering metaphor as a starting point: "This rich Slavic pudding is laced with Nabokov's undulating prose style, impossible to describe or parody" (Iglehart 4F). In this regard, the critic added, no one can be certain whether Nabokov writes the way he does because he chases butterflies or the other way around, "but I'm sure there is a connection. His sentences swoop and dart about, occasionally pausing while a stunningly colorful phrase dances in the beholder's eye—then, just as one closes in on the meaning, another zig-zag flight begins and the intention disappears in a thicket at the clearing edge" (Ibid.).

Despite a swarm of admissions that *The Gift* was all but incomprehensible, Nabokov's flock still expressed more admiration than disappointment. Praising Nabokov's "pyrotechnic prose" was a common motif in the critical reception of *The Gift* in 1963. Glendy Culligan noted (without much analysis or developed argumentation) that even the inclusion of Chernyshevski's biography, flanked by fictitious newspaper reviews, foreshadowed Nabokov's talent for complex literary parody, which would reach its apogee in *Pale Fire*:

In that incredibly involved story-within-a-story-within-a-story, much of the narrative was conveyed in mock footnotes to a mock-heroic poem. [...] With Nabokov, as with Fyodor, we can rarely be sure whose tongue is in whose cheek, so mercurial are both their moods and their modes.

In typical Nabokovism, this chameleon quality that Nabokov and his hero share is analyzed by another (almost certainly fictitious) critic in a discussion of Fyodor's work. [...] Such intellectual quick-sand is the essence of Nabokov, early or late, and a prime source of his power to amuse and bemuse us simultaneously. In vain does the real author, in a current preface, deny his identity with the young, fictional Fyodor, whose work as cited so echoes Nabokov's own.

Although the mature Nabokov, writing in English, would ultimately perfect some of the ingenious devices that his Fyodor only essays, their differences would be merely those of degree. Already in 1937, they were mastering together the pyrotechnic prose, the mordant, not quite morbid humor, the pathos and perversity of vision that would produce the unique works of Nabokov's maturity. This rare talent, 'the gift' that Fyodor sensed was his inheritance, is one that Nabokov has since 1937 shared with increasing numbers of admirers. (Culligan G8)

The English-language reader may have wondered at first why Nabokov wanted there to be an English translation of his book: "If so, he has his answer in the quality of Nabokov's English style—and it is his own style because he closely supervised and improved the translation. His volatile fancy and frequently scalding wit are found on almost every page. He is merciless, but he is also exuberant" (Sherman 4C). Amazement blended with praise: "*The Gift* is an impressive exercise in literary virtuosity—a showpiece of a master of lyrical prose" (Perley 7).

In Michele Murray's opinion, "Nabokov has been ignored, misinterpreted, abused and scorned" (Murray 5). But she believed this to be justified: "[In] the light of his books, it is not difficult to conclude that this unfriendly reception is due, not as much to his subject matter or difficult style, as to his originality both in subject and tone" (Ibid.). After all, Nabokov was "the high-wire artist who occasionally stumbles but who has not yet fallen" (Ibid.). The critic called the fourth chapter "the most audacious break with accepted fictional practices... an extremely subtle and clever parody of standard biographical writing" (Ibid.). Moreover, as if the story, moving from Fyodor's life to his books with easy recognition that both aspects of the young man are indeed one, is not sufficiently complex, Nabokov has employed his most brilliant style, replete with long descriptive and analytic passages, puns, verbal echoes, and imitations of other writers. The result, Murray stated, was a "book of utmost density and weight, for all its deliberate air of playfulness, a book paying tribute to the enduring splendor of art and imagination as opposed to ideology and the fictional depiction of 'the life of our times'" (Ibid.).

It was not only the puns and verbal echoes that gave the novel its charm as fiction—there was something alarming in it as well. Maie Perley noted that, despite Fyodor's general inactivity, he "manages to be a disturbing link in the chapters by constantly changing his manner of expression from the first person to the third, and it is only because of Nabokov's superb artistry that the reader is not thrown on his ear" (Perley 7). Similarly, Elaine Feinstein allowed that Nabokov's "control of language and the movement of time and plot (the movement even within a paragraph between one image to the next) is as clear, contrived, and absolute as the production of a poem" (Ibid.). The best parts of the book, she stated, were the magnificent descriptions of the figure of Fyodor's lost explorer-father and the imagined conversations between the two Berlin poets, because they again displayed Nabokov's delight in playing games with his reader, hypnotizing him into accepting shifts in time and space. The hypnotic quality of Nabokov's prose was a matter of consensus among critics, and his verbal games were often described as a show of a literary wizardry. Malcolm Forsyth wrote: "Nabokov's normal pace of writing seems to be the tour de force, and this novel... is no exception. [...] Which is not to say it is an easy book to read... [Nabokov's] performance is a fascinating one for those readers who like occasionally to pass up action-packed plots for the more contemplative delights of literary wizardry" (Forsyth 7).

In fact, the appearance of *The Gift* in 1963 did more to establish Nabokov's literary reputation in the long run than it did to strengthen his short-term popularity among the buyers of paperbacks. First and foremost it served as conclusive evidence of the lengthy career and creative durability of the writer: his *Lolita* now seemed not just a chance success but a logical development in the oeuvre of a mature artist. Bernard Share of *Irish Times* expressed his wonderment: "Nabokov, who must delight in this reversal of normal time-scale of authorship, shows that in 1937 he is still fascinating, as devious and as brilliantly original as he was in 1962. He was, and is, the greatest Slavonic gift to English since Conrad... and I would love to know how *Lolita* reads in Russian" (Share 10).

The mixed success of *The Gift* built expectations on the part of Nabokov's loyal American and British readers, who longed for more: "Each Nabokov novel differs from its fellows in many ways. *The Gift* comes from literary impulses that reach back into Russian history at the turn of the 20th century, and come forward in time to the strange inundations of Proust and Joyce. It is another chapter in the discovery of Nabokov and we can only hope that it is not the last" (Darack 10).

The critical discussion of the novel in 1963, with all its general bewilderment and occasional frustration, gave way to a clearly emerging consensus, something that Nelson Hayes rendered beautifully by paraphrasing Nabokov himself: "Midway in the novel, Fyodor remarks that 'genius is an African who dreams up snow.' Of such is the genius of Nabokov" (Hayes 6). Among those who fully appreciated the scale of the new translation were the *bilingual* readers and researchers. The first scholarly article on the novel, authored by Simon Karlinsky, stands out; Karlinsky flatly asserted that "not since *Evgenii Onegin* has a major Russian novel contained such a profusion of literary discussions, allusions and writers' characterizations"; he explained the most significant of them (Karlinsky

286). Less than a decade later, in another early example of Nabokov scholarship, Julian Moynahan recalled that the writer himself had called *The Gift* "the best, the most nostalgic of [his] Russian novels":

> It is also, even in the excellent English translation of 1963, the least accessible of Nabokov's major works to the general English-speaking reader. As a *Künstlerroman* ('artist's novel'), celebrating the life of literature and the literary life... *The Gift* is also a complex, playful, and creative work of literary criticism oriented toward the pre-Soviet Russian cultural tradition and aimed as a sidelong polemic against certain dubious values obtaining among literary and cultural pundits of the Russian émigré community in Western Europe. (Moynahan 37)

Without disputing his predecessors' claim that the audience would suffer from its lack of in-depth knowledge of the dozens of minor and major Russian writers the book alludes to, the critic added that, even so, the very same reader may well "feel he should acquire, along with a mastery of Russian literature, history, and the language, that ideal insomnia which Joyce recommended to the ideal reader of *Finnegans Wake*" (Ibid.).

Nabokov very rarely responded to his critics, but one curious testimony from his private correspondence sheds light on his own view of the critical reception of *The Gift*. When Stanley Edgar Hyman sent to Montreux a copy of his review recently printed in *The New Leader*, Véra, on behalf of her husband, declined the reviewer's invitation to speak at Bennington College (the critic taught at this women's college in Vermont for many years), and devoted the rest of the letter to a gracious but unequivocal denunciation of some key points in the article:

> Regarding your kind and admirable review: We do not think we have much chance of convincing you that my husband has no Oedipus complex; that Fyodor's mother is not his mother; that Zina has no resemblance to me; or that my husband has enough good taste never to put his wife, or his courtship, in his novels. After all, it would only be our word against Freud's. But one thing my husband would like to ask you. Who was your "consultant in Russian literature"? We strongly suspect that this person was pulling your leg—if he or she exists. It is a matter of historic record (and even Freud could do nothing about it) that my husband never signed any poems or indeed anything else with the name "Godunov-Cherdyntsev". (Are you sure your consultant did not confuse this name with that of a minor poet Golenishtshev-Kutuzov?). And it is of course absurd to equate Koncheyev with Khodasevich, a much older man whose reputation had been well established before the Revolution... (*Selected Letters* 351)

Although we might assume that the innocent Hyman did indeed not have help from any "consultant in Russian literature" whatsoever, for the matter of historic record, the truth, contrary to Véra Nabokov's insistence, is that in 1934 Nabokov printed a poem, "L'Iconnue de la Seine," with the subtitle "From F. G. Ch."—evidently meaning "from the poems of Fyodor Godunov-Cherdyntsev."

Dare to Reread *Dar*

Look at the Harlequins! (1974) turned out to be the last novel that Nabokov completed before his death in 1977. One of the recurrent themes taken up by Nabokov in *Look at the Harlequins!* is simultaneous identity and difference, shown in the phenomena of mirroring, doubling, twinning, symmetry of roles in physical, spiritual or emotional realms, and, last but not least, in the doubling of sense in puns and metaphors (Grabes 154). *The Gift* is full of physical and spiritual doubles: Yasha = Fyodor, Aleksandr Yakovlevich = Aleksandra Yakovlevna, Godunov = Koncheyev; a comic Gogolian pair "Chernolyubov and Dobroshevski" mimicking "Dobchinski and Bobchinski" from *The Inspector General*; or Dostoevsky, who becomes Chernyshevski's clownish double. In *Look at the Harlequins!*, *The Gift* appears in the disguise of a homonym, a novel titled *The Dare*, whose original title (*Podarok Otchizne*) can be translated as "a gift to the fatherland":

> The reader must have noticed that I speak only in a very general way about my Russian fictions of the Nineteen-Twenties and Thirties, for I assume that he is familiar with them or can easily obtain them in their English versions. At this point, however, I must say a few words about *The Dare*... When in 1934 I started to dictate its beginning to Annette, I knew it would be my longest novel. I did not foresee however that it would be almost as long as General Pudov's vile and fatuous "historical" romance about the way the Zion Wisers usurped St. Rus. It took me about four years in all to write its four hundred pages, many of which Annette typed at least twice. Most of it had been serialized in émigré magazines by May, 1939, when she and I, still childless, left for America; but in book form, the Russian original appeared only in 1950 (Turgenev Publishing House, New York), followed another decade later by an English translation, whose title neatly refers not only to the well-known device used to bewilder noddies but also to the daredevil nature of Victor, the hero and part-time narrator. (Nabokov, *Look at the Harlequins!* 99)

Nabokov's last finished novel is based on a 'shifting' device common in Nabokov's works, whereby the novel's slightly camouflaged reality remains largely recognizable, especially to the writer's devotees. For example, the Turgenev Publishing House stands in for the real-life Chekhov publishing enterprise; the protagonist's name, Victor, is even closer to that of his creator than "Fyodor" had been (the newborn Nabokov narrowly escaped being christened Victor by a bungling archpriest in a ceremony in the St. Petersburg church). Nabokov continues: "The novel begins with a nostalgic account of a Russian childhood (much happier, though not less opulent than mine). After that comes adolescence in England (not unlike my own Cambridge years); then life in émigré Paris, the writing of a first novel (*Memoirs of a Parrot Fancier*) and the tying of amusing knots in various literary intrigues" (Ibid, 100). The narrator of the novel goes on to say that Victor, "on a dare," wrote a brief biography and critical appraisal of Fyodor Dostoyevsky, which becomes an inset in the middle of the complete version of the book. Curiously, in *Look at the Harlequins!*, the crooked mirror Dostoyevsky becomes equated with his contemporary Chernyshevski, although the comparability of their aesthetic endeavors is dubious. The author and protagonist of *Look at the Harlequins!* finds hateful the politics of Dostoyevsky, "whose novels he condemns as absurd with their black-bearded killers presented as mere negatives of Jesus Christ's conventional image, and weepy whores borrowed from maudlin romances of an earlier age" (Nabokov, *Look at the Harlequins!* 100). The next chapter deals with the "rage and bewilderment" of émigré reviewers, all of them priests of the Dostoyevskian type. We also learn that in the last pages of *The Dare*, "the young hero accepts a flirt's challenge and accomplishes a final gratuitous feat by walking through a perilous forest into Soviet territory and as casually strolling back":

> I am giving this summary to exemplify what even the poorest reader of my *Dare* must surely retain, unless electrolysis destroys some essential cells soon after he closes the book. Now part of Annette's frail charm lay in her forgetfulness which veiled everything toward the evening of everything, like the kind of pastel haze that obliterates mountains, clouds, and even its own self as the summer day swoons. I know I have seen her many times, a copy of *Patria* in her languid lap, follow the printed lines with the pendulum swing of eyes suggestive of reading, and actually reach the "To be continued" at the end of the current installment of *The Dare*. [...] I must say I forgave her readily her attitude to my work. At public readings, I admired her public smile, the "archaic" smile of Greek statues. When her rather dreadful parents asked to see my books (as a suspicious physician might ask for a sample of semen), she gave them to read by mistake another man's novel because of a silly similarity of titles. The only real shock I experienced was when I overheard her informing some idiot woman friend that my *Dare* included biographies of "Chernolyubov and Dobroshevski"! She actually started to argue when I retorted that only a lunatic would have chosen a pair of third-rate publicists to write about—spoonerizing their names in addition! (Nabokov, *Look at the Harlequins!* 100-101)

In Emma Hamilton's characterization, *Look at the Harlequins!* is both a microcosm of Nabokov's oeuvre and its integral last piece that completes the circuit: "It is a refraction of Nabokov's earlier novels all of which appear within the text in varying degrees of mutation, disguised as Vadim's novels. *Look at the Harlequins!* abbreviates to LATH, as Vadim refers to his novel several times in the text. A lath is a thin strip of wood used in construction, but just one letter away and far more interesting, a *lathe* is a machine used to shape wood and metal, "chiefly used for circular or oval work" [Oxford English Dictionary]. Nabokov's final novel is indeed a lathe, a circular honing device for his corpus—all of his previous novels are processed through it, leaving different-sized shavings behind" (Hamilton 2008). One might also add that the lathe was leading to a TOOL, Nabokov's last unfinished novel, *The Original of Laura*.

Nabokov, it seems, was secretly hurt both by his Russian critics, who did not even have the opportunity to read the complete text of *The Gift* in the late 1930s, and by later readers who failed to penetrate the meaning of the book in translation. In response, he lynched the character's dull-witted soul mate: "I also know that she had typed every word of [the book] and most of its commas. Yet the fact remains that she retained nothing—perhaps in result of her having decided once for all that my prose was not merely 'difficult' but hermetic ('nastily hermetic,' to repeat the compliment Basilevski paid me the moment he realized—a moment which came in due time—that his manner and mind were being ridiculed in Chapter Three by my gloriously happy Victor)" (Nabokov, *Look at the Harlequins!* 100). The "gloriously happy" Nabokov applied the concept of distortion to his Russian short stories as early as in the 1920s. The same mechanism lies at the heart of *The Gift*, which obsessively explores the conflict between two modes of writing—the fictive and the autobiographical, or as John Burt Foster defines it even more precisely, "the vacillation between strict fidelity and creative reworking in the very constitution of the mnemonic image" (Foster 31-36).

CRITICAL RECEPTION: 1977–2000s

"And when will we return to Russia?"
The Gift in the Soviet Union and After

It was precisely the question in the title above that Nabokov put into the mouth of his programmatic hero in exile, Fyodor Godunov-Cherdyntsev (G350). Nabokov asked the same question when he was pondering the fate of his oeuvre in his own homeland.

The Gift is "the only Russian novel by Nabokov that I would not recommend to every reader," admits Alan Levy, "for *The Gift* is immensely difficult—and the best advice I have for getting through it, *if* you find yourself having difficulty, is to go on reading it in sequence, but take a day off between chapters and look upon *The Gift* as five different novellas with overlapping characters" (Levy 110). By way of confession, the critic says that when he first started reading *The Gift* in 1971, he gave it up in revulsion halfway through the first chapter, and raises a possibility that the Russian reader's experience might differ: *The Gift* is "the thick, old-fashioned, semi-Dickensian Russian novel many of us would dream of reading *if* we understood Nabokov's rich native tongue" (Ibid.; emphasis added). In fact, for many native Russian speakers reading the novel was akin to a revelation because they shared the same language with its creator only nominally—the Soviet official jargon is as close to Nabokov's style as unfiltered oil is to spring water.

Due to the growing circulation of *samizdat* literature, the earliest readers of Nabokov's *The Gift* in Russia appeared in the late 1960s and early 1970s. As noted earlier, the price for a paperback edition of *The Gift* on the Soviet black market was comparable with a worker's average monthly salary in the 1980s (Paperno, Hagopian 113).

In 1967 Nabokov "was amazed and delighted" by "a lengthy, intelligent, and subtle reaction to *The Gift*" that he received from a twenty-five-year-old in the Soviet Union (Boyd, *The American Years* 524). Véra admitted that they "really did not know that readers in this age bracket, nurtured on Sholokhov and his likes, *could* judge literature from the purely aesthetic point of view" (Ibid; italics in the original). It is now possible, four decades later, to name the young man—Alexander Gorianin, who would later co-translate with Mikhail Meilakh *The Real Life of Sebastian Knight* into Russian (Moscow, 1991). Gorianin gulped down a borrowed illegal copy of *The Gift* during three cold days and nights in January of 1967, while on a research trip to the Soviet capital. He was so deeply moved by his discovery that on the third night he went straight to the Moscow State University library and borrowed a fresh copy of "Who's Who" with Nabokov's publisher's address (care of G. P. Putnam's Sons, 210 Madison Ave., N.Y.C.), and sent "a long, muddled letter" (Gorianin). Because no answer ever came, Gorianin was convinced that it had been intercepted by the KGB. Then ten years later he received a message from Elena Sikorski, Nabokov's sister, who wrote: "Many years ago you sent an absolutely incredible letter to Vladimir Nabokov. He didn't respond because the least thing in the world he would want was to inflict any hardship upon you. But he was absolutely captivated by this letter. Now, after his death, I am visiting friends in Leningrad, and I've decided to finally write to you, so you wouldn't think that your wonderful words have gone unnoticed...I've preserved a photocopy of your letter and cherish it as the very first good news from Russia" (April 22, 1978; quoted in Gorianin, my translation).

The writer Aleksandr Konstantinovich Gladkov (1912–76), the laureate of the Stalin prize for literature, was arrested in 1949 and spent years in the GULAG. The diary that he kept after serving his term contains a curious note. While residing in Komarovo, on the outskirts of Leningrad, in the Writer's Union state sanatorium *Dom tvorchestva pisatelei* he confesses:

> All day I read Sirin's (Nabokov's) novel *The Gift*. I've read it before, in the serialized version in *Contemporary Annals*, i.e. without the Chernyshevski chapter, and not as attentively as now. The novel is splendid. In my opinion, this is the best novel

by this author. It is perfect in its conception, in its plot structure, intricate and not trivial, as well as in its mastery of words. But the main success of the novel is its protagonist who is convincing as a talent, as a man with the poetic gift. I am not aware of any other similar example in all world literature... (December 29, 1968; quoted in Martynov 1133, my translation)

In the climate of Khrushchev's post-Thaw Soviet Union it became almost impossible to deny Nabokov's presence in Russian literature any longer. An article on Nabokov was included in the fifth volume of the *Concise Literary Encyclopedia* (*Kratkaia Literaturnaia Entsiklopedia*) published in 1968 in Moscow. It was composed by a young humanities scholar named Leonid Chertkov (and supervised by Oleg Mikhailov), who soon immigrated to West Germany. In order to "smuggle" this biographical blurb into the official and highly authoritative *Encyclopedia*, the co-authors had to compromise—hence the infamous formula calling *Lolita* an "erotic bestseller" and defining Nabokov's basic trend as "literary snobbery" (*Kratkaia Literaturnaia Entsiklopedia* 5: 60). *The Gift* had been vouchsafed with a single sentence: "In the novel... Nabokov gives a tendentiously distorted image of N. G. Chernyshevski" (Ibid.). Six years later, when the ideological climate in the Soviet Union had cooled down, the same O. Mikhailov accused Nabokov of having a "mocking wit," seemingly hinting at the Chernyshevski chapter in *The Gift*, and of rejecting "everything that binds the artist with the ideas of homeland, state, and national continuity [*preemstvennost'*]" (*Nash Sovremennik* 1, 1974). While already in Europe, Leonid Chertkov met with Nabokov in person in 1976; a few months later he authored an obituary of the writer in an émigré newspaper in which, among a few other novels, he singled out *The Gift* for its "heart-wrenching pages about Father" ("Russkii pisatel'," *Russkaia Mysl'*, July 21, 1977).

The Moscow *Literaturnaia gazeta* allowed A. Chernyshev's article, "Vladimir Nabokov, in the first and in the second place..." (March 4, 1970), in which the full text of Fyodor's poem, "Blagodariu tebia, otchizna..." ("Thank you, my land..."; G29), is cited. Since that time Nabokov's name was, "curiously, mentioned quite freely by the establishment scholars. In 1982, it was cited in print at least five times—one sentence in an interview, half a sentence in a paper on literary translation, a mere reference tucked between Beckett and Joyce in an article on modernist literature in English" (Paperno, Hagopian 111).

Mikhail Lotman, son of the celebrated Tartu semiotician Yuri Lotman, composed a short article on a Russian poet named Godunov-Cherdyntsev. The still forbidden Nabokov's name does not surface throughout the piece; no one among the officials expected this sort of trick—the poet Vladimir Sirin-Nabokov disguised as a non-existing Russian author—and it was published in an academic journal (1979). The episode itself is rather symptomatic of "the odd distortions that occurred in a censor-controlled literary establishment of a police state" (Ibid.). Notwithstanding this bold challenge, the first truly serious research on Nabokov's work that had emerged in Russia before Perestroika was an article by another bright representative of the Tartu-Moscow Semiotic School, Iurii Iosifovich Levin (1935–2010), written in 1977 and published four years later in Holland (Levin).

The young generation of the Russian non-conformist poets read Nabokov's novel as attentively as their academic contemporaries. Aleksandr Kushner's writings present a rare case of unreserved acceptance of Nabokov. Kushner was an adherent of a sentimental current in the new Russian poetry:

> O, if only in our lifetime any novel could once again
> Captivate our hearts like *Werther* or *The Gift*,
> O, if only I could embrace the happy image,
> No matter whether he is young and you are old and sullen.
>
> *O, esli by pri nas kakoi-nibud' eshche raz*
> *Privlek serdtsa roman, kak Verter ili Dar,*
> *O, esli by k grudi prizhat' schastlivyi obraz,*
> *Ne vazhno, pust' on iun, a ty ugrium i star.*
>
> (Kushner 3)

Well-known contemporary Russian poet Olga Sedakova belongs to the same category: she responded to Nabokov's death with verses that played on the word "gift" and Nabokov's novel under the same title ("In Memory of Nabokov," 1979–80; Sedakova 166).

The 1990s cohort of Russian writers conceptualized the problem: Nabokov was transformed into a shining, mythical dissident and aesthete whose subversive discourse undermined the foundations of socialist realism (Leving 112-13).

At one of Nabokov's posthumous birthday celebrations, a post-Soviet author described an imaginary statue of "Nabokov Vladimir Vladimirovich, professor of pity and beauty, the Nobel non-laureate." According to this poet, his version of Nabokov's sculpture would bear no name or date. It would be just a figure of a thin young man in a light sweater, bent over the granite slate on his knees:

> [...] Approaching the monument a passer-by would suddenly stop
> not believing his eyes. He would turn around
> looking for a guide
> or a tablet with information
> about an avant-garde exhibition, —
> or a film crew, giggling behind the bushes.

> Then, forgetting his burger,
> or lowering the cornflower bouquet,
> should the passer-by be female,
> *would take the last step and make sure*
> *that the writing person is sitting on a w.c. pan.*
> He is sitting on a pan
> in a sweater and trousers,
> forever young,
> when he was writing *The Gift*.
> A poet on a pan is not a pun,
> not a trite challenge to a crowd.
> With his bent head he is above
> an angel on a column.
> The birch shadow falls on a Carrara page
> and moves up the hand.
> A raven burrs, and the day goes on.
> He is writing *The Gift* on a pan. (Dorman)

The text blends a number of basic archetypes of modern Russian poetic perception, among them the Alexander Column in St. Petersburg, Pushkin's poem "Exegi Monumentum" (1836), as well as a quotation from the infamous Nabokov's poem "What is the evil deed I have committed?" (*Kakoe sdelal ia durnoe delo*; in *Poems and Problems* 147).

Although in the inverted optics of postmodernism Nabokov has become part of official discourse, he still remains a dynamic commodity in the active readers' market. The famous finale of *The Gift*, with its paraphrase of an Onegin stanza, casts its shadow on the ending of Timur Kibirov's long poem "Johns" ("Sortiry"):

> The water washes down miserable sheets.
> Like mortal eyes, imagined ones must close some day —
>
> The lyrical hero rises from a toilet bowl,
> But the author retires. You can't squeeze out
> Even a single line...
>
> (*Voda smyvaet zhalkie listochki.*
> *I dlia videnii tozhe net otsrochki —*
>
> *liricheskii geroi vstaet s tolchka,*
> *no avtor udaliaetsia. Ni strochki*
> *uzhe ne vyzhmesh'.* [...])
>
> (Kibirov 212)

Compare this with Nabokov's: "Onegin from his knees will rise—but his creator strolls away...nor does this terminate the phrase" (G378). Restoring historical and literary order—bending the "straightened" prose back into poetic meter—Kibirov deflates an entire tradition and brings its semantics to naught.

Writing to his mother in Paris, Fyodor remarks that it is sheer sentimentality to expect ever to return to Russia. On the one hand, he can live more easily outside of his native country than some because he has taken away "the keys to her"—i.e. language, art, and memory—and because some day he "shall live there in [his] books" (G350). Indeed, *The Gift* is Nabokov's "happiest" novel, according to Julian Moynahan, "the work in which he frees himself from his Russian past, narrowly and nostalgically considered, by earning a free entry into the vital dialogue of Russian art over the centuries" (40). On the other hand, Fyodor fantasizes (albeit without much confidence) that the comeback is destined to happen—"no matter when, in a hundred, two hundred years" (G350).

This ended up happening much, much earlier than expected.

References

Abram, Lynwood. "Strangest Prose-Poet Russia Ever Produced," *Houston Chronicle*, June 2, 1963, Zest Magazine.

Adamovich, Georgii. [Review of *Sovremennye zapiski*, Book 64]. *Poslednie novosti* 6039 (October 7, 1937).

_____ [Review of *Sovremennye zapiski*, Book 65]. *Poslednie novosti* (January 20, 1938a).

_____ [Review of *Sovremennye zapiski*, Book 67]. *Poslednie novosti* 6437 (January 20, 1938b).

_____ *Odinochestvo i svoboda*. Moscow: Respublika, 1996.

Allsop, Kenneth. "Nabokov... Long Before *Lolita*," *London Daily Mail*, November 7, 1963.

B., A.G. "Nabokov Novel Not Up to Par," *News and Courier*. Charleston (South Carolina), July 28, 1963.

Barrett, William. "Dream of Russia," *Atlantic Monthly*, CCXI (May 1963).

Benedictus, David. "Before Lolita," *London Sunday Telegraph*, November 10, 1963.

Boyd, Brian. *Vladimir Nabokov: The Russian Years*. Princeton: Princeton University Press, 1990.

B[rady], C[harles] A., "Brilliant Novel By Nabokov Has Limited Appeal," *Buffalo Evening News*, May 25, 1963.

Brown, Alexander C. "Early Nabokov Novel Charms But Befuddles," *Newport News Daily Press*, July 7, 1963, Magazine Section.

Brown, Leonard. "*Lolita* Nabokov Offers *The Gift*," *Pasadena Independent Star News*, June 23, 1963, Scene Section.

Bryer, Jackson R. and Thomas J. Bergin, Jr. "A Checklist of Nabokov Criticism in English," *Wisconsin Studies in Contemporary Literature*, Vol. 8 (2). A Special Number Devoted to Vladimir Nabokov (Spring 1967): 353-358.

Butler, Henry. "Russia's Not What It Used to Be." *Indianapolis Times*, May 26, 1963.

Chertkov, Leonid. "Vladimir Nabokov," in *Kratkaia Literaturnaia Entsiklopedia*, Vol. 5. Moscow, 1968.

Coffey, Jerry. "Translation Shows Younger Nabokov," *Fort Worth Star-Telegram*, June 2, 1963, Sec. 2.

Cook, Bruce. *The Critic*, XXII (August-September 1963).

References

Crane, Milton. "Intricate Tale with Russian Literature as the Heroine," *Chicago Sunday Tribune Magazine of Books*, June 2, 1963.

Culligan, Glendy. "Nabokov's Early Gift," *Washington Post*, May 26, 1963.

Dance, Jim. "The Creator of Lolita Bares Writer's Soul," *Detroit Free Press*, June 2, 1963, Sec. B.

Darack, Arthur. "Nabokov's Newest Novel Is a Russian Translation," *Cincinnati Enquirer*, May 25, 1963.

Davie, Donald. "Reader in the Dock," *Manchester Guardian*, November 8, 1963.

Davydov, Sergei. *"Teksty-matreshki" Vladimira Nabokova*. Revised 2nd ed. St. Petersburg: Kircideli, 2004.

Desyatov, Vyacheslav. "Russkii postmodernism: Polveka s Nabokovym," in *Imperia N. 2006*, eds. Y. Leving and Soshkin, E. Moskva: Novoe literaturnoe obozrenie, 2006.

Dolinin, Alexander. "Pis'ma V.V. Nabokova k G. P. Struve. Chast' 2: 1931–1935 / Publ. E.B. Belodubrovskogo i A.A. Dolinina, komm. A.A. Dolinina. *Zvezda* 4, 2004: 139-63.

———. "*The Gift*: Addendum to Commentary," Part I, *Nabokov Online Journal*, Vol. I, 2007. <http://etc.dal.ca/noj/articles/volume1/DOLININ.pdf> Accessed July 19, 2010.

———. "*The Gift*: Addendum to Commentary," Part II, *Nabokov Online Journal*, Vol. II, 2008. <http://etc.dal.ca/noj/articles/volume2/13_Dolinin.pdf> Accessed July 19, 2010.

Dorman, Oleg. "If only I was asked to project a monument..." Publication at the electronic forum of the Nabokov Society, NABOKV-L (April 23, 2004).

Dwight, Ogden G. "Difficult but Absorbing is Early Nabokov Novel," *Des Moines Sunday Register*, July 28, 1963.

Feinstein, Elaine. "Fiction," *The Cambridge Review*. LXXXV, November 23, 1963.

Forsyth, Malcolm. "Old Nabokov Work Put Into English," New Orleans *Time's-Picayune*; June 9, 1963, Section Three.

Foster, John Burt Jr. *Nabokov's Art of Memory and European Modernism*. Princeton: Princeton University Press, 1993.

Garf, Andrei. "Literaturnye pelenki," *Novoe slovo* (March 20, 1938).

Gilmore, Jane L. "Early Nabokov Novel Paradoxical Wonder," *Omaha Sunday World-Herald*, July 14, 1963, Sec. G.

Gorianin, Alexander. "Kak pervuiu liubov'...," *Zvezda* 7, 2007. <http://magazines.russ.ru/zvezda/2007/7/go12.html> Accessed July 28, 2010.

Grabes, Herbert. "The Deconstruction of Autobiography: *Look at the Harlequins!*" *Cycnos* 10:1 (1993): 151-158.

Grant, Paul Benedict. "Humor and *Lolita* in the Classroom." *Approaches to Teaching Nabokov's* Lolita. Ed. by Z. Kuzmanovich and G. Diment. New York: The Modern Language Association of America, 2008.

Grayson, Jane. *Nabokov Translated: A Comparison of Nabokov's Russian and English Prose*. Oxford: Oxford University Press, 1977.

Griffin, Lloyd W. *Library Journal*, LXXXVII (April 15, 1963).

Hamilton, Emma. "*Look at the Harlequins!*: Nabokov's Corpus Compendium," *Nabokov Online Journal*, Vol. II, 2008.

Hayes, E. Nelson. "A Nabokov Definition: 'Genius Is an African Who Dreams Up Snow,'" *New Haven Register*, June 23, 1963, Part 4.

Hern, Anthony. "Clever Stuff From Nabokov," *London Evening Standard*, November 12, 1963.

Hilgenstuhler, Ted. "From *Lolita*'s Author," *Los Angeles Herald-Examiner*, June 16, 1963.

Hinde, Thomas. "Waugh's Oxford," *The Spectator*, No. 7063 (November 8, 1963).

Holley, Fred S. "Man's Self-Deception," *Norfolk Virginian-Pilot*, June 16, 1963.

H[unter], A[nna] C. "Autobiography Mystic Maze of Truth Whim and Fiction," *Savannah Morning News*, June 9, 1963, Magazine Section.

Hutchens, John K. "A Novel-But a Memoir, Too," *NY Herald Tribune*, May 27, 1963.

Hyman, Stanley Edgar. "Nabokov's Gift," *New Leader*, XLVI (October 14, 1963).

Idema, Jim. "Russian Exiles in Berlin," *Denver Post*, May 26, 1963, Roundup Section.

Iglehart, L.T., Jr. "Served By Vladimir Nabokov: A Rich, Slavic Pudding," *St. Louis Globe-Democrat*, June 1-2, 1963.

Iremonger, Lucille. *Housewife* (London), January 1964.

Karlinsky, Simon. "Vladimir Nabokov's Novel *Dar* as a Work of Literary Criticism: A Structural Analysis," *The Slavic and East European Journal* 7 (3), 1963: 284-296.

Khodasevich, Vladislav. [Review of *Sovremennye zapiski*, Book 63]. *Vozrozhdenie (Renaissance)* 4078 (May 15, 1937a).

_____ [Review of *Sovremennye zapiski*, Book 64]. *Vozrozhdenie* 4101 (October 15, 1937b).

_____ [Review of *Sovremennye zapiski*, Book 65]. *Vozrozhdenie* 4120 (February 25, 1938a).

_____ [Review of *Sovremennye zapiski*, Book 66]. *Vozrozhdenie* 4137 (June 24, 1938b).

_____ [Review of *Sovremennye zapiski*, Book 67]. *Vozrozhdenie* (November 11, 1938c).

_____ "On Sirin," trans. Michael H. Walker, in *Nabokov: The Critical Heritage*, ed. Norman Page. London: Routledge & Kegan Paul, 1982.

_____. *Sobranie sochinenii*. Vol. 4. Moskva: Soglasie, 1997.

Kibirov, Timur. "*Kto kuda—a ia v Rossiiu...*" Moscow: Vremia, 2001.

Kirsch, Robert R. "Four Newcomers: A Study in Extremes," *Los Angeles Times*, June 16, 1963, Calendar Section.

Kostelanetz, Richard. "The Gift," *Village Voice*, June 13, 1963.

Kushner, Aleksandr. "Eshche raz...," *Novyi mir* 1, 1998.

Levin, Iu. I. "Ob osobennostiakh povestvovatel'noi struktury i obraznogo stroia romana V. Nabokova *Dar*," *Russian Literature* 9 (2), 1981.

Levine, Paul. "Easterns and Westerns," *The Hudson Review*, XVI (Autumn 1963).

Leving, Yuri. "Plaster, Marble, Canon: The Vindication of Nabokov," *Ulbandus: The Slavic Review of Columbia University*. The Special Issue devoted to Vladimir Nabokov. No. 10, 2007: 101-121.

Levy, Alan. *The Velvet Butterfly*. Sag Harbor, New York: The Permanent Press, 1984.

References

Lotman, Mikhail. "Nekotorye zamechaniya o poezii i poetike F. K. Gudonova-Cherdyntseva" ["Several Remarks on the Poetry and Poetics of F. K. Gudonov-Cherdyntsev"], *Vtorichnye modeliruiushchie sistemy*. Tartu, 1979.

MacGillirray, Arthur, S.J. *Best Sellers*, XXIII (July 1, 1963): 123-124.

Malcolm, Donald. "A Retrospect," *New Yorker*, XL (April 25, 1964).

Malikova, Maria. "Pis'ma Gleba Struve Vladimiru i Vere Nabokovym 1942-1985 godov," *Russkaia literatura*. No. 1, 2007.

Malin, Irving. "Anti-Heroic Novel," *Louisville Courier-Journal*, June 2, 1963, Sec. 4.

Martynov, G.G. "V. Nabokov: Kratkaia letopis' zhizni i tvorchestva," in V. Nabokov, *Sobranie sochinenii*. Moscow: Dilia, 2007.

Mel'nikov, Nikolai. "Dar. Retsenzii i otzyvy." *Klassik bez retushi*. Moskva: Novoe literaturnoe obozrenie, 2000: 147-150.

Mercier, Jeanne. "Samovars in Berlin," *Milwaukee Journal*, June 30, 1963, Part 5.

Mitchell, Julian. "Dazzling Energy," *London Sunday Times*, November 10, 1963.

Moore, Harry T., "Early Novel of Nabokov Is Fine Fun," *Boston Sunday Herald*, June 2, 1963, Sec. 1.

Moynahan, Julian. *Vladimir Nabokov*. Minnesota: University of Minnesota Press, 1971.

Murray, Michele. "Gift From Nabokov Deserves Gratitude," *Catholic Reporter* (Kansas City, Mo.), June 28, 1963.

Nabokov, Vladimir. *Selected Letters: 1940-1977*. Ed. by D. Nabokov and M. J. Bruccoli. New York: Harcourt Brace Jovanovich, 1989.

_____ *Look at the Harlequins!* New York: McGraw-Hill, 1974.

_____ *Perepiska s sestroi*. Ann Arbor: Ardis, 1985.

_____ *Poems and Problems*. New York: McGraw Hill, 1970.

Page, James F. "A Professor Pure, Puzzled and Put Out," *Memphis Press Scimitar*, July 26, 1963.

Paperno S. and Hagopian J. "Official and Unofficial Responses to Nabokov in the Soviet Union," in *The Achievements of Vladimir Nabokov*. Eds. George Gibian and Stephen Jan Parker. Ithaca, New York: Center for International Studies, Cornell University, 1984.

Perlberg, Mark M. "A Novel of the Pursuit of Excellence-Eccentric, Hilarious, Splendid and Beautiful," *Chicago Daily News*, June 8, 1963, Panorama Section.

Perley, Maie E. "The Book Scene—A Glowing Work By Nabokov," *Louisville Times*, July 29, 1963, Sec. 1.

"Perepiska I. A. Bunina s M. A. Aldanovym," *Novyi zhurnal*, No. 150, 1983.

Pil'skii, Petr. [Review of *Sovremennye zapiski*, Book 63], *Segodnia* 117 (April 29, 1937).

"Pis'ma B. Zaitseva k I. i V. Buninym," *Novyi zhurnal* 149, 1982.

Pollock, Venetia. "New Fiction," *Punch*, CCXLV (December 4, 1963).

Rogers, W. G. "Nabokov Novel Not a Lolita," Gary *Post-Tribune*, May 26, 1963, Sec. D.

Rollow, Jack W. "Nabokov's Merry Pranks Hard to Follow in *Gift*," *Charlotte Observer*, June 2, 1963.

Ross, Maggie. "New novels," *The Listener*, LXX (November 21, 1963): 852-853.

Rowe, Percy. "Even the Mighty Can Fall," *Toronto Telegram*, October 5, 1963.

Sanders, Nicholas. "New Nabokov Novel Is Literary Event," *Nashville Banner*, June 7, 1963.

Sandrof, Nancy. "Work of Uncanny Lucidity," *Worcester Telegram*, May 26, 1963.

Sedakova, Olga. "Pamiati Nabokova." *Premiia Andreya Belogo: 1978–2004*. Anthology. Ed. by B. Ostanin. Moscow: Novoe literaturnoe obozrenie, 2005.

Share, Bernard. "The Moth and the Candle," *Irish Times* (Dublin), November 16, 1963.

Sherman, Thomas B. "Nabokov Nets Another Mixed Literary Bag," *St. Louis Sunday Post-Dispatch*, September 22, 1963.

Shrayer, Maxim. *Nabokov: Temy i variatsii*. St. Petersburg: Akademicheskii proekt, 2000.

Slonim, Marc. *Modern Russian Literature from Chekhov to the Present*. New York: Oxford University Press, 1953.

Smith, Miles. "Early Nabokov Tale Wordy, Confusing," *Toledo Blade*, May 26, 1963, Sec. 2.

Spender, Stephen. "and Demolished Truth" *New York Times*. May 26, 1963.

Stanley, Donald. "A Bizarre Tale by *Lolita*'s Creator," *San Francisco Examiner*, May 26, 1963, Highlight Section.

Struve, Gleb. *Russkaia literatura v izgnanii. Opyt istoricheskogo obzora zarubezhnoi literatury*. New York: Izdatel'stvo imeni Chekhova, 1956.

Sylvester, William. "Magnificent 'Gift'—Nabokov's Talent Shines Again," *Cleveland Plain Dealer*, June 2, 1963.

Taubman, Robert. "Near Zero," *New Statesman*, LXVI (November 8, 1963): 653-654.

Thorpe, Day. "Earlier Nabokov from the Russian," Washington (D.C.) *Sunday Star*, May 26, 1963.

[Unsigned]. "Lord of Language," *Time*, LXXXI (June 14, 1963).

[Unsigned]. "Russian Romp," *Times Literary Supplement*, November 7, 1963.

Vladimir Nabokov: The Critical Heritage, ed. Norman Page. London: Routledge & Kegan Paul, 1982.

Watkins, Sue. "On Russia," Austin (Texas) *American-Statesman*, June 16, 1963, Show World Section.

Weir, Sybil. "Nabokov's *The Gift* Reveals an Artist's Direction," *Oakland Tribune*, June 9, 1963.

W[eissblatt], H[arry] A. "The Poet in Exile," Trenton (N.J.) *Sunday Times*-Advertiser, June 23, 1963, Part Two.

Williams, Vera. "Book Reviews," Long Beach (Cal.) *Independent Press-Telegram*, June 13, 1963.

Wolff, Renate C. "Early Nabokov Novel—*The Gift* Not Up to *Lolita*," *Atlanta Journal and Constitution*, September 22, 1963.

Appendixes

Appendix I

Firing Practice to *The Gift*:
Nabokov's 1937 Letter to Samuil Rozov

As a "story of a great writer in the making" (Nabokov to James Laughlin, November 27, 1941; *Selected Letters* 39), *The Gift* would contain more autobiographical material than any of his other novels. Similar to Alexander Pushkin's letters, Nabokov's correspondence can provide the reader with a gateway to understanding his poetry and prose. In their entirety, Pushkin's letters are rightly considered a prose masterpiece: Pushkin is "ever the craftsman, the builder of harmonious literary structures; every detail counts, not only in its meaning, but also in the architecture of the line, stanza, paragraph, and the entire work" (Pushkin 5-6). The same can be said of Nabokov's correspondence; although he could be succinct and stark, especially in business matters and in his general correspondence in the later period of his life, the 1937 letter to Samuil Rozov is a happy exception.

Nabokov predicted that "the future specialist in such dull literary lore as autoplagiarism will like to collate a protagonist's experience in my novel *The Gift* with the original event" (*Speak, Memory* 37). Nabokov himself certainly did not consider such literary lore as "dull" when he was studying Pushkin's biography for his *Onegin* research. In the mid 1990s, I discovered a collection of twelve letters (1937–76) from Nabokov to Samuil Rozov in Israel. The originals, in Nabokov's hand, were preserved by Rozov's family. The entire correspondence has not been previously published, except for the three letters translated from Russian by Dmitri Nabokov in *Selected Letters: 1940–1977*. The most precious item is the letter dated September 4, 1937: eight pages of this fascinating text are reminiscent of the style in *Speak, Memory*. Rozov made a copy for Andrew Field in 1970, after Nabokov asked him to send some material to his first biographer; it was used by Brian Boyd in *The Russian Years*. The Russian original of this letter was published, with commentary, in *Nabokov: Pro et contra* (Leving).

There is the following passage in *Pnin*: "In reviewing his Russian friends throughout Europe and the United States Timofey Pahlch could easily count at least sixty dear people whom he had intimately known since say, 1920, and whom he never called anything but Vadim Vadimych, Ivan Khristoforovich, or Samuil Izrailevich as the case may be, and who called him by his name and patronymic with the same effusive sympathy" (76). Gene Barabtarlo, commenting on these lines in his A *Guide to Nabokov's* Pnin (1989), presents evidence that "Vadim Vadimych" is a reference to Nabokov himself. He did not, however, comment on the other two figures. Rozov is the most plausible prototype of Samuil Izrailevich, this seldom mentioned character, even more phantasmal than the mysterious Vadim Vadimych.

Samuil Rozov (1900–76), Nabokov's friend and Tenishev classmate, lived in Israel and maintained correspondence with Nabokov for forty years, up until his death. Their very special friendship can be reconstructed now thanks to the discovered correspondence. Placed in *Pnin* alongside such names as Samuil Lvovich Shpolyanski, Samuil Izrailevich seems to be simply another fictitious Jewish character, yet he is not. What, then, is he doing in Nabokov's novel, and why did the fastidious author decide to insert him here?

Samuil's father, Israel (Izrail) Rozov, was an active figure in the Zionist movement in St. Petersburg at the beginning of the century. He played a key role in the establishment of the Russian-language Jewish newspaper *Rassvet* (*The Daybreak*), where Khodasevich's translations of H. N. Bialik's poetry appeared in the early 1920s. The family lived in a large house on Kamenoostrovsky Street in downtown St. Petersburg before the Bolshevik revolution. A representative of the British oil company Shell in Russia, Samuil's father was strongly inclined towards English culture, a trait which he passed on to his son. In the same way Nabokov inherited an Anglophile disposition from his family. Of course, the choice of Tenishev school for a young Jew from a wealthy St. Petersburg family was not accidental. It was here that the boys' paths crossed.

Samuil Rozov, or *Mulya* (as Nabokov called his friend fondly), was invited on several occasions to dine with the Nabokovs. Just as Nabokov's St. Petersburg home was the meeting place for some of the best men among the Russian intelligentsia, so Rozov's house generously opened its doors to local Jewish society. Vladimir Jabotinsky, the well-known Zionist ideologue and Russian writer, made numerous visits.

After he emigrated to Britain in 1917, Rozov studied at the University of London for his engineering degree. There is a famous story about his "lending" Nabokov his Tenishev diploma in order to assist the latter in entering Cambridge (VN to Rozov, September 4, 1937; Boyd, *The Russian Years* 166n). In 1924, the Rozovs moved to Palestine.

Rozov's first known letter to Nabokov is dated 1937. In reply, Nabokov writes: "I should like to know more about you; you wrote too little. I am only about three hours away from you,—I mean, by airplane." In 1945, Nabokov notes in a similar vein, "I cannot tell you how I regret that there is constantly a bluish wall of space between us; as for time, I feel that we have achieved a great victory over it, and enjoy the harmony which connects us and which neither time nor seas can destroy." Nabokov says he is happy that Rozov lives in Palestine, and not in Europe. He writes that his brother Sergei and Ilya Fondaminsky, editor of *Sovremennye zapiski*, died in concentration camps, adding that all Germany would have to be "reduced to ashes several times over in order to quench my hatred of it, whenever I think of those who perished in Poland." In February 1946, Nabokov tried to meet Rozov's father in New York but when he arrived at the Savoy Hotel, Israel Rozov had already left.

[Ill. A-1] Nabokov and Rozov in Zermat, 1962.
Photograph by Horst Tappe, published by permission

A reunion became possible only in the 1960s. In one of his letters from that period, Nabokov concludes with these words: "I embrace you, my dear, and want to see you *very* much—in the eternal flourishing of our immutable youth!" Nabokov and Rozov finally saw each other in Zermat in 1962, recognizing one another at once, as if 40 years had not passed. In 1967, after the Six-Day War, Nabokov writes, "I have been with you with all my soul, deeply and anxiously, in the course of the latest events, and I triumph now, saluting the marvelous victory of Israel." In the 1970s, Nabokov regularly informs his friend about his newly published or planned books, which Rozov received directly from the publishers at Nabokov's request. Nabokov's query about Rozov's health at the end of his last letter, written in early 1976, strikes an odd note, for it reached Israel after its addressee had been dead for several weeks.

Rozov's family and friends remember him as an exceptionally kind-hearted and generous person. Nabokov's words from his last letter, "we are heartily enjoying your sunny grapefruits," means that even after his death Rozov managed to bring delight to others in a most literal sense. That *post mortem* exchange is emblematic in the overall context of their unique relationship, which Nabokov himself twice characterized as "a complete victory over time."

As it turns out, Rozov—and here we return to our starting point—already had received another life as a literary character. Combining the memories of the Jews who perished in the Holocaust with those of the survivors, Nabokov sets up in *Pnin* a complicated antinomic structure. Nabokov's insertion of his friend's name into the novel is a significant act, more than merely an expression of respect and love to an old pal, but rather a semi-fictitious documentary marker of the epoch.

Rozov's 1936 letter which had triggered Nabokov's wonderfully poetic response serves as yet another small satellite akin to the short story "The Circle," for descriptions of young Fyodor's Russian experiences in *The Gift*. Addressing the now famous prose writer Sirin, who—the rumors had it—is none other but his former classmate Volodya Nabokov, whom he had not seen for almost two decades, Rozov writes:

> Once, having a bet with Kiandzhuntsev, you have submerged into a frozen pool in the greenhouse—and have been sent off home immediately. In your novels you continue plunging into an icy depth. It takes my breath away.
> Do not catch cold, dear.
>
> (Leving and Shrayer)

Ignoring the metaphysical dimension and metaphoric language of the message, Nabokov breaks whatever "ice" could have accumulated during the years that passed. He sets the record straight by reprimanding his best friend of youth in the very opening paragraph: "Why do you write using the formal '*Vy*'"?

References

Boyd, Brian. *Vladimir Nabokov: The Russian Years*. Princeton: Princeton University Press, 1990.

Leving, Yuri. "Palestinskoe pis'mo V. Nabokova" ["V. Nabokov's Palestinian Letter of 1937"], in *V. V. Nabokov: Pro et contra*. Vol. 2. St. Petersburg: Russian Christian State Institute, 2001:12-33.

Leving, Yuri and Maxim D. Shrayer. "An Unknown 1936 Letter of S.I. Rozov to V.V. Nabokov," *Solnechnoe spletenie* [*The Plexus*] 16-17. Moscow–Jerusalem, 2001: 199-205.

Nabokov, Vladimir. *Pnin*. Everyman's Library Classics & Contemporary Classics. New York: Random House, 2004.

_____ *Selected Letters: 1940-1977*. Ed. by Dmitri Nabokov, Matthew Joseph Bruccoli. New York: Harcourt, Brace, Jovanovich, 1989.

_____ *Speak, Memory. An Autobiography Revisited*. New York: G.P. Putnam's Sons, 1966.

Pushkin, Alexander. *The Letters of Alexander Pushkin*. Three Volumes in One. Translated, with Preface, Introduction, and Notes by J. Thomas Shaw. Madison: University of Wisconsin Press, 1967.

[Ill. A-2] The first page of Nabokov's letter to Rozov

---————— Appendix I ————————

Letter to Rozov

Hôtel des Alpes,
Cannes A. M.
4 ix 1937

Dear friend,

I cannot tell you (no, let us suppose I can) how I was warmed by your kind, charming letter. But why do you write using the formal *"Vy"*? You are one of the few people with whom I would like to use the familiar *"Ty"* forever. I can't address you in any other way.

Several times over all these years I have heard about you (I already knew in broad outline where you were, what you were doing, and how you were doing). But the last time we saw each other was in London (along the streets of which on the first day after your arrival you were carrying your little sister[55] on the handlebars of your bicycle!) where we happened to play billiards with Pines[56] and where you rendered me a very great service by lending me your school diploma: I displayed it in Cambridge, prevaricated that I had one just like it (it even seems to me that people understood it to be my own)—that liberated me from taking the entrance examination. And it was then that I read you some of my poems in an ultra-Russian spirit; you condemned them.

When you and I were a little older, in the higher grades (the first [beginning—crossed out] years of school, which seemed to us to be so improbably two-digited!), you and I liked very much to visit the hall of the young children (who somehow birdlike, all together, squeaked, rushed about, sometimes plucked at one's sleeve, the motley piercing hubbub,[57] through which floated a head covered in gray fluff—what was his name? that tutor of the little ones, that old man who was also little?—[*you see, I also have forgotten names*—crossed out; written above: *Nikolai Platonych!*]) and with some sort of strange astonishment (the captivatingly mournful nuance of which I later in life was to experience frequently,—forgive the parentheses, but I need to include a great deal) you said: "Were we really like them not so long ago?"

I divide people into those who remember and those who don't remember, and the former are always better than the latter. You belong to the first group—the first of the first. How those boards, which you recollected, cracked under our feet! In "anatomy" classroom there stood a skeleton, strange as it might seem, that of a girl. The first experiments in the "laboratory"—the germination of the little

---

[55] Hertzlia Rozov (Levina) (1905–77).
[56] Roman Pines was born on March 13, 1901, and enrolled at the Tenishev School in January 1910.
[57] *Cf.* in *The Gift*: "Meanwhile the room had grown quite light and somewhere—most likely in the ivy—crazy sparrows, all together, not listening to each other, shrilled deafeningly: big recess in a little school" (G57).

pea, grape sugar, the blue of starch, the miracle of litmus paper. And further on into the depth: "sculpting," the dusty models, the plasticine lizard; and "manual labor"—the odor of glue and paint, the appetizing sensation of a plane with a perfect bite, the shuffling sound of sandpaper against wood, the little helicopters, which for some reason were called "flies," that flew up to the ceiling,—to this day I feel between my palms the rotation of the axle—and then—bzzt!

You were the Benjamin[58] of the school. You went about in a catskin hat with earflaps. Whenever you would run up against some difficulty in a problem, you swiftly pulled at the corners of your mouth. A figure-eight shaped divot on the side of your nose. Marvelous, clever eyes. Yellowish, short-cropped—and then a crew cut like Kerensky[59] had (who now touchingly rejoices when I tell him about such things or remind him of Kannegiser's poems: freedom, freedom, freedom, Kerensky on a white steed...[60]). I was a bit envious of how everybody loved you—and of how you bore it so lightly, as if you didn't notice it. I remember your mother (her first name was Sarah; I don't remember her patronymic[61]) just as petite as you were.

Popov![62] The cannon of our childhood, the only person I have ever feared in my life. His father had a cab business, and as a boy (that is, he was never a boy, but always a monster) Popov simply for <u>amusement</u> [underlining here and elsewhere is Nabokov's—*Y.L.*] rode in a draught-cart along the Bolshoi Prospekt. You remember how he would walk with his hands about his knees, the enormous soles of his feet barely parted from the floor, on his low forehead there was but a single wrinkle: of complete and hopeless incomprehension, incomprehension of his own existence. All in black, in a black Russian shirt, and the ponderous odor accompanying him everywhere like fate. Even at a mature age I sometimes have nightmares about Popov falling upon me. He ran off to the war—and suddenly

---

[58] Benjamin was the youngest of Jacob's twelve sons in the Book of Genesis, also known for its valor and military skills.

[59] Alexander Kerensky (1881–1970) was a controversial Russian politician who served as the Prime Minister of the Russian Provisional Government before the Bolsheviks overtook power in 1917. Nabokov knew Kerensky well during the émigré years in Europe.

[60] The poem Nabokov quotes is "The Review" by Leonid Ioakimovich Kannegiser (1896–1918) devoted to Kerensky ("O voice—to remember forever: / Russia, Freedom, War'); it contains a line: "Kerensky on white horseback."

[61] Sara Abramovna Rozov.

[62] Grigorii Popov was born on January 21, 1898. In fact, according to the Tenishev School records, Popov's father was a sculptor. This impressive gorilla-like classmate was depicted under different names in many Nabokov's writings: as Schshukin in the short story "Orache" (1932), Koldunov in "Lik" (1938), Koshmarenko in "Itch" ("Zud" in Russian; not translated into English, dated 1940), Kashmarin in *The Eye*, Petrishchev in *The Defense*, and as Paduk's unnamed classmate in *Bend Sinister*. As "Popov" he is featured in *Drugie berega* (*Other Shores*, the Russian version of the memoirs, *Speak, Memory*).

appeared in a hussar's pelisse, wounded in the behind. I think that he will have long ago sacrificed his stupid and unruly head.

I ran into some people afterwards, and heard about a few. From Shustov[63] about seven years ago I received a startling note from some northern wilderness — he was fighting there during Yudenich's[64] time. Stoianovich was killed somewhere in the south. Once, I think it was in 1925, Shmurlo[65] barged in on me after arriving from Siberia — the most boorish of louts, with some sort of energetic black-hundred spark in his eyes — and remembering absolutely nothing of school life, not even his own verses from then:

> Like a duchess there you went
> with flowers joined by thread
> blue and lilac, yellow, red,
> and you gave forth a fragrant scent!...

In Berlin he lived with a friend of his, a gynecologist, and slept on some sort of gynecological furniture, and spent all day drinking vodka that he made himself. Then he made quite a success of himself in Africa, on the Ivory Coast — and then suddenly appeared once again — calling in advance on the phone, but I was no longer so foolish, and, citing a case of the flu, avoided him.[66]

But once somehow in 1928 there was a sudden ring, and something very familiar entered — the first minute in the semidarkness it even seemed to me that there had been no change whatsoever: Nellis.[67] We liked to tease him by tangling him up with poor Shustov — the delicate stammering of the first against the explosive stuttering of the second. He and I began to reminisce. The main thing, and seemingly the only thing, he remembered was that "You and I were the only ones in the class with our own automobiles." Moreover he said it in a tone which implied that this connected us intimately and for all time! In parting he noted somewhat wistfully that there are encounters and encounters, but that one of our former comrades with whom he had also met in this manner had afterwards not even phoned him. The "automobile" gave me such a start that I entirely fulfilled his apprehensions.

---

63 Nikolai Shustov was one of Nabokov's playmates in school games. In the Russian version of autobiography, Nabokov calls him "a touching comrade, clumsy stammerer with a long pale face"; a couple of stammerers appear in Paduk's class as well.

64 Nikolai Yudenich (1862–1933), a commander of the Russian Caucasus Army, later one of the White Guard leaders fighting the Bolsheviks; he emigrated to France in 1920.

65 Vadim Shmurlo (b. April 7, 1899) joined the Tenishev School in the fall of 1911.

66 Nabokov and Shmurlo did meet once again. This time, Nabokov himself visited sick and drunk Schmurlo, who was dying in Nice in 1961.

67 Karl Nellis (born July 31, 1899, enrolled to the Tenishev School on September 1, 1909). About the same time a character named Nellis visits his mother in Berlin in Nabokov's short story "The Doorbell" (1927).

Kiandzhuntsev[68] I often saw in Paris. You are right about the cards, but along with that the thing that is ridiculously attractive about him is that he hasn't at all, even physically (well, a little, around the face [blue?]) changed. I have rarely had the opportunity to observe anything so infantile. He has no aspirations. He reads nothing and knows nothing. He has a cinema theatre in Paris, I was there a time or two with him: following the action with excitement, he lived out the film like a child, guessing what the hero would do next, wondering about the carelessness of one and the trustfulness of the other—and even yelling out some sort of warnings. There in Paris I also saw Lilienstern resembling a good little frog more than ever before.[69] He had a difficult romantic affair: his fiancée preferred someone else to him—and he tells about it, touchingly and at length. A first class chess player. He arranged a "banquet" for the Tenishev alumni, to pay me "honor."[70] There were about twelve people there—the majority of them I recalled only dimly. The rather repulsive curly-headed Rabinovich[71] with bulging eyes and outthrust jaw was there, and the younger Gurevich[72] that Sidorov once attacked for no reason in his capacity as director (because of which we had him removed—we wrote the manifesto at Beketov's[73] apartment). There was also a returning stray female, the offspring of a later generation of Tenishevites. Lilienstern pronounced a touching and very nice little speech, in the course of which Saba and his sister were shaking from their own weeping!

---

[68] Savely (Saba) Kiandzhuntsev was considered to be a wunderkind in childhood, but in the years of maturity he lost the former brilliance. The classmates' meeting in 1932 was very warm: Kiandzhuntsev, it turned out, had read all Nabokov's novels, and even loaned him a tuxedo for public appearances in Paris. Saba owned a small movie theater in Paris and in 1939 he supported Nabokov's family financially. Brian Boyd reports on 1,000 francs a month that Kiandzhuntsev was giving to Nabokov (*The Russian Years* 511).

[69] Faddey Lilienstern (b. 1900) was a son of the director of "Asia—Caoutchouc" corporation, Lev Lilienstern.

[70] A group photograph made at the Tenishev students restaurant gathering in Berlin (circa 1933) is reproduced in *Vladimir Nabokov: A Pictorial Biography*. Ed. by Ellendea Proffer. Ann Arbor: Ardis, 1991, p. 65.

[71] Grigorii Rabinovich (b. November 6, 1901; enrolled to the Tenishev School in 1909). His father, Ilya Grigorievich, was a pharmacist.

[72] The teacher noted in his report on Alexander Gurevich: "Not always tidy and not focused pupil, as well as very lighthearted compared to other boys of his age" (Central Historical Archive of St. Petersburg, f. 176, op. 1, d. 248, p. 201).

[73] There is a following record in the "Notes on academic success and behavior" (1912–13) on Beketov: "During the last semester he had really lagged behind; Beketov became awfully lighthearted, noisy, and talkative; very often he doesn't realize how childish, and even silly, his behavior is" (Central Historical Archive of St. Petersburg, f. 176, op. 1, d. 248, p. 260).

Appendix I

I met the other Rabinovich[74] as well—from the higher grades. A fat chemist and poet (He wrote "resonant" verses in the classical spirit under the pseudonym Raich); he had once in 1928 made a visit to Petersburg, and there encountered the old man Pedenko[75] on Mokhovaia street,[76] who apparently embraced him. Well, then there was Savely Grinberg[77] (much older than us), a most charming man, with whom I maintain very amicable relations. Not long ago he and I drove down to Cambridge in order to take a look at dear old locales, where the two of us studied together.[78] But these experiments ought not to be undertaken. By doing this I totally killed my Cambridge memories.

You remember how we were amused by the way some people changed in accordance with the passing of the semesters, how Kholmogorov,[79] who had been a clown and a face-puller about town, converted to taciturnity, and how Oks,[80] who, on the contrary, was at first unnoticeable, suddenly became the main attraction and wit. He had a good-looking sister, Tamara, who was infatuated with [illegible]. Oks was the first to reveal to me the existence of "houses where beautiful women give themselves to anyone who desires them"—I even recall where it was he said that—I was riding with him in a hansom cab directly across from Singer's (that glassy globe in the heavens).[81] In this same regard I remember what an impression Chekhov's story "Untitled"[82] made upon you [initially

---

[74] Evgenii Isaakovich Rabinovich (1898, Petersburg—1973, Albany, NY) was a biochemist and biophysicist who wrote poetry under a pen name Evgenii Raich. Emigrated from Soviet Russia in 1920; defended his PhD dissertation in Berlin University in 1926. Lived in the US since 1936, where he worked on the Manhattan nuclear project (1944–46). Nabokov could meet Rabinovich at the literary gatherings in Berlin; the latter was a member of the "Russian Poets' Circle" in Berlin since 1925 and contributed to its collections: *Novosel'e* [*Housewarming*] (1931), *Roshcha* [*Grove*] (1932), *Nevod* [*Seine*] (1933).

[75] Mokhovaya Street, 33 (lit. "the Street of Mosses"), is the address of the Tenischev School building in St. Petersburg.

[76] Dmitri Karpovich Pedenko (1876–1942) was one of the longest serving faculty members at the Tenishev School: a painter by profession, he also taught penmanship, drawing, and gymnastics.

[77] Savely Grinberg was born on February 19, 1896, and started his education at the Tenishev School in September of 1912.

[78] The joint trip to Cambridge was undertaken in February 1937. Apart from the desire to quench nostalgia for student years, Nabokov pursued a somewhat practical goal: he was hoping to find a teaching position in one of the British universities.

[79] Mikhail Kholmogorov (b. December 1, 1900; enrolled to the Tenishev School in September of 1909). His father, Ivan Mikhailovich, served as an engineer and was an adjunct professor.

[80] Evgeny Oks (b. March 13, 1900; enrolled to the Tenishev School in September of 1909). His father, Boris Abramovich, was a doctor but earned for living as an editor and publisher.

[81] A memorable globe still crowns the building on Nevsky Avenue, 28, where the Russian branch of a manufacturer of sewing machines, Singer Company, was located.

[82] Nabokov pretty accurately cites Anton Chekhov's short story in which a monk, who has just returned from the city, vividly describes to his peers an encounter with a young loose woman during the feast (A. P. Chekhov. *Sobranie sochinenii* in 12 vols. Moscow, 1955. Vol. 6, p. 8).

Nabokov writes 'nazvanie,' a different Russian word for "title," and then corrects it to 'zaglaviia'] and how you kept repeating a phrase from it: "that partially undraped tempting viper"—and how we envied the runaways! And can it be that Mitiushin's[83] face with its eyes screwed out and in a blue blouse left no mark in your memory—and dwarfish Shustov, next to whom he sat on the back bench, and stout peaceable Meerovich (who, during divinity lessons, would invariably request permission from Father to remain in the classroom, since he was no great fan of noise[84]), and Kharuzin,[85] who had a body like that of a fish (you were the one who somehow noted that), and muscular Kherkus,[86] and Gordon[87] (thrusting his arm out and forward and somehow predatorily and merrily casting his eyes upon those who didn't know the answer, and who maintained that position until he was called upon), etc. etc.... and even later the enigmatic Grossman, whom we did not find (or you found him and I did not) when we were enrolled, but who remained for a long time (like some sort of "dead soul") in the roll book. And those who sank like stones into the previous class and swiftly took upon themselves its protective coloration, and those during the war, seemingly chance arrivals, and that wise and disheveled (I've forgotten his last name[88]), who enrolled at the very, very end; during the revolution he clambered up onto the platform formed on the Field of Mars from crates in order to delivery a fiery speech (he was a *Cadet*), and who was mown from the platform the moment he uttered a word...

---

[83] The classmate has lent his surname to an episodic character of Nabokov's short story, "An Affair of Honor" (1927).

[84] David Meerovich (b. April 9, 1901), as all non-Orthodox students, would have been released from an obligatory attendance of the classes in Christian theology. The liberal Tenishev School had a special clause in its charter: "We accept the children of all faiths and social strata." The Jewish students had a great difficulty to enroll into public institutions beyond the Pale, but a liberal-minded board of the private Tenishev School was an exception. According to the 1915–16 statistics, 96 of 360 total students there were of the Jewish origin.

[85] Oleg Kharuzin (b. 1899) belonged to the gentry and became a student at Tenishev in the same year as Nabokov. In the record of pupils for 11th semester (October 1914–15) Nabokov is listed under number nine and Kharuzin is nineteenth (Central Historical Archive of St. Petersburg, f. 176, op. 3, d. 22). As usual, Nabokov incorporates the last name of the real acquaintance into a circle of fictitious personages in his short story "Music" (1932).

[86] Alexander Kherkus was born on March 21, 1898, and became the Tenishev student in 1908; he was a son of Vera Abramovna and Enokh Issakovich.

[87] Lev Gordon, son of a merchant, was born in 1900. He began his Tenishev education in 1910.

[88] The classmate's last name—Fridman—Nabokov suddenly remembered 34 years later, when he had an opportunity to reread the copy of his own letter. Nabokov called such a mechanism of remembrance "a beehive of memory" (VN to Rozov, January 28, 1971). Solomon Girshevich Fridman was born on October 22, 1898.

And the teachers! With unbelievable carefulness, with a sponge that had been moistened especially for him, blue-eyed, with an Assyrian beard, Fichtenholz[89] wiped the board, and then across that gleaming blackness, with divine rotundity executed the whitest of numerals. Kavun,[90] whose experiments wouldn't succeed—and who cheated to get them to turn out right, and who then suddenly on the day Peremyszl was taken[91] sat down to the piano and loftily played the national anthem. Gippius[92] in two vests, expectorating iambs: the poison dripping through its bark...[93] Puffy Vroblevsky[94] (a specialist in poplars and cypresses—but rather untalented), who would sit next to pupils to assist with ornamentation,—I see the rams-horn scrolls of the ornamentation and the heavy shading as if it were before me now. The female gymnastics teachers (whom Popov would terrorize,—especially during the spring when class took place outside) and then the agile well-built gentleman with a signet ring who replaced them. And Rozental',[95] who seemed not entirely to have discarded the shell of the sixteenth semester. And our marvelous ladies—Vera Leonidovna,[96]

---

[89] Grigorii Mikhailovich Fichtenholz was a teacher of mathematics at Tenishev; the same teacher is featured in *Bend Sinister*, and yet another former Tenishev student, Osip Mandelstam, ascribes an Assyrian beard to another instructor in his "The Noise of Time" (1928). "A handsome Assyrian with a black-bluish black beard" will later appear in *Lolita* (*The Annotated Lolita* 169).

[90] Ivan Nikitich Kavun (b. 1874) was a teacher of physics at Tenishev (Personal file in the Central Historical Archive of St. Petersburg, f. 176, op. 2, d. 68). Kavun's name "rebounded" into Nabokov's novel *The Defense*, disguised under the surname "Arbuzov": in Ukrainian, "kavun" means "watermelon" (*arbuz*). At a Russian ball Luzhin bumps into Petrishchev, a former classmate from the Balashov [sic!] School and the latter recalls the certain Arbuzov who once played the grand piano. As a result of establishing the prototype it is now possible not only to exactly date but also to name the opus that the episodic character Arbuzov-Kavun performs in the novel.

[91] The city of Peremyszl (Przemysl in Polish) was taken on March 22, 1915. This former Austrian fortress served as a junction of important railroads and highways leading to Budapest and Vienna.

[92] Vladimir Vasilievich Gippius (1876–1941) was a poet (pen name Vladimir Bestuzhev, Vladimir Neledinsky) and Nabokov's Russian literature teacher in the last two years of his studies at the Tenischev School. Staff member at Tenischev since 1906, he was appointed its principal in May of 1917; after the Bolshevik Revolution he served as a chair of the school board until July 1920. Nabokov admits that he "greatly admired" Gippius (*Speak, Memory* 238).

[93] A quote from Pushkin's poem "Anchar" (1828).

[94] Konstantin Kaetonovich Vroblevsky, an art teacher at Tenishev (Personal file in the Central Historical Archive of St. Petersburg, f. 176, op. 2, d. 36).

[95] Possibly, Lazar Vladimirovich Rozental' (1894–1900). Graduated the Tenshev School in 1912, he was tutoring Nabokov in 1916 in math. "Rozen" is one of the classmates who come to the future grand master's birthday in *The Defense*.

[96] Vera Leonidovna Simonova—the teacher of French language at Tenishev (Class schedules for 1914/15 academic year; Central Historical Archive of St. Petersburg, f. 176, op. 1, d. 159).

who seemed a beauty in comparison with the other teachers,—and the little blue books with Merimee's endless tale "Colomba."[97]

I have mentioned Tenishev soccer frequently in my novels. (Generally: I have been rather profligate in tucking in my school reminiscences—from the pink soap and the slap-damp-thwack of the towel in the lavatory to the silent figure of the belated pupil with his arm raised beyond the door glass.) Later I played a great deal in England and on the Russian team in Berlin until 1932, when I was removed from the field like a dead man,[98]—but nevertheless it is the school games that remain the most exciting. Like a little lion, you would often throw yourself upon Popov (who had only one kick, straight up, I hear his horrible foot thud against the ball, I see the ball rising...) The diverse composition of the goals (goals, not heads[99]): the maw of the tunnel leading to the street (with two tumbrels along the sides) and the door, or in the separate courtyard which was the dream of our childhood,—a door and an iron grate beyond which little steps led down beneath the overhang (with a sharp iron corner, against which the rubber ball tore and burst,—but which already dead, deadly flapping, was kicked and tortured for a long time anyway). When we played in the first place, sometimes a kick would result in a disappearance behind the side fence, on which with a shuffling sound someone would hang while another would run around into the neighboring courtyard. The hot slap of the ball fully against my goalkeeper's palm, the black traces it left on foreheads...the peculiar crunch beneath the feet on the iron covers at certain points in the courtyard. Bilinsky,[100] who has the ball, is agilely outfitted with slender but uncommonly strong legs. His straight arms move swiftly, his back is completely rounded—and then he shoots

---

[97] Nabokov's epithet "endless," as applied to Prosper Mérimée's (1803–70) tale "Colomba," most probably has to do with the length of its study during the literature course at Tenishev as well as with the French dramatist's general manner of writing (known for expected plots and slow narrative development) rather than with the novella's size (about 130 pages).

[98] The Russian sports club in Berlin was organized in November of 1931, and its major undertaking was an immediate organization of a football team with Vladimir Nabokov as a goalkeeper. On February 14, 1932, the first match against the German team was played. Just a few weeks later, during a game against an aggressive German team of factory workers, Nabokov was seriously injured (Michel Chenoweth. "On the Origins of Nabokov's Neuralgia," *The Nabokovian* 36, 1996, p. 13).

[99] Nabokov here is playing with the fact that the genitive plural forms of the Russian words for *head* (голова) and *goal* (гол) are identical (голов).

[100] Sigizmund Bilinsky (b. 1898). The class teacher noted in his personal file: "A good companion. His attitude toward elders is calm and proper" (Central Historical Archive of St. Petersburg, f. 176, op. 1, d. 248, p. 154). Kiandzhuntsev praised both the forward Bilinsky and the goalkeeper Nabokov as promising soccer players in his article "The Tenishev Students and Football," published in the school journal, *Youthful Thought* (*Iunaia Mysl'* 6, 1916, p. 25).

Appendix I

towards the goal. In the spring the teachers, I remember, would skip classes, leaving behind squares of light bluish sky with a soccer ball falling from the blue. This genuine soccer ball with a red liver beneath the lacing of a leather corset, was entirely different from a rubber one (obtained from the "Treugol'nik")! The vernal dust, a certain openness to the air, the sharpness of the sounds, the fatigue in one's legs, the ringing in one's head. "Ball in hands" or, as jokesters would put it, "hands in ball."

In a metaphysical sense I often later in life, and you, too, of course, also had to go one on one with the goalkeeper—after all, fate takes good aim. You can't always defend against it. You are holding on, and so am I.

You reminded me well of the flavor of our famous pie with meat and cabbage. The wild trading in bread-heels—during the early semesters. Pines's love of salt. The sour fruit gelatin and the aluminum spoon, on the wall there were some sort of damp patches, which prompted the wits to make a scurrilous and improbable guess about Linster's[101] potency. And do you remember when some sour milk appeared in cans and a representative for this sour milk paced, attentively and already hopelessly, in between the tables—and everyone spat on purpose—but, as I recall, you perceived his sorrow.

I could write many more pages like this, and yet it's such an inconsequential pittance—the mere upholstery, the fluff of a trembling creature whom I detain for a moment in my hands. I would like to know more about you, you have written very little. I am some three hours distance from you,—but of course, that's by plane. All these years my silliest concern has been the quotidian struggle with poverty—otherwise life has proceeded happily. Now we're living (I am married, I have a charming son,[102] more than pleasurable) in Cannes.[103] We have absolutely no idea what is to come, but in any event I shall <u>never</u> return to Germany. It is a foul and horrible country. I have never been able to stand Germans, the German bestial spirit, and in their current arrangements (those which suit them best) life there has become completely intolerable for me—and not just because I am married to a Jewish woman. Now I've reread it and see that there's a lot of fluff I still haven't picked up. The trembling in my memory continues still, a dreamy irritation. The buzzing pale lilac light in the classroom on dark winter mornings, when everything is somehow swarthy, and makes one slightly nauseous. The literary magazine with hectographed verses, the strange atmosphere of "the parties," when everything is illuminated in a different way,—beyond the windows it is night, and the classrooms seem somehow dismissed, gone to

---

[101] German Fyodorovich Linscer (Nabokov slightly misspells it as "Linster"), served as the Tenishev principal and resided in the school's building. He was succeeded by Gippius.
[102] The Nabokovs' only son, Dmitri, was born in Berlin on May 10, 1934.
[103] Nabokov moved to Cannes on June 7, 1937.

their rest, and everything is different, somehow, resonant and sad. Rashal',[104] who is reading Nadson with pathos: "and life will end up torn like that-ta-tata thread!,"[105] and the little geographer Mal'tsev,[106] who all of a sudden couldn't bear our behavior and broke into tears; he went to the window and ran his <u>finger</u> along the pane like a child whose feelings have been hurt. The gentleman who for a short time and unsuccessfully tried to teach art history — "the rectification of the columns." Ah, here's who else I happened to encounter — the stout, round-faced Iogolevich,[107] with a new American surname, agile and short, right out of Hollywood. An amusing dream, by the way: to put all of us in our present form in a classroom (if we would fit) and assign a problem from the last page of the problem book (there where it turned to garrulous fantasy, hitting its stride at last) or ask about the pedigree of the Russian princes... [108]

I shall not apologize for such a long letter — because it seems to have turned out rather interesting for us both; something has managed to be held onto — we should be grateful for small favors. I shake your dear unforgettable hand most firmly. It would be good to meet sometime![109]

Yours,
V. Nabokov

---

[104] Grigorii Leibovich Rashal' (b. October 8, 1899, admitted to the Tenishev School in May 1909). Rashal' is sitting next to Samuil Rozov and his sister, Yehudit, on a photograph displaying the members of the Zionist student club "Ha-Chaver" taken in 1915, in Petersburg.

[105] An inaccurate quotation from the ending of Semyon Nadson's poem "Believe — they say — torturous are doubts!.." ("Ver', — gvoriat oni, — muchitel'ny somnen'ia...").

[106] Nikolai Mal'tsev, a geography teacher at Tenishev School.

[107] Lazar Iogolevich (b. April 1, 1900) was the classmate of Nabokov's brother, Sergei. As an episodic character Iogolevich briefly appears in Nabokov's novel *Glory*.

[108] *Cf.* in *The Gift*: "But alas, even when you do happen, in a dream, to make such a return journey, then, at the border of the past your present intellect is completely invalidated, and amid the surroundings of a classroom hastily assembled by the nightmare's clumsy property man, you again do not know your lesson — with all the forgotten shades of those school throes of old" (G42).

[109] They managed to meet, but only after quarter of a century: in 1962, Rozov visited Nabokov in Zermatt, Switzerland. Nabokov intended to go to Israel with a reciprocal visit which was never realized. Rozov passed away in 1975, and Nabokov died two years after (Yuri Leving. "Phantom in Jerusalem: Or, the History of an Unrealized Visit," *The Nabokovian* 37, 1996: 30-44).

Appendix II

Nabokov's Summary of *The Gift*

This version of the plot summary was endorsed by the writer himself, when he was requested to prepare a preview for non-Russian editors. Usually reluctant to compose synopses, Nabokov made an exception in this case in the hope of having *The Gift* see the light of day. Posing as a neutral moderator, Véra submitted an unsigned précis to Lillian Dillon Plante of the Chekhov Publishing House along with a note stating: "I have finally managed to get one of the 'good' readers to make a synopsis of DAR" (January 28, 1952). Véra Nabokov's biographer, Stacy Schiff, has assumed that it was the Chekhov staff who needed a summary of the book (218). In fact, the request had nothing to do with the Russian-language edition (which had already been printed by that time), but rather with Nabokov's possible collaboration with Curtis Brown, the London-based literary agency. Lillian Plante had some connections with this reputable firm, and Nabokov hoped to lure the company into representing *The Gift* (once it had been translated) with either American or British publishers.

Five typed pages, previously unpublished, have been preserved in Nabokov's correspondence files at the Berg collection in the New York Public Library:

> "DAR," *The Gift*, is a novel in five chapters and has 411 pages. Its theme is a double one: the development of an artist's genius and the subtle workings of human fate. The development of Godunov-Cherdyntsev's literary talent is shown from its timid lyrical gropings in his first book of verse to his first real accomplishment: the controversial, highly original, youthfully bellicose yet mature in its style, psychology and erudition, "Biography of Chernyshevski." And the development of his fate is shown from his childhood which thoughtfully supplies all the ingredients necessary for the full realization of his complicated personality, through the early years of exile, his meeting with Zina, and the growth of their love.

Cable Address: CHEPUHO

CHEKHOV PUBLISHING HOUSE
OF THE EAST EUROPEAN FUND, INC.
387 FOURTH AVE., NEW YORK 16, N. Y., U.S.A.

January 30, 1953

Mrs. Vera Nabokov
Goldwin Smith Hall
Cornell University
Ithaca, New York

Dear Mrs. Nabokov:

    Thank you for the synopsis of DAR enclosed with your letter of January 28. I will pass it along to Curtis Brown and let you know their reactions.

    The $36.66 deducted from the last check to Mr. Nabokov covered copies of DAR which he ordered on his account.

Yours sincerely,

Lilian Dillon Plante

Lilian Dillon Plante

LDP:ib

[Ill. A-3] Letter to Nabokov from the Chekhov Publishing House acknowledging the receipt of the synopsis of *The Gift* (January 30, 1953)

So the first chapter starts with the little book of verse. Godunov's first published work, being ignored by the critics, while in chapter 5 the howl of adverse criticism which greets his "Biography of Chernyshevski," at least makes the author famous overnight. A friend calls up Godunov (so the book starts) at the dismal Berlin apartment, where the latter has just rented a repulsive furnished room, to tell him that a marvelous glowing review of his book of poems has just appeared in a Russian émigré periodical. This sends the young author back to reread and re-live his little book in an ecstasy and delight, and through his daydreams while he loses himself in it, we learn of his happy Russian childhood in the early years of the century, of his father, the eminent scientist-explorer of the fauna of little known regions in Central Asia, of his beautiful mother, whose life consisted of short spells of happiness and long spells of fearful waiting while her famous husband roams his Asian wilds; of the author's sister Tania; of Godunov himself, the future author, first as a little boy, then, in his teens, when he begins to grope, tremulously and delightedly, for the elusive words which would hold down and make tangible his individual poetic world. This was several years ago, but he has stubbornly pursued the same purpose in the following years, and it now seems to him, as he rereads the tiny booklet and it seems to him that just as it has the power to take him back through his verse to their source of inspiration, so this source should be conveyed by it to his unknown readers.

In his festive mood of fulfilled achievement Godunov goes to his friends' house: alas, there is no review waiting for him there, it was all an April's fool's joke.

But Godunov's friends are a story in themselves. Their only son has committed suicide—the result of an emotional storm involving a girl and two boys (of which he was one) in their late 'teens. They had been caught in a vortex of metaphysical and emotional confusion, tinged with a special German post-war brand of moral defeatism and defection.

But of the three who had signed a suicidal pact only one—Yasha—actually shot himself. While the two others, with the thoughtless elasticity of youth, revert to common everyday life, the dead boy's father seems to have taken a half-step into the other world, the new abode of the son he had worshiped, and teeters precariously between a mere philosophical speculation on the nature of that world and its actual gaping abyss.

We then follow Godunov on the tedious round of English-language lessons with which he makes his living, to the office of the émigré paper, where he takes his latest poem, to the shoe-store (and in between on the flights of his fancy that between chores take him back into his bright Russian past), and finally to the soirée littéraire, where a kindly elderly man of Russian-German origin reads (with a dreadful German accent) to a selected audience his solemn play, full of deep symbolism and appalling grammatical blunders.

Through this Chapter and the next one, Godunov's glorious gift keeps growing. He writes some new and lovely poems and spends a whole year painstakingly assembling materials for the biography of his father which he would like to write with the precision of a true artist and the fire of a true scientist—his father seems to him to embody both. This biography will remain unwritten, but in the process of preparation for it by Godunov we learn a number of things: what sort of man Godunov senior was, what his expeditions were all about, how he disappeared on his way back, early in the revolution, in some half-unexplored, half-uninhabited regions, amidst its wild fragrant beauty. And in the meantime Godunov the son's literary genius has served its apprenticeship, and when he abandons the project of writing his father's biography, he is quite ready to undertake his "Biography of Chernyshevski."

On it he goes to work in the middle of Chapter 3. The biography of Chernyshevski, the Russian revolutionary of the fifties and sixties, who has foreshadowed a whole generation of social dissenters, a socialist before socialism, a man who Lenin and his gang have claimed for a precursor, is written by Godunov with an approach so unorthodox, in a style so daring and iconoclastic, that its effect on the Russian émigré reader is just short of sensational. Godunov has shaken off his early youthful romanticism; he has mastered the language, has developed a style pervaded with a subtle sense... and with the new book emerges now as a writer of genius and an independent thinker.

But in the meantime, fate too has been at work. Slowly and diligently it has been trying to bring him together with Zina, and notwithstanding the failure of several carefully contrived plans, at long last fate succeeds. By a chain of interlinking circumstances, Godunov is made to rent a room from Zina's mother, a sloppy aging woman, who has known, with her first husband, a more graceful life in a cultured atmosphere, but now has married a vulgar and stupid cad and has willingly sunk to his level. Zina, who detests her stepfather and despises but pities her mother, won't have anything to do with Godunov in the dingy atmosphere of her home, and while there they exist side by side as complete strangers, their nightly roamings on the spellbound moonlit streets are full of magic and poetry.

The 4th chapter consists entirely of Godunov's book on Chernyshevski: his childhood, his youth, his 'prophetic' period, the incongruities and ineptitudes of Russianized Hegelianism and Fourierism[110] to produce that special brand of utilitarianism, positivism and materialism, to which the Nechayevs[111] and Lenins went in later years for a source of inspiration.

Chapter 5. The uproar caused by the book. The happy development of the Godunov–Zina relationship. Then the departure of her dreadful family. The

---

[110] The system of Charles Fourier (1772–1837), the French social reformer, under which society was to be organized into self-sufficient cooperatives.

[111] Sergey Nechayev (1847–82) was a Russian revolutionary associated with the Nihilist movement and known for his single-minded pursuit of revolution by any means necessary, including political violence. In 1872, Karl Marx produced the threatening letter Nechayev had written to the publisher at a meeting of the First International. Nechayev was sentenced to twenty years of hard labor in 1873, and, like Chernyshevski, locked up in a ravelin of the Peter and Paul Fortress. He served as the prototype for Petr Verkhovensky in Dostoevsky's novel, *The Devils* (aka *Demons* and *The Possessed*; 1872).

amusing episode of Godunov returning home through Berlin in his bathing trunks after being robbed of his clothes and money while swimming in the lake, and of the two pedantic policemen. The fascinating row at the general assembly of Russian émigrés equivalent of the Ameri[can] Literary Guild. And finally the return to the apartment of Godunov and Zina, each of whom has lost the keys and is relying on the other to get in.

This is, in the main, the 'story' of the book. But its stylistic atmosphere, its vivid details, the way Nabokov makes come to life the most incidental characters, is not as easily conveyed. The Russian readers who have read this book keep writing the author that they cannot keep away from it, read it again and again every time discovering new and delightful details. I think this is probably the best way to describe it and recommend it. Let us hope that the American readers will be given an opportunity to experience the same delight." ("Correspondence with the Chekhov Publishing House," Berg collection, NYPL)

Despite this moving summary, the opportunity that Véra and Vladimir both dreamt of for the American readership to discover *The Gift* did not present itself for another long decade.

Appendix III

TIMELINE

An internal chronology of the events mentioned in the narrative.

1790-1850

1792-95: The year of the National Convention to which N.G. Chernyshevski would draw the plan of the Hall (G232).

1828: The "first omnibus appeared"; July 12, in the third hour of the morning, Chernyshevski is born. On the morning of the 13, he is Christened (G300).

1833-1918: The dates of life and death of Olga Chernyshevski (G294).

1836: "Ch." (Fyodor's grandfather) quarrels with his family and sails off to Boston (G99).

1848: "What if, [Chernyshevksi] muses in 1848, one attached a pencil to a mercury thermometer, so that it moved according to temperature?" (G217). The exact date of the journal entry is August 19, according to *Letopis' zhizni i deiatel'nosti N.G. Chernyshevskogo* (Moscow-Leningrad, Academia, 1933, 33).

1848, May 19: The wedding date of the Lobodovskis, friends of Chernyshevski. It is also, notes Nabokov, the same day of Chernyshevksi's mock execution 16 years later (G220). In fact, Nabokov slightly retrofits chronology here in order to maintain the "patterns of Fate." According to the 1933 *Letopis'*, the actual wedding took place on May 18 (Chernyshevski described it in his diary entry of May 19 as taken place the day earlier); however, Chernyshevski made a slip—May 16 is the real date (See N.M. Chernyshevskaia. *Letopis' zhizni i deiatel'nosti N.G. Chernyshevskogo*. Moscow, 1953, 27).

1848: Cherynshevski's diary entry ("What if we are indeed living in the times of Cicero and Caesar...") (G247).

1851-1860

1853: G. Chernyshevski (N. Chernyshevski's father) advises his son "to write some tale or other" (G288).

1853: Chernyshevski attempts to develop perpetual motion device in January. Fearing aneurysm he visits a doctor in February prior to his wedding (G217).

1853, February: Chernyshevski begins "Diary of My Reflections with Her Who Now Constitutes My Happiness" (G229). Chernyshevski meets Olga Sokratovna Vasilieva, his future wife, on January 26, 1853, and begins the "Diary..." on February 19 (*Letopis'* 1953, 78-79).

1853, St. Olga's Day: Presumably, July 11 (St. Olga was born July 11, 969). According to Strannolyubski, the day Chernyshevski will start *What to do?* (G231).

1853, three August nights: The time frame in which Chernyshevski is to have written his dissertation (G238).

1853, 21 December: The date Chernyshevski's wife, Olga Sokratovna, conceives (G234). Firstborn Alexander is born on March 5, 1854.

1853-1862: Period in which Chernyshevski's works are "imbued with an aspiration to feed the lean Russians with a diet of the most variegated information..." (G233).

1854: Chernyshevski's critique in an issue of *The Contemporary* (G238).

1854: Chernyshevski teaches for several months in the Second Cadet Corps in St. Petersburg (G233).

1855, May 10: The date Chernyshevksi defends his dissertation (G237).

1855: Chernyshevki imparts his love of reading almanacs and noting the general information to the subscribers of *The Contemporary* (G234).

1855: Chernyshevksi attacks Pushkin's "colored hearing" (G240).

1856: Chernyshevski courts Turgenev hoping to enlist him for *The Contemporary* (G240).

1856: Chernyshevski writes about the Russian prosody in issue of *The Contemporary*, August 31, Vol. 59, No. 9 (G241).

1856, Summer: Dobrolyubov and Chernyshevski first meet (G259). *Letopis'* 1953 specifies the date: July 13 (123).

1858, Winter: Marks the unexpected visit of Kirill Ilyich Godunov-Cherdyntsev (Suhoshchokov's *Memoirs of the Past*) (G100).

1858, the second half: Chernyshevski's "final disillusionment" concerning the provincial committees (G248).

1858: *The Contemporary* has 4,700 subscribers under Chernyshevski's editorship (G251).

1858, July 12: Turgenev writes a letter on Chernyshevski's birthday. Coincidently, Fyodor's birthday is also the same day as Chernyshevski's: July 12 (G250).

1859, June 26-30: Period that Chernyshevski spends in London (G261).

1860: Chernyshevski critiques Turgenev after he is "no longer necessary" to *The Contemporary* (G250).

1860: Chernyshevski attacks Turgenev's *Rudin* (G250).

1860, July 8: The birth day of Fyodor's father, Konstantin Godunov-Cherdyntsev. It is also the day when many years later Fyodor "brings himself" to ask his mother about her relationship with his father (G102-103).

1861-1870

1861, October: Marks student unrest in St. Petersburg (G262). On September 25, over 900 students went to the streets and 26 were arrested. Chernyshevski expresses sympathy with these protests against the Russian government (*Letopis' 1953*, 219-222).

1861: Dobrolyubov is ailing (G262).

1861, November 17: Dobrolyubov dies (G263).

1862, January: Chernyshevski founds the St. Petersburg Chess Club (G265). The precise date is January 12 (*Letopis' 1953*, 235); the club also served as the headquarters for the illegal gatherings.

1862: The International fair, or Great London Exposition, is held at South Kensington in London, England. Dostoevsky mentions this exhibition several times in his writings (G228).

1862: Sixty Russian Old Believers with wives and children live in Lob-Nor for half a year (G124).

1862: Chernyshevski's misquotation and remark ("If people were able to announce all their ideas concerning public affairs...") (G257).

1862, March 2: Chernyshevski's first public address (G265).

1862, May 28: Whit Monday; also the day of the strongest May Fires (G267).

1862, June 10: Chernyshevski's family goes to Pavlosk and the incident with Lyubetski occurs (G268).

1862, July 5: Chernyshevski visits the Secret Police (G268). (June 15, according to *Letopis' 1953*, 260).

1862, July 7: Chernyshevski is arrested (G269).

1862, December 5: Chernyshevski's "famous letter" to his wife. He is imprisoned in the Alekseevski Ravelin of the Peter-and-Paul Fortress (G273).

1863: A revolution is expected (G264).

1863, January 15: Date Chernyshevski is to have already sent the first portion of *What to Do?* to Pypin (G274).

1863, January 28: Day the government refuses Chernyshevski permission to see his wife; the prisoner announces a hunger strike (G274).

1863, February 3: The military doctor examines Chernyshevski in the fortress (G275). The same day Nekrasov loses the manuscript of *What to Do?*

1863, Morning of February 6: Chernyshevski ends his hunger strike (G276).

1863, February 8: Nekrasov retrieves Chernyshevski's manuscript found on the street (N. Ashukin. *Letopis' zhizni i tvorchestva N.A. Nekrasova*. Moscow, 1935, 281).

1863, February 12: Chernyshevski is denied visitation of his wife for the second time (G276).

1863, March 23: Chernyshevski's confrontation with Kostomarov (G276). According to *Letopis' 1953*, this happened four days earlier (292).

1863, March: *The Contemporary containing beginning of* Chernyshevski's *novel is printed* (G277).

1863, October 8: Chernyshevski sends an article to the *Russian Word* (G277).

1863, April 4: The last part of *What to Do?* is completed (G283).

1864, May 4: Chernyshevski's sentence is announced (G280).

1864, May 19, 8:00 am: Chernyshevski's mock execution in Mytninski square (G280).

1864, May 20: Chernyshevski leaves St. Petersburg for Siberia (G283).

1864, July 23: Chernyshevski arrives at the mines of Nerchin mountain (G284).

1866, Summer: Olga Chernyshevski, her son Misha, and Dr. Pavlinov head on to Siberia. They arrive on August 23 (G284).

1866, August 27: Olga Chernyshevski leaves her husband after just four days (G285).

1866: The attempted assassination of Tsar Alexander II by the Karakozovites (G282).

1866: Chernyshevski writes *The Prologue* (G232).

1870, August 10: The date Chernyshevski's settlement was supposed to begin (G287).

1871-1880

1871, December 2: Chernyshevski is finally dispatched to Vilyuisk (G287) (December 7, according to *Letopis' 1953*, 391).

1871: Konstantin Kirillovich Godunov-Cherdyntsev catches his first peacock butterfly (G109).

1872: *Das Kapital* by Marx is sent to Chernyshevski (G245).

1872: Sophia Perovski tours Sebastopol (G283).

1872, July 10: Chernyshevski tries to break the door lock with a pair of tongs (G288).

1875, January: Pypin sends Chernyshevski an account of his son, Sasha (whom Chernyshevski writes off as a materialist) (G297).

1875: Chernyshevski dispatches "an ancient Persian poem" to Pypin (G290).

1876: Fyodor's father, Konstantin Godunov-Cherdyntsev, completes schooling in St. Petersburg (G102).

1876-1918: The period in Konstantin Godunov-Cherdyntsev's life devoted to traveling and scientific works. Works completed during this time include: *Lepidoptera Asiatica* (8 vol., 1890-1917); *The Butterflies and Moths of the Russian Empire* (6 vol., 1912-1916); *The Travels of a Naturalist* (7 vol., 1892-1912) (G102).

1877: Konstantin Godunov-Cherdyntsev's first scientific paper is published (G103).

1877: Sasha Chernyshevski joins the Nevski Infantry Regiment (G297).

1878: The year Fyodor's mother, Elizaveta Pavlovna Vezhin, is born. (Based on the given fact that she marries her husband in 1898 as the twenty-year-old lady, G103).

1879: Chernyshevski stops writing "learned letters" to his family for six months (G291).

1880: Chernyshevski sends "an ancient Persian poem" to Lavrov as he earlier did for Pypin (G290).

1881-1890

1881: Sophia Perovski is hanged on April 15 (new style) for the assassination of Tsar Alexander II (G283).

1881, March 15: Vitevski, the "unknown pupil" of Chernyshevski, sends him a supportive wire (G291).

1882: Sasha Chernyshevski's mental illness gets aggravated (G297).

1883, February: Chernyshevski is transferred to Irkutsk (G292).

1884, February: Review of Chernyshevski's translation of Weber's *Universal History* is published in issue of *The Examiner* (G294).

1885-1918: Konstantin Godunov-Cherdyntsev undertakes eight major expeditions (G103).

1888: "Another brief review" on Weber's tenth volume in Chernyshevski's translation appears in *The Messenger of Europe* (G295).

1888: Olga Chernyshevski's letter about her son, Sasha (G298).

1889: Chernyshevski goes to Saratov (G298).

1889: The year of *Exposition Universelle*, a World's Fair held in Paris, France (May 6—October 31, 1889). The main symbol of the Fair is the Eiffel Tower, which was completed the same year and served as the entrance arch to the Fair. The exhibitions had as "strong effect" on Chernyshevski (G228; 299).

1889, October 11: Chernyshevski sends money to Sasha to return to St. Petersburg (G299).

1889, October 12: Chernyshevski translates 18 pages of close print (G299).

1889, October 13: Chernyshevski wants to continue but is forced to stop (G299).

Appendix III

1889, October 14: Chernyshevski is in a state of delirium (G299).
1889, October 16: Chernyshevski has a stroke (G300).
1889, October 17: Chernyshevski utters his last words (G300).
1889, October 17: Chernyshevski dies shortly after midnight (G283).

1891-1910

1892: The year Zhaksybay saves Konstantin Godunov-Cherdyntsev's life (who was mauled by a bear) (G126).
1893: The year in which Fyodor's father meets Chinese cyclists in the Gobi (G120).
1896-1898: M.N. Chernyshevski compiles his father's works together (G296).
1898: The year Fyodor's father marries Elizaveta Pavlovna Vezhin (G103).
1900, July 12: Fyodor's date of birth (G12).
1903: Ivan Ivanovich Viskott, a chemist for Gatchina, dies of gangrene in Dyn-Kou (G116).
1909, November: An unsigned poem dedicated to N.G. Chernyshevski appears in *The Century* (G300).

1911-1920

1912, June: Konstantin Godunov-Cherdyntsev's final return from his travels (G125).
1914: After the start of World War I, Carl Lorentz's paintings loose their popular appeal (G58).
1914, Spring: Konstantin Godunov-Cherdyntsev begins preparations for his journey to Tibet (G127, 58).
1915: Death of Zhaksybay (G132).
1915, Spring: The Godunov-Cherdyntsev family moves to estate in the Crimea for the summer (G128).
1916: The year the last paper written by Konstantin Godunov-Cherdyntsev is published (G103).
1916, June: The day Konstantin Godunov-Cherdyntsev comes to bid farewell to the family prior to his last departure (G131).
1916, June: Fyodor meets his first love, the twenty-three-year-old girl (b. 1893 — d. after 1918 but not later than 1925) (G149).
1917, winter: Fyodor's first love leaves for Novorossisk (G149).
1918: Konstantin Godunov-Cherdyntsev's last letter is delivered to his family. The father indicates family should move to Finland (G135).
1919, winter: Marks the two summers spent waiting for Konstantin Godunov-Cherdyntsev's return (G135).
1919: The year Konstantin Godunov-Cherdyntsev is to have died, according to the Soviet Encylopedia (G136).

1921-1929

1922: Professor Anuchin says upon his arrest, "Gentlemen, history does not wait" (G305).

1923: Barruad describes his summer 1917 meeting with Konstantin Godunov-Cherdyntsev in *Exploration catholique* (G134).

1924: The year M.N. Chernyshevski dies (G296).

1926, April 1: The day *The Gift* begins. Referred to as "April 1st, 192–" (G3).

1929, June 28, around 3 p.m.: Fyodor swims (G336).

1929, June 29: The day *The Gift* ends (G366).

Appendix IV

BUTTERFLIES

Butterflies are listed in the order of their appearance in *The Gift*. The data used in the present section is gathered from the text and verified against the following sources: Joann Karges, *Nabokov's Lepidoptera: Genres and Genera* (Ann Arbor: Ardis, 1985); Dieter Zimmer, *A Guide to Nabokov's Butterflies and Moths* (Hamburg: Selbstverlag, 1996/1998), and *Nabokov's Butterflies*. Eds. Boyd, Brian and Robert Michael Pyle (Boston: Beacon Press, 2000).

Vanessa (*Vanessa atalanta*, Nymphalidae). The Red Admiral or Red Admirable, also known as the Alderman. Holarctic and quite common (G24).

Brimstone (*Gonepteryx rhamni*, Pieridae). A common sulphur butterfly in Europe; also North Africa, Asia (G24).

Limenitis populi (Nymphaliedae). The Poplar Admiral. Larval food plant is poplar, aspen. Widespread but uncommon in Europe (not in British Isles) and Asia. Nabokov also mentions L.*populi bucovinensis* Hormuzaki, the Russian Poplar Admiral (G78).

Catocalid (*Catocala fraxini*, Noctuidae). The Blue Underwing; the Clifden Non-pareil. Europe (G95).

Epicnaptera arborea (*Epicnaptera arborea*, Lasiocampidae). A lappet moth. Godunov brought back a specimen from Siberia only to find them also in St. Petersburg (G95).

Niobe Fritillary (*Fabriciana niobe*, Nymphalidae). Continental Europe, Asia Minor (G98).

Aspen Hawk Moth (*Laothoëpopuli*, Sphingidae). The Poplar Hawkmoth. Palearctic. Larval food plants are aspen and poplar (Populus); habitat is most woodland, river banks (G109).

Black Ringlet (*Erebia melas*, Satyridae). Southeastern Europe (G109).

Peacock Butterfly (*Inachia io*, Nymphalidae). Widely distributed throughout Europe, temperate Asia (G109).

Blue (*Maculinea arion*, Lycaenidae). The Large Blue is a species that has a symbiotic relationship with ants. Central Euope, local colonies elsewhere in Europe, Russia, Asia. Extinct in England (G110).

Malayan hawkmoth. A variety of Death's Head Hawk Moth (G110).

Death's Head Hawk Moth (*Acherontia atropos*, Sphingidae). The moth is called so because of the appearance of a human skull in the pattern of the scales on its thorax. Europe (G110).

Tiger Moths (*Arctiidae*). Circumpolar family of some 5000 species, many brightly colored and attractively marked (G110).

"A tropical geometrid colored in perfect imitation" (*Aletis libyssa*, Geometridae). The African moth that mimics *Danaus chrysippus* in a complex of mimicry that involves several other moths and several genera of butterflies (G110).

Painted Lady (*Vanessa cardui*, Nymphalidae) Cosmopolitan. Known also as the Cosmopolite and as the Thistle Butterfly. Nabokov found it most plentiful in the Crimea and also in the Snowy Range of Wyoming (G111).

African Swallowtail (*Papilio dardanus*, Papilionidae). Males of the species throughout their range have the long tails characteristic of the genus while the females vary greatly in coloration and in shape of their wings, mimicking in different localities various unpalatable species of other families of butterflies (G111).

Butler's Pierid (*Baltia butleri potanini*). "Potanin's subspecies of Butler's pierid" (G121).

"Elwes Swallowtail" (*Papilio elwesi*, Papilionidae). A "black wonder with tails in the shape of hooves." China, Formosa (G122).

Roborovski's White (Unidentified Pieridae) (G124).

Amandus Blue (*Plebicula Amanda*, Lycaenidae). Mountain butterfly found in the Pyrenees and the Alps this European Blue ranging into North Africa (G133).

Aphantopus Ringlets (*Aphantopus hyperantus*, Satyridae). Found through parts of Europe into Asia (G133).

Black-Veined Whites (*Aporia crataegi*, Pieridae). Continental Europe, North Africa, Asia. Extinct in England (G133).

Cabbage Butterfly (*Artogeia rapae*, Pieridae). Known in Europe as the Small White. Introduced into North America (G133).

Freya Fritillary (*Clossiana freija*, Nymphalideae). Northern Europe into Japan; also North America. The "dusky little fritillary" with the name of a Norse goddess (G133).

Selene Fritillary (*Boloria selene*, Nymphalidae). Europe, Asia, North America, where it is known as the Silver-Bordered Fritillary (G133).

Swallowtail (*Papilio machaon*, Papilionidae). The Swallowtail of Europe (G133).

Burnet Moth (Zygaenidae). There are a number of blue and red species with blue antennae among this family of European small, day-flying moths (G133).

Imperatorial Apollo (*Parnassium imperator*, Papilionidae). China, Tibet (G133).

Violet-Tinged Coppers (*Paleochrysaphanos hippothoe*, Lycaenidae). The males precede the females in emerging from winter diapause. Europe (G133).

Hummingbird Moth (Also called *Hummingbird Hawk Moth*). Some authorities make a distinction between those Sphingidae with rather longer proboscates, useful for probing into tubular flowers, a characteristic they share with hummingbirds, and the Hawk Moths of the same family. Other consider the terms synonymous. Like many hawks and to some extent hummingbirds, these moths hover. Among the various genera of Sphingidae, there are those with clear wings and those with densely scaled, opaque wings. The "glasslike" wings of the species described in *The Gift* lead to identification of *Hemaris fuciformis*, a common European species (G133).

"An Angle Wing butterfly." Possibly, refers to Comma Butterfly (*Polygonia c-album*, Nymphalidae). Throughout Europe into Asia. The North American Comma Butterfly is *P.comma* (G332).

"A golden, stumpy little butterfly, equipped with two black commas" (*Hesperis comma*, Hesperidae). Known as the Silver-Spotted Skipper in England, as the Comma Skipper in North America, it has many forms and subspecies (G334).

Thecla bieti (*Esakiozephrus bieti*, Lycaenidae). Native to Tibet (G354).

INDEX

A
Abbasi, Riza, 194
Abram, Lynwood, 438, 452, 462, 480
Adamovich, Georgii, 30, 187, 206, 219, 415, 419, 421, 422, 424, 428, 480
Adams, Tom, 56
Adrienne, Amalie A. K., 157
Aesop, 404
Aikhenvald, Yuly, 167, 343
Akhmatova, Anna, 44, 166
Aksakov, Sergei, 316
Aldanov, Mark, xxi, 29, 43, 44, 47, 75, 228, 319, 420, 424
Alekhine, Alexander, 425
Alekseev, Nikolai, 3
Aletrus, *See* 'Guadanini, Irina'
Alexandrov, Vladimir, 75, 163, 203, 213, 236-238, 240, 293, 305, 306, 308, 318, 327, 368, 370
Alexander *I*, 82, 111,
Alexander *II*, 89, 96, 103, 159, 320, 511, 520
Alexander *III*, 89, 93, 106
Alexandrova, Vera, 45
Alighieri, Dante, 7, 11, 132
Allen, Thomas Gaskell, 321
Alley, Ronald, 236
Alloy, Vladimir, 34
Allsop, Kenneth, 162, 236, 451, 480
Altman, Natan, 114

Amis, Kingsley W., 438 (*My Enemy's Enemy*), 443
Amundsen, Roald, 146
Anaximenes of Miletus, 316
Anschütz, Ernst, 345
Anderson, Paul, 48
Andreev, Leonid, 101, 232
Andrew, Joe, 121
Annenkov, Pavel, 216
Anthès, Georges-Charles d', 84, 278
Antipas, Herod, 228
Antokolski, Mark, 333
Appel, Alfred, 196, 236
Artsybashev, Mikhail, 241
Ashukin, N., 511
Austen, Jane, 444
Avinoff, Andrey, 190, 191
Avksentiev, Nikolai, 30, 37

B
Babel, Isaac, 337, 380
Bach, Johann Sebastian, 205, 206
Bacon, Francis, 326
Bakst, Léon, 109, 115
Bakunin, Mikhail, 86, 135, 431
Balanchine, George, 198 (*Apollon Musagète*)
Balmont, Konstantin, 42, 183, 231, 284
Baltrushaitis, Jurgis, 284
Balzac, Honoré de, 108, 380, 406 (*Les Chouans*)

Index

Bang-Haas, Andreas, 191
Barabtarlo, Gennady (Gene), 3, 34, 52, 75, 121, 131, 132, 162, 168, 236, 271, 317, 318, 319, 320, 368, 488
Baratynsky, Evgenii, 23
Bardeleben, Albrecht von, 153
Barnstead, John, xv
Barrett, William, 446, 454, 480
Barskova, Polina, 128, 185, 186, 296, 305
Barthes, Roland, 463
Bashkin, Andrei, xvi, 314
Batiushkov, Konstantin, 277, 284
Beckett, Samuel, 439, 440
Beckmann, Max, 203
Bedford, Sybille, 438 (*A Favorite of the Gods*)
Beerbohm, Max, 444
Beethoven, Ludwig van, 188, 316, 398
Belodubrovsky, Evgeny, 181, 236
Belinsky, Vissarion, 39, 53, 86, 87, 100, 109, 193, 448
Belleval, Guy de, 440
Bely, Andrey, *See* 'Bugaev, Boris N.'
Ben-Amos, Anat, 170, 172, 236, 260, 265, 266, 280, 289, 299, 300, 305, 368, 397, 398, 411
Benedictus, David, 444, 445, 462
Benjamin, Walter, 159, 236, 299
Bennett, Arnold, 380
Benois, Alexander, 109
Benton, Michael, 215, 236
Berberova, Nina, 30, 167, 179, 187, 219, 236
Berdiaev, Nikolai, 30, 85, 112
Berdjis, Nassim Winnie, 214, 217, 236, 324, 368, 396, 397, 411
Bergin, Thomas J., 480
Bergson, Henri-Louis, 325, 368
Berkman, Alexander, 104
Bernhardt, Sarah, 117
Bethea, David, xvi, 122, 212, 213, 165, 212, 236, 254, 305, 368
Beyle, Marie-Henri, 286, 308, 463
Bezrodny, Mikhail, 325
Bialik, Hayim Nahman, 488

Biet, Félix, 275
Bilinsky, Sigizmund, 500
Birney, Alice L., xvi
Bishop, Alison, 66, 67
Bishop, Morris, 66, 67
Bismarck, Otto von, 114
Blackwell, Stephen H., xvi, xvii, xviii, xviv, 17, 18, 75, 76, 206, 207, 236, 267-269, 279, 305, 343, 368, 384, 411
Blasing, Keith, xv
Bliumbaum, Arkady, 184, 185, 236
Blok, Alexander, 23 ("The Unknown Woman"), 128, 188, 189 ("O podvigakh, o doblestyakh, o slave..." ["Of feats, of braveries, of fame..."]), 192, 219, 283, 284, 332 ("Incognita")
Blum, Walter, 446
Bobrikov, Nikolai I., 281
Boldyrev, Ivan, *See* 'Shkott, Ivan'
Bonaparte, Napoleon, 154, 194, 278, 335
Boobbyer, Philip, 406, 411
Boris I (Borislav), 228
Boswell, James, 215, 216
Bowlt, John E., 114, 115
Boyd, Brian, xvii, 3-5, 7, 10, 13, 14, 17, 18, 29, 34, 38, 44, 51, 72, 73-75, 93, 104, 121, 129, 130, 132, 133, 153, 164, 170, 175, 197, 208, 214, 217, 237, 252, 271, 275, 281, 299, 300, 305, 319, 327, 328, 350, 368, 389, 411, 425, 441, 475, 480, 487, 488, 491, 496, 515,
Bozhnev, Boris, 261
Brady, Charles A., 440, 460, 461, 480
Breitensträter, Hans, 203
Brewer, Ebenezer Cobham, 225, 237
Brezhnev, Leonid, 51
Bristol, Evelyn, 118
Britan, Ilya, 219
Briusov, Valeri, 183, 231, 284
Brockhaus, Friedrich, 23
Brodsky, Anna, 183, 232, 237
Brooks, Jeffrey, 107
Brown, Alexander, 440, 459, 464, 480
Brown, Curtis, 503
Brown, Clarence, 177, 210, 237, 245, 305

Brown, Edward J., 87, 98, 103, 104, 121, 216, 237, 285, 305
Brown, Leonard, 462, 480
Brown, William E., 18, 75
Browning, Elizabeth, 281
Browning, John Moses, 280
Browning, Robert, 281, 305
Bryer, Jackson R., 480
Buchovetsky (Buchowetzki), Dimitri, 116
Buckler, Julie, 121
Budge, John Donald, 425
Bugaev, Boris N., 109, 203 (*Zapiski chudaka* [*Notes of an Eccentric*]), 231, 236, 252, 261, 262, 284, 305, 306, 322, 327, 380, 385
Bukharin, Nikolai, 166
Bunin, Ivan, 30, 44, 101, 120, 284, 374, 424, 483
    The Dreams of Chang and Other Stories, 368
    The Life of Arseniev, 218
    "Story with a Suitcase," 353
Butler, Henry, 333
Buyantuyev, Gantyp, 191
Byron, George, 4, 82, 104, 216

C

Caesar, Julius, 332, 508
Cagliostro, Alessandro, 228
Camus, Albert, 444
Cantor, Georg, 326, 368
Cantor, Rudolph, 326
Capote, Truman, 443
Carroll, Lewis, 292
Carr, Edward H., 135, 431
Carré, John le, *See* 'Cornwell, David J. M.'
Cervantes, Miguel de, 411
    Don Quixote, 98, 399
Chagall, Marc, 114, 124, 202, 205, 443
Chaikov, Iosif, 114
Chambers, D. L., 433
Chaplin, Charlie, 319
Chapman, Samuel B., 439
Chekhov, Anton, 44, 84, 101, 105, 106, 214, 239, 337, 344, 368, 452, 380
    The Cherry Orchard, 219
    "Gusev," 379
    "Ionych," 324
    "Untitled," 497
Chenoweth, Michel, 500
Chernov, S. N., 3
Chernyi, Sasha, 181, 259, 347, 350, 351, 368, 369
Chernyshev, Andrei, 476
Chernyshevskaia, Olga Sokratovna, 1, 140, 278, 508, 509, 511
Chernyshevskaia-Bystrova, Nina M., 340, 368, 508
Chernyshevski, Alexander N., 512
Chernyshevski, Gavriil I., 272, 380, 509
Chernyshevski, Mikhail N., 3, 4, 511, 513, 514
Chernyshevski, Nikolai G., x, xii, xiii, xix, xx, 3-5, 7, 8, 17, 20, 27, 30, 32, 34-39, 42, 46, 40, 52, 53, 87, 88, 90-94, 97, 98, 100-105, 107, 109, 112, 133-135, 139-142, 146-152, 156, 158, 163, 166, 172, 180, 181, 184, 188, 189, 193, 205, 206, 207, 209, 210-214, 216-218, 222-224, 226, 227, 229-231, 246, 248, 249, 251, 254-257, 265, 267-269, 271, 272, 276, 279, 282, 283, 289, 292, 294, 298, 301, 316, 320, 328, 332, 340, 347, 355, 409, 420, 421, 424, 426-42 8, 430-433, 448, 451, 454, 455, 459, 460, 467, 468, 472, 473, 475, 476, 503, 505, 506, 508-513
    Essays in the Gogolian Period of Russian Literature, 91
    Grammatika, 340
    Literaturnoe nasledie [*Literary Heritage*], 248
    "On the Aesthetic Relations of Art to Reality," 91
    The Prologue, 140, 511
    What to Do?, xvi, 93-104, 140, 146, 188, 217, 231, 347, 447, 509-511
Chertkov, Leonid, 476
Chouan, Jean, 405, 406
Chukovsky, Kornei, 259
Churchill, Winston, 458

Cicero, Marcus Tullius, 508
Clark, Katerina, 108
Coates, Steve, 160, 161, 169, 170, 190, 191, 239
Coen, Ethan Jesse, 265
Coen, Joel David, 265
Coffey, Jerry, 447, 466, 480
Connell, Richard, 281
Connolly, Julian, 76, 90, 121, 220, 221, 237, 241, 248, 266, 267, 305, 306, 337
Constantine, *See* 'Constantinus, Flavius V. A.'
Constantinus, Flavius V. A., 228
Cook, Bruce, 445, 448, 480
Cornwell, David J. M., 446
Corral, Rodrigo, 59
Coué, Émile, 145
Covici, Pascal, 376
Craft, Robert, 442
Crane, Milton, 441, 445, 456, 457, 481
Cui, César, 320 (*Feast in Time of Plague*)
Culler, Jonathan, 135
Culligan, Glendy, 450, 468, 469, 481
Curran, Michael W., 87, 96

D

Dahl, Vladimir, 19, 186, 225, 353, 363, 387
Dalí, Salvador, 195, 196
Dallwitz, Horst von, 153
Dance, Jim, 444, 465, 481
Danzas, Ekaterina D., 278, 280
Danzas, Konstantin K., 278, 280, 305
Danzas, Louis 278
Darack, Arthur, 462, 470, 481
Dark, Oleg, xxii
Darskii, Dmitrii, 132 (*Wondrous Fantasies*)
Darwin, Charles, 132, 170 (*The Origin of the Species*)
Dauben, Joseph W., 326
Davenport, Guy, 201, 203
David (King), 225, 226
Davie, Donald, 436, 438, 439, 442, 445
Davis, Natalie, 221, 237
Davydov, Sergei, 34, 75, 132, 146, 208, 212, 215, 237, 239, 462, 481

Debreczeny, Paul, 268
Deineka, Alexander, 203
Delalande, Pierre, xvi, 226, 327
Denner, M., 284
Derzhavin, Gavrila, 128, 222
Desyatov, Vyacheslav, 443, 481
Deutsch, Babette, 375
Diaghilev, Sergei, 106, 197, 375
Dickens, Charles, 116 (*Bleak House*), 380, 438, 444, 474
Dillon-Plante, Lillian, 46, 503
Dioneo, *See* 'Shklovsky, Isaak'
Döblin, Alfred, 159, 183, 232, 270, 299, 300
Dobuzhinsky, Mstislav, 47, 109
Dobrolyubov, Nikolai, 87, 140, 278, 509, 510
Dolgorukiy, Yuri, 145
Dolgorukov, Peter V., 146
Dolinin, Alexander, xv, xvi, xxii, xxiii, 10, 18, 19, 21-23, 27-30, 34, 39, 54, 76, 116, 119, 121, 128, 130, 144-146, 148, 149,152, 155, 157, 164, 175, 176, 179, 184, 186-189, 191, 222-224, 236-238, 266, 268, 270, 271, 277, 286, 287, 289-292, 300, 302, 306, 313, 317, 318, 321, 368, 395, 404, 411, 428, 481
Donets, Ia., 228
Dorman, Oleg, 478
Dostoevsky, Fyodor, 85, 100, 103, 106, 196, 238, 316, 337, 368, 376, 416, 422, 443, 448, 465, 472, 506, 510
    The Brothers Karamazov, 181, 459
    Crime and Punishment, 182, 385
    The Insulted and Humiliated, 354
    Notes from the Underground, 102
    The Possessed, 233, 235, 506
Doumer, Paul, 26
Dovlatov, Sergei, 353
Dragunoiu, Dana, xv
Drozd, Andrew, 104, 105, 122, 216, 238
Drozdov, Vasily M., 130
Druzhinin, Alexander V., 293
Dupin, Amantine-Lucile-Aurore, 316
Durantaye, Leland de la, 17

Index

Duse, Elenora, 145, 315
Dvyniatin, Fyodor, 294
Dwight, Ogden G., 450, 258, 465, 481
Dzhugashvili, Iosif, *See* 'Stalin, Joseph'

E

Eco, Umberto, ix (*The Limits of Interpretation*)
Efimov, Mikhail, 167, 238
Efron, Ilya, 22, 23
Eikhenbaum, Boris, 216, 246, 293, 294, 306, 343
Einstein, Albert, 113, 279
Eisenstein, Sergei, 303, 309, 345
  Strike, 280, 302
  The Battleship Potemkin, 302-304
El Greco, *See* 'Theotokópoulos, Doménikos'
Eliot, George, 380
Emerson, Ralph Waldo, 327
Engels, Friedrich, 85
Engelstein, Laura, 107
Ermolaev, Herman, 53
Ernst, Max, 114
Ershov, Petr P., 364
Eversmann, Alexander E. F., 191
Eyck, Jan van, 352

F

Faber, A. W., 335
Faberge, Peter Carl, 331
Faulkner, William, 441
Fedin, Konstantin, 377 (*Cities and Years*)
Feigin, Anna, xxi, 35, 46, 71, 377
Feinstein, Elaine, 466, 467, 470
Fel'zen, Iurii, 298
Ferrer, Daniel, 73
Fet, Afanasii, 23, 416, 448
Fet, Victor, 16, 76
Fichtenholz, Grigorii M., 499
Field, Andrew, 41, 487
Fielding, Henry, 380
Filonov, Pavel, 218
Fitzgerald, F. Scott, 434
Flaccus, Quintus Horatius, 222

Flaubert, Gustave, 380, 440
Fleishman, Lazar, xv
Fleming, Ian, 445
Florinsky, Michael, 81, 101, 122
Fondaminsky, Amalia, 489
Fondaminsky, Ilya, xix, xx, 3, 30, 32, 34, 38, 39, 44, 181
Forsh, Olga, 219 (*Sumasshedshii korabl'* [*The Crazy Ship*])
Forsyth, Malcolm, 470, 481
Foster, John Burt Jr., 171, 205, 238, 270, 474, 481
Fourier, Charles, *See* 'Fourier, François M.C.'
Fourier, François M. C., 506
Fowles, John, 75
  The Collector, 56, 438
France, Anatole, 145, 315
Frank, Joseph, 102
Freeborn, Richard, 86, 96, 100, 101, 122
Freidin, Gregory, 222, 238, 308, 337
Frenkel, Aleksei, 271
Freud, Sigmund, 181, 471
Frick, Henry C., 104
Fridman, Solomon G., 498
Funke, Sarah, 55, 61, 63, 64, 76

G

Gall, John, 53
Galsworthy, John, 432
Garf, Andrei, 422, 423
Garshin, Vsevolod, 231
Gasparov, Boris, 75, 83, 122, 237, 248
Gazdanov, Gaito, 20 (*An Evening with Claire*), 30, 298, 419
Genette, Gérard, 276
George, Stefan, 300
Gerard (German cartographer), 164
Gershenzon, Mikhail, 179, 241, 338, 369
Gessen, Georgii, 39, 46, 425
Gessen, Iosif, xix, 5, 6, 34, 76
Gewirtz, Isaac, xvi
Gezari, Janet, 208
Gide, André, 211 (*The Counterfeiters*), 270, 298
Gilmore, Jane L., 332, 339, 481

Index

Gippius, Vladimir V., 232, 284, 499, 501
Gippius, Zinaida, 24, 187, 232, 421, 499
Girard, Raymond, xxii, 68
Gladkov, Aleksandr K., 475
Glenny, Michael, 382
Glinka, K. A., 189
Glinka, Mikhail, 165 (*Life for the Tsar,* or *Ivan Susanin*), 189
Glushakov, P.S., 228
Glushanok, Galina, xxiii, 42, 48, 50, 76
Glynn, Michael, 302, 306
Godunov, Boris 90, 164, 165
Godunov, Fyodor II, 164
Goethe, Johann W. von, 17, 113, 280
Gofman, Victor, 231
Gogol, Nikolai, 45, 46, 84, 87, 91, 105, 128, 180, 212, 214, 221, 254, 288, 289, 292-296, 306, 337, 350, 380, 385, 438, 443, 447, 451, 464, 467
    Dead Souls, 84, 212, 292, 350, 361, 374
    "The Diary of a Madman," 289, 295
    The Inspector General, 84, 472
    "The Overcoat," 84
    Viy, 425
Goldenweizer, Alexander, 116, 122
Goldfrank, David, 81
Goldman, Emma, 104
Golenishtshev-Kutuzov, Arseny, 471
Goncharov, Ivan, 330 ("The Month of May in St. Petersburg"), 331, 369, 416 (*The Precipice*)
Goncharova, Natalia, 84, 202, 278
Goodenough, Ward H., 168
Gorbachev, Mikhail, 53
Gorchakov, Alexander, 160
Gordimer, Nadine, 61
Gordon, Lev, 498
Gorgulov, Paul, 26
Gorianin, Alexander, 475
Gorky, Maxim, 23, 101, 105, 374
Gorodetsky, Sergey, 232
Gourmont, Remy de, 439 ("Physique de l'Amour")
Grabes, Herbert, 472, 481
Grambow, Friedrich, 153

Grant, Paul Benedict, 481
Grass, Günter, 438 (*The Tin Drum*), 438 (*Cat and Mouse*)
Grayson, Jane, 10, 18-24, 27, 29, 76, 178, 238, 239, 241, 391-394, 397, 411, 412, 440, 481
Greene, Graham, 456 (*Sense of Reality*)
Greenleaf, Monika, 90, 119,122, 155, 165, 179, 183, 184, 186, 232, 238, 249, 306
Grey, Ian, 164, 238
Griffin, Lloyd W., 452, 464, 481
Grinberg, Savely, 497
Grishakova, Marina, 269, 270, 382, 383
Grishunin, Andrei, 74, 76
Gropius, Walter A., 113
Grosz, George, 203
Grumm-Grzhimaylo, Grigory, 190, 290, 291, 306, 319
Grynberg, Roman, 12, 46
Guadanini, Irina, 172, 173, 174, 175, 177, 229, 238
Guerney, Bernard Guilbert, xxi, 374, 376
Gukovsky, Alexander, 30
Gumbrecht, Hans Ulrich, 233, 238
Gurevich, Alexander, 496
Gurin, Olga, xv

H

Horace, *See* 'Flaccus, Quintus Horatius'
Horowitz, Glenn, xxiii, 61, 62, 64, 65, 66
Hosking, Geoffrey, 81, 101, 106
Huc, Évariste Régis, 317
Hughes, Robert, 75, 184
Hugo, Victor, 108, 406 (*Ninety-Three*), 463 (*Les Misérables*)
Humboldt, Alexander von, 156
Hunczak, Taras, 85
Hunter, Anna, 451, 452
Hutchens, John K., 440, 452, 454, 460, 462, 464, 465, 482
Hyman, Stanley E., 436, 439, 471

I

Idema, Jim, 471
Iglehart, L. T., Jr., 435, 482

Ilf, Ilya A.
  The Twelve Chairs, 182
  The Little Golden Calf, 359
Iogolevich, Lazar, 502
Iremonger, Lucille, 463
Irvine, Andrew, 145
Irving, Washington, 320 ("Rip Van Winkle")
Iser, Wolfgang, 369
Isherwood, Christopher, 444
Iswolsky, Hélène, 120
Ivannikov, Mikhail D., 420
Ivanov, Georgii, 76, 180
  Disintegration of the Atom, 24, 26
Ivanov, Viacheslav, 183
Ivleva, Victoria, 222, 238, 285, 292, 296

J
Jabotinsky, Vladimir (Ze'ev), 228, 488
  Chuzhbina [Strange Land], 259, 309
Jacob, Max, 332
Jannelli, Altagracia de, xx, 431-434
Jannings, Emil, 116
Jelavich, Peter, 122, 183, 238, 299, 300, 303, 306
Johnson, Donald Barton, 69, 128, 133, 164, 194, 207, 208, 212, 220, 238, 262, 274, 306, 309
Johnson, James P., 319
Johnson, Kurt, 64, 160-162, 169, 170, 190, 191, 239
Johnson, Samuel, 215, 216
Johnson, Uwe, 438 (*Speculations about Jacob*)
Jones, Sonya, 183, 239
Joyce, James, 74, 76, 101, 116, 132, 240, 254, 271, 299, 306, 309, 335, 366, 380, 440, 470, 476
  Finnegans Wake, 12, 61, 73, 471
  A Portrait of the Artist as a Young Man, 146, 300, 301, 323, 439
  Ulysses, ix, xx, 10, 61, 73, 133, 148, 299, 300-302, 322, 429, 432, 433, 439, 441
Juliar, Michael, 69, 70
Jutzi, Piel, 299

K
Kafka, Franz, 322 ("Metamorphosis")
Kagan, Abram, xx, 39-41
Kaminskaia, Valeria, 271-272
Kandinsky, Vassily, 113, 114, 202
Kannegiser, Leonid I., 184, 397, 494
Kant, Immanuel, 233, 316
Karakozov, Dmitri, 89, 511
Karamzin, Ekaterina N., 28
Karamzin, Nikolai,
  History of the Russian State, 28
  Letters of a Russian Traveler, 160
Karelin, S., 192
Kardakoff, Nikolai, 276
Karges, Joann, 515
Karlinsky, Simon, 196, 205, 206, 213, 219, 239, 304, 470, 482
Karpovich, Mikhail, xix, 5, 497
Kataev (Petrov), Yevgeni
  The Twelve Chairs, 257, 258, 260, 261, 295
Katsell, Jerome, 208
Katz, Boris, 329, 369
Katz, Michael, xvi, 94, 95, 102, 122
Kavun, Ivan N., 499
Kazantzakis, Nikos, 441
Kellerman, Bernard, 175
Kennedy, John F., 445
Kerensky, Alexander, 494
Kern, Anna P., 189
Kern, Catherine, 189
Kern, Otto, 318
Kerouac, Jack, 443
Kharuzin, Oleg, 498
Kherkus, Alexander, 498
Kherkus, Enokh I., 498
Kherkus, Vera A., 498
Khitrovo, Elizaveta, 129
Khlebnikov, Victor (Velemir), 263, 327
Khodasevich, Vladislav, 4, 24, 30, 53, 118, 128, 132, 167, 168, 179, 184, 218 ("The Life of Vasilii Travnikov"), 231, 238, 239, 261, 328, 369, 415, 418-421, 423, 426
Kholmogorov, Mikhail, 497

Index

Kiandzhuntsev, Savely (Saba), 490, 496, 500
Kibirov, Timur, 478, 479
Kirsch, Robert, 441, 444, 482
Kissel, V. S., 222, 239
Klee, Paul, 113
Kliuchevskii, Vasilii, 85
Knopf, Alfred A., 375
Knut, Dovid, 224
Kolerov, Modest, 52, 76
Koltsov, Alexei V., 388
Konishi, Masataka, 325-327, 369
Korabelnikov, G., 289
Korvin-Piotrovsky, Vladimir, 179
Kostalevsky, Marina, 216, 239, 245, 246, 294, 306, 343, 369
Kostelanetz, Richard, 447, 457, 482
Kostomarov, Nikolai, 511
Koussevitzky, Serge, 42
Krainii, Anton, *See* 'Gippius, Zinaida'
Kreitner, Gustav Ritter von, 275
Kricheldorff, Adolf, 276
Krupensky, P., 228
Krylov, Ivan, 404
Kryzhanovsky, Oleg, 191, 192, 239
Kubrick, Stanley, 377
Küchelbecker, Wilhelm von, 285
Kühnel, Ernst, 194
Kuprin, Alexander, 232, 374 (*The Pit*)
Kushner, Aleksandr, 477, 482
Kutik, Ilya, 284

L

L'vov, Lollii, 40, 41
L'vova, Nadezhda, 231
La Fontaine, Jean de, 404
Ladinsky, Anatonin, 179, 260
Lanchester, John, 314, 369
Laner, Joseph F. K., 277
Langhans, Carl G., 157
Langsdorff, G. I., 192
Latreille, Pierre A., 192
Laughlin, James, 374, 375, 487
Lavrov, Alexander, 262, 306
Lavrov, Peter, 512

Lawrence, David Herbert, 40 (*Lady Chatterly's Lover*), 380
Layton, Susan, 160, 161, 239
Ledenev, A. V., 284, 307
Leech, John H., 162, 190
Lemke, Mikhail, 4
Lenin, Vladimir, 53, 103 ("What is to be Done?"), 112, 134, 145, 147, 150, 304, 445, 506
Lepel, M. Von, 153
Lermontov, Mikhail, 82, 105, 190, 255, 316, 345, 354, 369
  "The Angel," 317
  "Bela," 354, 357
  A Hero of our Time, 354
Leskov, Nikolai, 316, 382, 416
Levavi, Arieh, 70, 72
Levin, Iurii I., 145, 239, 265, 266, 269, 307, 477, 482
Levine, Paul, 442, 443, 482
Leving, Yuri, 40, 42, 72, 107, 166, 176, 184, 294, 295, 314, 331, 350, 351, 377, 381, 385, 477, 487, 490, 502
  "Filming Nabokov," 176, 239
  "Nabokov i Sasha Chernyi," 351, 369
  "Phantom in Jerusalem: Or, the History of an Unrealized Visit," 502
  "Plaster, Marble, Canon: The Vindication of Nabokov," 482
  "Rakovinnyi gul," 184, 239
  "Samuel Izrailevich," 72, 77
  "Singing 'The Bells' and 'The Covetous Knight': Nabokov and Rachmaninoff's Operatic Translations of Poe and Pushkin," 76
  "Six Notes to *The Gift*," 307, 369
  "Tenishev Students," 166, 239
  "Translation is a Bastard Form," 308, 411
  Vokzal—Garazh—Angar. V. Nabokov i poetika russkogo urbanizma [*Train Station—Garage—Hangar. Vladimir Nabokov and Poetics of Russian Urbanism*], 122, 369
Levitan, Isaac, 193, 194

Levy, Alan, 245, 307, 474, 482
Liatskii, Evgenii, 50, 105, 122
Lichtenstein, Heinrich, 156
Likhachev, Dmitri, 73, 77
Lilienstern, Faddey, 496
Lilienstern, Lev, 496
Linscer, German F., 501
Lincoln, Bruce W., 112, 122
Linyov, I. L., 187
Lissitzky, El, 114
Livak, Leonid, 32, 77, 211, 239, 265, 286, 292, 298, 307
Lomonosov, Mikhail, 229 ("Evening Meditation on God's Greatness")
Lotman, Mikhail, xxii, 260, 283, 307, 476, 483
Lotman, Yuri, 73, 77
Lukash, Ivan, 228
Lukyanin, Valentin, 52
Lunceford, James Melvin, 319

M

MacGillirray, Aurthur, 460-462, 483
Mach, Ersnt, 279
MacKenzie, David, 87, 96, 123
MacLennan, Bud, 56
Magritte, René, 195, 196, 202
Maikov, Apollon, 223 ("Byvalo, ulovit' iz zhizni mig sluchainyi..." ["There was a time when to catch a chance moment of life..."]), 224 (*Mashen'ka [Mary]*)
Maksimovich, E., 259
Malcolm, Donald, 245, 249, 250, 307, 409, 411, 431, 436, 455-456, 461, 463, 483
Malevich, Kazimir, 114
Malia, Martin, 89, 123
Malikova, Maria, xvi, 22, 77, 130, 131, 218, 219, 239, 260, 261, 307, 425, 483
Malin, Irving, 454, 483
Mallarmé, Étienne, 438 ("L'Apres-midi d'un faune")
Mallarmé, Stéphane, *See* 'Mallarmé, Étienne.'
Mallory, George, 145, 315
Malmstad, John, 187, 239, 328, 369, 421

Mal'tsev, Nikolai, 502
Mandelstam, Osip, 44, 108, 109, 166, 167, 180, 222, 277, 282, 363
  Conversation about Dante, 7, 11
  Egyptian Stamp, 332
  "The Noise of Time," 499
  "Rakovina" ["A Conch"], 179
  The Slate Ode, 180, 277
  Stone, 260
Mander, John, 113, 115, 123
Mann, Thomas, 196 (*Doctor Faustus*)
Manolescu, Monica, 273-275, 307
Markov, Vladimir, 426, 428
Martinez, Juan, 57, 77
Martynov, G. G., 53, 77, 426, 476, 483
Marx, Karl, 85, 93, 96, 101-103, 109, 135, 181, 258, 259, 315, 432, 506
  Capital, 511
  Holy Family, 261
Maslov, Boris, 180, 189, 233, 240, 269, 277
Maupassant, Guy de, 198 ("The Necklace")
Maurier, Daphne du, 438 (*The Glass Blowers*)
Maurois, André, 4
Mauss, Marcel, 221, 222, 240
Max, Gabriel von, 279
Mazur, Natalia, 229, 240
McCormick, Richard W., 104, 183, 240
Mayakovsky, Vladimir, 109, 263, 351 ("Iubileinoe" ["Anniversary Poem"])
McCarthy, Mary, 430, 458,
Meerovich, David, 498
Meilakh, Mikhail, 475
Mel'nikov, Nikolai, 415, 423, 483
Melville, Herman, 443
Mendel, Gregor, 170
Menetriés, Eduard, 191, 192, 239
Mercier, Jeanne, 440, 459, 468, 483
Merezhkovsky, Dmitri, 30, 44, 228
Mérimée, Prosper, 500
Merwin, William, 61
Meyer, Priscilla, 104, 123, 287, 307
Mikhailov, Oleg, 476

Mikhailovsky, Nikolai K., 448
Mikhelson, M. I., 404
Miliukov, Pavel, 88, 123, 281
Milner-Gulland, R., 82, 84, 123
Milton, John, 188, 316, 398, 399
Minao, Maya, 170, 171, 240
Minton, Walter, 269
Mirsky, D. S., *See* 'Svyatopolk-Mirsky, Dmitri'
Mitchell, Julian, 250, 307, 439, 456, 457, 483
Möbius, August F., 177, 208-211, 340,
Mondri, Henrietta, 285, 307
Moore, Harry T., 465, 483
Moore, Thomas, 395
Morris, Paul D., 262, 263, 265, 307
Morson, Saul, 98, 123
Moser, Charles, 96-98, 100, 123
Moynahan, Julian, 102, 123, 148, 178, 215, 240, 471, 479, 483
Mozart, Wolfgang A., 132
Muchnic, Helen, xxi, 375, 376
Murdoch, Iris, 438 (*The Unicorn*)
Murray, Michele, 461, 463, 469, 483
Mussorgsky, Modest, 43, 165 (*Boris Godunov*)

N

Nabokov, Dmitri (grandfather), 93
Nabokov, Dmitri V. (son), xiii, xvi, 8, 10, 11, 55-57, 61, 62, 66-72, 131, 132, 153, 377-383, 399-401, 404, 405, 432, 487, 501
Nabokov, Elena I., 46, 338
Nabokov, Elena Vladimirovna, *See* 'Sikorski, Elena'
Nabokov, Nicolas, 46, 197, 240, 353, 369
Nabokov, Sergei, 44, 201, 489, 502
Nabokov, Vladimir D., 5, 89, 109, 111, 130, 165, 281
Nabokov, Vladimir, passim
  WORKS
    "A Busy Man," 6
    A Hero of our Time [trans.], 354
    Ada, 4, 50, 74, 190, 271, 332, 381
    The Aerial Path, 286

"An Affair of Honor," 498
"The Aurelian," 162
Bend Sinister, 44, 228, 409, 494, 499
"Cabbage Soup and Caviar," 376
"The Circle," xix, xxiii, 12, 40, 91, 168, 490
"Cloud, Castle, Lake," 39, 228,
Collected Works, 53, 54, 313
Conclusive Evidence, 46 (*See* also *Drugie berega* and *Speak, Memory*)
The Defense, 153, 182, 186, 207, 210, 251, 426, 436, 494, 499
Despair, 429, 431
"The Doorbell," 495
Drugie berega [Other Shores], 48, 494
The Enchanter, 457
Eugene Onegin [trans.], 6, 171, 205, 210, 322, 349-350, 377, 392, 394
"Evening in a Vacant Lot," 130
The Event, 230
The Eye, 210, 446, 494
"Father's Butterflies," xxiii, 10, 14, 15, 27, 40, 54, 129
Glory, 40, 51, 186, 203, 376, 381, 429, 502
"A Guide to Berlin," 119, 159,
"Hexameters," 130
"L'Inconnue De La Seine," 166
Invitation to a Beheading, xix, 4, 35, 340, 381, 419, 425, 461
"Itch," 494
"Iubilei," 294
King, Queen, Knave, 51, 158
"Lastochka" ["The Swallow"], 253
Laughter in the Dark, 251, 429, 433
Lectures on Russian Literature, 84, 144, 145, 184
"Lik," 494
"Lilac," 294
Lolita, xxii, 20, 29, 44, 52, 55, 72, 112, 157, 176, 245, 251, 271, 281, 313, 337, 377, 380, 381, 394, 409, 429, 436, 438, 446, 447, 450, 452, 455-458, 460-462, 464, 466, 470, 476, 499

Look at the Harlequins!, 472-474
"Lunnaia greza," 337
Mary, 51, 118, 186, 224, 382
"Mirror," 286
Nabokov-Wilson Letters, 44, 48, 281, 304, 322, 375, 376
Nabokov's Butterflies, 15, 16, 129, 515
Nikolai Gogol, 46
Notes on Prosody, 262
"On a Train," 294
"Orache," 130, 494
The Original of Laura, 11, 20, 23, 57, 69, 143, 314, 474
Pale Fire, xxii, 4, 16, 29, 55, 69, 209, 210, 213, 249, 314, 381, 430, 439, 441, 446, 451, 452, 455, 457, 458, 460, 461, 464, 466, 468
"Pamiati Amalii," 182
"The Parisian Poem," 26
"Pegasus," 336
Pnin, 44, 162, 168, 271, 318, 380, 409, 461, 467, 488, 490
Poems and Problems, 478
The Real Life of Sebastian Knight, 29, 177, 210, 382, 409, 466, 475
"Reply to My Critics," 392
"The Return of Chorb," 20
"The Reunion," 119
Selected Letters, 14, 56, 167, 373, 374, 376, 377, 419, 432, 433, 471, 483, 487
"Signs and Symbols," 218, 228
Solus Rex, 27, 29
The Song of Igor's Campaign [trans.], 377
Speak, Memory, 48, 55, 106, 108, 115, 119, 130, 147, 190, 195, 217, 278, 365, 441, 457, 487, 494, 499
Spring in Fialta [Collection], 48
"Spring in Fialta," 177, 196
Stikhotvoreniia (Poetry), 230
The Stories, 12, 27
Strong Opinions, 54, 90, 101, 115, 119, 152, 179, 181, 197, 202, 209, 246, 253, 281, 322, 323, 325

"To Count S. M. Kachurin," 427
"Tolstoy," 131
"Ultima Thule," 27
"What is the evil deed I have committed?," 478
"The Wood Sprite," 329
Nabokov, Véra, xxi, 6, 10, 13, 35, 44-46, 55, 56, 61-66, 69, 71, 135, 153, 154, 175-177, 251, 269, 276, 338, 377, 379-381, 384-388, 393, 402, 404, 419, 471, 475, 503, 507
Nadson, Semyon Y., 351, 502
Nagy, Moholy, 113
Naiman, Eric, xxiv (*Nabokov, Perversely*), 94, 123
Nakhimovsky, Alexander, 255-257, 307, 395, 398, 412
Narbut, Vladimir, 331 ("Alexandra Pavlovna")
Naso, Publius Ovidius, 205
Nazaroff, Alexander I., xx, 133, 428-433, 435
Nechayev, Sergey, 506
Nekrasov, Nikolai, 510, 511, 95, 282, 388, 420
Nellis, Karl, 495
Nemirovsky, Igor, xv
Nesbet, Anne, 231, 232, 272, 307
Nicol, Charles, 165, 241
Nicholas I, 157, 159, 320, 323
Nicholas II, 89, 109, 111, 112
Noel, Lucie Léon, 302, 308
Norman, Will, xvii, 76, 239
Novikov, A. A., 151
Numano, Mitsuyoshi, xxiii, 54

O

Oakes, Philip, 246
Oberthür, Charles, 190, 275
Offenbach, Jacques, 24
Ognyov, N., 375 (*The Diary of a Communist Schoolboy*)
Oks, Boris A., 497
Oks, Evgeny, 497
Oks, Tamara, 497

Olesha, Iurii, 216, 285,
Orlitsky, Yuri, 261, 308
Osorgin, Mikhail, 30
Ostrovsky, A. G., 323, 370
Ostrovsky, Alexander Nikolayevich, 329
Ovid, *See* 'Naso, Publius Ovidius'

P

Page, James F., 441, 453, 483
Painlevé, Paul, 316
Palimpsestov, Ivan U., 272, 273, 276
Papapulo, Alexander, 289, 308
Paperno, Irina, 96, 98, 103, 123, 193, 231, 241, 246, 248, 249, 271-273, 276, 282, 302, 308, 328
Paperno, S., 52, 77, 475, 476, 483
Pascal, Blaise, 406, 412
    Pensées, 403
Pasternak, Boris, 166, 180, 229, 374, 442, 444
    Doctor Zhivago, 442
Pedenko, Dmitri K., 497
Pepin, Maurice, 25
Pereira, Norman G., xvi, 94, 123
Perkins, Maxwell, 434
Perlberg, Mark, 438, 447, 451, 460, 463, 483
Perley, Maie E., 409, 412, 461, 462, 469, 470, 483
Pertzoff, Peter, xxi, 8, 373, 374, 376
Peter I (aka Peter the Great), 85, 111, 116, 268, 315
Peterson, Ronald E., 144, 145, 147, 241
Petrov, Yevgeni, *See* 'Kataev, Yevgeni Petrovich'
Petrovskaya, Nina, 231
Philaret, Metropolitan, *See* 'Drozdov, Vasily'
Phryna, 388
Picasso, Pablo, 197, 201, 442
Pichova, Hana, 257, 263, 308
Pilate, Pontius, 454
Pilnyak, Boris, 128
Pil'skii, Petr, 404, 405, 412, 415, 418, 424, 483
Pines, Roman, 493, 501

Pisarev, Dmitri, 87, 88, 140, 292
Piscator, Erwin, 116
Pisemsky, Alexey, 100, 316, 416
Planck, Max, 113
Platonov, Andrei, 337
Poe, Edgar Allan, 42 (*The Bells*), 438
Pollock, Venetia, 457, 483
Polo, Marco, 254, 274
    The Description of the World, 273, 274
    Li Livres du Graunt Caam, 274
Poplavsky, Boris, 30, 120, 179, 184, 231, 277, 298
Popov, Grigorii, 494, 499, 500
Potanin, Grigory, 333, 516
Pratt, Antwerp E., 162, 275, 276
Priestland, David, 102, 123
Proffer, Carl, 50, 51, 271, 313, 394, 412
Proffer, Ellendea, 50, 51, 496
Prokopoff, Stephen S., 198, 201, 241
Prokopov, Timofei, 232, 241
Propp, Vladimir, 135, 218, 241, 364, 370
Proskurina, Vera, 178, 179, 241
Proust, Marcel, 101, 171, 297, 440, 470
    In Search of Lost Time, 128, 298, 301, 322
Przhevalsky, Nikolai, 160, 191, 290, 317
Puccini, Giacomo, 145, 315
Pushkin, Alexander, 7, 14, 16, 17-19, 23, 24, 27-29, 38, 42, 53, 62, 73, 74, 77, 82-84, 87, 100, 103-106, 109, 111, 112, 128-132, 137, 138, 140, 146, 160, 161, 165-167, 171, 178, 179, 183, 184, 186-189, 193, 210, 212, 214, 215, 216, 218, 231, 245, 246, 248, 252, 254, 268, 278, 280, 285, 292-294, 296, 301, 316, 318, 320, 338, 341-343, 346, 351, 363, 375, 383, 386, 395, 419, 425, 438, 447, 451, 458, 464, 487, 509
    "Anchar," 499
    The Blackamoor of Peter the Great, 268
    Boris Godunov, 28, 82, 165, 225, 425
    "The Bronze Horseman," 111
    "A Canticle to Ekaterina Karamzin," 28

Index

The Captain's Daughter, 82, 146, 403
The Covetous Knight, ix, 42, 76, 165, 239
Egyptian Nights, 186
Eugene Onegin, 6, 82, 84, 87, 100, 106, 119, 171, 183, 205, 210, 213, 215, 230, 232, 263, 264, 292, 322, 349, 350, 362, 377, 392, 394, 398, 421, 447, 470, 478, 487
The Feast During the Plague, 42, 187, 320
History of the Pugachyov Rebellion, 403
"Ia pomnyu chudnoe mgnoven'e..." ("I Remember a Wondrous Moment..."), 189
Journey to Arzrum, 161, 212, 246
"Maria Schoning," 383
Mozart and Salieri, 132
Novel at a Caucasian Spa, 146
"Pamiatnik" ("Exegi Monumentum"), 178
"A Prisoner," 283
The Prisoner of the Caucasus, 160, 161
The Stone Guest, 23, 42
The Tale of Tsar Saltan, 16, 350
The Tales of Belkin, 146
"The Three Springs," 220
Rusalka (The Water-Nymph), 18, 19, 27-29, 42, 184
Ruslan and Lyudmila, 82
"To Count Gorchakov," 23
"Vain Gift," 129
"Verses Composed at Night during Insomnia," 229
Pyle, Robert M., 515
Pynchon, Thomas, 270, 441, 443
  V., 438, 441
Pypin, Alexander N., 510-512
Pythagoras of Samos, 316, 326

R

Rabelais, François, 439
Rabinovich, Evgenii I., 497
Rabinovich, Grigorii, 496
Rabinovich, Ilya G., 496
Rachmaninoff, Irina, 40
Rachmaninoff, Sergei, xx, 40-42
Rachmaninoff, Tatiana, 40
Raeff, Mark, 115, 123
Rampton, David, 104, 107, 123, 252, 253, 287, 288, 308, 398, 412
Randall, Francis, 93-96, 98, 103, 123
Rashal', Grigorii, 502
Reagan, Katherine, 62
Reni, Guido, 194
Riasanovsky, Nicholas V., 89, 91, 123
Rijn, Rembrandt van, 194, 217
Rilke, Rainer Maria, 300, 439 (*The Notebooks of Malte Laurids Brigge*)
Rimbaud, Arthur, 120, 270 ("Voyelles")
Rimsky-Korsakov, Nikolai, 43, 197 (*The Wedding Feast of the Boyar*), 329
Robbe-Grillet, Alain, 270
Roborovskii, Vsevolod I., 289, 308
Rochmilovich, A. S., 333
Rogers, W. G., 436, 438, 439, 451, 464, 483
Rohe, Mies van der, 113
Rölke, Erich, 153
Rollow, Jack W., 448, 461, 483
Ronen, Irena, 209, 241, 327, 370
Ronen, Omry, xv, 26, 77, 148, 159, 209, 241, 285, 288, 291, 308, 328, 330, 370
Rosengrant, Judson, 398
Ross, Maggie, 410, 412, 445, 461, 464, 484
Roth, Joseph, 114, 124, 158, 159, 241
Rousseau, Henri, 196, 203, 204
Rousseau, Jean-Jacques, 103 (*La Nouvelle Héloïse; Emile*)
Rowe, Percy, 442, 456, 484
Rozanov, A. I., 273
Rosanov, Mikhail G., 375
Rozanov, Vasily, 184, 229, 352
Rozental', Lazar V., 499
Rozov, Arieh, 3
Rozov, Hertzlia (Levina), 493
Rozov, Izrail, 488

Rozov, Samuil, xiii, xv, xx, 71, 72, 330, 487-492, 498, 502
Rozov, Sara A., 494
Rozov, Yehudit, 502
Rudnev, Vadim, xix, xx, 3, 30, 32, 34-39, 47, 230, 259
Russell, Bertrand, 327
Rustichello da Pisa, 274
Rutherford, Brendan, xvi

S
Sachtleben, William L., 321
Sadock, Benjamin, 168
Salieri, Antonio, 132
Salinger, Jerome D., 438 (*Raise High the Roof Beam, Carpenters*)
Salomon, Roger B., 217, 241, 254, 308
Samokhvalov, Alexander, 203
Sanders, Nicholas, 440, 454, 484
Sandrof, Ivan, 250
Sandrof, Nancy, 250, 308
Sarton, May, 62
Sartre, Jean-Paul, 444
Scammell, Michael, xvi, xxi, xxiii, 55, 132, 223, 251, 280, 308, 377, 379-396, 399, 401, 402, 404, 406-412
Schäfer, A., 279
Schauman, Eugen, 281
Scherr, Barry P., 215, 241, 253, 308
Schopenhauer, Arthur, 183
Schiff, Stacy, 77, 117, 124, 175-177, 241, 381, 503
Scott, Charles T., 264, 308
Scott, Walter, 82
Sedakova, Olga, 477, 484
Sedykh, Andrei, 440
Seifrid, Thomas, 337
Seitz, Adalbert, 190
Semiradski, Henryk, 388
Senderovich, Savely, xv, 178, 241
Shakespeare, William, 73, 82, 185, 241, 264, 296, 320
    Hamlet, 128, 185, 241, 296
    King Lear, 296
    Othello, 326

Shakhovskaya, Zinaida, 127, 188
Shakhovskoy, Zinaida, *See* Shakhovskaya
Shapiro, Gavriel, 188, 194, 201-203, 241, 279, 308, 370
Share, Bernard, 385, 412, 462, 470, 484
Shaw, George Bernard, 452 (*Man and Superman*)
Shcheglov, Iurii, 342, 370
Shchukin, Nikolai L., 351
Shchyogolev, Petr, 184, 185
Sherman, Thomas B., 410, 412, 448, 452, 461, 463, 469, 484
Shestov, Lev, 30
Shirinskii-Shikhmatov, Sergei, 188
Shklovskaia, Zinaida, 425
Shklovsky, Isaak, 425
Shklovsky, Victor, 135, 159, 193, 219, 246, 282, 289, 361
    A Sentimental Journey, 166
    Khod konia, 328
    Mater'ial i stil' v romane L'va Tolstogo 'Voina i mir', 355
    "Piat' fel'etonov ob Eizenshteine," 302
    Zoo, or Letters Not About Love, 156
Shkott, Ivan, 231
Shmurlo, Vadim, 495
Sholokhov, Mikhail A., 475
Shrayer, Maxim, 373, 412, 424, 484, 490, 491
Shukhaev, Vasilii, 115
Shul'gin, Vasilii, 228
Shustov, Nikolai, 495, 498
Sikorski, Elena, 14, 46, 72, 369, 426, 475
Siodmak, Robert, 24, 25
Sirin, Vladimir, *See* 'Nabokov, Vladimir V.'
Sitwell, Osbert, 196, 201, 241
Skonechnaia, Olga, 184, 187, 241
Skryabin, Alexander, 106
Slonim, Marc, 89, 124, 427, 485
Slonim, Sonia, 69
Slonim, Véra, *See* 'Nabokova, Véra'
Smirnovski, Petr V., 339-341, 363
Smith, Gerald, 240, 260, 261, 308
Smith, Miles, 446, 484

Smollet, Tobias, 399
Socrates, 333, 334
Sologub, Fydor, 184, 239,
  The Petty Demon, 286, 308
Solomon (King), 226, 228
Soloukhin, Vladimir, 52
Spender, Steven, 439, 452-454, 484
Spengler, Oswald, 119
Stackensneider, Andrei, 189
Stacy, R. H., 87, 102, 124
Stahl-Urach, Carl, 118
Stalin, Joseph, 16, 51, 53, 103, 150, 166, 194, 375, 405, 406, 411, 442, 475
Stanislavsky, Constantin, 116
Stanley, Donald, 451, 458, 466, 484
Stasov, Vladimir, 106, 107
Staudinger, Otto, 190, 191
Stein, Gertrude, 197, 201
Steinberg, Mark D., 108, 109, 124
Stendhal, *See* Beyle, Marie-Henri
Steklov, Yuri, 3, 50, 248, 249, 272, 273, 427
Sterne, Laurence, 98, 380, 439
Sternweiler, Andreas, 201, 242
Stites, Richard, 112, 122
Stowe, Harriet Beecher, 432 (*Uncle Tom's Cabin*)
Strakhovskii, Leonid I., 172, 224, 242
Stravinsky, Igor, 106, 205, 441 (*Rite of Spring*), 442
Stringer-Hye, Suellen, 69, 77
Strokes, Frederick A., 428
Struve, Gleb, xix, 4, 5, 77, 115, 124, 128, 224, 242, 382, 412, 425, 426, 428, 430, 481, 483, 484
Sumner, Benedict, 85, 124
Svyatopolk-Mirsky, Dmitri P., 105, 106, 123, 166, 167, 238, 240, 376
Sylvester, William, 459, 484
Széchenyi, Béla, 275

T

Tairov, Alexander, 115, 116
Tammi, Pekka, 147, 148, 220, 242, 266, 268, 269, 308, 394, 412
Tappe, Horst, 440, 489
Taranovsky, Kiril, 210, 242, 277, 286, 287, 309
Tarasov-Rodionov, Aleksandr, 187
Tarkovsky, Andrei, 341
Taubman, Robert, 441, 457, 458, 484
Tchaikovsky, Pyotr, 53
Tchelitchew, Pavel, 194, 196-201, 203-205, 218, 241, 242
Terapiano, Iurii, 120, 124, 180
Terras, Victor, 85, 87, 100, 124
Tertz, Abram, *See* 'Sinyavsky, Andrei'
Thackeray, William Makepeace, 380
Thales of Miletus, 316, 409
Theotokópoulos, Doménikos, 196
Thomas, Peter-John, 252, 309, 402, 403, 412
Thoreau, Henry David, 332
Thorpe, George Day, 409, 412, 445, 459-461, 484
Timenchik, Roman, xi, xv, 166, 194, 229, 238, 242
Toker, Leona, xv, 142, 163, 182, 209, 210, 220, 222, 242, 265, 270, 325, 370
Tolstaia, Sof'ia, 375
Tolstoy, Aleksei K., 231, 402
Tolstoy, Leo, 78, 84, 100, 101, 105, 124, 144, 214, 216, 234, 242, 246, 293, 316, 380, 385, 452
  Anna Karenina, 85, 101, 145, 337
  Childhood, 146
  Resurrection, 131
  "The Death of Ivan Ilych," 234
  War and Peace, 94, 337, 424
Tompa, Andrea, 181, 242
Tour, Georges de la, 194
Trotsky, Leo, 304, 405, 406
Tsetlin, Mikhail, 43, 229, 421
Tso-lin, Chang, 145, 146
Tsvetaeva, Marina, 180 ("Poem of the End"), 222, 294 ("Daybreak on the Rails")
Tsybikov, G. T., 318
Tucker, Benjamin, 104
Tumarkin, Nina, 103, 124

Turgenev, Ivan, 20, 22, 82, 87, 89, 103, 277, 323, 370, 416, 453, 472, 509, 510
   A Sportsman's Sketches, 288
   Dnevnik lishnego cheloveka [Diary of a Superfluous Man]), 146
   Fathers and Sons, 88, 316, 337, 354
   "Neshchastnaia" ["The Unhappy One"], 288
   Rudin, 287
   Smoke, 287
Tutankhamen, 145
Tyler, Parker, 197, 242
Tynyanov, Yuri, 246, 285, 307
Tyutchev, Fyodor, 229 ("Insomnia")

U

Urban, Thomas, 153
Uritsky, Moisei, 397
Uzcudun Eizmendi, Paolino, 203

V

Vaginov, Konstantin, 219, 279 (*Kozlinaya Pesn [Goat Song]*)
Vaiskopf, Mikhail, 259, 309
Vasilieva, Olga Sokratovna, See 'Chernyshevskaia, Olga S.'
Velázquez, Diego, 352
Vengerov, Semyon, 23
Verdi, Giuseppe, 324
Vereshchagin, Vasily, 194, 335
Verity, Ruggero, 190, 191
Vertov, Dziga, 352
Vishniak, Mark, 30, 32, 37, 38
Voitinsky, V., 259
Voloshin, Alexander, 442 (*Kuznetsk Land*)
Volynsky, Akim, 3
Vonnegut, Kurt, 61
Vorontsov, Mikhail, 16
Vries, Gerard de, 155, 156, 194, 213, 217, 218, 242, 274, 292, 293, 309
Vroblevsky, Konstantin K., 499
Vrubel, Mikhail, 106, 199
Vyazemsky, Pyotr, 161, 425

W

Wachtel, Andrew, 284
Wagner, William, 94, 95, 102, 122
Waite, Sarah Tiffany, 172, 211, 242
Waldheim, Johann G. F. Von, 191
Watkins, Sue, 440, 484
Weber, Lloyd, 452, 512
Weidenfeld, George, 56, 64, 65, 72, 377, 457
Weir, Sybil, 456, 484
Weissblatt, Harry A., 440, 458, 484
Wells, Herbert G., 330 ("The Crystal Egg")
Werner, Gösta, 302, 309
Werth, Alexander, xxi, 375, 376,
West, Morris L., 438 (*The Shoes of the Fisherman*)
West, Nathanael, 463 (*Miss Lonelyhearts*)
Wheelock, John Hall, 434
White, Duffield, 215, 220, 242, 253, 254, 309
White, Duncan, xvii, 76, 239
White, Frederick, xv
Wilde, Oscar, 444
Wilhelm, Friedrich IV, 156
Williams, Carol, See 'Williams, William Carlos'
Williams, Vera, 440, 484
Williams, William Carlos, 199, 242, 265, 309
Wilson, Colin H., 444 (*The Outsider*)
Wilson, Edmund, xxi, 44, 47, 48, 50, 77, 281, 303, 304, 307, 322, 369, 374-376, 392, 412
Wilson, Jay, 8
Woehrlin, William, 102, 124
Wolfe, Thomas, 434
Wolff, Renate C. 439, 450, 459, 468, 484
Woolf, Virginia, 216, 440
   Orlando, 441
Wreden, Nikolai, 44, 45
Wren, Melvin, 85, 100, 124, 160, 242

Y

Yakovlev, Nikolai, 163, 164, 166
Yangirov, Rashit, 12, 78

Yanovsky, Vassily, 298
Yarmolinsky, Avraham, xxi, 48, 50, 87, 124, 375, 376, 427
Yeltsin, Boris, 53
Young, Terence, 445
Yudenich, Nikolai, 495

Z

Zaitsev, Boris, 30, 424, 483
Zamyatin, Evgeny, 327, 380
Zanftleben, Tatian, 271, 272
Zanganeh, Lila Azam, 69, 78
Zelnik, Reginald, 111, 124
Zenzinov, Vladimir, xxi, 42-44, 47, 76
Zhabotinsky, Vladimir, *See* 'Jabotinsky, Vladimir (Ze'ev)'
Zharkoy, S., 191
Zhukovsky, Vassily, 23, 366
Zimmer, Dieter E., xxiii, 153, 154, 169, 190, 237, 242, 248, 271, 275, 276, 279, 289-291, 306, 309, 317, 318, 370, 515
Zoshchenko, Mikhail, 219
Zubarev, Dmitrii, 151, 242
Zverev, Alexei, xxii, 53

THE EUROPEAN NABOKOV WEB, CLASSICISM AND ELIOT
Robin Davies
235 pages
Cloth 978-1-936235-65-0
$69.00 / £47.00

Robin Davies here demonstrates that Nabokov's *Pale Fire* has a classical unity and represents a direct attack on T.S.Eliot's philosophical position, particularly as given in *The Waste Land* and as represented by Eliot's later tendency for conservatism in literature, politics and religion. After Nabokov was forced into exile from Germany and then France in the 1930s with his young son and Jewish wife, Eliot's passivism must have seemed to him the very antithesis of survival. The enigmatic *Pale Fire* and its surface triviality suggested that there could be self-consistent logic within the obvious commentary of Charles Kinbote and John Shade's poem. Davies places this work in its vast European context, forming a bridge between Russian and European literature which will be appreciated by scholars of both.

Robin Davies (D.Phil, Oxford University) is a senior research associate at Cardiff University. He has long studied Nabokov's literature.

"*The European Nabokov Web, Classicism and Eliot* is a very fine book by a person of great talent and expertise both in the humanities and sciences, a kind of work that Nabokov himself would love to read, a kind of commentary to *Pale Fire*, which goes to the very heart of Nabokov's view of what literature is about."
—Lazar Fleishman, Professor of Slavic Languages and Literature, Stanford University

RANK AND STYLE
Russians in State Service, Life, and Literature
Irina Reyfman
250 pages
Cloth 978-1-936235-51-3
$69.00 / £47.00

Rank and Style is a collection of essays by Irina Reyfman, a leading scholar of Russian literature and culture. Ranging from the eighteenth to the twentieth century, the essays focus on the interaction of life and literature. In the first part, Reyfman examines how obligatory state service and the Table of Ranks shaped Russian writers' view of themselves as professionals, raising questions about whether the existence of the rank system prompted the development of specifically Russian types of literary discourse. The sections that follow bring together articles on Pushkin, writer and man, as seen by himself and others, essays on Leo Tolstoy, and other aspects of Russian literary and cultural history. In addition to examining little-studied writers and works, *Rank and Style* offers new approaches to well-studied literary personalities and texts.

Irina Reyfman (PhD Stanford University) is a professor of Russian Literature at Columbia University. In her studies, Reyfman focuses on the interaction of literature and culture: how literature reflects cultural phenomena and how it contributes to the formation of cultural biases and forms of behavior. Reyfman is the author of *Vasilii Trediakovsky: The Fool of the 'New' Russian Literature* (Stanford, 1990) and *Ritualized Violence Russian Style: The Duel in Russian Culture and Literature* (Stanford, 1999; also in Russian, Moscow: NLO, 2002). She is also a co-editor (with Catherine T. Nepomnyashchy and Hilde Hoogenboom) of *Mapping the Feminine: Russian Women and Cultural Difference* (Bloomington, IN: Slavica, 2008).

FROM SYMBOLISM TO SOCIALIST REALISM
A Reader
Irene Masing-Delic
600 pages
Cloth 978-1-936235-42-1
$59.00 / £40.25

Developed as a reader for upper division undergraduates and beginning graduates, *From Symbolism to Socialist Realism* offers a broad variety of materials contextualizing the literary texts most frequently read in Russian literature courses at this level. These approaches range from critical- theoretical articles, cultural and historical analyses, literary manifestos and declarations of literary aesthetics, memoirs of revolutionary terrorism and arrests by the NKVD, political denunciations and "literary vignettes" capturing the spirit of its particular time in a nutshell. The voices of this "polyphonic" reader are diverse: Briusov, Savinkov, Ivanov-Razumnik, Kollontai, Tsvetaeva, Shklovsky, Olesha, Zoshchenko, Zhdanov, Grossman, Evtushenko and others.
The range of specialists on Russian culture represented here is equally broad: Clark, Erlich, Falen, Grossman, Nilsson, Peace, Poznansky, Siniavskii, Volkov and others. Together they evoke and illuminate a complex and tragic era.

Irene Masing-Delic (PhD University of Stockholm) is a Professor at The Ohio State University, Columbus, Ohio; author of *Abolishing Death* (1992).

JEWS IN THE EAST EUROPEAN BORDERLANDS
Essays in Honor of John D. Klier
Edited by Eugene M. Avrutin and Harriet Murav
350 pages
Cloth 978-1-936235-59-9
$79.00 / £53.99

John Doyle Klier's pioneering publications on the relations between Jews and the Russian social order—on topics such as public opinion, governance, conversion, Russification politics, antisemitism, and pogroms—have influenced an entire generation of new scholarship. *Jews in the East European Borderlands*, a collection of essays honoring Klier's life and work, brings together some of the most innovative scholarship in the field. Focusing on the complex, often violent, entanglements between Jews and Russians, historians and literary scholars critically reassess the artifacts of high culture, including Yiddish and Russian prose and poetry, as well as dimensions of daily life, including letter-writing, diaries, the work of philanthropy, photojournalism, and the mass circulation press.

Eugene M. Avrutin (PhD University of Michigan) is assistant professor of modern European Jewish history and Tobor family scholar in the Program of Jewish Culture and Society at the University of Illinois. He is the author of *Jews and the Imperial State: Identification Politics in Tsarist Russia* (2010). He and Harriet Murav co-edited, together with Petersburg Judaica, *Photographing the Jewish Nation: Pictures from S. An-sky's Ethnographic Expedition* (2009).

Harriet Murav (PhD Stanford University) is a professor in the Department of Slavic Languages and Literatures and Comparative and World Literature at the University of Illinois. She is the author of *Holy Foolishness: Dostoevsky's Novels & the Poetics of Cultural Critique* (1992), *Russia's Legal Fictions* (1998), *Identity Theft: The Jew in Imperial Russia and the Case of Avraam Uri Kovner* (2003), and *Music From a Speeding Train: Jewish Literature in Post-Revolution Russia* (2011).

www.ingramcontent.com/pod-product-compliance
Lightning Source LLC
Chambersburg PA
CBHW051551230426
43668CB00013B/1820